WILEY PLUS
www.wileyplus.com

W9-BZV-928

This online teaching and learning environment integrates the entire digital textbook with the most effective instructor and student resources to fit every learning style.

With **WileyPLUS:**

○ Students achieve concept mastery in a rich, structured environment that's available 24/7

○ Instructors personalize and manage their course more effectively with assessment, assignments, grade tracking, and more

• manage time better

• study smarter

• save money

From multiple study paths, to self-assessment, to a wealth of interactive visual and audio resources, *WileyPLUS* gives you everything you need to personalize the teaching and learning experience.

»Find out how to MAKE IT YOURS»

www.wiley**plus**.com

ALL THE HELP, **RESOURCES**, AND PERSONAL **SUPPORT** YOU AND YOUR STUDENTS NEED!

2-Minute Tutorials and all of the resources you & your students need to get started
www.wileyplus.com/firstday

Student support from an experienced student user Ask your local representative for details!

Collaborate with your colleagues, find a mentor, attend virtual and live events, and view resources
www.WhereFacultyConnect.com

Pre-loaded, ready-to-use assignments and presentations
www.wiley.com/college/quickstart

Technical Support 24/7 FAQs, online chat, and phone support
www.wileyplus.com/support

Your *WileyPLUS* Account Manager Training and implementation support
www.wileyplus.com/accountmanager

www.wiley**plus**.com

MAKE IT YOURS!

ACCOUNTING PRINCIPLES

FIFTH CANADIAN EDITION

→ Jerry J. Weygandt *Ph.D., C.P.A.*
University of Wisconsin—Madison

→ Donald E. Kieso *Ph.D., C.P.A.*
Northern Illinois University

→ Paul D. Kimmel *Ph.D., C.P.A.*
University of Wisconsin—Milwaukee

→ Barbara Trenholm *M.B.A., F.C.A.*
University of New Brunswick—Fredericton

→ Valerie A. Kinnear *M.Sc. (Bus. Admin.), C.A.*
Mount Royal University

In collaboration with
Joan Barlow, Mount Royal University
Brad Witt, Humber Institute of Technology & Advanced Learning

WILEY

John Wiley & Sons Canada, Ltd.

To our students—past, present, and future

Copyright © 2010 John Wiley & Sons Canada Ltd.

Copyright © 2009 John Wiley & Sons Inc. All rights reserved. No part of this work covered by the copyrights herein may be reproduced or used in any form or by any means—graphic, electronic, or mechanical—without the prior written permission of the publisher.

Any request for photocopying, recording, taping, or inclusion in information storage and retrieval systems of any part of this book shall be directed in writing to The Canadian Copyright Licensing Agency (Access Copyright). For an Access Copyright Licence, visit www.accesscopyright.ca or call toll-free, 1-800-893-5777.

Care has been taken to trace ownership of copyright material contained in this text. The publishers will gladly receive any information that will enable them to rectify any erroneous reference or credit line in subsequent editions.

Library and Archives Canada Cataloguing in Publication

Accounting principles / Jerry J. Weygandt ... [et al.]. -- 5th Canadian ed.

ISBN 978-0-470-16079-4 (pt. 1).--ISBN 978-0-470-67841-1 (pt. 2).--ISBN 978-0-470-16081-7 (pt. 3)
BRV ISBN: 978-0-470-67966-1

1. Accounting--Textbooks. I. Weygandt, Jerry J.

HF5636.A33 2009a   657'.044   C2009-903891-9

Production Credits

Acquisitions Editor: Zoë Craig
Vice President & Publisher: Veronica Visentin
Vice President, Publishing Services: Karen Bryan
Creative Director, Publishing Services: Ian Koo
Director, Market Development: Carolyn Wells
Marketing Manager: Aida Krneta
Editorial Manager: Karen Staudinger
Developmental Editor: Daleara Jamasji Hirjikaka
Media Editor: Channade Fenandoe
Editorial Assistant: Laura Hwee
Design & Typesetting: OrangeSprocket Communications
Cover Photo: ©David Evans/National Geographic/Getty Images
Cover Design: Natalia Burobina
Printing & Binding: Quad/Graphics.

Printed and bound in the United States
2 3 4 5 QG 14 13 12 11

John Wiley & Sons Canada, Ltd.
6045 Freemont Blvd.
Mississauga, Ontario L5R 4J3
Visit our website at: www.wiley.ca

Part One

Part Two

Part Three

Part Four

CONTENTS – PART THREE

CHAPTER 11
FINANCIAL REPORTING CONCEPTS

✔ THE NAVIGATOR

- ☐ Understand *Concepts for Review*
- ☐ Read *Feature Story*
- ☐ Scan *Study Objectives*
- ☐ Read *Chapter Preview*
- ☐ Read text and answer *Before You Go On*
- ☐ Work *Demonstration Problem*
- ☐ Review *Summary of Study Objectives*
- ☐ Answer *Self-Study Questions*
- ☐ Complete assignments

CONCEPTS FOR REVIEW:

Before studying this chapter, you should understand or, if necessary, review:

a. The external users of accounting information. (Ch. 1, pp. 3–4)

b. How accounting standards are set in Canada and internationally. (Ch. 1, p. 7)

c. The definition of generally accepted accounting principles (GAAP) (Ch. 1, p. 7)

d. The accrual accounting and going concern assumptions. (Ch. 1, p. 8 and Ch. 3, pp. 119–120)

e. The revenue recognition and expense recognition criteria. (Ch. 1, p. 12 and Ch. 3, p. 120)

Canadian Accounting Goes Global

As of January 2011, Canadian generally accepted accounting principles (GAAP) will no longer exist as a distinct set of accounting standards for publicly accountable enterprises. Instead, Canadian publicly accountable enterprises must follow International Financial Reporting Standards (IFRS), a set of global accounting standards developed by the International Accounting Standards Board (IASB).

There are a number of reasons why it is important for Canadian companies to adopt IFRS, says Ian Hague, principal in accounting standards at the Accounting Standards Board of Canada (AcSB). "It was very clear to us from the consultations we did with companies and others across the country that it was no longer going to be sustainable to have a unique set of Canadian GAAP for publicly accountable enterprises in what was becoming a global market." Canadian companies wanting access to foreign markets must follow international standards. As well, the recent financial crisis increased support for a single set of high-quality global accounting standards.

The AcSB had two options: adopting U.S. GAAP or IFRS. It chose IFRS because, among other reasons, the standards are more similar to Canadian standards in their style, length, and complexity, Hague explains. "They are written in a similar kind of way, they require a similar degree of judgement, and they don't have all the extra detailed guidance the U.S. standards often have in them." The United States may be following suit. Its Securities and Exchange Commission has proposed a "roadmap" to converging U.S. GAAP with IFRS from 2014 to 2016. The United States already allows foreign companies to file according to IFRS. So, following the move to IFRS, Canadian companies that list on U.S. markets will no longer have to reconcile their financial statements to U.S. GAAP.

While all Canadian publicly accountable companies must adopt IFRS, the AcSB anticipates that others will voluntarily do so as well. "We do expect quite a number of private companies to adopt: those that are subsidiaries of foreign operations that report in accordance with IFRS, those thinking of going public in the near future, and those that want to access international markets. So while there's one group of companies that must adopt, there's another group that probably will adopt," says Hague.

The IASB is also reviewing the conceptual framework underlying the accounting standards. This is a multi-stage project still in the early stages. "Our conceptual framework in Section 1000 [of the *CICA Handbook*] is quite similar to the IASB conceptual framework anyway," says Hague. "So as they update their conceptual framework, we will, for publicly accountable enterprises, update it at the same time because we will be onto IFRS by then, and for private enterprises and not-for-profits, we will also take into account those updates."

"The framework doesn't override accounting standards," Hague continues. "The fact that the framework has changed won't immediately change accounting policies." The changes will have an impact in two ways: if an accounting standard changes, it would need to reflect the new thinking in the framework; and when there's no accounting standard in place, the framework would need to be referred to in developing the new accounting policy. "I don't think there is going to be a pervasive effect of immediate change to accounting just because the framework has changed," says Hague. "What companies are going to see is the new thinking in the framework applied as new standards are developed."

The Navigator

STUDY OBJECTIVES:

After studying this chapter, you should be able to:

1. Explain the importance of having a conceptual framework of accounting, and list the components.

2. Identify and apply the objective of financial reporting and the underlying assumptions used by accountants.

3. Describe the fundamental and enhancing qualitative characteristics of financial reporting.

4. Identify and apply the constraints on financial reporting.

5. Identify and apply the basic recognition and measurement concepts of accounting.

The Navigator

In the first 10 chapters, in Parts 1 and 2, you learned the process that leads to the preparation of a company's financial statements. You also learned that users make decisions based on financial statements, and that to be useful, these statements must communicate financial information to users in an effective way. This means that generally accepted accounting principles must be used. Otherwise, we would have to be familiar with each company's particular accounting and reporting practices in order to understand its financial statements. It would be difficult, if not impossible, to compare the financial results of different companies.

This chapter explores the conceptual framework that is used to develop generally accepted accounting principles. The chapter is organized as follows:

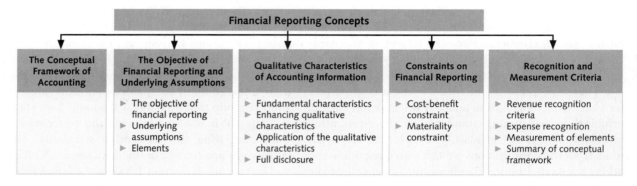

The Conceptual Framework of Accounting

STUDY OBJECTIVE 1

Explain the importance of having a conceptual framework of accounting, and list the components.

According to standard setters, the **conceptual framework of accounting** is "a coherent system of interrelated objectives and fundamentals that can lead to consistent standards and that prescribes the nature, function, and limits of financial accounting statements." In other words, the conceptual framework of accounting guides choices about what to present in financial statements, decisions about alternative ways of reporting economic events, and the selection of appropriate ways of communicating such information.

A conceptual framework ensures that we have a coherent set of standards. New standards are easier to understand and are more consistent when they are built on the same foundation as existing standards. By relying on an existing framework of basic theory, it should be possible to solve new and emerging problems more quickly.

As a foundation for accounting, the conceptual framework:

1. Ensures that existing standards and practices are clear and consistent.
2. Makes it possible to respond quickly to new issues.
3. Increases the usefulness of the financial information presented in financial reports.

Alternative terminology
Recall that, as we saw in Chapter 1, the words "standards" and "principles" mean the same thing in accounting.

However, it is impossible to create a rule for every situation. Canadian and international standards are therefore based mostly on general principles rather than specific rules. With the help of a conceptual framework and their professional judgement, it is hoped that accountants will be able to quickly determine an appropriate accounting treatment for each situation.

Accounting standards can differ significantly from country to country. This lack of uniformity has arisen over time because of differences in legal systems, in processes for developing standards, in government requirements, and in economic environments. The International Accounting Standards Board (IASB) was formed to try to reduce these areas of difference and unify global standard setting.

In Canada, accounting standards have been developed by the Accounting Standards Board (AcSB), an independent standard-setting body created by the Canadian Institute of Chartered Accountants (CICA). However, as noted in the opening story, the AcSB recognized the need to have globally uniform financial reporting and decided that, starting in 2011, publicly traded companies must follow International Financial Reporting Standards (IFRS).

As indicated in the feature story, the IASB and its U.S. counterpart, the Financial Accounting Standards Board (FASB), are also working on a joint project to improve and bring about convergence of their conceptual frameworks. Canada is participating in the project and the AcSB plans to adopt the improved IASB conceptual framework and to incorporate it into the *CICA Handbook*.

The six major components of the IASB conceptual framework are:

1. The objective of financial reporting
2. The underlying assumptions
3. The elements of financial statements
4. The qualitative characteristics of accounting information
5. The constraints on financial reporting
6. Recognition and measurement criteria

In 2008, the IASB issued an exposure draft recommending changes to two components of the conceptual framework: the objective of financial reporting and the qualitative characteristics of accounting information. These recommendations are expected to be approved and adopted. The IASB is continuing to improve the other components of the conceptual framework and we can expect to see further changes in the future.

This chapter includes the proposed changes to the objective of financial reporting and qualitative characteristics of accounting information, along with the other components of the IASB's current conceptual framework.

We will discuss the six components of the conceptual framework in the following sections.

> **Helpful hint** Accounting principles are affected by economic and political conditions, which change over time. As a result, accounting principles can and do change.

BEFORE YOU GO ON . . .

→ **Review It**

1. Describe the conceptual framework of accounting.
2. Why do we need a conceptual framework of accounting?
3. Why was the IASB formed?
4. What are the components of the IASB conceptual framework?

Related exercise material: BE11–1.

The Navigator

The Objective of Financial Reporting and Underlying Assumptions

The first step in establishing accounting standards is to decide on the purpose or objective of financial reporting. Once this is established, then the underlying assumptions can be determined.

STUDY OBJECTIVE 2

Identify and apply the objective of financial reporting and the underlying assumptions used by accountants.

The Objective of Financial Reporting

To decide what the objective of financial reporting should be, some basic questions need to be answered first: Who uses financial statements? Why? What information do the users need? How much do they know about business and accounting? How should financial information be reported so that it is best understood?

The main **objective of financial reporting** is to provide useful information for decision-making. More specifically, in the revised conceptual framework, accounting standard setters have decided that the objective for general purpose financial reporting is to provide financial information that is useful to present and potential investors, lenders, and other creditors in making decisions about a business. You will recall from earlier chapters that financial statements are prepared for an economic or business unit that is separate and distinct from its owners. This is referred to as the economic entity assumption. An economic (reporting) entity could be one company or a collection of companies consolidated under common ownership. We will learn more about consolidated companies in Chapter 16.

Although a wide variety of users rely on financial reporting, capital providers (investors and lenders) are identified as the main users of financial reporting. Capital providers play a fundamental role in the efficient functioning of the economy by providing capital (cash) to businesses. Businesses require cash to start up, to maintain operations, and to grow. Cash or capital comes from investors, lenders, and the company's revenue-generating activities.

To make decisions about allocating capital (e.g., about investing or lending), users look for information in the financial statements about a company's ability to earn a profit and generate future cash flows. To assess this ability, users read the financial statements to determine whether or not management acquired and used the company's resources in the best way possible. Consequently, financial statements must give information about the following:

1. Economic resources (assets), and claims on the economic resources (liabilities and equity)
2. Changes in economic resources and claims on the economic resources
3. Economic performance

Underlying Assumptions

Assumptions create a foundation for the accounting process. You already know the two major assumptions from earlier chapters: accrual accounting and going concern. We will review them here briefly.

Accrual Accounting Assumption

You learned in earlier chapters that the **accrual basis of accounting** is widely recognized as being significantly more useful for decision-making than the cash basis of accounting. Under accrual accounting, transactions are recorded in the period when the transaction occurs and not when cash is received or paid. For example, a law firm would record revenue in the accounting period when the legal services are provided to the client and not necessarily in the accounting period when the client pays for the services. Financial statements prepared on an accrual basis provide users with information on what cash will be received in the future and what cash will be paid out in the future.

As a result of the usefulness of the accrual basis in decision-making, it has become an underlying assumption that all financial statements are prepared using the accrual basis of accounting. Because of this **accrual accounting assumption**, there is no need to report that the accrual basis has been used. The basis of accounting (cash or accrual) will need to be explicitly stated only in the rare cases where the cash basis is used.

Going Concern Assumption

The **going concern assumption** is the assumption that the company will continue operating for the foreseeable future; that is, long enough to achieve its goals and respect its commitments. Although there are many business failures, most companies continue operating for a long time.

This assumption has important implications for accounting. If a company is assumed to be a going concern, then financial statement users will find it useful for the company to report assets, such as buildings and equipment, at their carrying amount (cost minus accumulated depreciation). If the company was not a going concern, then the carrying amount would not be relevant; instead the financial statement user would want to know what the assets can be sold for or their net realizable value. Furthermore, if the company is not a going concern, the classification of assets and liabilities as current or non-current would not matter. Labelling anything as long-term would be difficult to justify.

It is an underlying assumption that financial statements are prepared as if the company is a going concern. This means there is no need to report that the going concern assumption has been used. The only time the going concern assumption should not be used is when liquidation is likely. In that case, it will be explicitly stated that the going concern assumption is not being followed. Assets and liabilities should be revalued and stated at their net realizable value rather than at cost, and the current/non-current classifications will not be used. Accounting for liquidations is discussed in advanced accounting courses.

 ACCOUNTING IN ACTION: BUSINESS INSIGHT

Nortel is a global leader in delivering communications capabilities. On January 14, 2009, Nortel filed for bankruptcy protection in the United States, Canada, and other countries where Nortel has subsidiaries. Bankruptcy protection gives companies time to reorganize their operations and financial conditions and to develop a comprehensive restructuring plan. While bankruptcy protection is in place, creditors are prevented from taking any action against the company. While Nortel was operating under bankruptcy protection, its 2008 audited consolidated financial statements issued March 2, 2009, were prepared using the going concern basis, not a liquidation basis. In Nortel's notes to its financial statements, the company acknowledged that "it is not possible to predict whether the actions taken in any restructuring will result in improvements to Nortel's financial condition sufficient to allow it to continue as a going concern."

Source: Nortel Networks Corporation, audited consolidated financial statements for the year ended December 31, 2008

How did Nortel justify using the going concern assumption when it was so uncertain that the company would continue operating?

Elements of Financial Statements

Elements of financial statements are the basic categories used in the financial statements to meet the objective of financial reporting. These elements include assets, liabilities, equity, revenues, expenses, and other comprehensive income.

Because these elements are so important, they must be precisely defined and applied in the same way by all reporting entities. Currently the definitions are being reviewed by FASB and the IASB in their joint project to improve the conceptual framework. Finding the appropriate definition for many of these elements is not easy. For example, should the value of a company's employees be reported as an asset on a balance sheet? Should the death of the company's president be reported as a loss? A good set of definitions of financial statement elements should give answers to these types of questions. Because you have already read the current definitions for assets, liabilities, equity, revenues, and expenses in earlier chapters, they are not repeated here. Other comprehensive income is discussed in Chapters 13 and 14.

BEFORE YOU GO ON . . .

➡ Review It

1. What is the basic objective of financial information?
2. Identify the elements of the financial statements.
3. What are the accrual accounting assumption and going concern assumption?
4. When might the going concern assumption not be appropriate to use?

➡ Do It

Presented below are the underlying assumptions of accounting standards:

1. Going concern
2. Accrual accounting

Match the assumptions to the following statements:

(a) __ Sales revenue is recorded when the sale occurs, not when cash is collected.
(b) __ It is relevant to classify assets and liabilities as current and long-term.

Action Plan
- Review descriptions of the assumptions underlying accounting standards.

Solution

(a) 2 (b) 1

Related exercise material: BE11–2, BE11–3, and E11–1.

The Navigator

Qualitative Characteristics of Accounting Information

STUDY OBJECTIVE 3

Describe the fundamental and enhancing qualitative characteristics of financial reporting.

How does a company like The Forzani Group Ltd. decide how much financial information to disclose? In what format should its financial information be presented? How should assets, liabilities, revenues, and expenses be measured? Remember that the objective of financial reporting is to provide useful information for decision-making. Thus the main criterion for judging accounting choices is decision usefulness.

What makes information useful in decision-making? Accounting standard setters have decided that there are two fundamental characteristics that accounting information *must* have in order to be useful. In addition, there are other characteristics, complementary to the fundamental characteristics, that enhance the usefulness of accounting information. We discuss the qualitative characteristics in the following sections.

Fundamental Characteristics

In order for information to be useful in decision-making, accounting standard setters have agreed that the information should have two fundamental qualitative characteristics: relevance and faithful representation.

Relevance

Accounting information has **relevance** if it makes a difference in a decision. Relevant information has either predictive value or confirmatory value, or both. Predictive value helps users forecast future events. For example, when Forzani issues financial statements, the information in them is considered relevant because it gives a basis for predicting future profits or earnings. Confirmatory value confirms or corrects prior expectations. When Forzani issues financial statements, the company also confirms or corrects expectations about its financial health.

Faithful Representation

Once it is determined which information is relevant to financial statement users, then how the information is reported must be determined. To be useful, information must be a **faithful representation** of the economic reality of the events that it is reporting and not just the legal form. For example, a company may sign a lease agreement that requires periodic rental payments to be made over the life of the lease. If a company follows the legal form of the transaction, the periodic rental payments will be recorded as rent expense. However, for certain leases the economic reality is that an asset is purchased and the periodic payments are loan payments. For these leases, it is necessary to record an asset and a liability to show the economic reality. You will learn more about the accounting for lease agreements in Chapter 15.

Faithful representation is achieved when the information is (1) complete, (2) neutral, and (3) free from material error, as explained below.

1. Accounting information is **complete** if it includes all information necessary to show the economic reality of the transaction. If information is omitted, users will not be able to make appropriate resource allocation decisions. If Forzani did not disclose when payments are due on its long-term debt, users would not have the necessary information to predict future cash flows. The concept of completeness is discussed later in this chapter in the section on full disclosure.

2. Accounting information is **neutral** if it is free from bias that is intended to attain a predetermined result or to encourage a particular behaviour. For example, accounting information would be biased if the income statement was prepared so that it resulted in a high enough level of profit that the management team receives their bonuses.

3. An error is considered to be a **material error** if the error in the accounting information could have an impact on an investor's or creditor's decision. Accounting information includes estimates. If accounting information is to be free from material error, estimates must be based on the best available information and be reasonably accurate. Accountants must use professional judgement and caution when using estimates in financial reporting.

The fundamental qualitative characteristics of accounting information are summarized in Illustration 11-1.

Relevance
1. Provides a basis for forecasts
2. Confirms or corrects prior expectations

Faithful Representation
1. Is complete
2. Is neutral
3. Is free from material error

◀ Illustration 11-1

Fundamental qualitative characteristics of accounting information

Enhancing Qualitative Characteristics

Enhancing qualitative characteristics complement the two primary qualitative characteristics: relevance and faithful representation. The enhancing characteristics are said to help users distinguish more useful information from less useful information. Comparability, verifiability, timeliness, and understandability are enhancing characteristics.

Comparability

Accounting information about a company is most useful when it can be compared with accounting information about other companies. There is **comparability** when companies with similar circumstances use the same accounting principles. Comparability enables users to identify the similarities and differences between companies.

Comparability is reduced when companies use different methods of accounting for specific items. For example, there are different methods of determining the cost of inventory, which can result in different amounts of profit. But if each company states which cost determination method it uses, the external user can determine whether the financial information for two companies is comparable. This is known as the full disclosure concept, which we will learn about later in this chapter.

Comparability is easier when accounting policies are used consistently. **Consistency** means that a company uses the same accounting principles and methods from year to year. For example, if a company selects FIFO as its inventory cost formula in the first year of operations, it is expected to use FIFO in subsequent years. When financial information has been reported consistently, the financial statements make it possible to do a meaningful analysis of company trends.

This does not mean, however, that a company can never change its accounting policies. Sometimes changes in accounting policies are required by the CICA. For example, companies are required to change some accounting policies in 2011 when they adopt IFRS. At other times, management may decide that it would be better to change to a new accounting policy. To do this, management must prove that the new policy will result in more relevant information in the statements.

In the year of a change in an accounting policy, the change and its impact must be disclosed in the notes to the financial statements. This disclosure makes users of the financial statements aware of the lack of consistency. In addition, the financial statements for past years must be restated as if the new accounting policy had been used in those years. We will learn more about accounting for, and reporting, changes in accounting policies in Chapter 14.

Verifiability

Verifiability helps assure users that the financial information shows the economic reality of the transaction. Information is verifiable if two knowledgeable and independent people would generally agree that it faithfully represents the economic reality. In other words, there must be proof that the information is complete, an appropriate basis of measurement has been used, and there are no material errors and bias. Information must be verifiable for external professional accountants to audit financial statements and ensure that the financial statements reflect the financial reality of the company rather than the legal form of the transactions and events that underlie them.

Timeliness

Timeliness means that accounting information is provided when it is still highly useful for decision-making. In other words, it must be available to decision-makers before it loses its ability to influence decisions. Many people believe that by the time annual financial statements are issued—sometimes up to six months after a company's year end—the information has limited usefulness for decision-making. Timely *interim* financial reporting is essential to decision-making.

Understandability

For the information in financial statements to be useful, users must be able to understand it. **Understandability** enables users to gain insights into the company's financial position and results of operations. But users are expected to have a reasonable knowledge of business, economic, and financial activities, and of financial reporting. Users who do not have this level of understanding are expected to rely on professionals who do have an appropriate level of expertise. In making decisions, users should review and analyze the information carefully.

One of the benefits of Canada moving to a common set of international accounting standards is that Canadian companies' financial statements will be understood by global users.

Understandability is greater when the information is classified, characterized, and presented clearly and concisely.

The enhancing qualitative characteristics of accounting information are summarized in Illustration 11-2.

Illustration 11-2 ➡

Enhancing qualitative characteristics of accounting information

Apples   Apples

Comparability
1. Different companies use similar accounting principles.
2. A company uses the same accounting policies consistently from year to year.

Verifiability
3. Independent people agree that the economic reality is reported.

Timeliness
4. Information is provided when it is still useful.

Understandability
5. of accounting concepts and procedures.
6. of general business and economic conditions.

Application of the Qualitative Characteristics

The qualitative characteristics are complementary concepts; that is, they work together. Nonetheless, they must be applied in a certain order. The qualitative characteristic of relevance should be applied first because it will identify the specific information that would affect the decisions of investors and creditors and that should be included in the financial report.

Once relevance is applied, faithful representation should be applied to ensure that the economic information faithfully represents the economic events being described. Taken together, relevance and faithful representation make financial reporting information decision useful.

Then the enhancing qualitative characteristics—comparability, verifiability, timeliness, and understandability—are applied. They add to the decision usefulness of financial reporting information that is relevant and representationally faithful. They must be applied after the first two characteristics because they cannot, either individually or together, make information useful if it is irrelevant or not faithfully represented.

Full Disclosure

We have identified the characteristics that financial information must have to provide information that is useful for decisions. But companies must also provide **full disclosure** of circumstances and events that make a difference to financial statement users. It is important that investors be made aware of events that can affect the financial health of a company.

Full disclosure is respected through two elements in the financial statements: the data they contain and the accompanying notes. In most cases, the first note in the statements is a summary of significant accounting policies. The summary includes the methods used by the company when there are alternatives in acceptable accounting principles. For example, The Forzani Group's note on its significant accounting policies (see Note 2 in Appendix A at the end of this textbook) discloses that the company uses the weighted average cost method to determine the cost of its inventory and the declining-balance method to depreciate (or amortize, as Forzani calls it) its building.

The information that is disclosed in the notes to the financial statements generally falls into three additional categories. The information can:

1. Give supplementary detail or explanation (for example, a schedule of property, plant, and equipment)
2. Explain unrecorded transactions (for example, contingencies, commitments, and subsequent events)
3. Supply new information (for example, information about related party transactions)

Deciding how much disclosure is enough can be difficult. Accountants could disclose every financial event that occurs and every contingency that exists. But the benefits of giving this additional information may be less than the cost of making it available. We will discuss this problem in the following section.

BEFORE YOU GO ON . . .

➡ Review It

1. Describe the fundamental qualitative characteristics that make accounting information useful.
2. Describe the enhancing qualitative characteristics that make accounting information useful.
3. In what order are the qualitative characteristics to be applied?
4. What is meant by the concept of full disclosure?

➡ Do It

Presented below are some of the qualitative characteristics of financial information.

1. Relevance
2. Faithful representation
3. Complete
4. Neutral
5. Comparability
6. Verifiability
7. Timeliness
8. Understandability
9. Consistency

Match the qualitative characteristics to the following statements:

(a) ___ Information is available to decision-makers before the information loses its ability to influence decisions.
(b) ___ Information is free from bias that is intended to attain a predetermined result.
(c) ___ Information makes a difference in a decision.
(d) ___ Users are assured that the financial information shows the economic reality of the transaction.
(e) ___ The same accounting principles are used from year to year.
(f) ___ All of the information necessary to show the economic reality of transactions is provided.
(g) ___ Accounting information about one company can be evaluated in relation to accounting information from another company.
(h) ___ Accounting information reports the economic reality of a transaction, not its legal form.
(i) ___ Accounting information is prepared on the assumption that users have a general understanding of general business and economic conditions and are able to read a financial report.

Action Plan
- Review the two fundamental qualitative characteristics.
- Review the enhancing qualitative characteristics.

Solution
(a) 7   (b) 4   (c) 1   (d) 6   (e) 9   (f) 3   (g) 5   (h) 2   (i) 8

The Navigator

Related exercise material: BE11–4, E11–2, and E11–3.

Constraints on Financial Reporting

Identify and apply the constraints on financial reporting.

Two pervasive constraints limit the necessary information in financial statements and allow a company to modify GAAP without reducing the usefulness of the information it reports. These two constraints are cost-benefit and materiality.

Cost-Benefit Constraint

The **cost-benefit constraint** exists to ensure that the value of the information is more than the cost of providing it. As we discussed earlier in this chapter, when accountants apply the full disclosure principle, they could disclose every financial event that occurs and every contingency. However, giving more information increases reporting costs, and the benefits of giving this information may be less than the costs in some cases.

As there have been more and more changes to disclosure and reporting requirements, the costs of giving this information have increased. Because of these increasing costs, some critics have argued that the costs of applying GAAP to smaller or non-publicly traded companies are too high compared with the benefits. To respond to this problem, the CICA has developed Canadian GAAP for Private Enterprises for private companies, which is a simplified version of GAAP. As Paul Cherry, the chairman of the Accounting Standards Board, concluded, "One size does not necessarily fit all."

Materiality Constraint

The **materiality constraint** relates to an item's impact on a company's overall financial condition and operations. An item is material when it is likely to influence the decision of a reasonably careful investor or creditor. It is immaterial if including it or leaving it out has no impact on a decision-maker. In short, if the item does not make a difference in decision-making, GAAP does not have to be followed. To determine the materiality of an amount, the accountant usually compares it with such items as total assets, total liabilities, gross revenues, and cash and/or net profit.

To illustrate how the materiality constraint works, assume that Yanik Co. purchases several inexpensive pieces of office equipment, such as wastepaper baskets. Although it would appear that the proper accounting is to depreciate these wastepaper baskets over their useful lives, they would usually be expensed immediately instead. Doing this is justified because these costs are immaterial. Making depreciation schedules for these assets is costly and time-consuming. It will not make a material difference to total assets and profit. The materiality constraint is also applied in the non-disclosure of minor contingencies, and in the expensing of any long-lived assets under a certain dollar amount.

BEFORE YOU GO ON . . .

→ Review It

1. What is the cost-benefit constraint?
2. Why is it necessary to have a simpler GAAP for private enterprises?
3. Describe the materiality constraint. Give an example.

→ Do It

Presented below are the constraints on financial reporting.

1. Materiality
2. Cost-benefit

Match these constraints to the following accounting practices:

(a) ___ Private companies can follow a simplified version of GAAP.
(b) ___ Inexpensive repair tools that the company will use for several years are expensed when purchased.
(c) ___ The financial statements are not restated when a $100 error is found after the statements have been issued.
(d) ___ The company implements a perpetual inventory system that costs $50,000 and the expected cost savings is $20,000 annually in the current year and future years.

Action Plan
• Recall that an item is immaterial if leaving it out will have no impact on the financial statements.
• Recall that the value of the information should be more than the cost of providing it.

Solution
(a) 2   (b) 1   (c) 1   (d) 2

The Navigator

Recognition and Measurement Criteria

STUDY OBJECTIVE 5

Identify and apply the basic recognition and measurement concepts of accounting.

The objective of financial reporting, the elements of financial statements, and the qualitative characteristics of accounting information are very broad. Because accountants must solve practical problems, they need more detailed standards or criteria to help them decide when items should be included in the financial statements and how they should be measured. Recognition is the process of including an item in the financial statements. Recognition criteria help determine when items should be included or recognized in the financial statements. Measurement criteria outline how to measure or assign an amount to those items.

Generally an item will be included in the financial statements if it meets the definition of an asset, liability, equity, revenue, or expense; if it can be measured; and if a reasonable estimate of the amount can be made. The item is reported in the financial statements in a monetary amount. In Canada, the monetary unit used for financial reporting is generally the Canadian dollar.

There are two important concepts underlying the general criteria. The first concept is that if an asset is going to be recorded, then it must be probable that there will be a future economic benefit, and for a liability to be recognized, it is probable that economic resources will be given up. For example, a company does not have to be 100% certain that it will collect an account receivable to record the receivable; it just has to be probable that cash will be collected. The second concept is that estimates may be used to record the dollar amounts if the precise dollar amount is not known.

It would be easy to determine when to recognize revenues or expenses if the only determining factor was when the cash is received or paid. But since accounting standards require the use of accrual accounting, it is necessary to have criteria to determine when to record revenues and expenses. Should the revenue be recorded when the customer places an order with the company, or when the goods are delivered? How should the transaction be recorded if cash collection is uncertain? The revenue recognition criteria discussed in the next section provide guidance in answering these questions. Expense recognition will be discussed later in the chapter.

Revenue Recognition Criteria

In the opinion of many people, when to recognize revenue is the most difficult issue in accounting. And it is an issue that has been responsible for many of the accounting scandals of the past decade. There have been many high-profile cases that highlight improper use of the revenue recognition criteria. For example, when Afexa Life Sciences, the manufacturer of ColdFx, first started selling its products in the United States in 2006, it failed to recognize that there was considerable risk that a significant amount of the product would be returned by retailers. As a result, the company overstated its 2006 revenues (net sales) by $5.6 million because it recorded sales returns in 2007 that should have been recorded in 2006. As a result, Afexa Life Sciences was required to restate its 2006 financial statements.

Why is revenue recognition such a difficult concept to apply? In a few cases, revenue recognition has been intentionally abused in order to manage profits in a way that favours management or the shareholders. However, in most cases, revenue recognition is just a difficult concept because the activities that generate revenues have become a lot more innovative and complex than in the past. These include "swap" transactions, "bill and hold" sales arrangements, risk-sharing agreements, complex rights of return, price-protection guarantees, and post-sale maintenance contracts—all topics that go beyond an introductory accounting course. In these situations, professional judgement is required to determine if the criteria have been met before revenue can be recognized.

International Financial Reporting Standards provide the fundamental criteria to help accountants decide when revenue should be recognized. Basically, the **revenue recognition criteria** state that, revenue is recognized at the same time that an increase in an asset is recognized or a decrease in a liability is recognized for profit-generating activities. The question that needs to be answered is when assets have actually increased or liabilities decreased. We will see that professional judgement is often required to apply the basic criteria.

In the following sections, we will discuss revenue recognition criteria for the most common revenue-generating activities:

1. The sale of goods, and
2. Service contracts and construction contracts.

The Sale of Goods

Revenue from the sale of goods is recognized when all of the following conditions have been met:

1. The seller has transferred to the buyer the significant risks and rewards of ownership.
2. The seller does not have control over the goods or continuing managerial involvement.
3. The amount of the revenue can be reliably measured.
4. It is probable there will be an increase in economic resources (that is, cash will be collected).
5. Costs relating to the sale of the goods can be reliably measured.

For sales in a retail establishment, these conditions are generally met at the point of sale. Consider a sale by Forzani. At the point of sale, the customer pays the cash and takes the merchandise. The company records the sale by debiting Cash and crediting Sales Revenue. If the sale were on account rather than for cash (assuming the company accepts credit sales, and the customer has a good credit rating), the company would record the sale by debiting Accounts Receivable and crediting Sales Revenue. The cost of goods sold can be measured and directly matched to the sales revenue at the point of sale.

Typically the risks and rewards of ownership are transferred when legal title passes and the customer is in possession of the goods. For goods that are shipped, the shipping terms determine when the legal title passes. If the customer pays for the shipping (FOB shipping point), then revenue is recognized when the goods are shipped. If the company (the seller) pays for the shipping (FOB destination), then revenue is recognized when the goods are delivered.

When merchandise is sold on credit, revenue is recognized at the point of sale as long as it is reasonably sure that the cash will be collected. Of course, not all accounts are actually collected. However, as we learned in Chapter 8, revenue can be recognized as long as an estimate can be made of any possible uncollectible accounts and bad debts matched against revenue in the appropriate period.

Similarly, if a company provides refunds to customers for goods returned, revenue is recognized at point of sale if the company is able to reliably estimate future returns and recognizes a liability for the estimated returns.

Revenues and costs that relate to the sales transaction are recognized in the same accounting period. If a company provides free warranty service on its merchandise, revenue is recognized at point of sale if the company is able to reliably estimate the future warranty costs and it recognizes a warranty liability. If costs relating to the sale cannot be reliably measured, then the revenue cannot be recognized.

Service Contracts and Construction Contracts

Generally, in businesses that provide services, revenue is recognized when the service has been fully provided and it is probable that the cash will be collected. For example, when you visit your doctor for a routine checkup, the doctor will bill your provincial health care plan and recognize revenue when your checkup is completed.

In certain cases, revenue can be recognized before the service has been fully provided. Consider a law or accounting firm that provides services for a client over several months. Companies that provide services like this are different from retail companies, as the client is identified and the work is agreed upon (usually with an engagement letter) before the services are performed. In such cases, the client is usually billed every month for the hours of service provided during the particular month. These situations result in a continuing earnings process where revenue can be recognized as chunks of services are provided at a predetermined price (as long as it probable that cash will be collected).

Revenue recognition becomes even more difficult when the earnings process lasts years. This happens in the case of long-term service contracts and construction contracts for large projects, such as building bridges, roads, and aircraft. For example, the construction for the Richmond Olympic Oval, the venue for the speed skating events at the Vancouver 2010 Olympics, began in September 2005 and was completed in the fall of 2008.

Assume that Warrior Construction Co. has a contract to build a dam for the Province of British Columbia for $400 million. Construction is estimated to take three years (starting early in 2009) at a cost of $360 million. If Warrior recognizes revenue only when the construction is complete, it will report no revenues and no profit in the first two years. When completion and sale take place, at the end of 2011, Warrior will report $400 million in revenues, costs of $360 million, and the entire profit of $40 million. Did Warrior really produce no revenues and earn no profit in 2009 and 2010? Obviously not. The earnings process can be considered completed at various stages.

In situations like this, revenue can be partially recognized before the contract is completed if the following conditions are met:

1. The amount of revenue can be measured (an agreed price on the contract).
2. It is probable the company will receive the economic benefits (probable that cash will be collected).
3. The stage of completion of the contract can be reliably measured.
4. The costs to complete the contract can be reliably measured.

This is known as the percentage-of-completion method.

The **percentage-of-completion method** recognizes revenue on a long-term project based on reasonable estimates of the progress toward completion. Note that long-term construction and service contracts usually specify that the contractor (builder) may bill the purchaser at certain times throughout the contract period. However, revenue recognition should not be based on billings (this would be more similar to the cash basis of accounting). Rather, revenue should be recognized based on how much of the work has been performed to date.

There are three steps in the percentage-of-completion method. (1) Progress toward completion is measured by comparing the costs incurred in a period with the total estimated costs for the entire project. This results in a percentage that indicates the percentage of the work that is complete. (2) That percentage is multiplied by the total revenue for the current project, and the result is recognized as the revenue for the period. (3) The costs incurred are then subtracted from the revenue recognized to arrive at the gross profit for the current period. These three steps are presented in Illustration 11-3.

Illustration 11-3 ➡

Percentage-of-completion method

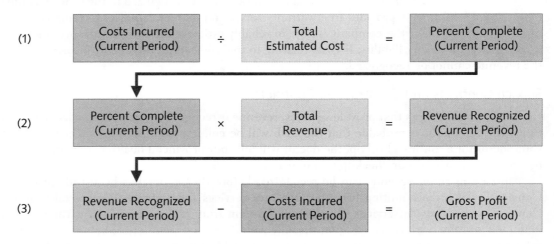

Let's look at an illustration of the percentage-of-completion method. Assume that Warrior Construction has costs of $54 million in 2009, $180 million in 2010, and $126 million in 2011 on the dam project mentioned earlier. The portion of the $400 million of revenue and gross profit that is recognized in each of the three years is shown below (all amounts are in millions):

Year	Costs Incurred (Current Period) ÷	Total Estimated Cost	Percentage Complete = (Current Period) ×	Total Revenue	Revenue Recognized = (Current Period) −	Costs Incurred (Current Period) =	Gross Profit (Current Period)
2009	$ 54	$360	15%	$400	$ 60	$ 54	$ 6
2010	180	360	50%	400	200	180	20
2011	126	360	35%	400	140	126	14
Total	$360				$400	$360	$40

In this example, the company's cost estimates were completely accurate. The costs incurred in the third year brought the total cost to $360 million—exactly what had been estimated. In reality, this does not always happen. As additional information becomes available, it may be necessary to revise estimates for what remains to be done in a project.

When an estimate is revised, the amounts incurred for the current period are changed so they include amounts incurred to date. Another step is added to the formulas shown in Illustration 11-3 to adjust for the revenue that has already been recognized. Illustration 11-4 shows this new step (now step 3), and it also shows, in red, minor adjustments to the wording of the formula.

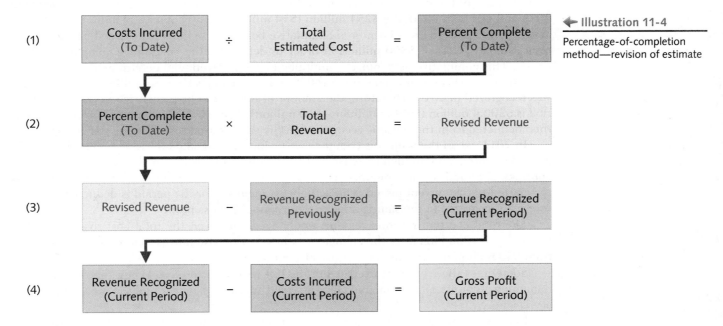

← Illustration 11-4

Percentage-of-completion method—revision of estimate

As when estimates are changed for useful lives or residual values for depreciation, the data for the percentage-of-completion method are only changed for current and future years, rather than for past years also. The percentage that is complete is revised according to the new total estimated costs. A **cumulative percentage** is used. It is calculated by dividing the costs incurred to date by the revised total estimated cost. This formula is similar to the one shown in step 1 of Illustration 11-3, except that the costs incurred are cumulative (to date) rather than just for the current period.

Similar to step 2 of Illustration 11-3, this cumulative percentage is then multiplied by total revenue to determine the revised revenue amount. In a new step—which is not used when actual costs equal estimated costs—the revenue that was recognized previously is now deducted from the revised revenue. This has to be done in order to account for previously recorded amounts and to "catch up" the difference in the estimate.

The remaining step (now step 4) is the same as step 3 demonstrated in Illustration 11-3, where actual costs are deducted from revenue to determine the amount of gross profit to recognize, as shown below.

To apply this formula for a change in estimate, assume the costs estimated to complete the dam project change partway through the three-year contract period for Warrior Construction. In 2010, the estimated total cost rises to $390 million, from its earlier estimate of $360 million. Actual costs incurred are $200 million in 2010 and $136 million in 2011.

The revised calculations for revenue, cost, and gross profit are as follows (all amounts in millions):

Year	Costs Incurred (To Date)	÷	Total Estimated Cost	=	Percentage Complete (To Date)	×	Total Revenue	=	Revised Revenue	−	Revenue Recognized (Previously)	−	Revenue Recognized (Current Period)	−	Costs Incurred (Current Period)	=	Gross Profit (Current Period)
2009	$ 54		$360		15.0%		$400		$ 60.0		$ 0.0		$ 60.0		$ 54		$ 6.0
2010	254		390		65.1%		400		260.4		60.0		200.4		200		0.4
2011	390		390		100.0%		400		400.0		260.4		139.6		136		3.6
Totals													$400.0		$390		$10.0

The calculations for 2009 are unchanged from the ones in the shaded table above. However, because of the change in estimate in 2010, the revenue, cost, and gross profit change in 2010 and 2011. In 2010, the $254 million ($54 million in 2009 and $200 million in 2010) of actual costs incurred are shown on a cumulative basis. These costs are divided by the revised total estimated cost of $390 million in order to determine the percentage complete to date, 65.1%. This cumulative percentage is multiplied by total revenue to determine the revised revenue amount. This revenue amount, $260.4 million, includes the $60 million of revenue that was recognized in 2010. Therefore, the amount of revenue to be recognized in the current period is $200.4 million ($260.4 million − $60 million). The actual cost incurred for the period is then deducted from the revenue recognized in the same period to determine the gross profit.

In 2011, when the project is complete, costs incurred to date now total $390 million ($54 million in 2009, $200 million in 2010, and $136 million in 2011). One hundred percent of the contract revenue less any amounts recognized previously ($400 million − $260.4 million) is recognized in the current period. The actual cost incurred for the period is deducted from the revenue recognized in the same period to determine the gross profit.

The total contract revenue remains unchanged. However, the total cost rose from $360 million to $390 million after the change in estimate. This also means that total gross profit fell from $40 million to $10 million because of the increased costs.

Sometimes there are cost overruns in the last year of a contract. When that happens, the remaining amounts of revenue and costs are recognized in that year and the relevant percentage is ignored.

In the percentage-of-completion method, it is necessary to be subjective to some extent. As a result, errors are possible in determining the amount of revenue to be recognized and gross profit to be reported. But to wait until completion would seriously distort each period's financial statements. Naturally, if it is not possible to get dependable estimates of costs and progress, then the percentage-of-completion method cannot be used. In this situation, revenue is recognized to the extent of the contract costs that have been incurred; no gross profit is recognized until reliable estimates can be made or the contract has been completed.

If we assume that Warrior Construction is a public company and it was not able to estimate its costs reliably, it would recognize revenue equal to the costs incurred for the first two years. In the third year, it would recognize the remaining revenue of $146 ($400 − $200 − $54). Gross profit would be zero in the first two years (because revenue equals expenses) and the full gross profit earned would be recognized in 2011, the final year of the project. This method is often referred to as the zero profit method.

If we compare the **zero profit method** and the percentage-of-completion method for the same contract data, Warrior Construction would have recognized the following amounts for revenue and gross profit.

	Zero Profit Method		Percentage-of-Completion Method	
	Revenue	Gross Profit	Revenue	Gross Profit
2009	$ 54	$ 0	$ 60.0	$ 6.0
2010	200	0	200.4	0.4
2011	146	10	139.6	3.6
Totals	$400	$10	$400.0	$10.0

For Canadian private companies that are not reporting under IFRS, if the revenues and costs on a long-term project cannot be reliably measured, the completed contract method would be used to recognize revenue and gross profit. Under the **completed contract method**, revenues and gross profit are recognized only when the contract is completed.

We have reviewed the timing of revenue recognition for common revenue-generating activities including the sale of goods, provision of services, and long-term service and construction contracts. Revenue recognition is a complex topic with many more dimensions than we have explored here.

Currently, revenue recognition is the topic of a substantial joint project between IASB and FASB. The boards want to eliminate weaknesses in the current approach, which is commonly referred to as the earnings approach and which emphasizes the income statement. At the time of writing this textbook, a discussion paper had been issued. It is proposed that a contract-based approach be adopted for recognizing revenue which emphasizes the balance sheet. However, it is not anticipated that new criteria will be established for several years.

ACCOUNTING IN ACTION: ACROSS THE ORGANIZATION INSIGHT

"Revenue recognition accounting remains one of the most troublesome reporting issues for many companies," according to *CAmagazine*. "In fact, more than 40% of respondents to a recent survey rated revenue as being more vulnerable to errors and inaccuracies than any other key finance and accounting process." Why is revenue recognition so troublesome? Well, many departments and individuals in a company may be involved in the revenue-generating activities. In large companies, these activities occur every day in many departments: sales, production, customer service, shipping, and billing. Revenue recognition is also affected when the customer accepts the product or agrees that the service is complete. All of these activities mean that the revenue reporting risk remains high.

Source: Gerry Murray, "Revenue reporting risk remains high," *CAmagazine.com*, December 2008, http://www.camagazine.com/archives/print-edition/2008/dec/upfront/value-added/camagazine4221.aspx [accessed March 29, 2009]

What is the manager of the shipping department's role in making sure revenue is recognized in the appropriate period?

Expense Recognition

The basic **expense recognition criteria** state that expenses are recognized when there is a decrease in an asset or increase in a liability, excluding transactions with owners. This is not necessarily when cash is paid. For example, as supplies are used, the asset Supplies is decreased and an expense is recognized. Alternatively, when a liability for wages payable is recorded, wage expense is recognized.

Expense recognition is tied to revenue recognition when there is a direct association between costs incurred and the earning of revenue. For example, there is a direct association between cost of goods sold and sales revenue. As we learned in Chapter 3, this process is commonly referred to as matching. Under matching, revenues and expenses that relate to the same transaction are recorded in the same accounting period.

Sometimes, however, there is no direct relationship between expenses and revenue. When it is hard to find a direct relationship, and assets are expected to benefit several accounting periods, a rational and systematic allocation policy can sometimes be developed instead.

To develop an allocation policy, assumptions have to be made about the benefits that will be received. Assumptions must also be made about the costs associated with those benefits. For example, the cost of a long-lived asset can be allocated to depreciation expense over the life of the asset because it can be determined that the asset contributes in some way to revenue generation during the asset's entire useful life.

In other cases, when expenditures are made that do not qualify for the recognition of an asset, an expense is recognized immediately. For example, expenditures for research do not qualify for recognition of an asset as it is impossible to determine the future benefits arising from the research, so the research costs are expensed immediately.

Sometimes a previously recognized asset ceases to have future benefit, and the asset must be expensed. For example, inventory that is obsolete and cannot be sold is expensed when it becomes apparent it cannot be sold.

In summary, costs need to be analyzed to determine whether it is probable there is a future benefit to the company or not. If there is a direct relationship between the revenues recognized and costs, the costs are recognized as expenses (matched against the revenue) in the period when the revenue is recognized. If it is hard to determine a direct relationship, but the costs are expected to benefit several periods, then it might be appropriate to systematically and rationally allocate the cost to expense over the periods that are expected to benefit. If there is no future benefit, or if the benefit is uncertain, the costs should simply be expensed in the current period.

Measurement of Elements

So far, we have looked at when items should be recognized or recorded in the accounting records. Now we will look at what dollar amounts should be used to record the items. There are a number of different measurements used in accounting. They include the following:

1. Cost
2. Fair value
3. Amortized cost

Assets are recorded at cost when they are acquired. Cost is used because it is both relevant and provides a faithful representation of the transaction. Cost represents the price paid, the assets sacrificed, or the commitment made at the date of acquisition. Cost is objectively measurable, factual, and verifiable. It is the result of an exchange transaction. Cost is relevant for reporting certain assets in the balance sheet because the assets are intended for use in the business and are not going to be sold.

Alternative terminology
Other common terms for fair value are market and realizable value.

However, for some assets it is more relevant to provide the assets' fair value: the amount of cash that is expected to be collected if the asset is sold. Users of financial information are better able to assess the impact of changes in fair value on the company's liquidity and solvency. For example, trading securities that are purchased for the purpose of resale are reported at their fair value in the financial statements. We will learn more about fair values used to report trading securities and some strategic long-term equity investments in Chapter 16.

Certain assets and liabilities, such as investments in bonds and bonds payable, are measured at amortized cost. We will learn more about amortized cost and investments in bonds and bonds payable in Chapters 15 and 16.

Cost is the most common basis used by companies in preparing their financial statements. Cost may be combined with other measurement bases. For example, you will recall from Chapter 6 that inventory is reported at the lower of cost and net realizable value.

ACCOUNTING IN ACTION: ALL ABOUT YOU

Before you started your post-secondary education, your parents may have invested cash in a Registered Education Savings Plan (RESP). An RESP is a special savings account registered with the Canadian government that helps families to save for students' education after high school. The plan allows the savings to grow tax-free and the government provides additional funds to the savings account through the Canada Education Savings Grant. The funds in the RESP may be invested in a simple cash savings account, a guaranteed investment certificate, or an equity investment fund. If the funds are invested in an equity investment fund, the value of the RESP will fluctuate with the market values of the equities in the investment fund.

The cost to your parents is the amount they have put into the RESP. However, combined with the contributions from your parents, the Canadian government grants, and the income earned on the amount invested in the RESP, the account's value may be significantly higher than the cost to your parents. On the other hand, if there is a significant portion in equity and the market fluctuates, it might be worth a lot less. An RESP is a valuable asset for you as a student as you pursue your education.

If you were preparing your personal financial report, what information about your RESP would be relevant: the cost of the RESP contributions or the fair value of the RESP?

Summary of Conceptual Framework

As we have seen, the conceptual framework for developing sound reporting practices starts with the objective of financial reporting. It then describes the underlying assumptions, the elements of the financial statements, the qualitative (fundamental and enhancing) characteristics of accounting information, and the constraints on financial reporting. Finally, more detailed recognition and measurement criteria are provided. The conceptual framework is summarized in Illustration 11-5.

The IASB and FASB are working on a joint project to improve the conceptual framework. At the time of writing this book, a discussion paper had been issued proposing new definitions for the financial statement elements. The standard-setting bodies are also working on a joint project to eliminate weaknesses in the current revenue recognition criteria. It is anticipated that there will be significant changes to GAAP in the next few years.

← **Illustration 11-5**

Conceptual framework

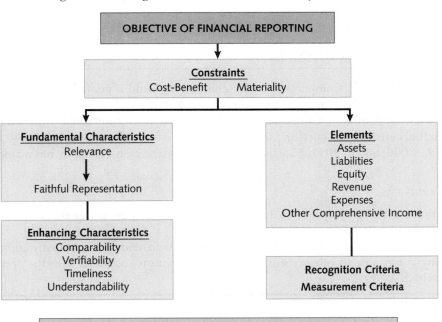

BEFORE YOU GO ON . . .

→ Review It

1. What is the basic criterion for revenue recognition under the current International Financial Reporting Standards?
2. What are the revenue recognition criteria for the sale of goods?
3. Describe when expenses are recognized.
4. What is stated about revenue recognition in Note 2 Significant Accounting Policies found in the financial statements of The Forzani Group Ltd.? The answer to this question is at the end of the chapter.

→ Do It

For each of the following independent situations, indicate if the revenue should be recognized in 2010 or 2011.

(a) Customer orders widgets on December 15, 2010; widgets are shipped FOB destination December 24, 2010; customer receives the goods January 15, 2011.
(b) Customer orders widgets on December 15, 2010; widgets are shipped FOB shipping point December 14, 2010; customer receives the goods January 15, 2011.

Action Plan
• Determine when all the significant risks and rewards of ownership have been transferred to the customer.

Solution
(a) Revenue should be recognized in 2011 as the seller retains ownership until the customer receives the goods.
(b) Revenue should be recognized in 2010 as ownership of the widgets is transferred to the customer when the goods are shipped.

The Navigator

Related exercise material: BE11–5, BE11–6, BE11–7, BE11–8, BE11–9, BE11–10, BE11–11, BE11–12, BE11–13, E11–4, E11–5, E11–6, E11–7, E11–8, E11–9, E11–10, and E11–11.

Demonstration Problems

Demonstration Problem

The Wu Construction Company is under contract to build a condominium building at a contract price of $2 million. The building will take 18 months to complete, at an estimated cost of $1.4 million. Construction begins in November 2009 and is finished in April 2011. Actual construction costs incurred in each year are as follows: in 2009, $140,000; in 2010, $910,000; and in 2011, $350,000. The Wu Construction Company has a December year end.

Instructions

(a) Calculate the gross profit to be recognized in each year using the percentage-of-completion method.
(b) Calculate the gross profit to be recognized in each year if Wu Construction Company is not able to reliably estimate the construction costs and uses the zero profit method.

Solution to Demonstration Problem

($ in thousands)

(a) Percentage-of-completion method

Year	Costs Incurred (Current Period)	÷	Total Estimated Cost	=	Percentage Complete (Current Period)	×	Total Revenue	=	Revenue Recognized (Current Period)	−	Costs Incurred (Current Period)	=	Gross Profit (Current Period)
2009	$ 140		$1,400		10%		$2,000		$ 200		$ 140		$ 60
2010	910		1,400		65%		2,000		1,300		910		390
2011	350		1,400		25%		2,000		500		350		150
Totals	$1,400								$2,000		$1,400		$600

(b) Zero profit method

Year	Revenue Recognized in Current Period	Costs Incurred in Current Period	Gross Profit Recognized in Current Period
2009	$ 140	$ 140	$ 0
2010	910	910	0
2011	950	350	600
Totals	$2,000	$1,400	$600

Action Plan

• The percentage-of-completion method recognizes revenue as construction occurs. The ongoing construction is viewed as a series of sales.
• Determine the percentage complete by dividing the costs incurred by total estimated costs.
• Multiply the percentage complete by the contract price to find the revenue to be recognized in the current period.
• Calculate gross profit: revenue recognized less actual costs incurred.
• If costs cannot be reliably estimated, no gross profit is recognized until the remaining costs can be reliably estimated.
• Record revenues equal to costs incurred each year until the year the contract is completed or cost can be reliably estimated.

The Navigator

Summary of Study Objectives

1. Explain the importance of having a conceptual framework of accounting, and list the components. The conceptual framework ensures that there is a consistent and coherent set of accounting standards. The key components of the conceptual framework are: (1) the objective of financial reporting, (2) the underlying assumptions, (3) the elements of financial statements, (4) the qualitative characteristics of accounting information, (5) the constraints on financial reporting, and (6) recognition and measurement criteria.

2. Identify and apply the objective of financial reporting and the underlying assumptions used by accountants. The objective of financial reporting is to provide useful information for investors and creditors in making decisions in their capacity as capital providers. The underlying assumptions are that, unless otherwise stated, the financial statements have been prepared using accrual accounting and the going concern assumption.

3. Describe the fundamental and enhancing qualitative characteristics of financial reporting. The fundamental qualitative characteristics are relevance and faithful representation. Accounting information has relevance if it makes a difference in a decision. Information is faithfully represented when it shows the economic reality.

The enhancing qualitative characteristics are comparability, verifiability, timeliness, and understandability.

Comparability enables users to identify the similarities and differences between companies. The consistent use of accounting policies from year to year is part of the comparability characteristic. Information is verifiable if two knowledgeable and independent people would generally agree that it faithfully represents the economic reality. Timeliness means that accounting information is provided when it is still highly useful for decision-making. Understandability enables users to gain insights into the company's financial position and results of operations.

4. Identify and apply the constraints on financial reporting. The major constraints are the cost-benefit and materiality constraints. The cost-benefit constraint exists to ensure the value of the information is more than the cost of providing it. If an item does not make a difference in decision-making, it is immaterial and GAAP does not have to be followed.

5. Identify and apply the basic recognition and measurement concepts of accounting. The revenue recognition criteria require that revenue be recognized when assets have increased or liabilities have decreased as a result of a transaction with a customer. Expenses are recognized when there is a decrease in an asset or increase in a liability, excluding transactions with owners. Three measurements used in accounting are cost, fair value, and amortized cost.

Glossary

Accrual accounting assumption The assumption that the accrual basis of accounting has been used. (p. 618)

Accrual basis of accounting The method of accounting where revenues are recorded in the period when the transaction occurs and not when cash is received or paid. (p. 618)

Comparability An enhancing qualitative characteristic that accounting information has if it can be compared with the accounting information of other companies because the companies all use the same accounting principles. (p. 621)

Completed contract method A method of recognizing revenue and gross profit on a project where they are recognized when the project is completed. (p. 631)

Complete The characteristic of accounting information when it provides all information necessary to show the economic reality of the transactions. Completeness is part of the faithful representation fundamental qualitative characteristic of accounting information. (p. 620)

Conceptual framework of accounting A coherent system of interrelated elements that guides the development and application of accounting principles: it includes the objective of financial reporting, underlying assumptions, elements of financial statements, qualitative characteristics of accounting information, constraints, and recognition and measurement criteria. (p. 616)

Consistency The use of the same accounting policies from year to year. Consistency is part of the comparability enhancing qualitative characteristic of accounting information. (p. 621)

Cost-benefit constraint The constraint that the costs of obtaining and providing information should not be more than the benefits that are gained. (p. 624)

Elements of financial statements The basic categories in financial statements: assets, liabilities, equity, revenue, expenses, and other comprehensive income. (p. 619)

Expense recognition criteria The criteria that state that expenses should be recognized when there is a decrease in an asset or increase in a liability, excluding transactions with owners. (p. 631)

Faithful representation A fundamental qualitative characteristic of accounting information that shows the economic reality of a transaction and not just its legal form. (p. 620)

Full disclosure The accounting concept that requires the disclosure of circumstances and events that make a difference to financial statement users. (p. 623)

Going concern assumption The assumption that the company will continue operating for the foreseeable future; that is, long enough to achieve its goals and respect its commitments. (p. 618)

Material error An error in the accounting information that could impact an investor's or creditor's decision. (p. 621)

Materiality constraint The constraint of determining whether an item is important enough to influence the decision of a reasonably careful investor or creditor. (p. 625)

Neutral The characteristic of accounting information when it is free from bias that is intended to attain a predetermined result or to encourage a particular behaviour. Neutrality is part of the faithful representation fundamental qualitative characteristic of accounting information. (p. 621)

Objective of financial reporting The goal of providing useful information for investors and creditors in making decisions in their capacity as capital providers. (p. 617)

Percentage-of-completion method A method of recognizing revenue on a long-term construction or service contract. When costs can be reliably estimated, a portion of the total revenue can be recognized in each period by applying a percentage of completion. This percentage is determined by dividing the actual costs incurred by the estimated costs for the entire project. (p. 628)

Relevance A fundamental qualitative characteristic that accounting information has if it makes a difference in a decision. (p. 620)

Revenue recognition criteria The criteria that state that revenue should be recognized when there is an increase in assets or decrease in liabilities from profit-generating activities. (p. 626)

Timeliness An enhancing qualitative characteristic that accounting information has if it is provided when it is still highly useful to decision-makers. (p. 622)

Understandability An enhancing qualitative characteristic of accounting information that enables users to gain insights into the company's financial position and results of operations. (p. 622)

Verifiability An enhancing qualitative characteristic of accounting information that assures users that the information shows the economic reality of the transaction. (p. 622)

Zero profit method A method of recognizing revenue where revenue is recognized to the extent of costs incurred and no gross profit is recognized until the contract is complete or costs can be estimated, (p. 630)

Self-Study Questions

WILEY PLUS Quizzes

Answers are at the end of the chapter.

(SO 1) K **1.** Which of the following is *not* one of the components of the conceptual framework?
(a) Underlying assumptions
(b) Qualitative characteristics
(c) The dimensions of the financial statements
(d) Recognition and measurement criteria

(SO 1) K **2.** Which of the following is *not* a reason for having a conceptual framework for financial reporting?
(a) To provide specific rules for every situation in accounting
(b) To ensure that existing standards and practices are clear and consistent
(c) To make it possible to respond quickly to new issues
(d) To increase the usefulness of the financial information presented in financial reports

(SO 2) K **3.** Which of the following is *not* information that is required to meet the objective of financial reporting?
(a) Information about the economic resources and claims on the economic resources
(b) Information about the company management's personal economic resources
(c) Information about the changes in economic resources and claims on the economic resources
(d) Information about the economic performance of the reporting entity

(SO 2) C **4.** Which of the following is *not* an example of accrual accounting?
(a) Sales revenue for goods sold on credit is recorded when the goods are shipped.
(b) Interest expense is debited and interest payable is credited on December 31.
(c) The utility expense for December is recorded in January when the bill is paid.
(d) Prepaid insurance is debited and cash is credited when the annual insurance bill is paid.

(SO 3) K **5.** The qualitative characteristics that must be applied first to ensure that information is useful are:
(a) relevance and comparability.
(b) relevance and faithful representation.
(c) faithful representation and verifiability.
(d) faithful representation and comparability.

(SO 3) K **6.** The full disclosure concept says that financial statements:
(a) should disclose all assets at their cost.
(b) should disclose only those events that can be measured in dollars.
(c) should disclose all events and circumstances that would matter to users of financial statements.
(d) should not be relied on unless an auditor has expressed an unqualified opinion on them.

(SO 4) C **7.** An item is considered material when:
(a) it is more than $500.
(b) it affects profits.
(c) not reporting it would influence or change a decision.
(d) it occurs infrequently.

(SO 5) K **8.** Which of the following is *not* a condition that must be met for revenue recognition on the sale of goods?
(a) The seller does not have control over the goods or continuing managerial involvement.
(b) The amount of the revenue can be reliably measured.
(c) Cash is collected.
(d) The seller has transferred to the buyer the significant risks and rewards of ownership.

(SO 5) C **9.** It is not appropriate to use the percentage-of-completion method for long-term construction contracts when:
(a) it is not possible to get reliable estimates of costs and progress.
(b) it is estimated that the project will take seven years to construct.
(c) cash is collected from the customer every month during construction.
(d) you are not 100% certain as to what the total costs to complete the project will be.

(SO 5) C **10.** Which of the following is *not* an appropriate time to recognize an expense?
(a) When cash is paid for the purchase of computer equipment
(b) When an expenditure is made that does not qualify for the recognition of an asset
(c) When the cost of computer equipment is allocated over its useful life
(d) When a previously recorded asset no longer has any future benefit

The Navigator

Questions

(SO 1) C 1. Describe the conceptual framework of accounting and explain how it helps financial reporting.

(SO 1) C 2. Why are principles-based standards better than rules-based standards?

(SO 2) K 3. What is the basic objective of financial reporting?

(SO 2) C 4. Explain the underlying assumptions of: (a) accrual accounting and (b) going concern.

(SO 2) C 5. (a) Why does it matter whether accountants assume an economic entity will remain a going concern? (b) How does the going concern assumption support reporting the cost of an asset instead of its fair value?

(SO 3) K 6. Identify and explain the two fundamental qualitative characteristics of accounting information.

(SO 3) K 7. Identify and explain the four enhancing qualitative characteristics of accounting information.

(SO 3) C 8. What is the difference between comparability and consistency?

(SO 3) K 9. The qualitative characteristics should be applied in a certain order. Identify the order and explain why it matters.

(SO 3) C 10. Explain the accounting concept of full disclosure.

(SO 4) C 11. Describe the two constraints that affect the accounting information reported in financial statements.

(SO 3, 4) C 12. Explain how the full disclosure concept relates to the cost-benefit constraint.

(SO 4) C 13. The controller of Mustafa Corporation rounded all dollar figures in the company's financial statements to the nearest thousand dollars. "It's not important for our users to know how many pennies we spend," she said. Do you believe rounded financial figures can provide useful information for decision-making? Explain why or why not.

(SO 4) C 14. Isabelle believes that the same GAAP should be used by every company, whether large or small and whether public or private. Do you agree? Explain your answer by referring to the appropriate accounting constraint.

(SO 5) C 15. Why is revenue recognition a difficult concept to apply in practice?

(SO 5) K 16. Describe the general criteria for revenue recognition under International Financial Reporting Standards.

(SO 5) K 17. What are the five conditions that must be met for revenue to be recognized from the sale of goods?

(SO 5) K 18. What are the four conditions that must be met for revenue and gross profit from long-term service and construction contracts to be recognized using the percentage-of-completion method?

(SO 5) C 19. What are the advantages of using the percentage-of-completion method to recognize revenue?

(SO 5) C 20. Explain how the percentage-of-completion method should be adjusted when a company's cost estimates change during the contract period.

(SO 5) AP 21. (a) Under what circumstances is it not appropriate to recognize revenue and gross profit using the percentage-of-completion method for long-term service and construction contracts? (b) Describe how revenue and gross profit would be recognized under these circumstances.

(SO 5) K 22. Describe when expenses should be recognized.

(SO 5) C 23. Explain why certain assets are reported at fair value not cost.

Brief Exercises

Identify items included in the conceptual framework.
(SO 1) K

BE11–1 Indicate which of the following items are included in the conceptual framework. (Write "Yes" or "No" beside each item.)

(a) The analysis of financial statement ratios
(b) The objective of financial reporting
(c) The qualitative characteristics of accounting information
(d) The elements of financial statements
(e) The rules for calculating taxable income
(f) The constraints on applying generally accepted accounting principles
(g) The measurement of the market value of a business

BE11–2 Presented below are the underlying assumptions of accounting standards.

1. Accrual accounting
2. Going concern

Identify assumptions in the conceptual framework.
(SO 2) C

For each of the following, indicate the assumption that has been violated.

(a) ___ All of the company's assets are reported in the balance sheet at the amount expected to be collected if the assets were sold.
(b) ___ The sale of goods received by the customer in December was recorded as revenue in January when the cash was collected from the customer.

BE11–3 Here are the basic elements of financial statements that we learned about in earlier chapters:

Identify elements of financial statements.
(SO 2) K

1. Assets	4. Revenues
2. Liabilities	5. Expenses
3. Owner's equity	6. Drawings

Instructions

Each statement that follows is an important aspect of an element's definition. Match the elements with the definitions. *Note*: More than one number can be placed in a blank. Each number may be used more than once or not at all.

(a) ___ Increases in assets or decreases in liabilities resulting from the main business activities of the organization
(b) ___ Existing debts and obligations from past transactions
(c) ___ Resources owned by a business
(d) ___ Goods or services used in the process of earning revenue
(e) ___ A residual claim on total assets after deducting liabilities
(f) ___ The capacity to provide future benefits to the organization

BE11–4 Presented below is a set of qualitative characteristics of accounting information:

Identify qualitative characteristics.
(SO 3) K

1. Predictive value	6. Comparability
2. Neutral	7. Feedback value
3. Verifiability	8. Consistency
4. Timeliness	9. Understandability
5. Faithful representation	

Instructions

Match these qualitative characteristics to the following statements, using numbers 1 to 9.

(a) ___ Accounting information must be available to decision-makers before the information loses its ability to influence their decisions.
(b) ___ Accounting information provides a basis to evaluate decisions made in the past.
(c) ___ Accounting information cannot be selected, prepared, or presented to favour one set of interested users over another.
(d) ___ Accounting information reports the economic substance of a transaction, not its legal form.
(e) ___ Accounting information helps reduce uncertainty about the future.
(f) ___ Accounting information must be provided in a way that knowledgeable and independent people agree that it faithfully represents the economic reality of the transaction or event.
(g) ___ Accounting information about one company can be evaluated in relation to accounting information from another company.
(h) ___ Accounting information is prepared based on the assumption that users have a reasonable understanding of accounting concepts and procedures, and of general business and economic conditions.
(i) ___ Accounting information in a company is prepared using the same principles and methods year after year.

Identify violation of concept or constraint.
(SO 4, 5) AP

BE11–5 For each of the following, indicate the accounting concept or constraint that has been violated, if any:

(a) The company currently records its accounting transactions and prepares its financial reports manually. The cost of using a new computerized accounting system to do these tasks is estimated at $25,000. Annual savings are expected to be $10,000.

(b) Inventory is reported at cost when market value is higher.

(c) Paper clips expense appears on the income statement, at $10.

(d) Bad debt expense is recorded in the period when the account receivable is written off.

(e) Small tools are recorded as long-lived assets and depreciated.

Identify concept, assumption, or constraint.
(SO 2, 3, 4, 5) C

BE11–6 Here are some of the accounting concepts, assumptions, and constraints discussed in this chapter:

1. Going concern
2. Economic entity
3. Matching
4. Full disclosure
5. Cost
6. Cost-benefit
7. Materiality

Instructions

Identify by number the accounting assumption, concept, or constraint that describes each situation below. Do not use a number more than once.

(a) ___ is why land is not reported at its liquidation value. (Do not use item 5, cost.)

(b) ___ indicates that personal and business record-keeping should be kept separate.

(c) ___ ensures that all relevant financial information is reported.

(d) ___ requires that GAAP be followed for all significant items.

(e) ___ requires expenses to be recognized in the same period as related revenues.

(f) ___ indicates the value at which an asset is recorded when acquired.

Identify concepts.
(SO 4, 5) C

BE11–7 A list of accounting concepts follows:

1. Revenue recognition
2. Matching
3. Full disclosure
4. Cost
5. Expense recognition
6. Fair value

Instructions

Match these concepts to the following statements, using numbers 1 to 6.

(a) ___ The Hirjikaka Company reports information about pending lawsuits in the notes to its financial statements.

(b) ___ The Sudin Company reduces prepaid insurance to reflect the insurance that has expired.

(c) ___ The Joss Company recognizes revenue at the point of sale, not when the cash is collected.

(d) ___ The Rich Bank reports its short-term investments that are held for resale at market.

(e) ___ The Hilal Company reports its land at the price it paid for it, not at what it is now worth.

(f) ___ The law firm Thériault, Lévesque, and Picard records interim billings and costs for its clients at the end of each month.

(g) ___ The Nickel Company depreciates its mining equipment using the units-of-production method.

Determine point of revenue and expense recognition.
(SO 5) AP

BE11–8 Howie, Price, and Whynot operate an accounting firm. In March, their staff worked a total of 2,000 hours at an average billing rate of $200 per hour. They sent bills to clients in the month of March that totalled $150,000. They expect to bill the balance of their time in April, when the work is complete. The firm's salary costs total $100,000 each month. How much revenue should the firm recognize in the month of March? How much salaries expense?

BE11–9 Mullen Manufacturing Ltd. sold $350,000 of merchandise on credit in the month of September to customers. All of the merchandise was sold FOB shipping point. At September 30, $25,000 of the merchandise was in transit. During September, the company collected $250,000 of cash from its customers. The company estimates that about 1% of the sales will become uncollectible and that about 2% of the sales will be returned by customers. How much revenue should the company recognize for the month of September? Describe how the uncollectible sales and returns by the customers should be accounted for.

Determine revenue to be recognized.
(SO 5) AP

BE11–10 Abbotsford Ltd., a sports equipment wholesaler, sold $275,000 of merchandise during November to customers. The cost of the merchandise shipped was $150,000. All of the merchandise was shipped FOB destination. At November 30, $35,000 of the merchandise was in transit. The cost of the merchandise in transit was $19,000. During November, Abbotsford purchased $100,000 of merchandise inventory and made cash payments for merchandise inventory of $125,000. How much revenue should the company recognize for the month of November? What is the gross profit recognized in November?

Determine revenue and expenses to be recognized.
(SO 5) AP

BE11–11 Flin Flon Construction Company is under contract to build a commercial building at a price of $4.2 million. Construction begins in January 2009 and finishes in December 2011. Total estimated construction costs are $2.8 million. Actual construction costs incurred in each year are as follows: in 2009, $840,000; in 2010, $1,120,000; and in 2011, $840,000. Calculate the revenue and gross profit to be recognized in each year, using the percentage-of-completion method.

Calculate revenue and gross profit—percentage-of-completion method.
(SO 5) AP

BE11–12 Refer to the data presented in BE11–11. Assume that the estimated total costs rose from $2.8 million to $3.1 million in 2010. Actual costs incurred are $840,000 in 2009, $1,260,000 in 2010, and $1 million in 2011. Calculate the revenue and gross profit that should be recognized each year, using the percentage-of-completion method.

Calculate revenue and gross profit with change in estimate—percentage-of-completion method.
(SO 5) AP

BE11–13 Refer to the data presented in BE11–11. Calculate the revenue and gross profit to be recognized in each year, assuming that Flin Flon is not able to reliably estimate the construction costs and uses the zero profit method.

Calculate revenue and gross profit—zero profit method.
(SO5) AP

Exercises

E11–1 The Skate Stop is owned by Marc Bélanger. It sells in-line skates and accessories. It shares space with another company, Ride Snowboards. Ride Snowboards is owned by Marc's wife, Dominique Maltais, who was an Olympic bronze medallist in snowboarding. Ride Snowboards sells snowboards and related accessories. The following transactions occurred during a recent year:

Apply the economic entity assumption.
(SO 2) AP

(a) In January, Marc purchased fire and theft insurance for the year to cover the rented space and inventory. He paid for all the insurance since he had more cash than Dominique.
(b) Dominique paid the rent for the month of July since she had more cash that month than Marc.
(c) Marc recorded skate sales for the month of September.
(d) Dominique purchased and paid for her winter inventory of snowboards in September.
(e) Marc and Dominique had such a successful year that they went out to a fancy restaurant to celebrate. They charged the bill to Marc's company.
(f) Dominique paid her annual membership fee to the local ski hill from company funds.
(g) Marc paid his annual membership fee to the curling club from company funds.

Instructions

Identify which of the above transactions should be recorded by Skate Stop, and which should be recorded by Ride Snowboards. State also if the transaction cost is a personal one or if it relates to both companies and should be allocated to each of them.

Discuss accounting policy choices and objective of financial reporting.
(SO 2, 3) C

E11–2 When they have to choose among generally accepted accounting principles, some managers may try to adopt policies that allow them to influence the company's profit.

Instructions

(a) Explain why a manager might be motivated to try to influence profit.
(b) Give an example of an accounting policy choice that management could use to (1) improve the company's profit, and (2) reduce the company's profit.
(c) How would this type of behaviour meet, or not meet, the objective of financial reporting?
(d) Explain how likely it is that a manager would be able to change accounting principles to manage profits as you describe in (b).

Identify qualitative characteristics.
(SO 3) C

E11–3 Presented below is a set of qualitative characteristics of accounting information.

1. Relevance
2. Neutrality
3. Verifiability
4. Timeliness
5. Faithful representation
6. Comparability
7. Consistency
8. Understandability

Instructions

For each of the following, indicate which qualitative characteristic was violated.

(a) ___ Allen Ltd. reported its merchandise inventory at a net realizable value of $25,000. The company's auditors disagree with this value and estimated the net realizable value to be $20,000.
(b) ___ Owens Corporation does not issue its annual financial statements for the year ended December 31, 2009, until November 2010.
(c) ___ Silver Mining Ltd. is the only company in the mining industry that uses the straight-line method to depreciate its mining equipment.
(d) ___ Chapman Ltd. switches inventory cost formulas from average to FIFO and back to average in a three-year period.
(e) ___ Enco Ltd. intentionally recorded revenue in 2009, for sales made in 2010, to ensure that management would receive their bonuses, which were based on profits.
(f) ___ World Talk Corporation used terminology in its financial statements and notes to the financial statements that is not commonly used in financial reporting and did not provide explanations of the terminology.
(g) ___ Precision R Us Ltd., a multinational drilling company, reported separately its paper, paper clips, and pens in the balance sheet rather than reporting a single line item for office supplies. Total office supplies were $5,000.
(h) ___ Community Health Foods Ltd. signed a legal agreement to finance the purchase of equipment. The agreement required annual payments of $15,000 for five years. The agreement referred to the payments as rental payments. The company records rent expense when the annual payments are made.

Identify assumption, constraint, or concept.
(SO 2, 3, 5) C

E11–4 Here are some assumptions, constraints, and concepts discussed in this chapter:

1. Going concern
2. Economic entity
3. Matching
4. Full disclosure
5. Cost
6. Cost-benefit
7. Materiality

Instructions

Identify by number the accounting assumption, principle, or constraint that describes each situation below. Do not use a number more than once.

(a) ___ Barb Denton runs her accounting practice out of her home. She separates her business records from her household accounts.

(b) ___ The cost should not be more than the benefits.

(c) ___ Significant accounting policies are reported in the notes to the financial statements.

(d) ___ Assets are not stated at their liquidation value.

(e) ___ Dollar amounts on financial statements are often rounded to the nearest thousand.

(f) ___ Bad debts expense is recorded using the allowance method of accounting.

(g) ___ Land is recorded at its cost of $100,000 rather than at its market value of $150,000.

E11–5 Several reporting situations follow:

1. Tercek Company recognizes revenue during the production cycle. The price of the product and how many items will be sold are not certain.

2. In preparing its financial statements, Seco Company left out information about its cost flow assumption for inventories.

3. Martinez Company amortizes patents over their legal life of 20 years instead of their economic life, which is usually about five years.

4. Ravine Hospital Supply Corporation reports only current assets and current liabilities on its balance sheet. Long-term assets and liabilities are reported as current. The company is unlikely to be liquidated.

5. Barton Company reports inventory on its balance sheet at its current market value of $100,000. The inventory has an original cost of $110,000.

6. Bonilla Company is in its third year of operations and has not yet issued financial statements.

7. Watts Company has inventory on hand that cost $400,000. Watts reports inventory on its balance sheet at its current market value of $425,000.

8. Steph Wolfson, president of the Download Music Company, bought a computer for her personal use. She paid for the computer with company funds and debited the computer account.

9. Smith Company decided not to implement a perpetual inventory system that would save $40,000 annually. The cost of the system was $100,000 and was estimated to have a 10-year life.

Identify qualitative characteristic, assumption, constraint, or concept violated.

(SO 2, 3, 4, 5) AP

Instructions

For each of the above, list the qualitative characteristic, assumption, constraint, or concept that has been violated, if any.

E11–6 Business transactions for Ellis Co. follow:

1. Equipment worth $100,000 is acquired at a cost of $85,000 from a company going out of business. The following entry is made:

Equipment	100,000	
Cash		85,000
Gain		15,000

2. The president of Ellis Co., Evan Ellis, purchases a truck for personal use and charges it to his expense account. The following entry is made:

Travel Expense	42,000	
Cash		42,000

Identify assumption, concept, or constraint violated and correct entries.

(SO 2, 4, 5) AN

3. An account receivable becomes a bad debt. The following entry is made:

Bad Debts Expense	5,000	
Accounts Receivable		5,000

4. Merchandise inventory with a cost of $255,000 is reported at its fair value of $280,000. The following entry is made:

Merchandise Inventory	25,000	
Gain		25,000

5. An electric pencil sharpener costing $40 is being depreciated over five years. The following entry is made:

Depreciation Expense	8	
Accumulated Depreciation—Pencil Sharpener		8

6. East Air sells an airline ticket for $650 in February for a trip scheduled in April. The following entry is made:

Cash	650	
Flight Revenue		650

Instructions

In each of the situations above, identify the assumption, concept, or constraint that has been violated, if any. If a journal entry is incorrect, give the correct entry.

Identify point of revenue recognition.
(SO 5) C

E11–7   The following situations require professional judgement to determine when to recognize revenue from the transactions:

(a) Air Canada sells you a nonrefundable Tango fare airline ticket in September for your flight home at Christmas.
(b) Leon's Furniture sells you a home theatre on a "no money down, no interest, and no payments for one year" promotional deal.
(c) The Toronto Blue Jays sell season tickets to games in the Rogers Centre on-line. Fans can purchase the tickets at any time, although the season doesn't officially begin until April. It runs from April through October.
(d) Babineau Company sells merchandise with terms of 2/10, n/30, FOB destination.
(e) In September, Centennial College collects tuition revenue for the term from students. The term runs from September through December.
(f) The College Bookstore has the following return policy for textbook sales: "Textbooks (new and used) may be returned for seven calendar days from the start of classes. After that time, textbooks (new and used) may be returned within 48 hours of purchase."

Instructions

Identify when revenue should be recognized in each of the above situations.

Identify point of revenue recognition.
(SO 5) C

E11–8   Over the winter months, the Green-Lawn Company pre-sells fertilizing and weed control lawn services to be performed from May through September, inclusive. If payment is made in full by April 1, a 10% discount is allowed. In March, 250 customers took advantage of the discount and purchased the summer lawn service package for $540 each. In June, 300 customers purchased the package for $600, and in July, 150 purchased it for the same price. For customers who pay after May 1 service starts in the month payment is made by the customer.

Instructions

How much revenue should be recognized by the Green-Lawn Company in each of the months of March, April, May, June, July, August, and September? Explain.

E11–9 Consider the following transactions of the Mitrovica Company, a diversified manufacturing and construction company, for the year ended December 31, 2009:

Determine amount of revenue to be recognized.
(SO 5) AP

(a) Leased office space for a one-year period beginning September 1. Three months of rent at $2,000 per month was received in advance.

(b) Received a sales order for merchandise that cost $9,000. It was sold for $16,000 on December 28 to Warfield Company. The goods were shipped FOB destination on December 31. Warfield received them on January 3, 2010.

(c) Signed a long-term contract to construct a building at a total price of $1.6 million. The total estimated cost of construction is $1.2 million. During 2009, the company incurred $300,000 of costs and collected $400,000 in cash.

(d) Mitrovica introduced a new product into the market. The company shipped product costing $25,000 to its regular customers. The customers were billed $50,000 for the product. To promote the product, Mitrovica does not require payment until June 2010 and if Mitrovica's customers do not sell all of the product by June 2010 they can return the unsold product to Mitrovica. The product is new and Mitrovica is uncertain if it will sell.

(e) Issued a $6,000, six-month, 5% note receivable on August 1, with interest payable at maturity.

(f) Received a sales order for $20,000 of merchandise that cost $10,000 from a new customer. The customer was required to prepay the invoice. On December 29, 2009, a cheque for $20,000 was received from the customer. The merchandise was shipped on January 4, 2010.

Instructions

For each item above, indicate the amount of revenue Mitrovica should recognize in 2009. Explain.

E11–10 Shen Construction Company had a long-term construction project that lasted three years. The project had a contract price of $150 million with total estimated costs of $100 million. Shen used the percentage-of-completion method. At the end of construction, the following actual costs had been incurred:

Calculate gross profit—percentage-of-completion method.
(SO 5) AP

	2009	2010	2011
Actual cost	$25 million	$55 million	$20 million

Instructions

(a) Calculate the gross profit that was recognized for each year of the construction contract.

(b) Assume instead that at the beginning of 2010, Shen revised the total estimated cost remaining for the last year of the contract to $25 million instead of $20 million. Actual costs incurred in 2011 were later determined to be $25 million. Calculate the gross profit that was recognized for each year of the construction contract.

E11–11 Refer to the data in E11–10(a) for Shen Construction Company. Assume that Shen was not able to reliably estimate the cost of the construction project.

Calculate gross profit—zero profit method.
(SO 5) AP

Instructions

Calculate the gross profit that should be recognized for each year of the construction contract if the zero profit method is used.

Problems: Set A

Comment on the objective of financial reporting, relevance, and faithful representation.
(SO 2, 3) C

P11–1A "Note 13. Commitments" in The Forzani Group Ltd.'s consolidated financial statements provides the following information on the future cash payments under lease agreements: "The Company is committed, at February 1, 2009, to minimum payments under long-term real property and data processing hardware and software equipment leases, for future years, as follows:

Year	Gross
2010	$87,523
2011	$77,283
2012	$65,083
2013	$52,753
2014	$40,403
Thereafter	$86,471"

Instructions

Explain why Forzani is required to disclose the future cash payments under its lease agreements. Support your answer with reference to the objective of financial reporting and the qualitative characteristics.

Taking It Further Refer to the Notes to Consolidated Financial Statements for The Forzani Group Ltd. in Appendix A and provide another example for which the company discloses required future cash payments.

Assumptions and concepts—going concern, full disclosure.
(SO 2, 3) AP

P11–2A General Motors Corporation reported significant losses from 2005 to 2008. General Motors acknowledged in its 2008 financial statements that with these losses, combined with the economic crisis in 2008 and the first part of 2009, it would not be able to meet its financial obligations. As a result, General Motors entered into an agreement with the United States government in which the government agreed to lend General Motors funds and the company made a commitment to restructure its operations. However, General Motors acknowledged that, due to the many uncertainties it faced, there was substantial doubt as to the company's ability to continue as a going concern.

Instructions

(a) What is the potential effect on a company's financial statements if the company files for bankruptcy?

(b) General Motors' 2008 consolidated financial statements were prepared under the assumption the company was a going concern. How did General Motors justify using the going concern assumption when it was so uncertain that the company would continue operating?

Taking It Further Describe the dilemma that a company's management faces in disclosing that a company may not be able to continue as a going concern.

Comment on objective of financial reporting, qualitative characteristics, and constraints.
(SO 1, 3, 4) C

P11–3A Starting in January 2011, Canadian public companies are required to follow International Financial Reporting Standards. The Canadian Accounting Standards Board recognized that a simpler approach to financial reporting was required for Canadian private enterprises and issued new Canadian GAAP specifically for private enterprises. Under the Canadian GAAP for Private Enterprises, there will be significantly less information required to be disclosed in the financial statements.

Instructions

Explain why it is appropriate that there are different reporting and disclosure standards for public and private companies. Support your answer with reference to the objective of financial reporting, qualitative characteristics, and the accounting constraints.

Taking It Further   Regardless of the new GAAP for Canadian private enterprises, a Canadian private company may choose to prepare its financial statements using International Financial Reporting Standards. In what circumstances might a Canadian private company choose to report under IFRS rather than under the simpler GAAP for private enterprises?

P11–4A   Czyz and Ng are accountants at Kwick Kopy Printers. Kwick Kopy has not adopted the revaluation model for accounting for its property, plant, and equipment. The accountants are having disagreements over the following transactions from the calendar year 2010:

Identify concept or assumption violated and prepare entries.
(SO 2, 4, 5) AN

1. Kwick Kopy bought equipment on January 1, 2010, for $80,000, including installation costs. The equipment has a useful life of five years. Kwick Kopy depreciates equipment using the double declining-balance method. "Since the equipment as installed in our system cannot be removed without considerable damage, it will have no resale value. It should not be depreciated but, instead, expensed immediately," Czyz argues.
2. Depreciation for the year was $43,000. Since the company's profit is expected to be low this year, Czyz suggests deferring depreciation to a year when there is higher profits.
3. Kwick Kopy purchased equipment at a fire sale for $36,000. The equipment would normally have cost $50,000. Czyz believes that the following entry should be made:

Equipment	50,000	
Cash		36,000
Gain		14,000

4. Czyz says that Kwick Kopy should carry its furnishings on the balance sheet at their liquidation value, which is $30,000 less than cost.
5. Kwick Kopy rented office space for one year, effective September 1, 2010. Six months of rent at $3,000 per month was paid in advance. Czyz believes that the following entry should be made on September 1:

Rent Expense	18,000	
Cash		18,000

6. Land that cost $41,000 was appraised at $59,000. Czyz suggests the following journal entry:

Land	18,000	
Gain on Appreciation of Land		18,000

7. On December 15, Kwick Kopy signed a contract with a customer to provide copying services for a six-month period at a rate of $1,500 per month starting January 1, 2011. The customer will pay on a monthly basis. Czyz argues that the contract should be recorded in December because the customer has always paid its bills on time in the past. The customer is legally obligated to pay the monthly amount because a contract has been signed. Czyz believes the following entry should be recorded:

Accounts Receivable	9,000	
Service Revenue		9,000

Ng disagrees with Czyz on each of the situations.

Instructions

(a) For each transaction, indicate why Ng disagrees. Support your answer with reference to the conceptual framework—definition of elements, characteristics, assumptions, constraints, recognition, and measurement criteria.
(b) Prepare the correct journal entry to record each transaction.

Taking It Further   Discuss the circumstances in which it is appropriate to record property, plant, and equipment at its liquidation value.

Identify assumption or
concepts and correct entries.
(SO 2, 5) AN

P11–5A Business transactions for Durkovitch Company from the current year follow. The company has not adopted the revaluation model of accounting for its property, plant, and equipment.

1. An order for $90,000 was received from a customer for products on hand. The customer paid a $10,000 deposit when the order was placed. The order is to be shipped on January 9 next year. The following entry was made:

Cash	10,000	
Accounts Receivable	80,000	
Sales		90,000

2. Because of a "flood sale," equipment worth $350,000 was acquired at a cost of $285,000. The following entry was made:

Equipment	350,000	
Cash		285,000
Gain on Acquisition of Equipment		65,000

3. Because the general level of prices decreased during the current year, Durkovitch determined that there was a $60,000 overstatement of depreciation expense on its equipment. The following entry was made:

Accumulated Depreciation	60,000	
Depreciation Expense		60,000

4. On December 31, merchandise purchased for resale was received. The following entry was made:

Cost of Goods Sold	78,000	
Accounts Payable		78,000

5. Land was purchased on April 30 for $230,000. The company plans to build a warehouse on the land. On December 31, the land would have cost $200,000. The following entry was made:

Loss on Decline in Value of Land	30,000	
Land		30,000

Instructions

(a) In each of the situations above, identify the assumption or concept that has been violated, if any.
(b) Prepare the journal entry to correct each incorrect transaction identified in (a).

Taking It Further   Would your answer for 5 have been different if the Durkovitch company was a real estate company and the land had been purchased for resale? Explain.

Identify point of revenue and
expense recognition.
(SO 5) C

P11–6A   Santa's Christmas Tree Farm grows pine, fir, and spruce trees. The company cuts and sells the trees for cash during the Christmas season. Most of the trees are exported to the United States. The remaining trees are sold to local tree lot operators.

It normally takes about 12 years for a tree to grow to a good size. The average selling price for a mature tree is $48. The owner of Santa's Christmas Tree Farm believes that the company should recognize revenue at the rate of $4 a year ($48 ÷ 12 years) for each tree that it cuts. The biggest cost of this business is the cost of fertilizing, pruning, and maintaining the trees over the 12-year period. These costs average $40 a tree and the owner believes they should also be spread over the 12-year period.

Instructions

Do you agree with the proposed revenue recognition policy for Santa's Christmas Tree Farms? Explain why or why not. Use the revenue recognition criteria to explain your argument for when the revenue should be recognized for this tree-farming business.

Taking It Further Explain how the costs of fertilizing, pruning, and maintaining the trees should be recorded.

P11–7A On February 11, 2010, Security Equipment was awarded a $6-million contract to develop a new security system for a nuclear plant. Work began on April 1 and estimated costs of completion at the contract date are $4.5 million over a two-year period. By December 31, 2010, Security Equipment's year end, costs of $1.8 million have been incurred. Contract payments totalling $2 million have been collected so far.

Calculate revenue at various points of recognition.
(SO 5) AP

Instructions

(a) Describe the two methods that may be used to recognize revenue for construction projects.

(b) Calculate the amount of revenue that would be recognized in fiscal 2010 for Security Equipment under each of the revenue recognition methods described in your response to (a).

Taking It Further Which method would you recommend that Security Equipment use? Explain why.

P11–8A Cosky Construction Company is involved in a long-term construction contract to build an office building. The estimated cost is $40 million and the contract price is $56 million. Additional information follows:

Calculate revenue, expense, and gross profit—percentage-of-completion and zero profit methods.
(SO 5) AP

Year	Cash Collections	Actual Costs Incurred
2009	$ 9,000,000	$ 6,000,000
2010	20,000,000	18,000,000
2011	14,000,000	10,000,000
2012	13,000,000	6,000,000
	$56,000,000	$40,000,000

The project is completed in 2012 as scheduled and all cash collections related to the contract have been received.

Instructions

(a) Prepare a schedule to determine the revenue, expense, and gross profit for each year of the contract, using the percentage-of-completion method.

(b) How would your answer in (a) change if Cosky Construction used the zero profit method?

Taking It Further Assume that Cosky can estimate costs reliably and that partway through the contract the customer encountered financial difficulty and fell behind in its cash payments, and Cosky is unsure if the customer will be able to pay the full amount owing. Would it still be appropriate to recognize revenue using the percentage-of-completion method? Explain.

P11–9A Refer to the data in P11–8A for Cosky Construction. Assume instead that the actual costs were $14 million in 2011. Because costs were higher than expected, Cosky revised its total estimated costs from $40 million to $48 million at the end of 2011. Actual costs incurred in 2012 were $10 million. All other data are unchanged.

Revise revenue, expense, and gross profit—percentage-of-completion.
(SO 5) AP

Instructions

Assuming Cosky Construction uses the percentage-of-completion method, prepare a revised schedule to determine the revenue, expense, and gross profit for each year of the long-term construction contract.

Taking It Further Assume that during 2010, Cosky Construction encountered difficulty in the construction of the office building as it discovered that the foundation was leaking and it was not able to estimate the costs to fix the foundation and complete the building reliably. Would it still be appropriate to use the percentage-of-completion method for the remaining years of the contract? Explain.

Calculate revenue, expense, and gross profit—percentage-of-completion method.
(SO 5) AP

P11–10A Kamloops Construction Company has a contract for the construction of a new health and fitness centre. It is accounting for this project using the percentage-of-completion method. The contract amount is $5.0 million and the cost of construction is expected to total $2.8 million. The actual costs incurred are as follows for the three-year life of the project:

Year	Actual Costs Incurred
2009	$1,120,000
2010	980,000
2011	700,000
	$2,800,000

Instructions

Calculate the amount of revenue, expense, and gross profit to be recognized in each year.

Taking It Further What if Kamloops Construction receives more cash in each of the first two years than the amount it has recognized as revenue? Is it still appropriate to recognize the amount of revenue as calculated? Explain.

Revenue recognition criteria—sale of goods.
(SO 5) AP

P11–11A Dave's Deep Discount Furniture Store opened for business October 1, 2009. To promote the store and develop a loyal customer base, customers could buy furniture with no money down and no payments for 12 months. Customers wishing to take advantage of the special promotion were required to pass a thorough credit check. Of the customers from October 1 to December 31, 2009, 75% took advantage of the special promotion; the other customers paid for the furniture in full when it was delivered. Total sales from October 1 to December 31, 2009, were $325,000, of which $250,000 was for customers who chose to delay payment for 12 months. Of the remaining $75,000 of sales, $60,000 worth had been delivered to the customers by December 31, 2009, and the remaining $15,000 would be delivered in January 2010. The accountant for the store made the following entry to record the sales.

Accounts Receivable	15,000	
Cash	60,000	
Sales Revenue		75,000

Dave disagreed with the accountant and argued that sales revenue of $325,000 should be recorded in 2009.

Instructions

(a) Identify the revenue recognition criteria that must be met before revenue is recorded for the sale of goods.
(b) Identify the critical factors relating to the Dave's Deep Discount Furniture Store's sales transactions that should be considered in determining how much revenue should be recognized.
(c) Indicate the amount of revenue that should be recognized for the period October 1 to December 31, 2009.

Taking It Further Would your response to (c) be different if the customers were not required to pass a thorough credit check? Explain why or why not.

Problems: Set B

Comment on relevance and faithful representation.
(SO 2, 3) C

P11–1B "Note 2. Significant Accounting Policies" in The Forzani Group Ltd.'s consolidated financial statements states: "The preparation of the financial statements in conformity with Canadian Generally Accepted Accounting Principles ('GAAP') requires management to make estimates and assumptions that affect the reported amounts of assets and liabilities and disclosures of contingent assets and liabilities at the date of the consolidated financial statements and the reported amounts of revenue and expenses during the reporting period. Actual results could differ materially from these estimates."

Instructions

Explain why Forzani's management is required to use estimates in the company's financial statements. Support your answer with reference to the objective of financial reporting and the qualitative characteristics.

Taking It Further   Which qualitative characteristics may be sacrificed when management is required to make estimates in the financial statements that may differ materially from actual results?

P11–2B   Air Canada reported a $1-billion loss for the year ended December 31, 2008. This loss, combined with increasing debt and pension obligations and reduced passenger travel during the first quarter of 2009, raised speculation by the financial markets that Air Canada's future is uncertain. If Air Canada is not able to meet its financial obligations, it may be forced into bankruptcy.

Comment on application of accounting assumptions and concepts.
(SO 2, 3) AP

Instructions

(a) What is the potential effect on a company's financial statements if the company files for bankruptcy?
(b) With the uncertainty facing Air Canada's future, should the company's financial statements be prepared under the assumption that it will continue to operate for the foreseeable future? Explain.

Taking It Further   Explain the implications of the full disclosure concept on Air Canada's financial statements in these circumstances.

P11–3B   Under Canadian GAAP prior to January 2008, Canadian companies were not required to separately disclose cost of goods sold in their financial statements. Because this disclosure was not specifically required, less than half of the Canadian companies that produced reports disclosed their cost of goods sold separately in their income statements. For fiscal years beginning after January 1, 2008, companies are required to disclose separately in their financial statements the amount of inventories recognized as an expense (cost of goods sold).

Comment on objective of financial reporting, qualitative characteristics, and constraints.
(SO 1, 3, 4) C

Instructions

In your opinion, will this new requirement improve financial statements? Include references to the objective of financial reporting and qualitative characteristics in your explanation.

Taking It Further   Why do you think companies have been reluctant to separately disclose cost of goods sold in their financial statements?

P11–4B   Jivraj and Juma are accountants at Desktop Computers. Desktop Computers has not adopted the revaluation model for accounting for its property, plant, and equipment. They disagree over the following transactions that occurred during the calendar year 2010:

Identify elements, assumptions, constraints, and recognition and measurement criteria.
(SO 2, 4, 5) AN

1. Desktop purchased equipment for $60,000 at a going-out-of-business sale. The equipment was worth $75,000. Jivraj believes that the following entry should be made:

Equipment	75,000	
Cash		60,000
Gain		15,000

2. Land costing $90,000 was appraised at $215,000. Jivraj suggests the following journal entry.

Land	125,000	
Gain on Appreciation of land		125,000

3. Depreciation for the year was $18,000. Since the company's profit is expected to be lower this year, Jivraj suggests deferring depreciation to a year when there is higher profit.

4. Desktop bought a custom-made piece of equipment for $54,000. This equipment has a useful life of six years. Desktop depreciates equipment using the straight-line method. "Since the equipment is custom-made, it will have no resale value," Jivraj argues. "So, instead of depreciating it, it should be expensed immediately." Jivraj suggests the following entry:

Equipment Expense	54,000	
Cash		54,000

5. Jivraj suggests that the company building should be reported on the balance sheet at the lower of cost and fair value. Fair value is $15,000 less than cost, although it is expected to recover its value in the future.

6. On December 20, 2010, Desktop hired a marketing consultant to design and implement a marketing plan in 2011. The plan will be designed and implemented in three stages. The contract amount is $60,000, payable in three instalments in 2011 as each stage of the plan is completed. Jivraj argues that the contract must be recorded in 2010 because there is a signed contract. Jivraj suggests the following:

Marketing Expense	60,000	
Accounts Payable		60,000

7. On December 23, Desktop received a written sales order for 10 computers. The computers will be shipped in January when the required software is installed. Jivraj suggests the following entries:

Accounts Receivable	103,000	
Sales Revenue		103,000
Cost of Goods Sold	53,000	
Inventory		53,000

* Juma disagrees with Jivraj on each of the situations.

Instructions

(a) For each transaction, indicate why Juma disagrees. Support your answer with reference to the conceptual framework (definition of elements, characteristics, assumptions, constraints, and recognition and measurement criteria).

(b) Prepare the correct journal entry to record each transaction.

Taking It Further   How would your response in (a) differ if Desktop adopted the revaluation model of accounting for its property, plant, and equipment?

P11–5B   Business transactions for SGI Company in the current year follow:

Identify assumptions and concepts and correct entries.
(SO 2, 5) AN

1. The company used the average cost formula to determine that the cost of the merchandise inventory at December 31 was $65,000. On December 31, it would have cost $80,000 to replace the merchandise inventory, so the following entry was made:

Merchandise Inventory	15,000	
Gain on Inventory		15,000

2. An order for $35,000 of goods on hand was received from a customer on December 27. The customer paid a $5,000 deposit when the order was placed. This order is to be shipped on January 9 next year. The following entry was made on December 27:

Cash	5,000	
Accounts Receivable	30,000	
Sales		35,000

3. On December 31, SGI Company's fiscal year end, a 12-month insurance policy for the following year was purchased. The following entry was made:

Insurance Expense	24,000	
Cash		24,000

4. At a fire sale, equipment worth $300,000 was acquired at a cost of $225,000. It had soot and smoke damage, but was otherwise in good condition. The following entry was made:

Equipment	300,000	
Cash		225,000
Gain on Acquisition of Equipment		75,000

5. The cost of utilities used during December was $4,200. No entry was made for the utilities in December as the bill was not received until January and was paid in February.

Instructions

(a) In each of the situations, identify the assumption or concept that has been violated, if any.
(b) Prepare the journal entry to correct each incorrect transaction identified in (a).

Taking It Further Would your response to item 5 be different if you did not know the cost of the December utilities?

P11–6B Superior Salmon Farm raises salmon that it sells to supermarket chains and restaurants. The average selling price for a mature salmon is $6. Many people believe that the selling price will increase in the future, because the demand for salmon is increasing as more people become aware of the health benefits of the omega-3 fatty acids in this fish.

Identify point of revenue and expense recognition.
(SO 5) C

It normally takes three years for the fish to grow to a saleable size. During that period, the fish must be fed and closely monitored to ensure they are healthy and free of disease. Their habitat must also be maintained. These costs average $4.50 per fish over the three-year growing period. The owner of Superior Salmon Farm believes the company should recognize revenue at a rate of $2 a year ($6 ÷ 3 years) for each fish that it harvests.

Instructions

Do you agree with the proposed revenue recognition policy for Superior Salmon Farm? Explain why or why not. Use the revenue recognition criteria to explain when you believe the revenue should be recognized for this salmon-farming business.

Taking It Further Explain how the costs of feeding, monitoring, and maintaining healthy fish and a proper habitat should be recorded.

P11–7B Devany Construction was awarded a $60-million contract on June 19, 2010, to build a civic centre. Construction began on August 1 and estimated costs of completion at the contract date are $50 million over a two-year period. By November 30, 2010, Devany's year end, construction costs of $13.5 million had been incurred. Contract payments totalling $20 million had been collected so far.

Calculate revenue at various points of recognition.
(SO 5) AP

Instructions

(a) Describe the two methods that may be used to recognize revenue for construction contracts.
(b) Calculate the amount of revenue and gross profit that would be recognized in fiscal 2010 for Devany Construction under each of the revenue recognition methods described in your response to (a).

Taking It Further Which method would you recommend that Devany Construction use? Explain why.

P11–8B MacNeil Construction Company has a long-term construction contract to build a shopping centre. The centre has a total estimated cost of $60 million, and a contract price of $76 million. Additional information follows:

Calculate revenue, expense, and gross profit—percentage-of-completion and zero profit methods.
(SO 5) AP

Year	Cash Collections	Actual Costs Incurred
2009	$12,000,000	$ 9,000,000
2010	16,000,000	12,000,000
2011	$25,000,000	$24,000,000
2012	23,000,000	15,000,000
	$76,000,000	$60,000,000

The shopping centre is completed in 2012 as scheduled. All cash collections for the contract have been received.

Instructions

(a) Prepare a schedule to determine the revenue, expense, and gross profit for each year of the long-term construction contract, using the percentage-of-completion method.

(b) How would your answer in (a) change if MacNeil Construction used the zero profit method?

Taking It Further Which of the revenue recognition methods used in (a) and (b) provides the most relevant information? Explain.

Revise revenue, expense, and gross profit—percentage-of-completion method.
(SO 5) AP

P11–9B Refer to the data in P11–8B for MacNeil Construction. Assume instead that the actual costs were $28 million in 2011. Because costs were higher than expected, MacNeil revised its total estimated costs from $60 million to $68 million at the end of 2011. Actual costs incurred in 2012 were $19 million. All other data are unchanged.

Instructions

Using the percentage-of-completion method, prepare a revised schedule to determine the revenue, expense, and gross profit for MacNeil Construction for each year of the long-term construction contract.

Taking It Further Explain why it is appropriate to use the percentage-of-completion method if actual costs differ from the estimated costs.

Calculate revenue, expense, and gross profit—percentage-of-completion method.
(SO 5) AP

P11–10B Hamilton Construction Company has a contract to build a new recreation centre. It accounts for this project using the percentage-of-completion method. The contract amount is $9 million and the cost of construction is expected to total $6.6 million. The actual costs incurred are shown below for the three-year life of the project:

Year	Actual Costs Incurred
2009	$1,980,000
2010	2,970,000
2011	1,650,000
	$6,600,000

Instructions

Calculate the amount of revenue, expense, and gross profit to be recognized in each year.

Taking It Further What if Hamilton Construction was uncertain about whether or not it would collect the full purchase price in cash from the customer: Is it still appropriate to recognize the amount of revenue calculated? Explain.

Determine when to recognize revenue when revenues are uncertain.
(SO 5) AP

P11–11B Vitamins R Us developed a new 100% organic multivitamin, Vita X, which is more easily absorbed by the body. Vita X is significantly more expensive than other vitamins on the market. In order to promote the product, Vitamins R Us shipped 50,000 bottles of Vita X, FOB destination, to retailers during December 2010. Retailers can return any Vita X not sold by March 31, 2011. As an added incentive, the retailers do not have to pay Vitamins R Us for any bottles of Vita X that they do not return to Vitamins R Us until March 31, 2011.

The selling price of the vitamins to the retailers is $45 per bottle. Vitamins R Us has not had previous promotions of this nature. Vitamins R Us has a December 31 fiscal year end.

The company's bookkeeper recognized the revenue on the vitamins when the vitamins were shipped to the retailers and made the following entry:

DR. Accounts Receivable	2,250,000	
CR. Sales Revenues		2,250,000

Instructions

(a) Indicate whether you agree or disagree with the bookkeeper's decision to recognize revenue when the vitamins were shipped. Support your answer with reference to the revenue recognition criteria.

(b) Indicate when the revenue for Vita X should be recognized.

Taking It Further Would your answers to (a) and (b) be different if Vitamins R Us had previously used the same promotion for Vita X and only 10% of the product was returned to Vitamins R Us? Explain your answer.

Continuing Cookie Chronicle

(*Note:* This is a continuation of the Cookie Chronicle from Chapters 1 through 10.)

Natalie's high school friend, Katy Peterson, has been operating a bakery for approximately 10 months, which she calls The Baker's Nook. Natalie and Katy usually meet once a month to catch up and discuss problems they have encountered while operating their respective businesses. Katy wishes to borrow from her bank so she can purchase a new state-of-the-art oven. She recognizes that the bank will be evaluating her income statement and wants to ensure that her profit is maximized. Katy thinks that she has found the solution to her problem.

Katy has recently negotiated a one-year contract with Coffee to Go to provide 1,500 cinnamon buns every week. Coffee to Go, upon receipt of a monthly invoice, will send Katy a cheque by the 15th of the following month. Katy has decided that, because she has signed this contract, she is able to record as revenue in her financial statements the contracted revenue that she is about to earn over the next 12 months. Katy assures Natalie that this is the right way to account for this revenue and is delighted because she is now sure that the bank will lend her the money that she needs to purchase this new oven.

Natalie is confused and comes to you with the following questions:

1. Is Katy accounting for this revenue correctly?
2. What other information will the bank be considering when deciding whether or not to extend the loan to Katy?
3. Do you think that Katy is being honest when she identifies this revenue as being earned on her income statement?

Instructions

(a) Answer Natalie's questions.
(b) How should Katy be recording this revenue?
(c) How could Katy ensure that the bank is aware of this contractual arrangement with Coffee to Go when it reads her financial statements?

Cumulative Coverage—Chapters 6 to 11

Johan Company and Nordlund Company are competing businesses. Both began operations six years ago and they are quite similar. The current balance sheet data for the two companies are as follows:

	Johan Company	Nordlund Company
Cash	$ 70,300	$ 48,400
Accounts receivable	309,700	312,500
Allowance for doubtful accounts	(13,600)	0
Merchandise inventory	463,900	520,200
Property, plant, and equipment	255,300	257,300
Accumulated depreciation	(112,650)	(189,850)
Total assets	$972,950	$948,550
Current liabilities	$440,200	$436,500
Long-term liabilities	78,000	80,000
Total liabilities	518,200	516,500
Owner's equity	454,750	432,050
Total liabilities and owner's equity	$972,950	$948,550

You have been hired as a consultant to do a review of the two companies. Your goal is to determine which one is in a stronger financial position. Your review of their financial statements quickly reveals that the two companies have not followed the same accounting policies. The differences, and your conclusions, are summarized below:

1. Johan Company has had good experience in estimating its uncollectible accounts. A review shows that the amount of its write offs each year has been quite close to the allowances the company provided.

   Nordlund Company has been somewhat slow to recognize its uncollectible accounts. Based on an aging analysis and review of its accounts receivable, it is estimated that $20,000 of its existing accounts will become uncollectible.

2. Johan Company has determined the cost of its merchandise inventory using the average inventory cost formula. The result is that its inventory appears on the balance sheet at an amount that is slightly below its current replacement cost. Based on a detailed physical examination of its merchandise on hand, the current replacement cost of its inventory is estimated at $477,000.

   Nordlund Company has used the FIFO inventory cost formula. The result is that its ending inventory appears on the balance sheet at an amount that is close to its current replacement cost.

3. Johan Company estimated a useful life of 12 years and a residual value of $30,000 for its property, plant, and equipment, and has been depreciating them on a straight-line basis. Nordlund Company has the same type of property, plant, and equipment. However, it estimated a useful life of 10 years and a residual value of $10,000. It has been depreciating its property, plant, and equipment using the double declining-balance method.

   Based on engineering studies of these types of property, plant, and equipment, you conclude that Nordlund's estimates and method for calculating depreciation are more appropriate.

Instructions

(a) Where would you find the above information on the two companies' accounting policies? Be specific about what information would be available and where you would find it.

(b) Using similar accounting policies for both companies, revise the balance sheets presented above.

(c) Has preparing the revised statements in (b) improved the quality of the accounting information for the two companies? How?

Financial Reporting and Analysis

Financial Reporting Problem

BYP11–1   Refer to the Notes to Consolidated Financial Statements for The Forzani Group Ltd. in Appendix A.

Instructions

(a) Note 2, Significant Accounting Policies, states that the preparation of the financial statements in conformity with Canadian generally accepted accounting principles requires management to make estimates. Indicate for which items reported in the financial statements estimates were made. Why are estimates required?

(b) Subsection (h) of Note 2, Significant Accounting Policies, describes Forzani's revenue recognition policy. Does this policy sound reasonable to you, given the types of goods Forzani sells?

(c) Subsection (i) of Note 2, Significant Accounting Policies, describes Forzani's treatment of its store opening expenses. Explain how the company's treatment of these expenses relates to the timing of recognition of revenue from new stores. Some costs are more directly associated with specific revenues than others. Would you consider there to be a direct association between these costs and the revenues to come in future accounting periods from the new stores? What alternative treatment for these expenses might you recommend according to the basic expense recognition criteria?

(d) Note 15, Contingencies and Guarantees, discloses several commitments by the company that are not recorded in the financial statements. Do you think this additional disclosure was necessary? Explain why or why not, referring to the appropriate concepts or items from the Conceptual Framework of accounting in your answer.

(e) Forzani's independent auditors' report is provided in Appendix A with the company's financial statements. What is the purpose of an independent audit? What did Forzani's auditors say about the company's financial statements?

Interpreting Financial Statements

BYP11–2   Today, companies must compete in a global economy. For example, Canada's oldest candy company, Ganong Bros., Limited, which has been making chocolates since 1873, must compete with Nestlé S.A., among others. Although Nestlé is best known for its chocolates and confections, this Swiss company is one of the largest food companies in the world.

Comparing companies such as Ganong and Nestlé can be challenging not only because of their size differences, but also because Ganong uses Canadian accounting principles and Nestlé uses international accounting principles. Consider the following excerpt from the notes to Nestlé's financial statements:

NESTLÉ S.A.
Notes to the Financial Statements (partial)
December 31, 2008

1. Accounting policies

Accounting convention and accounting standards

The Consolidated Financial Statements comply with International Financial Reporting Standards (IFRS) issued by the International Accounting Standards Board (IASB) and with the Interpretations issued by the International Financial Reporting Interpretations Committee (IFRIC).

The consolidated accounts have been prepared on an accruals basis and under the historical cost convention, unless stated otherwise.

Instructions

(a) Discuss the implications that Nestlé's (1) larger size with a more diversified product line, and (2) use of international financial reporting standards might have (positively or negatively) on your ability to compare Ganong with Nestlé.

(b) Ganong is a private corporation. Generally, Canadian private corporations will have the option of reporting under Canadian GAAP for Private Enterprises or reporting under IFRS starting January 1, 2011. What may be the benefits to Ganong of reporting under Canadian GAAP for Private Enterprises? What may be the benefits to Ganong of reporting under IFRS?

Critical Thinking

Collaborative Learning Activity

Note to instructor: Additional instructions and material for this group activity can be found on the Instructor Resource Site.

BYP11–3   Recognition and Measurement elements are major components of the conceptual framework of accounting. In this group activity, you will apply your knowledge by choosing the assumption, constraint, or recognition and measurement elements that applies in a situation and then explain your choice to your classmates.

Instructions

(a) Your instructor will divide the class into groups.

(b) Look around the classroom at the signs taped on the wall by your instructor. After reviewing the accounting situation presented by your instructor, choose one representative from your group to move to the sign that applies. Once each representative from each group has chosen a place, discuss with those in your group why you believe your choice is correct. The instructor will randomly select a student in each group to explain to everyone in the class why the members of the group selected their position. You may move to another sign if you are convinced by another group's explanation.

(c) Repeat the above activity for each situation presented by the instructor.

(d) You may be asked by your instructor to write a short quiz on this topic.

Communication Activity

BYP11–4 Junk R Us (Junk) is a wholesale distributor of goods. Junk purchases goods that are not selling from manufacturers and other wholesalers and sells them to discount retail outlets. You are a professional accountant and are preparing Junk's financial statements for the year ended September 30, 2010. The company had $110,000 of mini-disc players in inventory that were not selling. Junk has not had an order for mini-disc players for over a year. The president is reluctant to write off the inventory so the president signed an agreement with Cheap But Good, a retailer, to sell the mini-disc players to it for $150,000, with the understanding that Cheap But Good could return any mini-disc players not sold by December 31, 2010, to Junk and that Cheap But Good was not required to pay for any of the mini-disc players it sold to customers until December 31, 2010. The mini-disc players were shipped to Cheap But Good on September 29, 2010.

Writing Handbook

Instructions

Write a memo to the president of Junk R Us answering the following questions:

(a) When should revenue be recognized on the mini-disc players sold to Cheap But Good? Explain.
(b) How should the mini-disc players be reported in Junk R Us's financial statements for the year ended September 30, 2010? Explain.

Ethics Case

BYP11–5 When the IASB and ACSB issue new accounting recommendations, the required implementation date (the date when a company has to start applying the recommendations) is usually 12 months or more after the date of publication. For example, in November 2009, the IASB issued new recommendations for classifying and reporting investments: companies are required to implement the new recommendations for fiscal years starting January 1, 2013. This allows companies some time to change their accounting procedures. Nevertheless, early implementation is usually encouraged for those who are able to do so, because new rules are intended to provide better representation of the company's financial performance and position.

Ethics in Accounting

Carol DesChenes, an accountant at Grocery Online, discusses with her vice-president of finance the need for early implementation of a recently issued recommendation. She says it will result in a much more faithful representation of the company's financial position. When the vice-president of finance determines that early implementation will have a negative impact on the profits reported for the year, he strongly discourages Carol from implementing the recommendation until it is required.

Instructions

(a) Who are the stakeholders in this situation?
(b) What, if any, are the ethical considerations in this situation?
(c) What could Carol gain by supporting early implementation? Who might be affected by the decision against early implementation?

"All About You" Activity

BYP11–6 In the "All About You" feature, you learned about Registered Education Savings Plans (RESPs) and that the fair value of the RESP may be the most relevant information for some decisions and that cost may be the most relevant for other purposes.

To apply this concept further, assume that you are applying for a car loan. The loan application requires that you prepare two reports: (1) a projected cash budget and (2) information about your assets and liabilities. The information in the loan application will be used to determine if the bank manager will approve the loan or not.

Instructions

(a) Why would a bank manager ask you to complete a projected cash budget and provide information about your assets and liabilities in order to decide whether or not to approve your loan? What is the bank manager trying to determine about you?

(b) Recall from the chapter that there are different measurement bases used for different decisions. Two measurement bases we learned about in the chapter are cost (historical value), and fair value. Another measurement basis that is useful for some decisions is future replacement cost. For each item listed below, indicate (1) which of the two reports to the bank the item would be included in; (2) the measurement basis (cost, fair value, or future replacement cost) that is relevant to the bank manager's decision to approve or not approve your loan; and (3) the rationale for your specific choice of measurement basis.

1. Rent
2. Groceries
3. Cash in savings account
4. Tuition fees
5. RESP—equity fund
6. Textbooks
7. Clothes
8. Student loan
9. Summer earnings
10. Two-year-old mountain bike
11. Three-year-old furniture

ANSWERS TO CHAPTER QUESTIONS

Answers to Accounting in Action Insight Questions

Business Insight, p. 619

Q: How did Nortel justify using the going concern assumption when it was so uncertain that the company would continue operating?

A: Nortel used the going concern assumption because it was in the process of developing a plan to restructure its operations. It expected that the company would continue to operate in the foreseeable future.

Across the Organization, p. 631

Q: What is the manager of the shipping department's role in making sure revenue is recognized in the appropriate period?

A: The manager of the shipping department should ensure that the appropriate documentation is prepared for goods shipped and that it is sent to the accounting department. When the goods are shipped to the customer, the shipping department can prepare a shipping document that indicates what was shipped, the shipment date, and the terms of the shipping. A copy of the shipping document will be forwarded to the accounting department. The accounting department can review the shipping documents to determine what revenue should be recognized and when.

All About You, p. 633

Q: If you were preparing your personal financial report, what information about your RESP would be relevant: the cost of the RESP contributions or the fair value of the RESP?

A: The answer to the question depends on what the information is being used for. In the years that your parents were contributing to the RESP, the cost of the contributions may be the most relevant if they were deciding how much they could afford to contribute to the plan, and keeping track of how much they needed to contribute to collect the full Canada Education Savings Grant. Now that you have started your post-secondary education, the fair value of the RESP is probably more relevant because that is the amount that is available for you to use to pay for your education.

Answer to Forzani Review It Question 4, p. 634

Note 2 (h) Significant Accounting Policies, Revenue Recognition, states: "Revenue includes sales to customers through corporate stores operated by the Company and sales to, and service fees from, franchise stores and others. Sales to customers through corporate stores operated by the Company are recognized at the point of sale, net of an estimated allowance for sales returns. Sales of merchandise to franchise stores and others are recognized at the time of shipment. Royalties and administration fees are recognized when earned, in accordance with the terms of the franchise/license agreements."

Answers to Self-Study Questions

1. c   2. a   3. b   4. c   5. b   6. c   7. c   8. c   9. a   10. a

Remember to go back to the beginning of the chapter to check off your completed work!

←

CHAPTER 12
ACCOUNTING FOR PARTNERSHIPS

heagyllp.ca

CONCEPTS FOR REVIEW:

Before studying this chapter, you should understand or, if necessary, review:

a. The different forms of business organization. (Ch. 1, pp. 5–6)

b. The cost principle of accounting. (Ch. 1, p. 9)

c. The statement of owner's equity. (Ch. 1, pp. 21–22)

d. How to make closing entries. (Ch. 4, pp. 182–184)

e. The steps in the accounting cycle. (Ch. 4, p. 188)

f. The classified balance sheet. (Ch. 4, pp. 191–199)

Partners Work Together for Success

SASKATOON, Sask.—When chartered accountants Glen Bailey and Clare Heagy founded their partnership back in 1983, they knew that working together would be good for both them and their clients. Mr. Heagy had been a partner in a national firm and had clients who stayed loyal to him; Mr. Bailey was just starting out but had specialized training in taxation. By combining their talents and resources, they soon built a strong practice that served a wide range of Saskatchewan businesses.

Today, the firm they started more than 25 years ago has four partners and a staff of 13. Richard Altrogge, a partner in the firm, says the firm is successful because there is a clear understanding of what a partnership requires and everyone pulls their weight.

When they started, Mr. Bailey and Mr. Heagy drew up an agreement that basically covered how the business would be operated: splitting of profit; draws of money; and provisions concerning death, disability, or withdrawal of partners. The agreement also noted that Mr. Heagy had brought in the initial client base: as compensation for this, a provision stated that he would be paid a fee in addition to the value of his assets if he left the partnership.

A few years later, in 1988, Mr. Altrogge joined the partnership, initially as an associate. "After a while, I was admitted as a junior partner under a system that allowed me to become an equal partner by paying a specified amount of cash when my billings reached a certain percentage of total revenues," says Mr. Altrogge.

The firm was a three-way partnership for several years. When Mr. Heagy retired in 1998, Richard Matchett, who had been working for the firm as an employee, became a junior partner. By 2006, he had achieved equal status to Mr. Bailey and Mr. Altrogge. Mr. Bailey then left the firm in December 2006.

The firm had brought in another partner in 2001, Alan Ashdown, and added James Schemenauer in 2004. Each new partner's interest was determined by the volume of his client billings compared with the firm's total. When they were first admitted as partners, they were guaranteed a minimum share of the firm's profit. This was to recognize the fact that, while they were each growing their own practice, they were also working on the firm's other client files.

In 2002, the province of Saskatchewan passed legislation allowing professionals to incorporate. The partnership structure changed in response. "We each set up our own professional corporation and rolled our interests in the partnership into those," explains Mr. Altrogge. "We're still a partnership, but technically we're a partnership of corporations." The firm is now called Heagy Altrogge Matchett & Partners LLP.

"A partnership is much like a marriage," concludes Mr. Altrogge. "You're going to have problems, but if all the partners do their part and work together, you have the best chance of success."

The Navigator

STUDY OBJECTIVES:

After studying this chapter, you should be able to:

1. Describe the characteristics of the partnership form of business organization.
2. Account for the formation of a partnership.
3. Allocate and record profit or loss to partners.
4. Prepare partnership financial statements.
5. Prepare the entries to record the admission of a partner.
6. Prepare the entries to record the withdrawal of a partner.
7. Prepare the entries to record the liquidation of a partnership.

It is not surprising that Glen Bailey and Clare Heagy decided to use the partnership form of organization when they started their accounting practice. They saw an opportunity to combine their expertise and better leverage their resources. In this chapter, we will discuss why the partnership form of organization is often chosen. We will also explain the major issues in accounting for partnerships.

The chapter is organized as follows:

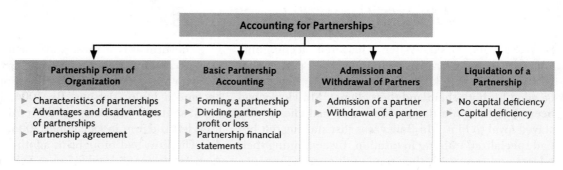

		Accounting for Partnerships		

Partnership Form of Organization	**Basic Partnership Accounting**	**Admission and Withdrawal of Partners**	**Liquidation of a Partnership**
▶ Characteristics of partnerships ▶ Advantages and disadvantages of partnerships ▶ Partnership agreement	▶ Forming a partnership ▶ Dividing partnership profit or loss ▶ Partnership financial statements	▶ Admission of a partner ▶ Withdrawal of a partner	▶ No capital deficiency ▶ Capital deficiency

Partnership Form of Organization

STUDY OBJECTIVE 1

Describe the characteristics of the partnership form of business organization.

All provinces in Canada have a *Partnership Act* that sets out the basic rules for forming and operating partnerships. These acts define a partnership as a relationship between people who do business with the intention of making a profit. This does not necessarily mean that there must be a profit—just that profit is the objective. Partnerships are common in professions such as accounting, advertising, law, and medicine. Professional partnerships can vary in size from two partners to thousands.

Characteristics of Partnerships

The main characteristics of the partnership form of business organization are shown in Illustration 12-1. They are explained after the illustration.

Illustration 12-1 ➡

Partnership characteristics

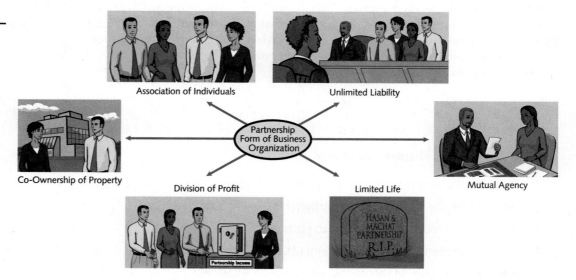

Association of Individuals

Unlimited Liability

Co-Ownership of Property

Division of Profit

Limited Life

Mutual Agency

Partnership Form of Business Organization

Association of Individuals

The association of two or more individuals in a partnership can be based on an act as simple as a handshake. However, it is much better to have a legal, written agreement that outlines the rights and obligations of the partners, as in the feature story. Partners who have not put their agreement in writing have found that the absence of a written agreement can sometimes cause later difficulties. In fact, some *Partnership Acts* state that if you receive a share of profit from a business, you will be considered a partner in the business unless there is contrary evidence. If there is no formal agreement that says who the partners of a business are, you may be part of a partnership without knowing it!

A partnership is a legal entity for certain purposes. For instance, property (land, buildings, and equipment) can be owned in the name of the partnership. The firm can sue or be sued. A partnership is also an accounting entity for financial reporting purposes. Thus, the personal assets, liabilities, and transactions of the partners are kept separate from the accounting records of the partnership, just as they are in a proprietorship.

However, a partnership is not taxed as a separate entity. It must file an information tax return that reports the partnership's profit and each partner's share of that profit. Each partner must then report his or her share of the partnership profit on their personal income tax returns. The partner's profit is taxed at his or her personal income tax rate, and does not depend on how much money the partner withdrew from the partnership during the year.

Co-Ownership of Property

Partnership assets are owned jointly by the partners. If the partnership is dissolved, an asset does not legally return to the partner who originally contributed it. The assets are normally sold and the partners share any gain or loss on disposition according to their profit and loss ratios. After partnership liabilities are paid, each partner then has a claim on any cash that remains: the claim is equal to the balance in the partner's capital account.

Similarly, if, in doing business, a partner invests a building in the partnership that is valued at $100,000 and the building is later sold at a gain of $20,000, that partner does not receive the entire gain. The gain becomes part of the partnership profit, which is shared among the partners, as described in the next section.

Division of Profit

Just as property is co-owned, so is partnership profit (or loss). The partners specify how the partnership profit (loss) will be divided when they form the partnership, as they did in the feature story. If the division is not specified, profit (loss) is assumed to be shared equally. We will learn more about dividing partnership profit in a later section of this chapter.

Limited Life

A partnership does not have an unlimited life. Any change in ownership ends the existing partnership. There is a **partnership dissolution** whenever a partner withdraws or a new partner is admitted. When a partnership is dissolved, this does not necessarily mean that the business ends. If the continuing partners agree, operations can continue without any interruption by forming a new partnership.

Mutual Agency

Mutual agency means that each partner acts for the partnership when he or she does partnership business. The action of any partner is binding on all other partners—in other words, the action cannot be cancelled by one of them. This is true even when partners exceed their authority, as long as the act looks appropriate for the partnership. For example, a partner of an accounting firm who purchases a building that is suitable for the business creates a binding contract in the name of the partnership. On the other hand, if a partner in a law firm decides to buy a snowmobile for the partnership, the act would not be binding on the partnership, because the purchase is unrelated to the business.

Unlimited Liability

Each partner is jointly and severally (individually) liable for all partnership liabilities. If one partner incurs a liability, the other partners are also responsible for it. For repayment, creditors first have claims on the partnership assets. If there are not enough assets to pay back the creditors, however, they can then claim the personal assets of any partner, regardless of that partner's equity in the partnership. Because each partner is responsible for all the debts of the partnership, each partner is said to have unlimited liability.

Unlimited liability and mutual agency can combine for disastrous results. An unethical or incompetent partner can commit the partnership to a deal that eventually bankrupts the partnership. The creditors may then be able to claim the partners' personal assets—the assets of all the partners, not just those of the partner who made the bad deal. As Mr. Altrogge says in the feature story, "A partnership is much like a marriage." Consequently, an individual must be extremely cautious in choosing a partner.

Because of concerns about unlimited liability, there are now special forms of partnership organization that modify liability. These include limited partnerships and limited liability partnerships, discussed in the next two sections.

Limited Partnerships (LP). In a **limited partnership**, or "LP," one or more of the partners have unlimited liability. This type of partner is called a general partner. A general partner normally contributes work and experience to the partnership and is authorized to manage and represent the partnership. The general partner's liability for the partnership's debts is unlimited.

In addition to the general partner(s), one or more partners have limited liability for the partnership's debts. This type of partner is called a limited partner. Limited partners normally give cash or assets to the partnership, but not services. The amount of debt that the limited partner is liable for in the partnership is limited to the amount of capital that he or she contributed to the partnership. In other words, a limited partner's personal assets cannot be sold to repay any partnership debt that is more than the amount that he or she contributed to the partnership.

A limited partnership is identified in its name with the words "Limited Partnership" or the abbreviation "LP." Limited partnerships are normally used by businesses that offer income tax shelters for investors, such as real estate investment trusts, rental properties, and sports ventures.

Limited Liability Partnerships (LLP). Most professionals, such as lawyers, doctors, and accountants, form a **limited liability partnership** or "LLP." In the feature story, Heagy Altrogge Matchett & Partners operates as a limited liability partnership.

A limited liability partnership is designed to protect innocent partners from the acts of other partners that result in lawsuits against the partnership. That is, partners in an LLP continue to have unlimited liability for their own negligence but have limited liability for other partners' negligence. In addition to being liable for their own actions, partners are also liable for the actions of employees whom they directly supervise and control.

Advantages and Disadvantages of Partnerships

Why do people choose partnerships? Often, it is to combine the skills and resources of two or more individuals. For example, the partners of Heagy Altrogge Matchett & Partners are able to work together and share office space and accounting knowledge. They can also divide among themselves different areas of responsibility and expertise—assurance, taxation, and business valuation, for example.

A partnership is easily formed and is controlled by fewer government regulations and restrictions than a corporation is. Also, decisions can be made quickly on important matters that affect the firm. This is also true in a proprietorship, but not in a corporation, where some decisions have to be approved by the board of directors.

Partnerships also have some disadvantages: mutual agency, limited life, and unlimited liability in general partnerships. Unlimited liability is particularly troublesome. Many individuals fear they may lose not only their initial investment but also their personal assets if those assets are needed to pay partnership creditors. As a result, partnerships often have difficulty getting large amounts of investment capital. That is one reason why the largest businesses in Canada are corporations, not partnerships.

The advantages and disadvantages of the general partnership form of business organization are summarized below.

Advantages	Disadvantages
• Combines skills and resources of two or more individuals • Easily formed • Fewer government regulations and restrictions • Easier decision-making	• Mutual agency • Limited life • Unlimited liability

Partnership Agreement

Ideally, when two or more individuals agree to organize a partnership, their agreement should be expressed as a written contract. Called a **partnership agreement**, this contract contains such basic information as the name and main location of the firm, the purpose of the business, and the date of inception. In addition, relationships among the partners must be specified, such as:

1. The names and capital contributions of partners
2. The rights and duties of partners
3. The basis for sharing profit or loss
4. Provisions for a withdrawal of assets
5. Procedures for submitting disputes to arbitration
6. Procedures for the withdrawal, or addition, of a partner
7. The rights and duties of surviving partners if a partner dies
8. Procedures for the liquidation of the partnership

Ethics note A partnership agreement that is carefully planned reduces ethical conflict among partners. It specifies, in clear language, the process for solving ethical and legal problems. This becomes especially important when the partnership is in financial distress.

As discussed in our feature story, Heagy Altrogge Matchett & Partners has a detailed partnership agreement that covers all of these areas. The importance of a written contract cannot be overemphasized. If there is no partnership agreement, the provisions of the *Partnership Act* will apply, and they may not be what the partners want. The partnership agreement should be written with care so that it considers all possible situations, contingencies, and future disagreements between the partners.

 ### ACCOUNTING IN ACTION: BUSINESS INSIGHT

Limited partnerships provide investment opportunities in a variety of industries, including agriculture and real estate. In 2005, Assiniboia Capital Corp., as the general partner, launched its first farmland limited partnership designed to provide Canadian investors with an opportunity to participate in farmland ownership in Saskatchewan. By 2008, there were four Assiniboia Farmland Limited Partnerships, which were merged into one entity in early 2009. The Assiniboia Farmland Limited Partnership now owns a diversified portfolio of approximately 80,000 acres (about 32,000 hectares) of farmland across Saskatchewan and continues to acquire more land. The partnership's business is renting the properties to farm operators. The goal is to maximize long-term total return through capital appreciation of the farmland, and to distribute cash to limited partners every June and December. Limited partners purchased units in the Assiniboia Farmland Limited Partnership for $25 per unit and the value of their units rises as the value of the farmland portfolio increases. The general partner expects the value of Saskatchewan farmland will benefit from a number of global trends including the environmental focus on biofuels.

Source: http://www.farmlandinvestor.ca/.

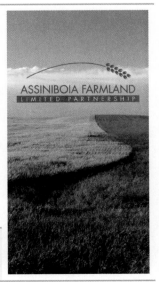

If an investor wants to own Saskatchewan farmland, why doesn't he or she simply buy the farmland instead of buying units of this limited partnership? Why is it important to the investors to invest in a limited partnership as opposed to just a partnership?

BEFORE YOU GO ON . . .

➜ Review It

1. What are the main characteristics of a partnership?
2. How can partners limit their liability?
3. What are the main advantages and disadvantages of a partnership?
4. What are the major items in a partnership agreement?
5. The Forzani Group Ltd. originally started as a partnership when Calgary Stampeder John Forzani and three of his teammates (two of them were his brothers) started Forzani's Locker Room in 1974. What could be the reason that it changed to the corporate form of organization in 1993? The answer to this question is at the end of the chapter.

The Navigator

Related exercise material: BE12–1 and E12–1.

Basic Partnership Accounting

We now turn to the basic accounting for partnerships. Accounting for a partnership is very similar to accounting for a proprietorship. Just as most proprietorships will choose to use Canadian GAAP for Private Enterprises, many partnerships are private and will also choose to follow these accounting standards. On the other hand, Limited Partnerships are often public enterprises and these companies will have to use International Financial Reporting Standards.

There are three accounting issues where there are some differences between partnerships and proprietorships: formation of a partnership, dividing the partnership profit or loss, and preparing partnership financial statements. We will examine each of these in the following sections.

Forming a Partnership

STUDY OBJECTIVE 2

Account for the formation of a partnership.

Each partner's initial investment in a partnership is entered in the partnership records. These investments should be recorded at the assets' fair value at the date of their transfer to the partnership. The values used must be agreed to by all of the partners.

To illustrate, assume that M. Gan and K. Sin combine their proprietorships on January 2 to start a partnership named Interactive Software. Gan and Sin each have the following assets before forming the partnership:

	M. Gan		K. Sin	
	Book Value	Fair Value	Book Value	Fair Value
Cash	$ 8,000	$ 8,000	$ 9,000	$ 9,000
Accounts receivable			4,000	4,000
Allowance for doubtful accounts			(700)	(1,000)
Office equipment	5,000	4,000		
Accumulated depreciation	(2,000)			
	$11,000	$12,000	$12,300	$12,000

The entries to record the investments in the partnership are:

		Investment of M. Gan		
Jan.	2	Cash	8,000	
		Office Equipment	4,000	
		M. Gan, Capital		12,000
		To record investment of Gan.		
		Investment of K. Sin		
	2	Cash	9,000	
		Accounts Receivable	4,000	
		Allowance for Doubtful Accounts		1,000
		K. Sin, Capital		12,000
		To record investment of Sin.		

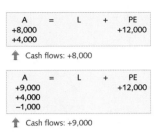

A	=	L	+	PE
+8,000				+12,000
+4,000				

↑ Cash flows: +8,000

A	=	L	+	PE
+9,000				+12,000
+4,000				
−1,000				

↑ Cash flows: +9,000

Helpful hint The fair value of the noncash assets at the date of acquisition becomes the cost of these assets to the partnership. The fair value is what the assets would have cost if they had been purchased at that time.

Note that neither the original cost of Gan's office equipment ($5,000) nor its accumulated depreciaton ($2,000) are recorded by the partnership. Instead, the equipment is recorded at its fair value of $4,000. Because the equipment has not yet been used by the partnership, there is no accumulated depreciation.

In contrast, Sin's gross claims on customers ($4,000) are carried into the partnership. The allowance for doubtful accounts is adjusted to $1,000 to arrive at a net realizable value of $3,000. A partnership may start with an allowance for doubtful accounts, because it will continue to track and collect existing accounts receivable and some of these are expected to be uncollectible. In addition, this procedure maintains the control and subsidiary relationship between Accounts Receivable and the accounts receivable subsidiary ledger that we learned about in Chapter 8.

After the partnership has been formed, the accounting for transactions is similar to the accounting for any other type of business organization. For example, all transactions with outside parties, such as the performance of services and payment for them, should be recorded in the same way for a partnership as for a proprietorship.

The steps in the accounting cycle that are described in Chapter 4 for a proprietorship are also used for a partnership. For example, a partnership journalizes and posts transactions, prepares a trial balance, journalizes and posts adjusting entries, and prepares an adjusted trial balance. However, there are minor differences in journalizing and posting closing entries and in preparing financial statements, as explained in the following sections. The differences occur because there is more than one owner.

BEFORE YOU GO ON . . .

→ Review It

1. How should assets that are invested into the partnership by a partner be valued?
2. Why is there no accumulated depreciation on property, plant, and equipment invested in a partnership?
3. Why is the gross value of accounts receivable carried forward to a partnership?

→ Do It

On June 1, Eric Brown and Erik Smistad decide to organize a partnership, E&E Painting. Eric Brown contributes painting equipment with a cost of $5,000 and $2,000 of accumulated depreciation. Erik Smistad contributes accounts receivable of $1,200. Eric and Erik agree that the equipment has a fair value of $2,500 and the accounts receivable a net realizable value of $1,000. Erik Smistad will also contribute the amount of cash required to make his investment equal to Eric Brown's. (a) How much cash must Erik Smistad contribute? (b) Prepare the journal entries to record their investments in the partnership.

Action Plan
- Use fair values for the assets invested in the partnership.
- Each partner's equity is equal to the fair value of the net assets he invested in the partnership.

Solution

(a)

Fair value of painting equipment contributed by Eric Brown	$2,500
Less: fair value of accounts receivable contributed by Erik Smistad	1,000
Cash investment required from Erik Smistad	$1,500

(b)

July 1	Painting Equipment	2,500	
	E. Brown, Capital		2,500
	To record investment of Eric Brown.		
1	Cash	1,500	
	Accounts Receivable	1,200	
	Allowance for Doubtful Accounts		200
	E. Smistad, Capital		2,500
	To record investment of Erik Smistad.		

The Navigator

Related exercise material: BE12–2, BE12–3, and E12–2.

Dividing Partnership Profit or Loss

STUDY OBJECTIVE 3

Allocate and record profit or loss to partners.

Partnership profit or loss is shared equally unless the partnership agreement indicates a different division. Usually, the same basis of division is used for both profit and losses, and it is typically called the **profit and loss ratio**. It is also known as the profit ratio, or the income and loss ratio. A partner's share of profit or loss is recognized in the accounts through closing entries.

Closing Entries

As in a proprietorship, there are four entries to prepare closing entries for a partnership:

1. To close revenue accounts: Debit each revenue account for its balance and credit Income Summary for total revenues.
2. To close expense accounts: Debit Income Summary for total expenses and credit each expense account for its balance.
3. To close Income Summary: Debit Income Summary for its balance (which should equal the profit amount) and credit each partner's capital account for his or her share of profit. Conversely, credit Income Summary and debit each partner's capital account for his or her share of a loss.
4. To close drawings: Debit each partner's capital account for the balance in that partner's drawings account, and credit each partner's drawings account for the same amount.

The first two entries are the same as in a proprietorship, as shown in Chapter 4. The last two entries are different because (1) it is necessary to divide profit (or loss) among the partners, and (2) there are two or more owners' capital and drawings accounts.

To illustrate the last two closing entries, we will assume that Interactive Software has a profit of $32,000 for the year. The partners, M. Gan and K. Sin, share profit and loss equally. Drawings for the year were $8,000 for Gan and $6,000 for Sin. The closing entries on December 31 are as follows:

A	=	L	+	PE
				−32,000
				+16,000
				+16,000

Cash flows: no effect

A	=	L	+	PE
				−8,000
				−6,000
				+8,000
				+6,000

Cash flows: no effect

Dec. 31	Income Summary	32,000	
	M. Gan, Capital ($32,000 × 50%)		16,000
	K. Sin, Capital ($32,000 × 50%)		16,000
	To close profit to capital accounts.		
31	M. Gan, Capital	8,000	
	K. Sin, Capital	6,000	
	M. Gan, Drawings		8,000
	K. Sin, Drawings		6,000
	To close drawings accounts to capital accounts.		

Recall from the previous section that both Gan and Sin had made investments in the partnership of $12,000 at the beginning of the year. After posting the closing entries, the capital and drawing accounts will appear as shown below:

M. Gan, Capital					K. Sin, Capital				
Dec. 31	Clos. 8,000	Jan. 2		12,000	Dec. 31	Clos. 6,000	Jan. 2		12,000
		Dec. 31	Clos.	16,000			Dec. 31	Clos.	16,000
		Dec. 31	Bal.	20,000			Dec. 31	Bal.	22,000

M. Gan, Drawings				K. Sin, Drawings			
Dec. 31	Bal. 8,000	Dec. 31 Clos.	8,000	Dec. 31	Bal. 6,000	Dec. 31 Clos.	6,000
Dec. 31	Bal. 0			Dec. 31	Bal. 0		

As in a proprietorship, the partners' capital accounts are permanent accounts, and their drawings accounts are temporary accounts. Normally the capital accounts will have credit balances and the drawing accounts will have debit balances. Drawing accounts are debited when partners withdraw cash or other assets from the partnership for personal use.

Profit and Loss Ratios

As noted earlier, the partnership agreement should specify the basis for sharing profit or loss. The following are typical profit and loss ratios:

1. A fixed ratio, expressed as a proportion (2:1), a percentage (67% and 33%), or a fraction ($^2/_3$ and $^1/_3$)
2. A ratio based either on capital balances at the beginning or end of the year, or on average capital balances during the year
3. Salaries to partners and the remainder in a fixed ratio
4. Interest on partners' capital balances and the remainder in a fixed ratio
5. Salaries to partners, interest on partners' capital balances, and the remainder in a fixed ratio

In each case, the goal is to share profit or loss in a way that fairly reflects each partner's capital investment and service to the partnership.

A fixed ratio is easy to use, and it may be a fair basis in some circumstances. Assume, for example, that Hughes and Lane are partners. Each contributes the same amount of capital, but Hughes expects to work full-time in the partnership, while Lane expects to work only half-time. Accordingly, the partners agree to a fixed ratio of two-thirds to Hughes and one-third to Lane.

A ratio that is based on capital balances may be the right choice when the funds invested in the partnership are the critical factor. Capital balances may also be fair when a manager is hired to run the business and the partners do not plan to take an active role in daily operations.

The three remaining profit and loss ratios (items 3, 4, and 5 in the list above) recognize specific differences among the partners. These ratios give salary allowances for time worked and interest allowances for capital invested. Any remaining profit or loss is divided using a fixed ratio.

Salaries to partners and interest on partners' capital balances are not expenses of the partnership. These ratios are used only for the calculations that divide profit or loss among partners. This means that for a partnership, as with other companies, salary expense is the cost of services performed by employees. Likewise, interest expense is the cost of borrowing from creditors. As owners, **partners are neither employees nor creditors.** Some partnership agreements allow partners to make monthly cash withdrawals based on their salary allowance. In such cases, the withdrawals are debited to the partner's drawings account, not salary expense.

Salaries, Interest, and Remainder in a Fixed Ratio

In three of the profit- and loss-sharing ratios, salaries and/or interest must be allocated before the remainder is divided according to a fixed ratio. This is true even if the salary and/or interest provisions are more than profit. It is also true even if the partnership has suffered a loss for the year. The same basic method of dividing (or allocating) profit or loss is used if there is only a salary allocation, or if there is only an interest allocation, or if both are used. In the illustration

Helpful hint It is often easier to work with fractions or percentages than proportions when allocating profit or loss. When converting to a fraction, determine the denominator for the fractions by adding the proportions. Then use the appropriate proportion to determine each partner's fraction. For example, (2:1) converts to $^2/_3$ and $^1/_3$; (3:5) converts to $^3/_8$ and $^5/_8$; and for three partners using (3:2:1), these proportions convert to $^3/_6$, $^2/_6$, and $^1/_6$.

that follows, we will use a profit and loss ratio that includes both salary and interest allocations before allocating the remainder (item 5 above).

Assume that Sara King and Ray Lee are partners in the Kingslee Company. The partnership agreement specifies (1) salary allowances of $8,400 for King and $6,000 for Lee, (2) interest allowances of 5% on capital balances at the beginning of the year, and (3) the remainder to be distributed equally. Capital balances on January 1, 2011, were King $28,000 and Lee $24,000. In 2011, partnership profit is $22,000. The division of profit for the year is shown in Illustration 12-2.

Helpful hint The total of the amounts allocated to each partner must equal the profit or loss.

Illustration 12-2 ➡

Division of profit when profit exceeds allowances

	S. King	R. Lee	Total
KINGSLEE COMPANY			
Division of Profit			
Year Ended December 31, 2011			
Profit			$22,000
Salary allowance			
S. King	$ 8,400		
R. Lee		$6,000	
Total			14,400
Profit remaining for allocation			7,600
Interest allowance			
S. King ($28,000 × 5%)	1,400		
R. Lee ($24,000 × 5%)		1,200	
Total			2,600
Profit remaining for allocation			5,000
Fixed ratio (*remainder shared equally*)			
S. King ($5,000 × 50%)	2,500		
R. Lee ($5,000 × 50%)		2,500	
Total			5,000
Profit remaining for allocation			0
Profit allocated to the partners	$12,300	$9,700	$22,000

The entry to record the division of profit is:

A	=	L	+	PE
				−22,000
				+12,300
				+9,700

Cash flows: no effect

Dec. 31	Income Summary	22,000	
	S. King, Capital		12,300
	R. Lee, Capital		9,700
	To transfer profit to partners' capital accounts.		

Let's now look at a situation where the salary and interest allowances are greater than profit. Assume that Kingslee Company reports profit of $14,000. In this case, the salary and interest allowances create a deficiency of $3,000 ($14,000 − $14,400 − $2,600). This deficiency is divided equally among the partners as in Illustration 12-3.

Illustration 12-3 ➡

Division of profit when allowances exceed profit

	S. King	R. Lee	Total
KINGSLEE COMPANY			
Division of Profit			
Year Ended December 31, 2011			
Profit			$14,000
Salary allowance			
S. King	$8,400		
R. Lee		$6,000	
Total			14,400
Profit (deficiency) remaining for allocation			(400)
Interest allowance			
S. King ($28,000 × 5%)	1,400		
R. Lee ($24,000 × 5%)		1,200	
Total			2,600
Profit (deficiency) remaining for allocation			(3,000)

◀ Illustration 12-3 (cont.)

Division of profit when allowances exceed profit

Fixed ratio (*remainder shared equally*)			
S. King ($3,000 × 50%)	(1,500)		
R. Lee ($3,000 × 50%)		(1,500)	
Total			(3,000)
Profit (deficiency) remaining for allocation			0
Profit allocated to the partners	$8,300	$5,700	$14,000

The entry to record the division of profit is:

Dec. 31	Income Summary	14,000	
	S. King, Capital		8,300
	R. Lee, Capital		5,700
	To transfer profit to partners' capital accounts.		

A	=	L	+	PE
				−14,000
				+8,300
				+5,700

Cash flows: no effect

Let's now look at a situation where there is a loss. Assume that Kingslee Company reports a loss of $18,000. The salary and interest allowances are still allocated first. After the salary and interest allowances, there is a deficiency of $35,000 ($18,000 + $14,400 + $2,600). The deficiency is then divided equally among the partners as in Illustration 12-4.

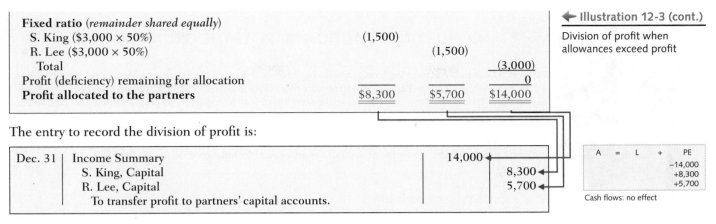

◀ Illustration 12-4

Division of loss

KINGSLEE COMPANY
Division of Loss
Year Ended December 31, 2011

	S. King	R. Lee	Total
Loss			$(18,000)
Salary allowance			
S. King	$ 8,400		
R. Lee		$6,000	
Total			14,400
Deficiency remaining for allocation			(32,400)
Interest allowance			
S. King ($28,000 × 5%)	1,400		
R. Lee ($24,000 × 5%)		1,200	
Total			2,600
Deficiency remaining for allocation			(35,000)
Fixed ratio (*remainder shared equally*)			
S. King ($35,000 × 50%)	(17,500)		
R. Lee ($35,000 × 50%)		(17,500)	
Total			(35,000)
Loss remaining for allocation			0
Loss allocated to the partners	$(7,700)	$(10,300)	$(18,000)

The salary and interest allowances are calculated first, as in the previous examples, whether the partnership reports a profit or a loss. Any remaining excess or deficiency is then allocated to the partners.

The journal entry to record the division of the loss would be as follows:

Dec. 31	S. King, Capital	7,700	
	R. Lee, Capital	10,300	
	Income Summary		18,000
	To transfer loss to partners' capital accounts.		

A	=	L	+	PE
				−7,700
				−10,300
				+18,000

Cash flows: no effect

 ACCOUNTING IN ACTION: ACROSS THE ORGANIZATION

Partners in large public accounting firms can make big incomes. A few senior partners may earn as much as $1 million a year. However, the average earnings of partners are more likely to be in the $300,000 range. The compensation of partners in most large partnerships is similar to the compensation of a proprietor in a proprietorship. Like proprietors, partners are not guaranteed an annual salary—compensation depends entirely on each year's operating results, which could be positive (profit) or negative (loss). Also, a large investment is required of each partner. This capital is at risk for the partner's entire career—often 25 to 30 years—and there is no rate of return on it. Upon leaving, the partner is simply repaid the investment without any adjustment for inflation or increase in value.

How is the profit earned by a partner in an accounting partnership different from the earnings of a staff accountant in the same partnership?

BEFORE YOU GO ON . . .

➜ **Review It**

1. What are the differences between closing entries for a partnership and a proprietorship?
2. What are some examples of profit and loss ratios used in a partnership?
3. What is the difference between a salary allowance and salary expense? Between an interest allowance and interest expense?

➜ **Do It**

LeMay Company reports profit of $72,000 for the year ended May 31, 2011. The partnership agreement specifies (1) salary allowances of $30,000 for L. Leblanc and $24,000 for R. May, (2) an interest allowance of 4% based on average capital account balances, and (3) sharing any remainder on a 60:40 basis (60% to Leblanc, 40% to May). Average capital account balances for the year were $40,000 for Leblanc and $30,000 for May. (a) Prepare a schedule dividing the profit between the two partners. (b) Prepare the closing entry for profit.

Action Plan
- First allocate the salary allowances and the interest allowances.
- Then apply the partners' fixed ratios to divide the remaining profit or the deficiency.
- In the closing entry, distribute profit or loss among the partners' capital accounts according to the profit and loss ratio.

Solution

(a)

LEMAY COMPANY Division of Profit Year Ended May 31, 2011			
	L. Leblanc	R. May	Total
Profit			$72,000
Salary allowance			
L. Leblanc	$30,000		
R. May		$24,000	
Total			54,000
Profit remaining for allocation			18,000
Interest allowance			
L. Leblanc ($40,000 × 4%)	1,600		
R. May ($30,000 × 4%)		1,200	
Total			2,800
Profit remaining for allocation			15,200
Fixed ratio (*remainder shared 60:40*)			
L. Leblanc (60% × $15,200)	9,120		
R. May (40% × $15,200)		6,080	
Total			15,200
Profit remaining for allocation			0
Profit allocated to the partners	$40,720	$31,280	$72,000

(b)

May 31	Income Summary	72,000	
	L. Leblanc, Capital		40,720
	R. May, Capital		31,280
	To close profit to partners' capital accounts.		

Related exercise material: BE12–4, BE12–5, BE12–6, BE12–7, BE12–8, E12–3, and E12–4.

The Navigator

Partnership Financial Statements

The financial statements of a partnership are very similar to those of a proprietorship. The differences are due to the additional owners involved in a partnership.

STUDY OBJECTIVE 4

Prepare partnership financial statements.

The income statement for a partnership is identical to the income statement for a proprietorship. The division of the partnership profit or loss is not an additional financial statement. It is simply a schedule that shows how the profit or loss was allocated to the partners. It is often disclosed as a separate schedule or in a note to the statement.

The statement of equity for a partnership is called the **statement of partners' equity**. Its function is to explain the changes in each partner's capital account and in total partnership capital during the year. As in a proprietorship, changes in capital may result from three causes: additional investments by owners, drawings, and each partner's share of the profit or loss.

The statement of partners' equity for Kingslee Company is shown in Illustration 12-5. It is based on the division of $22,000 of profit in Illustration 12-2. The statement includes assumed data for the investments and drawings.

KINGSLEE COMPANY
Statement of Partners' Equity
Year Ended December 31, 2011

	S. King	R. Lee	Total
Capital, January 1	$28,000	$24,000	$52,000
Add: Investments	2,000	0	2,000
Profit	12,300	9,700	22,000
	42,300	33,700	76,000
Less: Drawings	7,000	5,000	12,000
Capital, December 31	$35,300	$28,700	$64,000

← **Illustration 12-5**

Statement of partners' equity

The statement of partners' equity is prepared from the income statement and the partners' capital and drawings accounts.

The balance sheet for a partnership is the same as for a proprietorship, except for the equity section. In a proprietorship, the equity section of the balance sheet is called owner's equity. A one-line capital account is reported for the owner. In a partnership, the capital balances of each partner are shown in the balance sheet, in a section called partners' equity. The partners' equity section in Kingslee Company's balance sheet appears in Illustration 12-6.

KINGSLEE COMPANY
Balance Sheet (partial)
December 31, 2011

Liabilities and Partners' Equity		
Total liabilities (assumed amount)		$115,000
Partners' equity		
S. King, Capital	$35,300	
R. Lee, Capital	28,700	64,000
Total liabilities and partners' equity		$179,000

← **Illustration 12-6**

Partners' equity section of a partnership balance sheet

It is impractical for large partnerships to report each individual partner's equity separately. For reporting purposes, these amounts are usually aggregated in the balance sheet.

BEFORE YOU GO ON . . .

→ **Review It**

1. How are partnership financial statements similar to, and different from, proprietorship financial statements?
2. Identify the components reported in the statement of partners' equity.

→ **Do It**

The capital accounts of Mindy Dawson and Tara Pughes, partners in the Best Skate Company, had balances of $80,000 and $95,000, respectively, on January 1, 2011. During the year, Dawson invested an additional $15,000 and each partner withdrew $50,000. Profit for the year was $150,000 and was shared equally between the partners. Prepare a statement of partners' equity for the year ended December 31, 2011.

Action Plan

- Each partner's capital account is increased by the partner's investments and profit, and decreased by the partner's drawings.
- Allocate profit between the partners according to their profit-sharing agreement.

Solution

(a)

	M. Dawson	T. Pughes	Total
BEST SKATE COMPANY Statement of Partners' Equity Year Ended December 31, 2011			
Capital, January 1	$ 80,000	$ 95,000	$ 175,000
Add: Investments	15,000	0	15,000
Profit	75,000	75,000	150,000
	170,000	170,000	340,000
Less: Drawings	50,000	50,000	100,000
Capital, December 31	$120,000	$120,000	$240,000

The Navigator

Related exercise material: BE12–9, E12–5, and E12–6.

Admission and Withdrawal of Partners

We have seen how the basic accounting for a partnership works. We now look at how to account for something that happens often in partnerships: the addition or withdrawal of a partner.

Admission of a Partner

STUDY OBJECTIVE 5

Prepare the entries to record the admission of a partner.

The admission of a new partner legally dissolves the existing partnership and begins a new one. From an economic standpoint, the admission of a new partner (or partners) may have only a minor impact on the continuity of the business. For example, in large public accounting or law firms, partners are admitted without any change in operating policies. To recognize the economic effects, it is only necessary to open a capital account for each new partner. In most cases, the accounting records of the old partnership will continue to be used by the new partnership.

A new partner may be admitted by either (1) purchasing the interest of an existing partner, or (2) investing assets in the partnership, as shown in Illustration 12-7. The purchase of a partner's interest involves only a transfer of capital among the partners who are part of the transaction: the total capital of the partnership is not affected. The investment of assets in the partnership increases both the partnership's net assets (total assets less total liabilities) and its total capital.

1. Purchase of a partner's interest   2. Investment of assets in the partnership

◀ Illustration 12-7

Ways of adding partners

Purchase of a Partner's Interest

The admission by purchase of a partner's interest is a personal transaction between one or more existing partners and the new partner. Each party acts as an individual, separate from the partnership entity. The price paid is negotiated by the individuals involved. It may be equal to or different from the partner's capital in the partnership's accounting records. The purchase price passes directly from the new partner to the partner who is giving up part or all of his or her ownership claims. Any money or other consideration that is exchanged is the personal property of the participants and not the property of the partnership.

Accounting for the purchase of an interest is straightforward. In the partnership, only the transfer of a partner's capital is recorded. The old partner's capital account is debited for the ownership claims that have been given up. The new partner's capital account is credited with the ownership interest purchased. Total assets, total liabilities, and total capital remain unchanged, as do all individual asset and liability accounts.

To illustrate, assume that on July 1, L. Carson agrees to pay $8,000 each to two partners, D. Arbour and D. Baker, for one-third of their interest in the ABC partnership. At the time of Carson's admission, each partner has a $30,000 capital balance. Both partners, therefore, give up $10,000 ($\frac{1}{3} \times \$30,000$) of their capital. The entry to record the admission of Carson is as follows:

> **Helpful hint** In a purchase of an interest, the partnership is not a participant in the transaction. No cash is contributed to the partnership.

July 1	D. Arbour, Capital	10,000	
	D. Baker, Capital	10,000	
	L. Carson, Capital		20,000
	To record admission of Carson by purchase.		

A	=	L	+	PE
				−10,000
				−10,000
				+20,000

Cash flows: no effect

Note that the cash paid by Carson is not recorded by the partnership because it is paid personally to Arbour and Baker. The entry above would be exactly the same regardless of the amount paid by Carson for the one-third interest. If Carson pays $12,000 each to Arbour and Baker for one-third of their interest in the partnership, the above entry is still made.

The effect of this transaction on the partners' capital accounts is as follows:

D. Arbour, Capital		D. Baker, Capital		L. Carson, Capital	
	Bal. 30,000		Bal. 30,000		
July 1 10,000		July 1 10,000			July 1 20,000
	Bal. 20,000		Bal. 20,000		Bal. 20,000

Each partner now has a $20,000 ending capital balance and total partnership capital is $60,000 ($20,000 + $20,000 + $20,000). Net assets (assets − liabilities) and total partners' capital remain unchanged. Arbour and Baker continue as partners in the firm, but the capital interest of each has been reduced from $30,000 to $20,000.

Investment of Assets in a Partnership

The admission of a partner by an investment of assets in the partnership is a transaction between the new partner and the partnership. It is sometimes referred to simply as **admission by investment**. This transaction increases both the net assets and the total capital of the partnership. In the feature story, Richard Altrogge, Richard Matchett, Alan Ashdown, and James Schemenauer were admitted to their partnership by investment.

To illustrate, assume that instead of purchasing a partner's interest as illustrated in the previous section, Carson invests $30,000 in cash in the ABC partnership for a one-third capital interest. In this case, the entry is:

A	=	L	+	PE
+30,000				+30,000

↑ Cash flows: +30,000

July 1	Cash	30,000	
	L. Carson, Capital		30,000
	To record admission of Carson by investment.		

Both net assets and total capital increase by $30,000. The effect of this transaction on the partners' capital accounts is as follows:

D. Arbour, Capital		D. Baker, Capital		L. Carson, Capital	
	Bal. 30,000		Bal. 30,000		
					July 1 30,000
	Bal. 30,000		Bal. 30,000		Bal. 30,000

Remember that Carson's one-third capital interest might not result in a one-third profit and loss ratio. Carson's profit and loss ratio should be specified in the new partnership agreement. It may or may not be equal to the one-third capital interest.

The before and after effects of an admission by purchase of an interest or by investment are shown in the following comparison of the net assets and capital balances:

	Before Admission of Partner	After Admission of Partner	
		Purchase of a Partner's Interest	Investment of Assets in the Partnership
Net assets	$60,000	$60,000	$90,000
Partners' capital			
D. Arbour	$30,000	$20,000	$30,000
D. Baker	30,000	20,000	30,000
L. Carson		20,000	30,000
Total partners' equity	$60,000	$60,000	$90,000

When an interest is purchased, the partnership's total net assets and total capital do not change. In contrast, when a partner is admitted by investment, both the total net assets and the total capital change (increase) by the amount of cash invested by the new partner.

In an admission by investment, complications occur when the new partner's investment is not the same as the capital equity acquired. When those amounts are not the same, the difference is considered a bonus either (1) to the old (existing) partners or (2) to the new partner.

Bonus to Old Partners. The existing partners may want a bonus when admitting a new partner. In an established firm, existing partners may insist on a bonus as compensation for the work they have put into the partnership over the years. The fair value of the partnerships' assets may exceed their carrying value. Or if a partnership has been profitable, goodwill may exist. Recall that internally generated goodwill is not recorded as part of the company's net assets. In such cases, the new partner is usually willing to pay a bonus to become a partner. The bonus is allocated to the existing partners based on their profit and loss ratios before the admission of the new partner.

To illustrate, assume that on November 1, the Peart-Sampson partnership, owned by Sam Peart and Hal Sampson, has total partnership capital of $120,000. Peart has a capital balance of $72,000; Sampson has a capital balance of $48,000. The two partners share profits and losses as follows: Peart 60%, and Sampson 40%.

Peart and Sampson agree to admit Lana Trent to a 25% ownership (capital) interest in exchange for a cash investment of $80,000. Trent's capital balance on the new partnership books of $50,000 and the bonus to the old partners are calculated as follows:

Partnership capital before Trent is admitted ($72,000 + $48,000)	$120,000
Trent's investment in the partnership	80,000
Partnership capital after Trent is admitted	$200,000
Trent's capital in the partnership ($200,000 × 25%)	$ 50,000
Bonus to the old partners ($80,000 − $50,000)	$ 30,000

The bonus is allocated to the old partners based on their profit and loss ratios:

To Peart ($30,000 × 60%)	$ 18,000
To Sampson ($30,000 × 40%)	12,000
Total bonus allocated to old partners	$ 30,000

The entry to record the admission of Trent on November 1 is:

Nov. 1	Cash	80,000	
	S. Peart, Capital		18,000
	H. Sampson, Capital		12,000
	L. Trent, Capital		50,000
	To record admission of Trent and bonuses to old partners.		

A	=	L	+	PE
+80,000				+18,000
				+12,000
				+50,000

⬆ Cash flows: +80,000

The before and after effects of the admission of a partner who pays a bonus to the old partners are shown in the following comparison of the net assets and capital balances:

	Bonus to Old Partners	
	Before Admission of a Partner	After Admission of a Partner
Net assets	$120,000	$200,000
Partners' capital		
S. Peart	$ 72,000	$ 90,000
H. Sampson	48,000	60,000
L. Trent		50,000
Total capital	$120,000	$200,000

In summary, Lana Trent invests $80,000 cash in the partnership for a 25% capital interst of $50,000. The difference of $30,000 between these two amounts is a bonus that is allocated to the old partners based on their profit- and loss-sharing ratio as follows: $18,000 to Sam Peart and $12,000 to Hal Sampson.

Bonus to New Partner. If a new partner has specific resources or special attributes that the partnership wants, the partnership may be willing to give a bonus to the new partner. For example, the new partner may be able to supply cash that is urgently needed for expansion or to meet maturing debts. Or the new partner may be a recognized expert or authority in a relevant field. Or the new partner may be a celebrity whose name will draw more customers to the business.

A bonus to a new partner decreases the capital balances of the old partners. The amount of the decrease for each partner is based on the profit and loss ratios before the admission of the new partner.

To illustrate, assume instead that on November 1 the Peart-Sampson partnership admits Lana Trent to a 25% ownership (capital) interest in exchange for a cash investment of $20,000 (instead of $80,000 as in the previous illustration). Trent's capital balance on the new partnership books of $35,000 and allocation of the bonus from the old partners are calculated as follows:

Partnership capital before Trent is admitted ($72,000 + $48,000)	$120,000
Trent's investment in the partnership	20,000
Partnership capital after Trent is admitted	$140,000
Trent's capital in the partnership ($140,000 × 25%)	$ 35,000
Bonus to the new partner ($35,000 − $20,000)	$ 15,000

The bonus from the old partners is based on their profit and loss ratios:

From Peart ($15,000 × 60%)	$ 9,000
From Sampson ($15,000 × 40%)	6,000
Total bonus allocated to the new partner	$15,000

The entry to record the admission of Trent on November 1 in this case is:

A	=	L	+	PE
+20,000				−9,000
				−6,000
				+35,000

↑ Cash flows: +20,000

Nov. 1	Cash	20,000	
	S. Peart, Capital	9,000	
	H. Sampson, Capital	6,000	
	L. Trent, Capital		35,000
	To record Trent's admission and bonus to new partner.		

The before and after effects of the admission of a partner who is paid a bonus by the old partners are shown in the following comparison of the net assets and capital balances:

	Bonus to New Partner	
	Before Admission of a Partner	After Admission of a Partner
Net assets	$120,000	$140,000
Partners' capital		
S. Peart	$ 72,000	$ 63,000
H. Sampson	48,000	42,000
L. Trent		35,000
Total capital	$120,000	$140,000

In summary, $20,000 cash was invested in the partnership by Lana Trent for a $35,000 capital credit, and the $15,000 bonus was allocated from the partners' capital accounts as follows: $9,000 from Sam Peart and $6,000 from Hal Sampson.

BEFORE YOU GO ON . . .

→ **Review It**

1. How is the accounting for admission in a partnership by purchase of a partner's interest different from the accounting for admission by an investment of assets in the partnership?
2. How do net assets and total capital change before and after the admission of a partner (a) by purchase of a partner's interest, and (b) by an investment of assets in the partnership?
3. What are some reasons why a new partner may be willing to pay a bonus to the existing partners to join their partnership?
4. What are some reasons why the existing partners may be willing to give a new partner a bonus for joining a partnership?

→ **Do It**

I. Shandler and M. Rossetti have a partnership in which they share profit and loss equally. There is a $40,000 balance in each capital account. Record the journal entries on September 1 for each of the independent events below:

1. Shandler and Rossetti agree to admit A. Rachel as a new one-fourth interest partner. Rachel pays $16,000 in cash directly to each partner.
2. Shandler and Rossetti agree to admit A. Rachel as a new one-fourth interest partner. Rachel contributes $32,000 to the partnership.

Action Plan

• Recognize that the admission by purchase of a partnership interest is a personal transaction between one or more existing partners and the new partner.
• In an admission by purchase, no cash is received by the partnership and the capital credit for the new partner is not based on the cash paid.

- Recognize that the admission by investment of partnership assets is a transaction between the new partner and the partnership.
- In an admission by investment, determine any bonus to old or new partners by comparing the total capital of the new partnership with the new partner's capital credit. Allocate the bonus based on the old partners' profit and loss ratios.

Solution

1. Sept. 1	I. Shandler, Capital		10,000	
	M. Rossetti, Capital		10,000	
	A. Rachel, Capital			20,000[1]
	To record admission of Rachel by purchase.			
2. Sept. 1	Cash		32,000	
	I. Shandler, Capital ($4,000[2] × 50%)			2,000
	M. Rossetti, Capital ($4,000[2] × 50%)			2,000
	A. Rachel, Capital			28,000
	To record admission of Rachel by investment.			

[1] Total capital of partnership: $40,000 + $40,000 = $80,000
Rachel's capital credit: $80,000 × ¼ = $20,000
[2] Total capital of partnership: $40,000 + $40,000 + $32,000 = $112,000
Rachel's capital credit: $112,000 × ¼ = $28,000
Bonus to old partners: $32,000 − $28,000 = $4,000 (shared equally)

Related exercise material: BE12–10, BE12–11, E12–7, and E12–8.

The Navigator

Withdrawal of a Partner

Let's now look at the opposite situation, when a partner withdraws. A partner may withdraw from a partnership voluntarily, by selling his or her equity in the firm. He or she may withdraw involuntarily, by reaching mandatory retirement age, by expulsion, or by dying. The withdrawal of a partner, like the admission of a partner, legally dissolves the partnership. However, it is customary to record only the economic effects of the partner's withdrawal, while the partnership reorganizes itself and continues to operate.

STUDY OBJECTIVE 6

Prepare the entries to record the withdrawal of a partner.

As indicated earlier, the partnership agreement should specify the terms of withdrawal. Often, however, the withdrawal of a partner occurs outside of the partnership agreement. For example, when the remaining partners are anxious to remove an uncontrollable partner from the firm, they may agree to pay the departing partner much more than was specified in the original partnership agreement.

The withdrawal of a partner may be done by a payment from partners' personal assets or a payment from partnership assets, as shown in Illustration 12-8. Payment from personal assets affects only the remaining partners' capital accounts, not total capital. Payment from partnership assets decreases the total net assets and total capital of the partnership.

1. Payment from partners' personal assets

2. Payment from partnership assets

← Illustration 12-8

Ways of dropping partners

After a partner has withdrawn, profit and loss ratios for the remaining partners must be reviewed and specified again. If a new profit and loss ratio is not indicated in the partnership agreement, the remaining partners are assumed to share profit and losses equally.

Payment from Partners' Personal Assets

A **withdrawal by payment from partners' personal assets** is a personal transaction between the partners. It is the direct opposite of admitting a new partner who purchases a partner's interest. Payment to the departing partner is made directly from the remaining partners' personal assets. Partnership assets are not involved in any way, and total capital does not change. The effect on the partnership is limited to a transfer of the partners' capital balances.

To illustrate, assume that Javad Dargahi, Dong Kim, and Robert Viau have capital balances of $25,000, $15,000, and $10,000, respectively. The partnership equity totals $50,000 ($25,000 + $15,000 + $10,000). Dargahi and Kim agree to buy out Viau's interest. Each agrees to personally pay Viau $8,000 in exchange for one-half of Viau's total interest of $10,000 on February 1. The entry to record the withdrawal is as follows:

A	=	L	+	PE
				−10,000
				+5,000
				+5,000

Cash flows: no effect

Feb. 1	R. Viau, Capital	10,000	
	J. Dargahi, Capital		5,000
	D. Kim, Capital		5,000
	To record purchase of Viau's interest by other partners.		

The effect of this transaction on the partners' capital accounts is as follows:

J. Dargahi, Capital		D. Kim, Capital		R. Viau, Capital	
	Bal. 25,000		Bal. 15,000		Bal. 10,000
	5,000		5,000	10,000	
	Bal. 30,000		Bal. 20,000		Bal. 0

Net assets of $50,000 remain the same and total partnership capital is also unchanged at $50,000 ($30,000 + $20,000 + $0). All that has happened is a reallocation of capital amounts. Note also that the $16,000 paid to Robert Viau personally is not recorded because this is not partnership cash. Viau's capital is debited for only $10,000, not the $16,000 cash that he received. Similarly, both Javad Dargahi and Dong Kim credit their capital accounts for only $5,000, not the $8,000 they each paid. This is because we are showing the accounting for the partnership, not the partners' personal accounting.

Payment from Partnership Assets

A **withdrawal by payment from partnership assets** is a transaction that involves the partnership. Both partnership net assets and total capital are decreased. Using partnership assets to pay for a withdrawing partner's interest is the reverse of admitting a partner through the investment of assets in the partnership.

In accounting for a withdrawal by payment from partnership assets, asset revaluations should not be recorded. Recording a revaluation to the fair value of the assets at the time of a partner's withdrawal violates the cost principle, which requires assets to be stated at original cost. It would also ignore the going concern assumption, which assumes that the entity will continue indefinitely. The terms of the partnership contract should not dictate the accounting for this event.

To illustrate, assume that instead of Robert Viau's interest being purchased personally by the other partners, as illustrated in the previous section, his interest is bought out by the partnership. In this case, the entry is:

A	=	L	+	PE
−10,000				−10,000

↓ Cash flows: −10,000

Feb. 1	R. Viau, Capital	10,000	
	Cash		10,000
	To record purchase of Viau's interest by partnership.		

Both net assets and total partnership capital decrease by $10,000. The effect of this transaction on the partners' capital accounts is as follows:

J. Dargahi, Capital		D. Kim, Capital		R. Viau, Capital	
	Bal. 25,000		Bal. 15,000		Bal. 10,000
				10,000	
	Bal. 25,000		Bal. 15,000		Bal. 0

The before and after effects of the withdrawal of a partner when payment is made from personal assets or from partnership assets are shown in the following comparison of the net assets and capital balances:

	Before Withdrawal of Partner	After Withdrawal of Partner	
		Payment from Partners' Personal Assets	Payment from Partnership Assets
Net assets	$50,000	$50,000	$40,000
Partners' capital			
J. Dargahi	$25,000	$30,000	$25,000
D. Kim	15,000	20,000	15,000
R. Viau	10,000		
Total capital	$50,000	$50,000	$40,000

When payment is made from partners' personal assets, the partnership's total net assets and total capital do not change. In contrast, when payment is made from the partnership assets, both the total net assets and the total capital decrease.

In a payment from partnership assets, it is rare for the partnership to pay the partner the exact amount of his or her capital account balance, as was assumed above. When the amounts are not the same, the difference between the amount paid and the withdrawing partner's capital balance is considered a bonus either (1) to the departing partner, or (2) to the remaining partners.

Bonus to Departing Partner. A bonus may be paid to a departing partner in any of these situations:

1. The fair value of partnership assets is more than their carrying amount.
2. There is unrecorded goodwill resulting from the partnership's superior earnings record.
3. The remaining partners are anxious to remove the partner from the firm.

The bonus is deducted from the remaining partners' capital balances based on their profit and loss ratios at the time of the withdrawal.

In our feature story, Mr. Heagy received a bonus when he retired from the partnership. In his particular case, this bonus was specified in the partnership agreement to recognize the fact that he had brought in the initial client base for the firm in 1983.

To illustrate a bonus to a departing partner, assume the following capital balances in the RST partnership: Fred Roman, $50,000; Dee Sand, $30,000; and Betty Terk, $20,000. The partners share profit in the ratio of 3:2:1, respectively. Terk retires from the partnership on March 1 and receives a cash payment of $25,000 from the firm. The bonus to the departing partner and the allocation of the bonus to the remaining partners is calculated as follows:

Terk's capital balance in the partnership before departing	$20,000
Cash paid from partnership to Terk	25,000
Bonus paid to the departing partner—Terk	$ 5,000
Allocation of bonus from the remaining partners:	
From Roman ($5,000 × $^3/_5$)	$3,000
From Sand ($5,000 × $^2/_5$)	2,000
Total bonus to the departing partner—Terk	$5,000

The entry to record the withdrawal of Terk on March 1 is as follows:

A	=	L	+	PE
−25,000				−20,000
				−3,000
				−2,000

↓ Cash flows: −25,000

Mar. 1	B. Terk, Capital	20,000	
	F. Roman, Capital	3,000	
	D. Sand, Capital	2,000	
	Cash		25,000
	To record withdrawal of, and bonus to, Terk.		

The before and after effects of the withdrawal of a partner when a bonus is paid to the departing partner are shown in the following comparison of the net assets and capital balances:

	Bonus to Departing Partner	
	Before Withdrawal of Partner	After Withdrawal of Partner
Net assets	$100,000	$75,000
Partners' capital		
F. Roman	$ 50,000	$47,000
D. Sand	30,000	28,000
B. Terk	20,000	
Total capital	$100,000	$75,000

In summary, both net assets and capital decreased by $25,000 when $25,000 cash was paid by the partnership to Betty Terk to purchase her $20,000 equity interest. The $5,000 bonus was allocated from the remaining partners' capital accounts according to their profit and loss ratios. Fred Roman and Dee Sand, the remaining partners, will recover the bonus given to Terk as the undervalued assets are used or sold.

Bonus to Remaining Partners. The departing partner may give a bonus to the remaining partners in the following situations:

1. Recorded assets are overvalued.
2. The partnership has a poor earnings record.
3. The partner is anxious to leave the partnership.

In such cases, the cash paid to the departing partner will be less than the departing partner's capital balance. The bonus is allocated (credited) to the capital accounts of the remaining partners based on their profit and loss ratios.

To illustrate, assume, instead of the example above, that Terk is paid only $16,000 for her $20,000 equity when she withdraws from the partnership on March 1. The bonus to the remaining partners is calculated as follows:

Terk's capital balance in the partnership before departing	$20,000
Cash paid from partnership to Terk	16,000
Bonus to the remaining partners	$ 4,000
Allocation of bonus to the remaining partners:	
To Roman ($4,000 × ³/₅)	$2,400
To Sand ($4,000 × ²/₅)	1,600
Total bonus to the remaining partners	$4,000

The entry to record the withdrawal on March 1 follows:

A	=	L	+	PE
−16,000				−20,000
				+2,400
				+1,600

↓ Cash flows: −16,000

Mar. 1	B. Terk, Capital	20,000	
	F. Roman, Capital		2,400
	D. Sand, Capital		1,600
	Cash		16,000
	To record withdrawal of Terk and bonus to remaining partners.		

The before and after effects of the withdrawal of a partner when a bonus is paid by the departing partner to the remaining partners are shown in the following comparison of the net assets and capital balances:

	Bonus to Remaining Partners	
	Before Withdrawal of Partner	After Withdrawal of Partner
Net assets	$100,000	$84,000
Partners' capital		
F. Roman	$ 50,000	$52,400
D. Sand	30,000	31,600
B. Terk	20,000	0
Total capital	$100,000	$84,000

In summary, both net assets and capital decreased by $16,000 when $16,000 cash was paid by the partnership to Betty Terk to purchase her $20,000 equity interest. The $4,000 bonus was allocated to the remaining partners' capital accounts according to their profit and loss ratios.

Death of a Partner

The death of a partner dissolves the partnership. But there is generally a provision in the partnership agreement for the surviving partners to continue operations. When a partner dies, the partner's equity at the date of death normally has to be determined. This is done by (1) calculating the profit or loss for the year to date, (2) closing the books, and (3) preparing the financial statements.

The death of the partner may be recorded by either of the two methods described earlier in the section for the withdrawal of a partner: (1) payment from the partners' personal assets or (2) payment from the partnership assets. That is, one or more of the surviving partners may agree to use his or her personal assets to purchase the deceased partner's equity. Or, partnership assets may be used to settle with the deceased partner's estate. To make it easier to pay from partnership assets, many partnerships take out life insurance policies on each partner. The partnership is named as the beneficiary. The proceeds from the insurance policy on the deceased partner are then used to settle with the estate.

BEFORE YOU GO ON . . .

➡ Review It

1. Compare the withdrawal of a partner with the admission of a partner.
2. Contrast the accounting for the withdrawal of a partner by payment from (a) personal assets, and (b) partnership assets.
3. How do net assets and total capital change before and after the withdrawal of a partner when a bonus is paid (a) to the departing partner, and (b) to the remaining partners?
4. Explain how the accounting for the death of a partner is similar to, or differs from, the accounting for the withdrawal of a partner.

➡ Do It

S. Hosseinzadeh, M. Bélanger, and C. Laurin have a partnership in which they share profit and loss equally. There is a $40,000 balance in each capital account. Record the journal entries on March 1 for each of the independent events below:

1. Laurin withdraws from the partnership. Hosseinzadeh and Bélanger each pay Laurin $25,000 out of their personal assets.
2. Laurin withdraws from the partnership and is paid $30,000 of partnership cash.

Action Plan
- Recognize that the withdrawal by sale of a partnership interest is a personal transaction between one or more remaining partners and the withdrawing partner.

- Recognize that the withdrawal by payment of partnership assets is a transaction between the withdrawing partner and the partnership.
- In a withdrawal by payment of partnership assets, determine any bonus to the departing or remaining partners by comparing the amount paid with the amount of the withdrawing partner's capital balance. Allocate the bonus based on the remaining partners' profit and loss ratios.

Solution

1.	Mar. 1	C. Laurin, Capital	40,000	
		S. Hosseinzadeh, Capital ($40,000 × ½)		20,000
		M. Bélanger, Capital ($40,000 × ½)		20,000
		To record purchase of Laurin's interest.		
2.	Mar. 1	C. Laurin, Capital	40,000	
		Cash		30,000
		S. Hosseinzadeh, Capital ($10,000[1] × ½)		5,000
		M. Bélanger, Capital ($10,000[1] × ½)		5,000
		To record withdrawal of Laurin by payment of		
		partnership assets and bonus to remaining partners.		

[1] Bonus: $30,000 − $40,000 = $(10,000)

The Navigator

Related exercise material: BE12–12, BE12–13, E12–9, and E12–10.

Liquidation of a Partnership

STUDY OBJECTIVE 7

Prepare the entries to record the liquidation of a partnership.

The liquidation of a partnership ends the business. It involves selling the assets of the business, paying liabilities, and distributing any remaining assets to the partners. Liquidation may result from the sale of the business by mutual agreement of the partners or from bankruptcy. A **partnership liquidation** ends both the legal and the economic life of the entity.

Before the liquidation process begins, the accounting cycle for the partnership must be completed for the final operating period. This includes the preparation of adjusting entries, a trial balance, financial statements, closing entries, and a post-closing trial balance. Only balance sheet accounts should be open when the liquidation process begins.

In liquidation, the sale of noncash assets for cash is called **realization**. Any difference between the carrying amount and the cash proceeds is called the gain or loss on realization. To liquidate a partnership, it is necessary to follow these steps:

1. Sell noncash assets for cash and recognize any gain or loss on realization.
2. Allocate any gain or loss on realization to the partners, based on their profit and loss ratios.
3. Pay partnership liabilities in cash.
4. Distribute the remaining cash to partners, based on their capital balances.

Each of the steps must be done in sequence, and creditors must be paid before partners receive any cash distributions.

It sometimes happens, when a partnership is liquidated, that all partners have credit balances in their capital accounts. This situation is called **no capital deficiency**. Alternatively, one or more of the partners' capital accounts may have a debit balance. This situation is called a **capital deficiency**.

To illustrate each of these situations, assume that Ace Company is liquidated on April 15, 2011, when its post-closing trial balance shows the assets, liabilities, and partners' equity accounts in Illustration 12-9. The profit and loss ratios of the partners are 3:2:1 for R. Aube, P. Chordia, and W. Elliott.

ACE COMPANY Post-Closing Trial Balance April 15, 2011	Debit	Credit
Cash	$ 5,000	
Accounts receivable	33,000	
Equipment	35,000	
Accumulated depreciation—equipment		$ 8,000
Accounts payable		31,000
R. Aube, capital		15,000
P. Chordia, capital		17,800
W. Elliott, capital		1,200
Totals	$73,000	$73,000

No Capital Deficiency

No capital deficiency means that all partners have credit balances in their capital accounts prior to the final distribution of cash. An example of the steps in the liquidation process with no capital deficiency follows:

1. Assume the noncash assets (accounts receivable and equipment) are sold on April 18 for $75,000. The carrying amount of these assets is $60,000 ($33,000 + $35,000 − $8,000). Thus, a gain of $15,000 is realized on the sale, and the following entry is made:

(1)			
Apr. 18	Cash	75,000	
	Accumulated Depreciation—Equipment	8,000	
	Accounts Receivable		33,000
	Equipment		35,000
	Gain on Realization		15,000
	To record realization of noncash assets.		

A = L + PE
+75,000   +15,000
+8,000
−33,000
−35,000

↑ Cash flows: +75,000

2. The gain on realization of $15,000 is allocated to the partners based on their profit and loss ratios, which are 3:2:1 (or $\frac{3}{6}$, $\frac{2}{6}$, and $\frac{1}{6}$). The entry is:

(2)			
Apr. 18	Gain on Realization	15,000	
	R. Aube, Capital ($15,000 × $\frac{3}{6}$)		7,500
	P. Chordia, Capital ($15,000 × $\frac{2}{6}$)		5,000
	W. Elliott, Capital ($15,000 × $\frac{1}{6}$)		2,500
	To allocate gain to partners' capital accounts.		

A = L + PE
      −15,000
      +7,500
      +5,000
      +2,500

Cash flows: no effect

3. Partnership liabilities consist of accounts payable, $31,000. Creditors are paid in full on April 23 by a cash payment of $31,000. The entry is:

(3)			
Apr. 23	Accounts Payable	31,000	
	Cash		31,000
	To record payment of partnership liabilities.		

A = L + PE
−31,000   −31,000

↓ Cash flows: −31,000

Illustration 12-10 shows the account balances after the entries in the first three steps are posted. All of the accounts will have zero balances except for cash and the partners' capital accounts.

Illustration 12-10 →
Partnership liquidation—
no capital deficiency

		Assets			= Liabilities +	Partners' Equity		
	Cash	Accounts Receivable	Equipment	Accum. Dep. Equipment	Accounts Payable	R. Aube, Capital	P. Chordia, Capital	W. Elliott, Capital
Account balances prior to liquidation:	$ 5,000	$33,000	$35,000	$8,000	$31,000	$15,000	$17,800	$1,200
1. & 2. Sale of assets and share of gain	+75,000	–33,000	–35,000	–8,000		+7,500	+5,000	+2,500
Balances	80,000	0	0	0	31,000	22,500	22,800	3,700
3. Payment of accounts payable	–31,000				–31,000			
Balances	49,000	0	0	0	0	22,500	22,800	3,700
4. Distribution of cash to partners	–49,000					–22,500	–22,800	–3,700
Final balances	$ 0	$ 0	$ 0	$ 0	$ 0	$ 0	$ 0	$ 0

4. The remaining cash is distributed to the partners on April 25 based on their capital balances as shown in Illustration 12-10. The entry to record the distribution of cash on April 25 is:

A	=	L	+	PE
–49,000				–22,500
				–22,800
				–3,700

↓ Cash flows: –49,000

		(4)		
Apr. 25	R. Aube, Capital		22,500	
	P. Chordia, Capital		22,800	
	W. Elliott, Capital		3,700	
	Cash			49,000
	To record distribution of cash to partners.			

As shown in Illustration 12-10, after this entry is posted, all of the accounts have zero balances and the liquidation of the partnership is complete.

Two points to remember:

- Gains or losses on sale of assets are allocated to the partners based on the profit and loss ratio.
- The final cash payment to the partners is based on the balances in the partners' capital accounts.

Capital Deficiency

Capital deficiency means that at least one partner has a debit balance in his or her capital account before the final distribution of cash. This may be caused by recurring losses, excessive drawings, or losses from the realization during liquidation.

To illustrate, assume instead that Ace Company (see Illustration 12-9) is almost bankrupt. The partners decide to liquidate by having a going-out-of-business sale on April 18. Many of the accounts receivable cannot be collected, and the equipment is sold at auction at less than its fair value. Cash proceeds from the equipment sale and collections from customers total only $42,000. The loss on liquidation is $18,000 ($60,000 in carrying amount − $42,000 in proceeds). The steps in the liquidation process are as follows:

1. The entry for the realization of noncash assets is recorded on April 18:

A	=	L	+	PE
+42,000				–18,000
+8,000				
–33,000				
–35,000				

↑ Cash flows: +42,000

		(1)		
Apr. 18	Cash		42,000	
	Accumulated Depreciation—Equipment		8,000	
	Loss on Realization		18,000	
	Accounts Receivable			33,000
	Equipment			35,000
	To record realization of noncash assets.			

2. The loss on realization is allocated to the partners based on their profit and loss ratios of 3:2:1 and is recorded as follows:

(2)		
Apr. 18	R. Aube, Capital ($18,000 × 3/6)	9,000	
	P. Chordia, Capital ($18,000 × 2/6)	6,000	
	W. Elliott, Capital ($18,000 × 1/6)	3,000	
	Loss on Realization		18,000
	To allocate loss to partners' capital accounts.		

A	=	L	+	PE
				−9,000
				−6,000
				−3,000
				+18,000

Cash flows: no effect

3. Partnership liabilities are paid on April 23 and recorded:

(3)		
Apr. 23	Accounts Payable	31,000	
	Cash		31,000
	To record payment of partnership liabilities.		

A	=	L	+	PE
−31,000		−31,000		

⬇ Cash flows: −31,000

After posting of the three entries, as shown in Illustration 12-11, there is $16,000 of cash remaining. Two of the partners' capital accounts have credit balances: R. Aube, Capital $6,000; and P. Chordia, Capital $11,800. The illustration shows W. Elliott's capital account as a negative number, which represents a debit balance or capital deficiency of $1,800.

Illustration 12-11 ⬇

Partnership liquidation— capital deficiency

	Assets				= Liabilities +	Partners' Equity		
	Cash	Accounts Receivable	Equipment	Accum. Dep. Equipment	Accounts Payable	R. Aube, Capital	P. Chordia, Capital	W. Elliott, Capital
Account balances prior to liquidation:	$ 5,000	$33,000	$35,000	$8,000	$31,000	$15,000	$17,800	$1,200
1. & 2. Sale of assets and share of loss	+42,000	−33,000	−35,000	−8,000		−9,000	−6,000	−3,000
Balances	47,000	0	0	0	31,000	6,000	11,800	−1,800
3. Payment of accounts payable	−31,000				−31,000			
Balances	16,000	0	0	0	0	6,000	11,800	−1,800

W. Elliott's capital deficiency of $1,800 means that he owes the partnership $1,800. R. Aube and P. Chordia have a legally enforceable claim for that amount against Elliott's personal assets. The final distribution of cash depends on how Elliott's deficiency is settled. Two alternatives for settling are presented next.

Payment of Deficiency

If the partner with the capital deficiency pays the amount owed to the partnership, the deficiency is eliminated. To illustrate, assume that W. Elliott pays $1,800 to the partnership on April 24. The entry to record this payment is as follows:

(4)		
Apr. 24	Cash	1,800	
	W. Elliott, Capital		1,800
	To record payment of capital deficiency by Elliott.		

A	=	L	+	PE
+1,800				+1,800

⬆ Cash flows: +1,800

As shown in Illustrtion 12-12, after posting this entry, the cash balance of $17,800 is now sufficient to pay the two remaining partners with credit balances in the capital accounts ($6,000 + $11,800).

Illustration 12-12 →

Payment of deficiency

	Assets	=		Partners' Equity	
	Cash		R. Aube, Capital	P. Chordia, Capital	W. Elliott, Capital
Account balances after selling assets and paying liabilities:	$16,000		$6,000	$11,800	$−1,800
Payment of capital deficiency	+1,800				+1,800
Balances	17,800		6,000	11,800	0
Distribution of cash to partners	−17,800		−6,000	−11,800	
Final balances	$0		$0	$0	$0

Cash is distributed based on these balances on April 25. This was step 4 in the list when there was no capital deficiency on p. xxx. The following entry is made:

A	=	L	+	PE
−17,800				−6,000
				−11,800

↓ Cash flows: −17,800

		(5)		
Apr. 25	R. Aube, Capital		6,000	
	P. Chordia, Capital		11,800	
	Cash			17,800
	To record distribution of cash to partners.			

As shown in Illustration 12-12, after this entry is posted, all accounts will have zero balances and the partnership liquidation is finished.

Helpful hint The profit and loss ratio changes when the partner with the capital deficiency is not included. When allocating the loss from the sale of the assets, the profit and loss ratio was divided among the three partners as 3:2:1 or $^3/_6$, $^2/_6$, and $^1/_6$. When Elliott is excluded, the profit and loss ratio is now 3:2 or $^3/_5$ and $^2/_5$.

Nonpayment of Deficiency

If a partner with a capital deficiency is unable to pay the amount owed to the partnership, the partners with credit balances must absorb the loss. The loss is allocated based on the profit and loss ratios between the partners with credit balances. Recall that the profit and loss ratios of R. Aube and P. Chordia are 3:2 (or $^3/_5$ and $^2/_5$), respectively. The following entry would be made to remove W. Elliott's capital deficiency on April 25:

A	=	L	+	PE
				−1,080
				−720
				+1,800

Cash flows: no effect

		(4)		
Apr. 25	R. Aube, Capital ($1,800 × $^3/_5$)		1,080	
	P. Chordia, Capital ($1,800 × $^2/_5$)		720	
	W. Elliott, Capital			1,800
	To write off Elliott's capital deficiency.			

After posting this entry, the cash balance of $16,000 now equals the sum of the credit balances in the capital accounts ($4,920 + $11,080), as shown below:

Illustration 12-13 →

Nonpayment of deficiency

	Assets	=		Partners' Equity	
	Cash		R. Aube, Capital	P. Chordia, Capital	W. Elliott, Capital
Account balances after selling assets and paying liabilities:	$16,000		$6,000	$11,800	$−1,800
Write off of capital deficiency	0		−1,080	−720	+1,800
Balances	16,000		4,920	11,080	0
Distribution of cash to partners	−16,000		−4,920	−11,080	
Final balances	$0		$0	$0	$0

The entry to record the final distribution of cash is:

A	=	L	+	PE
−16,000				−4,920
				−11,080

↓ Cash flows: −16,000

		(5)		
Apr. 25	R. Aube, Capital		4,920	
	P. Chordia, Capital		11,080	
	Cash			16,000
	To record distribution of cash to partners.			

After this entry is posted, all accounts will have zero balances, as shown in Illustration 12-13, but Aube and Chordia still have a legal claim against Elliott for the deficiency. If Elliott is able to make a partial payment, it would be split between Aube and Chordia 3:2 in the same way as the deficiency was split.

 ## ACCOUNTING IN ACTION: ALL ABOUT YOU

Many successful businesses start as a simple partnership based on an inspiration, idea or dream shared by a couple of friends. Bill Hewlett and David Packard became close friends after graduating with degrees in electrical engineering from Stanford in 1934. Later they began working part-time on a product in a rented Palo Alto garage with $538 in cash and a used drill press. In 1939, the men formalized their partnership, flipping a coin to decide their startup's name.

In 1968, Bill Gates and Paul Allen met at a computer club meeting at Seattle's private Lakeside School. In Gates' dorm room at Harvard in 1974, they devised a BASIC platform for the Altair 8800 and sold it, earning Gates disciplinary charges from the university for running a business in his dorm. A year later, Gates and Allen formed Microsoft, now the world's largest software company.

Larry Page and Sergey Brin met while working on their doctorates in computer science at Stanford University in 1995. Together, they created a proprietary algorithm for a search engine on the Net that catalogued search results according to the popularity of pages. The result was Google, arguably the world's No. 1 Internet search engine.

Source: Stacy Perman, "Historic Collaborations – Business Partnerships That Changed the World", *BusinessWeek,* November 21, 2008

If you and a friend wanted to start a partnership, how might you use a partnership agreement to ensure that your partnership becomes successful, instead of ending in an unhappy liquidation?

BEFORE YOU GO ON . . .

➜ Review It

1. What are the steps in liquidating a partnership?
2. What basis is used for making the final distribution of cash to the partners when there is no capital deficiency?
3. What basis is used for making the final distribution of cash to the partners when there is a capital deficiency and the deficiency is paid? And when it is not paid?

➜ Do It

S. Anderson, J. Hinton, and R. Smit LLP dissolved their partnership as of August 31. Before liquidation, the three partners shared profit and losses in the ratio of 3:2:4. After the books were closed on August 31, the following summary accounts remained:

Cash	$ 6,000	S. Anderson, Capital	$30,000
Noncash assets	110,000	J. Hinton, Capital	20,000
Accounts payable	25,000	R. Smit, Capital	41,000

On September 24, the partnership sold the remaining noncash assets for $74,000 and paid the liabilities. If there is a capital deficiency, none of the partners will be able to pay it. Prepare the journal entries to record (1) the sale of noncash assets, (2) the allocation of any gain or loss on realization, (3) the payment of liabilities, and (4) the distribution of cash to the partners.

Action Plan

- Calculate the gain or loss by comparing cash proceeds with the carrying amount of assets.
- Allocate any gain or loss to each partner's capital account using the profit and loss ratios.
- Allocate the capital deficiency, if there is one, using the profit and loss ratio of the other partners.
- Record the final distribution of cash to each partner to eliminate the balance in each capital account. Do not distribute cash using the profit and loss ratio.

Solution

1. Sept. 24	Cash	74,000	
	Loss on Realization	36,000	
	Noncash Assets		110,000
	To record realization of noncash assets.		
2. Sept. 24	S. Anderson, Capital ($36,000 × ³/₉)	12,000	
	J. Hinton, Capital ($36,000 × ²/₉)	8,000	
	R. Smit, Capital ($36,000 × ⁴/₉)	16,000	
	Loss on Realization		36,000
	To allocate loss to partners' capital accounts.		
3. Sept. 24	Accounts Payable	25,000	
	Cash		25,000
	To record payment of liabilities.		
4. Sept. 24	S. Anderson, Capital ($30,000 – $12,000)	18,000	
	J. Hinton, Capital ($20,000 – $8,000)	12,000	
	R. Smit, Capital ($41,000 – $16,000)	25,000	
	Cash ($6,000 + $74,000 – $25,000)		55,000
	To record distribution of cash to partners.		

The Navigator

Related exercise material: BE12–14, BE12–15, BE12–16, E12–11, E12–12, E12–13, and E12–14.

WILEY PLUS

Demonstration Problems

Action Plan

- Allocate the partners' salaries and interest allowances, if any, first. Divide the remaining profit among the partners, based on the profit and loss ratio.
- Journalize the division of profit in a closing entry.
- Recognize the admission by purchase of a partnership interest as a personal transaction between an existing partner and the new partner.
- Recognize the admission by investment of partnership assets as a transaction between the new partner and the partnership.
- In an admission by investment, determine any bonus to old or new partners by comparing the total capital of the new partnership with the new partner's capital credit. Allocate the bonus based on the old partners' profit and loss ratios.

Demonstration Problem

On January 1, 2010, the partners' capital balances in Hollingsworth Company are Lois Holly, $26,000, and Jim Worth, $24,000. For the year ended December 31, 2010, the partnership reports profit of $32,500. The partnership agreement specifies (1) salary allowances of $12,000 for Holly and $10,000 for Worth, (2) interest allowances on opening capital account balances of 5%, and (3) the remainder to be distributed equally. Neither partner had any drawings in 2010.

In 2011, assume that the following independent transactions occur on January 2:

1. Donna Reichenbacher purchases one-half of Lois Holly's capital interest from Holly for $25,000.
2. Marsha Mears is admitted with a 25% capital interest by a cash investment of $37,500.
3. Stan Keewatin is admitted with a 30% capital interest by a cash investment of $32,500.

Instructions

(a) Prepare a schedule that shows the distribution of profit in 2010.
(b) Journalize the division of 2010 profit and its distribution to the partners on December 31.
(c) Journalize each of the independent transactions that occurred on January 2, 2011.

Solution to Demonstration Problem

(a)

HOLLINGSWORTH COMPANY Division of Profit Year Ended December 31, 2010			
	L. Holly	J. Worth	Total
Profit			$32,500
Salary allowance			
L. Holly	$12,000		
J. Worth		$10,000	
Total			22,000
Profit remaining for allocation			10,500

HOLLINGSWORTH COMPANY (cont.)
Division of Profit
Year Ended December 31, 2010

	L. Holly	J. Worth	Total
Interest allowance			
L. Holly ($26,000 × 5%)	1,300		
J. Worth ($24,000 × 5%)		1,200	
Total			2,500
Profit remaining for allocation			8,000
Fixed ratio (*remainder shared equally*)			
L. Holly ($8,000 × 50%)	4,000		
J. Worth ($8,000 × 50%)		4,000	
Total			8,000
Profit remaining for allocation			0
Profit allocated to the partners	$17,300	$15,200	$32,500

(b) 2010

Dec. 31	Income Summary		32,500	
	L. Holly, Capital			17,300
	J. Worth, Capital			15,200
	To close profit to partners' capital accounts.			

L. Holly, Capital			J. Worth, Capital		
	Bal.	26,000		Bal.	24,000
		17,300			15,200
	Bal.	43,300		Bal.	39,200

(c) 2011

1.	Jan. 2	L. Holly, Capital ($43,300 × 50%)	21,650	
		D. Reichenbacher, Capital		21,650
		To record purchase of one-half of Holly's interest.		

2.	Jan. 2	Cash	37,500	
		L. Holly, Capital ($7,500 × 50%)		3,750
		J. Worth, Capital ($7,500 × 50%)		3,750
		M. Mears, Capital		30,000
		To record admission of Mears by investment and bonus to old partners.		

Total capital after investment: ($43,300 + $39,200 + $37,500) $120,000
Mears's capital in the partnership: (25% × $120,000) $30,000
Bonus to old partners: ($37,500 − $30,000) $7,500

3.	Jan. 2	Cash	32,500	
		L. Holly, Capital ($2,000 × 50%)	1,000	
		J. Worth, Capital ($2,000 × 50%)	1,000	
		S. Keewatin, Capital		34,500
		To record admission of Keewatin by investment and bonus to new partner.		

Total capital after investment: ($43,300 + $39,200 + $32,500) $115,000
Keewatin's capital in the partnership: (30% × $115,000) $34,500
Bonus to Keewatin: ($34,500 − $32,500) $2,000

The Navigator

Summary of Study Objectives

1. *Describe the characteristics of the partnership form of business organization.* The main characteristics of a partnership are (1) the association of individuals, (2) mutual agency, (3) co-ownership of property, (4) limited life, and (5) unlimited liability for a general partnership.

2. *Account for the formation of a partnership.* When a partnership is formed, each partner's initial investment should be recorded at the assets' fair value at the date of their transfer to the partnership. If accounts receivable are contributed, both the gross amount and an allowance for doubtful accounts should be recorded. Accumulated depreciation is not carried forward into a partnership.

3. *Allocate and record profit or loss to partners.* Profit or loss is divided based on the profit and loss ratio, which may be any of the following: (1) a fixed ratio; (2) a ratio based on beginning, ending, or average capital balances; (3) salaries allocated to partners and the remainder in a fixed ratio; (4) interest on partners' capital balances and the remainder in a fixed ratio; and (5) salaries allocated to partners, interest on partners' capital balances, and the remainder in a fixed ratio.

4. *Prepare partnership financial statements.* The financial statements of a partnership are similar to those of a proprietorship. The main differences are that (1) the statement of owners' equity is called the statement of partners' equity, and (2) each partner's capital account is usually reported on the balance sheet or in a supporting schedule.

5. *Prepare the entries to record the admission of a partner.* The entry to record the admission of a new partner by purchase of a partner's interest affects only partners' capital accounts. The entry to record the admission by investment of assets in the partnership (1) increases both net assets and total capital, and (2) may result in the recognition of a bonus to either the old partners or the new partner.

6. *Prepare the entries to record the withdrawal of a partner.* The entry to record a withdrawal from the firm when payment is made from partners' personal assets affects only partners' capital accounts. The entry to record a withdrawal when payment is made from partnership assets (1) decreases net assets and total capital, and (2) may result in recognizing a bonus to either the departing partner or the remaining partners.

7. *Prepare the entries to record the liquidation of a partnership.* When a partnership is liquidated, it is necessary to record (1) the sale of noncash assets, (2) the allocation of the gain or loss on realization based on the profit and loss sharing ratio, (3) the payment of partnership liabilities, (4) the removal of any capital deficiency either by repayment or by allocation to the other partners, and (5) the distribution of cash to the partners based on their capital balances.

The Navigator

Glossary

Glossary
Key Term Matching Activity

Admission by investment Admission of a partner by an investment of assets in the partnership. Both partnership net assets and total capital increase. (p. 677)

Admission by purchase of a partner's interest Admission of a partner through a personal transaction between one or more existing partners and the new partner. It does not change total partnership assets or total capital. (p. 677)

Capital deficiency A debit balance in a partner's capital account after the allocation of a gain or loss on liquidation of a partnership. Capital deficiencies can be repaid, or allocated among the remaining partners. (p. 686)

Limited liability partnership (LLP) A partnership in which partners have limited liability for other partners' negligence. (p. 666)

Limited partnership (LP) A partnership in which one or more general partners have unlimited liability, and one or more partners have limited liability for the obligations of the partnership. (p. 666)

Mutual agency The concept that the action of any partner is binding on all other partners. (p. 665)

No capital deficiency A situation where all partners have credit balances after the allocation of a gain or a loss on liquidation of a partnership. (p. 686)

Partnership An association of individuals who operate a business for profit. (p. 664)

Partnership agreement A written contract that expresses the voluntary agreement of two or more individuals in a partnership. (p. 667)

Partnership dissolution A change in the number of partners that dissolves (ends) the partnership. It does not necessarily end the business. (p. 665)

Partnership liquidation An event that ends both the legal and economic life of a partnership. (p. 686)

Profit and loss ratio The basis for dividing both profit and loss in a partnership. (p. 670)

Realization The sale of noncash assets for cash on the liquidation of a partnership. (p. 686)

Statement of partners' equity The equity statement for a partnership that shows the changes in each partner's capital balance, and in total partnership capital, during the year. (p. 675)

Withdrawal by payment from partners' personal assets Withdrawal of a partner by a personal trans-

action between partners. It does not change total partnership assets or total capital. (p. 682)

Withdrawal by payment from partnership assets Withdrawal of a partner by a transaction that decreases both partnership net assets and total capital. (p. 682)

Self-Study Questions

Answers are at the end of the chapter.

(SO 1) K 1. Which of the following is not a characteristic of a partnership?
   (a) Taxable entity
   (b) Co-ownership of property
   (c) Mutual agency
   (d) Limited life

(SO 2) K 2. When a partnership is formed, each partner's initial investment of assets should be recorded at its:
   (a) carrying amount.
   (b) original cost.
   (c) fair value.
   (d) liquidation value.

(SO 3) AP 3. The ABC Company reports profit of $60,000. If partners A, B, and C have a salary allowance of $10,000 each and a fixed ratio of 50%, 30%, and 20%, respectively, what is B's share of the profit?
   (a) $16,000
   (b) $19,000
   (c) $20,000
   (d) $18,000

(SO 4) K 4. Which of the following statements about partnership financial statements is true?
   (a) Details on how profit is distributed are shown in the cash flow statement.
   (b) The distribution of profit is shown on the balance sheet.
   (c) Partner capital balances are usually shown in the income statement.
   (d) The statement of owners' equity is called the statement of partners' equity.

(SO 5) AP 5. R. Ranken purchases 50% of L. Lars's capital interest in the Kim & Lars partnership for $20,000. The capital balances of Kim and Lars are $40,000 and $30,000, respectively. Ranken's capital balance after the purchase is:

   (a) $15,000.
   (b) $20,000.
   (c) $22,000.
   (d) $35,000.

(SO 5) AP 6. Capital balances in the DEA partnership are Delano, Capital $60,000; Egil, Capital $50,000; and Armand, Capital $40,000. The profit and loss ratio is 5:3:2. The DEAR partnership is formed by admitting Ranger to the firm with a cash investment of $60,000 for a 25% capital interest. The bonus to be credited to Armand, Capital, in admitting Ranger is:
   (a) $1,500.
   (b) $3,750.
   (c) $7,500.
   (d) $10,000.

(SO 6) AP 7. Capital balances in the Alouette partnership are Tremblay, Capital $50,000; St-Jean, Capital $40,000; and, Roy, Capital $30,000. The profit and loss ratio is 5:4:3. Roy withdraws from the partnership after being paid $16,000 personally by each of Tremblay and St-Jean. Tremblay's capital balance after recording the withdrawal of Roy is:
   (a) $48,889.
   (b) $50,000.
   (c) $51,111.
   (d) $65,000

(SO 6) AP 8. Capital balances in the TERM partnership are Takako, Capital $50,000; Endo, Capital $40,000; Reiko, Capital $30,000; and Maeda, Capital $20,000. The profit and loss ratio is 4:3:2:1. Maeda withdraws from the firm after receiving $29,000 in cash from the partnership. Endo's capital balance after recording the withdrawal of Maeda is:
   (a) $36,000.
   (b) $37,000.
   (c) $37,300.
   (d) $40,000.

(SO 7) AP 9. Fontaine and Tomah were partners in the AFN partnership, sharing profit and losses in a ratio of 3:2. Fontaine's capital account balance was $30,000 and Tomah's was $20,000, immediately before the partnership liquidated on February 19. If noncash assets worth $60,000 were sold for $75,000, what was Fontaine's capital account balance after the sale?
(a) $14,000
(b) $21,000
(c) $26,000
(d) $39,000

10. Partners Aikawa, Ito, and Mori shared a profit and (SO 7) AP loss ratio of 2:1:3 in the AIM Company. After AIM was liquidated, $12,000 cash remained and the balances in the partners' capital accounts were as follows: Aikawa, $10,000 Cr.; Ito, $5,000 Cr.; and Mori, $3,000 Dr. How much cash would be distributed to Aikawa, assuming Mori does not repay his capital deficiency?
(a) $8,000
(b) $8,500
(c) $9,000
(d) $10,000

The Navigator

Questions

(SO 1) C 1. The characteristics of a partnership include the following: (a) association of individuals, (b) limited life, and (c) co-ownership of property. Explain each of these terms.

(SO 1) C 2. Carla Cardosa is confused about mutual agency and unlimited liability in partnerships. (a) Explain these two characteristics to Carla. (b) When they are combined, how can these two characteristics create problems in a partnership?

(SO 1) C 3. K. Nasser and T. Yoko are considering a business venture. They ask you to explain the advantages and disadvantages of the partnership form of organization.

(SO 1) K 4. Because of concerns over unlimited liability, there are now special forms of partnership organization that modify that characteristic. Describe these other forms of partnership.

(SO 1) K 5. What is the difference between a general partner and a limited partner?

(SO 1) K 6. (a) What items should be specified in a partnership agreement? (b) Why is it important to have this agreement in writing?

(SO 2) K 7. (a) For accounting purposes, when a partner invests assets in a partnership, how is the value of these assets determined? (b) Is this practice consistent with the cost principle? Explain.

(SO 2) C 8. Ingrid and Hartmut are transferring the assets from each of their sole proprietorships into a partnership. These assets include equipment, net of accumulated depreciation, and accounts receivable, net of allowance for doubtful accounts. (a) What amount should be used to record the transfer of the equipment to the partnership: the historic cost, carrying amount, or fair value? (b) What amount should be used to record the transfer of the receivables to the partnership?

9. R. Hay, S. Innis, and L. Joyce have a partnership (SO 3) C called Express Wings. There is a dispute among the partners. Hay has invested twice as much as the other two partners. She believes that profit and losses should be shared according to the capital contributions. The partnership agreement does not specify the division of profits and losses. How will profit and loss be divided?

10. S. Hark and R. Green are discussing how profit and (SO 3) C losses should be divided in a partnership they plan to form. What factors should they consider before reaching a decision?

11. What is the relationship between (a) a salary allow- (SO 3) C ance for allocating profit among partners and (b) partners' cash withdrawals?

12. What is difference between a salary allowance for (SO 3) C allocating profit among partners and salary expense? Between an interest allowance and interest expense?

13. Explain how each financial statement for a part- (SO 4) C nership is similar to, and different from, those of a proprietorship.

14. Holly Canter decides to pay $50,000 for a one-third (SO 5) AP interest in a partnership. What effect does this transaction have on the partnership net assets?

15. R. Minoa decides to invest $25,000 in a partner- (SO 5) C ship for a one-sixth capital interest. Will Minoa's capital balance be $25,000? Does Minoa also acquire a one-sixth profit and loss ratio through this investment?

16. Explain why a new partner may agree to pay a bo- (SO 5) C nus as part of the cost of investing in an existing partnership.

(SO 6) C 17. What is the impact on a partnership's balance sheet when (a) a partner withdraws by payment from partners' personal assets, and (b) a partner withdraws by payment from partnership assets?

(SO 6) C 18. Under what circumstances will a partner who is leaving a partnership give the remaining partners a bonus?

(SO 6) C 19. What is the purpose of a partnership's obtaining life insurance policies on each of the partners?

(SO 7) C 20. How is the liquidation of a partnership different from the dissolution of a partnership?

(SO 7) K 21. Identify the steps in liquidating a partnership.

(SO 7) C 22. How is the cash distribution to partners in the liquidation of a partnership different when (a) there is a capital deficiency, and (b) there is no capital deficiency?

(SO 7) C 23. Joe and Rajiv are discussing the liquidation of a partnership. Joe argues that all cash should be distributed to partners based on their profit and loss ratios. Is he correct? Explain.

Brief Exercises

BE12–1 The following terms were introduced in this chapter:

1. Profit and loss ratio
2. Admission by investment
3. Partnership liquidation
4. Mutual agency
5. Salary allowance
6. Withdrawal by payment from partners' personal assets
7. Capital deficiency
8. Limited liability partnership
9. General partnership
10. Partnership dissolution

Identity partnership terminology.
(SO 1) K

Match the terms with the following descriptions:

(a) ___ Partners have limited liability.
(b) ___ Partners have unlimited liability.
(c) ___ It is the basis for dividing profit and loss.
(d) ___ Partnership assets and capital increase with the change in partners.
(e) ___ Partnership assets and capital stay the same with the change in partners.
(f) ___ Actions of partners are binding on all other partners.
(g) ___ It is a compensation for differences in personal effort put into the partnership.
(h) ___ Partnership is changed by the addition or withdrawal of a partner.
(i) ___ There is a debit balance in a partner's capital account.
(j) ___ Partnership is ended.

BE12–2 R. Black and B. Rivers decide to organize the Blackriver partnership. Black contributes $10,000 cash and equipment having a carrying amount of $5,500. The equipment has an original cost of $8,000 and a fair value of $5,000. Rivers contributes $2,000 of accounts receivable, of which the partners agree that $900 is collectible. Rivers will also contribute the amount of cash required so both partners have the same amount in their capital accounts. Prepare the entry to record each partner's investment in the partnership on July 1 of the current year.

Record formation of partnership.
(SO 2) AP

BE12–3 C. Held and G. Kamp decide to merge their proprietorships into a partnership called Held-Kamp Company. Immediately before the merger, the balance sheet of Kamp Co. shows the following:

Prepare opening balance sheet.
(SO 2) AP

Accounts receivable	$16,000	
Less: allowance for doubtful accounts	1,200	$14,800
Equipment	$20,000	
Less: accumulated depreciation	7,000	13,000

The partners agree that the receivables' net realizable value is $14,000. The equipment's fair value is $12,000. Indicate how these items should appear in the opening balance sheet of the partnership on March 1 of the current year.

Convert proportions into fractions and percentages.
(SO 3) AP

BE12–4 Fixed profit and loss ratios can be expressed as proportions, fractions, or percentages. For each of the following proportions, determine the equivalent fractions or percentages:

	Proportions	Fractions	Percentages
(a)	2:1		
(b)	6:4		
(c)	3:5		
(d)	4:3:2		
(e)	1:1:2		

Calculate and record division of profit.
(SO 3) AP

BE12–5 Brung & Rohls Co. reports profit of $60,000 for the current year. The profit and loss ratios are A. Brung 60% and P. Rohls 40%. (a) Calculate the division of profit to each partner. (b) Prepare the entry to distribute the profit.

Calculate division of profit.
(SO 3) AP

BE12–6 MET Co. reports profit of $75,000 for the current year. Partner salary allowances are J. Moses $25,000; T. Eaton $15,000; and M. Talty $15,000. The profit and loss ratio is 5:3:2. Calculate the division of profit to each partner.

Calculate division of profit.
(SO 3) AP

BE12–7 The MillStone Partnership reported profit of $50,000 for the year ended February 28, 2011. Salary allowances are $30,000 for H. Mills and $25,000 for S. Stone. Interest allowances of 5% are calculated on each partner's opening capital account balance. Capital account balances at March 1, 2010, were as follows: H. Mills $70,000 (Cr.); and S. Stone $45,000 (Cr.). Any remainder is shared 60% by Mills and 40% by Stone. Calculate the division of profit to each partner.

Calculate division of loss.
(SO 3) AP

BE12–8 S & T Co. reports a loss of $44,000 for the current year. Salary allowances for the partners are J. Siebrasse $15,000 and S. Tong $10,000. Interest allowances are J. Siebrasse $8,000 and S. Tong $6,000. The remainder is shared equally. Calculate the division of loss to each partner.

Prepare financial statements.
(SO 4) AP

BE12–9 The medical practice of Dr. W. Jarratt and Dr. M. Bramstrup had the following general ledger account balances at April 30, 2011, its fiscal year end:

Cash	$25,000	W. Jarratt, drawings	$130,000
Equipment	75,000	M. Bramstrup, capital	50,000
Accumulated depreciation—		M. Bramstrup, drawings	120,000
equipment	20,000	Fees earned	365,000
Note payable, due Jan. 15, 2012	20,000	Operating expenses	145,000
W. Jarratt, capital	40,000		

Prepare financial statements for the partnership, assuming the doctors share profit or loss equally.

Record admission of partner.
(SO 5) AP

BE12–10 In ABC Co., the capital balances of the partners are A. Ali $30,000; S. Babson $25,000; and K. Carter $46,000. The partners share profit equally. On June 9 of the current year, D. Dutton is admitted to the partnership by purchasing one half of K. Carter's interest for $30,000. (a) Journalize the admission of Dutton on June 9. (b) How would the entry change if Dutton paid $20,000 instead of $30,000 to be admitted to the partnership?

Record admission of partner.
(SO 5) AP

BE12–11 In the EZ Co., the capital balances of the partners are J. Edie $45,000 and K. Zane $30,000. The partners share profit equally. On October 1 of the current year, when she invests $45,000 cash in the partnership, J. Kerns is admitted to the partnership with a 40% interest. (a) Journalize the admission of Kerns on October 1. (b) What would the journal entry be if Kerns had paid $70,000 for a 40% interest in the partnership?

Record withdrawal of partner.
(SO 6) AP

BE12–12 The capital balances of the partners in DEB Co. are M. Ditka $20,000; E. Embs $30,000; and B. Boyd $40,000. The partners share profit equally. Embs decides that he is going to leave the partnership. Ditka and Boyd each agree to pay Embs $18,000 from their personal assets to each receive 50% of Embs' equity. (a) Journalize the withdrawal of Embs on

December 31 of the current year. (b) How would the journal entry change if they paid Embs $13,000 each instead of $18,000?

BE12–13 Data for DEB Co. are presented in BE12–12. Instead of a payment from personal assets, assume that Embs receives $36,000 from partnership assets in withdrawing from the partnership. (a) Journalize the withdrawal of Embs on December 31. (b) What would the journal entry be if Embs received $26,000 cash instead of $36,000?

Record withdrawal of partner.
(SO 6) AP

BE12–14 On November 15 of the current year, the account balances in Greenscape Partnership were Cash $4,000; Other Assets $14,000; D. Dupuis, Capital $8,000; V. Dueck, Capital $9,000; and B. Veitch, Capital $1,000. The three partners share profit and losses equally. The other assets are sold for $17,000 cash. Prepare journal entries to (a) record the sale of the other assets, (b) distribute any resulting gain or loss to the capital accounts, and (c) record the final distribution of cash to the partners.

Record partnership liquidation.
(SO 7) AP

BE12–15 Data for Greenscape Partnership are presented in BE12–14. Assume that the other assets were sold for $11,000 cash instead of $17,000. Prepare journal entries to (a) record the sale of the other assets, (b) distribute any resulting gain or loss to the capital accounts, and (c) record the final distribution of cash to the partners.

Record partnership liquidation.
(SO 7) AP

BE12–16 Before the distribution of cash to the partners on April 30 of the current year, the accounts in LMN Enterprises are as follows: Cash $37,000; G. Lodge, Capital $22,000 (Cr.); L. McDonald, Capital $19,000 (Cr.); and A. Norin, Capital $4,000 (Dr.). The profit and loss ratios is 5:3:2. (a) Assuming Norin repays her capital deficiency, prepare the entry on April 30 to record (1) Norin's payment of $4,000 in cash to the partnership, and (2) the distribution of cash to the partners. (b) Assuming Norin is not able to repay her capital deficiency, prepare the entry on April 30 to record (1) the absorption of Norin's capital deficiency by the other partners, and (2) the distribution of cash to the partners.

Record partnership liquidation.
(SO 7) AP

Exercises

E12–1 Presented below are three independent situations:

1. Angelique Gloss and David Deutsch, two students looking for summer employment, decide to open a home meal replacement business. Each day, they prepare nutritious, ready-to-bake meals, which they sell to people on their way home from work.
2. Joe Daigle and Cathy Goodfellow own a ski repair business and a ski shop, respectively. They have decided to combine their businesses. They expect that in the coming year they will need a large amount of money to expand their operations.
3. Three business professors have formed a business to offer income tax services to the community. They expect to hire students during the busy season.
4. Myles Anawak would like to organize a company that buys and leases commercial real estate. Myles will need to raise a large amount of capital so that he can buy commercial property for lease.

Determine form of organization.
(SO 1) AN

Instructions

In each of the above situations, explain whether the partnership form of organization is the best choice for the business. Explain your reasoning.

E12–2 Ted Karl has owned and operated a proprietorship for several years. On January 1, he decides to end this business and become a partner in the firm of Kurl and Karl. Karl's investment in the partnership consists of $24,000 cash and the following assets from his proprietorship: accounts receivable of $28,000 less an allowance for doubtful accounts of $4,000, and equipment of $40,000 less accumulated depreciation of $8,000. The partners

Record formation of partnership.
(SO 2) AP

agree that the accounts receivable's net realizable value should be $22,000 for the partnership and that the equipment's fair value is $35,000. The partnership will also assume responsibility for Karl's accounts payable of $12,000.

Instructions

Journalize Karl's admission to Kurl and Karl on January 1.

Calculate and record division of profit.
(SO 3) AP

E12–3   R. Huma and W. How have capital balances on July 1, 2010, of $75,000 and $60,000, respectively. The partnership profit-sharing agreement specifies (1) salary allowances of $30,000 for Huma and $22,000 for How, (2) interest at 5% on beginning capital balances, and (3) for the remaining profit or loss to be shared 60% by Huma and 40% by How.

Instructions

(a) Prepare a schedule showing the division of profit for the year ended June 30, 2011, assuming profit is (1) $75,000, and (2) $35,000.
(b) Journalize the allocation of profit in each of the situations in (a).

Calculate and record division of loss.
(SO 3) AP

E12–4   Daisey Brodsky and Jim Leigh began a partnership on February 1, 2010, by investing $62,000 and $88,000, respectively. They agree to share profit and losses by allocating yearly salary allowances of $60,000 to Daisey and $40,000 to Jim, an interest allowance of 8% on their investments, and to split the remainder 55:45. During the year, Daisey withdrew $30,000 and Jim withdrew $22,000. During the first year, the partnership recorded a loss of $15,000.

Instructions

(a) Prepare a schedule showing the division of the loss for the year.
(b) Prepare the journal entry to close the income summary account at the end of the year.
(c) How much of the loss should be allocated to each partner if Daisey and Jim failed to agree on the method of sharing profit or loss?

Prepare partial financial statements.
(SO 4) AP

E12–5   In Schott Co., the partners' beginning capital balances on January 1, 2011, are M. Salz $20,000 and C. Toni $18,000. During the year, drawings were $8,000 by M. Salz and $5,000 by C. Toni. Profit was $32,000 for the year ended December 31, 2011. Salz and Toni share profit based on a 3:1 ratio.

Instructions

(a) Prepare the statement of partners' equity for the year.
(b) Prepare the partners' equity section of the balance sheet at year end.

Prepare financial statements and closing entries.
(SO 3, 4) AP

E12–6   Dr. J. Kovacik and Dr. S. Donovan have been operating a dental practice as a partnership for several years. The fixed profit and loss ratio is 60% for Dr. Kovacik and 40% for Dr. Donovan. The dental practice had the following general ledger account balances at November 30, 2011, its fiscal year end:

Cash	$32,000	J. Kovacik, drawings	$140,000
Supplies	15,750	S. Donovan, capital	32,000
Equipment	175,500	S. Donovan, drawings	90,000
Accumulated depreciation—equipment	41,250	Dental fee revenue	422,000
Accounts payable	15,000	Salaries expense	78,500
Note payable, due 2015	50,000	Other operating expenses	81,500
J. Kovacik, capital	58,000	Interest expense	5,000

Instructions

(a) Prepare financial statements for the partnership.
(b) Prepare closing entries.

Record admission of partner.
(SO 5) AP

E12–7   T. Halo, K. Rose, and J. Lamp share profit on a 5:3:2 basis, respectively. They have capital balances of $36,000, $28,000, and $16,000, respectively, when R. Zahn is admitted to the partnership on July 1 of the current year.

Instructions

Prepare the journal entry to record the admission of Zahn under each of the following independent assumptions:

(a) Zahn purchases $33\frac{1}{3}\%$ of Halo's equity for $20,000.
(b) Zahn purchases 50% of Rose's equity for $20,000.
(c) Zahn purchases 100% of Lamp's equity for $20,000.
(d) Zahn invests $20,000 cash in the partnership for a 20% interest.

E12–8   Jose Keho and Mike McLain share profit on a 4:2 basis, respectively. They have capital balances of $90,000 and $75,000, respectively, when Ed Kehler is admitted to the partnership on January 1 of the current year.

Record admission of partner. (SO 5) AP

Instructions

Prepare the journal entry to record the admission of Kehler on January 1 under each of the following independent assumptions:

(a) Kehler invests $75,000 cash for a 25% ownership interest.
(b) Kehler invests $45,000 cash for a 25% ownership interest.
(c) Calculate the amount Kehler would have to pay for a 25% ownership interest where there would be no bonus to the old partners nor to Kehler.

E12–9   Julie Lane, Sara Miles, and Amber Noll have capital balances of $50,000, $40,000, and $30,000, respectively. The profit and loss ratio is 5:3:2. Assume Noll withdraws from the partnership on December 31 of the current year under each of the following independent conditions:

Record withdrawal of partner. (SO 6) AP

1. Lane and Miles agree to purchase Noll's equity by paying $17,000 each from their personal assets. Each purchaser receives 50% of Noll's equity.
2. Miles agrees to purchase all of Noll's equity by paying $35,000 cash from her personal assets.
3. Lane agrees to purchase all of Noll's equity by paying $25,000 cash from her personal assets.
4. Noll withdraws $30,000 cash from the partnership.

Instructions

(a) Journalize the withdrawal of Noll under each of the above assumptions.
(b) Determine the balances in the partners' capital accounts and in total partners' equity after Noll has withdrawn, for conditions 1 and 4 above.

E12–10   Dale Nagel, Keith White, and Issa Mbango have capital balances of $95,000, $73,000, and $65,000, respectively. They share profit or loss on a 4:3:2 basis. White withdraws from the partnership on September 30 of the current year.

Record withdrawal of partner. (SO 6) AP

Instructions

(a) Journalize the withdrawal of White under each of the following assumptions.
  1. White is paid $85,000 cash from partnership assets.
  2. White is paid $69,000 cash from partnership assets.
(b) Determine the balances in the partners' capital accounts and in total partners' equity after White has withdrawn from the partnership for both of the above assumptions.

E12–11   Windl, Houghton, and Pesowski decided to liquidate their partnership on October 1. Before the noncash assets were sold, the capital account balances were Windl, $86,250; Houghton, $34,500; and Pesowski, $51,750. The partners divide profits and losses equally. After the noncash assets are sold and the liabilities are paid, the partnership has $172,500 of cash.

Calculate amounts paid on liquidation of partnership. (SO 7) AP

Instructions

(a) How much cash will each partner receive in the final liquidation?
(b) Assume instead that there is $139,500 of cash after the noncash assets are sold and the liabilities are paid. How much cash will each partner receive?

E12–12 At December 31, Baylee Company has cash of $30,000, equipment of $140,000, accumulated depreciation of $40,000, liabilities of $55,000, and the following partners' capital balances: H. Bayer $50,000 and J. Leech $25,000. The partnership is liquidated on December 31 of the current year and $120,000 cash is received for the equipment. Bayer and Leech have profit and loss ratios of 60% and 40%, respectively.

Instructions

Calculate how much will be paid to each of the partners when the company is liquidated on December 31.

E12–13 Data for the Baylee Company partnership are presented in E12–12.

Instructions

Prepare the entries to record (a) the sale of the equipment, (b) the allocation to the partners of the gain or loss on liquidation, (c) the payment of creditors, and (d) the distribution of cash to the partners.

E12–14 Ole Low, Arnt Olson, and Stig Lokum decided to liquidate the LOL partnership on December 31 of the current year, and go their separate ways. The partners share profit and losses equally. As at December 31, the partnership had cash of $15,000, noncash assets of $120,000, and liabilities of $20,000. Before selling their noncash assets, the partners had capital balances of $45,000, $60,000, and $10,000, respectively. The noncash assets were sold for $84,000 and the creditors were paid.

Instructions

(a) Calculate the loss on the sale of the noncash assets and the amount of cash remaining after paying the liabilities.
(b) Calculate the balance in each of the partner's capital accounts after allocating the loss from the sale of the noncash assets and paying the liabilities.
(c) Assume that all of the partners have the personal resources to cover a deficit in their capital accounts. Prepare journal entries to record any cash receipts from the partners to cover any existing deficit and to record the final distribution of cash.
(d) Now assume that the partners do not have the personal resources to cover a deficit in their capital accounts. Prepare journal entries to allocate any deficit to the remaining partners and to record the final distribution of cash.

Problems: Set A

P12–1A Patricia Derbyshire and Ann Dixon are interested in starting a marketing company that will focus on branding for performers and musicians in the entertainment industry. Patricia is very creative and understands how the entertainment industry operates. Ann has exceptional administrative and customer relations skills.

Instructions

(a) What are the advantages and disadvantages for these two individuals of forming a partnership as opposed to setting up a corporation?
(b) Assuming they decide to form a partnership, what should be included in their partnership agreement?

Taking It Further How can a partnership agreement help reduce the effects of mutual agency?

P12–2A The trial balances of two proprietorships on January 1, 2011, follow:

	Domic Company		Dasilva Company	
	Dr.	Cr.	Dr.	Cr.
Cash	$ 14,000		$12,000	
Accounts receivable	18,500		26,000	
Allowance for doubtful accounts		$ 3,000		$ 5,500
Merchandise inventory	26,500		18,500	
Equipment	45,000		30,000	
Accumulated depreciation—equipment		24,000		13,000
Notes payable		30,000		15,000
Accounts payable		11,000		28,000
I. Domic, capital		36,000		
P. Dasilva, capital				25,000
	$104,000	$104,000	$86,500	$86,500

Domic and Dasilva decide to form a partnership on January 1 and agree on the following valuations for the noncash assets that they are each contributing:

	Domic	Dasilva
Accounts receivable—net realizable value	$14,000	$22,000
Merchandise inventory	25,000	20,000
Equipment	23,000	15,000

All cash will be transferred to the partnership. The partnership will also assume all the liabilities of the two proprietorships. It is also agreed that Dasilva will invest the amount of cash required so their investments in the partnership are equal.

Instructions

(a) Prepare separate journal entries to record the transfer of each proprietorship's assets and liabilities to the partnership on January 1.
(b) Journalize the additional cash investment.
(c) Prepare a balance sheet for the partnership at January 1.

Taking It Further   What are some of the advantages of two individuals such as Domic and Dasilva operating as a partnership instead of as two separate proprietorships?

P12–3A   At the end of its first year of operations, on December 31, 2011, CNW Company's accounts show the following:

Calculate and record division of profit. Prepare statement of partners' equity.
(SO 3, 4) AP

Partner	Drawings	Capital
J. Chapman-Brown	$10,000	$30,000
C. Nelson	8,000	20,000
H. Weir	6,000	10,000

The capital balance represents each partner's initial capital investment. No closing entries for profit (loss) or drawings have been recorded as yet.

Instructions

(a) Journalize the entry to record the division of profit for the year ended December 31, 2011, under each of the following independent assumptions:
  1. Profit is $40,000. Profit is shared 3:2:1 by Chapman-Brown, Nelson, and Weir, respectively.
  2. Profit is $30,000. Nelson and Weir are given salary allowances of $8,000 and $12,000, respectively. The remainder is shared equally.
  3. Profit is $28,000. Each partner is allowed interest of 5% on beginning capital balances. Chapman-Brown, Nelson, and Weir are given salary allowances of $5,000, $15,000, and $15,000, respectively. The remainder is shared equally.

(b) Journalize the entry to close each partner's drawings account.
(c) Prepare a statement of partners' equity for the year under assumption (3) in (a) above.

Taking It Further   Explain why partnerships such as CNW Company include an interest allowance in their profit- and loss-sharing arrangements.

Calculate division of profit or loss. Prepare income statement, statement of partners' equity, and closing entries.
(SO 3, 4) AP

P12–4A Veda Storey and Gordon Rogers have a partnership agreement with the following provisions for sharing profit or loss:

1. A salary allowance of $30,000 to Storey and $40,000 to Rogers
2. An interest allowance of 4% on capital balances at the beginning of the year
3. The remainder to be divided between Storey and Rogers on a 2:3 basis

The capital balances on January 1, 2011, for Storey and Rogers were $80,000 and $100,000, respectively. For the year ended December 31, 2011, the Storey Rogers Partnership had sales of $340,000; cost of goods sold of $250,000; operating expenses of $130,000; V. Storey drawings of $24,000; and G. Rogers drawings of $32,000.

Instructions

(a) Prepare an income statement for Storey Rogers Partnership for the year.
(b) Prepare a schedule to show how the profit or loss will be allocated to the two partners.
(c) Prepare a statement of partners' equity for the year.
(d) Prepare closing entries at December 31.

Taking It Further   Assume that gross profit was lower than expected for 2011 because Rogers sold a significant amount of inventory to friends at substantially reduced prices. These arrangements were made without Storey's approval. She therefore argues that she should be allocated her salary allowance and the remaining loss should be allocated to Rogers. Is this reasonable?

Prepare financial statements and closing entries.
(SO 3, 4) AP

P12–5A Below is an alphabetical listing of the accounts in the general ledger of the Kant-Adder accounting firm at the partnership's fiscal year end, March 31, 2011. Adjusting entries for the year have been posted and included in these balances.

Accounts payable	$10,000	Prepaid insurance	$ 3,000
Accounts receivable	80,000	Professional fees	350,000
Accumulated depreciation—			
office equipment	12,000	Rent expense	24,000
Cash	16,000	Salaries expense	100,000
Demand bank loan payable	40,000	Salaries payable	8,000
Depreciation expense	6,000	Supplies	4,000
I. Kant, capital	15,000	Supplies expense	5,000
I. Kant, drawings	90,000	U. Adder, capital	10,000
Insurance expense	12,000	U. Adder, drawings	70,000
Interest expense	20,000	Unearned fees	15,000
Note payable	10,000	Utilities expense	10,000
Office equipment	30,000		

Additional information:

1. The balance in Kant's capital account includes an additional $5,000 investment during the year.
2. $1,500 of the note payable is due within the next year.
3. Kant and Adder share profit in the ratio of 60% and 40%, respectively.

Instructions

(a) Prepare an income statement, statement of partners' equity, and balance sheet.
(b) Journalize the closing entries.

Taking It Further   Each partner's drawings are larger than their respective capital account balances. Is this a problem?

Record admission of partner.
(SO 5) AP

P12–6A At April 30 of the current year, partners' capital balances and the profit- and loss-sharing ratio in the SOS Enterprises are as follows:

Partner	Capital Balance	Profit and Loss Ratio
R. Sanga	$40,000	3
K. Osborne	$20,000	2
W. Sanga	$60,000	4

On May 1, the SOSO Company is formed by admitting N. Osvald to the firm as a partner.

Instructions

Journalize the admission of Osvald under each of the following independent assumptions:

(a) Osvald purchases 50% of W. Sanga's ownership interest by paying W. Sanga $32,000 cash.
(b) Osvald purchases 50% of Osborne's ownership interest by paying Osborne $13,000 cash.
(c) Osvald invests $70,000 cash in the partnership for a 40% ownership interest.
(d) Osvald invests $40,000 in the partnership for a 20% ownership interest.
(e) Osvald invests $30,000 in the partnership for a 20% ownership interest.

Taking It Further Why would a new partner be willing to pay a bonus to the existing partners in order to join a partnership? Give an example of a situation where this might happen.

P12–7A At February 15, partners' capital balances in the MAD partnership are L. Meechum $62,500; D. Assad $50,000; and D. Dong $37,500. The profit and loss ratio is 5:4:3, in the same order. On February 16, S. Dionne is admitted to the MADD partnership by investment. After Dionne's admission, the total partnership capital is $170,000 and Assad's ownership interest has been reduced from $33^{1}/_{3}$% to 30% of total partnership capital. Dong's and Meechum's ownership interests have also been reduced proportionately.

Calculate investment and bonus on admission of partner.
(SO 5) AN

Instructions

(a) How much was Dionne's cash investment in the partnership?
(b) What was the total bonus allocated to the old partners?
(c) What is the balance in each partner's capital account after Dionne's admission to the partnership?

Taking It Further How will the partners determine the new profit and loss ratio?

P12–8A On December 31, the capital balances and profit and loss ratios in the FJA Company are as follows:

Record withdrawal of partner.
(SO 6) AP

Partner	Capital Balance	Profit and Loss Ratio
H. Fercho	$140,000	60%
P. Jiang	60,000	30%
R. Antoni	49,000	10%

Antoni is withdrawing from the partnership.

Instructions

Journalize the withdrawal of Antoni under each of the following independent assumptions:

(a) Each of the remaining partners agrees to pay $29,000 cash from personal funds to purchase Antoni's ownership equity. Each partner receives 50% of Antoni's equity.
(b) Jiang agrees to purchase Antoni's ownership interest for $58,000 cash.
(c) Antoni is paid $58,000 from partnership assets.
(d) Antoni is paid $38,200 from partnership assets.

Taking It Further What factors are important in deciding whether the withdrawing partner should be paid from the remaining partners' personal assets or from the partnership's assets?

P12–9A At April 30, partners' capital balances in the Children's partnership were K. Children $90,000; D. Picard $60,000; and V. Markle $75,000. The partners share profit equally. On May 1, Picard withdrew from the partnership. After Picard's exit, Markle's capital balance was $67,500.

Calculate bonus and payment on withdrawal of partner.
(SO 6) AN

Instructions

(a) What was the total partnership capital after Picard left the partnership?
(b) What is the percentage ownership of Children and Markle after Picard left the partnership?

(c) How much cash was paid by the partnership to Picard?

(d) What was the total bonus allocated to Picard?

Taking It Further   Why would the remaining partners agree to pay a bonus to a partner who is withdrawing from the partnership?

Prepare and post entries for partnership liquidation.
(SO 7) AP

P12–10A   The partners in Cottage Country Company decide to liquidate the company when the post-closing trial balance shows the following:

COTTAGE COUNTRY COMPANY
Post-Closing Trial Balance
April 30, 2011

	Debit	Credit
Cash	$ 39,200	
Accounts receivable	26,600	
Allowance for doubtful accounts		$ 1,400
Inventory	39,200	
Equipment	23,800	
Accumulated depreciation		14,000
Notes payable		29,400
Accounts payable		25,200
Wages payable		7,000
A. Hoffer, capital		35,000
K. Lonseth, capital		15,680
D. Posca, capital		1,120
Totals	$128,800	$128,800

The partners share profit and loss 5:3:2 for Hoffer, Lonseth, and Posca, respectively. During the process of liquidation, the transactions below were completed in the sequence shown:

1. A total of $67,200 was received from converting noncash assets into cash on May 5.
2. Liabilities were paid in full on May 7.
3. Posca paid his capital deficiency on May 9.
4. Cash was paid to the partners with credit balances on May 12.

Instructions

(a) Prepare the entries to record the transactions.

(b) Post the transactions to the cash and capital accounts.

(c) Assume that Posca is unable to repay his capital deficiency. Prepare the entry to record (1) the reallocation of his deficiency, and (2) the final distribution of cash.

Taking It Further   When determining how the cash is distributed to partners in a liquidation, the profit and loss ratio should be used. Is this correct or incorrect? Why?

Record liquidation of partnership.
(SO 7) AP

P12–11A   On June 2, 2011, the musical partnership of M. James, S. Lars, J. Kirk, and B. Robert ends and the partnership is to be liquidated. The partners have capital balances of $500,000 each except for Robert, whose capital balance is $250,000. Cash, noncash assets, and liabilities total $400,000, $2.9 million, and $1.55 million, respectively. The four partners share profit and loss equally.

Instructions

Journalize the liquidation of the partnership on June 2 under each of the following independent assumptions:

(a) The noncash assets are sold for $3 million cash, the liabilities are paid, and the remaining cash is paid to the partners.

(b) The noncash assets are sold for $1.7 million cash and the liabilities are paid. The partner with the debit capital balance pays the amount owed to the partnership and the remaining cash is paid to the partners.

(c) The noncash assets are sold for $1.7 million cash and the liabilities are paid. The partner with the debit capital balance is unable to pay the amount owed to the partnership. The cash is paid to the other three partners.

Taking It Further   What can partners do when a partnership is first created to reduce the possibility that one of the partners will have a deficit (debit balance) when the partnership is liquidated?

P12–12A   On March 2, 2010, Zoe Moreau, Karen Krneta, and Veronica Visentin start a partnership to operate a personal coaching and lifestyle consulting practice for professional women. Zoe will focus on work-life balance issues, Karen on matters of style, and Veronica on health and fitness. They sign a partnership agreement to split profits in a 3:2:3 ratio for Zoe, Karen, and Veronica, respectively. The following are the transactions for MKV Personal Coaching:

Account for formation of a partnership, allocation of profits, and withdrawal and admission of partners; prepare partial balance sheet. (SO 2, 3, 4, 5, 6) AP

2010

Mar. 2   The partners contribute assets to the partnership at the following agreed amounts:

	Z. Moreau	K. Krneta	V. Visentin
Cash	$15,000	$10,000	$20,000
Furniture		17,000	
Office equipment	18,000		
Fitness equipment			13,000
Total	$33,000	$27,000	$33,000

They also agree that the partnership will assume responsibility for Karen's note payable of $5,000.

Dec. 20   Zoe, Karen, and Veronica each withdraw $30,000 cash as a "year-end bonus." No other withdrawals were made during the year.

31   Total profit for 2010 was $110,000.

2011

Jan. 5   Zoe and Veronica approve Karen's request to withdraw from the partnership for personal reasons. They agree to pay Karen $15,000 cash from the partnership.

6   Zoe and Veronica agree to change their profit-sharing ratio to 4:5, respectively.

Dec. 20   Zoe and Veronica withdraw $42,750 and $45,000 cash, respectively, from the partnership.

31   Total profit for 2011 was $123,750.

2012

Jan. 4   Zoe and Veronica agree to admit Dela Hirjikaka to the partnership. Dela will focus on providing training in organizational skills to clients. Dela invests $31,000 cash for a 25% ownership in the partnership.

Instructions

(a) Record the above transactions. For the profit earned each year, calculate how it is to be allocated and record the closing of the income summary account.

(b) Prepare the partners' equity section of the balance sheet after Dela is admitted to the partnership.

Taking It Further   Every time a new partner is admitted to a partnership or a partner withdraws from a partnership, it is necessary to completely close the accounting records of the existing partnership and start new accounting records for the new partnership. Do you agree or disagree? Explain.

Problems: Set B

P12–1B   Canadian Equipment Rental Fund Limited Partnership operates under the trade-name 4-Way Equipment Rentals and is listed on the TSX Venture Exchange under the symbol CFL.UN. The company is located in Edmonton, Alberta, and is in the business of providing

Discuss partnership characteristics. (SO 1) C

equipment solutions including equipment rentals, sales, and service. Its main target market is the commercial and residential construction industry. As at December 31, 2008, there were 5.8 million partnership units issued and total partners' equity was just under $9 million.

Instructions

(a) What probably motivated Canadian Equipment Rental Fund Limited Partnership to organize as a limited partnership?
(b) In June 2007, the partnership issued 223,000 partnership units to certain employees for a total of $530,740. What amount are these employees liable for in the partnership?

Taking It Further What are the advantages to this limited partnership of being listed on a public stock exchange?

Record formation of partnership and prepare balance sheet.
(SO 2, 4) AP

P12–2B Here are the post-closing trial balances of two proprietorships on January 1 of the current year:

	Visanji Company Dr.	Visanji Company Cr.	Vanbakel Company Dr.	Vanbakel Company Cr.
Cash	$ 14,500		$ 6,000	
Accounts receivable	15,000		23,000	
Allowance for doubtful accounts		$ 2,500		$ 4,000
Merchandise inventory	28,000		18,000	
Equipment	52,500		30,000	
Accumulated depreciation—equipment		27,000		14,000
Notes payable		35,000		20,000
Accounts payable		15,000		17,000
F. Visanji, capital		30,500		
P. Vanbakel, capital				22,000
	$110,000	$110,000	$77,000	$77,000

Visanji and Vanbakel decide to form the Varsity partnership and agree on the following fair values for the noncash assets that each partner is contributing:

	Visanji	Vanbakel
Accounts receivable	$11,500	$18,000
Merchandise inventory	32,000	15,000
Equipment	28,000	15,000

All cash will be transferred to the partnership on January 1. The partnership will also assume all the liabilities of the two proprietorships. Further, it is agreed that Vanbakel will invest the amount of cash required so her investment in the partnership is one-half of Visanji's.

Instructions

(a) Prepare separate journal entries to record the transfer of each proprietorship's assets and liabilities to the partnership on January 1.
(b) Journalize the additional cash investment.
(c) Prepare a balance sheet for the partnership at January 1.

Taking It Further What are some of the advantages of two individuals such as Visanji and Vanbakel operating their businesses as a partnership instead of as two separate proprietorships?

Calculate and record division of profit. Prepare statement of partners' equity.
(SO 3, 4) AP

P12–3B At the end of its first year of operations, on December 31, 2011, LBS Company's accounts show the following:

Partner	Drawings	Capital
S. Little	$20,000	$60,000
L. Brown	15,000	30,000
G. Scholz	10,000	20,000

The capital balance represents each partner's initial capital investment. No closing entries have been recorded for profit (loss) or drawings as yet.

Instructions

(a) Journalize the entry to record the division of profit for the year ended December 31, 2011, under each of the following independent assumptions:

1. Profit is shared in the ratio of the partners' initial investments. Profit is $55,000.
2. Profit is $41,000. Little, Brown, and Scholz are given salary allowances of $5,000, $15,000, and $10,000, respectively. The remainder is shared equally.
3. Profit is $23,000. Each partner is allowed interest of 5% on beginning capital balances. Brown and Scholz are given salary allowances of $10,000 and $12,000, respectively. The remainder is shared equally.

(b) Journalize the entry to close each partner's drawings account.
(c) Prepare a statement of partners' equity for the year under assumption (3) in (a) above.

Taking It Further   Explain why partnerships such as LBS Company include a salary allowance in their profit- and loss-sharing arrangements.

P12–4B   Terry Lam and Chris Tan have a partnership agreement with the following provisions for sharing profit or loss:

1. A salary allowance of $25,000 to Lam and $35,000 to Tan
2. An interest allowance of 6% on capital balances at the beginning of the year
3. The remainder to be divided between Lam and Tan on a 3:4 basis

The capital balances on February 1, 2010, for T. Lam and C. Tan were $110,000 and $130,000, respectively. For the year ended January 31, 2011, the Lam Tan Partnership had sales of $395,000; cost of goods sold of $275,000; operating expenses of $150,000; T. Lam drawings of $25,000; and C. Tan drawings of $35,000.

> Calculate division of profit or loss. Prepare income statement, statement of partners' equity, and closing entries.
> (SO 3, 4) AP

Instructions

(a) Prepare an income statement for the Lam Tan Partnership for the year.
(b) Prepare a schedule to show how the profit or loss is allocated to the two partners.
(c) Prepare a statement of partners' equity for the year.
(d) Prepare closing entries on January 31.

Taking It Further   In general, what is the relationship between the salary allowance specified in the profit and loss ratio and a partner's drawings?

P12–5B   Below is an alphabetical listing of the accounts in the general ledger of Clay and Ogletree, LLP at the partnership's fiscal year end, September 30, 2011. Adjusting entries for the year have been posted and included in these balances.

> Prepare financial statements and closing entries.
> (SO 4) AP

Accounts payable	$ 15,000	Land	75,000
Accounts receivable	105,000	M. Ogletree, capital	$ 37,500
Accumulated depreciation—		M. Ogletree, drawings	150,000
building	112,500	Note payable	22,500
Accumulated depreciation—		Office equipment	60,000
office equipment	30,000	Professional fees	675,000
Bank loan payable (short-term)	67,500	Property tax expense	15,000
Building	225,000	Salaries expense	225,000
Cash	11,250	Salaries payable	7,500
Depreciation expense	22,500	Supplies	3,750
G. Clay, capital	75,000	Supplies expense	7,500
G. Clay, drawings	150,000	Unearned fees	37,500
Interest expense	5,000	Utilities expense	25,000

Additional information:
1. The balance in Clay's capital account includes an additional investment of $10,000 made during the year.

2. $5,000 of the note payable is due within the next year.
3. Clay and Ogletree share profit and loss in the ratio of 2:1, respectively.

Instructions

(a) Prepare an income statement, statement of partners' equity, and balance sheet.
(b) Journalize the closing entries.

Taking It Further Is it reasonable in this partnership for the partners to draw equal amounts each year? Both of them work full-time for the partnership.

Record admission of partner.
(SO 5) AP

P12–6B At September 30 of the current year, partners' capital balances and profit and loss rations in NEW Company are as follows:

Partner	Capital Balance	Profit and Loss Ratio
A. Nolan	$62,000	5
D. Elder	$48,000	4
T. Wuhan	$14,000	1

On October 1, the NEWS Company is formed by admitting C. Santos to the partnership.

Instructions

Journalize the admission of C. Santos under each of the following independent assumptions:

(a) Santos purchases 25% of Nolan's ownership interest by paying Nolan $20,000 cash.
(b) Santos purchases 33⅓% of Elder's ownership interest by paying Elder $20,000 cash.
(c) Santos invests $80,000 for a 30% ownership interest.
(d) Santos invests $36,000 for a 30% ownership interest.
(e) How much would Santos have to invest in the partnership for a 30% ownership interest so there is no bonus to the existing partners or the new partner?

Taking It Further Why would the existing partners be willing to give a bonus to the new partner? Give an example of a situation where this might happen.

Calculate investment and
bonus on admission of
partner.
(SO 5) AN

P12–7B At April 30, partners' capital balances in the DLM partnership are A. Donatella $100,000; M. Liebovitz $60,000; and K. Michaels $40,000. The profit and loss ratio is 5:3:2, in the same order. On May 1, S. Rafael is admitted to the partnership by investment. After Rafael's admission, the total partnership capital is $234,000. Donatella's ownership interest has been reduced from 50% to 40% of total partnership capital.

Instructions

(a) How much was Rafael's cash investment in the partnership?
(b) What was the total bonus allocated to Rafael by the old partners?
(c) What is the balance in each partner's capital account after Rafael's admission to the partnership?

Taking It Further If Donatella's ownership interest has been reduced to 40%, does this mean his share of the profits will also be reduced to 40%?

Record withdrawal of partner.
(SO 6) AP

P12–8B On December 31, the capital balances and profit and loss ratios in the VKD Company are as follows:

Partner	Capital Balance	Profit and Loss Ratio
B. Vuong	$75,000	50%
G. Khan	50,000	30%
R. Dixon	37,500	20%

Instructions

Journalize the withdrawal of Dixon under each of the following independent assumptions:

(a) Each of the continuing partners agrees to pay $22,500 cash from personal funds to purchase Dixon's ownership equity. Each partner receives 50% of Dixon's equity.
(b) Khan agrees to purchase Dixon's ownership interest for $45,000 cash.
(c) Dixon is paid $47,500 from partnership assets.
(d) Dixon is paid $29,500 from partnership assets.

Taking It Further   Assume that instead of any of the above options, Dixon withdraws from the partnership by selling her interest to S. Meyers. Do Vuong and Khan need to approve it? Why or why not?

P12–9B   At April 30, partners' capital balances in the Marckx Company partnership are G. Harper $96,000; F. Chiconi $64,000; and M. Gauchon $48,000. The profit and loss ratio is 5:4:2. On May 1, Gauchon withdrew from the partnership. After Gauchon's exit, Chiconi's capital balance was $76,800.

Calculate bonus and payment on withdrawal of partner.
(SO 6) AN

Instructions

(a) What was the total partnership capital after Gauchon left the partnership?
(b) What is the percentage ownership of Harper and Chiconi after Gauchon left the partnership?
(c) How much cash was paid by the partnership to Gauchon?
(d) What was the total bonus allocated to the remaining partners?

Taking It Further   Why would the partner who is withdrawing from a partnership agree to a cash payment that results in a bonus to the remaining partners?

P12–10B   The partners in Omni Company decide to liquidate the company when the post-closing trial balance shows the following:

Prepare and post entries for partnership liquidation.
(SO 7) AP

OMNI COMPANY Post-Closing Trial Balance May 31, 2011	Debit	Credit
Cash	$ 33,000	
Accounts receivable	30,000	
Allowance for doubtful accounts		$ 1,200
Inventory	41,400	
Equipment	25,200	
Accumulated depreciation		6,600
Notes payable		16,200
Accounts payable		32,400
Wages payable		4,560
L. Sciban, Capital		39,600
V. Subra, Capital		25,200
C. Werier, Capital		3,840
Totals	$129,600	$129,600

The partners share profit and loss 5:3:2 for Sciban, Subra, and Werier, respectively. During the process of liquidation, the following transactions were completed in the sequence shown:

1. A total of $60,000 was received from converting noncash assets into cash on June 2.
2. Liabilities were paid in full on June 4.
3. Werier paid her capital deficiency on June 6.
4. Cash was paid to the partners with credit balances on June 9.

Instructions

(a) Prepare the entries to record the transactions.
(b) Post the transactions to the cash and capital accounts.

(c) Assume that Werier is unable to repay her capital deficiency. Prepare the entry to record (1) the reallocation of her deficiency, and (2) the final distribution of cash.

Taking It Further   In a liquidation, why are the liabilities paid before the partners?

Record liquidation of partnership.
(SO 7) AP

P12–11B   On September 1, 2011, the accounting partnership of M. Broski and B. Hazle ended and the partnership was liquidated. The partners Broski and Hazle share profit and loss in a 1:3 ratio. Just before the liquidation, the post-closing trial balance showed the following: Cash, $160,000; Office Equipment, $170,000; Accumulated Depreciation—Office Equipment, $100,000; Accounts Payable, $110,000; M. Broski, Capital, $90,000; and B. Hazle, Capital, $30,000.

Instructions

Journalize the liquidation of the partnership on September 2 under each of the following independent assumptions:

(a) The equipment is sold for $78,000 cash, the accounts payable are paid, and the remaining cash is paid to the two partners.
(b) The equipment is scrapped and the accounts payable are paid. Hazle pays his capital deficiency and the remaining cash is distributed to the partners.
(c) The equipment is scrapped and the accounts payable are paid. Hazle does not pay his capital deficiency. The remaining cash is distributed to Broski.

Taking It Further   For what reasons would a partnership decide to liquidate?

Account for formation of a partnership, allocation of profits, and admission and withdrawal of partners; prepare partial balance sheet.
(SO 2, 3, 4, 5, 6) AP

P12–12B   On February 14, 2010, Isabelle Moreau, Aida Krneta, and Channade Fenandoe start a partnership to operate a marketing consulting practice. They sign a partnership agreement to split profits in a 2:3:4 ratio for Isabelle, Aida, and Channade, respectively. The following are transactions for MKF Marketing:

2010

Feb. 14 The partners contribute assets to the partnership at the following agreed amounts:

	I. Moreau	A. Krneta	C. Fenandoe
Cash	$ 9,000	$12,000	$18,000
Furniture	15,000		
Office equipment		24,000	
Graphic equipment			40,000
Total	$24,000	$36,000	$58,000

They also agree that the partnership will assume responsibility for Channade's accounts payable of $10,000.

Dec. 20 The partners agree to withdraw a total of $72,000 cash as a "year-end bonus." Each partner will receive a share proportionate to her profit-sharing ratio. No other withdrawals were made during the year.

   31 Total profit for 2010 was $81,900.

2011

Jan. 5 The three partners agree to admit Carolyn Wells to the partnership. Carolyn will pay Channade $30,000 cash for 50% of her interest in the partnership. The profit-sharing ratio will be changed so that Carolyn is allocated 50% of what was previously allocated to Channade. The partnership's name is changed to MKFW Marketing.

Dec. 20 The partners agree to pay another "year-end bonus." The total amount withdrawn is $91,800. Each partner will receive a share proportionate to her profit-sharing ratio. No other withdrawals were made during the year.

   31 Total profit for 2011 was $103,050.

2012

Jan. 2 Channade withdraws from the partnership. The partners agree the partnership will pay Channade $25,550 cash. The partnership's name is changed to MKW Marketing.

Instructions

(a) Record the above transactions. For the profit earned each year, calculate how it is to be allocated and record closing the income summary account.

(b) Prepare the statement of partners' equity for 2011.

(c) Calculate the balance in each partner's capital account on January 2, 2012, after Channade has withdrawn.

Taking It Further   Every time a new partner is admitted to a partnership or a partner withdraws from a partnership, it is necessary to change the name of the partnership to reflect the fact that a new partnership has been formed. Do you agree or disagree? Explain.

Continuing Cookie Chronicle

(*Note:* This is a continuation of the Cookie Chronicle from Chapters 1 through 11.)

Because Natalie has been so successful operating Cookie Creations, Katy would like to have Natalie become her partner. Katy believes that together they will create a thriving cookie-making business. Recall that Katy is Natalie's high school friend and has been operating her bakery for approximately 10 months.

Natalie is quite happy with her current business set-up. Up until now, she had not considered joining forces with anyone. From past meetings with Katy, however, Natalie has gathered the following information about Katy's business and compared it to her own results:

- The current fair values of the assets and liabilities of both businesses are as follows:

	The Baker's Nook	Cookie Creations
Cash	$ 1,500	$10,000
Accounts receivable	5,250	800
Merchandise inventory	500	1,200
Equipment	7,500	1,000
Bank loan payable	10,000	0

All assets would be transferred into the partnership. The partnership would assume all of the liabilities of the two proprietorships. The bank loan is due October 31, 2014.

- Katy operates her business from leased premises. She has just signed a lease for 12 months. Monthly rent will be $1,000. Katy's landlord has agreed to draw up a new lease agreement that would be signed by both partners.
- Katy has no assets and has a lot of student loans and credit card debt. Natalie's assets consist of investments in Canada Savings Bonds. Natalie has no personal liabilities.
- Katy is reluctant to have a partnership agreement drawn up. She thinks it's a waste of both time and money. As Katy and Natalie have been friends for a long time, Katy is confident that all problems can be easily resolved over a nice meal.

Natalie believes that it may be a good idea to establish a partnership with Katy. She comes to you with the following questions:

1. Do I really need a formalized partnership agreement drawn up? What would be the point of having one if Katy and I agree on all major decisions? What type of information should the partnership agreement contain?
2. I would like to have Katy contribute the same amount of capital as I am contributing. How much additional cash, in addition to the amount in Katy's proprietorship, would Katy have to borrow to invest in the partnership so that she and I have the same capital balances?
3. Katy has a lot of personal debt. Should this affect my decision about whether or not to go forward with this business venture? Why or why not?
4. What other issues should I consider before I say yes or no to Katy?

Instructions

(a) Answer Natalie's questions.

(b) Assume that Natalie and Katy go ahead and form a partnership called Cookie Creations and More on November 1, 2011, and that Katy is able to borrow the additional cash she needs to contribute to the partnership. Prepare a balance sheet for the partnership on November 1.

BROADENING YOUR PERSPECTIVE

Financial Reporting and Analysis

Financial Reporting Problem

BYP12–1 The Forzani Group Ltd. originally started as a partnership when Calgary Stampeder John Forzani and three of his teammates (including two of his brothers) started Forzani's Locker Room in 1974. The business grew steadily and expanded its initial athletic footwear business to include clothing and selected sports equipment. In 1991, the company purchased Sport-Check International Ltd., and in 1992 it purchased Hogarth's Sport & Ski. These companies were sports superstores that helped Forzani expand its business to include ski, golf, and bike equipment. In 1993, the partnership was liquidated and a corporation was formed in its place.

Instructions

(a) What probably motivated the Forzani partnership to reorganize as a corporation in 1993?

(b) Explain what is involved in liquidating a partnership.

(c) Explain how the Forzani partnership would record the transfer of its assets and liabilities into the new corporation.

(d) Look at The Forzani Group Ltd.'s corporate financial statements reproduced in Appendix A at the back of this textbook. In what ways would the partnership financial statements have been different from these corporation statements?

Interpreting Financial Statements

BYP12–2 The Sherobee Glen Limited Partnership was formed in 1982 to purchase rental properties. The balance sheet and notes to its financial statements include the following excerpts:

SHEROBEE GLEN LIMITED PARTNERSHIP Balance Sheet (partial) October 31, 2008	
Limited partners' equity	
Original investment, 200 limited partnership units	$2,500,000
Deficit	(807,296)
	$ 1,692,704

> **SHEROBEE GLEN LIMITED PARTNERSHIP**
> Notes to the Financial Statements (partial)
> October 31, 2008
>
> 6. Liability of Limited Partners
>
> The Limited Partnership Agreement provides that the General Partner has unlimited liability for the debts and obligations of the Limited Partnership. The liability of each Limited Partner is limited to the amount of capital contributed or agreed to be contributed plus the Limited Partner's share of undistributed profit.

Instructions

(a) What are the advantages to the company of operating as a limited partnership rather than as a general partnership?

(b) Use the balance sheet information to determine the limited partners' liability in dollars.

Critical Thinking

Collaborative Learning Activity

Note to instructor: Additional instructions and handout material for this group activity can be found on the Instructor Resource Site.

BYP12–3   In this group activity, you will review accounting for the admission of a new partner in the following situations: (1) Purchase of an existing partner's interest and (2) Investment of assets in partnership

(a) equal to a new partner's capital interest (b) with a bonus to the old partners (c) with a bonus to the new partner.

Working in Groups

Instructions

(a) Your instructor will divide the class into "home" groups and distribute a package to each. Select one page from the package, which will indicate a type of admission of a new partner. Join the "expert" group for that type of admission.

(b) In the "expert" group, review and discuss accounting for the addition of a new partner in your type of situation and ensure that each group member thoroughly understands the necessary entries and their effects.

(c) Return to your "home" group and explain accounting for the admission of a new partner in your situation to the other students in your group.

(d) You may be asked by your instructor to write a short quiz on this topic.

Communication Activity

BYP12–4   You are an expert in forming partnerships. Dr. Konu Chatterjie and Dr. Sheila Unger want to establish a partnership to practice medicine. They will meet with you to discuss their plans. However, you will first send them a letter that outlines the issues they need to consider beforehand.

Writing Handbook

Instructions

Write a letter, in good form, discussing the different types of partnership organizations and the advantages and disadvantages of each type so that the doctors can start thinking about their needs.

Ethics Case

Ethics in Accounting

BYP12–5   Susan and Erin operate a spa as partners and share profits and losses equally. Their business has been more successful than they expected and is operating profitably. Erin works hard to maximize profits. She schedules appointments from 8 a.m. to 6 p.m. daily and she even works weekends. Susan schedules her appointments from 9 a.m. to 5 p.m. and does not work weekends. Susan regularly makes much larger withdrawals of cash than Erin does, but tells Erin not to worry. "I never make a withdrawal without you knowing about it," she says to Erin, "so it's properly recorded in my drawings account and charged against my capital at the end of the year." To date, Susan's withdrawals are twice as much as Erin's.

Instructions

(a) Who are the stakeholders in this situation?

(b) Identify the problems with Susan's actions. In what ways are they unethical?

(c) What provisions could be put in the partnership agreement so that the differences in Susan's and Erin's work and withdrawal habits are no longer unfair to Erin?

"All About You" Activity

BYP12–6   In the "All About You" feature, we learned about the importance of having a partnership agreement. The Beatles and the Rolling Stones were popular music bands that started in the early sixties. However, the Beatles broke up in 1970 after disagreements, including a disagreement on who should be their financial advisor. In contrast, the Rolling Stones have continued to play together.

You and a couple of friends have decided to form an "indie" band. An indie band records and publishes its music independently from commercial record labels, thus maintaining control over its music and career. You play the guitar and sing; your friends are a bass player and a keyboard player. You have written the lyrics to a couple of songs and the music for the lyrics was composed by the band. After the songs are recorded, the band intends to register the recordings with SOCAN. SOCAN sells access to music registered with it by collecting licence fees from anyone playing or broadcasting live or recorded music. SOCAN then pays the musicians a royalty.

The three of you have decided to get together and discuss some of the issues that may arise and what should be addressed in the band's agreement.

Instructions

(a) Is the band a partnership even if a partnership agreement is never created?

(b) Identify the different types of revenues that the band may earn.

(c) Identify the costs that the band will incur to earn these revenues.

(d) Identify issues that may arise when the band is determining how the revenues and costs should be shared by the members.

(e) Identify issues that may arise if one of the band members wants to leave the band. How might this be addressed in the agreement?

(f) Identify issues that may arise if a new member joins the band after the band has already successfully recorded music and is receiving royalties.

(g) Identify issues that may arise if one of the band members does a solo recording or performance.

(h) Identify issues that may arise if the band decides to split up.

ANSWERS TO CHAPTER QUESTIONS

Answers to Accounting in Action Insight Questions

Business Insight, p. 667

Q: If an investor wants to own Saskatchewan farmland, why doesn't he or she simply buy the farmland instead of buying units of this limited partnership? Why is it important to the investors to invest in a limited partnership as opposed to just a partnership?

A: Most investors do not have sufficient cash to purchase a tract of farmland, nor would they have the expertise or even the time to oversee the partnership's operations and find a farm operator to rent the land. The limited partnership works because the general partner operates the business of the partnership and each of the limited partners contributes part of the cash necessary to buy the partnership's assets. That way, even investors with small amounts of funds are able to invest in Saskatchewan farmland.

Across the Organization, p. 674

Q: How is the profit earned by a partner in an accounting partnership different from the earnings of a staff accountant in the same partnership?

A: A staff accountant is an employee of the partnership and is paid a fixed salary for the year. A partner's profit varies depending on the partnership's earnings during the year and the profit sharing arrangements among all the partners. A partner can receive cash payments in the form of withdrawals during the year, but these are recorded as reductions of capital and not as salary expense.

All About You, p. 691

Q: If you and a friend wanted to start a partnership, how might you use a partnership agreement to ensure that your partnership becomes successful, instead of ending in an unhappy liquidation?

A: A partnership agreement should include: Who are the partners? What is each partner contributing? What are each partner's duties? How is profit/(loss)shared? How will disputes be resolved? Addressing these items in advance, may assist in resolving issues that might arise as the partnership evolves.

Answer to Forzani Review It Question 5, p. 668

Mutual agency, limited life, unlimited liability, and co-ownership of property are characteristics of a partnership. As a company grows in size, it is difficult for it to remain a partnership, because of these factors. The corporate form of organization separates ownership and management and makes it easier to raise capital. The unlimited liability of a partnership makes it harder to find investors because owners can lose not only their investment but also their personal assets if those assets are needed to pay the partnership's creditors.

Answers to Self-Study Questions

1. a   2. c   3. b   4. d   5. a   6. a   7. d   8. b   9. d   10. a

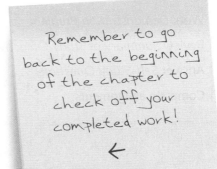

Remember to go
back to the beginning
of the chapter to
check off your
completed work!

CHAPTER 13
CORPORATIONS: ORGANIZATION AND SHARE CAPITAL TRANSACTIONS

ZERO EMISSION   NO NOISE

ZENN

zenncars.com

✓ THE NAVIGATOR

- ☐ Understand *Concepts for Review*
- ☐ Read *Feature Story*
- ☐ Scan *Study Objectives*
- ☐ Read *Chapter Preview*
- ☐ Read text and answer *Before You Go On*
- ☐ Work *Demonstration Problem*
- ☐ Review *Summary of Study Objectives*
- ☐ Answer *Self-Study Questions*
- ☐ Complete assignments

CONCEPTS FOR REVIEW:

Before studying this chapter, you should understand or, if necessary, review:

a. The differences between the forms of business organization. (Ch. 1, pp. 5 & 12–13)

b. The content of the equity section of the balance sheet for the different forms of organization. (Ch. 1, p. 21 and Ch. 4, pp. 196–197)

c. How to prepare closing entries for a proprietorship (Ch. 4, pp. 183–184) and for a partnership. (Ch. 12, pp. 686–687)

A Clean Driving Alternative Goes Public

TORONTO, Ont.—Tired of Toronto's traffic gridlock and breathing in its toxic fumes, Ian Clifford decided to do something about it. He founded Feel Good Cars Inc. in 2000 to develop a Neighborhood Electric Vehicle, or NEV. With a top speed of 40 kilometres per hour, the vehicle runs only on roads with speed limits of 50 kilometres per hour and is touted as a clean alternative for daily driving needs.

Feel Good Cars needed more cash to grow, so it took advantage of the TSX Venture Exchange's Capital Pool Company (CPC) program, which introduces investors with financial market experience to entrepreneurs whose growth and development-stage companies require capital and public company management expertise. The CPC program allows seasoned directors and officers to form a capital pool company with no assets other than cash and no commercial operations, list it on the TSX Venture Exchange, and raise a pool of capital. The CPC then uses these funds to invest in a growing business. Once the CPC has acquired an operating company that meets listing requirements, its shares continue trading as a regular listing on the Exchange.

In January 2006, the capital pool company MCL Capital Inc. acquired Feel Good Cars. MCL Capital Inc. took the call letters ZNN and, in 2007, officially changed its name to ZENN Motor Company Inc. ZENN is an acronym that reflects the branding of the company: zero emission, no noise. All of ZENN's shares are common shares—one share, one vote.

"Whether you follow the CPC route, or you do a straight IPO (initial public offering), going public requires considerable investment of time, money, and effort," says ZENN's Chief Financial Officer, Larry Schreiner. "For example, you will likely require two years of audited financial statements, a really solid business plan, and a management team with public company experience." So, even before going public, a private company needs to handle its financials as if it were already a public company.

And once a company is public, the requirements are even more demanding, Schreiner adds. The continuous disclosure requirements include holding an annual general meeting and preparing an information circular that meets prescribed disclosure requirements, including the top five executives' compensation, background information on the board members, and so on. A public company must also file its financial statements along with a management discussion and analysis (MD&A) on a quarterly basis, all of which have to be mailed to shareholders. "Another responsibility in being a public company is the investor relations function," says Schreiner. "You must communicate with your investors on a regular basis."

Like all Canadian public companies, effective January 2011, ZENN is required to follow International Financial Reporting Standards. The company has a project team assessing what this will mean for it; however, says Schreiner, "Since we're such a new company, I don't think you'll see significant restatements of our balance sheet because of IFRSs. The real issue with IFRS is meeting the need for more comprehensive disclosures in narrative form."

The Navigator

STUDY OBJECTIVES:

After studying this chapter, you should be able to:

1. Identify and discuss the major characteristics of the corporate form of organization.
2. Record common share transactions.
3. Record preferred share transactions.
4. Prepare the shareholders' equity section of the balance sheet and calculate return on equity.

The Navigator

Many incorporated companies start out small and then grow larger. ZENN Motor Company, for example, is well on its way down that path. The company, starting in 1995 as an idea in the mind of its now Chief Executive Officer, has successfully raised millions of dollars as an incorporated company by offering shares for sale to the public. Because of its advantages, the corporation dominates as the most common form of business organization. In this chapter, we will explain the essential features of a corporation and the accounting for a corporation's share capital transactions. In Chapter 14, we will look at other accounting issues for corporations.

The chapter is organized as follows:

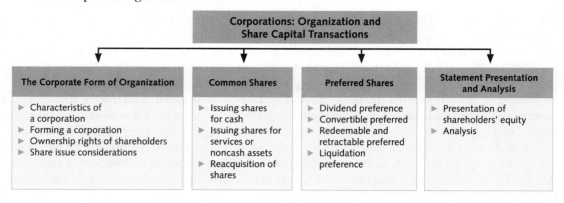

The Corporate Form of Organization

STUDY OBJECTIVE 1

Identify and discuss the major characteristics of the corporate form of organization.

A **corporation** is a legal entity that is separate from its owners, who are known as shareholders. As a legal entity, a corporation has most of the rights and privileges of a person. Like any citizen, it also has the obligation to respect laws and pay income tax. The major exceptions in its privileges are the ones that only a living person can exercise: corporations cannot vote or hold public office.

Corporations can be classified in a variety of ways. Two common classifications are by purpose and by ownership. For example, a corporation may be organized for the purpose of making a profit (such as ZENN Motor Company in our feature story) or it may be not-for-profit (such as the Canadian Cancer Society).

In classification by ownership, the difference is between publicly held and privately held corporations. A **publicly held corporation** may have thousands of shareholders. Its shares are usually traded in an organized securities market, such as the Toronto Stock Exchange. This type of organization is similar to a publicly accountable enterprise. A publicly accountable enterprise has a slightly broader definition as it also includes securities brokers and dealers, banks, and credit unions whose role is to hold assets for the public as part of their primary business. Most of the largest Canadian corporations are publicly held. Examples of publicly held corporations are Bombardier Inc., The Forzani Group Ltd., Magna International Inc., and, of course, ZENN Motor Company.

In contrast, a **privately held corporation**, often called a closely held corporation, usually has only a few shareholders. It does not offer its shares for sale to the general public. Privately held companies are generally much smaller than publicly held companies, although there are notable exceptions such as McCain Foods, The Jim Pattison Group, and the Irving companies. But a privately held corporation can also be a publicly accountable enterprise if it has bonds that are publicly held.

Helpful hint Stock exchanges are operated by publicly held corporations. In Canada in 2008, the TSX Group and the Montreal Exchange combined to form a publicly held corporation called the TMX Group. The TMX Group's operations include the Toronto Stock Exchange, the TSX Venture Exchange, and the Montreal Exchange, among other services.

ACCOUNTING IN ACTION: INTERNATIONAL INSIGHT

Corporations in North America are identified by "Ltd.," "Inc.," "Corp.," or in some cases, "Co." following their names. These abbreviations can also be spelled out. In Brazil and France, the letters used are "SA" (Sôciedade Anonima, Société Anonyme); in Japan, "KK" (Kabushiki Kaisha); in the Netherlands, "NV" (Naamloze Vennootschap); in Italy, "SpA" (Società per Azioni); and in Sweden, "AB" (Aktiebolag).

In the United Kingdom, public corporations are identified by "Plc" (Public limited company), while private corporations are denoted by "Ltd." The same designations in Germany are "AG" (Aktiengesellschaft) for public corporations and "GmbH" (Gesellschaft mit beschränkter Haftung) for private corporations.

Does IFRS make it more important for users of financial statements to identify whether a company is a corporation or not?

Characteristics of a Corporation

Regardless of the purpose or ownership of a corporation, there are many characteristics that make corporations different from proprietorships and partnerships. The most important ones are explained below.

Separate Legal Existence

As an entity that is separate from its owners, the corporation acts under its own name rather than in the name of its shareholders. ZENN Motor Company, for example, may buy, own, and sell property. It may borrow money and enter into legally binding contracts in its own name. It may also sue or be sued, and it pays income tax as a separate legal entity.

Remember that in a proprietorship or partnership, the acts of the owners (partners) bind the proprietorship or partnership. In contrast, the acts of owners (shareholders) do not bind a corporation unless these individuals are also official agents of the corporation. For example, if you owned shares of ZENN Motor Company, you would not have the right to purchase a new production facility unless you were an official agent of the corporation.

Limited Liability of Shareholders

Since a corporation is a separate legal entity, creditors have access to corporate assets only to have their claims repaid to them. The liability of each individual shareholder is limited to the amount that he or she invested in the shares of the corporation. This means that shareholders cannot be made to pay for the company's liabilities out of their personal assets, which can be done in the case of a proprietorship and a general partnership.

Limited liability is a significant advantage for the corporate form of organization, just as it is for a limited, or limited liability, partnership. However, in certain situations, creditors may demand a personal guarantee from a controlling shareholder. This makes the controlling shareholder's personal assets available for satisfying the creditor's claim if they are needed—and it eliminates or reduces the limited liability advantage.

Transferable Ownership Rights

Ownership of a corporation is held in shares of capital. These are transferable units. Shareholders may dispose of part or all of their interest in a corporation simply by selling their shares. Remember that the transfer of an ownership interest in a proprietorship or partnership requires the consent of each owner or partner. In contrast, in a corporation, the transfer of shares is entirely decided by the shareholder. It does not require the approval of either the corporation or other shareholders.

The transfer of ownership rights between shareholders has no effect on the corporation's operating activities. Nor does it affect the corporation's assets, liabilities, and total equity. The transfer of these ownership rights is a transaction between individual shareholders. The company is not involved in the transfer of ownership rights; it is only involved in the original sale of the share capital.

Ability to Acquire Capital

It is relatively easy for a large corporation to get capital by issuing shares. Buying shares in a corporation is often attractive to an investor because a shareholder has limited liability and shares are easily transferable. Also, because only small amounts of money need to be invested, many individuals can become shareholders. For these reasons, a successful corporation's ability to obtain capital is almost unlimited.

Note that the "almost unlimited" ability of a corporation to acquire capital is only true for large, publicly traded corporations. Small, or closely held, corporations can have as much difficulty getting capital as any proprietorship or partnership. Also, costs such as registration and legal fees related to incorporating (organization costs are discussed later in the chapter) and extensive public filing requirements and disclosures demanded by various securities exchanges can make incorporation an expensive option.

Continuous Life

Most corporations have an unlimited life. Since a corporation is a separate legal entity, its continuance as a going concern is not affected by the withdrawal, death, or incapacity of a shareholder, employee, or officer. As a result, a successful corporation can have a continuous and indefinite life. For example, the Hudson's Bay Co., Canada's oldest corporation, was founded in 1670 and is still going strong. Its shareholders have changed over the years, but the corporation itself continues. In contrast, proprietorships end if anything happens to the proprietor and partnerships must reorganize if anything happens to one of the partners and the other partners want to continue the partnership.

Corporation Management

Shareholders legally own the corporation. But they manage the corporation indirectly through a board of directors that they elect. The board, in turn, decides on the company's operating policies and selects officers—such as a president and one or more vice-presidents—to execute policy and to perform daily management functions. Ian Clifford is ZENN Motor Company's Chief Executive Officer. He and two other senior executives also sit on ZENN Motor Company's board of directors. The other four members of ZENN's board of directors are independent (outside) directors.

The organizational structure of a corporation makes it possible for it to hire professional managers to run the business. On the other hand, the separation of ownership and management prevents shareholders from having an active role in managing the company, which is difficult for some shareholders to accept.

Government Regulations

Canadian companies may be incorporated federally, under the terms of the *Canada Business Corporations Act*, or provincially, under the terms of a provincial business corporations act. Federal and provincial laws specify the requirements for issuing shares, distributing income to shareholders, and reacquiring shares. Similarly, provincial securities commissions' regulations control the sale of share capital to the general public. When a corporation's shares are listed and traded on foreign securities markets, the corporation must also respect the reporting requirements of these exchanges. Respecting international, federal, provincial, and securities regulations increases costs and complexity for corporations.

Distribution of Profit

Profits can be either reinvested by a company or distributed to its shareholders as dividends. Dividends are payments made by a corporation, on a pro rata basis, to its shareholders. There are certain conditions that must be met before a corporation can pay dividends. These conditions, as well as an explanation of various types of dividends, are discussed in Chapter 14.

To illustrate the entry for a payment of a cash dividend to shareholders, assume that Zaboschuk Inc. pays a dividend on January 24. If the total dividend payment is for $80,000, the entry to record the dividend payment is as follows:

Jan. 24	Dividends	80,000	
	Cash		80,000
	To record payment of dividend.		

| A | = | L | + | SE |
| -80,000 | | | | -80,000 |

↓ Cash flows: -80,000

Dividends in a corporation are the equivalent of drawings in a proprietorship or a partnership. Dividends reduce shareholders' equity, just as drawings reduce owner's equity in a proprietorship and partners' equity in a partnership.

Income Tax

Proprietorships and partnerships do not pay income tax as separate entities. Instead, each owner's (or partner's) share of profit from these organizations is reported on his or her personal income tax return. Income tax is then paid by the individual on this amount. In terms of income taxes, it does not matter how much cash a proprietor or partner withdraws from the business. The owner is taxed on the profit, not on the cash withdrawals.

Corporations, on the other hand, must pay federal and provincial income taxes as separate legal entities. These taxes can be substantial. They can amount to as much as 36% of taxable income. There are, however, income tax deductions for some corporations. With eligible deductions or other corporate tax incentives, a corporation's tax rate may be reduced to between 11% and 19% on certain kinds of active small business income. This tax rate is much lower than the tax rate for the same amount of income earned by an individual.

The shareholders of a corporation do not pay tax on corporate profit. Shareholders pay tax on cash dividends, which are pro rata distributions of profit. Thus, many people argue that corporate income is taxed twice: once at the corporate level and again at the individual level. This is not exactly true, however, as individuals receive a dividend tax credit to reduce some of the tax burden. On the other hand, an advantage of incorporation is being able to defer personal income tax when profit is held in the corporation and not paid to the owners.

To summarize, owners of proprietorships and partnerships can access funds generated by their business by simply withdrawing cash. But if an owner of a corporation wants to withdraw cash for personal use, it must be through payment of dividends or the payment of salary or wages, both of which are taxable. To determine whether incorporating will result in more or less income tax for a proprietorship or partnership, it is wise to get expert advice. Income tax laws are complex, and careful tax planning is essential for any business venture.

The following list summarizes the advantages and disadvantages of the corporate form of business organization:

Advantages	Disadvantages
• Corporation management—professional managers	• Corporation management—ownership separated from management
• Separate legal existence	• Increased cost and complexity to follow government regulations
• Limited liability of shareholders	• Potential for additional income tax
• Potential for deferred or reduced income tax	
• Transferable ownership rights	
• Ability to acquire capital	
• Continuous life	

As was noted earlier, many of these advantages and disadvantages depend on the size of the corporation. For example, compare Bob's Coffee Ltd. (a small, private, closely held corporation) with Tim Hortons Inc. (a large publicly traded corporation). Bob's Coffee finds it just as difficult to sell shares of ownership, or to acquire capital, as it would if it were an unincorporated business.

Forming a Corporation

As previously mentioned, a company can incorporate federally or provincially. The federal government and the majority of provinces file articles of incorporation to incorporate a company, although there are also other methods.

Articles of incorporation form the company's "constitution." They include information such as (1) the name and purpose of the corporation, (2) the amounts and kinds of share capital to be authorized and the number of shares, (3) the names and addresses of the incorporators, and (4) the location of the corporation's head office. Anyone can apply to incorporate a company, as long as he or she is over the age of 18, of sound mind, and not bankrupt.

After receiving its articles of incorporation, the corporation sets its bylaws. The bylaws are the internal rules and procedures for operations. Corporations that operate interprovincially must also get a licence from each province they do business in. The licence ensures that the corporation's operating activities respect the laws of the province.

The costs of forming a corporation are called **organization costs**. These costs include legal fees, accounting fees, and registration costs. In the past, it was sometimes argued that organization costs should be capitalized as they have an asset life equal to the life of the corporation. However, most companies expensed organization costs in the year they occurred. Expensing is now required under recent changes to Canadian accounting standards as well as under International Financial Reporting Standards.

Ownership Rights of Shareholders

Shareholders purchase ownership rights in the form of shares. The company's shares are divided into different classes, such as Class A, Class B, and so on. The rights and privileges for each class of shares are stated in the articles of incorporation. The different classes are usually identified by the generic terms *common shares* and *preferred shares*. When a corporation has only one class of shares, this class has the rights and privileges of **common shares**. Each common share gives the shareholder the ownership rights shown in Illustration 13-1.

Alternative terminology
Common shares are also known as *ordinary shares*.

Illustration 13-1 ➡

Ownership rights of common shareholders

Vote: Shareholders have the right to vote on certain matters, such as the election of the board of directors and appointment of external auditors. Each shareholder normally has one vote for each common share owned.

Dividends: Shareholders share in the distribution of the corporate income through dividends, proportionate to the number of shares owned.

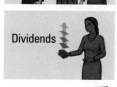

Liquidation: Shareholders share in any assets that remain after liquidation, in proportion to the number of shares owned. This is known as a residual claim because shareholders are paid only if any cash remains after all the assets have been sold and the liabilities paid.

ACCOUNTING IN ACTION: ALL ABOUT YOU

If you are starting a business, you need to ask if it is better to use a proprietorship or to incorporate. The best form of organization for a business start-up may not be the best as the business's profits increase. When you start your business, a proprietorship is generally more advantageous because it involves relatively low start-up costs, low regulatory costs, and tax savings. Also, if your proprietorship suffers losses in its early years, these losses may be deducted against your other personal income, thus reducing your personal tax. But as your business becomes profitable, there may be advantages if it is incorporated, especially in terms of tax savings. For example, some Canadian private corporations are eligible for a small business deduction that reduces the federal tax rate to 11% on the first $400,000 of taxable income. In comparison, your personal federal tax rate may be as high as 27% on $400,000. But most owners of a corporation will need to take some income out of the business and must decide if it should be a salary or dividends. If the owner is paid a salary, it will reduce corporate income taxes, but the owner will pay personal income taxes on employment income. Personal income taxes paid on dividends are less than those on employment income. But if an individual only has dividend income, he or she cannot contribute to the Canada Pension Plan (CPP) or a Registered Retirement Savings Plan (RRSP). As you can see, deciding whether to incorporate or not is a complex matter.

Given the complexity of tax planning, and the impact that taxes could have on the advantages of incorporating, what should you do before deciding to incorporate your business?

Share Issue Considerations

When a company first issues shares for sale, it has to make a number of decisions. How many shares should be authorized for sale? How should the shares be issued? At what initial price should the shares be issued? These kinds of questions are answered in the following sections.

Authorized Share Capital

A corporation's **authorized shares**—the total number of shares a company is allowed to sell—is indicated in its articles of incorporation. It may be specified as an unlimited number or a certain number (e.g., 500,000 shares authorized). ZENN Motor Company has unlimited common and preferred shares authorized. The majority of public companies with share capital in Canada have an unlimited number of authorized shares.

If a number is specified, the amount of authorized shares normally reflects the company's initial need for capital and what it expects to need in the future. **Issued shares** are the authorized shares that have been sold. At the time of writing, ZENN Motor Company had issued 34 million common shares and had no preferred shares issued.

If a corporation has issued all of its authorized shares, it must get legislative approval to change its articles of incorporation before it can issue additional shares. To find out how many shares can still be issued without changing the articles of incorporation, the total shares issued are subtracted from the total authorized. However, for ZENN Motor Company, this is not an issue because the company has an unlimited number of common shares authorized.

The authorization of share capital does not result in a formal accounting entry, because the event has no immediate effect on either assets or shareholders' equity. However, a company must disclose in the shareholders' equity section of its balance sheet or the notes to the financial statements how many authorized shares it has and how many have been issued.

Issue of Shares

A corporation can issue common shares in two ways: either directly to investors or indirectly through an investment dealer (brokerage house) that specializes in making potential investors aware of securities. Direct issue is typical in closely held companies. Indirect issue is typical for a publicly held corporation, such as ZENN Motor Company in our feature story.

The first time a corporation's shares are offered to the public, the offer is called an **initial public offering (IPO)**. In 2008, there were more than 50 IPOs on Canada's stock exchanges. With a traditional IPO, the company receives the cash from the sale of the IPO shares whether they are issued directly or indirectly. The company's assets (cash) increase, and its shareholders' equity (share capital) also increases. In our feature story, we explained how ZENN Motor Company used an alternative to the traditional IPO by taking advantage of a two-step Capital Pool Company (CPC) program offered by the TSX Venture Exchange. The company was able to raise $5 million using the CPC program.

Once these initial shares have been issued, they then trade on the **secondary market**. That is, investors buy and sell shares from each other, rather than from the company. When shares are sold among investors, there is no impact on the company's financial position. The only change in the company records is the name of the shareholder, not the number of shares issued.

Market Value of Shares

After the initial issue of new shares, the market price per share changes according to the interaction between buyers and sellers on the secondary market. To some extent, the price follows the trend of a company's income and dividends. The price also depends to some extent on how well the company is expected to perform in the future. Factors that a company cannot control (such as an embargo on oil, changes in interest rates, the outcome of an election, terrorism, and war) can also influence market prices.

For each listed security, the financial press reports the highest and lowest prices of the shares for the year; the annual dividend rate; the highest, lowest, and closing prices for the day; and the net change from the previous day. The total volume of shares traded on a particular day, the dividend yield, and price-earnings ratio are also reported. A recent listing for ZENN Motor Company from the TSX Venture Exchange is shown below:

365-day		stock	sym	div	high/bid	low/ask	close	chg	vol 100s	yld	pe ratio
high	low	Zenn Motor Co	ZNN	0.00	4.42	4.32	4.41	−.09	187	0.0	N/A
6.89	1.40										

ZENN Motor Company's shares have traded as high as $6.89 and as low as $1.40 during the past year. The stock's ticker symbol is "ZNN." ZENN Motor Company has not paid a dividend, shown as a "0.00" in the "div" column. The highest, lowest, and closing prices for the date shown were $4.42, $4.32, and $4.41 per share, respectively. The share price has decreased $0.09 from the previous day. The trading volume was 18,700 shares. And because ZENN Motor Company does not pay a dividend, the dividend yield ("yld") is 0.0%. The dividend yield reports the rate of return an investor earned from dividends, and is calculated by dividing the dividend amount by the share price. The price-earnings ("pe") ratio (share price divided by earnings per share) is shown as "N/A" for ZENN Motor Company because the company had a loss. We will learn more about the price-earnings ratio in the next chapter.

One commonly reported measure of fair value of a company's total equity is its market capitalization. The **market capitalization** of a company is calculated by multiplying the number of shares issued by the share price at any given date. ZENN Motor Company's market capitalization was $151 million at the time of writing. The largest market capitalization for any company in Canada was that of Royal Bank of Canada, whose market capitalization at June 3, 2009, was $63 billion.

Legal Capital

You may recall from Chapters 1 and 4 that the shareholders' equity section of a corporation's balance sheet includes (1) share capital (contributed capital) and (2) retained earnings (earned capital). **Share capital** is amounts paid or contributed to the corporation by shareholders in exchange for shares of ownership. **Retained earnings** are earned capital (cumulative profit less losses and amounts distributed to shareholders since incorporation) that has been retained for future use. We will study retained earnings in the next chapter.

The distinction between retained earnings and share capital is important for both legal and financial reasons. Retained earnings can be distributed to shareholders as dividends (similar to drawings in a proprietorship or partnership) or retained in the company for operating needs. On the other hand, share capital is **legal capital** that cannot be distributed to shareholders. It must remain invested in the company for the protection of corporate creditors.

Some countries, notably the United States, assign a par or stated value to shares to determine the amount of legal capital. The use of par value shares is rare in Canada, with fewer than 1% of publicly traded companies issuing par value shares. In fact, companies that are incorporated federally, as well as companies that incorporate in most Canadian provinces, are not allowed to issue shares with par values.

In Canada, **no par value shares**—shares that have not been assigned any specific value—are normally issued. When no par value shares are issued, all of the proceeds received from the sale of the shares are considered to be legal capital. Whenever shares are issued in this chapter, we will assume that they have no par value.

BEFORE YOU GO ON . . .

→ Review It

1. What are the advantages and disadvantages of a corporation compared with a proprietorship or partnership?
2. For a corporation, why is the amount of authorized shares important? Of issued shares?
3. How does the sale of shares affect a company in an initial public offering? Afterwards, in the secondary market?
4. What are the differences between share capital and retained earnings?
5. What is legal capital?

Related exercise material: BE13–1, BE13–2, E13–1, and E13–2.

The Navigator

Common Shares

As we learned in the preceding section, share capital is the amounts that have been contributed to the corporation by shareholders in exchange for shares of ownership. Other amounts can also be contributed by shareholders, or can accrue to them. Together, these other amounts and share capital form the total **contributed capital** of the corporation.

All corporations issue common shares. Some corporations also issue preferred shares, which have different rights and privileges than common shares. We will look at common shares in this section, and preferred shares in the next. We will also learn more about other sources of contributed capital.

> **STUDY OBJECTIVE 2**
>
> Record common share transactions.

Issuing Shares for Cash

Most of the time, shares are issued in exchange for cash. As discussed earlier, when no par value common shares are issued, the entire proceeds from the issue become legal capital. To illustrate the issue of common shares, assume that Hydroslide, Inc. is authorized to issue an unlimited number of no par value common shares. It issues 1,000 of these shares for $1 per share on January 12. The entry to record this transaction is as follows:

Jan. 12	Cash	1,000	
	Common Shares		1,000
	To record issue of 1,000 common shares.		

A	=	L	+	SE
+1,000				+1,000

 Cash flows: +1,000

Issuing Shares for Services or Noncash Assets

Although it is more usual to issue common shares for cash, they are sometimes issued in exchange for services (as compensation to lawyers or consultants) or for noncash assets (land, buildings, and equipment). When shares are issued for a noncash consideration, they should be recorded at the fair value of the goods or services received.

Helpful hint The asking price or the list price of land, buildings, or equipment is rarely the fair value of the asset. Fair value is the amount that would be agreed upon in an arm's-length transaction between knowledgeable, willing parties, or as the result of a bargaining process over the value of the asset. Appraised values are often used as a reasonable estimate of the fair value of the asset, assuming the appraiser has the appropriate independence and expertise.

A	=	L	+	SE
				−3,800
				+3,800

Cash flows: no effect

To illustrate, assume that the lawyer who helped Hydroslide incorporate billed the company $3,800 for her services. On January 18, when the shares were trading at a market price of $1, the lawyer agreed to accept 4,000 common shares in payment of her bill. If a company has limited cash, sometimes shares are offered instead to avoid using cash. In this case, the lawyer would likely be willing to accept the shares because she could immediately sell them for more than $3,800, or keep them if she thinks the shares will grow in value. The transaction is recorded at the fair value of the lawyer's services received, not at the value of the shares given up. Accordingly, the entry is recorded at $3,800 as follows:

Jan. 18	Legal Fees Expense	3,800	
	Common Shares		3,800
	To record issue of 4,000 common shares for legal services.		

Sometimes, however, the fair value of the goods or services received cannot be reliably measured. In these cases, the fair value of the common shares given up would instead be used to record the transaction. To illustrate, assume that a newly incorporated company issues 10,000 shares on October 1 to acquire refurbished bottling equipment. A fair value for this equipment cannot be established. However, at the time of the acquisition, the company's shares have a fair value of $7. In this case, the equipment would be recorded at the fair value of the shares given up, $70,000, as follows:

A	=	L	+	SE
+70,000				+70,000

Cash flows: no effect

Oct. 1	Equipment	70,000	
	Common Shares		70,000
	To record issue of 10,000 common shares for equipment.		

Reacquisition of Shares

Companies can purchase their own shares on the open market. A corporation may acquire its own shares for any number of reasons, including the following:

1. To increase trading of the company's shares in the securities market in the hope of increasing the company's fair value
2. To increase earnings per share by reducing the number of shares issued
3. To eliminate hostile shareholders by buying them out
4. To have additional shares available so that they can be reissued to officers and employees through bonus and stock compensation plans, or can be used to acquire other companies
5. To comply with percentage share ownership requirements (i.e., to respect limits on foreign ownership)

For federally incorporated companies, and most provincially incorporated companies, the repurchased shares must be retired and cancelled. This restores the shares to the status of authorized but unissued shares. In some Canadian provinces, in the United States, and internationally, reacquired shares can also be held for subsequent reissue. If the shares are not retired and cancelled, they are referred to as **treasury shares**.

The reacquisition of shares is a common practice and the financial press often contains announcements of "normal course issuer bids," which inform the public that a company plans to repurchase its shares. To record a reacquisition of common (or preferred) shares, the following steps are required:

1. **Remove the cost of the shares from the share capital account:** Recall that when a long-lived asset is retired, the cost of the asset must be deleted (credited) from the appropriate asset account. Similarly, the cost of the common shares that are reacquired and retired must be determined and this amount is then deleted (debited) from the Common Shares account.

In order to determine the cost of the common shares reacquired, it is necessary to calculate an **average cost per share**. It is impractical, and often impossible, to determine the cost of each individual common share that is reacquired. An average cost per common share is therefore calculated by dividing the balance in the Common Shares account by the number of shares issued at the transaction date.

2. **Record the cash paid:** The Cash account is credited for the amount paid to reacquire the shares. Note that a company has little choice in what it has to pay to reacquire the shares (it can only decide when to make the reacquisition). It must purchase the shares on the secondary market by paying whatever the current market price is on the date of purchase.

3. **Record the "gain" or "loss" on reacquisition:** The difference between the price paid to reacquire the shares and their original cost is basically a "gain" or "loss" on reacquisition. However, because companies cannot realize a gain or suffer a loss from share transactions with their own shareholders, these amounts are not reported on the income statement. They are seen instead as an excess or deficiency that belongs to the original shareholders. As a result, the amount is reported as an increase or decrease in the shareholders' equity section of the balance sheet.

The accounting for the reacquisition of shares differs depending on whether the shares are reacquired by paying less than the average cost or more than the average cost. We will examine each situation in the next two sections.

Reacquisition below Average Cost

To illustrate the reacquisition of common shares at a price less than average cost, assume that Cocagne Inc. has an unlimited number of common shares authorized, and a total of 25,000 common shares issued. It has a balance in its Common Shares account of $50,000. The average cost of Cocagne's common shares is therefore $2 per share ($50,000 ÷ 25,000).

On September 23, Cocagne reacquired 5,000 of its common shares at a price of $1.50 per share. Since the average cost of the shares was $2 per share, a $0.50 ($2.00 − $1.50), an additional contribution to shareholders' equity results and is recorded as follows:

Sept. 23	Common Shares (5,000 × $2)	10,000	
	Contributed Capital—Reacquisition of Shares		2,500
	Cash (5,000 × $1.50)		7,500
	To record reacquisition and retirement of 5,000 common shares.		

A	=	L	+	SE
−7,500				−10,000
				+2,500

↓ Cash flows: −7,500

In this entry, the difference between the average cost of the shares and the amount paid to repurchase them is credited to a new shareholders' equity account for the contributed capital from the reacquisition of the shares. This account is in the contributed capital section of the shareholders' equity section on the balance sheet, along with the share capital, to indicate the total capital contributed by the shareholders. The cash in the entry was paid to the various shareholders that the shares were repurchased from.

After this entry, Cocagne still has an unlimited number of shares authorized, but only 20,000 (25,000 − 5,000) shares issued, and a balance of $40,000 ($50,000 − $10,000) in its Common Shares account. The average cost is still $2 per share ($40,000 ÷ 20,000).

Reacquisition above Average Cost

Now assume that Cocagne paid $2.50 per share to reacquire 5,000 of its common shares, rather than $1.50 per share as assumed above. In this case, there would be a debit to the shareholders' equity account for the difference between the price paid to reacquire the shares and their average cost. If there is any balance in the contributed capital account from previous reacquisitions, this amount would first be reduced (debited). However, contributed capital cannot be reduced below zero. In other words, contributed capital can never have a negative, or debit, balance. Instead, if the debit amount is greater than the balance in contributed capital, the difference is recorded in Retained Earnings, which can go into a deficit (debit) position.

The journal entry to record the reacquisition and retirement of Cocagne's common shares at $2.50 per share is as follows:

A	=	L	+	SE
−12,500				+10,000
				−2,500

↓ Cash flows: −12,500

Sept. 23	Common Shares (5,000 × $2)	10,000	
	Retained Earnings	2,500	
	Cash (5,000 × $2.50)		12,500
	To record reacquisition and retirement of 5,000 common shares.		

In this entry, Cocagne is assumed to have no existing balance in a contributed capital account. After this entry, Cocagne still has 20,000 (25,000 − 5,000) shares issued and a balance of $40,000 ($50,000 − $10,000) in its Common Shares account.

In summary, the only difference in the accounting for a reacquisition at prices below or above the average cost has to do with recording the difference between the average cost of the shares and the amount of cash paid to reacquire them. If the shares are reacquired at a price below the average cost, the difference is credited to a contributed capital account. If the shares are reacquired at a price above their average cost, the difference is debited first to the contributed capital account that was used for any previous reacquisition below cost of the same class of shares, and then to the Retained Earnings account if there is no credit balance left in the contributed capital account.

 ACCOUNTING IN ACTION: ACROSS THE ORGANIZATION

A shocking aspect of the recent recession is the collapse of the stock prices of iconic companies, such as century-old General Motors, the lifeblood of Oshawa, Ontario. When times are good, most investors focus on profits and few look at the strength of a company's balance sheet; however, when times are bad, companies with little debt and lots of equity suffer the least. Before the recession hit, in an effort to appear to be more profitable, hundreds of companies spent billions of dollars buying back their own shares, often borrowing money to do so—a practice that pushed up the price of their stock. Few investors imagined that a lack of cash and too much debt could ultimately cause these companies to fail. In hindsight, the companies should have sold stock to generate cash when their shares were at record highs, rather than buy it back.

Source: David Baskin, "Share Buybacks Sparked Some of the Business World's Woes," CBC Money Talks (March 27, 2009), www.cbc.ca [accessed on May 25, 2009]

How can buying back its own shares make a company appear to be more profitable?

BEFORE YOU GO ON . . .

➔ Review It

1. Explain the accounting for an issue of common shares for cash.
2. Explain the accounting for an issue of common shares for services or noncash assets.
3. Distinguish between the accounting for a reacquisition of shares at a price lower than average cost and at a price higher than average cost.
4. Did The Forzani Group Ltd. repurchase any of its shares in fiscal 2009? The answer to this question is at the end of the chapter.

➔ Do It

Victoria Corporation begins operations on March 1 by issuing 100,000 common shares for cash at $12 per share. On March 15, it issues 5,000 common shares to its lawyers in settlement of their bill for $65,000. The shares continue to trade at $12 per share on March 15. On June 1, Victoria repurchases 10,000 of its shares at $10 per share. Record the share transactions.

Action Plan
- Credit the Common Shares account for the entire proceeds.
- When shares are issued for services, use the fair value of what is received. If this amount cannot be determined, use the fair value of what is given up.

- When shares are reacquired, calculate the average cost per share by dividing the balance in the Common Shares account by the number of shares issued.
- Debit the Common Shares account for the average cost of the reacquired shares. If the reacquisition price is below the average cost, credit the difference to a contributed capital account. If the reacquisition price is above the average cost, debit the difference to Retained Earnings unless there is already a balance in a contributed capital account from previous reacquisitions and retirements.

Solution

Mar. 1	Cash		1,200,000	
	Common Shares (100,000 × $12)			1,200,000
	To record issue of 100,000 shares at $12 per share.			
15	Legal Fees Expense		65,000	
	Common Shares			65,000
	To record issue of 5,000 shares for $65,000 of lawyers' fees.			
June 1	Common Shares (10,000 × $12.048)		120,480	
	Contributed Capital—Reacquisition of Shares			20,480
	Cash (10,000 × $10)			100,000
	To record reacquisition and retirement of 10,000 common shares at an average cost of $12.048 ($1,265,000 ÷ 105,000).			

Related exercise material: BE13-3, BE13-4, BE13-5, BE13-6, and E13-3.

The Navigator

Preferred Shares

STUDY OBJECTIVE 3

Record preferred share transactions.

A corporation may issue preferred shares in addition to common shares. **Preferred shares** have a preference, or priority, over common shares in certain areas. Typically, preferred shareholders have priority over (1) dividends (distributions of income) and (2) assets if the company is liquidated. They generally do not have voting rights. A recent survey indicated that nearly 20% of Canadian companies have preferred shares.

Like common shares, preferred shares may be issued for cash or for noncash assets or services. They can also be reacquired. The entries for all these transactions are similar to the entries for common shares. When a company has more than one class of shares, the transactions for each class should be recorded in separate accounts (e.g., Preferred Shares, Common Shares). As with common shares, no par value shares are normally issued.

Some typical features of preferred shares, including dividend and liquidation preferences, are discussed next.

Dividend Preference

Preferred shareholders have the right to share in the distribution of dividends before common shareholders do. For example, if the dividend rate on preferred shares is $5 per share, common shareholders will not receive any dividends in the current year until preferred shareholders have first received $5 for every share they own. The first claim to dividends does not, however, guarantee that dividends will be paid. Dividends depend on many factors, such as having enough retained earnings and available cash. In addition, all dividends must be formally approved by the board of directors.

Preferred shares may have a **cumulative** dividend feature. This means that preferred shareholders must be paid dividends from the current year as well as any unpaid dividends from past years before common shareholders receive any dividends. When preferred shares are cumulative, preferred dividends that are not declared in a period are called **dividends in arrears**. When preferred shares are not cumulative (known as **noncumulative**), a dividend that is not paid in any particular year is lost forever. Most preferred shares that are issued today are noncumulative.

To illustrate the cumulative dividend feature, assume that Staudinger Corporation has 10,000 $3-cumulative preferred shares. The $3 is the per-share dividend amount, which is usually expressed as an annual amount, similar to interest rates. So, Staudinger's annual total dividend is $30,000 (10,000 × $3 per share). If dividends are two years in arrears, preferred shareholders are entitled to receive the following dividends:

Dividends in arrears ($30,000 × 2)	$60,000
Current year dividends	30,000
Total preferred dividends	$90,000

No distribution can be made to common shareholders until this entire preferred dividend is paid. In other words, dividends cannot be paid on common shares while any preferred shares are in arrears.

Dividends in arrears are not considered a liability. There is no obligation to pay a dividend until one is declared by the board of directors. However, the amount of dividends in arrears should be disclosed in the notes to the financial statements. This allows investors to assess the potential impact of a future dividend declaration on the corporation's financial position.

Even though there is no requirement to pay an annual dividend, companies that do not meet their dividend obligations—whether cumulative or noncumulative—are not looked upon favourably by the investment community. When discussing one company's failure to pay its cumulative preferred dividend, a financial officer noted, "Not meeting your obligations on something like that is a major black mark on your record." The accounting entries for dividends are explained in Chapter 14.

Convertible Preferred

As an investment, preferred shares are even more attractive when there is a conversion privilege. Nearly half of the companies in Canada that report having preferred shares also have a conversion feature. **Convertible preferred shares** give preferred shareholders the option of exchanging their preferred shares for common shares at a specified ratio. They are purchased by investors who want the greater security of preferred shares but who also want the option of converting their preferred shares for common shares if the fair value of the common shares increases significantly.

To illustrate, assume that Ross Industries Inc. issues 1,000 convertible preferred shares at $100 per share. One preferred share is convertible into 10 common shares. The current market price of the common shares is $9 per share. At this point, holders of the preferred shares would not want to convert, because they would exchange preferred shares worth $100,000 (1,000 × $100) for common shares worth only $90,000 (10,000 × $9). However, if the price of the common shares were to increase above $10 per share, it would be profitable for shareholders to convert their preferred shares to common shares.

When the shares are converted, the cost of the preferred shares is transferred to the Common Shares account. As it is seldom possible to determine the original cost of the preferred shares that are involved in the conversion, the average cost per share of the preferred shares is used instead. For the preferred shares that are being converted, this is calculated by dividing the balance in the Preferred Shares account by the number of shares issued at the transaction date.

To illustrate, assume that the 1,000 preferred shares of Ross Industries Ltd. with an average cost of $100 per share are converted into 10,000 common shares when the fair values of the two classes of shares are $101 and $12 per share, respectively, on June 10. The entry to record the conversion is:

June 10	Preferred Shares	100,000	
	Common Shares		100,000
	To record conversion of 1,000 preferred shares into 10,000 common shares.		

A	=	L	+	SE
				−100,000
				+100,000

Cash flows: no effect

Note that the average cost (which is the same as the original cost in this example) of the preferred shares is used to record the conversion. The fair values of either the preferred or the common shares are *not* considered in recording the transaction, because the total amount of contributed capital has not changed. Therefore, the conversion of preferred shares will never result in either a gain or loss to the contributed capital.

Redeemable and Retractable Preferred

Many preferred shares are issued with a redemption or call feature. **Redeemable (or callable) preferred shares** give the issuing corporation the right to purchase the shares from shareholders at specified future dates and prices. The redemption feature gives a corporation some flexibility: it allows the corporation to eliminate the preferred shares when doing this will benefit the corporation.

Often, shares that are redeemable are also convertible. Sometimes, companies will redeem or call their preferred shares to force investors to convert those preferred shares into common shares.

Retractable preferred shares are similar to redeemable preferred shares except that the shareholders can redeem shares at their option instead of the corporation redeeming the shares at its option. The redemption usually occurs at an arranged price and date.

When preferred shares are redeemable or retractable, the distinction between equity and debt begins to blur. Redeemable and retractable preferred shares are similar in some ways to debt. They both offer a rate of return to the investor, and with the redemption of the shares, they both offer a repayment of the principal investment.

Contractual arrangements of this type are called **financial instruments**. A financial instrument is a contract that creates a financial asset for one company, and a financial liability or equity instrument for the other company. Amounts receivable and payable are simple examples of financial instruments. More complex examples include convertible bonds and redeemable or retractable preferred shares.

Financial instruments must be presented in accordance with their economic substance rather than their form. That is, redeemable and retractable preferred shares are usually presented in the *liabilities* section of the balance sheet rather than in the shareholders' equity section. This is because they have more of the features of debt than of equity.

Companies are issuing an increasing number of shares with innovative preferences. Some have the attributes of both debt and equity; others have the attributes of both common and preferred shares. Accounting for such financial instruments presents unique challenges to accountants. Further discussion of this topic is left to an intermediate accounting course.

Helpful hint The two features benefit different parties. Redeemable is at the option of the corporation. Retractable is at the option of the shareholder.

Liquidation Preference

In addition to having a priority claim on the distribution of income over common shares, preferred shares also have a priority claim on corporate assets if the corporation fails. This means that if the company is bankrupt, preferred shareholders will get money back before common shareholders do. The preference to assets can be for the legal capital of the shares or for a specified liquidating value. So, while creditors still rank above all shareholders in terms of preference, preferred shareholders rank above the common shareholders, and this is important as the money usually runs out before everyone gets paid.

Because of these two preferential rights—the right to dividends and assets—preferred shareholders generally do not mind that they do not have the voting right that common shareholders have.

BEFORE YOU GO ON . . .

→ Review It

1. Compare the normal rights and privileges of common and preferred shareholders.
2. What are the differences between cumulative and noncumulative preferred shares?
3. What are the differences between convertible, redeemable, and retractable preferred shares?

→ Do It

Turin Corporation issued 50,000 preferred shares on February 22 for $20 each. Each share was convertible into 10 common shares. On April 12, another 30,000 preferred shares were issued for $30 each. On June 5, when the price of the common shares was $4 and the price of the preferred shares was $35, shareholders converted 20,000 of the preferred shares into common. Record the share transactions.

Action Plan

- Credit the Preferred Shares account for the entire proceeds of the share issue.
- Use the average cost to record the conversion. Fair values are irrelevant.
- Calculate the average cost per share by dividing the balance in the Preferred Shares account by the number of shares issued.

Solution

Feb. 22	Cash	1,000,000	
	Preferred Shares (50,000 × $20)		1,000,000
	To record issue of 50,000 preferred shares at $20.		
Apr. 12	Cash	900,000	
	Preferred Shares (30,000 × $30)		900,000
	To record issue of 30,000 preferred shares at $30.		
June 5	Preferred Shares (20,000 × $23.75)	475,000	
	Common Shares		475,000
	To record conversion of 20,000 preferred shares into 200,000 (20,000 × 10) common shares at an average cost of $23.75 ($1,900,000 ÷ 80,000).		

The Navigator

Related exercise material: BE13–7, BE13–8, BE13–9, E13–4, E13–5, E13–6, and E13–7.

Statement Presentation and Analysis

STUDY OBJECTIVE 4

Prepare the shareholders' equity section of the balance sheet and calculate return on equity.

In this section, we will review the preparation and presentation of the shareholders' equity section of the balance sheet and then learn how to use this information to calculate an important profitability measure—the return on equity ratio.

Presentation of Shareholders' Equity

The shareholders' equity section of the balance sheet always includes two parts: (1) contributed capital, and (2) retained earnings. Corporations following International Financial Reporting Standards (IFRS) will also have a third section called accumulated other comprehensive income. We have already mentioned the first two categories and will illustrate them here. Accumulated other comprehensive income is a new concept that we will introduce here and look at in more detail in Chapter 14.

Contributed Capital

Recall that contributed capital is the amounts contributed by, or accruing to, the shareholders. Within contributed capital, there are two classifications:

1. **Share capital.** This is the amount invested in the company by the shareholders. The category consists of preferred and common shares. Because of the additional rights they possess, preferred shares are shown before common shares. The legal value (e.g., no par value), number of shares authorized, number of shares issued, and any particular share preferences (e.g., convertible) are reported for each class of shares.

2. **Additional contributed capital.** This category includes amounts contributed from reacquiring and retiring shares. Other situations not discussed in this textbook can also result in additional contributed capital. If a company has a variety of sources of additional contributed capital, it is important to distinguish each one. For many companies, there is no additional contributed capital. The category "share capital" is therefore used more often than "contributed capital."

Alternative terminology
Additional contributed capital is also known as *contributed surplus*.

Retained Earnings

Retained earnings are the cumulative profit (or loss) since incorporation that has been retained in the company (i.e., not distributed to shareholders). Each year, profit is added (or a loss is deducted) and dividends are deducted from the opening retained earnings balance to determine the ending retained earnings amount. As discussed earlier in the chapter, dividends are amounts distributed to shareholders—they are similar to drawings by an owner in a proprietorship.

To illustrate, assume that Zaboschuk Inc. had $928,000 of retained earnings at January 1, 2011, earned profits of $210,000 for the year, and paid cash dividends of $80,000. Retained earnings at the end of the year would be calculated as follows:

Retained earnings, January 1, 2011	$ 928,000
Add: Profit for 2011	210,000
	1,138,000
Less: Cash dividends	80,000
Retained earnings, December 31, 2011	$1,058,000

As in a proprietorship, revenue and expense accounts (which combine to produce profit or loss) and the Dividends account are temporary accounts that accumulate transactions for the period. At the end of each period, these accounts are closed, just as their corresponding accounts in a proprietorship are: (1) individual revenue and expense accounts are closed to Income Summary, (2) the Income Summary account is closed to Retained Earnings, and (3) Dividends is closed to Retained Earnings. Note that the Income Summary account is not closed to the owner's capital account, the way it is in a proprietorship. Instead, in a corporation, it is closed to the Retained Earnings account, as is the Dividends account.

For example, assume for simplicity that Zaboschuk Inc. has three temporary accounts at its December 31 year end: Service Revenue $500,000; Operating Expenses $290,000; and Dividends $80,000. The closing entries follow:

Dec. 31	Service Revenue	500,000	
	Income Summary		500,000
	To close revenue to income summary.		
31	Income Summary	290,000	
	Operating Expenses		290,000
	To close expenses to income summary.		
31	Income Summary	210,000	
	Retained Earnings		210,000
	To close income summary ($500,000 − $290,000) to retained earnings.		
31	Retained Earnings	80,000	
	Dividends		80,000
	To close dividends to retained earnings.		

A	=	L	+	SE
				−500,000
				+500,000

Cash flows: no effect

A	=	L	+	SE
				−290,000
				+290,000

Cash flows: no effect

A	=	L	+	SE
				−210,000
				+210,000

Cash flows: no effect

A	=	L	+	SE
				−80,000
				+80,000

Cash flows: no effect

After these entries are posted, the Retained Earnings account (a permanent account) is updated in the general ledger to equal $1,058,000, as previously calculated. It is this ending balance that is reported as an addition in the shareholders' equity section of the balance sheet, as shown in Illustration 13-2. The normal balance of the Retained Earnings account is a credit. If there is a negative, or deficit, balance, it is reported as a deduction from shareholders' equity, rather than as an addition.

This ending Retained Earnings balance becomes the opening balance for the next period. Companies are required to include in their financial statements a reconciliation of the opening and ending balances of retained earnings each period. Under Canadian GAAP for Private Enterprises, this information is included in the statement of retained earnings, similar to a statement of owner's equity in a proprietorship. Under IFRS, this reconciliation is part of the statement of shareholders' equity. We will learn how to prepare a statement of retained earnings and a statement of shareholders' equity in the next chapter.

Accumulated Other Comprehensive Income

Companies following IFRS are required to report comprehensive income in addition to profit. While most revenues, expenses, gains, and losses are included in profit, certain gains and losses bypass profit and are recorded as direct adjustments to shareholders' equity. **Comprehensive income** includes all changes in shareholders' equity during a period except for changes that result from the sale or repurchase of shares or from the payment of dividends. This means that it includes (1) the revenues, expenses, gains, and losses included in profit; *and* (2) the gains and losses that bypass profit but affect shareholders' equity. This second category is referred to as **other comprehensive income (loss)**.

There are several examples of other comprehensive income. One example that we will learn about in more detail in Chapter 16 is gains and losses on certain types of equity investments. Gains and losses are recorded when investments are adjusted up or down to their fair value at the end of each accounting period and when they are sold. You will learn more in Chapter 16 about equity investments including how to determine whether the gains and losses should be included in profit or in other comprehensive income. In Chapters 13 and 14, we will tell you how to classify these gains and losses.

If a company has other comprehensive income, it must report **accumulated other comprehensive income** as a separate component of shareholders' equity. Other comprehensive income is reported separately from profit (and accumulated other comprehensive income is reported separately from retained earnings) for two important reasons: (1) it protects profit from sudden changes that would simply be caused by fluctuations in fair value, and (2) it informs the financial statement user of the cash that would have been received if the investment had actually been sold at year end because the asset is reported at its fair value.

Under Canadian GAAP for Private Enterprises, there is no such concept as other comprehensive income. Thus, companies following these standards will not report accumulated other comprehensive income as part of shareholders' equity.

Sample Shareholders' Equity Section

The assumed shareholders' equity section of Zaboschuk Inc., shown in Illustration 13-2, includes most of the accounts discussed in this chapter. Zaboschuk's preferred shares section discloses that the dividend rate is $6 per year; 50,000 noncumulative preferred shares with no par value have been authorized; and 6,000 shares are issued. This means 44,000 shares are still available for issue at some point in the future.

The common shares are no par value with an unlimited amount of shares authorized. To date, 400,000 shares have been issued. Zaboschuk also reports additional contributed capital of $60,000 that was earned when reacquiring common shares, retained earnings of $1,058,000 (as previously shown), and accumulated other comprehensive income of $312,000.

← Illustration 13-2

Shareholders' equity section

ZABOSCHUK INC. Balance Sheet (partial) December 31, 2011		
Shareholders' equity		
Contributed capital		
Share capital		
$6-noncumulative preferred shares, no par value, 50,000 shares authorized, 6,000 shares issued	$ 770,000	
Common shares, no par value, unlimited shares authorized, 400,000 shares issued	2,800,000	
Total share capital		$3,570,000
Additional contributed capital		
Contributed capital—reacquisition of common shares		60,000
Total contributed capital		3,630,000
Retained earnings		1,058,000
Accumulated other comprehensive income		312,000
Total shareholders' equity		$5,000,000

Analysis

There are many ratios that can be determined from the shareholders' equity section of the balance sheet. We will learn about return on equity here. In the next chapter, we will learn about other ratios, like earnings per share, price-earnings, and the payout ratio.

Return on Equity

Return on equity, also known as return on investment, is considered by many to be *the* most important measure of a company's profitability. This ratio is used by management and investors to evaluate how many dollars are earned for each dollar invested by the shareholders. It can be used to compare investment opportunities in the marketplace.

Return on equity is a widely published figure. One of the highest return on equity numbers reported among Canada's top 500 corporations in a recent year was that of Bombardier, which reported a return on equity of 39%. The following illustration calculates the return on equity ratio for The Forzani Group ($ in thousands):

Profit	÷	Average Shareholders' Equity	=	Return on Equity
$29,325	÷	($333,179 + $355,483) ÷ 2	=	8.5%

← Illustration 13-3

Return on equity

Forzani's return on equity, at 8.5%, is well above the industry average, which was recently reported as 1.8% on Yahoo! Finance. Return on equity can vary significantly by company and by industry.

Calculations can be done to produce a return on equity for common shareholders only. This is done by dividing profit available to common shareholders by the average common shareholders' equity. Profit available to common shareholders is profit less any preferred dividends. Common shareholders' equity is total shareholders' equity less the legal capital of any preferred shares. Recall that everything else belongs to the common, or residual, shareholders.

BEFORE YOU GO ON . . .

Do It

1. Identify the classifications found in the shareholders' equity section of a balance sheet.
2. Why is accumulated other comprehensive income reported separately from retained earnings?
3. Explain how to calculate the return on equity.

Related exercise material: BE13–10, BE13–11, BE13–12, BE13–13, E13–8, E13–9, E13–10, and E13–11.

The Navigator

WILEY
PLUS

Demonstration Problem

Demonstration Problem

The Rolman Corporation is authorized to issue an unlimited number of no par value common shares and 100,000 no par value, $6-noncumulative, convertible preferred shares. Each preferred share is convertible into 7.5 common shares. In its first year, 2011, the company had the following share transactions:

Jan. 10	Issued 400,000 common shares at $8 per share.
July 1	Issued 100,000 common shares in exchange for land. The land had an appraised value of $900,000. The shares were selling on the Toronto Stock Exchange at $8.50 per share on that date.
Aug. 1	Issued 20,000 preferred shares at $50 each.
Oct. 12	Reacquired 50,000 common shares at $7 per share.
Nov. 15	Paid quarterly dividend to preferred shareholders and a $10,000 quarterly dividend to common shareholders.
Nov. 18	Reacquired 65,000 common shares at $9.20 per share.
Dec. 1	Converted 4,000 preferred shares into 30,000 common shares. The preferred shares were selling for $55 per share and the common shares for $9 per share on that date.
Dec. 19	Reacquired 10,000 common shares at $7.95 per share.

Instructions

(a) Journalize the transactions.

(b) Calculate retained earnings at December 31, 2011, assuming the company had a profit of $900,000 in 2011.

(c) Prepare the shareholders' equity section of the balance sheet at December 31, 2011, assuming the company had other comprehensive income of $100,000 in 2011.

Action Plan

- Credit the appropriate share capital account for the full amount of the proceeds from the issue of no par value shares.
- Fair value of consideration received should be used when shares are issued for noncash assets.
- Use separate accounts for each type or class of shares.
- Record the conversion of shares at average cost of the preferred shares.
- Keep track of the number of shares issued. Calculate the average cost per share by dividing the balance in the share account by the number of shares issued.
- Calculate the quarterly preferred dividend by dividing the annual dividend requirement by 4.
- Debit the common shares account for the average cost of the reacquired shares. If the reacquisition price is below the average cost, credit the difference to a contributed capital account. If the reacquisition price is above the average cost, debit the difference to Retained Earnings unless there is an existing balance in a contributed capital account from previous reacquisitions and retirements.

Solution to Demonstration Problem

(a)

Date	Account	Debit	Credit
Jan. 10	Cash	3,200,000	
	Common Shares (400,000 × $8)		3,200,000
	To record issue of 400,000 common shares at $8.		
July 1	Land	900,000	
	Common Shares		900,000
	To record issue of 100,000 common shares for land.		
Aug. 1	Cash	1,000,000	
	Preferred Shares (20,000 × $50)		1,000,000
	To record issue of 20,000 preferred shares at $50.		
Oct. 12	Common Shares (50,000 × $8.20)	410,000	
	Contributed Capital—Reacquisition of		
	Common Shares		60,000
	Cash (50,000 × $7)		350,000
	To record reacquisition of 50,000 common shares at an average cost of $8.20 ($4,100,000 ÷ 500,000).		
Nov. 15	Dividends [($6.00 ÷ 4) × 20,000 + $10,000]	40,000	
	Cash		40,000
	To record quarterly payment of common and preferred cash dividends.		
Nov. 18	Common Shares (65,000 × $8.20)	533,000	
	Contributed Capital—Reacquisition of Common Shares	60,000	
	Retained Earnings	5,000	
	Cash (65,000 × $9.20)		598,000
	To record reacquisition of 65,000 common shares at an average cost of $8.20 ($3,690,000 ÷ 450,000).		

Dec. 1	Preferred Shares (4,000 × $50)	200,000	
	Common Shares		200,000
	To record conversion of 4,000 preferred shares into 30,000 common shares.		
Dec. 19	Common Shares (10,000 × $8.089)	80,890	
	Contributed Capital—Reacquisition of Common Shares		1,390
	Cash (10,000 × $7.95)		79,500
	To record reacquisition of 10,000 common shares at an average cost of $8.089 ($3,357,000 ÷ 415,000).		

(b)

Retained earnings, January 1		$ 0
Add: Profit for the year		900,000
	900,000	
Less: Cash dividends	($40,000)	
Reacquisition of common shares	(5,000)	(45,000)
Retained earnings, December 31		$855,000

(c)

ROLMAN CORPORATION
Balance Sheet (partial)
December 31, 2011

Shareholders' equity		
Contributed capital		
Share capital		
Preferred shares, no par value, $6-noncumulative, convertible, 100,000 authorized, 16,000[1] issued	$ 800,000[2]	
Common shares, no par value, unlimited number of shares authorized, 405,000[3] issued	3,276,110[4]	
Total share capital		$ 4,076,110
Contributed capital—reacquisition of common shares		1,390[5]
Total contributed capital		4,077,500
Retained earnings		855,000
Accumulated other comprehensive income		100,000
Total shareholders' equity		$5,032,500

[1] 20,000 − 4,000 = 16,000
[2] $1,000,000 − $200,000 = $800,000
[3] 400,000 + 100,000 − 50,000 − 65,000 + 30,000 − 10,000 = 405,000
[4] $3,200,000 + $900,000 − $410,000 − $533,000 + $200,000 − $80,890 = $3,276,110
[5] $60,000 − $60,000 + 1,390 = $1,390

The Navigator

Summary of Study Objectives

1. *Identify and discuss the major characteristics of the corporate form of organization.* The major characteristics of a corporation are as follows: separate legal existence, limited liability of shareholders, transferable ownership rights, ability to acquire capital, continuous life, corporation management, government regulations, and corporate income tax. Corporations are incorporated federally or provincially, and may have shareholders of different classes. Each class of shares carries different rights and privileges.

2. *Record common share transactions.* When no par value shares are issued for cash, the entire proceeds from the issue become legal capital and are credited to the Common Shares account. When shares are issued for noncash assets or services, the fair value of the consideration received is used if it can be determined. If not, the fair value of the consideration given up is used.

When shares are reacquired, the average cost is debited to the Common Shares account. If the shares are reacquired at a price below the average cost, the difference is credited to a contributed capital account. If the shares are reacquired at a price above the average cost, the difference is debited first to a contributed capital account if a balance exists, and then to the Retained Earnings account.

3. **Record preferred share transactions.** The accounting for preferred shares is similar to the accounting for common shares. Preferred shares have priority over common shares in certain areas. Typically, preferred shareholders have priority over (1) dividends, and (2) assets, if the company is liquidated. They usually do not have voting rights. In addition, preferred shares may be convertible, redeemable, and/or retractable. Convertible preferred shares allow their holder to convert them into common shares at a specified ratio. The redemption feature gives the issuing corporation the right to purchase the shares from shareholders at specified future dates and prices. Retractable preferred shares give shareholders the option of selling their shares to the corporation at specified future dates and prices. Redeemable and retractable preferred shares are often more like debt than equity.

4. **Prepare the shareholders' equity section of the balance sheet and calculate return on equity.** Within the shareholders' equity section, the following are reported: contributed capital, retained earnings, and accumulated comprehensive income (if any). Within contributed capital, two classifications may be shown if applicable: share capital and additional contributed capital.

Return on equity is calculated by dividing profit by average shareholders' equity. It is an important measure of a company's profitability.

The Navigator

Glossary

Accumulated other comprehensive income The cumulative amount of other comprehensive income and losses over the life of the company reported as separate amount in shareholders' equity. (p. 736)

Authorized shares The amount of share capital that a corporation is authorized to sell, as indicated in its articles of incorporation. This amount may be specified or unlimited. (p. 725)

Common shares Shares where the owners have the right to (1) vote on the election of the board of directors, (2) share in the distribution of profit through dividends, and (3) share any assets that remain after all debts and shares with priority rights have been paid. If the corporation has only one class of shares, these are the common shares. (p. 724)

Comprehensive income All changes in shareholders' equity during a period except for changes resulting from the sale or repurchase of shares, or from the payment of dividends. Comprehensive income includes (1) the revenues, expenses, gains, and losses included in profit; and (2) the gains and losses that bypass profit but affect shareholders' equity. (p. 736)

Contributed capital The total amount of cash paid or other assets contributed by shareholders in exchange for share capital. (p. 727)

Convertible preferred shares Preferred shares that the shareholder can convert into common shares at a specified ratio. (p. 732)

Corporation A business organized as a separate legal entity, with most of the rights and privileges of a person. Shares are evidence of ownership. (p. 720)

Cumulative A feature of preferred shares that entitles the shareholder to receive current dividends and unpaid prior-year dividends before common shareholders receive any dividends. (p. 732)

Dividends in arrears Preferred dividends that were not declared during a period. (p. 732)

Financial instrument A contract between two or more parties that establishes financial rights or obligations. (p. 733)

Initial public offering (IPO) The initial offering of a corporation's shares to the public. (p. 725)

Issued shares The portion of authorized shares that has been sold. (p. 725)

Legal capital The amount per share that must be retained in the business for the protection of corporate creditors. (p. 726)

Market capitalization A measure of the value of a company's equity. It is calculated by multiplying the number of shares issued by the share price at any given date. (p. 726)

No par value shares Share capital that has not been given a specific value. All the proceeds from the sale of no par value shares are treated as legal capital. (p. 727)

Noncumulative Preferred shares that are entitled to the current dividend, but not to any unpaid amounts from previous years. (p. 732)

Organization costs Costs incurred in the formation of a corporation. (p. 724)

Other comprehensive income Gains and losses that bypass profit but affect shareholders' equity. (p. 736)

Preferred shares Shares that have contractual preferences over common shares. (p. 731)

Privately held corporation A corporation that has only a few shareholders. Its shares are not available for sale to the general public. (p. 720)

Publicly held corporation A corporation that may have thousands of shareholders. Its shares are usually traded on an organized securities market. (p. 720)

Redeemable (callable) preferred shares Preferred shares that give the issuer the right to purchase the shares from shareholders at specified future dates and prices. (p. 733)

Retained earnings Earned capital (cumulative profit less losses and amounts distributed to shareholders since incorporation) that has been retained for future use. If negative (i.e., a debit balance), it is called a deficit. (p. 726)

Retractable preferred shares Preferred shares that give the shareholder the right to sell the shares to the issuer at specified future dates and prices. (p. 733)

Return on equity A measure of profitability from the shareholders' point of view. It is calculated by dividing profit by average common shareholders' equity. (p. 737)

Secondary market A market where investors buy and sell shares from each other, rather than from the company. (p. 726)

Share capital The amount paid, or contributed, to the corporation by shareholders in exchange for shares of ownership. It can consist of preferred and common shares. (p. 726)

Treasury shares A corporation's own shares that have been reacquired and not yet retired or cancelled. They are held in "treasury" for later reissue or cancellation. (p. 728)

Self-Study Questions

Answers are at the end of the chapter.

(SO 1) K **1.** An important characteristic unique to a corporation is that:
(a) It is separate and distinct from its owners.
(b) Owner liability is unlimited.
(c) Owners personally manage the company.
(d) Ownership rights are not transferable.

(SO 1) AP **2.** Ilona Schiller purchased 1,000 common shares of Bombardier Inc. on the Toronto Stock Exchange for $2 per share. Bombardier had originally issued these shares at $3. This transaction will have what impact on Bombardier's Common Shares account?
(a) Decrease of $1,000
(b) Decrease of $2,000
(c) Decrease of $3,000
(d) No effect

(SO 2) AP **3.** ABC Corporation issues 1,000 common shares at $12 per share. In recording the transaction, a credit is made to:
(a) Gain on Sale of Shares for $12,000.
(b) Common Shares for $12,000.
(c) Investment in ABC Common Shares for $12,000.
(d) Contributed Capital for $12,000.

(SO 2) C **4.** To record the reacquisition of shares, the price used to record the shares is the:
(a) one-month average market price per share.
(b) average cost per share.
(c) most recent market price per share.
(d) par value.

(SO 2) AP **5.** Common shares are repurchased for $150,000 by a company with Contributed Capital—Reacquisition of Shares $75,000; and Retained Earnings $750,000. The repurchased shares have an average cost of $125,000. The journal entry to record the repurchase would include a:
(a) debit to Retained Earnings of $25,000.
(b) credit to Contributed Capital—Reacquisition of Shares of $25,000.
(c) debit to Contributed Capital—Reacquisition of Shares of $25,000.
(d) debit to Common Shares of $150,000.

(SO 3) K **6.** Which of the following is *not* true? Preferred shares:
(a) have priority over common shareholder dividends.
(b) have priority over common shareholders for assets in the event of liquidation.
(c) generally have voting rights.
(d) can be reacquired.

(SO 3) K **7.** A company converts 15,000 convertible preferred shares to 30,000 common shares. At the time of the conversion, the average cost of the preferred shares is $5 and the fair value is $7. Also at the time of conversion, the fair value of the common shares is $4. The entry to record this transaction would include a:
(a) credit to Common Shares for $120,000.
(b) debit to Common Shares for $120,000.
(c) credit to Preferred Shares for $75,000.
(d) debit to Preferred Shares for $75,000.

(SO 4) K 8. Which of the following is reported in the shareholders' equity section?
(a) Accumulated other comprehensive income
(b) Common shares
(c) Contributed capital—reacquisition of shares
(d) All of the above

(SO 4) AP 9. The shareholders' equity section of a balance sheet will never report:
(a) a debit balance in a contributed capital account.
(b) a debit balance in accumulated other comprehensive income.
(c) a debit balance in the Retained Earnings account.
(d) (a) and (c).

10. If a company's profit is $50,000, its total assets (SO 4) C $1 million, its average common shareholders' equity $500,000, and its net sales $800,000, its return on equity is:
(a) 3.3%.
(b) 5%.
(c) 6.25%.
(d) 10%.

The Navigator

Questions

(SO 1) C 1. Corporations can be classified in different ways. For example, they may be classified by purpose (e.g., profit or not-for-profit) or by ownership (e.g., public or private). Explain the difference between each of these types of classifications.

(SO 1) C 2. Pat Kabza, a student, asks for your help in understanding the following characteristics of a corporation: (a) limited liability of shareholders, (b) transferable ownership rights, and (c) ability to acquire capital. Explain how these characteristics work together to create a significant advantage for the corporate form of organization.

(SO 1) C 3. Your small business has been formed as a corporation and has several shareholders. After a very profitable year, it is decided that a special bonus will be paid to the owners. The company Sales Manager (who is also a shareholder) suggests to you that each shareholder take the bonus in the form of a drawing from equity.
(a) Explain to the Sales Manager the ways in which this bonus payment must be made.
(b) What are the differences to the owners' personal income tax if they receive a bonus from a corporation instead of a drawing from a partnership?

(SO 1) C 4. Explain why some of the advantages of the corporate form of organization may not apply to small, privately held corporations.

(SO 1) C 5. List the rights of preferred shareholders and compare them with those of a common shareholder.

(SO 1) C 6. Explain the difference between authorized and issued shares. Are both recorded in the general journal?

(SO 1) C 7. (a) What term is used to describe the portion of the shareholders' equity section of the balance sheet that accumulates earnings?

(b) What term is used to describe the portion of the shareholders' equity section of the balance sheet that records the amount contributed by shareholders? What constraints are tied to this portion of shareholders' equity?

8. List the types of information likely to be included (SO 1) C in a company's articles of incorporation.

9. Paul Joyce purchases 100 common shares of Tech- (SO 1) AP Top Ltd. for $12 per share from the company's initial public offering. Later, Paul Joyce purchases 200 more TechTop Ltd. common shares for $20 each on the Toronto Stock Exchange, using his own online brokerage account. Explain the impact of each of these transactions on TechTop's assets, liabilities, and shareholders' equity.

10. Open Text Corp.'s share price climbed more than (SO 1) AP 25% in one year from $29.80 to $37.38. Explain the effect of this increase in share price on Open Text's financial statements.

11. A delivery truck with an estimated fair value of (SO 2) AP $22,000 is acquired by issuing 1,000 common shares. The shares' market price at the time of the exchange is $24 per share. Should the truck be recorded at $22,000 or $24,000? Explain.

12. Why would a company repurchase some of its (SO 2) C shares? Give some reasons.

13. Wilmor, Inc. repurchases 1,000 of its own com- (SO 2) C mon shares. What effect does this transaction have on (a) total assets, (b) total liabilities, and (c) total shareholders' equity?

14. Explain how the accounting for the reacquisition of (SO 2) C shares changes depending on whether the reacquisition price is greater or lower than average cost.

(SO 2) C 15. Ciana Chiasson is confused. She says, "I don't understand why sometimes, when the price paid to reacquire shares is greater than their average cost, the 'loss on reacquisition' is debited to a contributed capital account. But at other times, it is debited to the Retained Earnings account. And sometimes it even is debited to both!" Help Ciana understand.

(SO 3) C 16. Identify the three areas in which preferred shares are given priority over common shares.

(SO 3) C 17. What is the difference between noncumulative and cumulative preferred shares? Between redeemable and retractable preferred shares?

(SO 3) C 18. Following two years of no dividend payments to either cumulative preferred or common shareholders, management decides to declare a dividend for all shareholders. (a) Is the company required to pay all shareholders for the previous two years of missed dividends? (b) Should the company report a liability for the years of missed dividends or are there any other reporting requirements?

(SO 3) C 19. A preferred shareholder converts her convertible preferred shares into common shares. What effect does this have on the corporation's (a) total assets, (b) total liabilities, and (c) total shareholders' equity?

20. The shareholders' equity is divided into major components. Identify and explain what each component represents. (SO 4) K

21. Indicate how each of the following accounts should be classified in the shareholders' equity section: (SO 4) C
   (a) Common Shares
   (b) Retained Earnings
   (c) Contributed Capital—Reacquisition of Shares
   (d) Accumulated Other Comprehensive Income
   (e) Preferred Shares

22. What is comprehensive income? Why is accumulated other comprehensive income reported separately from retained earnings? (SO 4) K

23. Two independent companies have the same annual earnings ($100,000); however, the companies have different amounts of shareholders' equity. Shareholders' equity for company 1 is $300,000 and for company 2 it is $350,000. Which company would you consider a better investment and why? (SO 4) C

24. Common shareholders may want a more precise measure of the company's performance. How could the return on equity formula be changed to meet this requirement? (SO 4) C

Brief Exercises

BE13–1 For each characteristic listed, identify which type of business organization best fits the description. There may be more than one answer in some cases. The first one has been done for you as an example.

Distinguish between characteristics of different business organizations. (SO 1) C

Characteristic	Proprietorship	Partnership	Corporation
1. Continuous life			X
2. Unlimited liability			
3. Ease of formation			
4. Income taxes			
5. Ability to acquire capital			
6. Shared skills and resources			
7. Fewer government regulations			
8. Separation of ownership and management			
9. Owners' acts are binding			
10. Easy transfer of ownership rights			

BE13–2 You were recently hired as an accountant for Victory Sports Ltd. The Vice President of Finance told you that he was excited about how much better the company's balance sheet will look given a recent increase in the fair value of the company's shares. Is the Vice President's conclusion correct? Who benefits from increasing share prices?

Evaluate impact of share price on financial position. (SO 1) AP

Record issue of common shares.
(SO 2) AP

BE13–3 On August 5, Hansen Corporation issued 1,000 common shares for $15 per share. On September 10, Hansen issued an additional 500 shares for $17 per share. (a) Record the share transactions. (b) What is the average cost per share of the common shares following the last transaction?

Record issue of common shares in noncash transaction.
(SO 2) AP

BE13–4 On March 8, Happy Hollow Inc. issued 3,000 common shares for cash of $18 per share. On April 20, when the shares were trading at $22, the company issued 5,500 common shares in exchange for land with a fair value of $125,000. (a) Prepare the journal entries for each transaction. (b) Would your answer change if you were unable to determine the land's fair value on April 20?

Discuss share repurchase.
(SO 2) AP

BE13–5 The Quebec-based international paper company Cascades Inc. repurchased 595,500 of its own common shares in 2008. The share repurchase resulted in a debit of $3 million to the Common Shares account and a debit of $1 million to the Retained Earnings account. (a) How much did Cascades pay, on average, to repurchase its shares? (b) What was the initial issue price of the shares, on average? (c) What was Cascades' likely reason for repurchasing some of its own shares?

Record reacquisition of shares.
(SO 2) AP

BE13–6 Ramsay Corporation reported having 25,000 common shares issued for a total share capital of $100,000 on its December 31, 2010, balance sheet. On February 15, 2011, it reacquired 4,000 of these shares. This is the first time Ramsay has reacquired any of its shares. Record the reacquisition of the shares assuming the company paid (a) $14,000, and (b) $18,000, to reacquire the shares.

Record issue of preferred shares.
(SO 3) AP

BE13–7 BuiltRight Ltd. had the following share transactions during the year:

March 18 Issued 1,000 preferred shares for $100 cash per share.
April 7 Issued 1,500 preferred shares for $125 cash per share.

For each of the transactions above, (a) journalize the transactions and (b) calculate the average cost per share after the April 7 transaction.

Record conversion of preferred shares.
(SO 3) AP

BE13–8 The Progressive Parts Corporation issued 25,000 preferred shares on May 10 for $25 each. Each share is convertible into two common shares. On November 21, the preferred shares had a fair value of $27 each, and the common shares $14 each. On this day, 5,000 of the preferred shares are converted into common shares. (a) Journalize the issue of the preferred shares on May 10. (b) Journalize the conversion of the preferred shares on November 21.

Determine dividends in arrears.
(SO 3) AP

BE13–9 Gushue Incorporated had 40,000 $2-cumulative preferred shares. It was unable to pay any dividend to the preferred shareholders in the current year. (a) What are the dividends in arrears, if any? (b) Would your answer change if the preferred shares were noncumulative rather than cumulative?

Prepare shareholders' equity section.
(SO 4) AP

BE13–10 As the new Accounting Manager at True Green Nurseries Ltd., you have been asked to prepare the shareholders' equity section of the company's balance sheet with the following December 31, 2011, account balances: common shares, no par value, unlimited number of shares authorized, 10,000 shares issued, $100,000; preferred shares, $7-noncumulative, no par value, unlimited number of shares authorized, 900 shares issued, $23,400; contributed capital—reacquisition of common shares, $8,000; and retained earnings, $45,000. Prepare the shareholders' equity section as requested.

Prepare shareholders' equity section with accumulated other comprehensive income.
(SO 4) AP

BE13–11 Refer to BE13–10. In addition to the information provided, assume that True Green Nurseries Ltd. also has accumulated other comprehensive income of $12,000. (a) Prepare the shareholders' equity section of the balance sheet. (b) What amount would True Green report as total shareholders' equity if it had an accumulated other comprehensive loss of $12,000 rather than accumulated other comprehensive income?

BE13–12 Dearborn Enterprises Ltd. reported its financial performance for the year ended December 31, 2011. During that year, the company generated revenues of $850,000 and expenses of $600,000. Having had a successful year, the company declared and paid dividends of $75,000. Prepare summary closing entries.

Record closing entries.
(SO 4) AP

BE13–13 For the year ended December 31, 2008, Canada Bread Company, Limited reported (in thousands) net revenue $1,708,330; profit $64,936; beginning shareholders' equity $635,043; and ending shareholders' equity $708,340. (a) Calculate the return on equity. (b) Canada Bread has no preferred shares. Would its return on common shareholders' equity be the same as, or different from, its return on equity?

Calculate return on equity.
(SO 4) AP

Exercises

E13–1 Here is a stock market listing for Maple Leaf Foods Inc. (MFI) common shares:

Interpret stock market listing.
(SO 1) AN

365-day		stock	sym	div	high	low	close	chg	vol 100s	yld	p/e ratio
high	low	Maple Leaf	MFI	0.16	8.48	8.41	8.48	−0.04	317	1.9	30.7
12.00	6.54										

Instructions

Answer the following questions:

(a) What is the highest price MFI shares traded for during the last year? The lowest price?
(b) What is the annual per-share dividend paid on these shares?
(c) If you had purchased 1,000 common shares at MFI's high price of the day in the above listing, what would be the total cost of your share purchase?
(d) What was the closing price of MFI common shares on the previous day?
(e) How many MFI common shares were sold on the trading day of the listing?
(f) What would be your likely motivation for purchasing these shares: dividend income or capital appreciation?

E13–2 As an accountant for the consulting firm Insite, you are asked by a client to provide advice on the form of organization her new business should take. After a brief conversation, you have learned the following about your client's needs:

Identify the characteristics of a corporation.
(SO 1) AP

1. The client has several children whom she expects to become involved in the business, and to whom she will want to transfer ownership in the future.
2. Companies in the industry segment in which this business will operate (the medical industry) tend to be sued frequently.
3. Profit (and taxable income) are expected to be significant in the early years.
4. The company is expected to grow significantly, and your client expects to need substantial funding in the next few years to manage this growth.

Instructions

Write a brief report to advise your client on why organizing as a corporation may, or may not, be the appropriate choice.

E13–3 As an accountant for the firm Stein and Partners, you encounter the following situations while doing the accounting for different clients:

Record issue of shares in noncash transactions.
(SO 2) AP

1. New Ventures is a closely held corporation whose shares just recently began trading on the TSX Venture Exchange. On August 7, the corporation acquired equipment by issuing 10,000 common shares. Because of the uniqueness of this equipment, appraisers were unable to determine a fair value. The company's shares were trading at $12 per share at the time of the exchange.

2. Forge Corporation is a publicly held corporation whose common shares are traded on the Toronto Stock Exchange. On September 21, it acquired land by issuing 15,000 shares. At the time of the exchange, the land had a fair value of $220,000. The shares were selling at $14 per share.

Instructions

Prepare the journal entries for each situation.

Record issue of shares in cash and noncash transactions.
(SO 2, 3) AP

E13–4 Santiago Corp. had the following share transactions during the year:

June 12 Issued 50,000 common shares for $5 per share.
July 11 Issued 1,000 preferred shares for $25 per share.
Oct. 1 Issued 10,000 common shares in exchange for land. The common shares were trading at $6 per share on that date. The land's fair value was estimated to be $65,000.
Nov. 15 Issued 1,500 preferred shares for $30 per share.

Instructions

(a) Journalize the share transactions.
(b) Calculate the average cost for the (1) preferred shares and (2) common shares.

Record issue and reacquisition of shares.
(SO 2, 3) AP

E13–5 Moosonee Co. Ltd. had the following share transactions during its first year of operations:

Jan. 6 Issued 200,000 common shares for $1.50 per share.
    12 Issued 50,000 common shares for $1.75 per share.
Mar. 17 Issued 1,000 preferred shares for $105 per share.
July 18 Issued 1 million common shares for $2 per share.
Nov. 17 Reacquired 200,000 common shares for $1.95 per share.
Dec. 30 Reacquired 150,000 common shares for $1.80 per share.

Instructions

(a) Journalize the transactions.
(b) How many common shares remain at the end of the year and what is their average cost?

Determine dividends in arrears.
(SO 3) AP

E13–6 Windswept Power Corporation issued 150,000 $4.50-cumulative preferred shares to fund its first investment in wind generators. In its first year of operations, it paid $450,000 of dividends to its preferred shareholders. In its second year, the company paid dividends of $900,000 to its preferred shareholders.

Instructions

(a) What is the total annual preferred dividend supposed to be for the preferred shareholders?
(b) Calculate any dividends in arrears in years 1 and 2.
(c) Explain how dividends in arrears should be reported in the financial statements.
(d) If the preferred shares were noncumulative rather than cumulative, how much dividend would the company likely have paid its preferred shareholders in year 2?

Determine conversion date and record conversion of preferred shares.
(SO 3) AP

E13–7 New Wave Pool Corporation issued 100,000 preferred shares for $110 per share on March 1, convertible into 8 common shares each. The common shares were trading at $12 on June 10, $13.75 on June 16, and $14 on June 20.

Instructions

(a) On which date or dates would the convertible preferred shareholders be willing to convert their shares into common shares? Why?
(b) Journalize the conversion of the preferred shares using the date chosen in part (a).

E13–8 Here are some of the terms discussed in the chapter:

Identify terminology.
(SO 1, 2, 3, 4) C

1. Retained earnings
2. Issued shares
3. Contributed capital
4. Liquidation preference
5. Authorized shares
6. Publicly held corporation
7. Convertible
8. Comprehensive income
9. Retractable preferred shares
10. Cumulative
11. Initial public offering
12. Redeemable preferred shares
13. Secondary market

Instructions

For each description, write the number of the term it best matches.

(a) ___ Preferred shares that give the shareholder the right to redeem shares at their option
(b) ___ The type of corporation whose shares are traded in an organized security market, such as the Toronto Stock Exchange
(c) ___ Preferred shares that give the issuing corporation the right to repurchase the shares at a specified price and date
(d) ___ The maximum number of shares a corporation is allowed to sell
(e) ___ The number of shares a corporation has actually sold
(f) ___ The first time a corporation's shares are offered to the public
(g) ___ Where investors buy and sell shares from each other, rather than from the company
(h) ___ The element of shareholders' equity that is increased by profit and decreased by losses
(i) ___ A preference to get money back before common shareholders if the company is bankrupt
(j) ___ Includes all changes in shareholders' equity during a period except for changes that result from the sale or repurchase of shares or from the payment of dividends
(k) ___ The amount contributed by, or accruing to, the shareholders
(l) ___ A feature that allows preferred shareholders to exchange their shares for common shares
(m) ___ A preference to collect unpaid dividends on preferred shares before common shareholders can receive a dividend

E13–9 The ledger of Val d'Or Corporation contains the following selected accounts:

Classify financial statement accounts.
(SO 4) AP

1. Cash
2. Common Shares
3. Contributed Capital—Reacquisition of Common Shares
4. Gain on Sale of Property, Plant, and Equipment
5. Long-Term Equity Investments
6. Gain on Equity Investments (other comprehensive income)
7. Preferred Shares
8. Retained Earnings
9. Legal Fees Expense
10. Dividends

Instructions

Using the following table headings, indicate whether or not each of the above accounts should be reported in the shareholders' equity section of the balance sheet. If yes, indicate whether the account should be reported as share capital, additional contributed capital, retained earnings, or accumulated other comprehensive income. If not, indicate in which financial statement (balance sheet or income statement) and in which section the account should be reported. The first account has been done for you as an example.

| | Shareholders' Equity | | | | | |
	Share Capital	Additional Contributed Capital	Retained Earnings	Accumulated Other Comprehensive Income	Financial Statement	Classification
Account						
1. Cash					Balance Sheet	Current assets

E13–10 The following accounts appear in the ledger of Ozabal Inc. after the books are closed at December 31, 2011:

Prepare shareholders' equity section of balance sheet.
(SO 4) AP

Accumulated other comprehensive income	$ 75,000
Common shares (no par value, unlimited number of shares authorized, 300,000 shares issued)	150,000
Contributed capital—reacquisition of common shares	25,000
Preferred shares ($4-noncumulative, no par value, 100,000 shares authorized, 30,000 shares issued)	150,000
Retained earnings	900,000

Instructions

Prepare the shareholders' equity section of the balance sheet.

E13–11 The shareholders' equity section of Sharma Corporation at December 31 is as follows:

Answer questions about shareholders' equity.
(SO 2, 3, 4) AN

SHARMA CORPORATION
Balance Sheet (partial)
December 31, 2011

Shareholders' equity	
Contributed capital	
Share capital	
Preferred shares, $4-cumulative, no par value, unlimited number of shares authorized, 15,000 shares issued	$ 825,000
Common shares, no par value, 800,000 shares authorized, 650,000 shares issued	2,600,000
Total share capital	3,425,000
Contributed capital—reacquisition of common shares	150,000
Total contributed capital	3,575,000
Retained earnings	1,959,000
Total shareholders' equity	$5,534,000

Instructions

(a) What is the average cost of the preferred shares? Of the common shares?
(b) How many additional common shares can Sharma sell if it wants to raise additional equity financing?
(c) If Sharma repurchased 100,000 common shares, and that is the only transaction that affected Contributed Capital—Reacquisition of Shares, how much did it pay to repurchase the shares?
(d) What is the total annual dividend on preferred shares?
(e) If dividends of $60,000 were in arrears on the preferred shares, rather than paid during 2011, what would be the balance reported for Retained Earnings?

Problems: Set A

Determine form of business organization.
(SO 1) AN

P13–1A Presented below are five independent situations:

1. After passing their final accounting exam, four students put together plans to offer bookkeeping services to small companies. The students have signed an agreement that details how the profits of this new business will be shared.
2. Darien Enns has had so many people ask about the new solar and wind equipment he recently added to his home, he has decided to start a company that will offer planning, design, and installation of alternative power technology. To launch the business, Darien will need substantial funding to purchase a service truck, a special crane, and the solar- and wind-generating equipment. He expects the business to grow quickly and that he will have to hire additional employees and triple the number of trucks and cranes owned by the business. Darien has no way to provide funding for the start of the business, and he also understands that the expected growth will require large additional investments.

3. Joanna Hirsh lives 12 months a year on Look About Bay, where most of her neighbours have summer cottages. To generate income in her retirement, Joanna has decided to offer cottage inspection services for residents while they are away. Joanna will need a snowmobile to access the buildings in the winter. She also hopes to expand her service to surrounding areas. Expansion will require hiring more inspectors and purchasing additional snowmobiles.

4. After working in the construction industry for several years, Joel Pal has decided to offer his own roofing services to homeowners.

5. Frank Holton owns a small two-seater airplane to fly hunters and hikers to remote areas in northern Ontario. Demand for Frank's services has grown so much that he plans to hire additional pilots and purchase four larger planes. Frank will also purchase liability insurance in case of accidents, and plans to maintain control of the company.

Instructions

In each case, explain what form of organization the business is likely to take: proprietorship, partnership, or corporation. Give reasons for your choice.

Taking It Further   Since a corporation is a separate legal entity, what gives employees the authority to complete a transaction on behalf of the company?

P13–2A   Advanced Technologies Inc. reported the following information related to its shareholders' equity on January 1:

> Determine impact of reacquired shares.
> (SO 2) AP

Common shares, 1,000,000 authorized, 500,000 shares issued	$1,500,000
Contributed capital—reacquisition of common shares	15,000
Retained earnings	720,000

During the year, the following transactions related to common shares occurred in the order listed:

1. Issued 35,000 shares at $4.20 per share.
2. Reacquired 10,000 shares at $3.00 per share.
3. Issued 5,000 shares at $4.50 per share.
4. Reacquired 18,000 shares at $4 per share.
5. Reacquired 75,000 shares at $3 per share.

Instructions

(a) Calculate the number of shares authorized and issued at the end of the year.

(b) Determine the ending balances in each of the following accounts: Common Shares; Contributed Capital—Reacquisition of Common Shares; and Retained Earnings.

Taking It Further   Why is it important to report the number of shares issued? The number authorized?

P13–3A   At the beginning of its first year of operations, Northwoods Limited has 5,000 no par value, $4 preferred shares and 50,000 no par value common shares.

> Allocate dividends between preferred and common shares.
> (SO 3) AP

Instructions

Using the format shown below, allocate the total dividend paid in each year to the preferred and common shareholders, assuming that the preferred shares are (a) noncumulative, and (b) cumulative. The first year has been done for you as an example.

		(a)		(b)	
Year	Dividend Paid	Noncumulative Preferred	Common	Cumulative Preferred	Common
1	$20,000	$20,000	$0	$20,000	$0
2	15,000				
3	30,000				
4	35,000				

Taking It Further Why would an investor choose to invest in common shares if preferred share dividends have a higher priority?

Allocate dividends between preferred and common shares and record conversion.
(SO 3) AP

P13–4A Pro Com Ltd. issues 8,000 no par value, $5-cumulative preferred shares (convertible into 2 common shares apiece) at $66, and 15,000 no par value common shares (at $30 each) at the beginning of 2009. During the years 2010 and 2011, the following transactions affected Pro Com's shareholders' equity accounts:

2010

Jan. 10 Paid $12,000 of annual dividends to preferred shareholders.

2011

Jan. 10 Paid annual dividend to preferred shareholders and a $4,000 dividend to common shareholders.

Mar. 1 The preferred shares were converted into common shares.

Instructions

(a) Journalize each of the transactions.
(b) Are there any additional reporting requirements regarding preferred share dividends in either 2010 or 2011?

Taking It Further What factors affect a preferred shareholder's decision to convert their shares into common shares?

Show impact of transactions on accounts.
(SO 2, 3, 4) AP

P13–5A The following shareholders' equity accounts are reported by Branch Inc. on January 1:

Common shares (no par value, unlimited authorized, 150,000 issued)	$2,400,000
Preferred shares ($4-cumulative, convertible, 100,000 authorized, 5,000 issued)	350,000
Contributed capital—reacquisition of common shares	30,000
Retained earnings	1,275,000
Accumulated other comprehensive income	45,000

Branch Inc. had the following transactions during the year:

1. Issued 1,000 common shares at $23.55 per share.
2. Reacquired 10,000 common shares at $20 per share.
3. Shareholders converted 1,000 preferred shares into 4,000 common shares. The fair value per preferred share was $80; per common share, $24.
4. Issued 1,000 common shares for land. The fair value of each common share was $25; of the land, $25,500.
5. Issued 100 preferred shares at $75 per share.
6. A $15,000 dividend was paid to the preferred shareholders at the end of the year.
7. The company reported a gain on an equity investment of $2,500 at the end of the year. The gain was included in other comprehensive income.

Instructions

For each of the above transactions, indicate whether it increases (+), decreases (–), or does not affect (n/a) each item in the table below and by how much. The first transaction has been done for you as an example.

		Shareholders' Equity				
Assets	Liabilities	Preferred Shares	Common Shares	Other Contributed Capital	Retained Earnings	Accumulated Other Comprehensive Income
1.+$23,550	n/a	n/a	+$23,550	n/a	n/a	n/a

Taking It Further Assume instead that Branch Inc.'s preferred shares were noncumulative and not convertible. Would that affect the price investors are prepared to pay for the shares? Explain.

P13–6A Wetland Corporation was organized on February 1, 2010. It is authorized to issue an unlimited number of $6-noncumulative, no par value preferred shares, and an unlimited number of no par value common shares. The following transactions were completed during the first year:

Record and post transactions. Prepare shareholders' equity section. (SO 2, 3, 4) AP

Feb. 10 Issued 80,000 common shares at $4 per share.
Mar. 1 Issued 5,000 preferred shares at $115 per share.
Apr. 1 Issued 22,000 common shares for land. The asking price of the land was $100,000 and its appraised value was $95,000. The fair value of the common shares was $4.25 per share on this date.
June 20 Issued 78,000 common shares at $4.50 per share.
Aug. 1 Issued 10,000 common shares to lawyers to pay for their bill of $50,000 for services they performed in helping the company organize. The fair value of the common shares was $4.75 on this date.
Sept. 1 Issued 10,000 common shares at $5 per share.
Nov. 1 Issued 1,000 preferred shares at $117 per share.
Jan. 31 Reported profit of $500,000 for the year.
31 Paid $24,000 of dividends to the preferred shareholders.

Instructions

(a) Journalize the transactions and summary closing entries.
(b) Open general ledger accounts and post to the shareholders' equity accounts.
(c) Prepare the shareholders' equity section of the balance sheet at January 31, 2011.

Taking It Further What is the likely impact on the company's stock price if a dividend is no longer paid? What conditions would likely cause a company to stop paying dividends?

P13–7A On January 1, 2011, Schipper Ltd. had the following shareholders' equity accounts:

Record and post transactions. Prepare shareholders' equity section. (SO 2, 3, 4) AP

Common shares (no par value, unlimited number of shares authorized, 1,000,000 issued)	$1,500,000
Retained earnings	1,800,000
Accumulated other comprehensive income (loss)	(25,000)

The company was also authorized to issue an unlimited number of no par value $4-noncumulative preferred shares. As of January 1, 2011, none had been issued. During 2011, the corporation had the following transactions and events related to its shareholders' equity:

Jan. 2 Issued 100,000 preferred shares for $50 per share.
Apr. 1 Paid quarterly dividend to preferred shareholders.
July 1 Paid quarterly dividend to preferred shareholders.
Aug. 12 Issued 100,000 common shares for $1.70 per share.
Oct. 1 Paid quarterly dividend to preferred shareholders and a $0.25 per share dividend to the common shareholders.
Dec. 31 Loss for the year was $100,000.

Instructions

(a) Journalize the transactions and the summary closing entries.
(b) Open general ledger accounts and post to the shareholders' equity accounts.
(c) Prepare the shareholders' equity section of the balance sheet at December 31, 2011, including the disclosure of any preferred dividends in arrears.

Taking It Further Who makes the final decision about the payment of a dividend and the amount?

P13–8A Cattrall Corporation is authorized to issue an unlimited number of no par value $5-noncumulative preferred shares and an unlimited number of no par value common shares. On February 1, 2011, the general ledger contained the following shareholders' equity accounts:

Record and post transactions. Prepare shareholders' equity section. (SO 2, 3, 4) AP

Preferred shares (8,000 shares issued)	$ 440,000
Common shares (70,000 shares issued)	1,050,000
Contributed capital—reacquisition of preferred shares	75,000
Retained earnings	1,000,000
Accumulated other comprehensive income	65,000

The following equity transactions occurred during the year ended January 31, 2012:

> Feb. 28 Issued 2,400 preferred shares for $150,000.
> Apr. 12 Issued 200,000 common shares for $3.2 million.
> May 25 Issued 5,000 common shares in exchange for land. At the time of the exchange, the land was valued at $75,000 and the common shares at $80,000.
> Sept. 12 Repurchased 75,000 common shares for $1,275,000.
> Jan. 1 Paid dividend of $2.50 per share to preferred shareholders.
> 31 A loss of $5,000 was incurred for the year.

Instructions

(a) Journalize the transactions and the closing entries.

(b) Enter the beginning balances in the accounts and post the journal entries to the shareholders' equity accounts.

(c) Prepare the shareholders' equity section of the balance sheet at January 31, including the disclosure of any preferred dividends that may be in arrears.

Taking It Further What is the key difference between redeemable and retractable preferred shares? If all other things were equal, on which type would you expect investors to pay a higher price?

Record closing entries and prepare balance sheet. (SO 4) AP

P13–9A The adjusted trial balance of Muskoka Manufacturing Ltd. as at December 31, 2011, is shown below:

MUSKOKA MANUFACTURING LTD.
Adjusted Trial Balance
December 31, 2011

	Debit	Credit
Cash	$ 18,000	
Accounts receivable	55,000	
Inventory	82,000	
Prepaid insurance	4,000	
Supplies	5,000	
Land	120,000	
Building	550,000	
Accumulated depreciation—building		$ 80,000
Equipment	300,000	
Accumulated depreciation—equipment		87,000
Accounts payable		52,000
Salaries payable		7,500
Interest payable		3,200
Income tax payable		8,300
Unearned sales revenue		21,000
Mortgage payable ($12,000 of this mortgage is due in the next year)		330,000
Preferred shares ($4-noncumulative, unlimited number authorized, 4,000 issued)		80,000
Common shares (unlimited number authorized, 120,000 issued)		180,000
Contributed capital—reacquisition of common shares		9,000

MUSKOKA MANUFACTURING LTD.
Adjusted Trial Balance
December 31, 2011 (cont.)

	Debit	Credit
Retained earnings		173,000
Accumulated other comprehensive income		22,200
Dividends	12,000	
Sales revenue		614,600
Salaries expense	161,000	
Cost of goods sold	159,000	
Depreciation expense	80,000	
Interest expense	29,500	
Rent expense	37,000	
Income tax expense	26,700	
Utilities expense	15,200	
Insurance expense	7,800	
Supplies expense	5,600	
	$1,667,800	$1,667,800

Instructions

(a) Journalize the closing entries.
(b) Prepare a balance sheet at December 31.

Taking It Further What are the differences between dividends paid to owners of corporations versus withdrawals by owners of proprietorships or partnerships?

P13–10A Brick Brewing Co. Limited is one of Ontario's microbreweries. It has the following selected accounts, listed in alphabetical order, as at January 31, 2009:

Prepare balance sheet and calculate return on equity. (SO 4) AP

BRICK BREWING CO. LIMITED
Selected Accounts
January 31, 2009

Accounts payable and accrued liabilities	$ 3,846,187
Accounts receivable	2,096,781
Accumulated depreciation—property, plant, and equipment	18,801,998
Cash	209,291
Common shares, unlimited authorized, 28,057,010 shares issued	34,657,984
Loss and comprehensive loss	(7,471,778)
Contributed surplus	673,593
Current portion of long-term debt and obligations under capital lease	1,343,282
Deferred costs and other assets (long-term asset)	419,220
Deficit, February 1, 2008	(6,852,240)
Future income taxes (long-term asset)	547,030
Future income taxes recoverable (short-term asset)	522,338
Inventories	5,309,474
Long-term debt	2,067,900
Other current liabilities	270,758
Prepaid expenses	507,518
Property, plant, and equipment	32,324,718
Trademarks and other intangibles	5,401,314

Instructions

(a) Prepare a classified balance sheet.
(b) Calculate the return on equity. Total shareholders' equity at January 31, 2008, was $25,311,285.

Taking It Further Why is it important to shareholders that retained earnings in the shareholders' equity section be tracked and presented separately from share capital?

Calculate return on equity.
(SO 4) AP

P13–11A Canadian Tire Corporation reported the following selected information:

CANADIAN TIRE CORPORATION
Fiscal years
(in millions)

	2009	2008	2007
Profit	$ 374.2	$ 411.7	$ 354.6
Shareholders' equity	3,568.1	3,108.1	2,785.2

Instructions

(a) Calculate Canadian Tire's return on equity for 2009 and 2008. Comment on whether its return on equity improved or deteriorated.

(b) Assume that the return on equity for Canadian Tire's industry was 9.9% in 2009 and 8.4% in 2008. Compare Canadian Tire's performance with the industry average.

Taking It Further Is the return on equity still a useful measurement if the company is not profitable? What changes to the formula would be appropriate in such a situation?

Answer questions about shareholders' equity section.
(SO 2, 3, 4) AP

P13–12A The shareholders' equity section of Maple Corporation reported the following information at November 30, 2011:

MAPLE CORPORATION
Balance Sheet (partial)
November 30, 2011

Shareholders' equity	
Contributed capital	
Share capital	
$3-noncumulative preferred shares, unlimited number authorized, 12,000 shares issued	$1,200,000
Common shares, no par value, 500,000 shares authorized, 100,000 shares issued	1,000,000
Total share capital	2,200,000
Additional contributed capital	
Contributed capital—reacquisition of common shares	40,000
Total contributed capital	2,240,000
Retained earnings[1]	675,000
Accumulated other comprehensive income	10,000
Total shareholders' equity	$2,925,000

[1] Opening balance ($500,000) + Profit ($175,000)

Instructions

(a) What was the average cost of the preferred shares, on a per-share basis? Of the common shares?

(b) What was the total amount of dividends, if any, paid by Maple Corporation for the year ended November 30, 2011?

(c) Assuming that there were no dividends in arrears at December 1, 2010, are there any dividends in arrears at November 30, 2011? If so, for what amount?

(d) Assume that the full amount in the Contributed Capital—Reacquisition of Common Shares account was for the reacquisition of 20,000 common shares and that no new common shares were issued during the year. How much did Maple Corporation pay to reacquire those shares?

(e) What is "accumulated other comprehensive income"?

Taking It Further Why are common shareholders sometimes referred to as "residual owners"?

Problems: Set B

P13–1B Five independent situations follow:

1. Kevin Roberts, President and CEO of Hanley Tools Inc., has just been notified that his company has been sued due to the failure of one of its key products. Although the lawsuit is for several million dollars, Kevin is not concerned that he will have to sell his new house to pay damages if his company is unsuccessful in defending itself against the lawsuit.
2. Salik Makkar has just negotiated a borrowing agreement with a bank. The completed borrowing agreement is a contract between two parties: the bank and the company that Salik works for as the Treasurer.
3. Ping Yu is in the top personal tax bracket due to a significant amount of investment income she earns each year. Ping has just started a new company and has organized it as a publicly held corporation. Sales for the first few years are expected to make her new company eligible for tax incentives and deductions as an active small business.
4. Marion Kureshi incorporated her business, Kureshi Fine Furniture Corporation, in 1964. The business has steadily grown every year, and now employs over 2,000 people. Kureshi Fine Furniture's common shares trade on a public stock exchange. Marion is currently the President of the company; however, due to deteriorating health, Marion can no longer be active in the business. Fortunately, Marion has put in place plans for her daughter to assume her role as President.
5. Matthew Antoine has been working on a new technology to improve cell phone reception in remote rural locations. Matthew knows that a significant amount of funding will be required to purchase the production equipment and inventory to manufacture his new antenna. In order to launch his new business, Matthew plans to organize the business as a publicly held corporation and issue shares on the TSX Venture Exchange.

Instructions

In each case, identify the characteristic being described in the situation that separates a corporation from a proprietorship or partnership, and explain how the situation might be different for a sole proprietor or partnership.

Taking It Further How does limited liability help investors sell shares in the secondary markets?

P13–2B The following is related to the shareholders' equity of Adanac Limited on January 1:

Common shares, 150,000 authorized, 14,000 shares issued	$490,000
Contributed capital—reacquisition of common shares	12,000
Retained earnings	220,000

During the year, the following transactions related to common shares occurred in the order listed:

1. Reacquired 600 shares at $44 per share.
2. Issued 3,600 shares at $47 per share.
3. Issued 1,000 shares at $64.50 per share.
4. Reacquired 1,200 shares at $58 per share.
5. Reacquired 1,500 shares at $36 per share.

Instructions

(a) Calculate the number of shares authorized and issued at the end of the year.
(b) Determine the ending balances in each of the following accounts: Common Shares; Contributed Capital—Reacquisition of Common Shares; and Retained Earnings.

Taking It Further It takes time and money to authorize shares, so why don't all companies just start with an unlimited number of shares authorized?

Allocate dividends between preferred and common shares. (SO 3) AP

P13–3B At the beginning of its first year of operations, Backwoods Limited has 3,000 no par value, $5 preferred shares and 50,000 no par value common shares.

Instructions

(a) Using the format shown below, allocate the total dividend paid in each year to the preferred and common shareholders, assuming that the preferred shares are (a) noncumulative, and (b) cumulative. The first year has been done for you as an example.

		(a)		(b)	
Year	Dividend Paid	Noncumulative Preferred	Common	Cumulative Preferred	Common
1	$15,000	$15,000	$0	$15,000	$0
2	12,000				
3	27,000				
4	35,000				

Taking It Further Why would an investor choose to invest in common shares if preferred share dividends have a higher priority?

Allocate dividends between preferred and common shares and record conversion. (SO 3) AP

P13–4B The Kari Corporation issues 5,000 no par value, $4-cumulative preferred shares (convertible into 4 common shares apiece) at $80, and 10,000 no par value common shares (at $18 each) at the beginning of 2009. During the years 2010 and 2011, the following transactions affected the Kari Corporation's shareholders' equity accounts:

2010

Jan. 10 Paid $12,000 of annual dividends to preferred shareholders.

2011

Jan. 10 Paid annual dividend to preferred shareholders and a $4,000 dividend to common shareholders.

Mar. 1 The 4,000 preferred shares were converted into common shares.

Instructions

(a) Journalize each of the transactions.
(b) Are there any additional reporting requirements regarding preferred share dividends in either 2010 or 2011?

Taking It Further Why might investors be willing to pay more for preferred shares that have a conversion option?

Show impact of transactions on accounts. (SO 2, 3, 4) AP

P13–5B The following shareholders' equity accounts are reported by Talty Inc. on January 1:

Common shares (no par value, unlimited authorized, 500,000 issued)	$4,000,000
Preferred shares ($4-noncumulative, convertible, 100,000 authorized, 4,000 issued)	600,000
Contributed capital—reacquisition of preferred shares	2,000
Retained earnings	1,958,000
Accumulated other comprehensive income	25,000

The following selected transactions occurred during the year:

1. Issued 10,000 common shares at $10 per share.
2. Issued 500 common shares in exchange for a piece of equipment. The fair value of the shares was $11 per share; of the equipment, $6,000.
3. Shareholders converted 2,000 preferred shares into 20,000 common shares. The fair value per preferred share was $160; per common share, $16.50.
4. Issued 1,000 preferred shares at $150 per share.
5. Reacquired 500 preferred shares at $145 per share.
6. The preferred share dividend was paid at the end of the year.
7. The company reported a loss on its equity investments of $5,000 at the end of the year. The loss is classified as other comprehensive income.

Instructions

For each of the transactions, indicate whether it will increase (+), decrease (–), or not affect (n/a) the items in the table below and by what amount. The first transaction has been done for you as an example.

		Shareholders' Equity				
Assets	Liabilities	Preferred Shares	Common Shares	Other Contributed Capital	Retained Earnings	Accumulated Other Comprehensive Income
1. +$100,000	n/a	n/a	+$100,000	n/a	n/a	n/a

Taking It Further Does the noncumulative feature of these preferred shares affect the fair value of the shares?

P13–6B Highland Corporation was organized on January 1, 2011. It is authorized to issue an unlimited number of $3-noncumulative, no par value preferred shares, and an unlimited number of no par value common shares. The following transactions were completed during the first year:

> Record and post transactions. Prepare shareholders' equity section.
> (SO 2, 3, 4) AP

Jan. 10 Issued 100,000 common shares at $2 per share.

Mar. 1 Issued 10,000 preferred shares at $42 per share.

Apr. 1 Issued 25,000 common shares for land. The land's appraised value was $67,000 and the common shares' fair value was $2.50 per share on this date.

May 1 Issued 75,000 common shares at $3 per share.

July 24 Issued 16,800 common shares for $60,000 cash and used equipment. The equipment originally cost $15,000. It now has a carrying amount of $7,500 and a fair value of $8,000. The common shares issued had a fair value of $4 per share on this date.

Nov. 1 Issued 2,000 preferred shares at $48 per share.

Dec. 31 Reported profit of $650,000 for the year.

31 Paid $36,000 of dividends to the preferred shareholders.

Instructions

(a) Journalize the transactions and the summary closing entries.

(b) Open general ledger accounts and post to the shareholders' equity accounts.

(c) Prepare the shareholders' equity section of the balance sheet at December 31.

Taking It Further Why would a company issue cumulative instead of noncumulative preferred shares if that creates a disclosure requirement for the dividends in arrears?

P13–7B On January 1, 2011, Conway Ltd. had the following shareholders' equity accounts:

> Record and post transactions. Prepare shareholders' equity section.
> (SO 2, 3, 4) AP

Preferred shares (no par value, $6-cumulative, unlimited authorized, none issued)	
Common shares (no par value, unlimited number of shares authorized, 1.5 million issued)	$16,500,000
Retained earnings	1,900,000
Accumulated other comprehensive income	25,000

During 2011, the corporation had the following transactions and events related to its shareholders' equity:

Jan. 2 Issued 100,000 preferred shares at $66 per share.

Apr. 1 Paid quarterly dividend to preferred shareholders.

Apr. 18 Issued 250,000 common shares at $13 per share.

July 1 Paid quarterly dividend to preferred shareholders.

Oct. 1 Paid quarterly dividend to preferred shareholders.

Dec. 31 Profit for the year were $3.6 million.

Instructions

(a) Journalize the transactions and the summary closing entries.

(b) Open general ledger accounts and post to the shareholders' equity accounts.

(c) Prepare the shareholders' equity section of the balance sheet at December 31, including the disclosure of any preferred dividends in arrears.

Taking It Further Who makes the final decision about the payment of a dividend and the amount?

Record and post transactions. Prepare shareholders' equity section. (SO 2, 3, 4) AP

P13–8B Largent Corporation is authorized to issue 200,000 no par value, $4-cumulative preferred shares and an unlimited number of no par value common shares. On January 1, 2011, the general ledger contained the following shareholders' equity accounts:

Preferred shares (8,000 shares)	$ 440,000
Common shares (70,000 shares)	1,050,000
Contributed capital—reacquisition of preferred shares	25,000
Retained earnings	800,000
Accumulated other comprehensive income	10,000

During 2011, the following transactions occurred:

Jan. 10 Repurchased 20,000 common shares for $240,000.

Feb. 6 Issued 10,000 preferred shares for $600,000.

Apr. 14 Issued 40,000 common shares for $560,000.

July 1 Paid a semi-annual dividend to the preferred shareholders.

Aug. 22 Issued 10,000 common shares in exchange for a building. At the time of the exchange, the fair value of the building was $165,000 and that of the common shares was $150,000.

Dec. 31 Profit for the year was $582,000.

Instructions

(a) Journalize the transactions and the closing entries.

(b) Enter the beginning balances in the accounts and post the journal entries to the shareholders' equity accounts.

(c) Prepare the shareholders' equity section of the balance sheet at December 31, including the disclosure of any preferred dividends that may be in arrears.

Taking It Further Describe a situation where the fair value of a company's shares cannot be determined.

Record closing entries and prepare balance sheet. (SO 4) AP

P13–9B The adjusted trial balance of Ramsden Environmental Corporation, as at July 31, 2011, follows:

RAMSDEN ENVIRONMENTAL CORPORATION Adjusted Trial Balance July 31, 2011		
	Debit	Credit
Cash	$ 46,600	
Accounts receivable	67,400	
Supplies	10,100	
Equipment	148,000	
Accumulated depreciation—equipment		$ 66,000
Inventory	195,000	
Accounts payable		32,000
Salaries payable		8,200
Interest payable		900
Income tax payable		4,500
Unearned consulting revenue		8,900
Note payable ($10,000 of this note is due within the next year)		70,000
Preferred shares ($3.75-noncumulative, unlimited number authorized, 500 issued)		40,000

RAMSDEN ENVIRONMENTAL CORPORATION Adjusted Trial Balance July 31, 2011 (cont.)		
	Debit	Credit
Common shares (unlimited number authorized, 35,000 issued)		120,000
Contributed capital—reacquisition of preferred shares		1,500
Retained earnings		75,000
Dividends	2,300	
Consulting revenue		125,500
Construction revenue		189,375
Salaries expense	160,180	
Rent expense	28,000	
Depreciation expense	33,020	
Supplies expense	18,200	
Utilities expense	11,475	
Interest expense	2,100	
Income tax expense	19,500	
	$741,875	$741,875

Instructions

(a) Journalize the closing entries.

(b) Prepare a balance sheet at July 31.

Taking It Further Are there any differences between the retained earnings account for corporations and the owner's capital account used for proprietorships?

P13–10B Andrew Peller Limited, headquartered in Ontario, is one of Canada's leading wine producers. It has the following balance sheet accounts, in alphabetical order, as at March 31, 2009:

Prepare balance sheet and calculate return on equity.
(SO 4) AP

ANDREW PELLER LIMITED Selected Accounts March 31, 2009 (in thousands)	
Accounts payable and accrued liabilities	$ 43,349
Accounts receivable	22,430
Accumulated depreciation—property, plant, and equipment	72,465
Bank indebtedness	52,192
Class A shares, nonvoting, unlimited authorized, 11,888 issued	6,975
Class B shares, voting, convertible into Class A shares, unlimited authorized, 3,004 issued	400
Current portion of long-term debt	8,877
Dividends	4,787
Dividends payable	1,197
Future income tax liability (long-term)	10,765
Goodwill	39,384
Income taxes recoverable	5,892
Inventories	104,157
Long-term debt	71,549
Net and comprehensive earnings	(125)
Other long-term assets	16,938
Other long-term liabilities	8,787
Prepaid expenses and other assets	2,339
Property, plant, and equipment	174,832
Retained earnings, April 1, 2009	94,328

Instructions

(a) Prepare a classified balance sheet.

(b) Calculate the return on equity. Total shareholder's equity at March 31, 2007, was $95,522,000.

Taking It Further   Is the return on equity ratio useful when a company reports a loss?

Calculate return on equity
(SO 4) AP

P13–11B   Sears Canada Inc. reported the following selected information:

SEARS CANADA INC.
December 31
(in millions)

	2008	2007	2006
Profit	$ 289	$ 306	$153
Shareholders' equity	1,508	1,093	785

Instructions

(a) Calculate Sears' return on equity for 2007 and 2008. Comment on whether its return on equity improved or worsened.

(b) Assume the return on equity for Sears' industry was 23.2% in 2008 and 26.4% in 2007. Compare Sears' performance with the industry average.

Taking It Further   Could the return on equity ratio be improved? How would the use of fair values of the company's shares versus average shareholder equity affect the usefulness of the ratio?

Answer questions about
shareholders' equity section.
(SO 2, 3, 4) AP

P13–12B   The shareholders' equity section of Moreau Corporation reported the following information at December 31, 2011:

MOREAU CORPORATION
Balance Sheet (partial)
December 31, 2011

Shareholders' equity	
Share capital	
$5-cumulative preferred shares, no par value, unlimited number of shares authorized, ? shares issued	$3,150,000
Common shares, no par value, unlimited number of shares authorized, 250,000 shares issued	1,000,000
Total share capital	4,150,000
Retained earnings[1]	468,750
Accumulated other comprehensive loss	(18,750)
Total shareholders' equity	$4,600,000

[1] Opening balance ($500,000) + Profit ($175,000) – Reacquisition of common shares ($56,250) – Preferred Dividends ($150,000)

There are no dividends in arrears at the end of 2010 or 2011.

Instructions

(a) How many preferred shares were issued at December 31?

(b) What was the average cost of the preferred shares, on a per-share basis? Of the common shares?

(c) Assume that the debit to retained earnings for the reacquisition of common shares was to reacquire 25,000 shares and that no new common shares were issued during the year. How much did Moreau Corporation pay to reacquire those shares?

(d) In terms of the limited liability characteristic of a corporation, what is the dollar amount that the preferred shareholders are potentially liable for? How much are the common shareholders potentially liable for?

(e) What is an "accumulated other comprehensive loss"?

Taking It Further   Similarly to debt, preferred shares have a stated rate (dividend rate), no voting rights, and preference over common shareholders. Why are preferred shares not presented as long-term debt instead of shareholders' equity?

Continuing Cookie Chronicle

(*Note:* This is a continuation of the Cookie Chronicle from Chapters 1 through 12.)

Natalie's friend, Curtis Lesperance, decides to meet with Natalie after hearing that her discussions about a possible business partnership with her friend Katy Peterson have failed. (Natalie had decided that forming a partnership with Katy, a high school friend, would hurt their friendship. Natalie had also concluded that she and Katy were not compatible to operate a business venture together.)

Because Natalie has been so successful with Cookie Creations and Curtis has been just as successful with his coffee shop, they both conclude that they could benefit from each other's business expertise. Curtis and Natalie next evaluate the different types of business organization, and because of the advantage of limited liability, decide to form a corporation.

Curtis has operated his coffee shop for two years. He buys coffee, muffins, and cookies from a local supplier. Natalie's business consists of giving cookie-making classes and selling fine European mixers. The plan is for Natalie to use the premises Curtis currently rents to give her cookie-making classes and demonstrations of the mixers that she sells. Natalie will also hire, train, and supervise staff to bake the cookies and muffins sold in the coffee shop. By offering her classes on the premises, Natalie will save on travel time going from one place to another. Another advantage is that the coffee shop will be a central location for selling the mixers.

The current fair values of the assets of both businesses are as follows:

	Curtis's Coffee	Cookie Creations
Cash	$7,500	$10,000
Accounts receivable	100	800
Merchandise inventory	450	1,200
Kitchen equipment	2,500	1,000

Combining forces will also allow Natalie and Curtis to pool their resources and buy a few more assets to run their new business venture.

Curtis and Natalie then meet with a lawyer and form a corporation on November 1, 2011, called Cookie & Coffee Creations Ltd. The articles of incorporation state that there will be two classes of shares that the corporation is authorized to issue: common shares and preferred shares. An unlimited number of common shares are authorized; 10,000 preferred shares with a $0.50-noncumulative dividend are authorized.

The assets held by each of their sole proprietorships will be transferred into the corporation at current fair value. Curtis will receive 10,550 common shares and Natalie will receive 13,000 common shares in the corporation.

Natalie and Curtis are very excited about this new business venture. They come to you with the following questions:

1. Curtis's dad and Natalie's grandmother are interested in investing $5,000 each in the business venture. We are thinking of issuing them preferred shares. What would be the advantage of issuing them preferred shares instead of common shares?
2. Our lawyer has sent us a bill for $1,200. When we talked the bill over with her, she said that she would be willing to receive common shares in our new corporation instead of cash. We would be happy to issue her shares, but we're not sure exactly how to do this. She told us that she wanted 1,300 shares. Does this seem reasonable or should we pay her $1,200 cash?

Instructions

(a) Answer their questions.
(b) Prepare the journal entries required on November 1, 2011, the date when Natalie and Curtis transfer the assets of their respective businesses into Cookie & Coffee Creations Ltd.

(c) Assume that Cookie & Coffee Creations Ltd. issues 1,000 $0.50-noncumulative preferred shares to Curtis's dad and the same number to Natalie's grandmother, in both cases for $5,000. Also assume that Cookie & Coffee Creations Ltd. issues 1,300 common shares to its lawyer. Prepare the journal entries for each of these transactions. They all occurred on November 1.

(d) Prepare the opening balance sheet for Cookie & Coffee Creations Ltd. as at November 1, 2011, including the journal entries in (b) and (c) above.

BROADENING YOUR PERSPECTIVE

Financial Reporting and Analysis

Financial Reporting Problem

BYP13–1 The shareholders' equity section for The Forzani Group Ltd. is shown in the Consolidated Balance Sheet in Appendix A. You will also find data related to this problem in the notes to the financial statements.

Instructions

(a) How many classes of shares does Forzani have? For each class of shares, specify how many shares are authorized and issued at February 1, 2009.

(b) Did Forzani issue any additional shares in fiscal 2009? If so, specify how many were issued, for what dollar amount, and for what purpose.

(c) Did Forzani repurchase any shares in fiscal 2009? If so, how much cash did it spend to reacquire the shares?

(d) What was the average cost of the common (Class A) shares at the end of fiscal 2009?

(e) Forzani's return on equity was calculated for fiscal 2009 in Illustration 13-3. Calculate the company's return on equity for fiscal 2008. The shareholders' equity at January 28, 2007, was $327,813,000. Did this ratio improve or worsen from 2008 to 2009?

Interpreting Financial Statements

BYP13–2 Talisman Energy Inc., headquartered in Calgary, is a large, international oil and gas producer. Talisman's authorized share capital includes an unlimited number of common shares.

During the 2007 fiscal year, Talisman repurchased 45,994,100 common shares for a total of $951 million. The following additional information is also available for the years ended December 31, 2007 and 2008:

	2008	2007
Profit margin	36.4%	28.1%
Asset turnover	0.4 times	0.3 times
Return on assets	15.4%	9.7%
Return on equity	36.8%	27.2%
Market price per share	$12.18	$18.39

Instructions

(a) What are some of the reasons why a company repurchases its own shares?

(b) During the 2007 year, Talisman debited Retained Earnings $839 million for the repurchase of its common shares. Were Talisman's common shares repurchased for more, or less, than their average cost? Prepare the journal entry to record this repurchase.

(c) Discuss the change in Talisman's profitability from 2007 to 2008.

(d) Is your assessment in (c) consistent with the change in market price per share? Explain why this would likely happen or not happen.

Critical Thinking

Collaborative Learning Activity

Note to instructor: Additional instructions and material for this group activity can be found on the Instructor Resource Site.

Working in Groups

BYP13–3 In this group activity, you will take on the role of either corporation or investor. As an investor, you will be given the opportunity to buy, convert, or redeem shares of four corporations during the month of November. Each company's shareholders' equity section will be available for you to make informed decisions.

Instructions

(a) Your instructor will divide the class into groups. If you are in a corporate group, your goal is to prepare the shareholders' equity section of the company's balance sheet for the end of the month. If you are in an investor group, your goal is to maximize your wealth.

(b) In the corporate groups, you will receive a one-page handout showing your shareholders' equity section and other corporate information as at November 1. In the investor groups, you will receive a handout showing your investment holdings as at the same date. Using this sheet as a starting point, you will then visit each corporate group and determine which company's shares to buy, convert, or redeem.

(c) Corporate groups will complete the shareholders' equity section as at November 30. Investor groups will determine their holdings as at the same date. Together, all the investor groups will complete an overhead summary chart, as directed.

(d) Each corporate group will present its shareholders' equity section to the class and compare it with the overhead summary chart prepared by the investor groups.

Communication Activity

BYP13–4 Under International Financial Reporting Standards (IFRS), companies must prepare a comprehensive income statement that includes other comprehensive income. Under Canadian GAAP for Private Enterprises, companies do not prepare a comprehensive income statement and do not report other comprehensive income.

Writing Handbook

Assume that you are a newly graduated professional accountant, working for a large private Canadian company that is considering going public within the next three years. If the company follows IFRS, it has had several transactions in 2011 that result in "other comprehensive income" items. The chief financial officer is preparing for a meeting with the company's board of directors to discuss the impact of using IFRS for its financial statements. He has asked you to explain how other comprehensive income affects the company's balance sheet. In particular, he would like to understand how reporting comprehensive income benefits the company's current and potential shareholders and why it is used under IFRS but not in Canadian GAAP for Private Enterprises.

Instructions

Write a memo to the chief financial officer, answering his questions.

Ethics Case

Ethics in Accounting

BYP13–5 The R&D division of Simplex Chemical Corp. has just developed a chemical to sterilize the voracious mountain pine beetles that are invading Western Canada's forests. The president of Simplex is anxious to get the new chemical to market and has already named it PinebeetleX101. Simplex's profits need a boost and his job is in jeopardy because of decreasing sales and profits. Simplex has an opportunity to sell this chemical in several Central American countries, where the laws are much more relaxed than in Canada about proving product safety before beginning to use it or sell it.

The director of Simplex's R&D division strongly recommends more laboratory testing for side effects of this chemical on other insects, birds, animals, plants, and even humans. He cautions the president, "We could be sued from all sides if the chemical has tragic side effects that we didn't even test for in the labs." The president answers, "We can't wait an additional year for your lab tests. We can avoid losses from such lawsuits by creating a new separate corporation called Simplex Central America Inc., which will be 100% owned by Simplex Chemical Corp., to operate our business in those countries. We will invest just the patent covering this chemical in Simplex Central America Inc. That corporation will have limited liability so we can't lose any more than the assets that we put into it. Since we will own 100% of the shares of Simplex Central America Inc., we can put ourselves on its board of directors, and then we can make it pay dividends to Simplex Chemical Corp. when it makes a profit. We'll reap the benefits if the chemical works and is safe, and avoid the losses from lawsuits if it's a disaster."

The following week Simplex Chemical Corp. creates the new 100%-owned corporation Simplex Central America Inc., sells it the chemical patent for PinebeetleX101 for $10, delivers a shipload of the chemicals, and watches the spraying begin.

Instructions

(a) Who are the stakeholders in this situation?
(b) Are the president's motives and actions ethical?
(c) Can Simplex Chemical Corp. be certain that it is protected against all losses related to the activities of Simplex Central America Inc.?

"All About You" Activity

BYP13–6 As you learned in the "All About You" feature, the decision to incorporate or not is complex. After you have completed your post-secondary business education, you may be an entrepreneur and may need to decide if and when to incorporate your business. And if you decide to incorporate, you will also need to know more about how.

Instructions

Go to the website of Corporations Canada, part of Industry Canada, at http://corporationscanada.ic.gc.ca. Click on "FAQ" (frequently asked questions).

(a) What are the benefits of incorporating with the federal government?
(b) What kinds of businesses can incorporate under the *Canada Business Corporations Act*?
(c) Who can form a corporation?
(d) Go to the FAQ "If I decide to incorporate, what next?" When are corporations formed? Describe the information required in the Articles of Incorporation (forms 1 and 2).
(e) What are the advantages of incorporating online?
(f) On the Corporations Canada homepage, go to "Incorporate a Business" and then click on the "Guide to Federal Incorporation." Go to Chapter 6, Other Obligations of the Corporation. Answer the following questions:

 1. When do the annual financial statements have to be prepared by?
 2. The financial statements are required to be prepared in accordance with generally accepted accounting principles (GAAP). For Canadian corporations, where is GAAP set out?

3. Does a company have to appoint auditors?
4. What corporate records are required to be kept by a corporation?

ANSWERS TO CHAPTER QUESTIONS

Answers to Accounting in Action Insight Questions

International Insight, p. 721

Q: Does IFRS make it more important for users of financial statements to identify whether a company is a corporation or not?

A: This information does become more important because public companies operating in countries that have adopted IFRS are required to adhere to international standards.

All About You, p. 725

Q: Given the complexity of tax planning, and the impact that taxes could have on the advantages of incorporating, what should you do before deciding to incorporate your business?

A: The business owner should seek expert tax advice to ensure the benefits of incorporating are greater than the costs.

Across the Organization, p. 730

Q: How can buying back its own shares make a company appear to be more profitable?

A: Spreading profit over a smaller number of shares (i.e., dividing profits by a smaller number) increases earnings per share. Investors will often divide the market price of a company's share by its earnings per share (known as the PE or price/earnings ratio); the greater the number, the more attractive the shares become.

Answer to Forzani Review It Question 4, p. 730

Forzani repurchased 2,694,376 Class A common shares in 2009 for $44,027,000, and 1,802,900 common shares in 2008 for $33,331,000 (see Note 11(e) to the financial statements).

Answers to Self-Study Questions

1. a   2. d   3. b   4. b   5. c   6. c   7. d   8. d   9. a   10. d

Remember to go back to the beginning of the chapter to check off your completed work!

←

sunlife.com

✓ THE NAVIGATOR

- ☐ Understand *Concepts for Review*
- ☐ Read *Feature Story*
- ☐ Scan *Study Objectives*
- ☐ Read *Chapter Preview*
- ☐ Read text and answer *Before You Go On*
- ☐ Work *Demonstration Problems*
- ☐ Review *Summary of Study Objectives*
- ☐ Answer *Self-Study Questions*
- ☐ Complete assignments

CONCEPTS FOR REVIEW:

Before studying this chapter, you should understand or, if necessary, review:

a. How to prepare an income statement and statement of owner's equity. (Ch. 3, pp. 136–137)

b. How to record cash dividends. (Ch. 13, p. 723)

c. How to account for share transactions. (Ch. 13, pp. 727–730 & 731–733)

d. Preferred shareholders' rights to dividends. (Ch. 13, pp. 731–733)

e. Comprehensive income. (Ch. 13, p. 736)

f. How to calculate ending retained earnings. (Ch. 13, pp. 735–736)

g. The form and content of the shareholders' equity section of the balance sheet. (Ch. 13, pp. 734–737)

h. How to calculate return on equity. (Ch. 13, p. 737)

Many Considerations Go into the Dividend Decision

Since becoming a public company in 2000, the financial services company Sun Life Financial Inc. has issued dividends to shareholders. Sun Life began selling life insurance in 1871; today, with its Canadian head office in Waterloo, Ontario, and worldwide corporate headquarters in Toronto, the company provides a range of insurance and investment products and services to individuals and corporations worldwide. Sun Life shares trade on the Toronto, New York, and Philippine stock exchanges under the symbol SLF.

The decision on whether to issue a dividend and for what amount is made each quarter by the Sun Life board of directors, after considering a range of alternatives and a recommendation presented by management, explains Stephen Kicinski, Senior Vice President, Treasurer. The board and management consider a number of factors when making their decision: the dividend's current yield; the dividend paid last quarter; share price volatility; the level of share buybacks; the dividend levels and yields of Sun Life's peers; shareholder composition (that is, whether its shareholders are income sensitive); the company's cash balances; the potential impact on its capital; market expectations; and, most importantly, the earnings run rate. Mr. Kicinski explains that the "earnings run rate" is "your view of what your earnings capacity is going forward." The company considers what future earnings might be and has historically targeted 30% to 40% as the payout ratio.

"We use all of that information to assess our current dividend levels, as well as any changes we might be considering," says Mr. Kicinski.

The company's dividends initially increased every year, then every six months from 2004 until 2009, when they remained the same in light of the unstable financial market. "Our payout ratio stayed within this 30% to 40% rate until the recent financial crisis," says Mr. Kicinski. Under these circumstances, the company looks through the crisis to assess whether the dividend is realistic in a future scenario with stable markets, based on the earnings run rate; that is, projected future earnings capacity.

Sun Life has never had a stock split, though Mr. Kicinski says the process used to consider one would be similar to that for a dividend. "We would try to optimize our share price vis-à-vis our shareholders." If the stock price got high enough to impede shareholders' ability to purchase, the company would need to consider whether to split the shares.

"As you look at your capital, you look at a range of alternatives," says Mr. Kicinski. One that has met with success is Sun Life's dividend reinvestment program (DRIP). This program currently provides shareholders with the option to receive their dividends in shares at a discounted price rather than in cash. "It's a win-win situation," he adds.

The Navigator

STUDY OBJECTIVES:

After studying this chapter, you should be able to:

1. Prepare the entries for cash dividends, stock dividends, and stock splits, and compare their financial impact.
2. Prepare a corporate income statement and statement of comprehensive income.
3. Prepare a statement of retained earnings including prior period adjustments.
4. Prepare a statement of changes in shareholders' equity.
5. Evaluate earnings and dividend performance.

The Navigator

This chapter discusses dividends, stock splits, corporate income statements, retained earnings, the statement of changes in shareholders' equity, and key earnings and dividend ratios. The chapter is organized as follows:

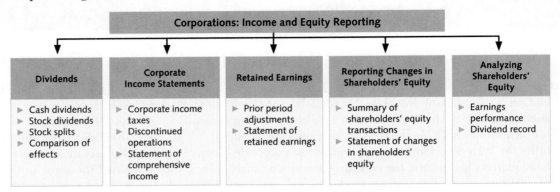

Dividends

STUDY OBJECTIVE 1

Prepare the entries for cash dividends, stock dividends, and stock splits, and compare their financial impact.

A dividend is a pro rata distribution of a portion of a corporation's retained earnings to its shareholders. "Pro rata" means that if you own, say, 10% of a corporation's shares, you will receive 10% of the total dividend paid to all shareholders. While there are different types of dividends, the most common are (1) cash dividends and (2) stock dividends. They are the focus of our discussion on dividends.

Investors are very interested in a company's dividend practices. Some companies are known for consistently paying dividends. The Bank of Montreal, for example, has the longest unbroken dividend record in Canadian history. It began paying dividends in 1829 and has not missed a year since then. For investors, dividends are an important part of any investment strategy. This is highlighted by the fact that the compounded return from reinvested dividends accounted for more than 60% of the total return from the Toronto Stock Exchange Index over the past 50 years.

In the financial press, dividends are reported as an annual dollar amount per share, even though it is usual to pay dividends quarterly.

Cash Dividends

A cash dividend is a distribution of cash to shareholders. For a corporation to pay a cash dividend, it must have all three of the following:

1. **Enough retained earnings.** Because dividends are distributed from retained earnings and therefore reduce retained earnings, a company must have enough retained earnings to pay a dividend. Companies rarely pay out dividends equal to their retained earnings, however. They must keep a certain portion of retained earnings to finance their operations. In addition, some level of retained earnings must be kept as a cushion or buffer against possible future losses. The laws determining how corporations pay cash dividends differ depending on the jurisdiction. However, in general, corporations are not allowed to create or increase a deficit (negative retained earnings) by the declaration of the dividend.

    In some cases, there may be specific retained earnings restrictions that make a portion of the Retained Earnings balance unavailable for dividends. For example, a company may have long-term debt contracts that restrict retained earnings as a condition of the loan. These restrictions are known as debt covenants, which, among other things, can limit the payment of dividends in order to make it more likely that the corporation will be able to meet required loan payments.

2. **Enough cash.** Having enough retained earnings does not necessarily mean that a company can pay a dividend. There is no direct relationship between the balance in the Retained Earnings account and the balance in the Cash account. So, in addition to having enough retained earnings, a company must also have enough cash before it can pay a dividend. To illustrate that the Retained Earnings and Cash balances may be quite different, the table below shows recent amounts of retained earnings and cash for selected companies.

Company	(in millions) Retained Earnings	Cash
Canadian Tire	$2,756	$ 429
George Weston Limited	5,299	1,465
Saputo	1,374	44
WestJet Airlines	611	820

How much cash is enough to declare a dividend? That is hard to say, but a company must keep enough cash on hand to pay for its ongoing operations and to pay its bills as they come due. Under the *Canada Business Corporations Act*, a corporation cannot pay a dividend if it would then become unable to pay its liabilities.

3. **A declaration of dividends by the board of directors.** A company cannot pay dividends unless its board of directors decides to do so, at which point the board "declares" the dividend to be payable. The board of directors has full authority to determine the amount of retained earnings to be distributed as a dividend and the amount to keep in the business. Dividends do not accrue like interest on a note payable. Even if the preferred shares are cumulative, dividends in arrears are not a liability until they are declared.

In order to remain in business, companies must honour their interest payments to creditors, bankers, and debt holders. But the payment of dividends to shareholders is another matter. Many companies can survive, and even thrive, without such payouts. For example, high-growth companies generally do not pay dividends. Their policy is to retain all of their earnings to finance their growth.

Investors must keep an eye on a company's dividend policy and understand what it may mean to existing and future shareholders. For example, regular increases in dividends when the company has irregular earnings can be a warning signal. Companies with high dividends and rising debt may be facing problems by borrowing money to pay shareholders. On the other hand, a small dividend or a missed dividend may lead to unhappiness among shareholders. Many shareholders purchase shares because they expect to regularly receive a reasonable dividend payment from the company.

Nonetheless, low dividends are not always a bad thing. Investors who receive low dividends could end up earning higher returns from a rising share price than from dividends. Presumably, investors who feel that regular dividends are important will buy shares in companies that pay periodic dividends, and those who feel that the share price is more important will buy shares in companies that retain earnings.

 ACCOUNTING IN ACTION: BUSINESS INSIGHT

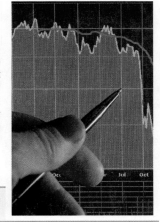

Vancouver's Teck Resources Ltd. produces and develops coal, copper, gold, and energy. In July 2008, Teck acquired Fording Canadian Coal Trust for about US$14 billion, securing bridge- and term-loan extensions and issuing bonds in order to do so. The company's share price fell from $42.85 on the day the deal was announced to $7.05 eight months later. At the end of the year, the company had $1 billion in cash, but $6 billion in debt due before the end of 2009. Something needed to be done. The board of directors came up with a 12-step plan to limit the damage. The first step was to suspend Teck's $486-million dividend—something that may seem obvious, but that many companies don't dare do. The reason for the dividend cut was to send a message to banks that the company will pay back the money it owes them. Teck also cut mine production, laid off 1,400 employees worldwide, and started to sell off non-core assets that weren't adding much to the cash flow.

Source: Sharda Prashad, "Teck Resources: Back from the Brink," *Canadian Business*, June 15, 2009.

Why would suspending its dividend send a message to Teck Resources' banks? What was the risk to Teck Resources of suspending its dividend?

Entries for Cash Dividends

There are three important dates for dividends: (1) the declaration date, (2) the record date, and (3) the payment date. Normally, there are several weeks between each date and the next one. Accounting entries are required on two of the dates: the declaration date and the payment date. In Chapter 13, we showed the journal entry for recording a cash dividend when the dividend is declared and paid on the same day. In this chapter, we expand our discussion of cash dividends by exploring the role of the board of directors in declaring dividends, and by showing how to record cash dividends when the dividend is paid after it is declared.

On the **declaration date**, a company's board of directors formally declares (authorizes) the cash dividend and announces it to shareholders. Declaring a cash dividend commits the corporation to a legal obligation. The obligation is binding and cannot be rescinded (reversed). An entry is required to recognize the increase in Cash Dividends (which results in a decrease in Retained Earnings) and the increase in the current liability Dividends Payable. Cash dividends can be paid to preferred or common shareholders. If dividends are paid to the common shareholders, remember that preferred shareholders have to be paid first.

To illustrate a cash dividend paid to preferred shareholders, assume that on December 1, the directors of Media General declare a $0.50-per-share quarterly cash dividend on the company's 100,000 $2-noncumulative preferred shares. The dividend totals $50,000 ($2 ÷ 4 = $0.50 × 100,000) and is payable on January 23 to shareholders of record on December 30. The entry to record the declaration is as follows:

A	=	L	+	SE
		+50,000		−50,000

Cash flows: no effect

Declaration Date		
Dec. 1	Cash Dividends—Preferred	50,000	
	Dividends Payable		50,000
	To record declaration of cash dividend.		

Note that the balance in Dividends Payable is a current liability. It will normally be paid within the next month or so. In the case of Media General, it will be paid on January 23.

On the **record date**, ownership of the shares is determined so that the corporation knows who to pay the dividend to. As discussed in Chapter 13, share ownership constantly changes as shares are bought and sold on the secondary market. Remember that these transactions are between investors, not between an investor and the company. Therefore, to keep track of constantly changing shareholders, a share register is maintained. In practice, larger companies typically hire a bank or trust company to manage this immense task. In the time between the declaration date and the record date, the corporation updates its share ownership records. For Media General, the record date is December 30. No entry is required on this date because the corporation's liability was recognized on the declaration date and is unchanged.

Helpful hint Between the declaration date and the record date, the number of shares remains the same. The purpose of the record date is to identify the persons or entities that will receive the dividend, not to determine the total amount of the dividend liability.

On the **payment date**, dividend cheques are mailed to shareholders and the payment of the dividend is recorded. The entry on January 23, the payment date, is as follows:

A	=	L	+	SE
−50,000		−50,000		

↓ Cash flows: −50,000

Payment Date		
Jan. 23	Dividends Payable	50,000	
	Cash		50,000
	To record payment of cash dividend.		

Note that the declaration of a cash dividend increases liabilities and reduces shareholders' equity. The payment of the dividend reduces both assets and liabilities, but has no effect on shareholders' equity. The cumulative effect of the declaration and payment of a cash dividend is to decrease both shareholders' equity (through the Retained Earnings account) and total assets (through the Cash account).

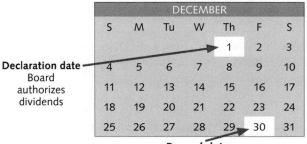

Illustration 14-1

Key dividend dates

Declaration date
Board authorizes dividends

Record date
Registered shareholders are eligible for dividend

Payment date
Dividend cheques are issued

Stock Dividends

A **stock dividend** is a distribution of the corporation's own shares to shareholders. Whereas a cash dividend is paid in cash, a stock dividend is distributed (paid) in shares. And while a cash dividend decreases assets and shareholders' equity, a stock dividend does not change either assets or shareholders' equity. A stock dividend results in a decrease in retained earnings and an increase in share capital, but there is no change in *total* shareholders' equity.

Note that since a stock dividend neither increases nor decreases the assets in the company, investors are not receiving anything they did not already own. In a sense, it is like ordering a piece of pie and cutting it into smaller pieces. You are no better or worse off, as you have the same amount of pie.

To illustrate a stock dividend for common shareholders, assume that you have a 2% ownership interest in IBR Inc. You own 1,000 of its 50,000 common shares. If IBR declares a 10% stock dividend, it will issue 5,000 additional shares (50,000 × 10%). You will receive 100 shares (2% × 5,000 or 10% × 1,000). Will your ownership interest change? No, it will remain at 2% (1,100 ÷ 55,000). You now own more shares, but your ownership interest has not changed. Illustration 14-2 shows the effect of a stock dividend for shareholders.

Before Stock Dividend   **After Stock Dividend**

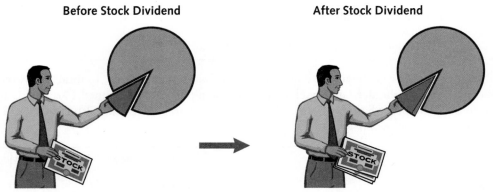

Illustration 14-2

Effect of stock dividend for shareholders

1,000 of 50,000 shares = 2% ownership   1,100 of 55,000 shares = 2% ownership

From the company's point of view, no cash has been paid, and no liabilities have been assumed. What are the purposes and benefits of a stock dividend? A corporation generally issues stock dividends for one or more of the following reasons:

1. To satisfy shareholders' dividend expectations without spending cash.
2. To increase the marketability of the corporation's shares. When the number of shares increases, the market price per share tends to decrease. Decreasing the market price makes it easier for investors to purchase the shares.

3. To emphasize that a portion of shareholders' equity has been permanently retained in the business and is unavailable for cash dividends.

The size of the stock dividend and the value to be assigned to each share are determined by the board of directors when the dividend is declared. It is common for companies to assign the fair value per share for stock dividends at the declaration date.

Entries for Stock Dividends

To illustrate the accounting for stock dividends, assume that IBR Inc. has a balance of $300,000 in Retained Earnings. On June 30, it declares a 10% stock dividend on its 50,000 common shares, to be distributed on August 5 to shareholders of record on July 20. The fair value of its shares on June 30 is $15 per share. On July 20, the fair value is $16 per share and on August 5, it is $14 per share. Note that for this transaction, the fair value at the declaration date is relevant, not the fair value on the record date or payment date. The number of shares to be issued is 5,000 (10% × 50,000). The total amount to be debited to Stock Dividends is $75,000 (5,000 × $15). The entry to record the declaration of the stock dividend is as follows:

A	=	L	+	SE
				+75,000
				−75,000

Cash flows: no effect

June 30	Stock Dividends—Common	75,000	
	Common Stock Dividends Distributable		75,000
	To record declaration of 10% stock dividend.		

At the declaration date, the Stock Dividends account is increased by the fair value of the shares to be issued, which results in a decrease in Retained Earnings similar to cash dividends. Common Stock Dividends Distributable, a shareholders' equity account, is increased by the same amount. Common Stock Dividends Distributable is not a liability, because assets will not be used to pay the dividend. Instead, it will be "paid" with common shares. If a balance sheet is prepared before the dividend shares are issued, the Dividends Distributable account is reported as share capital in the shareholders' equity section of the balance sheet.

Helpful hint Note that the dividend account title uses the word "Distributable," not "Payable."

As with cash dividends, no entry is required at the record date. When the dividend shares are issued on August 5, the account Common Stock Dividends Distributable is debited and the account Common Shares is credited:

A	=	L	+	SE
				+75,000
				−75,000

Cash flows: no effect

Aug. 5	Common Stock Dividends Distributable	75,000	
	Common Shares		75,000
	To record issue of 5,000 common shares in a stock dividend.		

Note that neither of the above entries changes shareholders' equity in total. However, the composition of shareholders' equity changes because a portion of Retained Earnings is transferred to the Common Shares account. The number of shares issued has also increased. These effects are shown below for IBR Inc.:

	Before Stock Dividend	After Stock Dividend
Shareholders' equity		
Common shares	$500,000	$575,000
Retained earnings	300,000	225,000
Total shareholders' equity	$800,000	$800,000
Total number of common shares issued	50,000	55,000

In this example, the account Common Shares is increased by $75,000 and Retained Earnings is decreased by the same amount. Total shareholders' equity remains unchanged at $800,000, the total before and after the stock dividend.

Stock Splits

Although stock splits are not dividends, we discuss them in this section because of their similarities to stock dividends. A **stock split**, like a stock dividend, involves the issue of additional shares to shareholders according to their percentage ownership. However, a stock split is usually much larger than a stock dividend.

The purpose of a stock split is to increase the shares' marketability by lowering the fair value per share. A lower fair value interests more investors and makes it easier for the corporation to issue additional shares. On the other hand, sometimes companies will decrease the number of shares outstanding by doing a **reverse stock split**. Instead of issuing two stocks for one, they issue one stock for two, to increase the fair value per share.

The effect of a split on fair value is generally inversely proportional to the size of the split. For example, in a 2-for-1 stock split, since there are twice as many shares, the fair value normally will decrease by half. Sometimes, due to increased investor interest, the share price will quickly rise beyond its split value.

In a stock split, the number of shares is increased by a specified proportion. For example, in a 2-for-1 split, one share is exchanged for two shares. A stock split does not have any effect on share capital, retained earnings, or shareholders' equity. Only the number of shares increases.

A stock split is illustrated below for IBR Inc.'s common shares. For the illustration, we assume that, instead of a 10% stock dividend, IBR splits its 50,000 common shares on a 2-for-1 basis.

	Before Stock Split	After Stock Split
Shareholders' equity		
Common shares	$500,000	$500,000
Retained earnings	300,000	300,000
Total shareholders' equity	$800,000	$800,000
Total number of common shares issued	50,000	100,000

Because a stock split does not affect the balances in any shareholders' equity accounts, it is not necessary to journalize it. Only a memo entry explaining the details of the split is needed.

Either common or preferred shares can be split. If preferred shares that have a stated dividend rate are split, then the dividend must also be adjusted for the effects of the split. For example, if 10,000 $6 preferred shares are split 3 for 1, then after the split there will be 30,000 preferred shares with a $2 annual dividend. The total dividend before and after the split remains unchanged at $60,000 (10,000 × $6 before and 30,000 × $2 after). After all, it is the same shareholders who held 10,000 shares before the split who now hold 30,000 shares.

Comparison of Effects

Significant differences between stock splits, stock dividends, and cash dividends (after payment) are shown below. In the illustration, "+" means increase, "–" means decrease, and "NE" means "no effect."

	Assets	Liabilities	Shareholders' Equity Share Capital	Retained Earnings
Cash dividend	–	NE	NE	–
Stock dividend	NE	NE	+	–
Stock split	NE	NE	NE	NE

Cash dividends reduce assets (the Cash account) and shareholders' equity (the Cash Dividends account, which reduces retained earnings). Stock dividends increase share capital (the Common Shares or Preferred Shares account) and decrease retained earnings (the Stock Dividends account, which reduces retained earnings). Stock splits do not affect any of the accounts. However, both a stock dividend and a stock split increase the number of shares issued.

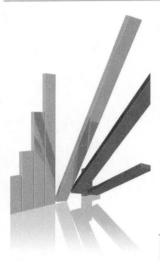

 ACCOUNTING IN ACTION: ACROSS THE ORGANIZATION

The value of shares in American International Group Inc. (AIG) tumbled in July 2009, despite a 1-for-20 reverse split of its stock, meaning investors who previously held 1,000 shares now owned 50. In the week following the July 1 announcement, AIG stock was down more than 50%. Shareholders approved the reverse stock split to prop up the share price while the company sold assets and spun off subsidiaries in an effort to repay a U.S. government loan and return to profitability. The government had bailed out the insurance company with a US$85-billion loan in September 2008, at the height of the financial crisis. By July 2009, AIG had received US$182.5 billion in loans from the government, which held an 80% stake in the company. In the early 2000s, AIG shares had traded at over $100 and they were near $70 when the financial crisis began in late 2007. However, the stock had fallen 89% since the government first bailed the company out. The day before the split, AIG's shares closed at $1.16; taking the split into account, they fell 21% on July 1, to $18.22.

Source: Associated Press, "AIG Shares Drop after 1-for-20 Reverse-Stock Split," Yahoo Finance, July 1, 2009, available at http://finance.yahoo.com/news/AIG-shares-drop-after-1for20-apf-2913886017.html?x=0&.v=2 [accessed on September 30, 2009]; Jonathan Ratner, "Market on the Short Side of AIG," *Financial Post* Trading Desk, July 10, 2009.

When senior managers were making a decision about the 1-for-20 reverse stock split, should they have expected the stock price to drop?

BEFORE YOU GO ON . . .

➡ **Review It**

1. What entries are made for cash dividends on (a) the declaration date, (b) the record date, and (c) the payment date?
2. What entries are made for stock dividends on (a) the declaration date, (b) the record date, and (c) the payment date?
3. What is the difference between a stock dividend and a stock split?
4. Contrast the effects of a cash dividend, stock dividend, and stock split on (a) assets, (b) liabilities, (c) shareholders' equity, and (d) the number of shares.
5. Did The Forzani Group declare any dividends or stock splits in fiscal 2009? The answer to this question is at the end of the chapter.

➡ **Do It**

Sing CD Corporation has had five years of record earnings. Due to this success, the market price of its 500,000 common shares tripled from $15 to $45 per share. During this period, the Common Shares account remained the same at $2 million. Retained Earnings increased from $1.5 million to $10 million. President Bill Zerter is considering either (1) a 10% stock dividend, or (2) a 2-for-1 stock split. He asks you to show the before-and-after effects of each option on the accounts Common Shares and Retained Earnings and on the number of shares.

Action Plan
- Calculate the stock dividend effect on Retained Earnings by multiplying the stock dividend percentage by the number of existing shares to determine the number of new shares to be issued. Multiply the number of new shares by the market price of the shares.
- A stock dividend increases the number of shares and affects both Common Shares and Retained Earnings.
- A stock split increases the number of shares but does not affect Common Shares and Retained Earnings.

Solution
1. With a 10% stock dividend, 50,000 new shares will be issued (500,000 × 10%). The stock dividend amount is $2,250,000 (50,000 × $45). The new balance in Common Shares is $4,250,000 ($2,000,000 + $2,250,000). In Retained Earnings, it is $7,750,000 ($10,000,000 − $2,250,000).

2. With a 2-for-1 stock split, 500,000 new shares will be issued. The account balances in Common Shares and Retained Earnings after the stock split are the same as they were before: $2 million and $10 million, respectively.

The effects in the shareholders' equity accounts of each option are as follows:

	Original Balances	After Stock Dividend	After Stock Split
Common shares	$ 2,000,000	$ 4,250,000	$ 2,000,000
Retained earnings	10,000,000	7,750,000	10,000,000
Total shareholders' equity	$12,000,000	$12,000,000	$12,000,000
Total number of common shares issued	500,000	550,000	1,000,000

The Navigator

Related exercise material: BE14–1, BE14–2, BE14–3, BE14–4, E14–1, and E14–2.

Corporate Income Statements

Income statements for corporations are very similar to the statements for proprietorships or partnerships except for the reporting of income taxes. There are also two other topics that may affect corporate income statements: the reporting of discontinued operations, and the reporting of other comprehensive income.

STUDY OBJECTIVE 2

Prepare a corporate income statement and statement of comprehensive income.

Corporate Income Taxes

For income tax purposes, a corporation is a separate legal entity. As a result, income tax expense is reported in a separate section of the corporate income statement, just before profit. The condensed, multiple-step income statement for Leads Inc. in Illustration 14-3 shows a typical presentation.

◄ Illustration 14-3

Corporate income statement

LEADS INC. Income Statement Year Ended December 31, 2011	
Sales	$800,000
Cost of goods sold	600,000
Gross profit	200,000
Operating expenses	40,000
Profit from operations	160,000
Other expenses	4,000
Profit before income tax	156,000
Income tax expense	46,800
Profit	$ 109,200

Income taxes not only affect the income statement (through the Income Tax Expense account) but also the balance sheet (through the Income Tax Payable account). Companies prepare a corporate income tax return (called a T2) annually to determine their taxable income and income tax payable. However, the Canada Revenue Agency requires income tax to be estimated in advance and paid (remitted to taxing authorities) in monthly instalments, rather than waiting until the end of the company's fiscal year.

After a company determines its total income tax payable at year end, it compares this amount with the total income tax instalments paid during the year. The difference between the income tax paid and income tax payable results in either an additional amount payable or a refund. Companies have six months after their fiscal year end to submit their corporate income tax return, or else they will incur late filing penalties on any balance due.

Once the additional liability (or receivable) has been determined, an adjusting entry is required. Assume Leads had originally estimated that its taxable income would be $140,000. It has a 30% income tax rate, so its income tax was anticipated to be $42,000 ($140,000 × 30%).

Leads remitted monthly instalments in the amount of $3,500 per month ($42,000 ÷ 12). At year end, Leads actually reports taxable income (profit before income taxes) of $156,000. Its total income tax liability is $46,800 ($156,000 × 30%), and not $42,000 as estimated. Assuming it has already recorded and remitted $42,000 of income tax, the required adjusting entry is for $4,800 ($46,800 − $42,000) and is recorded as follows:

A	=	L	+	SE
		+4,800		−4,800

Cash flows: no effect

Dec. 31	Income Tax Expense	4,800	
	Income Tax Payable		4,800
	To adjust estimated income tax expense to actual.		

Leads' income statement reports profit before income tax of $156,000 and income tax expense of $46,800. The balance sheet reports a current liability of $4,800.

Income Tax Allocation

Income taxes are, in reality, more complicated than the preceding discussion implies. As discussed in earlier chapters, the objectives for revenues and expenses for accounting purposes are not the same as the objectives for income tax purposes. Because of this, there are often temporary differences. Transactions can be recorded in one period for accounting purposes (in order to determine income tax expense) and in another period for income tax purposes (to determine income tax payable). These temporary differences result in deferred income taxes, which can be classified on the balance sheet as an asset (current or noncurrent) and/or a liability (current or noncurrent).

Alternative terminology
Deferred income taxes are referred to as *future* income taxes under Canadian GAAP for Private Enterprises.

Deferred income taxes are discussed at length in intermediate accounting courses. For now, it should be said that the income tax expense amount presented in many financial statements is usually divided between the amount that is due or receivable now and the amount that is due or receivable in the future. The act of dividing the amounts is called **interperiod tax allocation**. An illustration of interperiod income tax allocation is presented in the income statement of The Forzani Group. Note that Forzani uses the term "future income taxes" instead of "deferred income taxes."

Helpful hint *Intra* means within the current year's income statement; *inter* means between two or more income statements.

Intraperiod tax allocation is the process of associating income taxes in a specific period with their related item of income. Interperiod tax allocation, on the other hand, is when income taxes are allocated between two or more periods. In intraperiod tax allocation, the income tax expense or saving is associated with certain items or categories, and the items are reported net of applicable income tax. The general concept is "let the tax follow the profit or loss."

In the following sections, we will apply intraperiod tax allocation to discontinued operations and other comprehensive income. You will also see similar treatment in later sections on corrections of prior period errors and changes in accounting policy. Intraperiod tax allocation gives statement users useful information about the income tax effects of these items.

Discontinued Operations

Discontinued operations refer to the disposal or reclassification to "held for sale" of a component of an entity. A component of an entity is a separate major line of business or geographic area of operations. It must be possible to clearly separate operations and cash flows from the rest of the entity in order to be considered a component of an entity.

Most large corporations have multiple separate major lines of business. For example, Forzani reports that it operates principally in two business segments: corporately owned and operated retail stores and as a wholesale business selling to franchises and others.

When a component of an entity is disposed of, the disposal is reported separately on the income statement as a nonrecurring item called discontinued operations. The profit (or loss) reported in the discontinued operations section consists of two parts: the profit (loss) from these operations and the gain (loss) on disposal of the segment. Both items are presented net of applicable income tax so that the income tax related to continuing operations is clearly separated from the income tax for discontinued operations.

To illustrate, we will continue using Leads Inc. as an example and assume the company discontinued and sold its unprofitable kayak manufacturing division in 2011. The loss from operating this manufacturing division during 2011 (prior to selling it) is $70,000. Using intra-period income tax allocation, this loss will be shown on the income statement net of $21,000 ($70,000 × 30%) of income taxes, at $49,000 ($70,000 − $21,000).

The loss from selling the kayak manufacturing division is $50,000. It is also shown on the income statement net of $15,000 ($50,000 × 30%) of income taxes, at $35,000 ($50,000 − $15,000). Illustration 14-4 shows how this information is reported in Leads' income statement.

LEADS INC.
Income Statement (partial)
Year Ended December 31, 2011

Profit before income tax		$156,000
Income tax expense		46,800
Profit from continuing operations		109,200
Discontinued operations		
Loss from manufacturing operations, net of $21,000 income tax savings	$49,000	
Loss on disposal of manufacturing operations, net of $15,000 income tax savings	35,000	84,000
Profit		$ 25,200

Illustration 14-4

Income statement presentation of discontinued operations

Note that the caption "Profit from continuing operations" is used, and that a section called "Discontinued operations" is added. In the new section, both the operating loss and the loss on disposal are reported net of applicable income tax. This presentation clearly indicates the separate effects of continuing operations and discontinued operations on profit. This allows us to separate the effects of operations that are not relevant to the company's ongoing performance.

It is not uncommon to find companies reporting discontinued operations. For example, George Weston Limited reported a gain from discontinued operations of $187 million in its calendar year ending December 31, 2008, after selling its U.S. fresh bakery business.

Statement of Comprehensive Income

In Chapter 13, we learned that companies following IFRS must report comprehensive income. Recall that comprehensive income includes all items that result in changes in shareholders' equity during a period except for those related to the sale or repurchase of shares, or the payment of dividends. It is reported in a **statement of comprehensive income**.

Under IFRS, a company has the option of preparing the statement of comprehensive income in one of two possible formats:

1. **All-inclusive format.** A statement of comprehensive income can include all components of profit or loss and other comprehensive income in a single statement. In this case, the traditional profit or loss is shown as a subtotal in arriving at comprehensive income. By showing all of the revenues and expenses and resulting profit or loss found in the traditional income statement, in combination with other sources of income, the statement of comprehensive income makes it easier to evaluate a company's profitability on an "all-inclusive" basis.

2. **Separate statement.** The other option is to present the traditional income statement, followed by a separate statement of comprehensive income. In this case, the statement of comprehensive income starts with the profit or loss that was reported on the income statement. Then the other comprehensive income gains or losses are added to, or deducted from, profit to calculate comprehensive income.

Similar to discontinued operations, other comprehensive income must be reported net of income taxes. Each item of other comprehensive income can be shown net of income taxes, or if a company has several items in other comprehensive income, it can show the total income taxes on the other comprehensive items as one number. In this textbook, we will show each other comprehensive income item net of income taxes.

To illustrate a comprehensive income statement, we will continue our example with Leads Inc. Recall that Leads Inc. has prepared a separate traditional income statement, with profit of $25,200, as shown in Illustration 14-4. Assume that Leads Inc. also has equity investments where the gains and losses are recognized as other comprehensive income and that in 2011, Leads had a loss on these equity investments of $5,000. This will be shown in the statement of comprehensive income net of $1,500 ($5,000 × 30%) of income taxes at $3,500 ($5,000 − $1,500). This information is presented in Illustration 14-5 in a statement of comprehensive income for Leads Inc.

Illustration 14-5 ➡

Statement of comprehensive income

LEADS INC. Statement of Comprehensive Income Year Ended December 31, 2011	
Profit	$25,200
Other comprehensive income (loss)	
Loss on equity investments, net of $1,500 of income tax savings	(3,500)
Comprehensive income	$21,700

Recall from Chapter 13 that profit is added to retained earnings. Also recall that other comprehensive income is added to (losses are deducted from) accumulated other comprehensive income. We will see how this is presented in the financial statements, as part of the statement of changes in shareholders' equity, later in the chapter.

As discussed in Chapter 13, there is no such concept as other comprehensive income under Canadian GAAP for Private Enterprises. Therefore, companies following these standards will not prepare a statement of comprehensive income.

BEFORE YOU GO ON . . .

➡ Review It

1. What is the unique feature of a corporate income statement?
2. What is the difference between interperiod and intraperiod tax allocation?
3. Why are gains or losses from discontinued operations recorded separately on an income statement?
4. What is a statement of comprehensive income and how is it different from a traditional income statement?
5. What is the difference between other comprehensive income reported on the statement of comprehensive income, and accumulated other comprehensive income reported on the balance sheet?

➡ Do It

Qu Ltd. reports comprehensive income in a single statement of comprehensive income. In 2011 the company reported profit before income tax of $400,000; a pre-tax loss on discontinued operations of $75,000; a pre-tax gain on the disposal of the assets from the discontinued operations of $30,000; and other comprehensive income from a gain on an unrealized foreign currency translation adjustment of $14,000. The company has a 25% income tax rate. Prepare a statement of comprehensive income, beginning with profit before income tax.

Action Plan
- Allocate income tax between income from continuing operations, income from discontinued operations, and other comprehensive income items.
- Separately disclose (1) the results of operations of the discontinued division, and (2) the disposal of the discontinued operation.

- A statement of comprehensive income presents other comprehensive income amounts, net of taxes, following the profit for the year.

Solution

QU LTD. Statement of Comprehensive Income (partial) Year Ended December 31, 2011		
Profit before income tax		$400,000
Income tax expense		100,000[1]
Profit from continuing operations		300,000
Discontinued operations		
Loss from operations, net of $18,750[2] income tax savings	$56,250[3]	
Gain on disposal of assets, net of $7,500[4] income tax expense	22,500[5]	33,750
Profit		266,250
Other comprehensive income		
Unrealized gain on foreign currency translation adjustment,		
net of $3,500[6] income tax expense		10,500[7]
Comprehensive income		$ 276,750

[1] $400,000 × 25% = $100,000   [5] $30,000 − $7,500 = $22,500
[2] $75,000 × 25% = $18,750   [6] $14,000 × 25% = $3,500
[3] $75,000 − $18,750 = $56,250   [7] $14,000 − $3,500 = $10,500
[4] $30,000 × 25% = $7,500

Related exercise material: BE14–5, BE14–6, BE14–7, and E14–3.

The Navigator

Retained Earnings

As you learned in Chapter 13, retained earnings are the cumulative total since incorporation of profit (less losses) less any declared dividends. In other words, they are the profit (or earnings) that have been retained in the business. Each year profit is added to (or a loss is deducted from) and dividends are deducted from opening Retained Earnings to determine the ending Retained Earnings amount.

STUDY OBJECTIVE 3

Prepare a statement of retained earnings including prior period adjustments.

As in a proprietorship, revenue and expense accounts (which make up profit) and dividends accounts are temporary accounts and are closed to Retained Earnings at the end of each period to bring the Retained Earnings account up to date. The ending Retained Earnings balance at December 31, 2010, will become the opening Retained Earnings amount, dated January 1, for the 2011 fiscal year.

Prior Period Adjustments

Suppose that a corporation's books have been closed and the financial statements have been issued. The corporation then discovers that a material error has been made in reporting profit of a prior year. Or suppose that the corporation changes an accounting policy that affects the comparison of prior-year figures. How should these situations be recorded in the accounts and reported in the financial statements of the previous periods?

When there is a correction of an error or a change in accounting policy, the accounting treatment is similar:

1. The corrected amount or new policy should be used in reporting the results of operations of the current year.
2. The cumulative effect of the correction or change should be disclosed as an adjustment to opening retained earnings net of (after subtracting) applicable income tax. Since prior period earnings are affected, this effect is not reported in the current period's income statement.

3. All financial statements for prior periods should be corrected or restated to make it easier to compare them.
4. The effects of the change should be detailed and disclosed in a note to the statements.

An adjustment of financial results for prior periods is only appropriate in these two circumstances: (1) when correcting an error related to a prior period, and (2) when changing an accounting policy. Now let's look in more detail at the accounting for each of these.

Correction of Prior Period Errors

Helpful hint Normally, errors made in the year are discovered and corrected before the financial statements for the year are issued. Thus, corrections of prior period errors rarely happen.

The **correction of a prior period error** in previously issued financial statements is made directly to Retained Earnings since the effect of the error is now in this account. The revenues and expenses (profit) for the previous period have been recorded in Retained Earnings through the journalizing and posting of closing entries.

To illustrate the correction of a prior period error, assume that Graber Inc. discovers in 2011 that it overstated its cost of goods sold in 2010 by $10,000 as a result of errors in counting inventory. Because cost of goods sold (an expense account) was overstated, profit before income tax was understated by the same amount, $10,000. If we assume an income tax rate of 30%, income tax expense would also be understated, but by $3,000 ($10,000 × 30%). The overall effect on profit is to understate it by $7,000 ($10,000 – $3,000). In other words, profit is understated by the difference after tax [$10,000 × (100% – 30%)]. If profit is understated, then retained earnings at the end of 2010 would also be understated by the same amount, $7,000.

The following table details the effect of this error on the income statement, using assumed data for revenues and expenses:

	Incorrect	Correct	Difference
Revenues	$900,000	$900,000	$ 0
Expenses	550,000	540,000	10,000
Profit before income tax	350,000	360,000	10,000
Income tax expense (30%)	105,000	108,000	3,000
Profit	$245,000	$252,000	$ 7,000

In addition to overstating cost of goods sold by $10,000, the error will result in merchandise inventory being understated by the same amount. You will recall that we learned about the pervasive impact of inventory errors in Chapter 6.

The entry for the correction of this error, discovered on February 12, 2011, is as follows:

A	=	L	+	SE
+10,000		+3,000		+7,000

Cash flows: no effect

Feb. 12	Merchandise Inventory	10,000	
	Income Tax Payable		3,000
	Retained Earnings		7,000
	To adjust for overstatement of cost of goods sold in a prior period.		

A credit to an income statement account, in this case Cost of Goods Sold, instead of Retained Earnings, would be incorrect because the error is for a prior year. Recall that income statement accounts are temporary accounts that are closed at the end of each year to the Retained Earnings account.

Change in Accounting Policy

To make comparisons easier, financial statements for the current period are prepared using the same accounting policies that were used for the preceding period. This improves comparability, an important characteristic of accounting information that we learned about in Chapter 11. However, an accounting policy used in the current year can be different from the one used in the previous year only if the change (1) is required by generally accepted accounting principles or (2) results in the financial statements providing more reliable and relevant information. This is called a **change in accounting policy**.

The transition to International Financial Reporting Standards and Canadian GAAP for Private Enterprises is an example of a change in accounting policy because of a change in generally accepted accounting principles. When there is a change in accounting policy, companies are required to retroactively apply the new standards except if it is impractical to do so. For example, if significant estimates are required, or if the required information is not available, then it is not possible for prior financial statements to be restated for comparative purposes.

If the company starts using a new accounting method because of a change in circumstances, this is not considered a change in accounting policy. Because it is not a change in accounting policy, the company will not retroactively change prior periods as it will in the case of a change in accounting policy. For example, in Chapter 9 we explained that companies must review their choice of depreciation methods each year. If a change in circumstances indicates the method must be changed, then the company will simply start using the new method in the current and future periods.

Presentation of Prior Period Adjustments

Prior period adjustments—whether they are for corrections of prior period errors or changes in accounting policies—are added to (or deducted from, depending on the direction of the adjustment) the beginning Retained Earnings balance. This must be reported in the financial statements. Similar to gains or losses from discontinued operations, prior period adjustments are reported net of the associated income taxes.

To illustrate, using the adjustment we journalized above—the correction for the overstatement of cost of goods sold—assume that Graber had reported $750,000 of retained earnings at December 31, 2010. Note that the ending balance in Retained Earnings on December 31, 2010, is the beginning balance in Retained Earnings on January 1, 2011.

Also note that, as the error was found in 2011, it will be reported as a correction in the 2011 financial statements. Thus, Graber Inc. will show the following information about its retained earnings in its 2011 financial statements:

Retained earnings, January 1, 2011, as previously reported	$750,000
Add: Correction for overstatement of cost of goods sold in 2010,	
net of $3,000 income tax expense	7,000
Retained earnings, January 1, 2011, as adjusted	757,000

Any financial statements from the prior year that are presented for comparison would be restated using the correct cost of goods sold expense and inventory amounts. There would also be a note that is cross-referenced to the statements: it would give details about the impact of both the correction of the error and, if applicable, any changes in policy and it would say that statements from previous years have been restated.

Statement of Retained Earnings

Companies are required to provide information on each of the transactions and events that changed retained earnings during the period and to show how ending retained earnings has been calculated. This information was traditionally reported in a **statement of retained earnings**.

A statement of retained earnings is similar to the statement of owner's equity prepared for a proprietorship. The income statement must be prepared before the statement of retained earnings in order to determine the profit that will be added to (or loss that will be deducted from) beginning retained earnings. As in the statement of owner's equity, the statement of retained earnings starts with the beginning balance, and then shows all of the changes in order to calculate the ending balance.

In Chapter 13, and earlier in this chapter, we learned about the transactions and events that change retained earnings. These include earning profit (or incurring a loss), declaring cash and stock dividends, making prior period adjustments, and sometimes incurring losses from the reacquisition of shares. Recall that losses occur when shares are reacquired at a price higher than the average issue price. The loss is first deducted from contributed capital. But if the loss is greater than an existing balance in contributed capital, retained earnings is reduced by the remaining loss.

Companies following Canadian GAAP for Private Enterprises prepare a statement of retained earnings. Companies following IFRS include the information on changes in retained earnings in their statement of changes in shareholders' equity, as opposed to preparing a separate statement of retained earnings.

Under the assumption that Graber Inc. is following Canadian GAAP for Private Enterprises, its statement of retained earnings for 2011 is shown in Illustration 14-6 using assumed data for profit and dividends, and incorporating the prior period adjustment just discussed.

Illustration 14-6 ➡

Statement of retained earnings

GRABER INC. Statement of Retained Earnings Year Ended December 31, 2011	
Balance, January 1, 2011, as previously reported	$ 750,000
Add: Correction for overstatement of cost of goods sold in 2010, net of $3,000 income tax expense	7,000
Balance, January 1, 2011, as adjusted	757,000
Add: Profit	549,000
	1,306,000
Less: Cash dividends	100,000
Balance, December 31, 2011	$1,206,000

Companies following Canadian GAAP for Private Enterprises are much less likely to have stock dividends or to reacquire shares on a regular basis. We will illustrate how to show these changes in retained earnings in the section on the statement of changes in shareholders' equity. Some companies combine the statement of retained earnings with their income statement instead of presenting them separately. For example, in its 2009 financial statements included in Appendix A, The Forzani Group does this in its Consolidated Statements of Operations and Retained Earnings.

BEFORE YOU GO ON . . .

➡ **Review It**

1. What is the difference between a correction of a prior period error and a change in accounting policy?
2. How is the correction of a prior period error shown in the financial statements?
3. What information is included in a statement of retained earnings?

➡ **Do It**

Vega Corporation reported retained earnings of $5,130,000 at December 31, 2010. In 2011, the company earns $2 million of profit. It declares and pays a $250,000 cash dividend. Vega also records a pre-tax prior period adjustment of $275,000 for an overstatement resulting from a mathematical error that affected 2010 ending inventory. The company also incurs a $25,500 charge to retained earnings for the reacquisition of common shares. Its income tax rate is 30%. Prepare a statement of retained earnings for the year ended December 31.

Action Plan
- To calculate retained earnings, begin with retained earnings, as reported at the end of the previous year.
- Add or subtract any prior period adjustments, net of applicable income tax, to arrive at the adjusted opening Retained Earnings balance.
- Add profit and subtract dividends declared and any other debits (e.g., from a reacquisition of shares) to arrive at the ending balance in Retained Earnings.

Solution

VEGA CORPORATION		
Statement of Retained Earnings		
Year Ended December 31, 2011		
Balance, January 1, as previously reported		$ 5,130,000
Less: Correction for overstatement of ending inventory,		
net of $82,500[1] applicable income tax		(192,500)[2]
Balance, January 1, as adjusted		4,937,500
Add: Profit		2,000,000
		6,937,500
Less: Cash dividend	$250,000	
Reacquisition of common shares	25,500	275,500
Balance, December 31		$6,662,000

[1] $275,000 × 30% = $82,500   [2] $275,000 − $82,500 = $192,500

Related exercise material: BE14–8, BE14–9, BE14–10, E14–4, E14–5, and E14–6.

The Navigator

Reporting Changes in Shareholders' Equity

STUDY OBJECTIVE 4

Prepare a statement of changes in shareholders' equity.

Recent changes in Canadian accounting standards require companies to disclose all changes affecting shareholders' equity in a statement of changes in shareholders' equity. This statement shows the changes in total shareholders' equity during the year, as well as changes in each shareholders' equity account, including contributed capital, retained earnings, and accumulated other comprehensive income.

Prior to that, the financial statements included a statement of retained earnings, with detail about changes in other equity accounts disclosed in the notes to the statements. As previously mentioned, this is the approach that will continue to be used by companies following Canadian GAAP for Private Enterprises. It is considered sufficient for private enterprises as they have less complex shareholders' equity transactions. But companies following IFRS must prepare a statement of changes in shareholders' equity.

In the following sections, we will first review the transactions that affect shareholders' equity and then show how to prepare a statement of changes in shareholders' equity.

Alternative terminology
The statement of changes in shareholders' equity is also called the *statement of shareholders' equity* or *statement of changes in equity*.

Summary of Shareholders' Equity Transactions

In Chapters 13, and earlier in this chapter, you have learned several transactions and events that affect shareholders' equity accounts. These are summarized in Illustration 14-7.

Illustration 14-7

Summary of transactions affecting shareholders' equity

Transaction	Impact on Shareholders' Equity Accounts
1. Issuance of share capital	1. Common or Preferred Shares is increased.
2. Reacquisition of share capital	2. Common or Preferred Shares is decreased. Contributed Capital may be increased or decreased. Retained Earnings may be decreased.
3. Correction of a prior period error that affected the prior year's ending retained earnings.	3. Opening Retained Earnings is either increased or decreased as required to make the correction.
4. Cumulative effect of a change in accounting policy on the prior year's ending retained earnings.	4. Opening Retained Earnings is either increased or decreased as required to make the adjustment.
5. Profit (loss)	5. Retained Earnings is increased (decreased).
6. Other comprehensive income (loss)	6. Accumulated Other Comprehensive Income is increased (decreased).
7. Cash dividends are declared	7. Retained Earnings is decreased.
8. Stock dividends are declared	8. Retained Earnings is decreased and Stock Dividends Distributable is increased.
9. Stock dividends are distributed	9. Stock Dividends Distributable is decreased and Common Shares is increased.
10. Stock split	10. Number of shares issued increases; there is no effect on account balances.

It is important to review this summary and make sure you understand each of these transactions and their impact on the shareholders' equity accounts. This is the information that is included in the statement of changes in shareholders' equity.

Statement of Changes in Shareholders' Equity

To explain and illustrate the preparation of a statement of changes in shareholders' equity, we will use financial information from Tech International Inc. Illustration 14-8 presents Tech International's prior-year shareholders' equity section of the balance sheet and its current-year statement of comprehensive income.

Illustration 14-8 ➡

Tech International's financial information

TECH INTERNATIONAL INC. Balance Sheet (partial) December 31, 2010	
Shareholders' equity	
Share capital	
Common shares, no par value, unlimited number authorized, 1,000,000 shares issued	$2,980,000
Contributed capital—reacquired shares	20,000
	3,000,000
Retained earnings	190,000
Accumulated other comprehensive income	385,700
Total shareholders' equity	$ 3,575,700

TECH INTERNATIONAL INC. Statement of Comprehensive Income Year Ended December 31, 2011	
Profit	$349,800
Other comprehensive income	
Gain on equity investments, net of $132,000 of income tax expense	198,000
Comprehensive income	$547,800

During 2011, Tech International entered into a number of transactions that affected its shareholder equity accounts as follows:

1. On January 21, Tech International reacquired 25,000 common shares for $115,000. As you learned in Chapter 13, Common Shares is decreased $74,500 [($2,980,000 ÷ 1,000,000) × 25,000]. Contributed Capital—Reacquired Shares is decreased by its balance of $20,000. Retained Earnings is decreased $20,500 ($115,000 − $74,500 − $20,000).
2. On March 4, Tech International declared a 4% stock dividend to be distributed on April 10 to shareholders of record on March 20. The fair value of its shares on March 4 was $4.75. As the total shares issued at that point amounted to 975,000 (1,000,000 − 25,000), 39,000 shares are distributed (975,000 × 4%) at $185,250 (39,000 × $4.75).
3. On September 22, Tech International sold 50,000 common shares at $5 per share for a total of $250,000 cash.
4. On November 9, Tech International declared cash dividends of $100,000 to be paid on January 2, 2012, to shareholders of record on December 7, 2011.

It was also determined that cost of goods sold had been overstated by $70,000 in 2010. Tech International has an income tax rate of 40%. The income tax impact of the overstatement was $28,000 ($70,000 × 40%). The net impact of the error on opening retained earnings was $42,000 ($70,000 − $28,000).

In the statement of changes in shareholders' equity, this information is organized by shareholders' equity account. For each account, the beginning balance from the prior-year balance sheet is shown, followed by the increases and decreases during the year. The ending balance is calculated for each shareholders' equity account and then the overall total of shareholders' equity is determined.

Remember that comprehensive income is divided into profit and other comprehensive income in terms of its impact on shareholders' equity. Profit is added to Retained Earnings, and Other Comprehensive Income is added to Accumulated Other Comprehensive Income.

In Illustration 14-9, Tech International's statement of changes in equity for 2011 has been prepared using the above information.

← **Illustration 14-9**

Statement of changes in shareholders' equity

TECH INTERNATIONAL INC. Statement of Changes in Shareholders' Equity Year Ended December 31, 2011	
Share capital, common shares	
Balance, January 1, 1,000,000 shares issued	$2,980,000
Reacquired 25,000 shares	(74,500)
Stock dividend issued, 39,000 shares	185,250
Issued for cash, 50,000 shares	250,000
Balance, December 31, 1,064,000 shares issued	3,340,750
Stock dividends distributable	
Balance, January 1	0
Common stock dividend declared	185,250
Common stock dividend distributed	(185,250)
Balance, December 31	0
Contributed capital—reacquired shares	
Balance, January 1	20,000
Reacquired common shares	(20,000)
Balance, December 31	0
Retained earnings	
Balance, January 1, as previously reported	190,000
Correction for overstatement of cost of goods sold in 2010, net of $28,000 of income tax expense	42,000
Balance, January 1, as adjusted	232,000
Profit	349,800
Reacquired common shares	(20,500)
Stock dividends	(185,250)
Cash dividends	(100,000)
Balance, December 31	276,050
Accumulated other comprehensive income	
Balance, January 1	385,700
Other comprehensive income	198,000
Balance, December 31	583,700
Shareholders' equity, December 31	$4,200,500

Note that the end-of-year balances shown in the statement of changes in shareholders' equity are the amounts that are reported on the shareholders' equity section of the December 31, 2011, balance sheet.

BEFORE YOU GO ON . . .

→ Review It

1. What transactions increase shareholders' equity? What shareholders' equity account does each of these transactions affect?
2. What transactions decrease shareholders' equity? What shareholders' equity account does each of these transactions affect?
3. Where is comprehensive income shown in the statement of changes in shareholders' equity?
4. Explain how the statement of shareholders' equity relates to the balance sheet.

→ Do It

Grand Lake Corporation had the following shareholders' equity balances at January 1, 2011:

Common shares, unlimited number authorized, no par value, 500,000 issued	$1,000,000
Retained earnings	600,000
Accumulated other comprehensive income	100,000

The following selected information is available for the year ended December 31, 2011:

1. Issued 100,000 common shares for $300,000 cash.
2. Declared dividends of $50,000.
3. Reported profit of $360,000.
4. Reported a loss on equity investments of $25,000 as other comprehensive loss.

Action Plan

- The statement of shareholders' equity covers a period of time, starting with the opening balances and ending with the ending balances for the period.
- Include all of the changes in each shareholders' equity account, as well as total shareholders' equity.
- Recall that comprehensive income consists of both profit and other comprehensive income.

Solution

GRAND LAKE CORPORATION
Statement of Changes in Shareholders' Equity
Year Ended December 31, 2011

Share capital, common shares	
Balance, January 1, 500,000 shares issued	$1,000,000
Issued for cash, 100,000 shares	300,000
Balance, December 31, 600,000 shares issued	1,300,000
Retained earnings	
Balance, January 1	600,000
Profit	360,000
Cash dividends	(50,000)
Balance, December 31	910,000
Accumulated other comprehensive income	
Balance, January 1	100,000
Other comprehensive loss	(25,000)
Balance, December 31	75,000
Shareholders' equity, December 31	$2,285,000

The Navigator

Related exercise material: BE14–11, BE14–12, E14–7, E14–8, and E14–9.

Analyzing Shareholders' Equity

STUDY OBJECTIVE 5

Evaluate earnings and dividend performance.

Shares are generally purchased by investors for potential capital gains (increases in the shares' market price) or for potential income (dividends). Consequently, investors are interested in both a company's earnings performance and its dividend record.

Earnings Performance

When shareholders want to analyze their investment in a company, they can measure the company's earnings performance, or profitability, in several different ways. We learned about one measure in Chapter 13: the return on equity ratio. Two other ratios are widely used by existing shareholders and potential investors: earnings per share and the price-earnings ratio.

Earnings per share is useful because shareholders usually think in terms of the number of shares they own—or plan to buy or sell—so determining profit per share makes it easier for the shareholder to understand the return on his or her investment.

Investors and others also link earnings per share to the market price per share. This relationship produces the second ratio: the price-earnings ratio.

Earnings Per Share

Earnings per share (EPS) indicates the profit earned by each common share. Thus, earnings per share is reported only for common shares. When a company has both preferred and common shares, the current year's dividend declared on preferred shares is subtracted from profit to determine the income available to common shareholders. Illustration 14-10 shows the formula for calculating EPS.

Profit Minus Preferred Dividends	÷	Weighted Average Number of Common Shares	=	Earnings per Share
($29,325 – $0)	÷	31,298	=	$0.94

← Illustration 14-10

Earnings per share formula

To show the calculation of earnings per share, the illustration uses data (in thousands) from Forzani's 2009 financial statements. Forzani's net earnings of $29,325,000 is divided by the weighted average number of common shares, 31,298,000, to determine its earnings per share of $0.94.

In determining the numerator of the earnings per share calculation ($29,325,000), note that Forzani had no preferred dividends to subtract from profit. If it did, any preferred dividends declared for the current year would be subtracted from profit to determine the income available for the common shareholders. In addition, note that if preferred shares are cumulative, the dividend is deducted whether or not it is declared.

For the denominator of the earnings per share calculation (31,298), the **weighted average number of shares** is used instead of the ending balance, or a straight average. If there is no change in the number of common shares issued during the year, the weighted average number of shares will be the same as the ending balance. If new shares are issued in the year, these shares are adjusted for the fraction of the year they are outstanding to determine the weighted average number of shares. This is done because the issue of shares during the period changes the amount of net assets that income can be earned on.

To illustrate the calculation of the weighted average number of common shares, assume that a company had 100,000 common shares on January 1, and issued an additional 10,000 shares on October 1. The weighted average number of shares for the year would be calculated as follows:

Date	Actual Number	Fraction of Year	Weighted Average
Jan. 1	100,000	× $^{12}/_{12}$ =	100,000
Oct. 1	10,000	× $^{3}/_{12}$ =	2,500
	110,000		102,500

As illustrated, 110,000 shares were actually issued by the end of the year. Of these, 100,000 were outstanding for the full year and are allocated a full weight, 12 months out of 12. As 10,000 of the shares have only been outstanding for three months (from October 1 to December 31), they are weighted for $^{3}/_{12}$ of the year, resulting in 2,500 weighted shares. In total, the company's weighted average number of shares is 102,500 for the year. In the next calendar year, the 110,000 shares would receive a full weight (unless some of these shares are repurchased) because all 110,000 shares would be outstanding for the entire year.

The disclosure of the earnings per share is required for companies reporting under IFRS. This disclosure is so important that EPS must be reported directly on the statement of comprehensive income or income statement if presented separately, and it also has to be explained in the notes to the financial statements. It is the only ratio that is reported in this way. Companies reporting under Canadian GAAP for Private Enterprises do not report EPS.

Complex Capital Structure. When a corporation has securities that may be converted into common shares, it has what is called a complex capital structure. One example of a convertible security is convertible preferred shares. When the preferred shares are converted into common shares, the additional common shares will result in a reduced, or diluted, earnings per share figure.

Two earnings per share figures are calculated when a corporation has a complex capital structure. The first earnings per share figure is called **basic earnings per share**. The earnings per share amount we calculated in Illustration14-10, $0.94, is known as basic earnings per share, which is what Forzani reported on its income statement for fiscal 2009.

The second earnings per share figure is called **fully diluted earnings per share**. This figure calculates *hypothetical* earnings per share as though *all* securities that can be converted into, or exchanged for, common shares have been (even though they really have not). Forzani, which has other securities that can be converted into common shares (stock options, in this case) is considered to have a complex capital structure. It reports fully diluted earnings per share of $0.93 for fiscal 2009. Note that fully diluted earnings per share will never be higher than basic earnings per share.

The calculation of fully diluted earnings per share is complex. In addition, the determination of the weighted average number of shares for both basic and fully diluted earnings per share becomes more complicated when there are stock dividends and stock splits during the year. Further discussion of these and other earnings per share complexities is left to an intermediate accounting course.

Price-Earnings Ratio

Comparing the earnings per share amounts of different companies is not very helpful, because there are big differences in the numbers of shares in companies and in the share prices. In order to compare earnings across companies, we instead calculate the **price-earnings (PE) ratio**. The price-earnings ratio is a frequently quoted statistic that gives the ratio of the market price of each common share to its earnings per share.

To illustrate, we will calculate the price-earnings ratio for The Forzani Group Ltd. Forzani's earnings per share for the year ended February 1, 2009, was $0.94, as shown in Illustration 14-10. Its market price per share at year end was $9.51. Illustration 14-11 shows Forzani's price-earnings ratio.

← **Illustration 14-11**

Price-earnings ratio formula

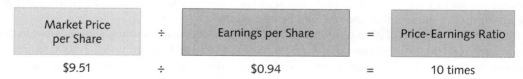

Market Price per Share	÷	Earnings per Share	=	Price-Earnings Ratio
$9.51	÷	$0.94	=	10 times

This ratio indicates that Forzani's shares are trading at 10 times earnings. The PE ratio reflects investors' assessment of a company's future earnings. The ratio of price to earnings will be higher if investors think that current income levels will continue or increase. It will be lower if investors think that income will decrease.

The price-earnings ratio is not relevant for private companies. Private companies will not have a readily available market price per share, and, as discussed above, they do not report earnings per share in their financial statements.

Dividend Record

One way that companies reward shareholders for their investment is to pay dividends. The **payout ratio** tells you what percentage of income the company is distributing to its shareholders. If the number is very high, it could be a warning signal—it could mean the company is failing to reinvest enough of its income in its operations. A high payout ratio can also mean the company's income is falling or that it is trying to attract investors who find little else to get excited about.

The payout ratio is calculated by dividing cash dividends by profit. This ratio can also be expressed on a per share basis by dividing dividends per share by earnings per share. The payout ratio can be calculated for total dividends, for common dividends, or for preferred dividends. The formula to calculate the payout ratio is shown in Illustration 14-12.

Cash Dividends	÷	Profit	=	Payout Ratio
$9,327	÷	$29,325	=	.32

Forzani's payout ratio is .32. This indicates that for every dollar of profit earned during the fiscal year, the company has paid approximately $0.32 to the owners. Prior to fiscal 2009, Forzani did not pay a dividend.

Like most ratios, the payout ratio varies with the industry. For example, utilities have high payout ratios. But companies that have high growth rates generally tend to have low payout ratios because they reinvest their profit in the company.

ACCOUNTING IN ACTION: ALL ABOUT YOU

Many of the jobs that students have just pay a straightforward hourly wage. But after you graduate, you may encounter companies that include stock options or stock savings plans as part of their employees' compensation. Both stock options and stock savings plans provide employees with the opportunity to be shareholders of the company. Microsoft and Google both created numerous millionaire employees through stock options. The engineers, software developers, and even office administrators who joined the companies in the startup years took a risk by taking stock options and lower salaries. In Canada, WestJet's first 15 pilots who gave up their steady-paying jobs at other airlines for slightly lower salaries and company stock options all became millionaires as WestJet turned into a major player in the airline industry. Not everybody is as lucky with stock options. As the economy and stock markets crashed in the fall of 2008, stock options issued to many Canadian employees became worthless and they were left with no benefits from the options.

Source: Anthony A. Davis, "The Sky's the Limit," *Alberta Venture*, September 2008, page 164.

Why do companies use stock options and stock savings plans to partially compensate employees?

BEFORE YOU GO ON . . .

→ Review It

1. Why is profit available to the common shareholders not always the same as net income?
2. Explain how to calculate earnings per share.
3. How is the weighted average number of shares calculated?
4. Explain how the price-earnings ratio relates to the earnings per share ratio.
5. What ratio gives information about a company's dividend record?

→ Do It

Shoten Limited reported profit of $249,750 on its October 31 year-end income statement. The shareholders' equity section of its balance sheet reported 3,000 $2-noncumulative preferred shares and 50,000 common shares. Of the common shares, 40,000 had been issued since the beginning of the year, 15,000 were issued on March 1, and 5,000 were repurchased on August 1. The preferred dividend was declared and paid during the year.

(a) Calculate Shoten's earnings per share.
(b) Assuming the fair value of Shoten's shares was $40 per share at the year end, calculate Shoten's price-earnings ratio.

Action Plan
- Subtract the preferred dividends from profit to determine the income available for common shareholders.
- Adjust the shares for the fraction of the year they were outstanding to determine the weighted average number of shares.
- Divide the income available for common shareholders by the weighted average number of shares to calculate the earnings per share.

Solution
(a) Weighted average number of common shares:

Date	Actual Number	Fraction of Year	Weighted Average
Nov. 1	40,000	$\times\ ^{12}/_{12} =$	40,000
Mar. 1	15,000	$\times\ ^{8}/_{12} =$	10,000
Aug. 1	(5,000)	$\times\ ^{3}/_{12} =$	(1,250)
	50,000		48,750

Earnings per share: $\dfrac{\$249,750 - \$6,000\ [3,000 \times \$2]}{48,750} = \$5$

(a) Price-earnings ratio: $\$40 \div \$5 = 8$

The Navigator

Related exercise material: BE14–13, BE14–14, BE14–15, E14–10, E14–11, E14–12, and E14–13.

Demonstration Problem

WILEY PLUS
Demonstration Problems

On January 1, 2011, Fuso Corporation had the following shareholders' equity accounts:

Preferred shares, $5-noncumulative, no par value, unlimited number authorized, 9,500 issued	$ 950,000
Common shares, no par value, unlimited number authorized, 260,000 issued	3,120,000
Retained earnings	3,200,000
Accumulated other comprehensive income	30,000

During the year, the following transactions occurred:

Jan. 18   Issued 500 preferred shares for $100 per share.

Feb. 14   Reacquired 10,000 common shares for $13 per share.

Mar. 10   Declared quarterly cash dividend to preferred shareholders of record on March 31, payable April 15.

June 1   Announced a 2-for-1 stock split of the preferred shares. Immediately before the split, the share price was $100 per share. After the split, the dividend was adjusted from $5 to $2.50 per share.

10   Declared quarterly cash dividend to preferred shareholders of record on June 30, payable July 15.

Sept. 10   Declared quarterly cash dividend to preferred shareholders of record on September 30, payable October 15.

Nov. 30   Declared a 5% stock dividend to common shareholders of record on December 20, distributable January 8. On November 30, the share price was $15 per share. On December 20, it was $16 per share and on January 8, it was $17 per share.

Dec. 10   Declared quarterly cash dividend to preferred shareholders of record on December 31, payable January 15.

31   A loan agreement entered into on December 31 restricts the payment of future dividends to 75% of profit.

In addition, Fuso Corporation reported profit of $590,000 and other comprehensive income of $10,000 for the year.

Instructions

(a) Record the transactions and the closing entries for dividends.
(b) Prepare a statement of changes in shareholders' equity.
(c) Prepare the shareholders' equity section of the balance sheet.

Solution to Demonstration Problem

(a)

Jan. 18	Cash	50,000	
	Preferred Shares		50,000
	To record issuing 500 preferred shares for $100 per share.		
Feb. 14	Common Shares [($3,120,000 ÷ 260,000) × 10,000]	120,000	
	Retained Earnings ($130,000 − $120,000)	10,000	
	Cash ($13 × 10,000)		130,000
	Reacquired 10,000 common shares.		
Mar. 10	Cash Dividend—Preferred	12,500	
	Dividend Payable		12,500
	To record quarterly preferred dividend ($5 ÷ 4 = $1.25; $1.25 × 10,000).		
Apr. 15	Dividend Payable	12,500	
	Cash		12,500
	To record payment of quarterly preferred dividend.		
June 1	Memo entry only about 2-for-1 stock split. Now 20,000 (10,000 × 2) preferred shares.		
10	Cash Dividend—Preferred	12,500	
	Dividend Payable		12,500
	To record quarterly preferred dividend ($2.50 ÷ 4 = $0.625; $0.625 × 20,000).		
July 15	Dividend Payable	12,500	
	Cash		12,500
	To record payment of quarterly preferred dividend.		
Sept.10	Cash Dividend—Preferred	12,500	
	Dividend Payable		12,500
	To record quarterly preferred dividend ($2.50 ÷ 4 = $0.625; $0.625 × 20,000).		
Oct. 15	Dividend Payable	12,500	
	Cash		12,500
	To record payment of quarterly preferred dividend.		
Nov. 30	Stock Dividend—Common	187,500	
	Stock Dividend Distributable		187,500
	To record stock dividend to common shareholders (250,000 × 5% = 12,500; 12,500 × $15).		
Dec. 10	Cash Dividend—Preferred	12,500	
	Dividend Payable		12,500
	To record quarterly preferred dividend ($2.50 ÷ 4 = $0.625; $0.625 × 20,000).		
31	Retained Earnings	237,500	
	Cash Dividend—Preferred		50,000
	Stock Dividend—Common		187,500
	To close dividend accounts. Cash dividend account = $50,000 ($12,500 + $12,500 + $12,500 + $12,500).		
31	No entry required.		

Action Plan

- Keep a running total of the number of shares issued.
- Remember that dividend rates are expressed as annual amounts.
- Make journal entries for dividends on the declaration and payment dates, but not on the record date.
- Adjust the number of shares for the stock split, but make no journal entry.
- Apply the stock dividend percentage to the number of shares issued. Multiply the new shares to be issued by the shares' fair value.
- Recall that the statement of changes in shareholders' equity explains the changes for the period in the beginning and ending balances of each shareholders' equity account.
- The balance sheet reports shareholders' equity at the end of the period. These numbers should be taken from the ending balances on the statement of changes in shareholders' equity.

(b)

FUSO CORPORATION Statement of Changes in Shareholders' Equity Year ended December 31, 2011	
Preferred shares	
Balance, January 1, 9,500 preferred shares issued	$ 950,000
Issued 500 preferred shares	50,000
Issued 10,000 preferred shares in a 2-for-1 stock split	0
Balance, December 31, 20,000 preferred shares issued (*Note X*)	1,000,000
Common shares	
Balance, January 1, 260,000 common shares issued	3,120,000
Reacquired 10,000 common shares	(120,000)
Balance, December 31, 250,000 common shares issued	3,000,000
Stock dividends distributable	
Balance, January 1	0
Common stock dividend declared	187,500
Balance, December 31	187,500
Retained earnings	
Balance, January 1	3,200,000
Profit	590,000
Reacquired common shares	(10,000)
Preferred dividends—Cash	(50,000)
Common dividends—Stock	(187,500)
Balance, December 31	3,542,500
Accumulated other comprehensive income	
Balance, January 1	30,000
Other comprehensive income	10,000
Balance, December 31	40,000
Shareholders' equity, December 31	$7,770,000

Note X: A 2-for-1 stock split was declared on June 1. After the split, the dividend was adjusted from $5 to $2.50 per share.

(c)

FUSO CORPORATION Balance Sheet (partial) December 31, 2011	
Shareholders' equity	
Share capital	
Preferred shares, $2.50-noncumulative, no par value, unlimited number authorized, 20,000 issued	$1,000,000
Common shares, no par value, unlimited number authorized, 250,000 issued	3,000,000
Common stock dividend distributable, 12,500 shares	187,500
Total contributed capital	4,187,500
Retained earnings (*Note Y*)	3,542,500
Accumulated other comprehensive income	40,000
Total shareholders' equity	$7,770,000

Note Y: A loan agreement contains a restrictive covenant that limits the payment of future dividends to 75% of profit.

The Navigator

Summary of Study Objectives

1. Prepare the entries for cash dividends, stock dividends, and stock splits, and compare their financial impact. Entries for both cash and stock dividends are required at the declaration date and the payment or distribution date. There is no entry for a stock split. Cash dividends reduce assets and shareholders' equity (retained earnings). Stock dividends reduce retained earnings and increase common shares, but have no impact on total shareholders' equity. Both stock dividends and stock splits increase the number of shares issued. Stock splits reduce the fair value of the shares, but have no impact on the company's financial position.

2. Prepare a corporate income statement and statement of comprehensive income. Corporate income statements are similar to the income statements for proprietorships and partnerships, with one exception. Income tax expense must be reported in a separate section before profit in the corporation's income statement. Gains or losses on discontinued operations must be presented net of income taxes after profit (or loss) from continuing operations. Companies following IFRS must prepare a statement of comprehensive income that reports all increases and decreases to shareholders' equity during a period except changes resulting from the sale or repurchase of shares and from the payment of dividends. The statement of comprehensive income can be prepared on an all-inclusive basis, or can start with profit or loss as shown on a separate income statement.

3. Prepare a statement of retained earnings including prior period adjustments. A correction to beginning retained earnings is required if an error in the prior year's income and retained earnings is found after the temporary accounts have been closed and the statements have been issued. Beginning retained earnings is also adjusted to reflect the cumulative effect of a change in accounting policy. These are called prior period adjustments and are shown net of the related income tax impact. Retained earnings is changed when a company earns profit (or incurs a loss), declares cash and stock dividends, makes prior period adjustments, and sometimes, when it incurs a loss on the reacquisition of shares. All of these changes in retained earnings are reported in a statement of retained earnings for a company following Canadian GAAP for Private Enterprises. Companies following IFRS will report this information in the statement of changes in shareholders' equity.

4. Prepare a statement of changes in shareholders' equity. A statement of changes in shareholders' equity explains all of the changes in each of the shareholders' equity accounts, and in total, for the reporting period. This includes changes in contributed capital (common shares, preferred shares, and any other contributed capital accounts), retained earnings, and accumulated other comprehensive income. The statement of changes in shareholders' equity is a requirement for companies reporting under IFRS.

5. Evaluate earnings and dividend performance. Profitability measures that are used to analyze shareholders' equity include return on equity (discussed in Chapter 13), earnings per share, the price-earnings ratio, and the payout ratio. Earnings (loss) per share is calculated by dividing profit (loss) available to the common shareholders by the weighted average number of common shares. The price-earnings ratio is calculated by dividing the market price per share by the earnings per share. The payout ratio is calculated by dividing cash dividends by profit.

Glossary

Basic earnings per share The profit (or loss) earned by each common share. It is calculated by subtracting any preferred dividends declared from profit and dividing the result by the weighted average number of common shares. (p. 788)

Cash dividend A pro rata (equal) distribution of cash to shareholders. (p. 768)

Change in accounting policy The use of a generally accepted accounting policy in the current year that is different from the one used in the preceding year. (p. 780)

Component of an entity A separate major line of business or geographic area of operations. (p. 776)

Correction of a prior period error The correction of an error in previously issued financial statements. (p. 780)

Debt covenant A restriction in a loan agreement that, among other things, may limit the use of corporate assets for the payment of dividends. (p. 768)

Declaration date The date when the board of directors formally declares a dividend and announces it to shareholders. (p. 770)

Discontinued operations A component of an enterprise that has been disposed of or is reclassified as "held for sale." (p. 776)

Dividend A distribution of cash or shares by a corporation to its shareholders on a pro rata basis. (p. 768)

Earnings per share (EPS) The profit (or loss) earned by each common share. (p. 787)

Fully diluted earnings per share Earnings per share adjusted for the maximum possible dilution that would occur if securities were converted, or changed, into common shares. (p. 788)

Interperiod tax allocation The allocation of income tax expense between two or more periods to record the amount that is currently due and the amount that is due in the future (deferred). (p. 776)

Intraperiod tax allocation The procedure of associating income tax expense with the specific item that directly affects the income tax for the period. (p. 776)

Payment date The date when cash dividend cheques are mailed to shareholders. For a stock dividend, the date when the shares are distributed to shareholders. (p. 770)

Payout ratio A ratio that measures the percentage of income distributed as cash dividends. It is calculated by dividing cash dividends by profit. (p. 788)

Price-earnings (PE) ratio The ratio of the price of a common share to earnings per common share. (p. 788)

Record date The date when ownership of shares is determined for dividend purposes. (p. 770)

Retained earnings restrictions Circumstances that make a portion of retained earnings currently unavailable for dividends. (p. 768)

Reverse stock split A decrease in the number of shares outstanding. A 1-for-3 reverse stock split would reduce the amount of shares owned by a shareholder to one for every three shares owned before the split. (p. 773)

Statement of changes in shareholders' equity A statement that reports all increases and decreases to shareholders' equity during a period except changes resulting from the sale or repurchase of shares and from the payment of dividends. (p. 783)

Statement of comprehensive income A statement that reports all increases and decreases to shareholders' equity during a period except changes resulting from the sale or repurchase of shares and from the payment of dividends. (p. 777)

Statement of retained earnings A financial statement that shows the changes in retained earnings during the year. (p. 781)

Stock dividend A pro rata distribution of the corporation's own shares to shareholders. (p. 771)

Stock split The issue of additional shares to shareholders in a multiple, such as 2 for 1. A 2-for-1 stock split means that two new shares are issued in exchange for one old share. (p. 773)

Weighted average number of shares The number of common shares outstanding during the year, with any shares purchased or issued during the year weighted by the fraction of the year that they have been outstanding. (p. 787)

Self-Study Questions

Answers are at the end of the chapter.

(SO 1) K 1. For a corporation to pay a dividend, what must be present?
   (a) Enough profit for the year, cash, and retained earnings.
   (b) Enough profit for the year, cash, and contributed capital.
   (c) Enough cash, retained earnings, and a board declaration.
   (d) All authorized shares must be issued.

2. The date on which the company's board of directors (SO 1) K authorizes a cash dividend is the:
   (a) payment date.
   (b) record date.
   (c) annual general meeting date.
   (d) declaration date.

3. The following describes the entry to record issuing (SO 1) K a stock dividend:
   (a) Debit to dividends payable and credit to cash.
   (b) Debit to common stock dividends distributable and credit to common shares.

(c) Debit to common shares and credit to cash.

(d) Debit to common shares and credit to contributed surplus.

(SO 2) K 4. Discontinued operations:

(a) are reported as part of operating expenses on the income statement.

(b) are reported separately on the income statement as a nonrecurring item.

(c) are never presented net of applicable income taxes.

(d) result in an entry to retained earnings directly.

(SO 2) K 5. A statement of comprehensive income:

(a) must include all components of profit and loss and other comprehensive income.

(b) does not include profit or loss from the traditional income statement.

(c) is required for companies reporting under IFRS and Canadian GAAP for Private Enterprises.

(d) is required for companies reporting under IFRS only.

(SO 3) K 6. Canadian public companies' adoption of IFRS is best described as a:

(a) change in accounting policy and should be applied retroactively.

(b) correction of prior period errors and should be applied prospectively.

(c) correction of a prior period error and is applied retroactively.

(d) change in accounting policy and should not be applied retroactively.

(SO 3, 4) K 7. A prior period adjustment is:

(a) reported in the income statement.

(b) reported directly in the shareholders' equity section of the balance sheet.

(c) reported in either the statement of retained earnings or the statement of changes in shareholders' equity as an adjustment to the opening balance of retained earnings.

(d) reported in either the statement of retained earnings or the statement of changes in shareholders' equity as an adjustment to the ending balance of retained earnings.

8. Which of the following is not included in a statement of changes in shareholders' equity? (SO 4) AP

(a) A reacquisition of share capital

(b) Other comprehensive income

(c) Bond repayment

(d) Stock dividend

9. The Sonic Corporation reported profit of $42,000; (SO 5) AP its weighted average number of common shares as 12,000; and a market price per share of $66.50. It had no preferred shares. What were its earnings per share and price-earnings ratios?

(a) $8 and 12 times

(b) $6.50 and 6 times

(c) $2 and 15 times

(d) $3.50 and 19 times

10. Bernard Dupuis is nearing retirement and would (SO 5) C like to invest in shares that will give him a steady income. Bernard should choose shares with a:

(a) high earnings per share.

(b) high price-earnings ratio.

(c) high payout ratio.

(d) high return on equity.

The Navigator

Questions

(SO 1) K 1. A dividend is a "pro rata" distribution of retained earnings. Explain what "pro rata" means.

(SO 1) C 2. Why is having enough retained earnings a requirement for paying a cash dividend, even if the company has sufficient cash to make the payment?

(SO 1) K 3. What is the purpose of a retained earnings restriction? Why might a retained earnings restriction be included in a debt covenant?

(SO 1) K 4. At what point does a cash dividend become a liability of a company?

5. Freddy Investor says, "The shares I recently (SO 1) C bought just declared a 2-for-1 stock split. Now I've doubled my investment!" Is Freddy correct—is he any better off after the stock split?

6. Contrast the effects of a cash dividend, stock divi- (SO 1) C dend, and stock split on a company's (a) assets, (b) liabilities, (c) share capital, (d) retained earnings, and (e) number of shares.

7. What is the main difference between income state- (SO 2) C ments for corporations and income statements for proprietorships and partnerships? Why does this difference exist?

(SO 2, 4) K 8. Explain the difference between interperiod income tax allocation and intraperiod income tax allocation.

(SO 2) C 9. What are discontinued operations? Why is it important to report discontinued operations separately from profit or loss from continuing operations?

(SO 2) C 10. What is the difference between other comprehensive income and comprehensive income?

(SO 2) C 11. Explain how comprehensive income is reported on (a) the statement of comprehensive income, and (b) the balance sheet.

(SO 3) C 12. "I don't understand the difference between a correction of a prior period error and a change in accounting policy," Joss said. "It looks to me like they're accounted for and reported in exactly the same way." Explain the similarities and differences to Joss.

(SO 3) K 13. Under what circumstances is it appropriate to record an adjustment to the results of prior periods? How are these adjustments reported in the financial statements?

(SO 3, 4) K 14. Why is a statement of retained earnings not necessary if a statement of changes in shareholders' equity is prepared?

(SO 4) K 15. Provide examples of transactions that increase shareholders' equity and transactions that decrease shareholders' equity.

(SO 2) C 16. How does the reporting of comprehensive income and accumulated other comprehensive income improve the usefulness of a company's financial statements?

(SO 5) C 17. Distinguish between basic earnings per share and fully diluted earnings per share.

(SO 5) C 18. Franklin Corporation has both common and preferred shares. The company's accountant argues that because common shares pay dividends too, it is not necessary to subtract the amount of preferred dividends declared or paid to calculate earnings per share. Is the accountant correct? Discuss.

(SO 5) AP 19. Company A has a price-earnings ratio of 9 times and a payout ratio of 40%. Company B has a price-earnings ratio of 22 times and a payout ratio of 5%. Which company's shares would be better for an investor interested in large capital gains versus steady income? Why?

(SO 5) C 20. If all other factors stay the same, indicate whether each of the following is generally considered favourable or unfavourable by a potential investor: (a) a decrease in return on equity, (b) an increase in earnings per share, (c) a decrease in the price-earnings ratio, and (d) an increase in the payout ratio.

Brief Exercises

Record cash dividend.
(SO 1) AP

BE14–1 The board of directors of the Blue Heron Corporation met on December 12 and voted in favour of declaring the annual preferred share dividend to shareholders of record on January 1. The dividend will be paid on January 23. The company has 30,000 $4-non-cumulative preferred shares. Prepare the entries on the appropriate dates to record the cash dividend.

Record stock dividend.
(SO 1) AP

BE14–2 Lighthouse Corporation has 100,000 common shares. It declares a 5% stock dividend on April 1 to shareholders of record on April 16, to be distributed on April 30. The fair value per share was $7 on April 1, $9 on April 16, and $14 on April 30. Prepare the entries on the appropriate dates to record the stock dividend.

Analyze impact of stock dividend.
(SO 1) AP

BE14–3 The shareholders' equity section of Ferndale Corporation's balance sheet consists of 175,000 common shares for $2 million, and retained earnings of $600,000. A 10% stock dividend is declared when the fair value per share is $12. Show the before-and-after effects of the dividend on (a) share capital, (b) retained earnings, (c) total shareholders' equity, and (d) the number of shares.

BE14–4 Indicate whether each of the following transactions would increase (+), decrease (–), or have no effect (NE) on total assets, total liabilities, total shareholders' equity, and the number of shares:

Compare cash dividend, stock dividend, and stock split.
(SO 1) AP

Transaction	Assets	Liabilities	Shareholders' Equity	Number of Shares
(a) Declared a cash dividend.				
(b) Paid the cash dividend declared in (a).				
(c) Declared a stock dividend.				
(d) Distributed the stock dividend declared in (c).				
(e) Split stock 2 for 1.				

BE14–5 For the year ended June 30, 2011, Viceron Inc. earned $4 million in revenues and had $3.2 million of expenses. The company has a 30% income tax rate. Prepare (a) the journal entry to record income taxes, assuming that $180,000 had been previously accrued, and (b) the income statement.

Record income tax and prepare income statement.
(SO 2) AP

BE14–6 Olivier Corporation reported the following pre-tax amounts for the current year: profit before income tax (on the company's continuing operations), $500,000; loss from operations of discontinued operations, $154,000; and gain on disposal of assets of discontinued operations, $60,000. Olivier is subject to a 25% income tax rate. Calculate (a) the income tax expense on continuing operations, (b) any income tax expense or savings on discontinued operations, and (c) profit.

Calculate income tax on continuing and discontinued operations.
(SO 2) AP

BE14–7 Jet Set Airlines reported profit of $180,000. The company also reported the following other comprehensive income item: a gain on an equity investment of $40,000. This amount is before tax; Jet Set has a tax rate of 30%. All numbers are for the year ended December 31, 2011. (a) Prepare a statement of comprehensive income. (b) Jet Set had an accumulated other comprehensive loss of $11,914 at January 1, 2011. What amount would it report in the shareholders' equity section of its balance sheet on December 31, 2011?

Prepare statement of comprehensive income.
(SO 2) AP

BE14–8 For the year ending December 31, 2011, Grayfair Inc. reports profit of $250,000. The company declared dividends of $90,000 and paid $80,000 of these dividends during the year. Prepare a statement of retained earnings for the year, assuming the balance in Retained Earnings on January 1, 2011, was $190,000.

Prepare a statement of retained earnings.
(SO 3) AP

BE14–9 On March 1, 2011, Broadfoot Bakeries, Inc. discovered an error in its inventory count on December 31, 2010. The error had caused the prior year's cost of goods sold to be overstated by $120,000. The income tax rate is 32%. Prepare the journal entry to correct this error.

Record correction of prior period error.
(SO 3) AP

BE14–10 Broadfoot Bakeries, Inc. reported retained earnings of $280,000 on December 31, 2010. For the year ended December 31, 2011, the company had profit of $85,000, and it declared and paid dividends of $12,000. Using this information and the data for Broadfoot Bakeries in BE14–9, prepare a statement of retained earnings.

Prepare a statement of retained earnings with prior period adjustment.
(SO 3) AP

BE14–11 Peninsula Supply Corporation reported the following statement of changes in shareholders' equity for the years ended December 31, 2010, and 2011. Determine the missing amounts.

Complete a statement of changes in shareholders' equity.
(SO 4) AP

PENINSULA SUPPLY CORPORATION
Statement of Changes in Shareholders' Equity
Year Ended December 31

	2011		2010	
	Number of Shares	Amount	Number of Shares	Amount
Common shares, no par value, unlimited authorized				
Balance, January 1	500,000	$ (b)	500,000	$600,000
Issued shares for cash	50,000	32,500		0
Reacquired shares	(25,000)	(c)		0
Balance, December 31	(a)	603,750	500,000	600,000
Contributed capital—reacquired shares				
Balance, January 1		15,000		15,000
Reacquired common shares		8,000		0
Balance, December 31		(d)		15,000
Retained earnings				
Balance, January 1, as previously reported		179,500		190,000
Correction for overstatement of cost of goods sold (net of taxes)		18,000		
Balance, January 1, restated		197,500		190,000
Profit (loss)		22,500		(h)
Common dividends—Cash		(e)		(30,000)
Balance, December 31		190,000		179,500
Accumulated other comprehensive income				
Balance, January 1		51,000		(i)
Other comprehensive income (loss)		(f)		(3,000)
Balance, December 31		68,000		51,000
Shareholders' equity, December 31		$ (g)		$ (j)

Prepare a comprehensive income statement and shareholders' equity section of balance sheet.
(SO 2, 4) AP

BE14–12   A statement of changes in shareholders' equity for Peninsula Supply Corporation is presented in BE14–11. (a) Prepare the comprehensive income statement for 2011. (b) Prepare the shareholders' equity section of the balance sheet at December 31, 2011.

Calculate weighted average number of shares.
(SO 5) AP

BE14–13   Franklin Corporation had 25,000 common shares on January 1, 2011. On March 15, 5,000 shares were repurchased. On July 29 and September 30, 6,000 and 10,000 shares were issued, respectively. Calculate (a) the number of shares issued, and (b) the weighted average number of shares at December 31.

Calculate earnings per share.
(SO 5) AP

BE14–14   Northlake Limited reports profit of $454,000 and 220,000 common shares. (a) Calculate the earnings per share. (b) Assume that Northlake also has 8,000 $3-cumulative preferred shares, on which the dividend for the current year was declared and paid. Recalculate the earnings per share. (c) Assume that the preferred dividends referred to in part (b) were not declared and paid. What difference would this make in calculating the earnings per share?

Calculate price-earnings and payout ratios.
(SO 5) AP

BE14–15   Highlink, Inc. reported earnings per share of $3. Its common shares were selling at $24.10 per share. During the same year, the company paid a $0.40 per share cash dividend. Calculate the price-earnings ratio and the payout ratio.

Exercises

E14–1 Smart Mart Inc. is considering one of three options: (1) paying a $0.40 cash dividend, (2) distributing a 5% stock dividend, or (3) effecting a 2-for-1 stock split. The current fair value is $14 per share.

Compare cash dividend, stock dividend, and stock split.
(SO 1) AP

Instructions

Help Smart Mart decide what to do by completing the following chart (treat each possibility independently):

	Before Action	After Cash Dividend	After Stock Dividend	After Stock Split
Total assets	$1,875,000			
Total liabilities	$ 75,000			
Common shares	1,200,000			
Retained earnings	600,000			
Total shareholders' equity	1,800,000			
Total liabilities and shareholders' equity	$1,875,000			
Number of common shares	60,000			

E14–2 Before preparing financial statements for the current year, the chief accountant for Patel Ltd. discovered the following errors in the accounts:

Prepare correcting entries for dividends and stock split.
(SO 1) AP

1. Patel has 20,000 $4-noncumulative preferred shares issued. It paid the preferred shareholders the quarterly dividend, and recorded it as a debit to Dividends Expense and a credit to Cash.
2. A 5% stock dividend (1,000 shares) was declared on the common shares when the fair value per share was $12. To record the declaration, Retained Earnings was debited and Dividends Payable was credited. The shares have not been issued yet.
3. The company declared a 2-for-1 stock split on its 20,000 $4-noncumulative preferred shares. The average cost of the preferred shares before the split was $70. The split was recorded as a debit to Retained Earnings of $1.4 million and a credit to Preferred Shares of $1.4 million.
4. After the stock split described in (3) above, the declaration of the quarterly dividend was recorded as a debit to Cash Dividends—Preferred for $40,000 and a credit to Dividends Payable for $40,000.

Instructions

Prepare any correcting entries that are needed.

E14–3 Top Brands Limited reported the following selected information for the year ended March 31, 2011:

Prepare income statement and statement of comprehensive income.
(SO 2) AP

Advertising expense	$ 7,000	Interest expense	$ 5,500
Cash dividends	5,000	Loss on discontinued operations	18,000
Depreciation expense	3,000	Loss on equity investments	3,000
Fees earned	62,000	Rent revenue	34,000
Gain on sale of equipment	1,500	Retained earnings, April 1, 2010	19,000
Income tax payable	6,600	Training programs expense	8,000

The company's income tax rate is 30%. The company reports gains and losses on its equity investments as other comprehensive income.

Instructions

Prepare an income statement and a separate statement of comprehensive income for Top Brands Limited.

Prepare presentation of discontinued operations and prior period adjustment.
(SO 2, 3) AP

E14-4 Shrink Ltd. has profit from continuing operations of $320,000 for the year ended December 31, 2011. It also has the following items (before considering income taxes): (1) a net gain of $60,000 from the discontinuance of a component of the entity, which includes a $90,000 profit from the operation of the segment and a $30,000 loss on its disposal; and (2) the correction of an error which had understated the prior period's cost of goods sold by $20,000. Assume that the income tax rate on all items is 30%.

Instructions

(a) Prepare a partial income statement, beginning with "Profit from continuing operations."
(b) Indicate the statement presentation of any items not included in (a).

Indicate effects of transactions on shareholders' equity.
(SO 1, 3) AP

E14-5 Kettle Creek Corporation had the following transactions and events:

1. Declared a cash dividend.
2. Paid the cash dividend declared in (1).
3. Issued common shares for cash.
4. Completed a 2-for-1 stock split of the common shares.
5. Declared a stock dividend on the common shares.
6. Distributed the stock dividend declared in (5).
7. Made a prior period correction for an understatement of profit.
8. Adopted a new accounting policy that resulted in the recording of a gain on a long-lived asset revaluation.
9. Repurchased common shares for less than their initial issue price.
10. Restricted $50,000 of retained earnings.

Instructions

Indicate the effect(s) of each of the above items on the subdivisions of shareholders' equity. Present your answer in tabular form with the following columns. Use "I" for increase, "D" for decrease, and "NE" for no effect. Item 1 is given as an example.

Item	Contributed Capital		Retained Earnings	Accumulated Other Comprehensive Income	Total Shareholders' Equity
	Share Capital	Additional			
1.	NE	NE	D	NE	D

Prepare a statement of retained earnings with a prior period adjustment.
(SO 1, 2, 3) AP

E14-6 On January 1, 2011, Fyre Lite Corporation had retained earnings of $650,000. During the year, Fyre Lite had the following selected transactions:

1. Declared and paid cash dividends, $125,000.
2. Earned profit before income taxes, $200,000.
3. Corrected a prior period error of $42,000, before income taxes, which resulted in an understatement of profit in 2010.
4. Reacquired 25,000 common shares for $20,000 more than the original issue price. This was the first time the company had ever reacquired its own shares.
5. Fyre Lite has a debt covenant that restricts it from declaring cash dividends if that would reduce its retained earnings below $200,000.

Instructions

Prepare a statement of retained earnings for the year ended December 31, 2011. Assume the company has a 20% income tax rate.

Record share and dividend transactions; indicate statement presentation.
(SO 1, 4) AP

E14-7 On January 1, Zhou Corporation had 80,000 common shares issued. During the year, the following occurred:

May 15   Issued 6,000 additional common shares for $10 per share.

June 22   Declared a cash dividend of $0.30 per share to common shareholders of record on June 30, payable on July 12.

Aug. 19   Declared a 5% stock dividend to the common shareholders of record on August 31, distributable on September 18. The shares' fair value was $10 on August 19, $12 on August 31, and $14 on September 18.

Nov. 21 Issued 4,000 additional common shares for $16 per share.

Dec. 15 Declared a cash dividend of $0.22 per share to common shareholders of record on December 31, payable on January 14.

Instructions

(a) Journalize the transactions.

(b) Prepare the entry to close dividends at December 31, Zhou's year end.

(c) Assume Zhou follows IFRS. Explain where each of the following would be reported in the financial statements: (1) cash, (2) common shares, (3) dividends, (4) dividends payable, and (5) retained earnings.

E14–8 On January 1, 2011, Hopkins Corporation had an unlimited number of no par value common shares authorized, and 120,000 of them issued for $1.2 million; it also had retained earnings of $750,000. The company issued 60,000 common shares at $15 per share on July 1, and declared a 3-for-2 stock split on September 30 when the fair value was $19 per share. On December 9, it declared a 5% stock dividend to common shareholders of record at December 30, distributable on January 16, 2012. At the declaration date, the fair value of the common shares was $22 per share. The company earned profit of $390,000 for the year.

Record share and dividend transactions; prepare statement of changes in shareholders' equity.
(SO 1, 4) AP

Instructions

(a) Journalize the transactions. Ignore closing entries.

(b) Prepare a statement of changes in shareholders' equity for 2011.

E14–9 Agrium Inc. reported the following selected accounts and information (in US$ millions), as at December 31, 2008:

Prepare statement of comprehensive income and statement of changes in shareholders' equity.
(SO 2, 4) AP

Accumulated other comprehensive income, January 1	$ 84
Retained earnings, January 1	1,024
Cumulative effect of a change in inventory accounting policy, net of income tax—gain	4
Profit	1,322
Cost of shares reacquired (1 million shares)	15
Loss on reacquisition of shares	20
Other comprehensive loss items (net of taxes)	256
Dividends	17
Common shares, unlimited number authorized, 158 million issued	1,972
Stock compensation plan (increase to common share account—no shares issued)	4
Contributed capital, January 1	8

Instructions

Prepare a statement of comprehensive income and a statement of changes in shareholders' equity.

E14–10 Ruby Red Rental Corporation had the following balances in its shareholders' equity accounts at January 1, 2011:

Prepare statement of changes in shareholders' equity and calculate payout ratio.
(SO 4, 5) AP

Accumulated other comprehensive income	$ 40,000
Other contributed capital—reacquired shares	540,000
Retained earnings	1,500,000
Common shares (32,000 shares)	800,000

Ruby Red had the following transactions and events during 2011:

Feb. 2 Repurchased 1,000 shares for $44,500.

Apr. 17 Declared and paid cash dividends $70,000.

Oct. 29 Issued 2,000 shares for $104,000.

Dec. 31 Reported comprehensive income of $425,000, which included other comprehensive income of $25,000.

Instructions

(a) Prepare a statement of changes in shareholders' equity at December 31, 2011.

(b) Calculate Ruby Red Rental's payout ratio.

Calculate earnings per share.
(SO 5) AP

E14–11 Chinook Corporation reported profit of $343,125 for its November 30, 2011, year end. Cash dividends of $75,000 on the common shares and of $45,000 on the noncumulative preferred shares were declared and paid during the year. There were also the following changes in common shares:

Dec. 1, 2010 The opening number of common shares was 60,000.
Feb. 28, 2011 Sold 10,000 common shares for $200,000 cash.
May 31, 2011 Reacquired 5,000 shares for $90,000 cash.
Nov. 1, 2011 Issued 15,000 common shares in exchange for land with a fair value of $310,000.

Instructions

(a) Calculate the profit available for the common shareholders.

(b) Calculate the weighted average number of common shares for the year.

(c) Calculate the earnings per share for the year.

(d) Why is it necessary to calculate a weighted average number of shares? Why not use the average number of shares (beginning balance plus ending balance divided by two)? After all, we use averages for other ratio calculations.

Calculate the earnings per share.
(SO 5) AP

E14–12 At December 31, Morse Corporation has 2,000 $4 preferred shares and 100,000 common shares. Morse's profit for the year is $547,000.

Instructions

Calculate the earnings per share under each of the following independent assumptions.

(a) Assume that the preferred shares are cumulative and that the dividend to the preferred shareholders was (1) declared, and (2) not declared.

(b) Assume that the preferred shares are noncumulative and that the dividend to the preferred shareholders was (1) declared, and (2) not declared.

Calculate ratios.
(SO 5) AP

E14–13 The following financial information is available for Bank of Montreal as at October 31 (in millions, except for per share amounts):

	2008	2007	2006
Profit	$1,978	$2,131	$2,663
Preferred share dividends (total)	$73	$43	$30
Weighted average number of common shares	502	500	501
Dividends per common share	$2.80	$2.63	$2.13
Market price per common share	$43.02	$63.00	$68.99

Instructions

(a) Calculate the earnings per share, price-earnings ratio, and payout ratio for the common shareholders for each of the three years.

(b) Using the information in (a), comment on Bank of Montreal's earnings performance and dividend record.

Problems: Set A

Indicate impact of share and dividend transactions.
(SO 1) AP

P14–1A Savary Island Development Inc. has 200,000 common shares issued on November 1, 2010, the beginning of its fiscal year. Juanita Tolentino is the president and largest shareholder, owning 20% of the common shares. On November 1, the shares were trading on the Toronto Stock Exchange for $8 per share. The November 1 balances in Common Shares and Retained Earnings were $1 million and $500,000, respectively.

You have the following information about selected events and transactions that occurred during the fiscal year ended October 31, 2011:

Jan. 2 Savary Island issued 50,000 common shares for $10 per share in order to finance a new development project. Juanita purchased 10,000 of these shares in order to keep her 20% interest in the company.

May 1 The company effected a 3-for-2 stock split when the company's shares were trading at $12 per share. After the split, each share was trading at $8.

Aug. 31 Savary Island declared and issued a 3% stock dividend. The shares were trading at $9 on that day.

Oct. 31 The share price at the close of business was $11.

Instructions

Starting with the November 1 opening balances, indicate the impact of each transaction on the following:
(a) The balance in the Common Shares account
(b) The number of common shares issued by the company
(c) The balance in the Retained Earnings account
(d) The number of shares held by Juanita Tolentino
(e) The share price
(f) The fair value of Juanita Tolentino's portfolio of common shares

Taking It Further Why would Savary Island issue a stock dividend?

P14–2A The condensed balance sheet of Laporte Corporation reports the following:

Compare impact of cash dividend, stock dividend, and stock split.
(SO 1) AP

LAPORTE CORPORATION Balance Sheet (partial) June 30, 2011	
Total assets	$12,000,000
Liabilities and shareholders' equity	
Total liabilities	$ 4,000,000
Shareholders' equity	
Common shares, no par value, unlimited number authorized, 400,000 issued	2,000,000
Retained earnings	6,000,000
Total shareholders' equity	8,000,000
Total liabilities and shareholders' equity	$12,000,000

The market price of the common shares is currently $30 per share. Laporte wants to assess the impact of three possible alternatives on the corporation and its shareholders. The alternatives are:

1. Payment of a $1.50 per share cash dividend
2. Distribution of a 5% stock dividend
3. A 3-for-2 stock split

Instructions

(a) For each alternative, determine the impact on (1) assets, (2) liabilities, (3) common shares, (4) retained earnings, (5) total shareholders' equity, and (6) the number of shares.
(b) Assume a Laporte shareholder currently owns 1,000 common shares at a cost of $28,000. What is the impact of each alternative for the shareholder, assuming that the shares' market price changes proportionately with the alternative?

Taking It Further What are the advantages and disadvantages to the company of a stock split?

P14–3A On December 31, 2010, LeBlanc Corporation had the following shareholders' equity accounts:

Record and post transactions; prepare shareholders' equity section.
(SO 1, 2) AP

```
                        LEBLANC CORPORATION
                         Balance Sheet (partial)
                          December 31, 2010

Shareholders' equity
  Common shares (no par value, unlimited number of shares authorized,        $1,100,000
    90,000 issued)
  Retained earnings                                                             540,000
Total shareholders' equity                                                   $1,640,000
```

During the year, the following transactions occurred:

Jan. 15   Declared a $1 cash dividend per share to shareholders of record on January 31, payable February 15.

July 1   Announced a 3-for-2 stock split. The market price per share on the date of the announcement was $15.

Dec. 15   Declared a 10% stock dividend to shareholders of record on December 30, distributable on January 15. On December 15, the market price of each share was $10; on December 30, $12; and on January 15, $11.

31   Determined that profit before income taxes for the year was $450,000. The company has a 30% income tax rate.

Instructions

(a) Journalize the transactions and closing entries.
(b) Enter the beginning balances and post the entries in part (a) to the shareholders' equity accounts. (*Note*: Open additional shareholders' equity accounts as needed.)
(c) Prepare the shareholders' equity section of the balance sheet at December 31, 2011.

Taking It Further   Stock splits and stock dividends do not change the company's total assets. Given that, why does share price change after a stock split or stock dividend?

Prepare income statement and statement of retained earnings.
(SO 2, 3) AP

P14–4A   The ledger of Zurich Corporation at December 31, 2011, contains the following summary data:

Net sales	$1,700,000
Cost of goods sold	1,100,000
Operating expenses	260,000
Other revenues	20,000
Other expenses	28,000
Retained earnings, January 1	560,000
Dividends	40,000

Your analysis reveals the following additional information that is not included in the above data:

1. The Communication Devices division was discontinued on August 31. The profit from operations for the division up to that day was $20,000 before income taxes. The Communication Devices division was sold at a loss of $75,000 before income tax.

2. During the year, Zurich had a change in an accounting policy as a result of adopting Canadian GAAP for Private Enterprises. The cumulative effect of the change on prior years' profit was an increase of $60,000 before income taxes.

3. The company's income tax rate is 20%.

Instructions

(a) Prepare an income statement for 2011.
(b) Prepare a statement of retained earnings for 2011.

Taking It Further   Why report profit or losses from discontinued operations separate from profit or losses from continuing operations?

Prepare income statement and statement of retained earnings.
(SO 2, 3) AP

P14–5A   The ledger of Hyperchip Corporation at November 30, 2011, contains the following summary data:

Depreciation expense	$ 355,000	Other expenses	$ 83,000
Cash dividends	162,500	Other revenues	48,000
Common shares	325,000	Net sales	9,124,000
Cost of goods sold	7,280,000	Retained earnings,	
Operating expenses	1,120,000	December 1, 2010	755,000

Your analysis reveals the following additional information:

1. The company has a 25% income tax rate.
2. During the year, Hyperchip discovered a bookkeeping error that had recorded several months of interest expense twice. The cumulative effect of the error on prior years' income was an increase of $57,000 before income tax.

Instructions

(a) Prepare a multiple-step income statement for the year.
(b) Prepare a statement of retained earnings for the year ended November 30, 2011.

Taking It Further If an error from a previous period is found and corrected, why is it also important to restate the prior years' data shown for comparative purposes?

P14–6A The post-closing trial balance of Jajoo Corporation at December 31, 2011, contains the following shareholders' equity accounts:

Reproduce accounts and prepare a statement of retained earnings.
(SO 1, 2, 3) AP

$5-noncumulative preferred shares (10,000 issued)	$1,100,000
Common shares (400,000 issued)	2,000,000
Retained earnings	3,146,000

A review of the accounting records reveals the following:

1. The January 1, 2011, balance in Common Shares was $1,280,000 (320,000 shares), the balance in Contributed Capital—Reacquisition of Shares was $30,000, and the balance in Retained Earnings was $2,443,500.
2. One of the company's shareholders needed cash for a personal expenditure. On January 15, the company agreed to reacquire 20,000 shares from this shareholder for $7 per share.
3. On July 1, the company corrected a prior period error that resulted in a cumulative increase to the Investments account, as well as to the prior year's profit of $250,000 before income taxes.
4. On October 1, 100,000 common shares were sold for $8 per share.
5. The preferred shareholders' dividend was declared and paid in 2011 for two quarters. Due to a cash shortage, the last two quarters' dividends were not paid.
6. Profit for the year before income taxes was $760,000. The company has a 25% income tax rate.
7. On December 31, there was a $500,000 restriction of retained earnings as required by a debt covenant.

Instructions

(a) Starting with the January 1 balance, reproduce the Common Shares, Contributed Capital—Reacquisition of Common Shares, and Retained Earnings general ledger accounts for the year.
(b) Prepare a statement of retained earnings for the year.

Taking It Further Why is the correction of the prior period error recorded in the Retained Earnings account instead of being presented as a gain in the financial statements?

P14–7A The shareholders' equity accounts of Cedeno Inc. at December 31, 2010, are as follows:

Record and post transactions; prepare a statement of changes in shareholders' equity and shareholders' equity section.
(SO 1, 3, 4) AP

CEDENO INC.
Balance Sheet (partial)
December 31, 2010

Shareholders' equity

Common shares, no par value (unlimited number of shares authorized, 1,000,000 issued)	$3,000,000
Stock dividends distributable	400,000
Contributed capital—reacquired common shares	5,000
Retained earnings	1,200,000
Total shareholders' equity	$4,605,000

Cedeno has a 30% income tax rate. During 2011, the following transactions and events occurred:

Jan. 20 Issued 100,000 common shares as a result of a 10% stock dividend declared on December 15, 2010. The shares' fair value was $4 on December 15 and $5 on January 20.

Feb. 12 Issued 50,000 common shares for $5 per share.

Mar. 31 Corrected an error that had overstated the cost of goods sold for 2010 by $60,000.

Nov. 2 Reacquired 25,000 shares for $2.50 each.

Dec. 31 Declared a cash dividend to the common shareholders of $0.50 per share to shareholders of record at January 15, payable January 31.

31 Determined that profit $280,000.

31 Determined that other comprehensive loss was $28,000.

Instructions

(a) Journalize the transactions and summary closing entries.

(b) Enter the beginning balances, and post the entries in (a) to the shareholders' equity accounts. (*Note*: Open additional shareholders' equity accounts as needed.)

(c) Prepare a statement of changes in shareholders' equity.

(d) Prepare the shareholders' equity section of the balance sheet at December 31, 2011.

Taking It Further Why is the statement of changes in shareholders' equity not required of companies following Canadian GAAP for Private Enterprises?

Prepare a statement of changes in shareholders' equity.
(SO 4) AP

P14–8A The shareholders' equity accounts of Tmao, Inc. at December 31, 2010, are as follows:

TMAO INC.
Balance Sheet (partial)
December 31, 2010

Shareholders' equity

Preferred shares, $3-noncumulative, no par value, unlimited number authorized, 4,000 issued	$ 400,000
Common shares, no par value, unlimited number authorized, 160,000 issued	800,000
Retained earnings	450,000
Accumulated other comprehensive loss	(50,000)
Total shareholders' equity	$1,600,000

Tmao has a 35% income tax rate. During the following fiscal year, ended December 31, 2011, the company had the following transactions and events:

Feb. 1 Discovered a $70,000 understatement of 2010 depreciation expense.

July 12 Announced a 2-for-1 preferred stock split. The market price of the preferred shares at the date of announcement was $150.

Oct. 1 Adopted a new accounting policy that resulted in a cumulative decrease to prior years' profit of $30,000 before income tax.

Dec. 1 Declared a 10% stock dividend to common shareholders of record at December 20, distributable on January 12. The fair value of the common shares was $12 per share.

18 Declared the annual cash dividend ($1.50 post-split) to the preferred shareholders of record on January 10, 2012, payable on January 31, 2012.

31 Determined that for 2011, profit before income taxes was $350,000 and other comprehensive income, net of income tax expense of $35,000, was $65,000.

Instructions

Prepare a statement of changes in shareholders' equity for the year ended December 31, 2011.

Taking It Further Why is a statement of retained earnings no longer a requirement for companies reporting under IFRS?

P14–9A Suncor Energy Inc. reported the following selected accounts and information (in US$ millions), for the year ended December 31, 2008:

Prepare statement of comprehensive income, statement of changes in shareholders' equity, and shareholders' equity section.
(SO 2, 4) AP

Accumulated other comprehensive income (loss), January 1	$ (253)
Contributed capital, January 1	194
Share-based compensation expense (increase to contributed capital)	130
Profit	2,137
Shares issued under stock option plan (9,823 thousand shares)	226
Reduction to contributed capital for shares issued under stock option plan	36
Other comprehensive income items	350
Retained earnings, January 1	11,074
Dividends	180
Share capital, January 1 (925,566 thousand shares issued)	881
Stock dividend distributed (135 thousand shares)	6

Instructions

Prepare a statement of comprehensive income, a statement of changes in shareholders' equity, and the shareholders' equity section of the balance sheet.

Taking It Further Explain the two methods of preparing a statement of comprehensive income. Is one method better than the other?

P14–10A The shareholders' equity accounts of Blue Bay Logistics Ltd. on April 1, 2010, the beginning of the fiscal year, are as follows:

Calculate earnings per share.
(SO 5) AP

$6-preferred shares (20,000 issued)	$1,800,000
Common shares (500,000 issued)	3,750,000
Retained earnings	1,550,000
Total shareholders' equity	$7,100,000

During the year, the following transactions occurred:

2010
June 1 Reacquired 12,000 common shares for $9 per share.
July 1 Issued 50,000 common shares for $10 per share.
Sept. 30 Reacquired 8,000 common shares for $9.50 per share.

2011
Jan. 31 Issued 60,000 common shares in exchange for land. The land's fair value was $600,000.
Mar. 31 Profit for the year ended March 31, 2011, was $973,600.

Instructions

(a) Calculate the weighted average number of common shares for the year.
(b) Assuming the preferred shares are cumulative and one year in arrears:
   1. Calculate the earnings per share if no preferred dividends are declared during the year.
   2. Calculate the earnings per share if the preferred share dividends for the current and prior year are declared during the year.

(c) Assuming the preferred shares are noncumulative:
1. Calculate the earnings per share if no preferred share dividends are declared during the year.
2. Calculate the earnings per share if the company declares a preferred share dividend of $80,000.

Taking It Further Why is earnings per share an important measure for common shareholders but not for preferred shareholders?

Calculate ratios and comment.
(SO 5) AN

P14–11A The following selected information is available for Saputo Inc. for the year ended March 31:

(in millions, except market price)	2009	2008
Weighted average number of common shares	208	208
Profit	$ 279	$ 288
Total common cash dividends	112	95
Average shareholders' equity	1,796	1,576
Market price per common share	$20.94	$27.88

Saputo has no preferred shares.

Instructions

(a) Calculate the following ratios for 2009 and for 2008:
1. Return on equity
2. Earnings per share
3. Price-earnings ratio
4. Payout ratio

(b) Comment on the ratios for 2009 compared with the results for 2008.

Taking It Further Why is the presentation of fully diluted earnings per share required under IFRS, given that it is a *hypothetical* number?

Calculate and evaluate ratios with discontinued operations.
(SO 2, 5) AP

P14–12A Highlander Inc. reported the following selected information for the last three years (in millions, except for per share amounts):

	2011	2010	2009
Net sales	$4,000	$3,100	$2,600
Average shareholders' equity	3,400	2,400	1,800
Preferred dividends	20	20	15
Profit from continuing operations	$ 1,160	$ 810	$ 570
Loss on disposal of discontinued operations	340		
Loss from discontinued operations	110	80	70
Profit	$ 710	$ 730	$ 500
Weighted average number of common shares	300	290	280
Market price per share	$ 45.50	$33.65	$44.80

Instructions

(a) Calculate Highlander's return on equity, earnings per share, and price-earnings ratios before and after discontinued operations for 2011, 2010, and 2009.
(b) Evaluate Highlander's performance over the last three years before and after discontinued operations.
(c) Explain how reporting discontinued operations separately would affect your analysis of Highlander's performance.

Taking It Further Why is it important that discontinued operations be reported separately only if the operations qualify as a *component of an entity*?

Problems: Set B

P14–1B Gull Lake Enterprises Inc. had 100,000 common shares at July 1, 2010, the beginning of its fiscal year. Mark Bradbury is the president and largest shareholder, owning 25% of the common shares. On July 1, the common shares were trading on the Toronto Stock Exchange for $25 per share. Gull Lake Enterprises' Common Shares and Retained Earnings accounts had opening balances of $2 million and $350,000, respectively.

Indicate impact of share and dividend transactions.
(SO 1) AP

You have the following information about selected events and transactions that occurred during the year ended June 30, 2011:

Aug. 31   The company declared a 4% stock dividend to shareholders of record on September 15, distributable on September 30. The shares were trading at $28 per share on August 31, $30 on September 15, and $29 on September 30.

Dec. 1   The company issued 20,000 common shares for $30 per share. Mark Bradbury acquired 5,000 of these shares to keep his 25% interest in the company.

Mar. 31   The company's shares were trading at $26 per share and the company effected a 2-for-1 stock split. After the split, each share was trading at $13.

June 30   The share price at the close of business on June 30 was $15.

Instructions

Starting with the July 1 opening balances, indicate the impact of each transaction on the following:

(a) The balance in the Common Shares account
(b) The number of common shares issued by the company
(c) The balance in the Retained Earnings account
(d) The number of shares held by Mark Bradbury
(e) The share price
(f) The fair value of Mark Bradbury's portfolio of common shares

Taking It Further   Why would Gull Lake Enterprises issue a stock dividend?

P14–2B   The condensed balance sheet of Erickson Corporation reports the following:

Compare impact of cash dividend, stock dividend, and stock split.
(SO 1) AP

ERICKSON CORPORATION Balance Sheet (partial) January 31, 2011		
Total assets		$9,000,000
Liabilities and shareholders' equity		
Liabilities		$2,500,000
Shareholders' equity		
Common shares, no par value, unlimited number authorized, 500,000 issued	$3,000,000	
Retained earnings	3,500,000	6,500,000
Total liabilities and shareholders' equity		$9,000,000

The market price of the common shares is currently $30 per share. Erickson wants to assess the impact of three possible alternatives on the corporation and its shareholders. The alternatives are:

1. Payment of a $1.50 per share cash dividend
2. Distribution of a 5% stock dividend
3. A 2-for-1 stock split

Instructions

(a) For each alternative, determine the impact on (1) assets, (2) liabilities, (3) common shares, (4) retained earnings, (5) total shareholders' equity, and (6) the number of shares.

(b) Assume an Erickson shareholder currently owns 2,000 common shares at a cost of $50,000. What is the impact of each alternative for the shareholder, assuming that the market price of the shares changes proportionately with the alternative?

Taking It Further   What are the advantages and disadvantages to the company of a stock split?

Record and post transactions; prepare shareholders' equity section.
(SO 1, 2) AP

P14–3B   On December 31, 2010, Asaad Corporation had the following shareholders' equity accounts:

ASAAD CORPORATION
Balance Sheet (partial)
December 31, 2010

Shareholders' equity
  Common shares (no par value, unlimited number of shares authorized,
    75,000 shares issued) $1,700,000
  Retained earnings   600,000
  Total shareholders' equity $2,300,000

During the year, the following transactions occurred:

Feb. 1   Declared a $1 cash dividend to shareholders of record on February 15 and payable on March 1.

Apr. 1   Announced a 2-for-1 stock split. The market price per share was $36 on the date of the announcement.

Dec. 1   Declared a 5% stock dividend to shareholders of record on December 20, distributable on January 5. On December 1, the shares' market price was $16 per share; on December 20, it was $18 per share; and on January 5, it was $15 per share.

   31   Determined that profit before income taxes for the year was $400,000. The company has a 25% income tax rate.

Instructions

(a) Journalize the transactions and closing entries.
(b) Enter the beginning balances, and post the entries in (a) to the shareholders' equity accounts. (*Note*: Open additional shareholders' equity accounts as needed.)
(c) Prepare the shareholders' equity section of the balance sheet at December 31, 2011.

Taking It Further   Stock splits and stock dividends do not change the company's total assets. Given that, why does share price change after a stock split or stock dividend?

Prepare an income statement and statement of retained earnings.
(SO 2, 3) AP

P14–4B   The ledger of Hyperchip Corporation at November 30, 2011, contains the following summary data:

Net sales	$1,500,000
Cost of goods sold	800,000
Operating expenses	240,000
Other revenues	40,000
Other expenses	30,000
Retained earnings, December 1, 2010	1,050,000
Dividends	45,000

Your analysis reveals the following additional information that is not included in the above data:

1. The ceramics division was discontinued on August 31. The loss from operations for this division before income tax was $150,000. The ceramics division was sold at a pre-tax gain of $70,000.
2. During the year, Hyperchip changed an accounting policy as the result of adopting Canadian GAAP for Private Enterprises. The cumulative effect of the change on prior years' profit was a decrease of $30,000 before income tax.
3. The income tax rate on all items is 25%.

Instructions

(a) Prepare an income statement for the year ended November 30, 2011.

(b) Prepare a statement of retained earnings for the year ended November 30, 2011.

Taking It Further Why report profit or losses from discontinued operations separately from profit or losses from continuing operations?

P14–5B The ledger of Coquitlam Corporation at December 31, 2011, contains the following summary data:

Prepare income statement and statement of retained earnings.
(SO 2, 3) AP

Cash dividends—common	$ 125,000	Other revenues	$ 47,000
Cost of goods sold	1,088,000	Retained earnings,	
Operating expenses	551,000	January 1, 2011	642,000
Other expenses	28,000	Net sales	1,750,000

Your analysis reveals the following additional information:

1. The company has a 25% income tax rate.
2. In 2010, the company incorrectly recorded sales revenue of $66,000 that should have been recorded as revenue in 2011. This error has not been corrected in the above amounts.

Instructions

(a) Prepare a multiple-step income statement for the year.

(b) Prepare a statement of retained earnings for the year.

Taking It Further If an error from a previous period is found and corrected, why is it also important to restate the prior year's data shown for comparative purposes?

P14–6B The post-closing trial balance of Michaud Corporation at December 31, 2011, contains the following shareholders' equity accounts:

Reproduce accounts and prepare statement of retained earnings.
(SO 1, 2, 3) AP

$4-cumulative preferred shares (15,000 shares issued)	$ 850,000
Common shares (250,000 shares issued)	3,200,000
Contributed capital—reacquisition of common shares	20,000
Retained earnings	1,418,000

A review of the accounting records reveals the following:

1. The January 1 opening balance in Common Shares was $3,210,000 (255,000 shares) and the balance in Retained Earnings was $980,000.
2. On March 1, 20,000 common shares were sold for $15.50 per share.
3. One of the company's shareholders needed cash for personal reasons. On July 1, the company agreed to reacquire 25,000 shares from this shareholder for $12 per share.
4. On September 1, the company discovered a $60,000 error that overstated sales in 2010. The net-of-tax effect was properly debited to Retained Earnings. The company has a 30% income tax rate.
5. The preferred shareholders' dividend was declared and paid in 2011 for three quarters. Due to a cash shortage, the last quarter's dividend was not paid.
6. Profit for the year before income taxes was $750,000.
7. On December 31, there was a $250,000 restriction of retained earnings, as required by a debt covenant.

Instructions

(a) Starting with the January 1 balance, reproduce the Common Shares and Retained Earnings general ledger accounts for the year.

(b) Prepare a statement of retained earnings for the year.

Taking It Further Why is the prior period adjustment for the error in 2010 sales recorded in the Retained Earnings account instead of being a correction to sales in the 2011 financial statements?

Record and post transactions; prepare a statement of changes in shareholders' equity and the shareholders' equity section of the balance sheet.
(SO 1, 3, 4) AP

P14–7B The shareholders' equity accounts of Fryman Ltd. at December 31, 2010, are as follows:

FRYMAN LTD.	
Balance Sheet (partial)	
December 31, 2010	
Shareholders' equity	
Preferred shares, $4-noncumulative, no par value, unlimited	
number authorized, 12,000 issued	$ 800,000
Common shares, no par value, unlimited number authorized, 250,000 issued	500,000
Contributed capital—reacquired common shares	100,000
Retained earnings	900,000
Accumulated other comprehensive loss	(50,000)
Total shareholders' equity	$2,250,000

During 2011, the company had the following transactions and events:

Aug. 1   Discovered a $45,000 understatement of 2010 cost of goods sold. The company has a 30% income tax rate.

Oct. 15 Declared a 10% stock dividend to common shareholders of record on October 31, distributable on November 10. The fair value of the common shares was $18 per share on October 15, $19 per share on October 31, and $20 per share on November 10.

Dec. 15 Declared the annual cash dividend to the preferred shareholders of record on December 31, payable on January 15, 2012.

31   Determined that other comprehensive income for the year was $12,000 and profit was $395,000.

31   Recognized a $200,000 restriction of retained earnings for a plant expansion.

Instructions

(a) Journalize the transactions and summary closing entries.

(b) Enter the beginning balances in the accounts and post to the shareholders' equity accounts. (*Note*: Open additional shareholders' equity accounts as needed.)

(c) Prepare a statement of changes in shareholders' equity for the year.

(d) Prepare the shareholders' equity section of the balance sheet at December 31, 2011.

Taking It Further Why is the statement of changes in shareholders' equity not required for companies following Canadian GAAP for Private Enterprises?

Prepare a statement of changes in shareholders' equity.
(SO 4) AP

P14–8B The shareholders' equity accounts of Kanada Inc. at September 30, 2010, are as follows:

KANADA INC.	
Balance Sheet (partial)	
September 30, 2010	
Shareholders' equity	
Preferred shares, $5-noncumulative, no par value,	
unlimited number authorized, 6,000 issued	$ 465,000
Common shares, no par value, unlimited number authorized, 25,000 issued	900,000
Retained earnings	540,000
Accumulated other comprehensive income	95,000
Total shareholders' equity	$2,000,000

Kanada has a 30% income tax rate. During the following fiscal year, ended September 30, 2011, Kanada had the following transactions and events:

Mar. 14 Declared a 4% common stock dividend to shareholders of record at March 31, distributable on April 5. The fair value of the common shares was $10 per share on March 14, $11 on March 31, and $12 on April 5.

July 7 It was discovered that the computer system was incorrectly aging accounts receivable and therefore overestimating bad debts. The total effect of the error on prior years' profit was an increase of $33,000 before income tax.

Aug. 1 Discovered a $54,000 overstatement of cost of goods sold in the prior year's income statement.

Sept. 20 Declared the annual dividend payable to the preferred shareholders of record on October 5, payable on October 31.

25 Announced a 2-for-1 common stock split. The market price of the common shares at the date of announcement was $15 per share.

30 Determined that other comprehensive income for the year was $27,000 and profit before income taxes was $325,000.

Instructions

Prepare a statement of changes in shareholders' equity for the year ended September 30, 2011.

Taking It Further Why is a statement of retained earnings no longer a requirement for companies reporting under IFRS?

P14–9B Canadian National Railway Company reported the following selected accounts and information (in millions) for the year ended December 31, 2008:

Accumulated other comprehensive loss, January 1	$ 31
Common shares, January 1 (485.2 million shares issued)	4,283
Dividends	436
Average cost of shares reacquired (19.4 million shares)	172
"Loss" on reacquisition of shares	849
Shares issued under stock option plan (2.4 million shares)	68
Profit	1,895
Other comprehensive loss items	124
Retained earnings, January 1	5,925

Prepare statement of comprehensive income, statement of changes in shareholders' equity, and shareholders' equity section. (SO 2, 4) AP

Instructions

Prepare a statement of comprehensive income, a statement of changes in shareholders' equity, and the shareholders' equity section of the balance sheet.

Taking It Further Explain the two methods of preparing a statement of comprehensive income. Is one method better than the other?

P14–10B The shareholders' equity accounts of Gualtieri Inc. on August 1, 2010, the beginning of its fiscal year, are as follows:

Calculate earnings per share. (SO 5) AP

$4-preferred shares (25,000 issued)	$1,250,000
Common shares (350,000 issued)	3,750,000
Retained earnings	2,250,000
Total shareholders' equity	$7,250,000

During the year, the following transactions occurred:

Nov. 30 Issued 37,500 common shares for $12 per share.

Feb. 1 Reacquired 6,000 common shares for $10 per share.

Mar. 1 Issued 30,000 common shares in exchange for equipment. The equipment's fair value was $40,000.

July 31 Profit for the year ended July 31, 2011, was $1,022,800.

Instructions

(a) Calculate the weighted average number of common shares for the year.

(b) Assuming the preferred shares are cumulative and one year in arrears:
1. Calculate the earnings per share if no preferred dividends are declared during the year.
2. Calculate the earnings per share if the preferred share dividends for the current and prior year are declared during the year.

(c) Assuming the preferred shares are noncumulative:
1. Calculate the earnings per share if no preferred share dividends are declared during the year.
2. Calculate the earnings per share if the company declares a preferred share dividend of $60,000.

Taking It Further Why is it important to use a weighted average number of shares in the earnings per share calculations? Why not just use the average number of shares during the year?

Calculate ratios and comment.
(SO 5) AN

P14–11B The following selected information is available for National Bank of Canada for the year ended October 31:

(in millions, except market price)	2008	2007
Weighted average number of common shares	159	160
Profit	$ 776	$ 541
Total common cash dividends	394	364
Total preferred cash dividends	$ 32	$ 21
Average common shareholders' equity	4,598	4,439
Market price per common share	$45.21	$54.65

Instructions

(a) Calculate the following ratios for 2008 and for 2007:
1. Return on common shareholders' equity   3. Price-earnings ratio
2. Earnings per share   4. Payout ratio for common shareholders

(b) Comment on the ratios for 2008 compared with the results for 2007.

Taking It Further Why is the presentation of fully diluted earnings per share required under IFRS, given that it is a *hypothetical* number?

Calculate and evaluate ratios with discontinued operations.
(SO 2, 5) AP

P14–12B All Care Inc. reported the following selected information for the last three years (in millions, except for per share amounts):

	2011	2010	2009
Sales and operating revenues	$20,300	$24,900	$23,800
Average shareholders' equity	3,400	2,400	1,900
Preferred dividends	80	80	60
Profit from continuing operations	$ 1,250	$ 1,130	$ 990
Loss on disposal of discontinued operations	620		
Loss from discontinued operations	200	150	180
Profit	$ 430	$ 980	$ 810
Weighted average number of common shares	450	470	460
Market price per share	$ 24.40	$ 19.88	$ 21.60

Instructions

(a) Calculate All Care's return on equity, earnings per share, and price-earnings ratios before and after discontinued operations for 2011, 2010, and 2009.

(b) Evaluate All Care's performance over the last three years before and after discontinued operations.

(c) How would reporting discontinued operations affect your analysis of All Care's performance.

Taking It Further Why is it important that discontinued operations be reported separately only if the operations qualify as a *component of an entity*?

Continuing Cookie Chronicle

(*Note*: This is a continuation of the Cookie Chronicle from Chapters 1 through 13.)

After deciding that their company's fiscal year end was going be October 31, Natalie and Curtis begin operating Cookie & Coffee Creations Ltd. on November 1, 2011. As at that date, after the issue of shares, the share capital section of the company's balance sheet is as follows:

Share capital	
Preferred shares, $0.50-noncumulative, no par value,	
10,000 shares authorized, 2,000 issued	$10,000
Common shares, no par value, unlimited number of shares	
authorized, 24,850 issued	24,750

The company has the following selected transactions during its first year of operations:

Dec. 1 Issues an additional 500 preferred shares to Natalie's brother for $2,500.

Apr. 30 Declares a semi-annual dividend to the preferred shareholders of record on May 15, payable on June 1.

June 30 Repurchases 1,200 shares issued to the lawyer, for $1,300. The lawyer had decided to retire and wanted to liquidate all of her assets.

Oct. 31 The company has had a very successful first year of operations. It earned revenues of $475,000 and incurred expenses of $385,000 (excluding income tax).

31 Records income tax expense (the company has a 20% income tax rate).

31 Declares a semi-annual dividend to the preferred shareholders of record on November 15, payable on December 1.

Instructions

(a) Prepare the journal entries to record the above transactions.

(b) Prepare the statement of retained earnings for the year ended October 31, 2012.

(c) Prepare the shareholders' equity section of the balance sheet as at October 31, 2012.

(d) Prepare the closing entries.

(e) Cookie & Coffee Creations Ltd. reports its financial statement information using Canadian GAAP for Private Enterprises. If Cookie & Coffee Creations Ltd. were to report this information using IFRS, what changes to the financial statements would be required?

(f) Do you think the additional information IFRS provides would make any difference to those using the financial statements of Cookie & Coffee Creations Ltd.? Do you think that using Canadian GAAP for Private Enterprises is the better choice for Cookie & Coffee Creations Ltd.? Why or why not?

BROADENING YOUR PERSPECTIVE

Financial Reporting and Analysis

Financial Reporting Problem

BYP14–1 Refer to the consolidated financial statements and accompanying notes for The Forzani Group Ltd. reproduced in Appendix A.

Instructions

(a) Did Forzani pay, or distribute, any dividends in fiscal 2009? If yes, how much? If no, why might a company choose not to pay dividends?
(b) Did Forzani report any of the following in fiscal 2009: (1) other comprehensive income, (2) prior period adjustments, or (3) restricted retained earnings?
(c) Did Forzani provide a statement of changes in shareholders' equity for fiscal 2009? If not, where did it tell users about the changes in shareholders' equity items?
(d) Basic EPS of $0.94 for 2009 was reported in the chapter in Illustration 14-10. How much was basic EPS for 2008? Did EPS improve or weaken in 2009?
(e) Did Forzani report any fully diluted EPS in fiscal 2009 and 2008? If yes, what was the difference between these amounts and the basic EPS in each year?
(f) Forzani's price-earnings ratio for 2009 was reported in the chapter in Illustration 14-11. Its price-earnings ratio for 2008 was 11.1 times. Did the price-earnings ratio improve or weaken in 2009? Is your answer consistent with your findings in part (c)? Explain.

Interpreting Financial Statements

BYP14–2 Newfoundland Capital Corporation Limited (NCC), known as Newcap Radio, is one of Canada's leading radio broadcasters, with 81 licences across the country. On November 24, 2009, the company declared a 3-for-1 stock split on its Class A and B shares, for shareholders of record on November 25, 2009, to be distributed November 27, 2009. Financial information for NCC for the years ended December 31, 2008 and 2007, follows (in thousands, except per share data):

	2008	2007
Profit (loss) for the year	$(4,369)	$20,313
Shareholders' equity at December 31	90,677	104,952
Cash dividends declared during the year	3,298	3,327
Cash dividends per share declared during the year	$0.30	$0.30
Class A share price per share at December 31	$17.00	$20.05
Number of shares outstanding (at year end)	10,991	11,091
Weighted average number of shares outstanding	11,016	11,460

Instructions

(a) Explain the different effects that a cash dividend, stock dividend, and stock split would have on NCC's assets, liabilities, shareholders' equity, and the number of shares outstanding.
(b) What is the likely reason that NCC has split its shares?
(c) The market price for the Class A shares before the stock split November 24, 2009, was $22. What do you think the market price for a share would be immediately after the stock split?
(d) The cash dividend declared on Class A shares in 2008 was $0.30 before the stock split. How much would you expect it to be after the stock split?
(e) Calculate the return on shareholders' equity, earnings per share, and payout ratio for the shareholders for 2008 and 2007. Comment on the company's profitability. Shareholders' equity at December 31, 2006, was $90,922.

Critical Thinking

Collaborative Learning Activity

Note to instructor: Additional instructions and material for this group activity can be found on the Instructor Resource Site.

BYP14–3 In this group activity, you will review the impact of dividend and share transactions on shareholders' equity.

Instructions

(a) Your instructor will divide the class into groups. Each student will receive information on a company's shareholders' equity accounts, and dividend and share transactions. Each group will be divided into two subgroups. One of the subgroups will complete the instructions in the first item below; the other subgroup will follow the second set of instructions:

1. Prepare journal entries for each of the transactions. Then prepare the shareholders' equity section of the balance sheet at the end of the year without preparing a statement of changes in shareholders' equity.
2. Prepare a statement of changes in shareholders' equity without preparing journal entries. Then prepare the shareholders' equity section of the balance sheet at the end of the year.

(c) The two subgroups will return to their group and compare the shareholders' equity section of the balance sheet prepared by each subgroup. The group will also compare the journal entries prepared by the first subgroup to the statement of changes in shareholders' equity prepared by the second subgroup. Based on the comparison, the group will correct its journal entries and statements if necessary.

(d) Each group will hand in the journal entries, the statement of changes in shareholders' equity and the shareholders' section of the balance sheet at the end of the year.

Communication Activity

BYP14–4 Earnings per share is the most commonly cited financial ratio. Indeed, share prices rise and fall in reaction to a company's earnings per share. The price-earnings ratio is also published in many newspapers' stock market listings.

WILEY PLUS

Writing Handbook

Instructions

Write a memo explaining why earnings per share and the price-earnings ratio are so important to investors. Explain how both ratios are calculated and how they relate to each other. Include in your memo an explanation of how to interpret a high or low price-earnings ratio. Also comment on why you think earnings per share is not required to be reported under Canadian GAAP for Private Enterprises.

Ethics Case

BYP14–5 Flambeau Corporation has paid 40 consecutive quarterly cash dividends (10 years' worth). Increasing competition over the last six months has greatly squeezed profit margins. With only enough cash to meet day-to-day operating needs, the president, Vince Ramsey, has decided that a stock dividend instead of a cash dividend should be declared. He tells Flambeau's financial vice-president, Janice Rahn, to issue a press release stating that the company is extending its consecutive dividend record with the issue of a 5% stock dividend. "Write the press release to convince the shareholders that the stock dividend is just as good as a cash dividend," he orders. "Just watch our share price rise when we announce the stock dividend. It must be a good thing if that happens."

WILEY PLUS

Ethics in Accounting

Instructions

(a) Who are the stakeholders in this situation?
(b) Is there anything unethical about Ramsey's intentions or actions?
(c) As a shareholder, would you rather receive a cash dividend or a stock dividend? Why?

"All About You" Activity

BYP14–6 In the "All About You" feature, we learned about stock compensation plans. When employees are granted stock options, they are given the opportunity to purchase shares at a date in the future at a specific price referred to as the exercise price. If the share price is higher than the exercise price, the employees will buy the shares and sell them on the market at a profit. However, if the stock price falls, employees are left with little or no benefit.

You are a recent graduate from a post-secondary business school and you have been offered a position at Technology Is Us, a start-up private company that has developed and patented a new technology to use solar energy. The company hopes to go public in about a year. You have been offered a choice of compensation packages. Option #1 is an annual salary of $50,000, and health benefits. Option #2 is an annual salary of $38,000, health benefits, and 25,000 stock options with an exercise price of $5.00. The options can be exercised one year after the company goes public.

Instructions

(a) What are the advantages and disadvantages of Option #1?
(b) What are the advantages and disadvantages of Option #2?
(c) What would you need to know about your personal finances before choosing a compensation package?
(d) What information would you want to know about the company and the industry it is in before deciding to accept Option #2?

If Technology Is Us were an established company already trading on the public markets, would the advantages and disadvantages of Option #2 be different? Explain.

ANSWERS TO CHAPTER QUESTIONS

Answers to Accounting in Action Insight Questions

Business Insight, p. 769

Q: Why would suspending its dividend send a message to Teck Resources' banks? What was the risk to Teck Resources of suspending its dividend?

A: The amount and timing of paying a dividend is completely under a corporation's control, but companies cannot control if and when they pay their debts. In this case, because of the collapse in the markets, Teck Resources not only needed to show it had a plan to repay its debt, it also needed to make sure that none of the banks would ask for early repayment of the debt. This could have pushed the company into bankruptcy. Cutting a dividend can result in unhappy shareholders and reduced stock prices, but the bigger threat to the company's immediate survival was unhappy creditors. Thus, by suspending its dividend, Teck Resources was sending a message that the banks were its priority.

Across the Organization, p. 774

Q: When senior managers were making a decision about the 1-for-20 reverse stock split, should they have expected the stock price to drop?

A: Theoretically, if the shares were trading at $1.16 the day before the 1-for-20 reverse stock split, they should have traded at 20 times that amount, or $23.20, the day after. Neither a stock split nor a reverse stock split changes the percentage ownership of any of the shareholders, and should not, in theory, affect the share price. The fact that the share price was $18.22 the day after the reverse split (down 21% from $23.20) indicates that investors felt the reverse split was a negative signal. Some investors may have been concerned about the impact on future dividend payments. Others may not have fully understood a reverse split and may have seen it as an attempt to reduce their holdings. Senior management may have anticipated this reaction, but might have gone ahead with the split hoping to stop the slide in the value of the company's shares.

All About You, p. 789

Q: Why do companies use stock options and stock savings plans to partially compensate employees?

A: Stock options and stock savings plans give the employees an opportunity to share in the company's future success as the share price increases. Employees' ability to share in corporate success helps companies attract and keep motivated and loyal employees. Stock-based compensation plans also help companies conserve cash by reducing salaries.

Answer to Forzani Review It Question 5, p. 774

Forzani declared and paid dividends of $9.3 million in 2009. Each Class A common share received an annual dividend of $0.30 per share, paid in quarterly instalments of $0.075 per share. There were no stock splits.

Answers to Self-Study Questions

1. c   2. d   3. b   4. b   5. d   6. a   7. c   8. c   9. d   10. c

Remember to go
back to the beginning
of the chapter to
check off your
completed work!

←

CHAPTER 15
LONG-TERM LIABILITIES

hydroquebec.com

THE NAVIGATOR

- ☐ Understand *Concepts for Review*
- ☐ Read *Feature Story*
- ☐ Scan *Study Objectives*
- ☐ Read *Chapter Preview*
- ☐ Read text and answer *Before You Go On*
- ☐ Work *Demonstration Problems*
- ☐ Review *Summary of Study Objectives*
- ☐ Answer *Self-Study Questions*
- ☐ Complete assignments

CONCEPTS FOR REVIEW:

Before studying this chapter, you should understand or, if necessary, review:

a. How to record adjusting entries for interest expense. (Ch. 3, pp. 130–131)

b. What a current liability is, and what a long-term liability is. (Ch. 4, pp. 195–196 and Ch. 10, pp. 558–563)

c. How to record entries for the issue of notes payable and related interest expense. (Ch. 10, pp. 559-560)

d. How to calculate return on equity and earnings per share. (Ch. 13, p. 737 and Ch. 14, pp. 787–788)

Debt Issue Injects Power into Electric Company

Hydro-Québec generates, transmits, and distributes electricity for residents and businesses throughout the province of Quebec. This requires developing hydro-electric power to meet growing demand. The company conducts energy-related research and develops new generation, transmission, and distribution technologies. Its projects may include building hydroelectric facilities, refurbishing generating stations, adding transmission capacity, connecting communities to the grid, expanding energy interchanges with Ontario, or purchasing wind power from independent producers.

This type of development obviously requires a significant amount of capital. As Hydro-Québec's sole shareholder, the Quebec government guarantees most of its borrowings, which can be quite substantial.

The company raises funds by issuing bonds. For example, two issues were launched in January 2009, each for $500 million. These debentures, which will mature on February 15, 2050, were issued at premium prices; that is, prices that are above their face value. The coupon rate was 5%, but the yield rates were 4.907% and 4.990%. Having a yield rate that is less than the coupon rate reduces the cost of borrowing for the company since the net proceeds will be slightly more than $500 million for each issue.

Hydro-Québec's decision to take on this long-term debt is simply "a question of cost," says Jean-Hugues Lafleur, Vice President, Financing, Treasury and Pension Fund. "[To have a rate] below 5% is a good opportunity to finance the company... Considering that inflation on a long-term basis is around 2% and being able to finance the company at below 5%, the real cost of the interest rate is something like 3%."

The funds will be used for Hydro-Québec's investment program and the refinancing of debt. "Our company has very long-term assets, so it just makes sense in terms of asset-liability management to issue long-term paper," Mr. Lafleur continues. "Most of our investment program is to build long-term facilities such as dams or generating stations. The depreciation periods for these assets are 50 years or more."

Hydro-Québec's financing program is set at approximately $2 billion, so the company expected to issue another $1 billion in bonds in 2009. Part of its financing and debt management strategy is to stagger debt maturities to maintain the stability of the annual financing program. These recent bond issues are added to others issued in previous years, all maturing on different dates. They are reported on the financial statements as liabilities, and will be amortized over the duration of the debt at the yield to maturity rate, not the coupon rate.

The electricity company's investment and financing strategy has been effective. Credit rating agencies such as Moody's and Standard & Poor's all give Hydro-Québec an A rating or better.

The lead manager for Hydro-Québec's bond issues was National Bank Financial Inc., with CIBC World Markets Inc., Scotia Capital Inc., BMO Nesbitt Burns Inc., Casgrain & Company Limited, Desjardins Securities Inc., Laurentian Bank Securities Inc., Merrill Lynch Canada Inc., RBC Dominion Securities Inc., and the Toronto Dominion Bank acting as other managers. With that type of backing, coupled with its success in debt management and research and investment, the Quebec utility will no doubt be able to continue to finance itself easily on the bond markets.

The Navigator

STUDY OBJECTIVES:

After studying this chapter, you should be able to:

1. Compare the impact of issuing debt instead of equity.
2. Account for bonds payable.
3. Account for long-term notes payable.
4. Account for leases.
5. Explain and illustrate the methods for the presentation and analysis of long-term liabilities.
6. Apply the effective-interest method of amortizing bond discounts and premiums (Appendix 15A).

The Navigator

As you can see from the feature story, Hydro-Québec borrowed $1 billion in January 2009 by issuing bonds. The bonds will mature on February 15, 2050, and the funds borrowed will be used to finance long-term assets such as dams or generating stations. The bonds are classified as long-term liabilities because they are obligations that are not due within the next year. In this chapter, we will explain the accounting for the major types of long-term liabilities reported on the balance sheet. These liabilities include bonds, long-term notes, and lease obligations.

The chapter is organized as follows:

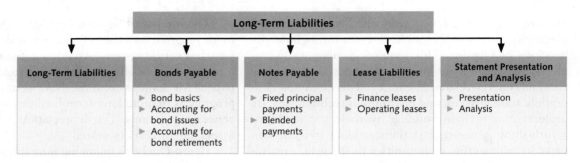

Long-Term Liabilities

STUDY OBJECTIVE 1

Compare the impact of issuing debt instead of equity.

Alternative terminology
Long-term liabilities are also referred to as *non-current liabilities*.

You will recall from Chapter 10 that a current liability is an obligation (debt) that is expected to be settled within one year from the balance sheet date or the company's normal operating cycle, whichever is longer. Debt that is not current is a **long-term liability**. Common examples of long-term liabilities include bonds payable, notes payable, and finance leases. These are all examples of financial instruments, which were introduced in Chapter 13. More specifically, long-term liabilities such as these are referred to as *financial liabilities* because there is a contract between two or more parties to pay cash in the future.

Just as people need money for long periods of time, so do companies. Sometimes, large corporations need much more money than the average bank can lend for certain types of projects, such as purchasing another company or constructing dams and generating stations like Hydro-Québec does. The solution is to raise money by issuing debt securities (e.g., bonds payable) or equity securities (e.g., common shares) to the investing public. In this way, thousands of investors each lend part of the capital that is needed. By issuing bonds, Hydro-Québec was able to raise $1 billion in January 2009 and planned to raise an additional $1 billion in 2009.

Whenever a company decides that it needs long-term financing, it must first decide if it should issue debt or equity. For a corporation that wants long-term financing, debt offers some advantages over equity, as shown in Illustration 15-1.

To show the potential effect on earnings per share and return on equity, assume that Microsystems Inc. is considering two plans for financing the construction of a new $5-million plant. Plan A is to use equity by issuing 200,000 common shares for $25 per share. Plan B is to use debt by issuing $5 million of 6% bonds payable. Once the new plant is built, Microsystems expects to earn an additional $1.5 million of profit before interest and income tax. The income tax rate is expected to be 30%. Microsystems has 100,000 common shares and shareholders' equity of $2.5 million, before including the common shares and profit expected to be generated by each plan.

	1. Shareholder control is not affected. Debtholders do not have voting rights, so shareholders keep full control of the company.
	2. Income tax savings result. Interest expense is deductible for income tax purposes. Dividends are not.
	3. Earnings per share may be higher. Although interest expense reduces net income, earnings per share is often higher under debt financing because no additional common shares are issued.
	4. Return on equity may be higher. Although net income is lower, return on equity is often higher under debt financing because shareholders' equity is proportionately lower than net income.

◄ Illustration 15-1

Advantages of debt over equity financing

The effects on earnings per share and return on equity for each plan are shown in Illustration 15-2.

	Plan A: Issue Equity	Plan B: Issue Debt
Profit before interest and income tax	$1,500,000	$1,500,000
Interest expense	0	300,000[6]
Profit before income tax	1,500,000	1,200,000
Income tax expense	450,000[1]	360,000[7]
Profit	$1,050,000	$ 840,000
Number of shares	300,000[2]	100,000
Earnings per share	$3.50[3]	$8.40[8]
Shareholders' equity	$8,550,000[4]	$3,340,000[9]
Return on equity	12%[5]	25%[10]

Calculations:
[1] 30% × $1,500,000 = $450,000
[2] 100,000 + 200,000 = 300,000
[3] $1,050,000 ÷ 300,000 = $3.50
[4] $2,500,000 + $5,000,000 + $1,050,000 = $8,550,000
[5] $1,050,000 ÷ $8,550,000 = 12%

[6] $5,000,000 × 6% = $300,000
[7] 30% × $1,200,000 = $360,000
[8] $840,000 ÷ 100,000 = $8.40
[9] $2,500,000 + $840,000 = $3,340,000
[10] $840,000 ÷ $3,340,000 = 25%

◄ Illustration 15-2

Comparison of effects of issuing equity vs. debt

Profit is $210,000 ($1,050,000 − $840,000) lower with long-term debt financing. But when this profit is spread over 200,000 fewer shares, earnings per share jumps from $3.50 per share to $8.40 per share. We learned about earnings per share in Chapter 14. Earnings per share is calculated by dividing the profit available for the common shareholders by the weighted average number of shares. For this illustration, we have assumed that the shares were issued for the entire period.

After seeing the effect of debt on earnings per share, one might ask why companies do not rely exclusively on debt financing rather than equity financing. The answer is that debt is riskier than equity because interest must be paid regularly each period and the principal (face value) of the debt must be paid at maturity. If a company is unable to pay its interest or principal, creditors could force the company to sell its assets to repay its liabilities. In contrast, if equity is issued, a company is not required to pay dividends or repay the shareholders' investment.

Even if it is riskier, most companies still choose to issue debt. They do this because money that is borrowed increases earnings per share and it also produces a higher return on equity for the shareholders. You may have heard the saying about "using other people's money to make money." In general, debt can increase the return on equity if the company can borrow at one rate and invest the borrowed money in company operations that earn a higher rate. Borrowing at one rate and investing at a different rate is known as **financial leverage**. Financial leverage is said to be "positive" if the rate of return is higher than the rate of borrowing. It is said to be "negative" if the rate of return is lower than the rate of borrowing.

As we can see in Illustration 15-2, Microsystems' return on equity increases from 12% in Plan A, where equity financing is used, to 25% in Plan B, where debt financing is used. Even though profit is lower under debt financing, there is much less equity to spread the profit across. If equity financing is used, shareholders' equity is $8,550,000. If debt financing is used, shareholders' equity is only $3,340,000. In Chapter 13, we learned that the return on equity ratio is calculated by dividing profit by average shareholders' equity. For this illustration, we have assumed that the shareholders' equity is the average amount.

Each company must decide what the right mix of debt and equity is for its particular circumstances. There is a risk with debt financing, and the risk increases with the amount of debt a company has. The risk that goes with debt must be compared with the return that can be generated by using debt. As we have just seen, earnings per share and return on equity can improve with the use of debt. Later in this chapter, we will introduce some ratios that will help us evaluate whether a company has too much debt or if the debt is reasonable.

 ### ACCOUNTING IN ACTION: ALL ABOUT YOU

Having enough cash to pay for education and living expenses while going to college or university is often a problem for students. One of the options for students is to use student loans. The federal, provincial, and territorial governments as well as private financial institutions all offer student loan programs.

Just like a business, a student can benefit from financial leverage, by borrowing for an education that will result in higher future earnings. Research released by the Canada Millennium Scholarship Foundation in June 2009, shows that post-secondary graduates are more likely to be employed, and they earn more than those who do not continue their studies past high school. Over their working life, a college graduate will earn $394,000 more than a high school graduate, while a bachelor's degree holder will earn $745,800 more.

While student loan programs offer interest-free financing while the student is in school, eventually they have to be paid. Just as with businesses, too much leverage can result in graduates struggling to make their loan payments.

Source: Joseph Berger and Andrew Parkin, *The Price of Knowledge: Access and Student Finance in Canada,* Vol. 4, Chapter 1: "The Value of a Degree: Education and Earnings in Canada," June 2009. Available at: http://www.millenniumscholarships.ca/images/Publications/090623_POKIV_Ch1_EN.pdf

What should you consider in your decision about how much is appropriate to borrow for your education?

BEFORE YOU GO ON . . .

➡ Review It

1. What is the difference between a current and a long-term liability?
2. What are the advantages of debt financing over equity financing?
3. Why can debt financing result in an improved earnings per share and return on equity ratio?

➡ Do It

Nuens Ltd. is considering two alternatives to finance the purchase of new manufacturing equipment at the beginning of the year. The new equipment will increase profit before interest and tax by $3 million annually. The alternatives are:

(a) issue 100,000 shares at a market price of $20 per share, or
(b) issue $2 million of 5% bonds at face value.

Nuens has 400,000 common shares outstanding and $4 million of shareholders' equity. The tax rate is 30%.

Calculate the effects of each of the alternatives on earnings per share.

Action Plan

Alternative (a): Issue 100,000 common shares at a market price of $20 per share

- Apply the tax rate to the increase in profit to determine the income tax expense.
- Deduct the income tax expense calculated from the increase in profit before interest and tax to determine the profit.

- Add the additional shares issued to the shares outstanding to determine the weighted average number of shares.
- Divide profit by the weighted average number of shares.

Alternative (b): Issue $2 million of 5% bonds at face value

- Apply the interest rate on the bonds to the amount of bonds issued to determine the interest expense.
- Deduct the interest expense from the increase in profit before interest and tax to determine the profit before tax.
- Apply the tax rate to the profit before tax to determine income tax expense.
- Deduct the income tax expense calculated from the increase in profit before tax to determine the profit.
- Divide the profit by the number of shares outstanding.

Solution

	Alternative (a) Issue shares	Alternative (b) Issue bonds
Profit before interest and tax	$3,000,000	$3,000,000
Interest expense	0	100,000
Profit before income tax	3,000,000	2,900,000
Income tax expense	900,000	870,000
Profit	$2,100,000	$2,030,000
Number of shares	500,000	400,000
Earnings per share	$4.20	$5.08

The Navigator

Related exercise material: BE15–1, E15–1, and E15–12.

Bonds Payable

Like other kinds of long-term debt, **bonds** represent a promise to repay a principal amount at a specific maturity date. In addition, periodic interest is paid (normally semi-annually) at a specified rate on the principal amount. Bonds are also similar to shares: they are sold to, and purchased by, investors on organized securities exchanges. Bonds are usually sold in small denominations ($1,000 or multiples of $1,000). As a result, bonds attract many investors.

Bond credit-rating agencies help investors assess the risk level or creditworthiness of bonds. The highest-quality bonds are graded as AAA bonds, superior quality as AA, and good quality as A. Credit rating agencies all give Hydro-Québec an A rating or higher. The credit-rating scale goes down to C, and finally to the D or default category. Generally, bonds rated below BBB (or its equivalent) are called *junk bonds*. Junk bonds are considered speculative and have a higher risk of default (of not being repaid).

The Standard & Poor's credit rating agency also adds a plus or a minus to each grade category from A to C to distinguish credit risk even more. Hydro-Québec's bonds were rated A+ by Standard & Poor's, which indicates that the bonds are of good quality and have a low credit risk.

Interest rates are linked to credit ratings. Normally, the higher the credit rating, the lower the interest rate. For example, banks might pay 1% or 2% on a term deposit, because there is almost no risk. On the other hand, a corporate bond rated AAA might pay 5% or 6%. A corporate bond rated BBB will likely have to pay an even higher rate—say 9% or 10%—because the risk is higher. Interest rates vary with risk, but they also vary with duration, the general state of the economy, and many other factors. So, although some interest rates have been given here as examples, they may be quite different right now in practice. Hydro-Québec took advantage of low interest rates in January 2009 and issued bonds at interest rates below 5%. With the general decline in the global economy in 2008 and 2009, interest rates decreased.

STUDY OBJECTIVE 2

Account for bonds payable.

WILEY PLUS

Bonds Tutorial

Bond Basics

In the next few sections, we will look at some basic questions about bonds, including how they are issued and traded. We will also show you how to calculate market value and introduce you to some different types of bonds.

Issuing Procedures

In a corporation, approval by the board of directors is required before bonds can be issued. In authorizing the bond issue, the board of directors must state the number of bonds to be authorized, the total face value, the contractual interest rate, and the maturity date. As happens with issues of share capital, the total bond authorization is often more than the number of bonds actually issued. This is done intentionally to help ensure that the company will have the flexibility it needs to meet future cash requirements by selling more bonds.

The **face value** is the amount of principal that the company (known as the *issuer*) must pay at the maturity date. The **contractual interest rate** is the rate that is used to determine the amount of interest the borrower pays and the investor receives. Usually, the contractual rate is stated as an annual rate and interest is paid semi-annually. For example, the contractual interest rate on Hydro-Québec's bonds is 5% a year, but interest is paid semi-annually at a rate of 2.5% (5% × $^6/_{12}$). The **maturity date** is the date when the final payment is due to the investor from the company. The maturity date for Hydro-Québec's bonds is February 15, 2050. All of these details are included in a **bond certificate**, which is issued to investors to provide evidence of an investor's credit claim against the company.

> **Alternative terminology**
> Face value is also called *par value* and *maturity value*. The contractual interest rate is commonly known as the *coupon interest rate* or *stated interest rate*.

Bond Trading

Corporate bonds, like share capital, are traded on organized securities exchanges. Thus, bondholders have the opportunity to convert their bonds into cash at any time by selling the bonds at the current market price. Illustration 15-3 shows one example of bond prices and yields, which are published daily in the financial press:

> **Illustration 15-3 ➡**
> Bond price and yield

Issuer	Coupon	Maturity Date	Price	Yield
Bell CDA	6.100	2035-Mar-16	82.813	7.632

This bond listing for Bell Canada (Bell CDA) bonds indicates that these bonds have a contractual (coupon) interest rate of 6.1% per year. However, as is the norm, interest is paid semi-annually at a rate of 3.05% (6.1% × $^6/_{12}$). The listing also states that the bonds mature on March 16, 2035.

Bond prices are quoted as a percentage of the face value of the bonds, which are usually sold in denominations of $1,000. You can assume that bonds are issued in $1,000 denominations unless you are told otherwise. In this particular case, the price of 82.813 means $828.13 ($1,000 × 82.813%) was the selling price of the bonds on the date of the above listing. The yield, or market interest rate, on the bonds is 7.632% on the date of the above listing. Note that because the market interest rate is higher than the contractual interest rate, these bonds are currently selling at a discount. We will learn more about market interest rates and bond discounts in the next section.

> **Helpful hint** Bonds are normally in denominations of $1,000, but they can be of any value, such as $100 or $5,000 or $10,000.

As is the case with share transactions, transactions between a bondholder and other investors are not journalized by the issuing corporation. If Vinod Thakkar sells his Bell Canada bonds to Julie Tarrel, the issuing corporation, Bell Canada, does not journalize the transaction. While the issuer (or its trustee) does keep records of the names of bondholders in the case of registered bonds, a corporation only makes journal entries when it issues or buys back bonds and pays interest.

Determining the Market Value of Bonds

If you were an investor wanting to purchase a bond, how would you determine how much to pay? To be more specific, assume that Candlestick Inc. issues a zero-interest bond (pays no interest) with a face value of $1 million due in five years. For this bond, the only cash you receive is $1 million at the end of five years. Would you pay $1 million for this bond? We hope not! One million dollars received five years from now is not the same as $1 million received today.

The reason you should not pay $1 million relates to the **time value of money**. If you had $1 million today, you could invest it. From that investment, you would earn interest. At the end of five years, your investment would be worth much more than $1 million. If someone were to pay you $1 million five years from now, you would want to find out its equivalent today. In other words, you would want to determine how much must be invested today at current interest rates to have $1 million in five years. That amount—what must be invested today at a specific rate of interest over a specific amount of time—is called the present value.

The present value of a bond is the value at which it should sell in the marketplace. Market value (present value), therefore, depends on the three factors that determine present value: (1) the dollar amounts to be received, (2) the length of time until the amounts are received, and (3) the market interest rate. The **market interest rate** is the rate that investors demand for lending their money. The process of finding the present value is called *discounting the future amounts*.

Alternative terminology
Market interest rate is also referred to as the *effective rate* or *yield*.

To illustrate, assume that on January 1, 2011, Candlestick issues $1 million of 5% bonds due in five years, with interest payable semi-annually. The purchaser of the bonds would receive two cash inflows: (1) the principal of $1 million to be paid at maturity, and (2) 10 interest payments of $25,000 ($1,000,000 × 5% × $^6/_{12}$) received semi-annually over the term of the bonds. Illustration 15-4 shows the time diagram for both cash flows.

← Illustration 15-4

Time diagram of bond cash flows

Note that there is no interest payment on January 1, 2011—time period 0—because the bonds have not been outstanding for any period of time, so no interest has been incurred.

The current market value of a bond is equal to the present value of all the future cash flows promised by the bond. The current market value of Candlestick's bonds is equal to the face value of the bonds if the market interest rate on the Candlestick bonds is the same as the contractual interest rate. This is shown below in the present value calculation:

Present value of $1 million received in 10 periods	
$1,000,000 × 0.78120 ($n = 10, i = 2.5\%$)[1]	$ 781,200
Present value of $25,000 received for each of 10 periods	
$25,000 × 8.75206 ($n = 10, i = 2.5\%$)	218,800
Present value (current market price) of bonds	$1,000,000
[1] When n = number of interest periods and i = interest rate.	

There are standard tables to determine the present value factors that are used (e.g., 0.78120 and 8.75206). We have reproduced these tables in the Present Value Appendix at the end of this book and you should look at them as you read the following procedures for calculating the present value of a bond:

1. Use Table PV–1 (the present value of $1) to determine the correct factor to use to calculate the present value of the principal, which is a single payment, paid at maturity.
2. Use Table PV–2 (the present value of an annuity of $1) to calculate the present value of the interest, which is paid every six months.
3. To find the correct factor in each table, locate the factor at the intersection of the number of periods and the interest rate. When interest is paid semi-annually, remember to double the number of periods and halve the annual interest rate. For instance, in our Candlestick example above, the five-year term of the bonds means that there are 10 semi-annual interest periods. In addition, the annual interest rate of 5% becomes 2.5% (5% × $^6/_{12}$) when adjusted for the semi-annual period.

4. The bonds' face value and contractual interest rate are used to calculate the interest payment. Note that while the contractual interest rate is used to determine the interest payment, the market interest rate is used to determine the present value.

Present value can also be determined mathematically using a financial calculator or spreadsheet program such as Excel. There is further discussion of present value concepts in the Present Value Appendix at the end of this book.

The present value illustration above assumed that the market interest rate and the contractual interest rate paid on the bonds were the same. The present value of the bonds always equals the face value when the two rates are the same. However, this is rarely the case because market interest rates change daily. They are influenced by the type of bond issued, the state of the economy, current industry conditions, and the company's performance. The market and contractual interest rates are often quite different. As a result, bonds sell below or above face value.

To illustrate, suppose that investors have one of two options: (1) purchase bonds that have just been issued with a contractual interest rate of 6%, or (2) purchase bonds issued at an earlier date with a lower contractual interest rate of 5%. If the bonds are of equal risk, investors will choose the 6% investment. To make the investments equal, investors will therefore demand a rate of interest higher than the 5% contractual interest rate provided in option 2. But investors cannot change the contractual interest rate. What they can do, instead, is pay less than the face value for the bonds. By paying less for the bonds, investors can effectively get the market interest rate of 6%. In these cases, bonds sell at a **discount**. You will recall that the Bell CDA bonds described in Illustration 15-3 are listed at a discount. This is because the market interest rate was 7.632% while the contractual interest rate was 6.1%.

On the other hand, the market interest rate may be lower than the contractual interest rate. In that case, investors will have to pay more than face value for the bonds. That is, if the market interest rate is 4% and the contractual interest rate is 5%, the issuer will require more funds from the investors. In these cases, bonds sell at a **premium**. You will recall from the feature story that Hydro-Québec issued bonds with a contractual interest rate of 5% at market rates of interest of 4.907% and 4.990%. Hydro-Québec sold these bonds at a premium because the market interest rate was lower than the contractual interest rate. The relationship between bond contractual interest rates and market interest rates, and the resultant selling price, is shown in Illustration 15-5.

Illustration 15-5 ➡

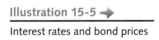

Interest rates and bond prices

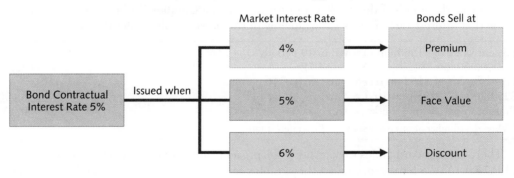

As was the case with Hydro-Québec's bond issue described in the feature story, issuing bonds at an amount different from face value is quite common. By the time a company prints the bond certificates and markets the bonds, it will be a coincidence if the market rate and the contractual rate are the same. Thus, the sale of bonds at a discount does not mean that the issuer's financial strength is questionable. Nor does the sale of bonds at a premium indicate superior financial strength. After the bonds are issued, the difference between the contractual rate and the market rate of interest may be larger as the market rate of interest fluctuates. This is shown in Illustration 15-3 where the contractual rate of interest on the Bell CDA bonds is 6.1% and the market rate of interest on the date of the listing is 7.632%.

Types of Bonds

There are many different kinds of bonds. Some of the more common types are described below.

Secured and Unsecured Bonds. Secured bonds have specific assets of the issuer pledged as collateral for the bonds. Unsecured bonds are issued against the borrower's general credit. There are no assets used as collateral. These bonds, also called debenture bonds, are used by large corporations with good credit ratings. For example, Hydro-Québec's bonds are unsecured debenture bonds.

Term and Serial Bonds. Bonds that mature (are due for payment) at a single specified future date are called term bonds. In contrast, bonds that mature in instalments are called serial bonds. The Hydro-Québec bonds in the feature story are term bonds, due in 41 years.

Registered and Bearer Bonds. Bonds issued with the name of the owner are called registered bonds. Interest payments on registered bonds are made by cheque or direct deposit to registered bondholders. Canada Savings Bonds, issued by the federal government each fall, are an example of registered bonds. Bonds that are not registered are called bearer (or coupon) bonds. Holders of bearer bonds must send in coupons to receive interest payments. Bearer bonds may be transferred directly to another party. In contrast, the transfer of registered bonds requires the cancellation of the bonds by the institution and the issue of new ones. Most bonds that are issued today are registered bonds.

Convertible Bonds. Bonds that can be converted into shares by the bondholder are called convertible bonds. Convertible bonds have features that are attractive to both the bondholder and the issuer. The conversion gives bondholders an opportunity to benefit if the market price of the common shares increases. The bondholder also receives interest on the bond until a decision is made to convert it. For the issuer, the bonds sell at a higher price and pay a lower rate of interest than similar debt securities that do not have a conversion option.

Because convertible bonds have both debt and equity features, these are considered to be a complex type of financial instrument. Accounting for complex financial instruments such as these is left to an intermediate accounting course.

Redeemable/Retractable Bonds. Bonds that can be retired (redeemed) by the issuer at a stated dollar amount before they mature are known as redeemable bonds or callable bonds. Retractable bonds are bonds that can be retired before maturity by the bondholder. Both redeemable and retractable bonds can be retired at a specified amount before they mature. The key distinction is that redeemable bonds can be retired at the option of the issuer (the borrower) and retractable bonds can be retired at the option of the bondholder (the investor).

Accounting for Bond Issues

Bonds can be issued at face value, below face value (at a discount), or above face value (at a premium).

Issuing Bonds at Face Value

To illustrate the accounting for bonds, let's continue the example discussed in the last section, where Candlestick Inc. issues five-year, 5%, $1 million bonds on January 1, 2011, to yield a market interest rate of 5%. Because the contractual interest rate and the market interest rate are the same, these bonds are issued at 100 (100% of face value).

The entry to record the sale is as follows:

Jan. 1	Cash	1,000,000	
	Bonds Payable		1,000,000
	To record sale of bonds at face value.		

A = L + SE
+1,000,000 +1,000,000

↑ Cash flows: +1,000,000

These bonds payable are reported in the long-term liabilities section of the balance sheet because the maturity date (January 1, 2016) is more than one year away.

Over the term (life) of the bonds, entries are required for bond interest. The interest payment on bonds payable is calculated in the same way as interest on notes payable, as explained in Chapter 10. Interest is payable semi-annually on January 1 and July 1 on the bonds described above. Interest of $25,000 ($1,000,000 × 5% × 6/12) must be paid on July 1, 2011, the first interest payment date. The entry for the interest payment, assuming no previous accrual of interest, is:

July 1	Bond Interest Expense	25,000	
	Cash		25,000
	To record payment of bond interest.		

At December 31, Candlestick's year end, an adjusting entry is needed to recognize the $25,000 of interest expense incurred since July 1. The entry is as follows:

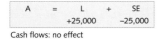

Dec. 31	Bond Interest Expense	25,000	
	Bond Interest Payable		25,000
	To accrue bond interest.		

Bond interest payable is classified as a current liability because it is scheduled for payment within the next year (in fact, it is due the next day in this case). When the interest is paid on January 1, 2012, Bond Interest Payable is debited and Cash is credited for $25,000.

Issuing Bonds at a Discount

To illustrate the issue of bonds at a discount (below face value), assume that on January 1, 2011, the Candlestick bonds are issued to yield a market interest rate of 6% rather than 5%, as we assumed in the previous section.

Using the present value tables in Appendix D, we can determine that the bonds will sell for $957,345. The selling price (present value) is determined as follows:

Present value of $1 million received in 10 periods	
$1,000,000 × 0.74409 ($n = 10$, $i = 3\%$)[1]	$744,090
Present value of $25,000 received for each of 10 periods	
$25,000 × 8.53020 ($n = 10$, $i = 3\%$)	213,255
Present value (market price) of bonds	$957,345

[1] When n = number of interest periods and i = market interest rate per period.

Sometimes you will be asked to calculate the market price as we have done above. Other times, you will be told that the bonds have been issued at a stated percentage amount (95.7345 in this situation), in which case you can calculate the market price by multiplying this percentage by the face value ($1,000,000 × 95.7345% = $957,345). Regardless, you will end up with the same issue price—$957,345 in this case.

The entry to record the bond issue is as follows:

Jan. 1	Cash	957,345	
	Bonds Payable		957,345
	To record sale of bonds at a discount.		

Rather than crediting the Bonds Payable account for the issue price of $957,345, some companies use a separate contra liability account to keep track of the bond discount. In this case the bond discount is $42,655, which is the difference between the face value and the issue price ($1,000,000 − $957,345). If following this method, one would credit Bonds Payable for $1 million, and debit a separate account, Bond Discount, for $42,655, instead of crediting Bonds Payable for $957,345. For reporting purposes, however, accounting standards require the presentation of bonds net of any discounts (or premiums, as we will learn in the next section). Consequently, many companies record their journal entries on a net basis as well. Although both ways of recording bond transactions are acceptable, we will illustrate in this text the recording of the journal entries net of any discount or premium, which is what is required for reporting purposes.

The issue of bonds at a discount (below face value) will result in a total cost of borrowing that is higher than the bond interest paid. That is, the issuing corporation must pay not only the contractual interest rate over the term of the bonds, but it must also repay the face value (rather than the issue price) at maturity. Therefore, the difference between the issue price ($957,345) and the face value ($1,000,000) of the bonds—the discount ($42,655)—is an additional cost of borrowing. That is, Candlestick must repay $1 million at maturity even though it only received $957,345 from the sale of the bonds.

The total cost of borrowing—the interest payment and bond discount—must be allocated to interest expense over the life of the bonds. The interest payment, $25,000, is recorded as one component of the interest expense every semi-annual period for five years (10 semi-annual periods). The bond discount is also allocated to interest expense over the 10 semi-annual periods—this allocation is called **amortizing the discount**. Consequently, the amortization of the discount increases the amount of interest expense that is reported each period. The higher interest expense reflects the cost of borrowing (economic reality).

The discounts (and premiums, which will be discussed in the next section) on all financial liabilities, such as bonds payable, must be amortized using the effective-interest method of amortization. We will explain this method in detail in Appendix 15A of this chapter. For now, we will assume that the discount amortization is $3,720 for the first interest period. Consequently, interest expense is the total of the interest payment ($25,000) plus the discount amortization ($3,720).

We record the interest expense, amortization of the discount, and payment of interest on the first interest payment date, July 1, as follows:

July 1	Interest Expense	28,720	
	Bonds Payable		3,720
	Cash		25,000
	To record semi-annual interest payment.		

A	=	L	+	SE
−25,000		+3,720		−28,720

Cash flows: −25,000

The face value of the bonds less any unamortized discount or plus any unamortized premium is referred to as the **amortized cost** of the bonds. The amortized cost of the bonds will increase as the discount is amortized, until at maturity the bonds' amortized cost equals their face value. In the Candlestick bonds example, the amortized cost will be $1 million on January 1, 2016, the maturity date.

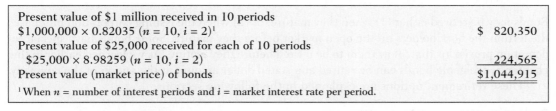

Issuing Bonds at a Premium

To illustrate the issue of bonds at a premium (above face value), assume that on January 1, 2011, the Candlestick bonds are issued to yield a market interest rate of 4% rather than 5%, as we assumed in the previous section. Using the present value tables in Appendix D, we can determine that the bonds will sell for $1,044,915. The issue price (present value) is determined as follows:

Present value of $1 million received in 10 periods	
$1,000,000 × 0.82035 ($n = 10, i = 2$)[1]	$ 820,350
Present value of $25,000 received for each of 10 periods	
$25,000 × 8.98259 ($n = 10, i = 2$)	224,565
Present value (market price) of bonds	$1,044,915

[1] When n = number of interest periods and i = market interest rate per period.

We could also say that these bonds have been issued at 104.4915 (104.4915% of face value). This issue price results in a premium of $44,915 ($1,044,915 − $1,000,000). Notice that the cash payments are the same as in the previous example. The only thing that has changed is the market interest rate.

The entry to record the sale would be as follows:

Jan. 1	Cash	1,044,915	
	Bonds Payable		1,044,915
	To record sale of bonds at a premium.		

A	=	L	+	SE
+1,044,915		+1,044,915		

Cash flows: +1,044,915

Rather than crediting the Bonds Payable account for the issue price of $1,044,915, some companies use a separate adjunct account to keep track of the bond premium. An adjunct account is the opposite of a contra account. A contra account reduces a related account while an adjunct account increases or adds to a related account. If an adjunct account were used, one would credit Bonds Payable $1 million and credit Bond Premium $44,915 instead of crediting Bonds Payable $1,044,915.

As we explained in the "Issuing Bonds at a Discount" section, accounting standards require the presentation of bonds net of any premiums (or discounts, as we learned in the previous section), so we will illustrate in this text the recording of the journal entries net of any discount or premium.

The issue of bonds above face value causes the total cost of borrowing to be less than the bond interest paid. The bond premium is considered a reduction in the cost of borrowing. Candlestick must only repay $1 million at maturity, even though it received $1,044,915 from the sale of the bonds.

The total cost of borrowing—the interest payment and bond premium—must be allocated to interest expense over the life of the bonds. The interest payment, $25,000, is recorded as one component of the interest expense every semi-annual period for five years (10 semi-annual periods). The bond premium is also allocated as a reduction of interest expense over the 10 semi-annual periods—this allocation is called **amortizing the premium**. Consequently, the amortization of the premium decreases the amount of interest expense that is reported each period. The lower interest expense reflects the cost of borrowing (economic reality).

To illustrate the recording of the interest expense and amortization of the premium on the first interest payment date, we will assume that the premium amortization is $4,102. Consequently, interest expense is the interest payment ($25,000) reduced by the premium amortization ($4,102). It is recorded as follows:

A	=	L	+	SE
−25,000		−4,102		−20,898

↓ Cash flows: −25,000

July 1	Interest Expense	20,898	
	Bonds Payable	4,102	
	Cash		25,000
	To record semi-annual interest payment.		

The same method—the effective-interest method—used to allocate bond discounts is also used to allocate bond premiums to interest expense. This method is described in Appendix 15A of this chapter, where we also show how the $4,102 premium amortization amount is calculated.

As the premium is amortized, the amortized cost of the bonds will decrease until at maturity the bonds' amortized cost equals their face value. In the Candlestick bonds example, the amortized cost will be $1 million on January 1, 2016, the maturity date.

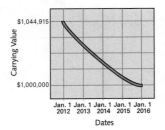

Accounting for Bond Retirements

Bonds may be retired either (1) when they mature, or (2) when the issuing corporation purchases them from the bondholders on the open market before they mature. Some bonds have special redemption provisions that allow them to be retired before they mature. As we learned earlier in this chapter, redeemable bonds can be retired at a stated dollar amount at the option of the company.

These retirement options are explained in the following sections.

Redeeming Bonds at Maturity

Regardless of the issue price of bonds, the amortized cost of the bonds at maturity will equal their face value. By the time the bonds mature, any discount or premium will be fully amortized.

Assuming that the interest for the last interest period has been paid and recorded, the entry to record the redemption of the Candlestick bonds at maturity, January 1, 2016, is as follows:

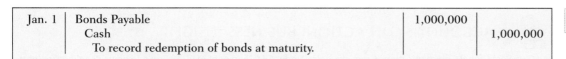

Jan. 1	Bonds Payable	1,000,000	
	Cash		1,000,000
	To record redemption of bonds at maturity.		

A = L + SE
−1,000,000 −1,000,000

↓ Cash flows: −1,000,000

Because the amortized cost of the bonds equals the face value at maturity, there is no gain or loss.

Redeeming Bonds before Maturity

Why would a company want to have the option to retire its bonds early? If interest rates drop, it can be a good idea financially to retire the bond issue and replace it with a new bond issue at a lower interest rate. Or, a company may become financially able to repay its debt earlier than expected. When a company purchases non-redeemable bonds on the open market, it pays the going market price. If the bonds are redeemable, the company will pay the bondholders an amount that was specified at the time of issue, known as the **redemption price**. To make the bonds more attractive to investors, the redemption price is usually a few percentage points above the face value.

Alternative terminology
Redemption price is also referred to as the *call price*.

If the bonds are redeemed between semi-annual interest payment dates, it will be necessary to pay the required interest and record the related amortization of any premiums or discounts. To record the redemption of bonds, it is necessary to (1) eliminate the amortized cost of the Bonds Payable (balance in Bonds Payable account), (2) record the cash paid, and (3) recognize the gain or loss on redemption.

A loss on redemption is recorded if the cash paid is more than the amortized cost of the bonds. There is a gain on redemption when the cash paid is less than the amortized cost of the bonds.

To illustrate, assume that Candlestick sells its bonds that were issued at a premium as described in the last section. It retires its bonds at 101 at the end of the fourth year (eighth period) after paying the semi-annual interest. Assume also that the bonds' amortized cost at the redemption date is $1,009,709. That is, the bonds' face value is $1 million and the unamortized premium is $9,709. The entry to record the redemption on January 1, 2012 (end of the eighth interest period) is:

Jan. 1	Bonds Payable	1,009,709	
	Loss on Bond Redemption	291	
	Cash ($1,000,000 × 101%)		1,010,000
	To record redemption of bonds at 101.		

A = L + SE
−1,010,000 −1,009,709 − 291

↓ Cash flows: −1,010,000

The loss of $291 is the difference between the cash paid of $1,010,000 and the amortized cost of the bonds of $1,009,709. This is very similar to the calculation of a loss or gain on the sale of property, plant, and equipment. In the case of property, plant, and equipment, cash is compared with the carrying amount. In the case of bonds, cash is compared with the amortized cost. However, the determination of whether a loss or a gain results is of course different, depending on whether you are selling property, plant, and equipment (assets) or repurchasing bonds (liabilities). For example, when you sell an asset, you gain when the cash received is greater than the carrying amount. When you retire a liability, you gain when the cash paid is less than the amortized cost. These differences are shown in Illustration 15-6.

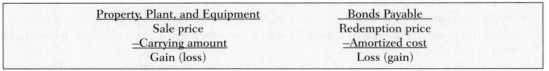

Property, Plant, and Equipment	Bonds Payable
Sale price	Redemption price
−Carrying amount	−Amortized cost
Gain (loss)	Loss (gain)

← **Illustration 15-6**

Comparison of asset and liability gain and loss

Similar to gains and losses on the sale of property, plant, and equipment, gains and losses on bond redemption are reported separately in the income statement as other expenses or other revenues.

ACCOUNTING IN ACTION: BUSINESS INSIGHT

As CanWest Global Communications Corp. struggled under $4 billion debt in 2009 and missed its deadlines for interest payments to its bondholders, it initiated negotiations with its bondholders on a financial restructuring that would involve a debt for equity swap whereby the bondholders would receive shares in the company. CanWest, owner of newspapers across Canada, Global Television and several cable TV channels, also needs the approval of the Canadian Radio-television and Telecommunications Commission to restructure. At issue, according to several sources involved in the restructuring, is whether the company can stay within Canadian ownership rules for broadcasting assets if they convert the debt into equity in the new restructured firm. Two of the debt funds that held CanWest's bonds are American.

Source: Grant Robertson and Andrew Willis, "CanWest, CRTC," *The Globe and Mail*, August 9, 2009.

In terms of Canadian ownership rules for broadcasting assets, why was CanWest able to have foreign debt holders? Why does it matter if these investors own debt or equity in CanWest? Why would the bondholders want to swap the bonds for equity in the company?

BEFORE YOU GO ON . . .

→ Review It

1. How is the market price of bonds determined?
2. Why do bonds sell at a discount? At a premium? At face value?
3. Explain the differences between each of these types of bonds: secured versus unsecured, term versus serial, registered versus bearer, and redeemable versus retractable.
4. Explain why bond discounts and premiums are amortized.
5. Explain the accounting for the redemption of bonds at maturity and before maturity.

→ Do It

On January 1, 2008, R & B Inc. issues $500,000 of 10-year, 4% bonds to yield a market interest rate of 5%, which resulted in an issue price of 92.2. Interest is paid semi-annually on January 1 and July 1. On July 1, 2012, the company records the semi-annual interest payment (the semi-annual amortization amount for this period is $1,859). The amortized cost of the bonds after the semi-annual interest payment is recorded is $476,214. On this same date, the company redeems the bonds at 99.

(a) Using present value factors, prove the issue price of the bonds of 92.2.
(b) Prepare the entries to record (1) the issue of the bonds on January 1, 2008; (2) the payment of interest and amortization of any bond discount or premium on July 1, 2012; and (3) the redemption of the bonds on July 1, 2012. Round all calculations to the nearest dollar.

Action Plan

- To calculate the present value (issue price), use Table 1 (the present value of $1) in Appendix D to find the factor to use to calculate the present value for the principal (face value), which is a single sum. Use Table 2 (the present value of an annuity of $1) in Appendix D to calculate the present value of the interest, which recurs periodically (as an annuity). Remember to double the number of periods and halve the annual interest rate when the interest is paid semi-annually.
- Apply the issue price as a percentage (e.g., 92.2%) to the face value of the bonds to determine the proceeds that are received. Prove this number to the present value (issue price) that is calculated.
- Remember that amortization of a bond discount increases interest expense and increases the amortized cost of the bond.
- To record the redemption, eliminate the amortized cost of the bonds, record the cash paid, and calculate and record the gain or loss (the difference between the cash paid and the amortized cost).

Solution

(a)

Issue price of the bonds ($500,000 × 92.2%)	$461,000
Present value of $500,000 received in 20 periods	
$500,000 × 0.61027 (n = 20, i = 2.5)	$305,135
Present value of $10,000 received for each of 20 periods	
$10,000 × 15.58916 (n = 20, i = 2.5)	155,892
Present value (issue price)	$461,027

(b)

(1) Jan. 1, 2008	Cash ($500,000 × 92.2%)	461,000	
	Bonds Payable		461,000
	To record issue of bonds at 92.2.		
(2) July 1, 2012	Interest Expense ($10,000 + $1,859)	11,859	
	Bonds Payable		1,859
	Cash ($500,000 × 4% × 6/12)		10,000
	To record payment of interest and		
	amortization of discount.		
(3) July 1, 2012	Bonds Payable	476,214	
	Loss on Bond Redemption		
	($495,000 − $476,214)	18,786	
	Cash ($500,000 × 99%)		495,000
	To record redemption of bonds at 99.		

Related exercise material: BE15–2, BE15–3, BE15–4, BE15–5, BE15–6, E15–2, E15–3, E15–4, E15–5, and E15–6.

The Navigator

Notes Payable

STUDY OBJECTIVE 3

Account for long-term notes payable.

You will recall that we first learned about notes payable in Chapter 10, where they were included as an example of a current liability. Long-term notes payable are similar to short-term notes payable except that the terms of the notes are for more than one year.

Notes and bonds are also quite similar. Both have a fixed maturity date and pay interest. However, whereas bonds have a contractual or fixed interest rate, notes may have either a fixed interest rate or a floating interest rate. A **fixed interest rate** is constant for the entire term of the note. A **floating (or variable) interest rate** changes as market rates change. A floating interest rate is often based on the prime borrowing rate. Prime is the interest rate that banks charge their most creditworthy customers. This rate is usually increased by a specified percentage that matches the company's risk profile—in other words, it depends on how risky the company is judged to be.

Similar to bonds, a long-term note may be unsecured or secured. A secured note pledges title to specific assets as security for the loan, often known as *collateral*. Secured notes are commonly known as *mortgages*. A **mortgage note payable** is widely used by individuals to purchase homes. It is also used by many companies to acquire property, plant, and equipment. Unsecured notes are issued against the general credit of the borrower. There are no assets used as collateral.

One difference between notes and bonds is that bonds are often traded on a stock exchange, as shares are. Notes are rarely traded on stock exchanges. Small and large corporations issue notes, whereas only large corporations issue bonds. You will recall that bonds help a company borrow when the amount of financing is too large for one lender.

While short-term notes and bonds are normally repayable in full at maturity, most long-term notes are repayable in a series of periodic payments. These payments are known as *instalments* and are paid monthly, quarterly, semi-annually, or at another defined period. Each payment consists of (1) interest on the unpaid balance of the loan, and (2) a reduction of loan principal. Payments generally take one of two forms: (1) fixed principal payments plus interest, or (2) blended principal and interest payments. Let's look at each of these payment patterns in more detail.

Fixed Principal Payments

Instalment notes with fixed principal payments are repayable in **equal periodic amounts, plus interest**. To illustrate, assume that on January 1, 2011, Bélanger Ltée issues a $120,000, five-year, 7% note payable to finance a new research laboratory. The entry to record the issue of the note payable is as follows:

A	=	L	+	SE
+120,000		+120,000		

↑ Cash flows: +120,000

Jan. 1	Cash	120,000	
	Notes Payable		120,000
	To record five-year, 7% note payable.		

The terms of the note provide for equal monthly instalment payments of $2,000 ($120,000 ÷ 60 monthly periods) on the first of each month, plus interest of 7% on the outstanding principal balance. Monthly interest expense is calculated by multiplying the outstanding principal balance by the interest rate. The calculation of interest expense for notes payable is similar to that of bonds payable—both use the effective-interest method.

For the first payment date—February 1—interest expense is $700 ($120,000 × 7% × $\frac{1}{12}$). Note that the 7% is an annual interest rate and must be adjusted for the monthly time period. The cash payment of $2,700 for the month of February is the sum of the instalment payment, $2,000, which is applied against the principal, plus the interest, $700.

The entry to record the first instalment payment on February 1 is as follows:

A	=	L	+	SE
–2,700		–2,000		–700

↓ Cash flows: –2,700

Feb. 1	Interest Expense ($120,000 × 7% × $\frac{1}{12}$)	700	
	Notes Payable	2,000	
	Cash ($2,000 + $700)		2,700
	To record monthly payment on note.		

An instalment payment schedule is a useful tool to help organize this information and prepare journal entries. The instalment payment schedule for the first few months for Bélanger Ltée, rounded to the nearest dollar, is shown in Illustration 15-7.

Illustration 15-7 →

Instalment payment schedule—fixed principal payments

	BÉLANGER LTÉE			
	Instalment Payment Schedule—Fixed Principal Payments			
Interest Period	(A) Cash Payment (B + C)	(B) Interest Expense (D × 7% × $\frac{1}{12}$)	(C) Reduction of Principal ($120,000 ÷ 60)	(D) Principal Balance (D –C)
Jan. 1				$120,000
Feb. 1	$2,700	$700	$2,000	118,000
Mar. 1	2,688	688	2,000	116,000
Apr. 1	2,677	677	2,000	114,000

Column A, the cash payment, is the total of the instalment payment, $2,000, plus the interest. The cash payment changes each period because the interest amount changes. Column B determines the interest expense, which decreases each period because the principal balance, on which interest is calculated, decreases. Column C is the instalment payment of $2,000, which is applied against the principal. The instalment payment (the reduction of the principal) is constant each period in a "fixed principal payment" pattern. Column D is the principal balance, which decreases each period by the amount of the instalment payment.

In summary, with fixed principal payments, the interest decreases each period (as the principal decreases). The portion applied to the reduction of loan principal stays constant, but because of the decreasing interest, the total cash payment decreases.

Blended Payments

Instalment notes with blended payments are repayable in **equal periodic amounts that include the principal and the interest**. With blended payments, the amounts of interest and principal that are applied to the loan change with each payment. Specifically, as happens with fixed principal payments, the interest decreases each period (as the principal decreases). In contrast to fixed principal payments, however, the portion that is applied to the loan principal increases each period.

To illustrate, assume that instead of fixed principal payments, Bélanger Ltée repays its $120,000 note payable in blended payments of $2,376 each month. As with the fixed principal payments illustrated in the previous section, monthly interest expense is calculated by multiplying the outstanding principal balance by the interest rate. For the first payment date—February 1—interest expense is $700 ($120,000 × 7% × $^1/_{12}$ months). The instalment payment of $2,376 is fixed for each month, and includes interest and principal amounts, which will vary. In February, the principal balance will be reduced by $1,676, which is the difference between the instalment payment of $2,376 and the interest amount of $700.

The entry to record the issue of the note payable is the same as in the previous section. The amounts in the journal entry to record the instalment payment on February 1 change as follows:

Feb. 1	Interest Expense ($120,000 × 7% × 1/12)	700	
	Notes Payable ($2,376 − $700)	1,676	
	Cash		2,376
	To record monthly payment on note.		

A	=	L	+	SE
−2,376		−1,676		−700

⬇ Cash flows: −2,376

An instalment payment schedule can also be prepared for blended principal and interest payments. Illustration 15-8 shows the instalment payment schedule for the first few months for Bélanger Ltée, rounded to the nearest dollar.

			BÉLANGER LTÉE Instalment Payment Schedule—Blended Payments	
Interest Period	(A) Cash Payment	(B) Interest Expense (D × 7% × $^1/_{12}$)	(C) Reduction of Principal (A − B)	(D) Principal Balance (D − C)
Jan. 1				$120,000
Feb. 1	$2,376	$700	$1,676	118,324
Mar. 1	2,376	690	1,686	116,638
Apr. 1	2,376	680	1,696	114,942

⬅ **Illustration 15-8**

Instalment payment schedule—blended payments

Column A, the cash payment, is specified and is the same for each period. The amount of this cash payment can be calculated using present value techniques discussed earlier in the chapter and in the companion website to this textbook. Column B determines the interest expense, which decreases each period because the principal balance on which interest is calculated also decreases. Column C is the amount by which the principal is reduced. This is the difference between the cash payment of $2,376 and the interest for the period. Consequently, this amount will increase each period. Column D is the principal balance, which decreases each period by an increasing amount; that is, by the reduction of the principal amount from Column C.

In summary, with blended payments, the interest decreases each period as the principal decreases. The cash payment stays constant, but because of the decreasing interest, the reduction of principal increases.

There are two key differences between a fixed principal payment and a blended payment schedule. With a fixed principal payment, the cash payment varies; with a blended payment, it is constant. Second, with a fixed principal payment, the reduction of principal is a constant amount; with a blended payment, it increases. The interest expense decreases each period in both payment situations because the principal balance varies.

With both types of instalment notes payable, as with any other long-term note payable, the reduction in principal for the next year must be reported as a current liability, and is normally called "Current portion of long-term note payable." The remaining unpaid principal is classified as a long-term liability. No journal entry is necessary; it is simply a reclassification of amounts for the balance sheet.

BEFORE YOU GO ON . . .

➡ Review It

1. What is the difference between short-term and long-term notes payable?
2. What is the difference between bonds and notes payable?
3. Why is the cash payment different each period for a note with fixed principal payments?
4. How is the reduction of principal different in a note with fixed principal payments compared with a note with blended payments?

➡ Do It

On December 31, 2010, Tian Inc. issued a $500,000, 15-year, 8% mortgage note payable. The terms provide for semi-annual blended payments of $28,915, on June 30 and December 31. (a) Prepare an instalment payment schedule for the first two years of the note (through to December 31, 2012). (b) Prepare the journal entries required to record the issue of the note on December 31, 2010, and the first two instalment payments. (c) Show the presentation of the liability on the balance sheet at December 31, 2011.

Action Plan

- For the instalment payment schedule, multiply the interest rate by the principal balance at the beginning of the period to determine the interest expense. Remember to adjust for the partial period ($\%_{12}$ months). The reduction of principal is the difference between the cash payment and the interest expense.
- Record the mortgage payments, recognizing that each blended payment consists of (1) interest on the unpaid loan balance, and (2) a reduction of the loan principal.
- Remember to separate the current and long-term portions of the note so that they are presented correctly in the balance sheet. The current portion is the amount of principal that will be repaid in the next year.

Solution

(a)

Interest Period	Cash Payment	Interest Expense	Reduction of Principal	Principal Balance
Dec. 31, 2010				$500,000
June 30, 2011	$28,915	$20,000	$8,915	491,085
Dec. 31, 2011	28,915	19,643	9,272	481,813
June 30, 2012	28,915	19,273	9,642	472,171
Dec. 31, 2012	28,915	18,887	10,028	462,143

(b)

Dec. 31, 2010	Cash		500,000	
	Mortgage Note Payable			500,000
	To record issue of 15-year, 8% mortgage note payable.			
June 30, 2011	Interest Expense ($500,000 × 8% × $\%_{12}$)		20,000	
	Mortgage Note Payable ($28,915 − $20,000)		8,915	
	Cash			28,915
	To record semi-annual payment on note.			
Dec. 31, 2011	Interest Expense [($500,000 − $8,915) × 8% × $\%_{12}$]		19,643	
	Mortgage Note Payable ($28,915 − $19,643)		9,272	
	Cash			28,915
	To record semi-annual payment on note.			

(c)

TIAN INC. December 31, 2011 Balance Sheet (partial)	
Current liabilities	
Current portion of mortgage note payable ($9,642 + $10,028)	$ 19,670
Long-term liabilities	
Mortgage note payable	462,143
Total liabilities	$481,813

Related exercise material: BE15–7, BE15–8, BE15–9, E15–7, E15–8, and E15–9.

The Navigator

Lease Liabilities

A **lease** is a contractual arrangement between two parties. A party that owns an asset (the **lessor**) agrees to allow another party (the **lessee**) to use the specified property for a series of cash payments over an agreed period of time. Why would anyone want to lease property rather than buy it? There are many advantages to leasing an asset instead of purchasing it:

STUDY OBJECTIVE 4
Account for leases.

1. **Reduced risk of obsolescence.** Obsolescence is the process by which an asset becomes out of date before it physically wears out. Frequently, lease terms allow the party using the asset (the lessee) to exchange the asset for a more modern or technologically capable asset if it becomes outdated. This is much easier than trying to sell an obsolete asset.
2. **100% financing.** To purchase an asset, most companies must borrow money, which usually requires a down payment of at least 20%. Leasing an asset does not usually require any money down, which helps to conserve cash. In addition, interest payments are often fixed for the term of the lease, unlike other financing, which often has a floating interest rate.
3. **Income tax advantages.** When a company owns a depreciable asset, it can only deduct the depreciation expense (called *capital cost allowance* for income tax purposes) on its income tax return. However, when a company leases an asset, it can deduct 100% of the lease payment on its income tax return.

The two main types of leases are finance leases and operating leases. Whether a lease is a finance lease or an operating lease depends on the economic reality of the transaction rather than the legal form of the lease agreeement. We will discuss these two types of leases in the next sections.

Alternative terminology
Finance leases are also referred to as *capital leases*.

Finance Leases

In a **finance lease** contract, substantially all of the benefits and risks of ownership are transferred to the lessee. This is essentially the same as if the company had purchased an asset and financed the purchase by issuing debt. Therefore, under a finance lease, both an asset and a liability are shown on the balance sheet.

Finance leases are a good example of the application of the "faithful representation" characteristic of accounting information. In order for accounting information to be a faithful representation of the transaction, it must show the economic reality, and not just the legal form, of the transaction. If the economic reality of a lease agreement results in substantially all of the benefits and risks of ownership being transferred to the lessee, the faithful representation characteristic requires the accounting information to show the asset and a liability.

Accountants must use professional judgement in deciding if a lease should be classified as a finance lease. Under International Financial Reporting Standards (IFRS), the lessee must classify the lease as a finance lease and record the purchase of an asset and a lease liability if any of the following qualitative conditions exists:

1. **Transfer of ownership:** If, during or at the end of the lease term, the lease transfers ownership of the asset to the lessee, the leased asset and lease liability should be recorded on the lessee's books.

2. **Option to buy:** If, during the term of the lease, the lessee has an option to purchase the asset at a price that is much below its fair value (called a *bargain purchase option*), we can assume that the lessee will choose to use this option. Thus, the leased asset and lease liability should be recorded on the lessee's books.

3. **Lease term:** If the lease term is for the major part of the economic life of the leased property, the asset has effectively been purchased and should be recorded as an asset along with the lease liability by the lessee.

4. **Purchase price:** If the present value of the lease payments amounts to substantially all of the fair value of the leased property, the lessee has essentially paid for the asset. As a result, the leased asset and lease liability should be recorded on the books of the lessee.

5. **Specialized asset:** If the leased asset is of such a specialized nature that only the lessee can use it, the leased asset and lease liability should be recorded on the lessee's books.

To illustrate, assume that Fortune Ltd. decides to lease new equipment on November 27. The lease period is 10 years and the economic life of the leased equipment is estimated to be 14 years. The present value of the lease payments is $170,000 and the fair market value of the equipment is $200,000. There is no transfer of ownership during the lease term.

In this example, Fortune has essentially purchased the equipment. Conditions (3) and (4) have both been met. First, the lease term is for the major part of the economic life of the asset (10 years ÷ 14 years = 71.43%). Second, the present value of cash payments amounts to substantially all of the equipment's fair market value ($170,000 ÷ $200,000 = 85%). The present value of the cash payments in a finance lease is calculated in the same way that was explained earlier in the chapter for bond interest payments.

Note that while two conditions were met in this case, only one condition has to be met for the lease to be treated as a finance lease. The entry to record the transaction is as follows:

A	=	L	+	SE
+170,000		+170,000		

Cash flows: no effect

Nov. 27	Leased Asset—Equipment	170,000	
	Lease Liability		170,000
	To record leased asset and lease liability.		

The leased asset is reported on the balance sheet under property, plant, and equipment. The portion of the lease liability that is expected to be paid in the next year is reported as a current liability. The remainder is classified as a long-term liability.

After it is acquired, the leased asset is depreciated just as any other long-lived asset is. In addition, the liability is reduced each period by the lease payment. The payment is allocated between interest expense and the principal amount of the lease liability, which is like what was shown earlier in the chapter for blended principal and interest payments on notes payable.

Canadian GAAP for Private Enterprises

While accounting for leases under Canadian GAAP for Private Enterprises is very similar to accounting for leases under IFRS, there are a few differences worth noting.

1. **Terminology:** Finance leases are called capital leases.

2. **Classification as capital or operating lease based on lease term:** Under IFRS, professional judgement needs to be used to assess whether the lease term is for the major part of the economic life. In comparison, under Canadian GAAP for Private Enterprises, specific benchmarks are used to assess if the conditions are met. A lease is classified as a capital lease if the lease term is equal to 75% or more of the economic life of the leased property.

3. **Classification as capital or operating lease based on lease payments:** Similar to lease term, professional judgement needs to be used under IFRS to assess whether the present value of the lease payments amounts to substantially all of the fair value of the property. In Canadian GAAP for Private Enterprises, if the present value of the lease payments is equal to or greater than 90% of the fair value of the leased property, then the lease is a capital lease.

4. **Classification of leases of specialized assets as finance leases under IFRS:** Canadian GAAP for Private Enterprises does not include the condition that leases of specialized assets that only the lessee can use be treated as capital leases.

Operating Leases

If the benefits and risks of ownership are not transferred to the lessee, and from an economic point of view the lease is a rental agreement, the lease is classified as an operating lease. Rental of an apartment and rental of a car are examples of **operating leases**. Under an operating lease, the lease (or rental) payments are recorded as an expense by the lessee and as revenue by the lessor. For example, assume that a sales representative for Western Inc. leases a car from Hertz Car Rental at the airport on July 17. Hertz charges a total of $275. The entry by the lessee, Western Inc., would be as follows:

July 17	Car Rental Expense	275	
	Cash		275
	To record payment of lease rental charge.		

Helpful hint *Financial Reporting in Canada* reports that 97% of the companies surveyed have operating leases and 45% have capital (finance) leases.

A	=	L	+	SE
−275				−275

⬇ Cash flows: −275

Many operating leases are short-term, such as the rental of an apartment or car as described above. Others are for an extended period of time. Operating leases that cover a long period of time are sometimes seen as a form of off–balance sheet financing. **Off–balance sheet financing** occurs when liabilities are kept off of a company's balance sheet. Many people argue that if an operating lease results in the long-term use of an asset and an unavoidable obligation, it should be recorded as an asset and a liability. To reduce these concerns, companies are required to report their operating lease obligations in detail in a note to the financial statements. This allows analysts and other financial statement users to adjust ratios such as debt to total assets (which we will learn about in the next section of this chapter) by adding leased assets and lease liabilities if this treatment is considered more appropriate.

To address the concern about off–balance sheet financing, the International Accounting Standards Board and Financial Accounting Standards Board are currently working on a joint project on leases that recognizes that, under any lease agreement, the right to use property by the lessee meets the definition of an asset and the related obligation to make periodic rental payments meets the definition of a liability. The boards are therefore proposing that all leases be accounted for by recording an asset and liability.

Illustration 15-9 summarizes the major difference between an operating and a finance lease.

Finance Lease

Lessee has substantially all of the benefits and risks of ownership.

Operating Lease

Lessor has substantially all of the benefits and risks of ownership.

◄ Illustration 15-9

Types of leases

For a finance lease, both an asset and a liability are reported in the balance sheet. Two expenses—depreciation expense related to the leased asset and interest expense related to the lease liability—are reported in the income statement. For an operating lease, no asset or liability is reported in the balance sheet. The only expense that is reported in the income statement is rental expense.

BEFORE YOU GO ON . . .

→ Review It

1. What is the difference in accounting for a finance lease and an operating lease?
2. Why is an operating lease sometimes considered to be an example of off–balance sheet financing?
3. Does The Forzani Group have any finance (capital) or operating leases? The answer to this question is at the end of the chapter.

→ Do It

The Alert Company has the following two leasing options to acquire a new machine:

	Lease Option 1	Lease Option 2
Transfer of ownership	No	No
Bargain purchase option	No	No
Lease term	8 years	2 years
Estimated useful life	11 years	5 years
Fair market value	$20,000	$20,000
Present value	$17,000	$9,000

Discuss how each lease option would affect Alert's financial statements.

Action Plan

- Know the five qualitative conditions to distinguish between an operating and a finance lease. A lease is considered to be a finance lease if any one of the following conditions are met: (1) there will be a transfer of ownership, (2) there is a bargain purchase option, (3) the lease term is for the major part of the economic life, (4) the present value of the lease payments amounts to substantially all of the fair value of the leased property, and (5) the asset is a specialized asset.
- Understand the impact of an operating and a finance lease on the income statement and balance sheet. With an operating lease, no asset or liability is recorded; with a finance lease, both an asset and a liability are recorded.

Solution

Lease option 1 would be recorded as a finance lease because the lease term is a major part of the economic life of the machinery (8 years ÷ 11 years = 72.7%). Because of this, an asset and a liability would be reported on the balance sheet. Depreciation expense and interest expense would be reported on the income statement.

Lease option 2 would be recorded as an operating lease as none of the five conditions of a finance lease have been met. There would be no impact on the balance sheet, but the lease payments would be reported as rental expense on the income statement.

The Navigator

Related exercise material: BE15–10, BE15–11, BE15–12, and E15–10.

Statement Presentation and Analysis

STUDY OBJECTIVE 5

Explain and illustrate the methods for the presentation and analysis of long-term liabilities.

Liabilities are a significant amount on the financial statements and they have to be disclosed in detail so they can be properly understood by investors and creditors. These and other users are very interested in assessing a company's solvency (its ability to pay) with regard to its long-term liabilities. We will look at the presentation and analysis of liabilities in the next sections.

Presentation

Long-term liabilities are reported in a separate section of the balance sheet, immediately after current liabilities, as here with assumed data:

ANY COMPANY LTD. Balance Sheet (partial) December 31, 2011	
Long-term liabilities	
Bonds payable, 6%, due in 2015	$ 920,000
Mortgage notes payable, 8%, due in 2021	500,000
Lease liability	540,000
Total long-term liabilities	$1,960,000

Full disclosure of debt is very important. Summary data are usually presented in the balance sheet, and detailed data (interest rate, maturity date, redemption price, convertibility, and any assets pledged as collateral) are shown in a supporting schedule or in the notes to the financial statements. The amount of long-term debt maturing within 12 months of the balance sheet date should be reported under current liabilities.

Analysis

A company's investors and creditors are interested in analyzing its liquidity and solvency. Short-term creditors are interested in liquidity ratios, which measure a company's ability to repay its short-term debt and to meet unexpected needs for cash. We learned about liquidity ratios such as the current ratio, inventory turnover, and receivables turnover in earlier chapters.

Long-term creditors and investors are more interested in solvency ratios, which measure a company's ability to repay its long-term debt and survive over a long period of time. They are particularly interested in a company's ability to pay interest when it is due and to repay its debt at maturity. Two examples of solvency ratios are debt to total assets and the interest coverage ratio. They are explained next.

Debt to Total Assets

Debt to total assets measures the percentage of the total assets that is financed by creditors rather than by shareholders. Financing provided by creditors is riskier than financing provided by shareholders, because debt must be repaid at specific points in time whether the company is doing well or not.

Illustration 15-10 shows how the debt to total assets ratio is calculated. Using data from Forzani's financial statements (in thousands), the ratio is calculated by dividing total liabilities (both current and long-term) by total assets.

Helpful hint Some users measure the percentage of the total assets that is financed by shareholders. This ratio is called the *debt to equity ratio.*

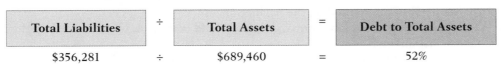

Total Liabilities	÷	Total Assets	=	Debt to Total Assets
$356,281	÷	$689,460	=	52%

← Illustration 15-10

Debt to total assets

This means that 52% of Forzani's assets are financed by creditors. The remainder, 48% (100% − 52%), has been financed by shareholders. In general, the higher the percentage of debt to total assets, the greater the risk that the company may be unable to meet its maturing obligations.

While you may assume that having no, or a low, debt to total assets ratio is ideal, recall that we learned at the beginning of this chapter that some debt may be good for a company. In some circumstances, a company can increase its earnings per share and return on equity by increasing how much debt financing it relies on.

Interest Coverage

The debt to total assets ratio must be interpreted in light of the company's ability to handle its debt. That is, a company might have a high debt to total assets ratio but still be able to easily pay its interest payments. Alternatively, a company may have a low debt to total assets ratio and struggle to cover its interest payments.

Alternative terminology
The interest coverage ratio is also commonly known as the *times interest earned ratio.*

The **interest coverage ratio** indicates the company's ability to meet interest payments as they come due. It is calculated by dividing profit before interest expense and income tax expense by interest expense. The numerator is often abbreviated and called **EBIT**, which stands for "earnings before interest and tax." EBIT can be calculated by adding back interest expense and income tax expense to profit. Because these amounts were originally deducted to determine profit, adding them back has the effect of cancelling them.

Illustration 15-11 calculates interest coverage for Forzani ($ in thousands).

Illustration 15-11 →

Interest coverage

Profit + Interest Expense + Income Tax Expense (EBIT)	÷	Interest Expense	=	Interest Coverage
$29,325 + $5,175 + $14,989	÷	$5,175	=	9.6 times

Even though Forzani's debt to total assets ratio is 52%, the company appears well equipped to handle its interest payments. Its EBIT can cover interest charges 9.6 times.

ACCOUNTING IN ACTION: ACROSS THE ORGANIZATION

Unions, retirees, and the government all got involved to help Air Canada avoid filing for bankruptcy in 2009. Air Canada faced a cash crunch when its pension plan's deficit rose to $2.9 billion, and it was required to pay $570 million into the plan, at a time when reduced demand for travel threatened Air Canada's future. Air Canada's unions, retirees, and the Canadian government supported a delay in payments to the pension plan for 21 months and the unions agreed to extend their current labour contracts. Air Canada agreed to give its unions a 15% equity interest in the company and a seat on the board of directors in exchange for the delay in pension payments and extension of current contracts. Both the delay of pension payments and labour stability were critical to the airline's securing $600 million in financing it needed to stay afloat.

Sources: Scott Deveau, "Air Canada Gets Key Backing on Pensions," *Financial Post*, July 25, 2009, Scott Deveau, "Air Canada Fights Financial Headwinds," *Financial Post*, May 9, 2009.

Do you think that delaying payments to the pension plan and borrowing an additional $600 million are all that Air Canada will have to do to avoid bankruptcy?

BEFORE YOU GO ON . . .

→ Review It

1. How are liabilities presented on the balance sheet?
2. What information about long-term liabilities should be disclosed in the notes to the
3. financial statements?
4. How are the debt to total assets and interest coverage ratios calculated? Explain why they should always be interpreted together.

→ Do It

Gleason Ltd. reported the following selected data at December 31, 2010.

Total assets	$529,000
Total liabilities	302,000
Interest expense	12,000
Income tax expense	25,000
Profit	75,000

Calculate Gleason Ltd.'s (a) debt to total assets, and (b) interest coverage ratios.

Action Plan

- Divide the total liabilities by the total assets to calculate the debt to total assets ratio.
- Add the interest expense and income tax expense to profit to calculate earnings before interest and income tax.
- Divide the earnings before interest and income tax expense by the interest expense to calculate the interest coverage ratio.

Solution

(a) Debt to total assets = 57% ($302,000 ÷ $529,000)
(b) Interest coverage ratio = 9.3 times ($75,000 + $25,000 + $12,000) ÷ $12,000

Related exercise material: BE15–13, BE15–14, BE15–15, E15–11, E15–12, and E15–13.

The Navigator

APPENDIX 15A ▶ EFFECTIVE-INTEREST AMORTIZATION

We learned earlier in the chapter that bond discounts and premiums must be allocated to expense over the life of the bonds using the **effective-interest method** of amortization. The effective-interest method uses the market interest rate when the bonds were issued to calculate periodic interest expense. We will see that the amount of interest expense will change each period as the amortized cost of the bonds changes. But the result is that interest expense will be a constant percentage of the amortized cost of the bonds over the life of the bonds.

There are three steps required to calculate amortization using the effective-interest method:

1. **Bond interest paid (or accrued):** Calculate the bond interest paid by multiplying the face value of the bonds by the contractual interest rate.
2. **Bond interest expense:** Calculate interest expense by multiplying the amortized cost of the bonds at the beginning of the interest period by the market (effective) interest rate.
3. **Amortization amount:** The amortization amount is the difference between the amounts calculated in steps (1) and (2).

Illustration 15A-1 shows how amortization is calculated with the effective-interest method.

STUDY OBJECTIVE 6

Apply the effective-interest method of amortizing bond discounts and premiums.

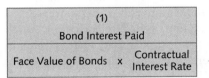 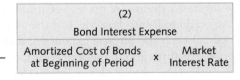

◀ **Illustration 15A-1**

Calculation of amortization using effective-interest method

We will explain each of these steps in the next two sections—first for a bond discount and then for a bond premium.

Amortizing a Bond Discount

To illustrate the effective-interest method of bond discount amortization, we will continue to use Candlestick Inc. from earlier in the chapter as our example. As you recall from the "Issuing Bonds at a Discount" section, Candlestick issued $1 million of five-year, 5% bonds at $957,345 to yield a market interest rate of 6%. This resulted in a bond discount of $42,655 ($1,000,000 − $957,345). Interest is payable semi-annually on July 1 and January 1.

The interest payment, $25,000, is calculated by multiplying the bonds' face value by the contractual interest rate ($1,000,000 × 5% × $^6/_{12}$). For the first interest period, the bond interest expense is $28,720, calculated by multiplying the amortized cost of the bonds at the beginning of the period by the market interest rate ($957,345 × 6% × $^6/_{12}$). The discount amortization is then calculated as the difference between the interest expense and the interest paid ($28,720 − $25,000 = $3,720).

A bond discount amortization schedule, as shown in Illustration 15A-2, makes it easier to record the interest expense and the discount amortization. For simplicity, amounts have been rounded to the nearest dollar in this schedule.

Illustration 15A-2 ➡

Bond discount amortization schedule—effective-interest method

		CANDLESTICK INC.			
		Bond Discount Amortization Schedule			
		Effective-Interest Method			
	(A)	(B)	(C)	(D)	(E)
	Interest Payment	Interest Expense	Discount Amortization	Unamortized Discount	Bond Amortized Cost
Semi-Annual Interest Period	($1,000,000 × 5% × $6/_{12}$)	(E × 6% × $6/_{12}$)	(A – B)	(D – C)	($1,000,000 – D)
Issue date (Jan. 1, 2011)				$42,655	$ 957,345
1 (July 1)	$ 25,000	$ 28,720	$ 3,720	38,935	961,065
2 (Jan. 1, 2012)	25,000	28,832	3,832	35,103	964,897
3 (July 1)	25,000	28,947	3,947	31,156	968,844
4 (Jan. 1, 2013)	25,000	29,065	4,065	27,091	972,909
5 (July 1)	25,000	29,187	4,187	22,904	977,096
6 (Jan. 1, 2014)	25,000	29,313	4,313	18,591	981,409
7 (July 1)	25,000	29,442	4,442	14,149	985,851
8 (Jan. 1, 2015)	25,000	29,576	4,576	9,573	990,427
9 (July 1)	25,000	29,713	4,713	4,860	995,140
10 (Jan. 1, 2016)	25,000	29,860[1]	4,860	0	1,000,000
	$250,000	$292,655	$42,655		
		[1] $6 difference due to rounding			

We have highlighted columns A, B, and C in the amortization schedule shown in Illustration 15A-2 to emphasize their importance. These three columns give the numbers for each period's journal entries. They are the main reason for preparing the schedule, although all the columns give useful information.

- Column A gives the amount of the credit to Cash (or Interest Payable). Note that the amounts in this column stay the same because the face value of the bonds ($1,000,000) is multiplied by the same semi-annual contractual interest rate each period.
- Column B shows the debit to Bond Interest Expense. It is calculated by multiplying the bond's amortized cost at the beginning of the period by the semi-annual market interest rate. Note that while the semi-annual market interest rate (3%) stays constant each interest period, the interest expense increases because the bond's amortized cost increases.
- Column C is the credit to Bonds Payable. It is the amortization of the bond discount, which is the difference between the interest expense and the interest payment. The amounts in this column increase throughout the amortization period because the interest expense increases. Notice that the total of this column—$42,655—is equal to the discount when the bond was issued on January 1, 2011.
- Column D shows the unamortized discount. It decreases each period by the discount amortization amount from Column C until it reaches zero at maturity.
- Column E is the bond's amortized cost (its face value less the unamortized discount). Note that the amortized cost of the bonds increases by the discount amortization amount each period until it reaches the face value of $1 million at the end of period 10 (January 1, 2013), when the discount is fully amortized.

Columns A, B, and C give information for the required journal entries. For the first interest period, the entry to record the payment of interest and amortization of the bond discount by Candlestick is as follows:

A	=	L	+	SE
−25,000		+3,720		−28,720

⬇ Cash flows: −25,000

July 1	Bond Interest Expense ($957,345 × 6% × $6/_{12}$)	28,720	
	Bonds Payable		3,720
	Cash ($1,000,000 × 5% × $6/_{12}$)		25,000
	To record payment of bond interest and amortization of bond discount.		

Recall from our chapter discussion that issuing a bond at a discount increases the cost of borrowing above the contractual interest rate. Consequently, the interest expense includes both the interest payment ($25,000) and the bond discount amortization ($3,720).

For the second interest period, at Candlestick's year end, the following adjusting entry is made:

Dec. 31	Bond Interest Expense ($961,065 × 6% × %12)	28,832	
	Bonds Payable		3,832
	Bond Interest Payable ($1,000,000 × 5% × %12)		25,000
	To record payment of bond interest and amortization of bond discount.		

A	=	L	+	SE
		+3,832		−28,832
		+25,000		

Cash flows: no effect

Note that Bond Interest Payable is credited rather than Cash because the next interest payment date is January 1. On January 1, the Bond Interest Payable account will be debited and the Cash account credited.

Amortizing a Bond Premium

Using our previous example, we will now assume that Candlestick Inc. issues its bonds at $1,044,915. You will recall from the "Issuing Bonds at a Premium" section in the chapter that the market interest rate of 4% resulted in selling the bonds at a premium of $44,915 ($1,044,915 − $1,000,000). Interest is payable semi-annually on July 1 and January 1.

The amortization of a bond premium by the effective-interest method is similar to the procedures described for a bond discount. The bond premium amortization schedule is shown in Illustration 15A-3. Figures have been rounded to the nearest dollar for simplicity.

← Illustration 15A-3

Bond premium amortization schedule—effective-interest method

	(A) Interest Payment	(B) 	(C) Premium	(D) Unamortized	(E) Bond
Semi-Annual Interest Period	($1,000,000 × 5% × %12)	Interest Expense (E × 4% × %12)	Amortization (A − B)	Premium (D −C)	Amortized Cost ($1,000,000 + D)
Issue date (Jan. 1, 2011)				$44,915	$1,044,915
1 (July 1)	$ 25,000	$ 20,898	$ 4,102	40,813	1,040,813
2 (Jan. 1, 2012)	25,000	20,816	4,184	36,629	1,036,629
3 (July 1)	25,000	20,733	4,267	32,362	1,032,362
4 (Jan. 1, 2013)	25,000	20,647	4,353	28,009	1,028,009
5 (July 1)	25,000	20,560	4,440	23,569	1,023,569
6 (Jan. 1, 2014)	25,000	20,471	4,529	19,040	1,019,040
7 (July 1)	25,000	20,381	4,619	14,421	1,014,421
8 (Jan. 1, 2015)	25,000	20,288	4,712	9,709	1,009,709
9 (July 1)	25,000	20,194	4,806	4,903	1,004,903
10 (Jan. 1, 2016)	25,000	20,097[1]	4,903	0	1,000,000
	$250,000	$205,085	$44,915		

[1] $1 difference due to rounding

Each column in the premium amortization schedule gives the following information:

- Column A gives the amount of the credit to Cash (or Interest Payable). The amounts in this column stay the same because the face value of the bonds ($1,000,000) is multiplied by the same semi-annual contractual interest rate each period.
- Column B shows the debit to Bond Interest Expense. It is calculated by multiplying the bonds' amortized cost at the beginning of the period by the semi-annual market interest rate. Note that while the semi-annual market interest rate (2%) stays constant each interest period, the interest expense decreases because the bond's amortized cost decreases. When we amortized a discount in Illustration 15A-2, the interest expense increased because the bond's amortized cost also increased.

- Column C is the debit to Bonds Payable. It is the difference between the interest payment and the interest expense. The amounts in this column increase throughout the amortization period because the interest expense decreases as the amortized cost of the bonds decreases. Notice that the total of this column—$44,915—is equal to the premium when the bond was issued on January 1, 2011.

  Note that for both a discount and a premium, the amortization amount is calculated as the difference between the interest payment (column A) and the interest expense (column B). However, for a discount, because the interest expense is greater than the interest payment, we subtract column A from column B. For a premium, where the interest payment is greater than the interest expense, we subtract column B from column A.
- Column E is the bond's amortized cost (its face value plus the unamortized premium). Note that the amortized cost of the bonds decreases by the premium amortization amount each period until it reaches the face value of $1 million at the end of period 10 (January 1, 2013). In the discount situation shown in Illustration 15A-2, the amortized cost *increased* but both amortization schedules end up with the same face value amount at maturity. Regardless of the original market interest rate, the face value of the bonds is the same in both examples.

The entry on the first interest payment date is as follows:

A	=	L	+	SE
−25,000		−4,102		−20,898

↓ Cash flows: −25,000

July 1	Bond Interest Expense ($1,044,915 × 4% × %₁₂)	20,898	
	Bonds Payable	4,102	
	Cash ($1,000,000 × 5% × %₁₂)		25,000
	To record payment of bond interest and amortization of bond premium.		

As we learned earlier in the chapter, issuing a bond at a premium reduces the cost of borrowing below the contractual interest rate. Consequently, the interest expense account is basically increased (debited) for the interest payment ($25,000) and decreased (credited) for the bond premium amortization ($4,102) in the same entry.

For the second period, the following adjusting entry is made. While the interest expense and amortization amounts vary, the cash payment is a constant $25,000 every interest period.

A	=	L	+	SE
		−4,184		−20,816
		+25,000		

Cash flows: no effect

Dec. 31	Bond Interest Expense ($1,040,813 × 4% × %₁₂)	20,816	
	Bonds Payable	4,184	
	Bond Interest Payable ($1,000,000 × 5% × %₁₂)		25,000
	To record payment of bond interest and amortization of bond premium.		

Illustration 15A-4 summarizes some of the differences between issuing a bond at a discount and a premium under the effective-interest method of amortization.

Illustration 15A-4 ➡

Differing effects of issuing a bond at a discount and a premium

	Discount	Preminm
Periodic interest payment	Same each period	Same each period
Periodic interest expense	Increases each period	Decreases each period
Bond's amortized cost	Increases to face value at maturity	Decreases to face value at maturity

Under the effective-interest method, the interest payment is the same whether the bonds were issued at a discount or at a premium. This is because the interest payment is calculated by multiplying the bonds' face value by the contractual interest rate, which does not change over the life of the bond.

However, interest expense is calculated by multiplying the bond's amortized cost by the market interest rate. The same market interest rate is used over the life of the bond, but the amortized cost changes as the premium or discount is amortized. Consequently, interest expense changes proportionately with the amortized cost. It increases with a discount because the amortized cost also increases. It decreases with a premium because the amortized cost also decreases.

BEFORE YOU GO ON . . .

→ **Review It**

1. How is the amount of bond interest paid calculated?
2. How is the interest expense on Bonds Payable calculated?
3. How is the amount of the amortization of the discount (premium) calculated?
4. Why is the interest expense higher than the interest paid when bonds are issued at a discount?
5. Why is the interest expense less than the interest paid when bonds are issued at a premium?

→ **Do It**

On January 1, 2010, Leonard Company issued $200,000, 10-year, 4% bonds, with interest payable semi-annually on July 1 and January 1. Leonard Company's fiscal year end is December 31.

(a) Assume the bonds were issued at $184,411 to yield 5%. (1) Record the issuance of the bonds. (2) Prepare a bond discount amortization schedule for the first four interest periods. (3) Record the interest expense and the payment of interest on July 1, 2010, December 31, 2010, and January 1, 2011.

(b) Assume the bonds were issued at $217,169 to yield 3%. (1) Record the issuance of the bonds. (2) Prepare a bond premium amortization schedule for the first four interest periods. (3) Record the interest expense and the payment of interest on July 1, 2010, December 31, 2010, and January 1, 2011.

Action Plan

- Debit cash and credit bonds payable for the amount the bonds were issued at.
- Calculate the semi-annual interest payment by multiplying the bonds' face value by the semi-annual contractual interest rate (contractual rate $\times$ $^6/_{12}$).
- Calculate the interest expense by multiplying the semi-annual market rate (yield rate $\times$ $^6/_{12}$) by the amortized cost of the bonds payable.
- The amount of the discount (premium) amortization is the difference between the interest payment and the interest expense.
- The amortized cost of the bonds issued at a discount increases by the amount of the discount amortization each interest period.
- The amortized cost of the bonds issued at a premium decreases by the amount of the premium amortization each interest period.

Solution

(a)

(1)

Jan. 1, 2010	Cash	184,411	
	Bonds Payable		184,411
	To record issue of bonds.		

(2)

LEONARD COMPANY
Bond Discount Amortization Schedule
Effective-Interest Method

Semi-Annual Interest Period	(A) Interest Payment ($200,000 $\times$ 4% $\times$ $^6/_{12}$)	(B) Interest Expense (E $\times$ 5% $\times$ $^6/_{12}$)	(C) Discount Amortization (A – B)	(D) Unamortized Discount (D – C)	(E) Bond Amortized Cost ($200,000 – D)
Issue date (Jan. 1, 2010)				$15,589	$ 184,411
1 (July 1)	$ 4,000	$ 4,610	$ 610	14,979	185,021
2 (Jan. 1, 2011)	4,000	4,626	626	14,353	185,647
3 (July 1)	4,000	4,641	641	13,712	186,288
4 (Jan. 1, 2012)	4,000	4,657	657	13,055	186,945

(3)

July 1, 2010	Bond Interest Expense		4,610	
	Bonds Payable			610
	Cash			4,000
	To record payment of interest and amortization of discount.			
Dec. 31, 2010	Bond Interest Expense		4,626	
	Bonds Payable			626
	Bond Interest Payable			4,000
	To record accrual of interest and amortization of discount.			
Jan. 1, 2011	Bond Interest Payable		4,000	
	Cash			4,000
	To record payment of interest.			

(b)

(1)

Jan. 1, 2010	Cash		217,169	
	Bonds Payable			217,169
	To record issue of bonds.			

(2)

LEONARD COMPANY Bond Premium Amortization Schedule Effective-Interest Method					
Semi-Annual Interest Period	(A) Interest Payment ($200,000 × 4% × 6/12)	(B) Interest Expense (E × 3% × 6/12)	(C) Premium Amortization (A – B)	(D) Unamortized Premium (D – C)	(E) Bond Amortized Cost ($200,000 – D)
Issue date (Jan. 1, 2010)				$17,169	$ 217,169
1 (July 1)	$ 4,000	$ 3,258	$ 742	16,427	216,427
2 (Jan. 1, 2011)	4,000	3,246	754	15,673	215,673
3 (July 1)	4,000	3,235	765	14,908	214,908
4 (Jan. 1, 2012)	4,000	3,224	776	14,132	214,132

(3)

July 1, 2010	Bond Interest Expense		3,258	
	Bonds Payable		742	
	Cash			4,000
	To record payment of interest and amortization of premium.			
Dec. 31, 2010	Bond Interest Expense		3,246	
	Bonds Payable		754	
	Bond Interest Payable			4,000
	To record accrual of interest and amortization of premium.			
Jan. 1, 2011	Bond Interest Payable		4,000	
	Cash			4,000
	To record payment of interest.			

The Navigator

Related exercise material: BE15–16, BE15–17, BE15–18, E15–14, E15–15, and E15-16.

Demonstration Problem 1

Demonstration Problems

On January 1, 2006, Feng Inc. issued $500,000 of 10-year, 7% bonds at 93.205 because the market interest rate was 8%. Interest is payable semi-annually on January 1 and July 1. Feng's year end is June 30. Five years later, on January 1, 2011, Feng redeemed all of these bonds at 98. The amortized cost of the bonds at that time was $479,724.

Instructions

(a) Calculate the total issue price of the bonds using (1) the market rate of interest and (2) the present value tables in Appendix D. Round your answers to the nearest dollar.

(b) Prepare the journal entry to record the issue of the bonds on January 1, 2006.

(c) Prepare the journal entry to accrue the first interest payment on June 30. Assume that the amortization amount for the first interest period is $1,141.

(d) Show the presentation of the liability on Feng's balance sheet on June 30, 2006.

(e) Prepare the journal entry to record the interest payment and amortization on January 1, 2011. Assume that the amortization amount for the period is $1,624.

(f) Prepare the journal entry to record the payment of the interest on January 1, 2011, and the redemption of the bonds on January 1, 2011.

Solution to Demonstration Problem 1

(a)

(1) $500,000 × 93.205%	$466,025
(2) Present value of $500,000 received in 20 periods	
$500,000 × 0.45639 ($n = 20, i = 4\%$)	$228,195
Present value of $17,500 received for each of 20 periods	
$500,000 × 7% × $^{6}/_{12}$ = $17,500;	
$17,500 × 13.59033 ($n = 20, i = 4\%$)	237,830
Present value (market price) of bonds	$466,025

(b)

Jan. 1, 2006	Cash	466,025	
	Bonds Payable		466,025
	To record issue of 10-year, 7% bonds.		

(c)

June 30	Bond Interest Expense ($17,500 + $1,141)[1]	18,641	
	Bonds Payable		1,141
	Bond Interest Payable ($500,000 × 7% × $^{6}/_{12}$)		17,500
	To record accrual of semi-annual interest.		

[1] Under the effective interest method, the calculation for Bond Interest Expense is ($466,025 × 8% × $^{6}/_{12}$)

(d)

FENG INC.
Balance Sheet (partial)
June 30, 2006

Long-term liabilities	
Bonds payable ($466,025 + $1,141)	$467,166

(e)

Jan. 1, 2011	Bond Interest Expense ($17,500 + $1,624)	19,124	
	Bonds Payable		1,624
	Bond Interest Payable ($500,000 × 7% × $^{6}/_{12}$)		17,500
	To record accrual of semi-annual interest.		

(f)

Jan. 1, 2011	Bonds Payable	479,724	
	Loss on Bond Redemption ($490,000 − $479,724)	10,276	
	Cash ($500,000 × 98%)		490,000
	To record redemption of bonds.		

Action Plan

- To calculate the proceeds using the stated percentage rate, multiply the face value by the issue price expressed as a percentage (e.g., 93.205%).
- To calculate the proceeds using the present value tables in Appendix D, use Table PV–1 for the face value and Table PV–2 for the interest payment. Don't forget to double the number of interest periods and halve the interest rate for semi-annual interest.
- If the proceeds are greater than the face value, the difference is a premium. If the proceeds are less than the face value, the difference is a discount.
- Record and report bonds payable at their present value.
- Amortization of a bond discount increases interest expense; amortization of a bond premium decreases interest expense.
- To record the redemption: (1) update any partial period interest and amortization if required, (2) eliminate the amortized cost of the bonds by removing the balance from the Bonds Payable account, (3) record the cash paid, and (4) calculate and record the gain or loss (the difference between the cash paid and the amortized cost).

The Navigator

Demonstration Problem 2

Note: This demonstration problem uses the same facts as those shown in the "Do It" problem on p. 838, but the nature and amount of the payment are changed.

On December 31, 2010, Tian Inc. issued a $500,000, 15-year, 8% mortgage note payable. The terms provide for semi-annual fixed principal payments of $16,667 on June 30 and December 31. Tian's year end is December 31.

Instructions

Round your answers to the nearest dollar.

(a) Prepare a payment schedule for the first two years of the note (through to December 31, 2012).

(b) Prepare the journal entries to record the issue of the note on December 31, 2010, and the first two instalment payments.

(c) Indicate the current and noncurrent amounts for the mortgage note payable at December 31, 2011.

(d) What is the difference between your results here using a fixed principal payment and the results shown using a blended payment for the same situation illustrated in the "Do It" problem on p. 838?

Solution to Demonstration Problem 2

Action Plan

- Determine the interest expense for the mortgage by multiplying the semi-annual interest rate by the principal balance at the beginning of the period. The cash payment is the total of the principal payment and interest expense. The reduction of principal is the amount of the fixed principal payment.
- Record the reduction of principal and interest expense separately.
- The current portion of the mortgage note payable is the amount of principal that will be repaid in the next year. The long-term portion is the remaining balance.

(a)

Semi-Annual Interest Period	Cash Payment	Interest Expense	Reduction of Principal	Principal Balance
Issue Date (Dec. 31, 2010)				$500,000
1 (June 30, 2011)	$36,667[1]	$20,000[2]	$16,667[3]	483,333[4]
2 (Dec. 31)	36,000	19,333	16,667	466,666
3 (June 30, 2012)	35,334	18,667	16,667	449,999
4 (Dec. 31)	34,667	18,000	16,667	433,332

[1] $20,000 + $16,667 = $36,667
[2] $500,000 × 8% × $^6/_{12}$ = $20,000
[3] $500,000 ÷ 30 periods = $16,667
[4] $500,000 − $16,667 = $483,333

(b)

Dec. 31, 2010	Cash	500,000	
	Mortgage Note Payable		500,000
	To record issue of 15-year, 8% mortgage note payable.		
June 30, 2011	Interest Expense ($500,000 × 8% × $^6/_{12}$)	20,000	
	Mortgage Note Payable	16,667	
	Cash		36,667
	To record semi-annual payment on note.		
Dec. 31, 2011	Interest Expense ($483,333 × 8% × $^6/_{12}$)	19,333	
	Mortgage Note Payable	16,667	
	Cash		36,000
	To record semi-annual payment on note.		

(c) The current liability is $33,334 ($16,667 + $16,667).
The long-term liability is $433,332.
The total liability is $466,666, the balance at the end of the second period, December 31, 2011.

(c) In a blended payment situation, the cash payment stays constant. In a fixed principal payment situation, the reduction of the principal stays constant. In both situations, the same amount of principal is repaid over the same period of time—just in a different payment pattern.

The Navigator

Summary of Study Objectives

1. *Compare the impact of issuing debt instead of equity.* Debt offers the following advantages over equity: (1) shareholder control is not affected, (2) income tax savings result, (3) earnings per share may be higher, and (4) return on equity may be higher.

2. *Account for bonds payable.* The market value of bonds is determined using present value factors: these factors determine the value of the interest and principal cash flows generated by the bond relative to the current market interest rate.

When bonds are issued, the Bonds Payable account is credited for the bonds' market value (present value). Bonds are issued at a discount if the market interest rate is higher than the contract interest rate. Bonds are issued at a premium if the market interest rate is lower than the contract interest rate. Bond discounts and bond premiums are amortized to interest expense over the life of the bond using the effective-interest method of amortization. The amortization of a bond discount increases interest expense. The amortization of a bond premium decreases interest expense.

When bonds are retired at maturity, Bonds Payable is debited and Cash is credited. There is no gain or loss at retirement. When bonds are redeemed before maturity, it is necessary to (1) pay and record any unrecorded interest, (2) eliminate the amortized cost of the bonds at the redemption date, (3) record the cash paid, and (4) recognize any gain or loss on redemption.

3. *Account for long-term notes payable.* Long-term notes payable are repayable in a series of instalments. Each payment consists of (1) interest on the unpaid balance of the note, and (2) a reduction of the principal balance. These payments can be either (1) fixed principal plus interest payments or (2) blended principal and inter-est payments. With fixed principal payments, the reduction in principal is constant but the cash payment and interest decreases each period (as the principal decreases). Blended payments result in a constant cash payment but changing amounts of interest and principal.

4. *Account for leases.* For a finance lease, the transaction is considered to be equivalent to a purchase of an asset. The lessee records the asset and the related obligation at the present value of the future lease payments. The income statement reflects both the interest expense and depreciation expense. For an operating lease, lease (or rental) payments are recorded as an expense by the lessee (renter).

5. *Explain and illustrate the methods for the presentation and analysis of long-term liabilities.* The current portion of the long-term debt is reported as a current liability in the balance sheet, and the remaining portions are reported as long-term liabilities. The nature of each liability should be described in the notes accompanying the financial statements. A company's long-term solvency may be analyzed by calculating two ratios. Debt to total assets indicates the proportion of company assets that is financed by debt. Interest coverage measures a company's ability to meet its interest payments as they come due.

6. *Apply the effective-interest method of amortizing bond discounts and premiums (Appendix 15A).* Amortization is calculated under the effective-interest method as the difference between the interest paid and the interest expense. Interest paid is calculated by multiplying the face value of the bonds by the contractual interest rate. Interest expense is calculated by multiplying the amortized cost of the bonds at the beginning of the interest period by the market interest rate.

Glossary

 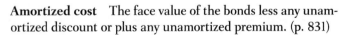

Amortized cost The face value of the bonds less any unamortized discount or plus any unamortized premium. (p. 831)

Bearer (coupon) bonds Bonds that are not registered. (p. 829)

Bond A debt security that is traded on an organized securities exchange, is issued to investors, and has these properties: the principal amount will be repaid at a designated maturity date and periodic interest is paid (normally semi-annually) at a specified rate on the principal amount. (p. 825)

Bond certificate A legal document indicating the name of the issuer, the face value of the bond, and other data such as the contractual interest rate and maturity date of the bond. (p. 826)

Contractual interest rate The rate that determines the amount of interest the borrower pays and the investor receives. (p. 826)

Convertible bonds Bonds that permit bondholders to convert them into common shares. (p. 829)

Debenture bonds Bonds issued against the general credit of the borrower. Also called *unsecured bonds.* (p. 829)

Debt to total assets The ratio of total liabilities to total assets. Indicates the proportion of assets that is financed by debt. (p. 843)

Discount (on bonds payable) The difference that results when bonds' selling price is less than their face value. This occurs when the market interest rate is greater than the contractual interest rate. (p. 828)

EBIT Earnings before interest and tax, calculated as profit + interest expense + income tax expense. (p. 844)

Effective-interest method of amortization A method of calculating interest expense and of amortizing a bond discount or bond premium that results in periodic interest expense equal to a constant percentage of the amortized cost of the bonds. (p. 845)

Face value The amount of principal that the issuer must pay at the bond's maturity date. (p. 826)

Finance lease A lease that transfers all the benefits and risks of ownership to the lessee, so that the lease effectively results in a purchase of the asset. (p. 839)

Financial leverage Borrowing at one rate and investing at a different rate. (p. 823)

Fixed interest rate An interest rate that is constant (unchanged) over the term of the debt. (p. 835)

Floating (or variable) interest rate An interest rate that changes over the term of the debt with fluctuating market rates. (p. 835)

Interest coverage ratio A measure of a company's ability to meet its interest obligations. It is calculated by dividing profit (earnings) before interest expense and income tax expense (EBIT) by interest expense. (p. 844)

Lease A contractual arrangement between two parties where the party that owns an asset agrees to allow another party to use the specified property for a series of cash payments over an agreed period of time. (p. 839)

Lessee The renter of a property. (p. 839)

Lessor The owner of an asset for rent. (p. 839)

Market (effective) interest rate The rate that investors require for lending money to a company. (p. 827)

Maturity date The date on which the final payment on a debt security is due to be repaid by the issuer to the investor. (p. 826)

Mortgage note payable A long-term note that pledges title to specific assets as security for a loan. (p. 835)

Off–balance sheet financing The intentional effort by a company to structure its financing arrangements to avoid showing liabilities on its books. (p. 841)

Operating lease A lease where the benefits and risks of ownership are not transferred to the lessee. (p. 841)

Premium (on bonds payable) The difference that results when bonds' selling price is greater than their face value. This occurs when the market interest rate is less than the contractual interest rate. (p. 828)

Present value The amount that must be invested today at a specified interest rate to have a certain amount in the future. (p. 827)

Redeemable bonds Bonds that the issuer can retire at a stated dollar amount before maturity. Also known as *callable bonds*. (p. 829)

Redemption price An amount that a company pays to buy back bonds that is specified at the time the bonds are issued. (p. 833)

Registered bonds Bonds issued in the name of the owner. (p. 829)

Retractable bonds Bonds that the bondholder can retire at a stated dollar amount before maturity. (p. 829)

Secured bonds Bonds that have specific assets of the issuer pledged as collateral. (p. 829)

Serial bonds Bonds that mature in instalments. (p. 829)

Term bonds Bonds that mature at a single specified future date. (p. 829)

Unsecured bonds Bonds that are issued against the general credit of the borrower. Also called *debenture bonds*. (p. 829)

Note: All questions, exercises, and problems below with an asterisk (*) relate to material in the appendix in this chapter.

Self-Study Questions

Answers are at the end of the chapter.

(SO 1) K 1. Which of the following are advantages of issuing debt securities instead of equity securities?
  (a) Voting control of the company is not affected.
  (b) Savings in income tax result because interest expense is tax-deductible.
  (c) Earnings per share and return on equity will be higher.
  (d) All of the above

2. If bonds are issued at a premium, it indicates that: (SO 2) K
  (a) the contractual interest rate is higher than the market interest rate.
  (b) the market interest rate is higher than the contractual interest rate.
  (c) the contractual interest rate and the market interest rate are the same.
  (d) the bonds have an AAA rating.

(SO 2) AP   3. On January 1, Scissors Corp. issues $200,000 of five-year, 7% bonds at 97. The entry to record the issue of the bonds is:
(a) debit to Cash for $200,000 and credit to Bonds Payable for $200,000.
(b) credit to Cash for $200,000 and debit to Bonds Payable for $200,000.
(c) credit to Cash for $194,000 and debit to Bonds Payable for $194,000.
(d) debit to Cash for $194,000 and credit to Bonds Payable for $194,000.

(SO 2) AP   4. The Marshlands Corporation has bonds issued at a premium. The entry to record the payment of semi-annual interest would include a:
(a) credit to Interest Expense, credit to Bonds Payable, and debit to Cash.
(b) debit to Interest Expense, debit to Bonds Payable, and credit to Cash.
(c) debit to Interest Expense, credit to Bonds Payable, and credit to Cash.
(d) debit to Cash, credit to Interest Expense, and debit to Bonds Payable.

(SO 2) AP   5. Gester Corporation redeems its $100,000 face value bonds at 105 on January 1, after the payment of semi-annual interest. The amortized cost of the bonds at the redemption date is $103,745. The entry to record the redemption will include a:
(a) credit of $103,745 to Bonds Payable.
(b) debit of $1,255 to Loss on Bond Redemption.
(c) credit of $1,255 to Gain on Bond Redemption.
(d) debit of $105,000 to Cash.

(SO 3) AP   6. Zhang Inc. issues a $497,000, three-year, 7% instalment note payable on January 1. The note will be paid in three annual blended payments of $189,383 each. What is the amount of interest expense that should be recognized by Zhang in the second year?
(a) $11,597
(b) $23,123
(c) $23,968
(d) $34,790

(SO 3) AP   7. Assume that the note issued by Zhang Inc. in question 6 above will be paid with fixed principal payments of $165,667 each. What is the amount of interest expense that should be recognized by Zhang in the second year?
(a) $11,597
(b) $23,193
(c) $23,968
(d) $34,790

(SO 4) C   8. The lease term for Lease A is equal to 72% of the estimated economic life of the leased property. The lease term for Lease B is equal to 45% of the estimated economic life of the leased property. Assuming no other conditions are met, how should the lessee classify these leases?

	Lease A	Lease B
(a)	Operating lease	Finance lease
(b)	Operating lease	Operating lease
(c)	Finance lease	Operating lease
(d)	Finance lease	Finance lease

(SO 5) AN   9. Which of the following ratio combinations indicates that a company's solvency position is improving?
(a) Debt to total assets ratios of 55% in year 2 and 45% in year 1
(b) Interest coverage ratios of 7 times in year 2 and 10 times in year 1
(c) Debt to total asset ratios of 55% in year 2 and 45% in year 1 and interest coverage ratios of 7 times in year 2 and 10 times in year 1
(d) Debt to total asset ratios of 45% in year 2 and 55% in year 1 and interest coverage ratios of 10 times in year 2 and 7 times in year 1

(SO 6) AP   *10. On January 1, Dias Corporation issued $2 million of five-year, 7% bonds with interest payable on July 1 and January 1. The bonds sold for $1,918,880. The market rate of interest for these bonds was 8%. On the first interest date, the debit entry to Bond Interest Expense (rounded to the nearest dollar) is for:
(a) $67,161.
(b) $76,755.
(c) $80,000.
(d) $70,000.

The Navigator

Questions

(SO 1) C   1. What is the difference between a current liability and a long-term liability? Give two examples of each type of liability.

(SO 1) C   2. As a source of long-term financing, what are the major advantages of using debt over equity? Disadvantages?

(SO 1) C   3. Explain how a company can increase its earnings per share and return on equity by issuing debt instead of equity.

(SO 2) C   4. Explain how bonds are similar to (a) notes payable and (b) common shares.

(SO 2) C 5. (a) Explain the difference between a contractual interest rate and market interest rate. (b) Explain why one rate changes over the term of the bonds and the other stays the same.

(SO 2) C 6. Explain how a bond's market value is determined using present value factors.

(SO 2) AP 7. Assume that Stoney Inc. sold bonds with a face value of $100,000 for $98,000. Was the market interest rate equal to, less than, or greater than the bonds' contractual interest rate? Explain.

(SO 2) C 8. How will the total cost of borrowing be affected if a bond is sold (a) at a discount and (b) at a premium? Explain when this cost of borrowing should be recorded.

(SO 2) C 9. Why is there no gain or loss when bonds are redeemed at maturity, but there usually is a gain or loss when bonds are redeemed before maturity?

(SO 3) C 10. What are the similarities and differences between short-term and long-term notes payable?

(SO 3) C 11. Canada Student Loans charge interest at prime plus an added percentage, such as 2.5%, on the student loans. Is this a fixed or floating rate? Explain.

(SO 3) C 12. What is the difference between instalment notes payable with fixed principal payments and those with blended payments?

(SO 3) C 13. When students borrow money for their post-secondary education under the Canada Student Loans Program, they sign an instalment note payable, which is repaid in monthly blended payments, starting six months following graduation. What is the advantage of blended payments to students repaying their loans?

(SO 3) AP 14. Doug Bareak, a friend of yours, has recently purchased a home for $200,000. He paid $20,000 down and financed the remainder with a 20-year, 5% mortgage, payable in blended payments of $1,290 per month. At the end of the first month,

Doug received a statement from the bank indicating that only $390 of the principal was paid during the month. At this rate, he calculated that it will take over 38 years to pay off the mortgage. Explain why this is not true.

15. (a) What is a lease? (b) Distinguish between a finance lease and an operating lease. (SO 4) C

16. What is off–balance sheet financing? Why are long-term operating leases considered to be a form of off–balance sheet financing? (SO 4) C

17. What is the impact on a company's balance sheet and income statement if it accounts for a lease as an operating lease instead of as a finance lease? (SO 4) AP

18. In general, what are the requirements for the financial statement presentation of long-term liabilities? (SO 5) K

19. How are the current and noncurrent portions of a mortgage note payable determined for presenting them in the liabilities section of the balance sheet? (SO 5) K

20. Distinguish between liquidity and solvency. Mention two ratios that are used to measure each. (SO 5) K

21. Huan Yue is wondering why the debt to total assets and interest coverage ratios are calculated. Answer her question and explain why the debt to total assets ratio should never be interpreted without also referring to the interest coverage ratio. (SO 5) C

*22. Explain how amortization is calculated using the effective-interest method of amortization when bonds are issued at a discount, and at a premium. (SO 6) K

*23. Compare the effects of the effective-interest method of amortization on interest paid, interest expense, and the bond amortized cost when bonds are issued at (a) a discount, and (b) a premium. (SO 6) C

*24. Explain why the bond's amortized cost (a) decreases over time when bonds are issued at a premium, and (b) increases when the effective-interest method of amortization is applied to bonds issued at a discount. (SO 6) C

Brief Exercises

Compare debt and equity financing alternatives.
(SO 1) AP

BE15–1 Olga Inc. is considering two alternatives to finance its construction of a new $4-million plant at the beginning of the year: (a) issue 200,000 common shares at a market price of $20 per share, or (b) issue $4 million of 6% bonds at face value.

It has 500,000 common shares and $10 million of shareholders' equity before the new financing. Complete the following table for the year, and indicate which alternative is better:

	(a) Issue Equity	(b) Issue Debt
Profit before interest and income tax	$1,000,000	$1,000,000
Interest expense	_____	_____
Profit before income tax	_____	_____
Income tax expense (25%)	_____	_____
Profit	_____	_____
Number of shares	_____	_____
Earnings per share	_____	_____
Shareholders' equity	_____	_____
Return on equity	_____	_____

BE15–2 Carvel Corp. issued $500,000 of five-year, 5% bonds with interest payable semi-annually. How much did Carvel receive from the sale of these bonds if the market interest rate was (a) 4%, (b) 5%, and (c) 6%?

Calculate present value of bond. (SO 2) AP

BE15–3 Keystone Corporation issued $1 million of five-year, 4% bonds dated April 1, 2011, at 100. Interest is payable semi-annually on October 1 and April 1. Keystone has a December 31 year end.

Record bond transactions. (SO 2) AP

(a) Prepare the journal entry to record the sale of these bonds on April 1, 2011.
(b) Prepare the journal entry to record the first interest payment on October 1, 2011.
(c) Prepare the adjusting journal entry on December 31, 2011, to accrue the interest expense.
(d) Prepare the journal entry to record the second interest payment on April 1, 2012.
(e) Prepare the journal entry to record the redemption of these bonds at maturity on April 1, 2016.

BE15–4 Refer to data presented in BE15–3 for Keystone Corporation's bond issue.

Record issue of bonds; show balance sheet presentation. (SO 2) AP

(a) Record the sale of these bonds assuming that the bonds were issued at 98, rather than 100.
(b) Record the sale of these bonds assuming that the bonds were issued at 102, rather than 100.
(c) Show the balance sheet presentation of the bonds on April 1, 2011, if the bonds were issued at (1) 100, (2) 98, and (3) 102.
(d) What will the amortized cost be at maturity, April 1, 2016, under each of the three different issue prices?

BE15–5 The Town of Moosonee issued $1 million of five-year, 5% bonds dated January 1. Interest is payable semi-annually on July 1 and January 1.

Record bond transactions. (SO 2) AP

(a) Record the sale of these bonds on January 1 and the first interest payment on July 1, assuming that the bonds were issued at 98 and that the semi-annual amortization amount for the first interest period is $1,766.
(b) Record the sale of these bonds on January 1 and the first interest payment on July 1, assuming that the bonds were issued at 100.
(c) Record the sale of these bonds on January 1 and the first interest payment on July 1, assuming that the bonds were issued at 102 and that the semi-annual amortization amount for the first interest period is $1,804.

BE15–6 Hathaway Corporation's July 1, 2011, balance sheet showed a balance in Bonds Payable of $980,000.

Record redemption of bonds. (SO 2) AP

Interest is payable semi-annually on June 30 and December 31.

(a) Assuming Hathaway redeems these bonds at 101 on July 1, prepare the journal entry to record the redemption.
(b) Assuming Hathaway redeems these bonds at 97 on July 1, prepare the journal entry to record the redemption.

Prepare instalment schedule.
(SO 3) AP

BE15–7 You qualify for a $10,000 loan from the Canada Student Loans Program to help finance your education. Once you graduate, you start repaying this note payable at an interest rate of 6%. The monthly cash payment is $111.02, principal and interest, for 120 payments (10 years). Prepare an instalment payment schedule for the first four payments.

Record note transactions.
(SO 3) AP

BE15–8 Eyre Inc. issues a $360,000, 10-year, 6% mortgage note payable on November 30, 2010, to obtain financing for a new building. The terms provide for monthly instalment payments. Prepare the journal entries to record the mortgage loan on November 30, 2010, and the first two payments on December 31, 2010, and January 31, 2011, assuming the payment is (a) a fixed principal payment of $3,000, and (b) a blended payment of $3,997.

Record note transaction; show balance sheet presentation.
(SO 3, 5) AP

BE15–9 Bow River Inc. issues a $500,000, four-year, 5% note payable on March 31, 2010. The terms provide for fixed principal payments annually of $125,000.

(a) Prepare the journal entries to record the note on March 31, 2010, and the first payment on March 31, 2011.
(b) Show the balance sheet presentation of the current and long-term liability related to the note as at March 31, 2011.

Analyze lease.
(SO 4) AN

BE15–10 Paget Ltd. signed a five-year lease agreement with Equipco Ltd. for manufacturing equipment that had been specifically designed for a specialized patented manufacturing process. Paget holds the exclusive rights to the manufacturing process. The equipment's estimated economic life is seven years. The equipment will be returned to Equipco at the end of the lease term. Indicate if the lease is a finance lease or operating lease. Explain.

Record lease.
(SO 4) AP

BE15–11 P. Paquin leases office space for $2,500 per month from Privateer Commercial Realty Ltd. The lease agreement is for five years.

(a) Prepare the journal entry to record the monthly lease payment by the lessee.
(b) Prepare the journal entry to record the receipt of the monthly lease payment by the lessor.

Record lease.
(SO 4) AP

BE15–12 Chang Corp. leases new manufacturing equipment from Bracer Construction, Inc. The present value of the lease payments is $300,000 and the fair value is $320,000.

(a) Which company is the lessor and which company is the lessee?
(b) Prepare the journal entry to record the lease for the lessee.

Balance sheet presentation.
(SO 5) AP

BE15–13 Cooke Inc. issued a $240,000, 10-year, 8% note payable on October 1, 2010. The terms provide for blended payments of $8,773 payable in quarterly instalments on January 1, April 1, July 1, and October 1. Below is a partial instalment schedule for the note payable.

Interest Period	Cash Payment	Interest Expense	Reduction of Principal	Principal Balance
Oct. 1, 2010				$240,000
Jan. 1, 2011	$8,773	$4,800	$3,973	236,027
Apr. 1, 2011	8,773	4,721	4,052	231,975
Jul. 1, 2011	8,773	4,639	4,134	227,841
Oct. 1, 2011	8,773	4,557	4,216	223,625
Jan. 1, 2012	8,773	4,472	4,301	219,324

Show the balance sheet presentation of the current and long-term liability related to the note as at December 31, 2010.

Prepare liabilities section of balance sheet.
(SO 5) AP

BE15–14 Selected liability items for Waugh Corporation at December 31, 2011, follow. Prepare the liabilities section of Waugh's balance sheet.

Accounts payable	$ 55,000	Income tax payable	$12,000
Bonds payable, due 2028	935,000	Total lease liability	50,000
Current portion of notes payable	15,000	Total notes payable, due 2015	
Current portion of lease liability	15,000	(net of current portion)	120,000

BE15–15 Molson Coors Brewing Company reported the following selected data at December 28, 2008 (in US$ millions):

Calculate solvency ratios.
(SO 5) AP

Total assets	$10,416.6
Total liabilities	4,426.9
Interest expense	103.3
Income tax expense	102.9
Profit	388.0

Calculate the company's (a) debt to total assets, and (b) interest coverage ratios.

*BE15–16 Niagara Corporation issued $100,000 of five-year, 5% bonds on April 1, 2011, with interest payable semi-annually on October 1 and April 1. The bonds were issued at $95,735 and yield a market interest rate of 6%. Prepare an amortization schedule to April 1, 2012.

Prepare amortization schedule.
(SO 6) AP

*BE15–17 A partial bond discount amortization schedule for Chiasson Corp. is presented below:

Complete amortization schedule and answer questions.
(SO 2, 6) AP

Semi-Annual Interest Period	Interest Payment	Interest Expense	Premium Amortization	Unamortized Premium	Bond Amortized Cost
Issue Date				$74,387	$1,074,387
1 (Apr. 30)	$35,000	(1)	$2,768	(2)	1,071,619
2 (Oct. 31)	35,000	$32,149	(3)	68,767	(4)

(a) Fill in the missing amounts for items (1) through (4).
(b) What is the face value of the bonds?
(c) What is the bonds' contractual interest rate? The market interest rate?
(d) Explain why interest expense is less than interest paid.
(e) Explain why interest expense will decrease each period.
(f) Prepare the journal entry to record the payment of interest on April 30 and October 31.

*BE15–18 On May 1, 2011, Jianhua Corporation issued $120,000 of 10-year, 6% bonds, with interest payable semi-annually on November 1 and May 1. The bonds were issued to yield a market interest rate of 5%.

Record bond transactions using effective-interest amortization.
(SO 2, 6) AP

(a) Calculate the issue price of the bonds.
(b) Record the issue of the bonds on May 1, 2011.
(c) Record the payment of interest on November 1, 2011.

Exercises

E15–1 East-West Airlines is considering two alternatives to finance the purchase of a fleet of airplanes. These alternatives are (1) to issue 120,000 common shares at $45 per share, and (2) to issue 10-year, 5% bonds for $5.4 million. It is estimated that the company will earn $1.2 million before interest and income tax as a result of this purchase. The company has an income tax rate of 30%. It has 200,000 common shares issued and shareholders' equity of $12 million before the new financing.

Compare debt and equity financing alternatives.
(SO 1) AP

Instructions

(a) Calculate the profit for each financing alternative.
(b) Calculate the earnings per share and return on equity for each alternative.
(c) Which financing alternative would you recommend for East-West Airlines? Why?

E15–2 Central College is about to issue $1 million of 10-year bonds that pay a 6% annual interest rate, with interest payable semi-annually.

Instructions

Record the issue of these bonds if the market interest rate is (a) 5%, (b) 6%, and (c) 7%.

E15–3 The following information about two independent bond issues was reported in the financial press on the same day:

1. George Weston Ltd.: 7.1% bonds, maturing February 5, 2032, were issued at a price of 85.45 to yield a market interest rate of 8.54%.
2. Greater Toronto Airport Authority (GTAA): 7.1% bonds maturing June 4, 2031, were issued at a price of 120.75 to yield a market interest rate of 5.5%.

Instructions

(a) Are the George Weston Ltd. bonds trading at a premium or a discount?
(b) Are the GTAA bonds trading at a premium or a discount?
(c) Explain how bonds, both paying the same contractual interest rate (7.1%), could be trading at different prices on the same date.
(d) Record the issue of $1,000 of each of these two bonds.

E15–4 On July 31, 2010, Laramie Corporation issued $400,000 of 10-year, 4% bonds at 102. Interest is payable semi-annually on July 31 and January 31. Laramie's fiscal year end is January 31.

Instructions

(a) Is the market rate of interest higher or lower than 4%? Explain.
(b) Record the issue of the bonds on July 31, 2010.
(c) Record the payment of interest on January 31, 2011, assuming the semi-annual amortization amount for this interest period is $333.
(d) Show how the bonds would be reported on Laramie's balance sheet on January 31, 2011.

E15–5 On July 1, 2010, BrightLight Corporation issued $800,000 of five-year, 5% bonds at 98. Interest is payable semi-annually on July 1 and January 1. BrightLight's fiscal year end is December 31.

Instructions

(a) Record the issue of the bonds on July 1, 2010.
(b) Record the accrual of interest on December 31, 2010, assuming the semi-annual amortization amount for this interest period is $1,413.
(c) Record the payment of interest on January 1, 2011.
(d) Show how the bonds would be reported on BrightLight's balance sheet on December 31, 2010.

E15–6 The following independent transactions occurred on June 30, 2011:

1. Ernst Corporation redeemed $140,000 of 7% bonds at 103. The amortized cost of the bonds at the date of redemption was $136,500.
2. Takase Corporation redeemed $150,000 of 5% bonds at 98. The amortized cost of the bonds at the redemption date was $152,000.
3. Young, Inc. redeemed $175,000 of 8% bonds at their maturity date, June 30, 2011.

Instructions

Record the transactions. Assume for each of the transactions that the interest expense and amortization has been updated to the redemption date.

E15–7   Ste. Anne Corp. receives $200,000 on December 31, 2011, when it issues a 20-year, 5% mortgage note payable to finance the construction of a building. The terms provide for semi-annual instalment payments on June 30 and December 31.

Record mortgage note payable.
(SO 3) AP

Instructions

Prepare the journal entries to record the mortgage note payable and the first two instalment payments assuming the payment is:

(a) a fixed principal payment of $5,000.
(b) a blended payment of $7,967

E15–8   The following instalment payment schedule is for a long-term note payable:

Analyze instalment payment schedule. Identify balance sheet presentation.
(SO 3) AP

Interest Period	Cash Payment	Interest Expense	Reduction of Principal	Principal Balance
Jan. 1, 2010				$50,000
Jan. 1, 2011	$12,500	$2,500	$10,000	40,000
Jan. 1, 2012	12,000	2,000	10,000	30,000
Jan. 1, 2013	11,500	1,500	10,000	20,000
Jan. 1, 2014	11,000	1,000	10,000	10,000
Jan. 1, 2015	10,500	500	10,000	0

Instructions

(a) Is this a fixed principal or blended payment schedule?
(b) What is the interest rate on the note?
(c) Prepare the journal entry to record the first instalment payment.
(d) What are the long-term and current portions of the note at the end of period 2?

E15–9   On January 1, 2011, Wolstenholme Corp. borrows $15,000 by signing a three-year, 6% note payable. The note is repayable in three annual blended payments of $5,612 on December 31 of each year.

Prepare instalment payment schedule and record note payable. Identify balance sheet presentation.
(SO 3, 5) AP

Instructions

(a) Prepare an instalment payment schedule for the note.
(b) Prepare journal entries to record the note and the first instalment payment.
(c) What amounts would be reported as current and long-term in the liabilities section of Wolstenholme's balance sheet on December 31, 2011?

E15–10   Two independent situations follow:

Analyze and record leases.
(SO 4) AP

1. Ready Car Rental leased a car to Dumfries Company for one year. Terms of the lease agreement call for monthly payments of $750, beginning on May 21, 2011.
2. On January 1, 2011, InSynch Ltd. entered into an agreement to lease 60 computers from HiTech Electronics. The terms of the lease agreement require three annual payments of $43,737 (including 5.5% interest), beginning on December 31, 2011. The present value of the three payments is $118,000 and the market value of the computers is $120,000.

Instructions

(a) What kind of lease—operating or finance—should be recorded in each of the above situations? Explain your rationale.
(b) Prepare the journal entry, if any, that each company must make to record the lease agreement.

E15–11   Shoppers Drug Mart Corporation reported the following selected data (in millions):

Analyze solvency.
(SO 4, 5) AP

	2008	2007
Total assets	$6,419.3	$5,621.9
Total liabilities	2,841.2	2,433.1
Profit	565.2	490.4
Income tax expense	253.3	242.9
Interest expense	63.9	52.8

Instructions

(a) Calculate the debt to total assets and interest coverage ratios for 2008 and 2007. Did Shoppers' solvency improve, worsen, or remain unchanged in 2008?

(b) The notes to Shoppers Drug Mart's financial statements show that the company has future operating lease commitments totalling $3.7 billion. What is the significance of these unrecorded obligations in an analysis of Shoppers Drug Mart's solvency?

Calculate ratios under financing alternatives.
(SO 1, 5) AP

E15–12 The Utopia Paper Company requires $5 million of financing to upgrade its production facilities. It has a choice to finance the upgrade with a 6% long-term loan or to issue additional shares. The company currently has total assets of $12 million, total liabilities of $8 million, shareholders' equity of $4 million, and profit of $2 million. It projects that profit will be $315,000 higher if debt is issued and $525,000 higher if shares are issued. Assume the project is invested in at the beginning of the year.

Instructions

(a) Calculate the debt to total assets and return on equity ratios under each financing alternative.

(b) Which financing alternative would you recommend for Utopia Paper? Why?

Prepare long-term liabilities section of balance sheet.
(SO 5) AP

E15–13 The adjusted trial balance for Priya Corporation at July 31, 2011, contained the following:

Interest payable	$ 15,000	Bonds payable, due 2018	$176,400
Note payable	165,000	Accounts payable	129,000
Lease liability	56,000	Accounts receivable	135,000
Note receivable, due 2011	35,000		

Of the lease liability amount, $14,000 is due within the next year. Of the note payable amount, $25,000 is due on January 31, 2012.

Instructions

(a) Prepare the long-term liabilities section of the balance sheet as at July 31, 2011.

(b) Some of the accounts above belong in the balance sheet but not in its long-term liabilities section. What is the correct classification for them?

Answer questions about amortization schedule.
(SO 2, 6) AP

E15–14 Creek Corporation issued 10-year bonds on January 1, 2008. Interest is paid semi-annually on January 1 and July 1 and the company's year end is December 31. Below is a partial amortization schedule for the first few years of the bond issue.

Semi-Annual Interest Period	Interest Payment	Interest Expense	Amortization	Unamortized Amount	Bond Amortized Cost
Jan. 1, 2008				$15,589	$215,589
July 1, 2008	$6,000	$5,390	$610	14,979	214,979
Jan. 1, 2009	6,000	5,374	626	14,353	214,353
July 1, 2009	6,000	5,359	641	13,712	213,712
Jan. 1, 2010	6,000	5,343	657	13,055	213,055
July 1, 2010	6,000	5,326	674	12,381	212,381
Jan. 1, 2011	6,000	5,310	690	11,691	211,691

Instructions

(a) Were the bonds issued at a discount or at a premium?

(b) What is the face value of the bonds?

(c) What will the bonds' amortized cost be at the maturity date?

(d) What is the bonds' contractual interest rate? The market interest rate?

(e) What will be the total interest payment over the 10-year life of the bonds? Total interest expense?

(f) Would your answers in (e) change if the bonds had been issued at a premium instead of a discount or at a discount instead of a premium? Explain.

*E15–15 Québec Corporation issued $650,000 of 10-year, 6% bonds on January 1, 2010, when the market interest rate was 7%. Interest is payable semi-annually on July 1 and January 1. Québec has a December 31 year end.

Prepare amortization schedule. Show balance sheet presentation.
(SO 2, 6) AP

Instructions

(a) Calculate the issue price of the bonds.
(b) Record the issue of the bonds.
(c) Prepare an amortization schedule through to December 31, 2011 (four interest periods).
(d) Record the accrual of the interest on December 31, 2011.
(e) Show the balance sheet presentation of the bonds at December 31, 2011.

*E15–16 Tagawa Corporation issued $600,000 of 10-year, 8% bonds on January 1, 2011, for $642,637. This price resulted in a market interest rate of 7% on the bonds. Interest is payable semi-annually on July 1 and January 1. Tagawa has a December 31 year end. On January 1, 2012, the bonds were redeemed at 104.

Record bond transactions.
(SO 2, 6) AP

Instructions

(a) Record the issue of the bonds on January 1, 2011.
(b) Record the payment of interest on July 1, 2011.
(c) Record the accrual of interest on December 31, 2011.
(d) Record the redemption of the bonds on January 1, 2012.

Problems: Set A

P15–1A The following is from Disch Corp.'s balance sheet:

Record bond transactions.
(SO 2) AP

DISCH CORP
Balance Sheet (partial)
December 31, 2010

Current liabilities	
Bond interest payable	$ 45,000
Long-term liabilities	
Bonds payable, 5%, due January 1, 2014	1,800,000

Interest is payable semi-annually on January 1 and July 1. The bonds were issued at par.

Instructions

(a) Record the payment of the bond interest on January 1, 2011.
(b) Assume that on January 1, 2011, after paying interest, Disch redeems $450,000 of the bonds at 99. Record the redemption of the bonds.
(c) Record the payment of the bond interest on July 1, 2011, on the remaining bonds.
(d) Prepare the adjusting entry on December 31, 2011, to accrue the interest on the remaining bonds.

Taking It Further Was the market rate of interest higher or lower than the contractual rate of interest on January 1, 2011, when the bonds were redeemed? Explain.

P15–2A On May 1, 2010, MEM Corp. issued $900,000 of five-year, 7% bonds at 103. The bonds pay interest annually on May 1. MEM's year end is April 30.

Record bond transactions; show balance sheet presentation.
(SO 2) AP

Instructions

(a) Record the issue of the bonds on May 1, 2010.
(b) Record the accrual of interest on April 30, 2011, assuming the amortization amount is $4,763.

(c) Show the balance sheet presentation on April 30, 2011.

(d) Record the payment of interest on May 1, 2011.

(e) Assume that on May 1, 2011, after payment of the interest, MEM redeems all of the bonds at 99. Record the redemption of the bonds.

Taking It Further What was the market rate of interest on May 1, 2010, when MEM issued the bonds?

Record bond transactions; show balance sheet presentation. (SO 2) AP

P15–3A On July 1, 2010, Energy Power Corporation issued $1.2 million of 10-year, 6% bonds at 98. The bonds pay interest semi-annually on July 1 and January 1. Energy Power's year end is December 31.

Instructions

(a) Record the issue of the bonds on July 1, 2010.

(b) Record the accrual of interest on December 31, 2010, assuming the amortization amount is $881.

(c) Show the balance sheet presentation on December 31, 2010.

(d) Record the payment of interest on January 1, 2011.

(e) What will be the total interest payment over the 10-year life of the bonds? What will be the total interest expense over the 10-year life of the bonds?

Taking It Further Explain why the total interest payment over the 10-year life of the bonds is equal to or different than the total interest expense over the 10-year life of the bonds.

Record note transactions. (SO 3) AP

P15–4A A local company has just approached a venture capitalist for financing to develop a ski hill. On April 1, 2010, the venture capitalist loaned the company $1 million at an interest rate of 7%. The loan is repayable over five years in fixed principal payments of $200,000 a year. The first payment is due March 31, 2011. The ski hill operator's year end will be December 31.

Instructions

(a) Record the issue of the note payable on April 1, 2010.

(b) Record the accrual of interest on December 31, 2010, and the instalment payment on March 31, 2011.

(c) Record the accrual of interest on December 31, 2011, and the instalment payment on March 31, 2012.

Taking It Further Explain how the interest expense and reduction of the note payable would change in (b) and (c) if the note had been repayable in blended payments of $243,890, rather than in fixed principal payments.

Record note transactions. (SO 3) AP

P15–5A On July 31, 2011, Myron Corporation purchased a piece of equipment for $750,000. The equipment was purchased with a $100,000 cash down payment and through the issue of a $650,000, four-year, 6% mortgage note payable for the balance. The terms provide for the mortgage to be repaid in monthly blended payments of $15,265 starting on August 31.

Instructions

(a) Record the issue of the note payable on July 31.

(b) Record the first two instalment payments on August 31 and September 30.

(c) Repeat part (b) assuming that the terms provided for monthly fixed principal payments of $13,542, rather than blended payments of $15,265.

Taking It Further If the instalments are fixed principal payments of $13,542, will the interest expense over the life of the note be greater than, the same as, or less than if the instalments are a blended payment of $15,265? Explain.

P15–6A   Kinyae Electronics issues a $700,000, 10-year, 7% mortgage note payable on December 31, 2010, to help finance a plant expansion. The terms of the note provide for semi-annual blended payments of $49,253. Payments are due on June 30 and December 31.

Prepare instalment payment schedule and record note transactions. Show balance sheet presentation.
(SO 3) AP

Instructions

(a) Prepare an instalment payment schedule for the first two years. Round all calculations to the nearest dollar.
(b) Record the issue of the mortgage note payable on December 31, 2010.
(c) Show how the mortgage liability should be reported on the balance sheet at December 31, 2010. (*Hint*: Remember to report any current portion separately from the long-term liability.)
(d) Record the first two instalment payments on June 30, 2011, and December 31, 2011.
(e) If Kinyae made instalments of fixed principal payments on a semi-annual basis, what would the fixed principal payment be?
(f) Record the first two instalments.

Taking It Further   Indicate the advantages and disadvantages of making fixed principal payments versus blended payments.

P15–7A   Three different lease transactions are presented below for Manitoba Enterprises. Assume that all lease transactions start on January 1, 2011. Manitoba does not receive title to the properties, either during the lease term or at the end of it. The yearly rental for each of the leases is paid on January 1 starting on January 1, 2011.

Analyze lease situations. Discuss financial statement presentation.
(SO 4) AP

	Bulldozer	Truck	Photocopier
Lease term	5 years	6 years	3 years
Estimated economic life	15 years	7 years	6 years
Yearly rental payment	$14,000	$14,981	$3,900
Fair market value of leased asset	$98,000	$85,000	$17,500
Present value of lease rental payments	$55,000	$74,800	$9,500

Instructions

(a) Which of the above leases are operating leases and which are finance leases? Explain.
(b) How should the lease transaction for each of the above assets be recorded on January 1, 2011?
(c) Describe how the lease transaction would be reported on the 2011 income statement and balance sheet for each of the above assets.

Taking It Further   For each of the leases, prepare any required adjusting journal entries on December 31, 2011. Assume that Manitoba Enterprises would pay 8% interest if it borrowed cash and purchased the equipment instead of leasing it.

P15–8A   Loblaw Companies Limited reported the following selected information (in millions):

Calculate and analyze solvency ratios.
(SO 4, 5) AN

	2008	2007
Total assets	$13,985	$13,674
Total liabilities	8,155	8,129
Interest expense	263	252
Income tax expense	228	150
Profit	545	330

Instructions

(a) Calculate Loblaw's debt to total assets and interest coverage ratios for each year.
(b) Based on the ratios calculated in (a), what conclusions can you make about Loblaw's solvency?

Taking It Further Loblaw has total operating lease commitments of $1,623 million in 2008 and $1,423 million in 2007. Explain the impact that an operating lease has on a company's solvency ratios. Does this information change any of your conclusions in (b)?

Analyze leverage.
(SO 1, 5) AN

P15–9A Two competitors in the retail industry, Rona Inc. and The Home Depot, Inc., recently reported the following selected ratios:

	Rona	Home Depot
Debt to total assets	40.44%	56.8%%
Interest coverage	8.7 times	6.7 times
Return on equity	11.4%	12.7%

Instructions

(a) Based on the debt to total assets and interest coverage ratios, which company is more solvent? Explain.

(b) Which company is making better use of debt to produce a higher return? Explain.

Taking It Further What other information would help in the analysis of the companies' solvency?

Record bond transactions and prepare amortization schedule. Show balance sheet presentation.
(SO 2, 6) AP

*P15–10A On July 1, 2010, Global Satellites issued $1.4 million of 10-year, 6% bonds to yield a market interest rate of 7%. The bonds pay semi-annual interest on July 1 and January 1, and Global has a December 31 year end.

Instructions

(a) Calculate the issue price of the bonds.

(b) Record the issue of the bonds on July 1, 2010.

(c) Prepare an amortization table through December 31, 2011 (three interest periods) for this bond issue.

(d) Record the accrual of interest on December 31, 2011.

(e) Show the balance sheet presentation of the bonds at December 31, 2011.

Taking It Further If Global Satellites redeemed the bonds at par on December 31, 2011, would there be a gain or loss recorded? Calculate the amount of the gain or loss.

Record bond transactions and answer questions.
(SO 2, 6) AP

*P15–11A On July 1, 2010, Webhancer Corp. issued $4 million of 10-year, 5% bonds at $4,327,029. This price resulted in a 4% market interest rate on the bonds. The bonds pay semi-annual interest on July 1 and January 1, and Webhancer has a December 31 year end.

Instructions

(a) Record the following transactions:
   1. The issue of the bonds on July 1, 2010
   2. The accrual of interest on December 31, 2010
   3. The payment of interest on January 1, 2011
   4. The payment of interest on July 1, 2011

(b) Answer the following questions:
   1. What amount of interest expense is reported for 2010?
   2. Would the bond interest expense reported in 2010 be the same as, greater than, or less than the amount that would be reported if the bonds had been issued at a discount rather than at a premium? Explain.
   3. Determine the total cost of borrowing over the life of the bonds.
   4. Would the total bond interest expense be greater than, the same as, or less than the total interest expense that would be reported if the bonds had been issued at a discount rather than at a premium? Explain.
   5. Assuming that the bonds were issued at a market interest rate of 6%, calculate the issue price of the bonds. Determine the total cost of borrowing over the life of the bonds.

Taking It Further   Explain what the impact would be on interest expense if the market rate of interest changed to 4.5% in December 2010 after the bonds were issued.

Problems: Set B

P15–1B   The following selected information is from Tri Corporation's balance sheet:

Record bond transactions.
(SO 2) AP

TRI CORPORATION Balance Sheet (partial) December 31, 2010	
Current liabilities	
Bond interest payable	$ 12,000
Long-term liabilities	
Bonds payable, 6%, due January 1, 2012	400,000

Interest is payable semi-annually on January 1 and July 1. The bonds were issued at par.

Instructions

(a) Record the payment of the bond interest on January 1, 2011.
(b) Assume that on January 1, 2011, after paying interest, Tri Corporation redeems $150,000 of the bonds at 101. Record the redemption of the bonds.
(c) Record the payment of the bond interest on July 1, 2011, on the remaining bonds.
(d) Prepare the adjusting entry on December 31, 2011, to accrue the interest on the remaining bonds.

Taking It Further   Was the market rate of interest higher or lower than the contractual rate of interest on January 1, 2011, when the bonds were redeemed? Explain.

P15–2B   On October 1, 2010, PFQ Corp. issued $800,000 of 10-year, 5% bonds at 98. The bonds pay interest annually on October 1. PFQ's year end is September 30.

Record bond transactions;
show balance sheet
presentation.
(SO 2) AP

Instructions

(a) Record the issue of the bonds on October 1, 2010.
(b) Record the accrual of interest on September 30, 2011, assuming the amortization amount is $1,257.
(c) Show the balance sheet presentation on September 30, 2011.
(d) Record the payment of interest on October 1, 2011.
(e) Assume that on October 1, 2011, after payment of the interest, PFQ redeems all of the bonds at 101. Record the redemption of the bonds.

Taking It Further   What was the market rate of interest on October 1, 2010, when PFQ issued the bonds?

P15–3B   On July 1, 2010, Alternate Corporation issued $1.5 million of 10-year, 7% bonds at 101. The bonds pay interest semi-annually on July 1 and January 1. Alternate's year end is December 31.

Record bond transactions;
show balance sheet
presentation.
(SO 2) AP

Instructions

(a) Record the issue of the bonds on July 1, 2010.
(b) Record the accrual of interest on December 31, 2010, assuming the amortization amount is $534.
(c) Show the balance sheet presentation on December 31, 2010.
(d) Record the payment of interest on January 1, 2011.
(e) What will be the total interest payment over the 10-year life of the bonds? What will be the total interest expense over the 10-year life of the bonds?

Taking It Further Explain why the total interest payment over the 10-year life of the bonds is equal to or different than the total interest expense over the 10-year life of the bonds.

Record note transactions.
(SO 3) AP

P15–4B Peter Furlong has just approached a venture capitalist for financing for his sailing school. The lenders are willing to lend Peter $100,000 in exchange for a note payable at a high-risk interest rate of 9%. The note is payable over three years in blended payments of $6,381. Payments are due at the end of every other month (that is, six times per year). Peter receives the $100,000 on May 1, 2011, the first day of his fiscal year, and makes the first payment on June 30.

Instructions

(a) Record the issue of the note payable on May 1.
(b) Record the first two instalment payments on June 30 and August 31.
(c) If the note had been repayable in fixed principal payments, rather than in blended payments, calculate how much the cash payments would have been on June 30 and August 31.

Taking It Further Indicate which instalment payment method (blended or fixed) results in the largest principal repayment on April 30, 2014 (the date of the last payment). Explain.

Record note transactions.
(SO 3)AP

P15–5B On September 30, 2010, Atwater Corporation purchased a new piece of equipment for $600,000. The equipment was purchased with a $50,000 down payment and the issue of a $550,000, four-year, 6% mortgage note payable for the balance. The terms provide for quarterly blended payments of $38,921 starting on December 31. Atwater's year end is December 31.

Instructions

(a) Record the purchase of equipment on September 30, 2010.
(b) Record the first two instalment payments on December 31, 2010, and March 31, 2011.
(c) Repeat part (b) assuming that the terms provided for quarterly fixed principal payments of $34,375, rather than blended payments of $38,921.

Taking It Further What will be the total interest expense over the life of the note if blended payments of $38,921 are made on a quarterly basis over four years?

Prepare instalment payment schedule and record note transactions. Show balance sheet presentation.
(SO 3) AP

P15–6B Elite Electronics issues a $450,000, 10-year, 7.5% mortgage note payable on December 31, 2010. The terms of the note provide for semi-annual fixed principal payments of $22,500, plus interest, on June 30 and December 31. Elite Electronics' year end is December 31.

Instructions

(a) Prepare an instalment payment schedule for the first two years. Round all calculations to the nearest dollar.
(b) Record the issue of the mortgage note payable on December 31, 2010.
(c) Show how the mortgage liability should be reported on the balance sheet at December 31, 2010. (*Hint*: Remember to report any current portion separately from the long-term liability.)
(d) Record the first two instalment payments on June 30, 2011, and December 31, 2011.

Taking It Further If the semi-annual payments were blended, would the amount of cash paid on a semi-annual basis be greater than, equal to, or less than if fixed principal payments are made for the first two instalments? For the last instalment?

Analyze lease situations.
Discuss financial statement presentation.
(SO 4) AP

P15–7B Presented below are three different lease transactions that occurred for Klippert Inc. Assume that all lease contracts start on January 1, 2011. Klippert does not receive title to any of the properties, either during the lease term or at the end of it. Annual lease payments are made on January 1 of each year starting on January 1, 2011.

	Manufacturing Equipment	Delivery Equipment	Automobile
Annual lease rental payment	$8,823	$4,800	$7,000
Lease term	6 years	3 years	3 years
Estimated economic life	7 years	7 years	7 years
Fair market value of lease asset	$51,000	$19,000	$21,000
Present value of lease rental payments	$45,000	$11,000	$11,000

Instructions

(a) Which of the leases above are operating leases and which are finance leases? Explain.

(b) How should the lease transaction for each of the above assets be recorded on January 1, 2011?

(c) Describe how the lease transaction would be reported on the income statement and balance sheet for each of the above assets for 2011.

Taking It Further For each of the leases, prepare any required adjusting journal entries on December 31, 2011. Assume that Klippert Inc. would pay 7% interest if it borrowed cash and purchased the equipment instead of leasing the equipment.

P15–8B Maple Leaf Foods Inc. reported the following selected information (in thousands):

Calculate and analyze solvency ratios.
(SO 4, 5) AN

	2008	2007
Total assets	$3,452,101	$2,997,844
Total liabilities	2,234,684	1,769,043
Interest expense	88,651	94,122
Income tax expense (recovery)	(8,538)	801
Profit (loss)	(36,857)	194,964

Instructions

(a) Calculate Maple Leaf Foods' debt to total assets and interest coverage ratios for each year.

(b) Based on the ratios calculated in (a), what conclusions can you make about Maple Leaf Foods Inc.'s solvency?

Taking It Further Maple Leaf Foods Inc. had total operating lease commitments of nearly $247,735 thousand in 2008 and $280,671 thousand in 2007. Explain the impact that an operating lease has on a company's solvency ratios. Does this information change any of your conclusions in (b)?

P15–9B Two companies in the oil industry, Petro-Canada and Suncor Energy, recently reported the following selected ratios:

Analyze leverage.
(SO 1, 5) AN

	Petro-Canada	Suncor Energy
Debt to total assets	49.1%	55.4%
Interest coverage	24.8 times	4.4 times
Return on equity	22.9%	16.2%

Instructions

(a) Based on the debt to total assets and interest coverage ratios, which company is more solvent? Explain.

(b) Which company is making better use of debt to produce a higher return? Explain.

Taking It Further Suncor and Petro-Canada announced in March 2009 that the two companies would merge into one and operate under the name Suncor. The merger will be accounted for as a purchase of Petro-Canada by Suncor. The net assets of Petro-Canada will be recorded by Suncor at their fair value, resulting in total assets being higher for the combined company than the two individual companies. Assuming the debt of the combined company is equal to Suncor's and Petro-Canada's existing debt, is the debt to total assets ratio for the combined company likely to be less than, greater than, or equal to Suncor's debt to total assets ratio? Explain.

Record bond transactions
and prepare amortization
schedule. Show balance
sheet presentation.
(SO 2, 6) AP

*P15–10B   On July 1, 2010, Ponasis Corporation issued $2.5 million of 10-year, 4% bonds to yield a market interest rate of 5%. The bonds pay semi-annual interest on July 1 and January 1, and Ponasis has a December 31 year end.

Instructions

(a) Calculate the issue price of the bonds.
(b) Record the issue of the bonds on July 1, 2010.
(c) Prepare an amortization schedule through December 31, 2011 (three interest periods) for this bond issue.
(d) Record the accrual of interest on December 31, 2011.
(e) Show the balance sheet presentation of the bonds at December 31, 2011.

Taking It Further   If Ponasis redeemed the bonds on December 31, 2011, at a market rate of interest of 4%, what is the amount of cash the company would pay to redeem the bonds? Would a gain or a loss be recorded? Indicate the amount of the gain or loss.

Record bond transactions and
answer questions.
(SO 2, 6) AP

*P15–11B   On July 1, 2010, Waubonsee Ltd. issued $3.2 million of 10-year, 6% bonds at $3,449,423. This price resulted in a market interest rate of 5%. The bonds pay semi-annual interest on July 1 and January 1, and Waubonsee has a December 31 year end.

Instructions

(a) Record the following transactions:
  1. The issue of the bonds on July 1, 2010
  2. The accrual of interest on December 31, 2010
  3. The payment of interest on January 1, 2011
  4. The payment of interest on July 1, 2011

(b) Answer the following questions:
  1. What amount of interest expense is reported for 2010?
  2. Would the bond interest expense reported in 2010 be the same as, greater than, or less than the amount that would be reported if the bonds had been issued at a discount rather than at a premium? Explain.
  3. Determine the total cost of borrowing over the life of the bonds.
  4. Would the total bond interest expense be greater than, the same as, or less than the total interest expense that would be reported if the bonds had been issued at a discount rather than at a premium? Explain.
  5. Assuming that the bonds were issued at a market interest rate of 7%, calculate the issue price of the bonds. Determine the total cost of borrowing over the life of the bonds.

Taking It Further   Explain what the impact would be on interest expense if the market rate of interest changed to 5.5% in December 2010 after the bonds were issued.

Continuing Cookie Chronicle

(*Note:* This is a continuation of the Cookie Chronicle from Chapters 1 through 14.)

Natalie and Curtis anticipate great demand for their cookies and muffins. As a result, they are making plans to purchase a commercial oven. The cost of this oven is estimated at $15,000, and the company already has $4,500 set aside for the purchase. Natalie and Curtis have met with their bank manager. She is willing to lend Cookie & Coffee Creations Ltd. $10,500 on May 1, 2012, for a period of three years at a 4% interest rate. The bank manager has set out the following two payment alternatives:

Alternative 1:   The terms provide for fixed principal payments of $1,750 on November 1 and May 1 of each year.

Alternative 2: The terms provide for blended payments of $1,875 on November 1 and May 1 of each year.

Natalie and Curtis ask you to help them decide which alternative is better for them.

Instructions

(a) Prepare instalment payment schedules for each of the alternatives for the full term of the loan.

(b) Prepare the journal entry for the purchase of the oven and the issue of the note payable on May 1, 2012.

(c) Prepare the journal entries for the first two instalment payments under each alternative.

(d) Determine the current portion of the note payable and the long-term portion of the note payable as at October 31, 2012, under each alternative.

(e) Which payment plan alternative do you recommend? Why?

BROADENING YOUR PERSPECTIVE

Financial Reporting and Analysis

Financial Reporting Problem

BYP15–1   Refer to the consolidated financial statements and notes of The Forzani Group Ltd. in Appendix A.

Instructions

(a) Refer to Note 8, what was the total debt reported by Forzani's in the schedule at February 1, 2009 and February 3, 2008? By how much has Forzani's total debt increased (decreased) since February 3, 2008?

(b) Does Forzani separate the current portion of its debt from its long-term debt? If so, how much of its long-term debt is currently due?

(c) What kind of long-term debt does Forzani have?

(d) Note 8 indicates that the company renewed its credit agreement with GE Finance Holding Company. The new agreement provides Forzani with a $250-million revolving loan. What is a revolving loan? Is the interest rate fixed or floating? What is the amount for the revolving loan reported in the balance sheet? Why is the total $250-million revolving loan not reported in Forzani's February 1, 2009, balance sheet? How is the loan classified in the balance sheet? Explain why it is classified as it is.

(e) Does Forzani have any off–balance sheet financing that you can determine? Consider the information in Note 13 to the financial statements.

(f) Forzani's debt to total assets and interest coverage ratios for fiscal 2009 were calculated in Illustrations 15-10 and 15-11, respectively, in the chapter. Calculate these ratios for fiscal 2008. Comment on whether Forzani's solvency improved or worsened in 2009.

Interpreting Financial Statements

BYP15–2   Reitmans (Canada) Limited and Le Château Inc. are two specialty clothing merchandisers. Here are financial data for both companies for their fiscal years ending in 2009 (in thousands):

	Reitmans	Le Château
Balance sheet data	January 31, 2009	January 31, 2009
Total assets	$633,239	$216,431
Total liabilities	110,700	74,017
	Year ended	Year ended
Income statement data	January 31, 2009	January 31, 2009
Interest expense	921	1,798
Income tax expense	41,371	19,095
Profit	85,806	38,621

Instructions

(a) Calculate the debt to total assets and interest coverage ratios for each company.

(b) Discuss the solvency of each company compared with the other.

(c) The notes to the financial statements for Reitmans and Le Château, indicate that the companies have significant operating lease commitments. Discuss the implications of these operating leases for each company's solvency.

Critical Thinking

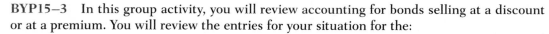

Collaborative Learning Activity

Note to instructor: Additional instructions and material for this group activity can be found on the Instructor Resource Site.

BYP15–3 In this group activity, you will review accounting for bonds selling at a discount or at a premium. You will review the entries for your situation for the:

1. Issue of the bonds
2. Payment of interest
3. Redemption of the bonds before maturity

Instructions

(a) Your instructor will divide the class into "home" groups. Each member of your group will select either bonds selling at a discount or bonds selling at a premium and then move to join the "expert" group for that particular situation.

(b) In the "expert" group, you will be given a handout to help you in your discussion of the accounting for the issue of bonds, payment of interest, and redemption of bonds. Ensure that each group member thoroughly understands these three journal entries for your situation.

(c) Return to your "home" group and explain your entries to the other students in the group.

(d) You may be asked by your instructor to write a short quiz on this topic.

Communication Activity

BYP15–4 Financial statement users are interested in the obligations that a company has from past transactions. It is important to determine which liabilities are current and which are long-term. Some company obligations are not recorded on the balance sheet itself, however; instead they are disclosed in the notes to the financial statements.

Instructions

Write a memorandum to a friend of yours who has inherited some money and would like to invest in some companies. Your friend plans to get professional advice before investing but would like you to review some basics with her. For instance, she is trying to determine the amount of cash that a company will have to pay within the next five years. She knows she should start with the liabilities that are on the balance sheet, but she is wondering if any of those can be settled without the company having to write a cheque. She would also like to know what kinds of liabilities could be buried somewhere in the notes to the financial statements.

Ethics Case

BYP15–5 Enron Corporation—once the world's largest electronic trader in natural gas and electricity—was one of the largest corporate bankruptcies in American history. Just weeks before it filed for bankruptcy, the company admitted that it had shifted billions of dollars of debt off its balance sheets and into a variety of complex partnerships.

Ethics in Accounting

One journalist wrote: "The Enron practice of shifting liabilities off the books to more than 3,500 subsidiaries raised so many red flags that you'd think you were in a military parade somewhere in China." Yet, Enron and its auditors argued vehemently that the "special purpose entity" partnerships they used were in accordance with GAAP and fully disclosed, even if they were not recorded in the books.

Instructions

(a) Who are the stakeholders in this situation?
(b) Explain how shifting debt off the balance sheet might mislead investors.
(c) Do you think that management has an obligation to ensure that a company's accounting and disclosure provides a faithful representation of the company's financial position and performance over and above following specific recommendations under GAAP?

"All About You" Activity

BYP15–6 As indicated in the "All About You" feature in this chapter, a student can benefit from financial leverage by borrowing to pay for an education. However, too much leverage can result in graduates struggling to make their loan payments. With most government student loan programs, you have at least six months' grace after your post-secondary education before you have to start paying back your loan. Normally the maximum number of monthly payments is 114; however, you may request an extended amortization period of up to 174 months by revising the terms of your loan agreement.

Instructions

Go to the Loan Repayment Estimator found at www.canlearn.ca to answer the following questions regarding monthly payments and the total interest payable on student loans. To find the Loan Repayment Calculator on the website, click on "After Post Secondary Education" and click on the link "Loan Repayment Estimator."

(a) Interest on loans may be a fixed interest rate or a floating interest rate. What is the difference between the two interest rates? Are there any advantages of having one over the other if interest rates rise over your payment period?
(b) What is the prime rate of interest indicated in the Loan Repayment Estimator? How is the fixed rate of interest calculated in the Loan Repayment Estimator? Assuming the prime rate of interest indicated in the calculator, what will be the fixed rate of interest?
(c) Under Option 1 in the Loan Repayment Estimator, enter the loan amount of $20,000 and assume a fixed interest rate and 114 months of repayment.

1. What is the amount of each monthly payment?
2. How much interest is payable over the 114 months?

(d) Under Option 2 in the Loan Repayment Estimator, enter the amount of $30,000 and assume a fixed interest rate and 114 months of repayment.

1. What is the amount of each monthly payment?
2. How much interest is payable over the 114 months?

(e) Under Option 1 in the Loan Repayment Estimator, enter the amount of $30,000 and assume a fixed interest rate and 174 months of repayment.

1. What is the amount of each monthly payment?
2. How much interest is payable over the 174 months?

(f) Assume that you accept a position when you graduate that pays you an annual salary of $48,000. After the required deductions for income tax, CPP, EI, and health benefits, your monthly paycheque is $2,800. You rent an apartment for $750 a month, have monthly payments on a car loan of $300, and your other costs for groceries, cable, Internet, insurance, gas, and phone total $1,100. How much will you have left at the end of the month to make payments on your student loan and other expenditures, such as clothes and entertainment? Can you afford to repay a $20,000 student loan? A $30,000 student loan?

ANSWERS TO CHAPTER QUESTIONS

Answers to Accounting in Action Insight Questions

All About You p. 824

Q: What should you consider in your decision about how much is appropriate to borrow for your education?

A: You should consider the cost of tuition and books; living expenses; other sources of cash, such as parents, part-time job, and scholarships and grants; expected income upon graduation; living expenses and other financial commitments after graduation; and expected interest rates and payment schedule on the student loan.

Business Insight, p. 834

Q: In terms of Canadian ownership rules for broadcasting assets, why was CanWest able to have foreign debt holders? Why does it matter if these investors own debt or equity in CanWest? Why would the bondholders want to swap the bonds for equity in the company?

A: CanWest was able to have foreign debt holders because debt holders do not own the company and do not have voting rights therefore they do not have a say in what the company does or in what it broadcasts.. The Canadian Radio-television and Telecommunications Commission (CRTC), operating under the Canadian Broadcasting Act, is mandated to ensure that broadcasting in Canada serves the Canadian public and that Canadians are provided with high quality Canadian programming. It recognizes that programming should reflect Canadian attitudes, values and creativity, display Canadian talent and provide information and analysis about Canada and other countries from a Canadian viewpoint. The concern is whether or not a company controlled by foreigners will fulfill these requirements.

The bondholders will want to swap debt for equity because the company struggling under $4 billion debt and unable to meet its interest payment deadlines. Swapping debt for equity maybe the only way the bondholders will be able to recover their investment.

Across the Organization, p. 844

Q: Do you think that delaying payments to the pension plan and borrowing an additional $600 million are all that Air Canada will have to do to avoid bankruptcy?

A: No, at some point in the future Air Canada will have to have sufficient cash to make payments to the pension plan and to pay off the additional debt. Air Canada will still have to make changes to its operations so that costs are reduced and revenues are increased, which will allow the pension plan payment and the loan repayments to be made.

Answer to Forzani Review It Question 3, p. 842

Forzani does not have any finance (capital) leases. It does, however, have an operating lease for land (see Building on Leased Land reported in note 5). Note 13 reports the company's commitments for this lease, as well as for equipment leases, over the next five years.

Answers to Self-Study Questions

1. d   2. a   3. d   4. b   5. b   6. c   7. b   8. c   9. d   *10. b

Remember to go back to the beginning of the chapter to check off your completed work!

←

CHAPTER 16
INVESTMENTS

scotiabank.com

CONCEPTS FOR REVIEW:

Before studying this chapter, you should understand or, if necessary, review:

a. How to calculate and record interest. (Ch. 3, pp. 130–131, Ch. 8, p. 449, and Ch. 15, pp. 836–837)

b. Where short- and long-term investments are classified on a balance sheet. (Ch. 4, pp. 191–194)

c. What comprehensive income is. (Ch. 13, p. 736)

d. The statement of comprehensive income. (Ch. 14, pp. 777-778)

e. How to record bond transactions. (Ch. 15, pp. 829–833)

Managing Money for Clients and the Company

Like all large organizations, Scotiabank manages its money through a number of investment vehicles. It has two main areas of investments—its regular banking operations and strategic acquisitions.

"In banks, we're always changing the mix of financial assets, looking for different opportunities," says Sean McGuckin, Senior Vice President and Head, Risk Policy & Capital Markets, "whereas for non-financial organizations, financial assets may not be their primary assets. It could be property, plant, and equipment, oil in the ground—what have you. So those companies may take a longer-term view on some of their investments." Scotiabank is like an individual investor who reviews and changes his or her portfolio regularly, rather than one who buys stocks and holds them over time with little change.

In its regular banking operations, Scotiabank holds investments in trading portfolios and treasury portfolios. In its trading environment, Scotiabank buys and sells securities, primarily to facilitate customer requests, and invests in certain securities to adjust its trading risk profile. These may be debt instruments like bonds, or equity instruments like common and preferred shares. Scotiabank's treasury investments strengthen the organization's liquidity profile because it has some assets on hand that it could quickly convert into cash if needed. The bank also uses various investments in fixed-term securities or variable-rate securities to help adjust its interest rate exposure. These investments can be held for a few days or longer. As well, the bank may also invest in long-term—for example, five-year—government bonds.

Scotiabank also invests strategically by acquiring all or a portion of other companies if a business is a good fit. "Our strategy, like most companies, is to grow," McGuckin explains. "You can grow either organically over time by continuing to build out your business, or there are opportunities where you can acquire growth; i.e., buy a company." In 2008, Scotiabank bought 100% of E*TRADE Canada's shares, doubling its hold on the Canadian on-line investing market. When more than 50% of a company's stock is purchased, it becomes consolidated with the purchaser; E*TRADE (now called Scotia iTRADE) became controlled by Scotiabank.

The organization may also acquire less than 50% of a company, which provides a significant interest but not control of the other company's operations. Scotiabank recently bought 19% of the shares in DundeeWealth Inc. and 37% of CI Financial Income Fund. These investments are all part of Scotiabank's wealth management business. "From a strategic standpoint, we identified opportunities to build our wealth management capability on an accelerated basis with specific acquisitions," explains McGuckin. When it buys a non-controlling interest in another company, Scotiabank will often share its business knowledge and expertise that helps the company grow. As well, Scotiabank often negotiates potential future rights for additional share purchases or the first right of refusal to purchase more shares, which may increase its future ownership stake.

The Navigator

STUDY OBJECTIVES:

After studying this chapter, you should be able to:

1. Identify reasons to invest, and classify investments.
2. Account for debt investments that are reported at amortized cost.
3. Account for trading investments.
4. Account for strategic investments.
5. Indicate how investments are reported in the financial statements.

The Navigator

Investments can include debt and equity, and can be made by individuals or corporations. As indicated in our feature story on Scotiabank, investments are made to generate investment income or for strategic purposes. They can be held for a short or long period of time. The way in which a company accounts for its investments is determined by the nature and purpose of the investment.

The chapter is organized as follows:

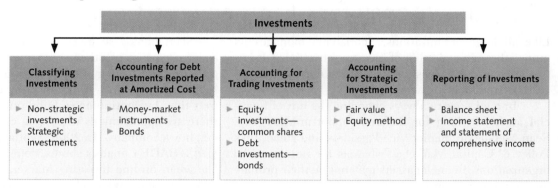

	Investments			
Classifying Investments	**Accounting for Debt Investments Reported at Amortized Cost**	**Accounting for Trading Investments**	**Accounting for Strategic Investments**	**Reporting of Investments**
▶ Non-strategic investments ▶ Strategic investments	▶ Money-market instruments ▶ Bonds	▶ Equity investments—common shares ▶ Debt investments—bonds	▶ Fair value ▶ Equity method	▶ Balance sheet ▶ Income statement and statement of comprehensive income

Classifying Investments

STUDY OBJECTIVE 1

Identify reasons to invest, and classify investments.

Helpful hint Debt and equity instruments are also referred to as *debt and equity securities* and these terms will be used interchangeably throughout the chapter.

Illustration 16-1 ➡

Why businesses invest

Corporations generally purchase **debt instruments** (debt obligations such as money-market instruments, bonds, commercial paper, or similar items that can be bought and sold) and **equity instruments** (an ownership interest in a company such as preferred and common shares) for one of two reasons: (1) as a **non-strategic investment** to generate investment income, or (2) as a **strategic investment** with the intention of establishing and maintaining a long-term operating relationship with another company. These reasons are shown in Illustration 16-1.

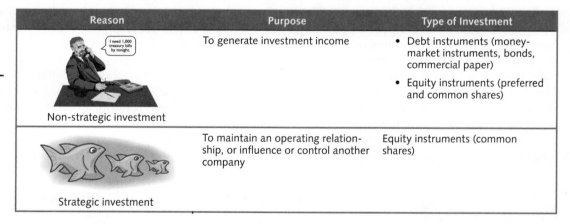

Reason	Purpose	Type of Investment
Non-strategic investment	To generate investment income	• Debt instruments (money-market instruments, bonds, commercial paper) • Equity instruments (preferred and common shares)
Strategic investment	To maintain an operating relationship, or influence or control another company	Equity instruments (common shares)

Non-Strategic Investments

Alternative terminology Non-strategic investments are also referred to as *passive investments*.

There are several reasons for a company to purchase debt or equity **securities** of another company as a non-strategic investment. A corporation may have cash that it does not immediately need. For example, many companies have seasonal fluctuations in sales, which can lead to idle cash until purchases are made for the next busy season. Until the cash is needed, these companies may decide to invest it to earn a higher return than they would get if they just kept the excess cash in the bank. As indicated in our feature story, Scotiabank's treasury investments are investments that can be quickly converted to cash when needed.

When investing excess cash for short periods of time, corporations invest in debt securities—usually money-market instruments, which are low-risk and highly liquid. **Money-market instruments** include money-market funds, banker's acceptances, term deposits, and treasury bills. It is not wise to invest short-term excess cash in equity securities, because share prices can drop suddenly and dramatically. If a company does invest excess cash in shares and the price of the shares falls just before the company needs the cash again, it will be forced to sell its equity securities at a loss. Money-market instruments do not change in fair value. Their value comes from the interest they generate.

Excess cash may also be invested for the longer term in debt securities to generate a steady source of interest income (e.g., bonds). Or, it may be invested in equity securities to generate dividend income. Preferred shares are usually purchased for dividend purposes, but both common and preferred shares can and do pay dividends.

Companies also invest in debt and equity securities hoping that they can sell them at a higher price than they originally paid for them. They speculate that the investment will increase in value and result in a gain when it is sold. Some companies, such as financial institutions like Scotiabank, are in the business of actively buying and selling securities in the hope of generating investment income from price fluctuations. Debt and equity securities that are purchased for the purpose of selling in the short term at a gain are referred to as **trading investments** or **trading securities**.

Classifying Non-Strategic Investments

Investments should be classified and reported in the financial statements in such a way as to provide users of financial statements with relevant information for decisions. This includes information that allows financial statement users to predict a company's future cash flows.

The classification and reporting of investments in recent years has changed significantly as standard setters moved away from reporting investments at cost to reporting many investments at fair value. It is anticipated that there will be more changes as to how specific investments are classified and reported as standard setters continue to study this issue.

Generally a non-strategic investment is classified and reported based on the purpose of the investment and on whether it is debt or equity, as shown in Illustration 16-2.

Type of Instrument	Purpose of Investment	Balance Sheet Classification and Valuation	
Short-term debt instruments	Held to earn interest income	Current assets	Amortized cost
Long-term debt instruments	Held to earn interest income	Non-current	Amortized cost
Short- or long-term debt instruments	Trading	Current	Fair value
Equity instruments	Trading	Current	Fair value

◄ Illustration 16-2

Classification and reporting of non-strategic investments

Note that the purpose of the investment is the more important factor in determining the balance sheet classification and valuation. The type of instrument does have an impact, as shown above, but the main consideration is why management purchases the investment.

It is also theoretically possible to report a non-strategic equity investment at cost. But IFRS requires that non-strategic equity investments be reported at fair value, and Canadian GAAP for Private Enterprises will allow cost only in limited circumstances. Reporting non-strategic equity investments at cost is not addressed in this chapter. The two methods of reporting non-strategic investments are briefly introduced here and will be covered in more detail later in the chapter.

Debt Investments Reported at Amortized Cost

If a company invests in a debt instrument for the purpose of holding the investment and earning interest, it is relevant to report the amount of interest earned on the investment and therefore it is relevant to report the investment at amortized cost. Examples of investments that may be reported at amortized cost are bonds and money-market instruments that are held to earn interest.

You will recall from Chapter 15 that amortized cost is the maturity value or principal less any unamortized discount or plus any unamortized premium and that the effective interest method is used to record interest and amortize any discount or premium. The time value of money concept is recognized in the use of the amortized cost measurement.

Debt and Equity Investments Reported at Fair Value

Alternative terminology Another common term for fair value is *market value*.

If a debt investment is not going to be held for the purpose of earning interest, then the time value of money concept is irrelevant and it is relevant to report the investment at fair value. Fair value is the amount of cash that is expected to be collected if the investment is sold. The fair value concept in accounting assumes that the exchange transaction is between knowledgeable, willing, and independent parties. The advantage of using fair value is that it allows users to better predict the future cash flows and assess the company's liquidity and solvency. As indicated in our feature story, Scotiabank buys bonds for the purposes of trading. These bonds are reported and recorded at fair value.

Investments in equity securities bought for purposes of trading (selling in the short term at a gain) are also reported at fair value.

Strategic Investments

While either debt or equity securities can be purchased as a non-strategic investment, only equity securities (normally common shares) can be purchased as a strategic investment. Only equity securities give the investor the right to vote at shareholders' meetings. Thus only investments in equity securities can result in either some level of influence or control over another company.

A company may make a strategic investment to become part of a different industry when it buys some or all of the common shares of another company in a related or new industry. In our feature story, we learned that Scotiabank bought 100% of E*TRADE Canada's shares, to have a presence in the on-line investment business. A company might also make a strategic investment to buy another company in the same industry as itself, as Scotiabank did when it bought shares in DundeeWealth Inc. and CI Financial Income Fund to increase its wealth management business.

Classifying Strategic Investments

The percentage of ownership or the degree of influence determines how a strategic investment is classified. More about the degree of influence and how it affects the classification and reporting of an investment will be discussed later in this chapter. Note also that, while non-strategic investments can be either short- or long-term, strategic investments can only be long-term.

ACCOUNTING IN ACTION: BUSINESS INSIGHT

Limited availability of investment capital and a rapid deterioration in profits drove acquisitions of Canadian companies to a six-year low in the first quarter of 2009. A total of 153 acquisitions were announced in the first three months of 2009, with a total value of $41.5 billion. The merger of Suncor and Petro-Canada announced in the first quarter was valued at $19.2 billion and accounted for almost half of the total value of the acquisitions. The merger will allow Petro-Canada and Suncor to cut costs by $1.3 billion and the combined company will be a more efficient player and will be better insulated from a foreign takeover. The combination will result in the largest energy company in Canada and the fifth largest in North America. The combined company will be the second largest company trading on the Toronto Stock Exchange, trailing only the Royal Bank of Canada. The combined company will operate under the Suncor name.

Sources: "Canadian M&A Activity: First Quarter 2009 Report," Crosbie & Company Inc. news release, June 9, 2009, available at: http://www.crosbieco.com/pdf/press_release/PR_Q109.pdf; "Merged Suncor, Petro-Canada Ready to Compete with 'Global Supermajors,'" CBC News, June 4, 2009, available at: http://www.cbc.ca/money/story/2009/06/04/suncor-petrocanada-merger.html

Was the merger of Suncor and Petro-Canada a non-strategic or strategic investment? What are some of the advantages the combined company might have now that it will be the largest energy company in Canada and the fifth largest in North America?

BEFORE YOU GO ON . . .

→ Review It

1. What are the reasons that corporations invest in debt and equity securities?
2. Distinguish between a non-strategic investment and a strategic investment.
3. When is it appropriate to classify and report an investment at amortized cost?

→ Do It

ABC Corp. engaged in the following investment activities during the year.

1. Purchased 20% of the common shares of the company's supplier to ensure that there is a reliable source of raw materials.
2. Purchased bonds to earn interest income.
3. Purchased common shares of a company, to be sold if the share price increases.
4. Purchased bonds with the intent to trade at a gain.
5. Purchased 100% of the common shares of the company's major competitor.

(a) For each investment, indicate if it is a strategic investment or a non-strategic investment.
(b) For each non-strategic investment, indicate if it should be reported at amortized cost or fair value.

Action Plan

- Non-strategic investments are purchased to earn investment income.
- Strategic investments are purchased with the intention of establishing a long-term relationship with the company.

Solution

(a)	(b)
1. Strategic	
2. Non-strategic	amortized cost
3. Non-strategic	fair value
4. Non-strategic	fair value
5. Strategic	

Related exercise material: BE16–1, BE16–2, E16–1, and E16-2.

The Navigator

Accounting for Debt Investments Reported at Amortized Cost

STUDY OBJECTIVE 2

Account for debt investments that are reported at amortized cost.

As mentioned in the previous section, debt instruments that are held for the purpose of earning interest are generally reported at amortized cost. This can include both short-term and long-term debt instruments. **Short-term debt instruments** are instruments that will mature within 12 months of the balance sheet date. **Long-term debt instruments** are instruments with a maturity of longer than 12 months after the balance sheet date. Regardless of the term of the debt, the accounting for all debt instruments reported at amortized cost has some basic similarities. Entries are required to record (1) the acquisition, (2) interest revenue and amortization of any discount or premium, and (3) the sale or disposition at maturity.

At acquisition, these debt instruments are recorded at the purchase price paid for the instrument. Subsequent to acquisition, interest revenue is recognized as it accrues and any discount or premium is amortized using the effective-interest method. The investment is reported at amortized cost on the balance sheet.

When the instrument matures or is sold, the cash received is recorded and its carrying amount is eliminated. If the instrument is sold before maturity, a gain is recorded if the cash received is greater than the carrying amount of the instrument. A loss is recorded if the cash received is less than the carrying amount of the instrument.

You will recall that debt instruments include money-market instruments as well as bonds, commercial paper, and a large variety of other debt securities. The following sections illustrate accounting for debt investments at amortized cost for both money-market instruments and bonds.

Money-Market Instruments

As we have learned, money-market instruments can be reasonably safe investments that allow a company to earn a higher interest rate than can normally be earned on a regular bank account balance. Money-market instruments include term deposits, treasury bills, money-market funds, and banker's acceptances. The following looks at the accounting for two types of money-market instruments: term deposits and treasury bills.

Term Deposits

Recording Acquisitions of Term Deposits. Assume that on November 30, 2010, Cheung Corporation purchases a $5,000, three-month, 2% term deposit. Most term deposits pay a fixed interest rate on maturity, although variable interest rates are also possible. The entry to record the investment is as follows:

A = L + SE
+5,000
−5,000

Cash flows: −5,000

Nov. 30	Short-Term Investment—Term Deposit	5,000	
	Cash		5,000
	To record purchase of three-month, 2% term deposit.		

Note that the debit entry above uses the account name Term Deposit. Some companies simply maintain each investment account separately in their general ledger, and then group them into the right investment portfolio category at year end for reporting purposes. Other companies maintain a subsidiary ledger for each category of investment. You will recall from Chapter 4 that current assets include assets that will be converted to cash or sold within one year from the balance sheet date. The term deposit is classified as a short-term investment and is reported in the current asset section of the balance sheet as it will mature within 12 months of the balance sheet date.

Recording Interest Revenue. Cheung Corporation's year end is December 31, so it is necessary to accrue $8 of interest for the month of December ($5,000 × 2% × $^1/_{12}$, rounded to the nearest dollar).

A = L + SE
+8 +8

Cash flows: no effect

Dec. 31	Interest Receivable	8	
	Interest Revenue		8
	To accrue interest on term deposit.		

Interest revenue is reported under other revenues in the income statement.

Recording the Maturity of Term Deposits. On February 28, 2011, when the term deposit matures, it is necessary to (1) update the interest for the latest period, (2) record the receipt of cash, and (3) remove the term deposit. Most banks credit the company's bank account directly for the interest and principal amounts when a term deposit matures.

A = L + SE
+5,025 +17
−8
−5,000

Cash flows: +5,025

Feb. 28	Cash	5,025	
	Interest Receivable		8
	Interest Revenue ($5,000 × 2% × $^2/_{12}$)		17
	Short-Term Investment—Term Deposit		5,000
	To record maturation of term deposit.		

If a term deposit, or other money-market instrument, is sold before it matures, it does not usually result in any gain or loss—just less interest revenue. Some term deposits are not cashable before their maturity date and some are. Before purchasing them, it is wise to look carefully at any penalties or conditions attached to money-market instruments that will be purchased for short-term use.

Treasury Bills

Government of Canada treasury bills are short-term debt instruments issued by the federal government. These instruments are a safe investment with a wide variety of maturity dates up to a maximum of one year. Treasury bills may be sold before their maturity date and quickly converted to cash because there is a well-established resale market. Treasury bills are sold at a discount to the face value (maturity value), and the difference between purchase price and value at maturity or date sold is the interest earned on the investment.

Recording Acquisitions of Treasury Bills. Assume that on October 1, 2010, Sulphur Research Limited purchases a $10,000, 150-day treasury bill for $9,756. The treasury bills are trading at a market rate of interest of 6% annually. The entry to record the investment is as follows:

Oct. 1	Short-Term Investment—Treasury Bill	9,756	
	Cash		9,756
	To record purchase of 150-day treasury bill at 6%.		

A	=	L	+	SE
+9,756				
−9,756				

↓ Cash flows: −9,756

Note that the treasury bill is recorded at the fair value (purchase price) on October 1. The treasury bill was purchased at a discount of $244, the difference between face value ($10,000) and the purchase price ($9,756). The discount is amortized over the remaining term of the treasury bill using the effective-interest method. The treasury bill will be reported in the current assets on the balance sheet.

Recording Interest Revenue and Amortizing the Discount. As shown in Chapter 15's Appendix A, when the effective-interest method is used, the interest expense on Bonds Payable is calculated by multiplying the market rate of interest by the bonds' carrying value. Similarly, with debt investments reported at amortized cost, interest revenue is calculated by multiplying the market rate of interest by the carrying value of the instrument.

Sulphur Research Limited's year end is December 31, so it is necessary to accrue $146 of interest for the months of October, November, and December ($9,756 × 6% × $3/12$ rounded to the nearest dollar).

Dec. 31	Short-Term Investment—Treasury Bill	146	
	Interest Revenue		146
	To accrue interest revenue and amortize discount.		

A	=	L	+	SE
+146				+146

Cash flows: no effect

Note that the debit is to the treasury bill investment account. The discount has been reduced or amortized by the amount of the interest revenue. The treasury bill is reported on the December 31 balance sheet at its amortized cost of $9,902 ($9,756 + $146). Interest revenue is reported under other revenues in the income statement.

Recording the Maturity of Treasury Bills. On February 28, 2011, when the treasury bill matures, it is necessary to (1) update the interest and amortize the discount for the latest period, (2) record the receipt of cash, and (3) remove the treasury bill investment account. The interest revenue of $98 is equal to the difference between the face value ($10,000) and the amortized cost ($9,902) of the bonds at December 31. The entry to record the interest revenue and amortize the discount is as follows:

Feb. 28	Short-Term Investment—Treasury Bill	98	
	Interest Revenue		98
	To accrue interest revenue and amortize discount.		

A	=	L	+	SE
+98				+98

Cash flows: no effect

Note that the amortized cost of the treasury bill is now $10,000 ($9,902 + $98), equal to its maturity value. The entry to record the receipt of cash and eliminate the treasury bill is as follows:

Feb. 28	Cash	10,000	
	Short-Term Investment—Treasury Bill		10,000
	To record the receipt of cash and eliminate the treasury bill.		

A	=	L	+	SE
+10,000				
−10,000				

↑ Cash flows: +10,000

Bonds

Bonds were discussed in Chapter 15 from the liability side; that is, from the issuer's perspective. Corporations, governments, and universities issue bonds that are then purchased by investors. The issuer of the bonds is known as the **investee**. The purchaser of the bonds, or the bondholder, is known as the **investor**. We learned earlier in the chapter that bonds can be held for purposes of earning interest revenue or for purposes of trading. It is relevant to report debt instruments that are held to earn interest revenue at amortized cost. The accounting for bonds reported at amortized cost is illustrated below.

Recording Acquisitions of Bonds

Like money-market instruments, at acquisition, a bond is recorded at its fair value, which is equal to the purchase price. The following example illustrates the accounting of bonds reported at amortized cost. Khadr Inc. purchases $100,000 of ABC Corporation five-year, 7% bonds at 101 on January 1, 2010. Recall from Chapter 15 that bonds will sell at a premium (purchase price is above face value) if the market interest rate was lower than the contract rate of 7%. Bonds are sold at a discount (purchase price is below face value) if the market interest rate is higher than the contract rate of 7%. In this case, if Khadr Inc. pays 101 for the bonds, the total purchase price is $101,000, and it will record the purchase as follows:

A = L + SE
+101,000
−101,000

↓ Cash flows: −101,000

Jan. 1	Long-Term Investment—ABC Bonds	101,000	
	Cash		101,000
	To record purchase of ABC bonds.		

Given that the bonds are held to earn interest revenue and not to trade, and the term of the bonds is five years, the bonds will be reported in long-term assets on the balance sheet date.

Recording Interest Revenue and Amortizing the Discount or Premium

When bonds are reported at amortized cost, any premium or discount recorded in the investment account is amortized to interest revenue over the remaining term of the bonds. If there is a bond premium, interest revenue is reduced by the amortization amount. If there is a bond discount, interest revenue is increased by the amortization amount. Like the issuer of the bonds, the investor uses the effective-interest method of amortization (explained in Appendix 15A to Chapter 15).

To continue our Khadr example, assume that interest is payable semi-annually on July 1 and January 1. The semi-annual amortization of the premium is assumed to be $86 for the first interest period in this example. The entry required to record the receipt of the interest and amortization of the premium on July 1, 2010, is as follows:

A = L + SE
+3,500   +3,414
−86

↑ Cash flows: +3,500

July 1	Cash	3,500	
	Long-Term Investment—ABC Bonds		86
	Interest Revenue		3,414
	To record receipt of interest on ABC bonds.		

Note that the Cash account is debited as interest is received semi-annually on the bonds, unlike money-market instruments, where interest is generally received when the instrument matures. The interest received is $3,500 ($100,000 × 7% × 6/12). Interest revenue of $3,414 includes the interest received, $3,500, less the amortization of the premium, $86. Interest revenue is reported under other revenues in the income statement.

If the investor purchases the bonds directly from the investee, the investor's accounting for the bonds will effectively be the "mirror image" of the investee's accounting for the bonds. Illustration 16-3 compares the recording of the bonds as an investment for Khadr Inc. (the investor) and as a liability for ABC Corporation (the investee) for the bond issue and first interest payment date.

Khadr Inc. (Investor)		
Jan. 1	Long-Term Investment—ABC Bonds	101,000	
	Cash		101,000
July 1	Cash	3,500	
	Long-Term Investment—ABC Bonds		86
	Interest Revenue		3,414

ABC Corporation (Investee)		
Jan. 1	Cash	101,000	
	Bonds Payable		101,000
July 1	Interest Expense	3,414	
	Bonds Payable	86	
	Cash		3,500

← Illustration 16-3

Comparison of bond investment and liability

Note that when Khadr's investment account is debited, ABC Corporation's liability is credited for the same amount and vice versa.

Recording the Maturity of Bonds

Regardless of the bonds' purchase price, their amortized cost at maturity will equal their face value. By the time the bonds mature, any discount or premium will be fully amortized. Assuming that the interest for the last interest period has been received and recorded, the entry to record the receipt of cash for the ABC Bonds at maturity, January 1, 2015, is as follows:

Jan. 1	Cash	100,000	
	Long-Term Investment—ABC Bonds		100,000
	To record maturity of ABC bonds.		

A	=	L	+	SE
+100,000				
−100,000				

↑ Cash flows: +100,000

Because the amortized cost of the bonds equals the face value at maturity, there is no gain or loss.

Sale of Bonds before Maturity

Although the company purchased the bonds to earn interest revenue, it may be necessary to sell the bonds before maturity if the company needs the cash or the company may choose to sell the bonds because interest rates have increased and it can earn a higher return.

To record the sale of bonds, it is necessary to (1) update any unrecorded interest and the amortization of the discount or premium, (2) record the cash received, (3) remove the amortized cost of the bonds, and (4) recognize the gain or loss on sale. Interest must be updated if the bonds are sold between semi-annual interest payment dates.

To illustrate, assume Khadr sells its investment in ABC Bonds on January 1, 2013, for $99,500. The amortized cost of the bonds on January 1, 2013, is $100,440. Assuming that the interest for the interest date of January 1, 2013, has been received and recorded, the entry to record the sale of the bonds is as follows:

Jan. 1	Cash	99,500	
	Loss on Sale of ABC Bonds	940	
	Long-Term Investment—ABC Bonds		100,440
	To record sale of ABC bonds.		

A	=	L	+	SE
+99,500				−940
−100,440				

↑ Cash flows: +99,500

A loss is recognized on the sale of the bonds as the bonds were sold at a price ($99,500) that was less than the amortized cost ($100,440). The loss is reported in other expenses in the income statement.

BEFORE YOU GO ON . . .

→ Review It

1. What entries are required for an investment in term deposits? In treasury bills? In bonds?
1. What are the differences between accounting for investments in money-market instruments, and investments in bonds, if both are reported at amortized cost?

→ Do It

Wang Corporation had the following transactions for debt investments held for purposes of earning interest revenue:

Jan. 1   Purchased five-year, 5% Hillary Corp. bonds with a face value of $30,000 for $30,660. Interest is payable semi-annually on July 1 and January 1.
Apr. 1   Purchased a $20,000, 120-day treasury bill for $19,600.
July 1   Received semi-annual interest on Hillary Corp. bonds. The semi-annual amortization of the premium is assumed to be $60.
    31   Received cash for the maturity of the treasury bill.
Dec. 1   Purchased a $10,000, three-month, 2% term deposit.

(a) Record the above transactions for Wang Corporation.
(b) Prepare the adjusting entry for the accrual of interest on December 31, Wang's year end. The semi-annual amortization of the bond premium is assumed to be $62.

Action Plan

- When investments are purchased, they are recorded at their fair value.
- Interest revenue is recognized as it accrues.
- The investments are reported at amortized cost on the balance sheet; therefore, premiums and discounts on these investments are amortized when interest revenue is recognized.
- When the investments mature, the cash received is recorded and the investment account is eliminated.

Solution

(a)

Jan. 1	Long-Term Investment—Hillary Bonds	30,660	
	Cash		30,660
	To record purchase of Hillary bonds.		
Apr. 1	Short-Term Investment—Treasury Bill	19,600	
	Cash		19,600
	To record purchase of treasury bill.		
July 1	Cash ($30,000 × 5% × $^6/_{12}$)	750	
	Long-Term Investment—Hillary Bonds		60
	Interest Revenue ($750 – 60)		690
	To record receipt of semi-annual interest on Hillary bonds.		
31	Short-Term Investment—Treasury Bill	400	
	Interest revenue		400
	To record interest revenue on treasury bill.		
	Cash	20,000	
	Short-Term Investment—Treasury Bill		20,000
	To record maturity of treasury bill.		
Dec. 1	Short-Term Investment—Term Deposit	10,000	
	Cash		10,000
	Record purchase of term deposit.		

(b)

Dec. 31	Interest Receivable ($30,000 × 5% × $^6/_{12}$)	750	
	Interest Revenue ($750 − $62)		688
	Long-Term Investment—Hillary Bonds		62
	To accrue semi-annual interest on Hillary bonds.		
	Interest Receivable	17	
	Interest Revenue ($10,000 × 2% × $^1/_{12}$)		17
	To accrue interest for December on the term deposit.		

Related exercise material: BE16–3, BE16–4, BE16–5, E16–3, and E16–4.

The Navigator

Accounting for Trading Investments

Earlier in the chapter, it was stated that debt and equity instruments purchased principally for selling in the near term are reported at fair value on the balance sheet. This includes investments in common or preferred shares and debt instruments such as bonds that are purchased with the intent of selling the instrument at a gain. These debt instruments are reported at fair value, not amortized cost.

STUDY OBJECTIVE 3

Account for trading investments.

In accounting for trading investments reported at fair value, entries are required to record (1) the acquisition, (2) interest and dividend revenue, (3) fair value adjustments, and (4) the sale of the investment.

At acquisition, trading investments are recorded at their fair value (purchase price). Transaction costs incurred to purchase the investment are expensed.

Subsequent to acquisition, interest revenue is recognized as it accrues and dividend revenue is recognized when the company receives the cash dividend or becomes entitled to the cash dividend. You will recall from Chapter 14 that an investor will be entitled to receive a dividend from the company paying dividends (investee) if the investor holds the shares on the date of record.

Because trading investments are reported at fair value on the balance sheet, accounting entries are required to adjust the investment's carrying value for any increases or decreases in its fair value. This is referred to as a **fair value adjustment**. As previously mentioned, fair value is the amount of cash to be received if the investment is sold. A gain is recorded if the fair value is higher than the carrying value and a loss is recorded if the fair value is less than the carrying value. Gains and losses for trading securities are reported in the income statement. When the investment is sold, the cash received is recorded, the investment account is eliminated, and a gain or loss is recorded. The gain or loss is equal to the difference between the cash received and the carrying value of the investment.

As mentioned earlier, either debt or equity investments can be made for the purpose of trading and any gains and losses on these investments are reported in profit. We will look at the accounting for trading investments in both equity and debt instruments.

Equity Investments—Common Shares

Recording Acquisitions of Shares

When an equity instrument is purchased, the investment is recorded at fair value, which is equal to the price paid for the shares. Assume, for example, that on July 1, 2010, Leonard Corporation purchases 500 common shares of Gleason Ltd. at $30 per share. Leonard Corporation purchased the shares with the intent of selling them to make a profit.

The entry to record the equity investment is as follows:

Helpful hint The entries for investments in common shares are also used for investments in preferred shares.

July 1	Trading Securities—Gleason Common Shares	15,000	
	Cash (500 × $30)		15,000
	To record purchase of 500 Gleason common shares.		

You will recall that investments that are purchased principally for selling in the near term are referred to as trading securities. Also, since this investment was made with the intent of selling it at a profit, the investment is reported as a current asset on the balance sheet.

Recording Dividend Revenue

During the time the shares are held, entries are required for any cash dividends that are received. If a $2 per share dividend is received by Leonard on December 1, the entry is as follows:

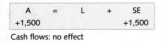

Dec. 1	Cash (500 × $2)	1,000	
	Dividend Revenue		1,000
	To record receipt of cash dividend.		

Dividend revenue is reported under other revenues in the income statement.

Recording Fair Value Adjustments at the Balance Sheet Date

On December 31, 2010, Leonard's fiscal year end, Gleason Ltd.'s shares are trading on the stock exchange at $33. The entry to record the adjustment to fair value is as follows:

Dec. 31	Trading Securities—Gleason Common Shares (500 × $3)	1,500	
	Gain on Fair Value Adjustment of Trading Securities		1,500
	To record adjustment of Gleason shares to fair value.		

The investment in Gleason shares will be reported on the balance sheet at its fair value of $16,500 ($15,000 + $1,500), which is the new carrying value of the investment. The gain on fair value adjustment is reported under other revenues in the income statement.

Recording Sales of Shares

When shares are sold, the difference between the proceeds from the sale and the carrying value of the shares is recognized as a gain or loss. Assume that Leonard receives proceeds of $17,000 on the sale of its Gleason common shares on October 10, 2011. Because the shares' carrying value is $16,500, there is a gain of $500 ($17,000 − $16,500). The entry to record the sale is as follows:

Oct. 10	Cash	17,000	
	Trading Securities—Gleason Common Shares		16,500
	Gain on Sale of Trading Securities ($17,000 − $16,500)		500
	To record sale of Gleason common shares.		

This gain is reported under other revenue in the income statement.

Debt Investments—Bonds

Recording Acquisitions of Bonds

At acquisition, an investment in bonds for trading purposes is recorded at its fair value, which is equal to its purchase price. To illustrate the accounting for an investment in bonds for trading purposes, assume that Kuhl Corporation acquires $50,000 face value of Doan Inc. 10-year, 6% bonds on January 1, 2011, for $49,000. Assuming that Kuhl purchased these bonds for the purpose of selling at a profit, the entry to record the investment is as follows:

Jan. 1	Trading Securities—Doan Bonds	49,000	
	Cash		49,000
	To record purchase of Doan bonds.		

A = L + SE
+49,000
−49,000

⬇ Cash flows: −49,000

Recording Interest Revenue

The bonds pay interest of $1,500 ($50,000 $\times$ 6% $\times$ $^6/_{12}$) semi-annually on July 1 and January 1. As discussed in Chapter 15, interest is paid on face value and not on acquisition cost or carrying value. The following entry records the receipt of interest on July 1:

July 1	Cash	1,500	
	Interest Revenue		1,500
	To record receipt of interest on Doan bonds.		

A = L + SE
+1,500   +1,500

⬆ Cash flows: +1,500

Note that any premium or discount on bonds (recorded net as part of the acquisition cost, as shown in the January 1 journal entry above) is not amortized to interest revenue for a trading investment in a debt instrument reported at fair value. The discount or premium is not amortized because the bonds were purchased for the purpose of selling at a profit and therefore are held for a short period of time. Any misstatement of interest revenue from not amortizing the premium or discount is not considered significant.

Assuming Kuhl's financial year end is December 31, an entry is required to accrue interest revenue for the interest earned. The following entry records the accrual of interest on December 31:

Dec. 31	Interest Receivable	1,500	
	Interest Revenue		1,500
	To record accrual of interest on Doan bonds.		

A = L + SE
+1,500   +1,500

Cash flows: no effect

Note that on January 1, 2012, when the interest payment is received from Doan, interest receivable will be credited.

Recording Fair Value Adjustments at the Balance Sheet Date

You will recall from Chapter 15 that bonds trade on the public market at prices that reflect the current market rate of interest. If the market rate of interest changes after a company purchases bonds, the bonds' fair value will be different from their purchase price. If the market rate of interest increases, the bonds' fair value will decrease, and if the market rate of interest decreases, the bonds' fair value will increase. Assume that on December 31, 2011, Kuhl's financial year end, the market rate of interest increased and the bonds are trading at $48,000. The entry to record the adjustment to fair value is as follows:

Dec. 31	Loss on Fair Value Adjustment of Trading Securities	1,000	
	Trading Securities—Doan Bonds		1,000
	To record adjustment to fair value.		

A = L + SE
−1,000   −1,000

Cash flows: no effect

The investment in Doan bonds will be reported on the balance sheet at its fair value of $48,000, which is the new carrying value of the bonds. The loss on fair value adjustment is reported under other expenses in the income statement.

Recording Sales of Bonds

When the bonds are sold, it is necessary to (1) update any unrecorded interest up to the date of sale, (2) debit Cash for the proceeds received, (3) credit the investment account for the carrying value of the bonds, and (4) record any gain or loss on sale. Any difference between the proceeds from the sale of the bonds and the carrying value is recorded as a gain or loss.

Assume, for example, that Kuhl receives $47,500 on the sale of the Doan bonds on July 1, 2012, after receiving (and recording) the interest due. Since the bonds' carrying value is $48,000, a loss of $500 is recorded. Assuming the interest payment for the period has been recorded, the entry to record the sale is as follows:

A	=	L	+	SE
+47,500				−500
−48,000				

↑ Cash flows: +47,500

July 1	Cash	47,500	
	Loss on Sale of Trading Securities	500	
	Trading Securities—Doan Bonds		48,000
	To record sale of Doan bonds.		

The loss on the sale of the bonds is reported as other expenses in the income statement.

Recording Bonds for Investor and Investee

Using the Kuhl Corporation example, Illustration 16-4 compares the recording of the bonds as a short-term investment reported at fair value for Kuhl (the investor) and the recording of the bonds as a long-term liability for Doan (the investee). For the purpose of this illustration, we have assumed that the discount amortization is $150 for the first interest period, $140 for the second interest period, and $130 for the third interest period.

Illustration 16-4 ➡

Comparison of debt trading investment and long-term liability

Kuhl Corporation (Investor)			
Jan. 1	Trading Securities—Doan Bonds	49,000	
	Cash		49,000
July 1	Cash	1,500	
	Interest Revenue		1,500
Dec. 31	Interest Receivable	1,500	
	Interest Revenue		1,500
31	Loss on Fair Value Adjustment of Trading Securities	1,000	
	Trading Securities—Doan Bonds		1,000
Jan. 1	Cash	1,500	
	Interest Receivable		1,500
July 1	Cash	1,500	
	Interest Revenue		1,500
1	Cash	47,500	
	Loss on Sale of Trading Securities	500	
	Trading Securities—Doan Bonds		48,000

Doan Inc. (Investee)			
Jan. 1	Cash	49,000	
	Bonds Payable		49,000
July 1	Interest Expense	1,650	
	Bonds Payable		150
	Cash		1,500
Dec. 31	Interest Expense	1,640	
	Bonds Payable		140
	Interest Payable		1,500
Jan. 1	Interest Payable	1,500	
	Cash		1,500
July 1	Interest Expense	1,630	
	Bonds Payable		130
	Cash		1,500

Recording a trading investment in bonds (an asset) for an investor differs from the recording of bonds payable (a liability) for an investee in several ways. First, any premium or discount is not amortized by the investor as it is for the investee. Second, there is no fair value adjustment for the investee. Last, assuming that Kuhl sold its bonds on the open market, the issuer,

Doan Inc., is not affected by this transaction. It would only be affected if the bonds were re-deemed before maturity or repaid at maturity.

BEFORE YOU GO ON . . .

→ Review It

1. When is it appropriate to report an investment in bonds at fair value?
2. What entries are required for trading investments in (a) equity instruments and (b) bonds?
3. What is a fair value adjustment? Under what circumstances is this reported for trading investments?

→ Do It

Lang Corporation had the following transactions:

Jan. 2   Purchased an investment in Utility Corp. $20,000, five-year, 4% bonds for $20,455. The market rate of interest is 3.5%. The bonds were purchased to trade.
July 1   Received semi-annual interest on the Utility Corp. bonds.
    2   Sold half of the Utility Corp. bonds for $10,500.
Sept. 1   Purchased 1,000 common shares of Electric Ltd. for $15 per share. The shares were purchased to trade.
Nov. 1   Received a $2 dividend on the Electric Ltd. shares.
Dec. 31   The Utility Corp. bonds' fair value was $9,750. The Electric Ltd. shares were trading at $14 per share.

(a) Record the above transactions.
(b) Prepare the required adjusting journal entries at December 31, Lang's financial year end.
(c) Identify where the investments would be reported in the balance sheet.
(d) Identify where the interest revenue, dividend revenue, and gains and losses will be reported.

Action Plan
- Record the interest received as the amount of interest revenue.
- When the bonds are sold, the difference between the bonds' carrying value and the proceeds is reported as a gain or loss.
- Record the interest accrued on the bonds held for the period July 2 to December 31.
- Fair value adjustments are the difference between the investments' carrying value and fair value.

Solution
(a)

Jan. 2	Trading Securities—Utility Corp. Bonds	20,455	
	Cash		20,455
	To record purchase of Utility Corp. bonds.		
July 1	Cash	400	
	Interest Revenue		400
	To record receipt of interest.		
2	Cash	10,500	
	Trading Securities—Utility Corp. Bonds		10,228
	Gain on Sale of Trading Securities		272
	To record sale of half of Utility Corp. bonds.		
Sept. 1	Trading Securities—Electric Ltd. Common Shares	15,000	
	Cash		15,000
	To record purchase of Electric Ltd. common shares.		
Nov. 1	Cash	2,000	
	Dividend Revenue		2,000
	To record dividends received (1,000 × $2).		

(b)

Dec. 31	Interest Receivable ($10,000 × 4% × ⁶/₁₂)	200	
	Interest Revenue		200
	To accrue semi-annual interest on Utility Corp. bonds.		
31	Loss on Fair Value Adjustment on Trading Securities	477	
	Trading Securities—Utility Corp. Bonds		477
	To record fair value adjustment on bonds ($10,227 − $9,750).		
31	Loss on Fair Value Adjustment on Trading Securities	1,000	
	Trading Securities—Electric Ltd. Common Shares		1,000
	To record fair value adjustment on Electric Ltd. common shares [1,000 × ($15 − $14)].		

(c) The investments will be reported in current assets on the balance sheet.

(d) Interest revenue, dividend revenue, and gain on sale will be reported in other revenues in the income statement. The losses from the fair value adjustments will be reported in other expenses in the income statement.

The Navigator

Related exercise material: BE16–6, BE16–7, BE16–8, BE16–9, E16–5, E16–6, E16–7, E16–8, and E16–9.

Accounting for Strategic Investments

STUDY OBJECTIVE 4

Account for strategic investments.

Recall from the start of the chapter that strategic investments are always long-term investments in equity securities. The accounting for strategic investments is based on how much influence the investor has over the operating and financial affairs of the issuing corporation (the investee). The degree of influence depends primarily on the percentage of common shares owned by the investor. Illustration 16-5 shows the guidelines for the levels of influence.

Illustration 16-5 ➡

Financial reporting guidelines for strategic investments

Investor's Ownership Interest in Investee's Common Shares	Presumed Influence on Investee	Financial Reporting Guidelines
Less than 20%	Insignificant	Fair value
20% to 50% or more	Significant	Equity method
Greater than 50%	Control	Consolidation

A company may invest in equity securities to maintain a long-term operating relationship. An investor company that owns less than 20% of the common shares of another company is generally presumed not to have significant influence over the decisions of the investee company. A long-term equity investment where there is no significant influence is reported at fair value.

When an investor owns 20% to 50% of the common shares of another company, the investor is generally presumed to have a significant influence over the decisions of the investee company and the equity method is used to account for and report the investment in the company's financial statements.

The influence that an investor is assumed to have may be weakened by other factors. For example, an investor that acquires a 25% interest as the result of a "hostile" takeover may not have significant influence over the investee. Among the questions that should be answered to determine an investor's influence are:

1. Does the investor have representation on the investee's board of directors?
2. Does the investor participate in the investee's policy-making process?
3. Are there material transactions between the investor and investee?
4. Are the common shares that are held by other shareholders concentrated among a few investors or dispersed among many?

In other words, companies are required to use judgement when determining if significant influence exists instead of blindly following the guidelines. If circumstances exist that indicate the investor does not have significant influence, regardless of the amount owned, the investment is reported at fair value.

In our feature story, Scotiabank purchased 37% of the equity of CI Financial Income Fund and 19% of the common shares of DundeeWealth Inc. Although Scotiabank owns only 19% of the common shares of DundeeWealth, it was determined that Scotiabank has significant influence over both of these companies and the equity method was used to account for these investments in the bank's 2008 annual financial statements.

When an investor owns more than 50% of the common shares of a corporation, it has more than significant influence—it has control. When one company (known as the **parent company**) controls another company (known as the **subsidiary company**), **consolidated financial statements** must be prepared for financial reporting purposes. For example, in our feature story, Scotiabank acquired 100% of the common shares of E*TRADE Canada in 2008. Scotiabank, the parent, gained control of E*TRADE Canada, the subsidiary.

Consolidated financial statements present the total assets and liabilities controlled by the parent company. They indicate the size and scope of operations under common control. Most publicly traded companies in Canada, including The Forzani Group Ltd., present consolidated financial statements.

Consolidated statements are prepared in addition to the financial statements for the parent company and each subsidiary company. For internal accounting purposes, the parent company will account for the investment using the equity method. For example, Scotiabank uses the equity method to account for its investment in E*TRADE Canada (now called Scotia iTRADE) in its own individual statements. But, for external reporting, Scotiabank consolidates Scotia iTRADE's results with its own financial statements. Under this approach, the individual assets and liabilities of Scotia iTRADE are included with those of Scotiabank's.

Consolidation is a complex topic and is discussed in greater detail in advanced accounting courses.

ACCOUNTING IN ACTION: ACROSS THE ORGANIZATION

In the fall of 2009, under pressure from Canada's institutional shareholders, the Toronto Stock Exchange approved a new rule giving shareholders of public companies the right to vote on takeover deals if their ownership level will be diluted by more than 25% as a result of the transaction. Canadian shareholders had been urging for reform on voting on takeover deals for several years. This ruling came after a shareholder of HudBay Minerals Inc. complained that there should be a vote on HudBay's planned takeover of Lundin Mining Corp. because HudBay was proposing to pay for the purchase in shares, diluting its outstanding shares by 100%. HudBay Minerals Inc. abandoned its takeover of Lundin after a shareholder appealed to the Ontario Securities Commission to call for a shareholder vote on the deal and the commission demanded that a vote should be held.

Sources: Janet McFarland, "Shareholders Urge Early Adoption of New TSX Takeover Rules," *The Globe and Mail*, September 25, 2009; "Hudbay Minerals and Lundin Mining Agree to Terminate Arrangement Agreement," Reuters, February 23, 2009.

Why should a company's management and the board of directors have to consult with their own shareholders if they are planning on issuing shares to take over another company?

Fair Value

For a strategic investment where there is no significant influence or control (normally a long-term investment with less than 20% of the total common shares), the investment in common shares is reported at fair value. This is similar to equity investments for trading purposes, except that equity securities purchased for trading are classified as current assets, and equity securities purchased as strategic investments are classified as long-term, or non-current, assets.

At the time of writing this textbook, the International Accounting Standards Board (IASB) was in the process of issuing new recommendations on the accounting for investments under IFRS. The IASB recognized that, if the investment is going to be held and not sold, then it may be inappropriate to affect a company's profit with the gains and losses on fair value adjustments caused by market fluctuations. Instead, it was proposed that these gains and losses may be reported in other comprehensive income if a company chooses to do so. Companies may also choose to report the gains and losses on fair value adjustments for these investments in profit.

If a company decides to report the gains and losses on fair value adjustments in other comprehensive income, then the cumulative net gain or loss on that investment is transferred to retained earnings when the investment is sold. Dividends earned on the investment are reported in other revenues in the income statement as they are earned.

As mentioned previously, if a company chooses to report the gains or losses on fair value adjustments in profit, the accounting is identical to the accounting for trading investments.

The following section illustrates how to account for long-term strategic investments, where the investor does not have significant influence or control, and where the company chooses to report the gains and losses from fair value adjustments in other comprehensive income. But we will not illustrate how to account for the gain or loss on the sale of an investment, where previous fair value adjustments have been included in other comprehensive income, because the accounting is relatively complex, and thus beyond the scope of an introductory accounting textbook. Also, if an investment is held for strategic reasons, it is expected that selling such an investment will happen infrequently.

The entries for an investment in common shares where gains and losses on fair value adjustments are reported in other comprehensive income are illustrated with the following example.

Recording Acquisitions of Shares

Assume that Cooke Ltd. purchases 5,000 common shares of Depres Company for $20 per share on October 1, 2010. Cooke Ltd. intends to hold the investment for strategic reasons, but does not have significant influence over Depres. Cooke Ltd. also decides to report the gains and losses resulting from the fair value adjustments in other comprehensive income. The entry to record the acquisition is as follows:

A = L + SE
+100,000
−100,000

↓ Cash flows: −100,000

July 1	Long-Term Investment—Depres Common Shares	100,000	
	Cash (5,000 × $20)		100,000
	To record purchase of 5,000 Depres common shares.		

Recording Dividend Revenue

Assume that on November 1, 2010, Depres pays a dividend of $3 per share. The entry to record the dividend revenue is as follows:

A = L + SE
+15,000   +15,000

↑ Cash flows: +15,000

Nov. 1	Cash (5,000 × $3)	15,000	
	Dividend Revenue		15,000
	To record receipt of cash dividend.		

The dividend revenue is reported under other revenues in the income statement.

Recording the Fair Value Adjustment at Balance Sheet Date

Assume that on December 31, 2010, Cooke Ltd.'s financial year end, Depres common shares are trading at $22, an increase of $2 per share since the shares were purchased on July 1. The entry to record the change in fair value is as follows:

Dec. 31	Long-Term Investment—Depres Common Shares (5,000 × $2)	10,000	
	Other Comprehensive Income—Gain on Fair Value Adjustment		10,000
	To record adjustment to fair value.		

A	=	L	+	SE
+10,000				+10,000

Cash flows: no effect

Recall from Chapter 14 that gains and losses included in other comprehensive income are reported in the statement of comprehensive income net of tax. Assuming a 30% tax rate, $7,000 [($10,000 − ($10,000 × 30%)] will be reported as other comprehensive income in the statement. As a result, Accumulated Other Comprehensive Income will be increased by the fair value adjustment of $7,000. You will recall from Chapters 13 and 14 that Accumulated Other Comprehensive Income is reported in shareholders' equity.

Equity Method

As noted earlier, when an investor company has significant influence over the investee, the equity method is used to account for the investment.

Under the **equity method**, the investment in common shares is initially recorded at cost, which includes the purchase price of the shares and any transaction costs paid to purchase them. After that, the investment account is adjusted annually to show the investor's equity in the investee. An alternative might be to delay recognizing the investor's share of profit until a cash dividend is declared. But doing that would ignore the fact that the investor and investee are, in some sense, one company, which means the investor benefits from the investee's profit.

Helpful hint Under the equity method, revenue is recognized on the accrual basis; i.e., when it is earned by the investee.

Each year, the investor adjusts the investment account to do the following:

1. **Record its share of the investee's profit (loss):** Increase (debit) the investment account and increase (credit) revenue for the investor's share of the investee's profit. Conversely, when the investee has a loss, the investor increases (debits) a loss account and decreases (credits) the investment account for its share of the investee's loss.
2. **Record the dividends received:** Decrease (credit) the investment account when dividends are received. The investment account is reduced for dividends received because the investee's net assets are decreased when a dividend is paid.

Recording Acquisitions of Shares

Assume that Milar Corporation (the investor) acquires 30% of the common shares of Beck Corporation (the investee) for $120,000 on January 1, 2011, and that Milar has significant influence over Beck. The following entry records this transaction:

Jan. 1	Equity Method Investment—Beck Common Shares	120,000	
	Cash		120,000
	To record purchase of Beck common shares.		

A	=	L	+	SE
+120,000				
−120,000				

 Cash flows: −120,000

Recording Investment Revenue

For the year ended December 31, 2011, Beck reports profit of $100,000. It declares and pays a $40,000 cash dividend. Milar is required to record (1) its share of Beck's profit, $30,000 (30% × $100,000), and (2) a reduction in the investment account for the dividends received, $12,000 ($40,000 × 30%). The entries are as follows:

A	=	L	+	SE
+30,000				+30,000

Cash flows: no effect

A	=	L	+	SE
+12,000				
−12,000				

↑ Cash flows: +12,000

	(1)		
Dec. 31	Equity Method Investment—Beck Common Shares	30,000	
	Revenue from Equity Investment in Beck		30,000
	To record 30% equity in Beck's profit.		
	(2)		
31	Cash	12,000	
	Equity Method Investment—Beck Common Shares		12,000
	To record dividends received.		

After the transactions for the year have been posted, the investment and revenue accounts will show the following:

Equity Method Investment—Beck Common Shares				Revenue from Equity Investment in Beck	
Jan. 1	120,000			Dec. 31	30,000
Dec. 31	30,000	Dec. 31	12,000		
Dec. 31 Bal.	138,000				

During the year, the investment account has increased by $18,000 ($138,000 − $120,000). This $18,000 is Milar's 30% equity in the $60,000 increase in Beck's retained earnings ($100,000 − $40,000). In addition, Milar will report $30,000 of revenue from its investment, which is 30% of Beck's profit of $100,000.

The difference between profits reported when an investment is reported at fair value and when the equity method is used can be significant. If Milar were assumed not to have significant influence, it would report $12,000 of dividend revenue (30% × $40,000) as part of profit. It would also have to report a gain or loss from the fair value adjustment in either profit or in other comprehensive income.

BEFORE YOU GO ON . . .

→ **Review It**

1. When is it appropriate to report a strategic investment at fair value? When is it appropriate to use the equity method?
2. When is it appropriate to prepare consolidated financial statements?
3. Compare the journal entries for long-term strategic investments where the investor has significant influence with those when the investor does not have significant influence.
4. Are The Forzani Group's financial statements consolidated? If they are, what percentage does Forzani own of its subsidiary companies? The answers to these questions are at the end of the chapter.

→ **Do It**

CJW Inc. made the following two investments during 2011:

1. Acquired 20% of the 400,000 common shares of Stillwater Corp. for $6 per share on January 2, 2011. On August 30, 2011, Stillwater paid a $0.10 per share dividend. On December 31, 2011, Stillwater reported profit of $244,000 for the year. Prepare all necessary journal entries for 2011 assuming there is significant influence.
2. Acquired 10% of the 200,000 common shares of Roughwater Ltd. for $5 per share on September 15, 2011. CJW intends to hold the investment for strategic reasons but does not have significant influence, and reports gains or losses on fair value adjustments as other comprehensive income. On December 31, the shares were trading at $4 per share.

Action Plan
- Use the equity method for ownership when there is significant influence (normally ownership of 20% or more of the common shares of another corporation).

- Under the equity method, recognize investment revenue when the investee declares a profit. The distribution of dividends is not income; rather, it reduces the equity investment.
- Use the fair value method for a strategic long-term investment where there is not significant influence and record the gain or loss in other comprehensive income.

Solution

Jan. 2	Equity Method Investment—Stillwater Common Shares	480,000	
	Cash (80,000 × $6)		480,000
	To record purchase of 80,000 Stillwater common shares (400,000 × 20% = 80,000 shares).		
Aug. 30	Cash	8,000	
	Equity Method Investment—Stillwater Common Shares		8,000
	To record receipt of cash dividend ($0.10 × 80,000).		
Sept. 15	Long-Term Investment—Roughwater Common Shares	100,000	
	Cash (20,000 × $5)		100,000
	To record purchase of 20,000 Roughwater common shares (200,000 × 10%).		
Dec. 31	Equity Method Investment—Stillwater Common Shares	48,800	
	Revenue from Equity Investment in Stillwater		48,800
	To record 20% equity in Stillwater's profit ($244,000 × 20%).		
31	Other Comprehensive Income—Loss on Fair Value Adjustment	20,000	
	Long-Term Investment—Roughwater Common Shares		20,000
	To record adjustment to fair value [20,000 × ($5 − $4)].		

Related exercise material: BE16–10, BE16–11, E16–10, E16–11, and E16–12.

The Navigator

Reporting of Investments

This section reviews the presentation of investments in the balance sheet, income statement, and statement of comprehensive income.

STUDY OBJECTIVE 5

Indicate how investments are reported in the financial statements.

Balance Sheet

As stated earlier in this chapter, all debt and equity investments are classified as one of the following: (1) trading investments, (2) debt investments reported at amortized cost, (3) long-term equity investments reported at fair value, or (4) equity investments accounted for using the equity method. These different types of investments will be reported on the balance sheet in either current assets or long-term investments.

Investments Classified as Current Assets

Trading investments are always classified as current assets, because management purchased the investment for the purpose of selling it in the near future at a gain. Recall that trading investments may include short-term and long-term debt instruments and equity securities. These assets are always reported at their fair value.

Short-term debt instruments, such as term deposits and government treasury bills, are included in current assets and reported at amortized cost, because the company plans to hold them to maturity. If the company has more than one such investment, they are either grouped together or presented in current assets in order of their liquidity. IFRS requires that trading investments and investments reported at amortized cost be separately disclosed.

If the short-term debt investment that is being held to earn interest is very short-term (usually the time to maturity is less than three months or 90 days), it may be viewed as "near" cash. These types of short-term investments are typically in money-market instruments and are generally combined with cash and reported as a single line item called "cash and cash equivalents." As discussed in Chapter 7, some accounting standard setters believe that these short-term investments should be reported with the other short-term investments and should not be considered cash equivalents. Companies following Canadian GAAP for Private Enterprises will continue to be allowed to report these investments as cash equivalents.

Illustration 16-6 shows one possible presentation of short-term investments on the balance sheet for Skaweniio Corporation.

Illustration 16-6 ➡

Presentation of short-term investments

SKAWENIIO CORPORATION Balance Sheet (partial) December 31, 2011	
Assets	
Current assets	
Cash and cash equivalents	$ 28,000
Treasury bills—at amortized cost	15,000
Trading securities—at fair value	143,000

Long-Term Investments

Long-term debt instruments, such as bonds, that are held to earn interest income are classified as long-term investments until they are about to mature. Any portion that is expected to mature within the year is classified as a current asset. In addition, all equity securities that are purchased for strategic purposes are also classified as long-term investments.

IFRS requires separate disclosure of long-term investments reported at fair value and amortized cost and investments accounted for using the equity method. In addition, for equity investments reported at fair value, those investments where gains and losses are reported in other comprehensive income and those where gains and losses are reported in the income statement should be separately disclosed.

Illustration 16-7 summarizes the reporting and valuation requirements of both short- and long-term investments on the balance sheet.

Illustration 16-7 ➡

Reporting and valuation of investments

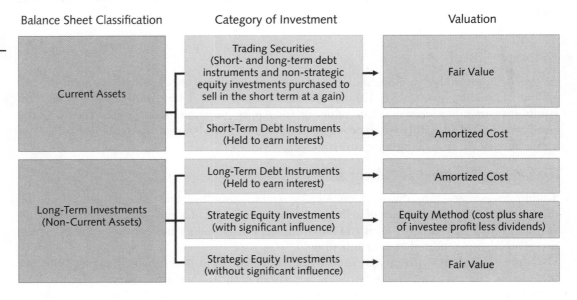

Income Statement and Statement of Comprehensive Income

This chapter has shown that companies can earn different types of income on investments, including (1) interest revenue, (2) dividend revenue, (3) gains or losses on fair value adjustments, (4) gains or losses on sale of the investment, and (5) equity income from a strategic investment with significant influence. Most of these items are included in profit in the non-operating section of the income statement. But you will recall that a company may choose to include gains and losses on fair value adjustments of strategic investments without significant influence in other comprehensive income. This is summarized in Illustration 16-8.

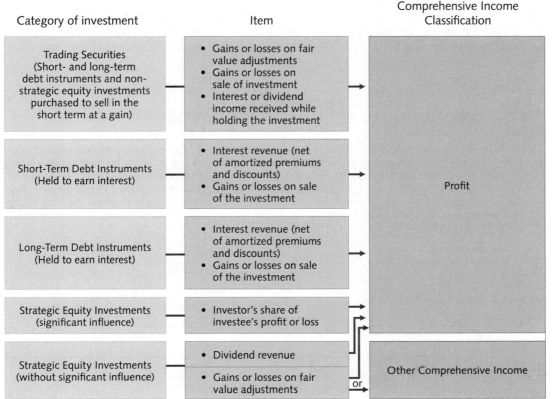

Illustration 16-8

Reporting income from investments

By combining items that are reported in the income statement with items reported in other comprehensive income when calculating comprehensive income, the financial statement users are provided with information that will help them to predict the company's future profitability and cash flows as well as evaluate how the company has performed.

Canadian GAAP for Private Enterprises

As discussed in Chapters 13 and 14, under Canadian GAAP for Private Enterprises, there is no such thing as other comprehensive income or accumulated other comprehensive income. Thus there are some differences in accounting for investments for companies using Canadian GAAP for Private Enterprises, as follows:

1. All investments in debt instruments are reported at amortized cost.
2. For equity investments where there is no significant influence, only those equity instruments where there is a quoted fair value from an active market are reported at fair value. If there is no active market, the equity investment is reported at cost.
3. There are no gains and losses reported in other comprehensive income.
4. All transaction costs are recorded as an expense.

Available-for-Sale Investments

This chapter has illustrated the accounting for a variety of different types of investments. We have focused on the investment classifications that are currently used and will continue to be used in the future. There is one investment classification not shown in this chapter: available-for-sale investments. **Available-for-sale investments** are defined as debt or equity securities that are held with the intention of selling them sometime in the future and are neither trading securities nor held to maturity for the purpose of earning interest income. Available-for-sale investments are reported at fair value as either current or long-term assets and the gains and losses from fair value adjustments are reported in other comprehensive income. This text does not illustrate the accounting for these investments because, when the new accounting standards for investments are adopted, companies will not be allowed to designate an investment as available for sale. Until 2013, you may continue to see this classification of investments in financial statements.

ACCOUNTING IN ACTION: ALL ABOUT YOU

Canadians need to save for many different things over their lifetimes. To reduce taxes on savings and help individuals achieve their goals, the Canadian government introduced a new investment vehicle, the tax-free savings account (TFSA), starting in 2009. Canadians aged 18 and older can contribute up to $5,000 every year to a TFSA. Investment income on the TFSA is not taxable. If an individual is not able to contribute the allowed $5,000 per year, they are able to carry forward any unused contribution to future years. Funds can be withdrawn from the TFSA at any time and for any purpose. The amount withdrawn can be put back in the TFSA at a later date. Canadians from all income levels can participate.

Source: http://www.tfsa.gc.ca

Assume that you are an 18-year-old student with no taxable income and, through the generosity of your grandparents, you will be able to save $2,000 a year while you are a student. Is it beneficial for you to contribute to a TFSA? Would you classify your investment in a TFSA as a long-term or short-term investment?

BEFORE YOU GO ON . . .

➡ Review It

1. How are investments reported on the balance sheet?
2. What are the different types of income that can be earned from investments? Are these items included in profit on the income statement? Or as other comprehensive income on the statement of comprehensive income?

➡ Do It

Zaboschuk Corporation has the following asset account balances at December 31, 2011. Prepare the assets section of Zaboschuk's balance sheet at December 31.

Accounts receivable	$ 84,000
Accumulated depreciation—buildings	200,000
Accumulated depreciation—equipment	54,000
Allowance for doubtful accounts	4,000
Buildings	800,000
Cash	21,000
Equipment	180,000
Equity investments—equity method	150,000
Goodwill	170,000
Inventory	130,000
Land	200,000

Long-term bond investment—amortized cost	$50,000
Long-term equity investment—fair value	90,000
Money-market instruments (maturity 120 days—amortized cost)	15,000
Prepaid insurance	23,000
Trading securities	65,000

Action Plan

- Organize each asset account into its proper classification: current assets; long-term investments; property, plant, and equipment; and intangible assets.
- Remember that contra asset accounts reduce the related account balance and asset accounts increase the related account balance.

Solution

ZABOSCHUK CORPORATION
Balance Sheet (partial)
December 31, 2011

Assets

Current assets			
Cash			$ 21,000
Money-market instruments—amortized cost			15,000
Trading securities—fair value			65,000
Accounts receivable		$ 84,000	
Less: Allowance for doubtful accounts		4,000	80,000
Inventory			130,000
Prepaid insurance			23,000
Total current assets			334,000
Long-term investments			
Equity investment—fair value			90,000
Bond investment—amortized cost			50,000
Equity investments—equity method			150,000
Total long-term investments			290,000
Property, plant, and equipment			
Land		$200,000	
Buildings	$800,000		
Less: Accumulated depreciation	200,000	600,000	
Equipment	$180,000		
Less: Accumulated depreciation	54,000	126,000	
Total property, plant, and equipment			926,000
Goodwill			170,000
Total assets			$1,720,000

Related exercise material: BE16–12, BE16–13, BE16–14, E16–13, E16–14, and E16–15.

The Navigator

Demonstration Problem

In its first year of operations, which ended December 31, 2011, Northstar Finance Corporation had the following selected transactions.

Jan. 1   Purchased 25% of the common shares of Southview Finance Ltd. for $125,000. Northstar purchased the investment for strategic purposes.

Mar. 14   Purchased $10,000 of treasury bills.

May 5   Purchased 15% of the common shares of Eastgate Financial Co. for $28,000. Northstar purchased the investment for strategic purposes.

June 1   Purchased 600 Sanburg common shares for trading at $24.50 per share.

    29   Treasury bill matured and the company received $10,000, plus $50 interest.

Demonstration Problems

July 1	Purchased $100,000 of Lower Corporation 10-year, 6% bonds for 98 to hold to earn interest.		
1	Purchased 800 Cey common shares for trading at $33.75 per share.		
Sept. 1	Received a $1 per share cash dividend from Cey Corporation.		
Oct. 8	Received dividends of $5,000 from Southview Finance Ltd.		
Nov. 1	Sold 200 Sanburg common shares for $26.25 per share.		
Dec. 15	Received a $0.50 per share cash dividend on Sanburg common shares.		
31	The fair values per share were $25 for Sanburg and $30 for Cey.		
31	Accrued interest revenue on the Lower Corporation bonds. The semi-annual amortization of the discount is $73.		
31	The fair value of the Eastgate common shares is $26,000. Northstar has chosen to record the gains and losses on the fair value adjustment in other comprehensive income.		
31	Southview reported profit of $90,000 for the year ended December 31, 2011.		
31	Northstar reported profit from operations of $250,000 for the year ended December 31, 2011. Northstar's income tax rate is 30%.		

Instructions

(a) Record the transactions.

(b) Prepare the adjusting entries at December 31 to report the securities at their fair value.

(c) Show the presentation of the investment accounts, and accumulated other comprehensive income in the balance sheet.

(d) Prepare a statement of comprehensive income starting with profit from operations.

Solution to Demonstration Problem

(a)

Date	Account	Debit	Credit
Jan. 1	Equity Method Investment—Southview Finance Co.	$125,000	
	Cash		$125,000
	To record purchase of strategic investment in Southview.		
Mar. 14	Short-Term Investment—Treasury Bills	10,000	
	Cash		10,000
	To record purchase of treasury bills.		
May 5	Long-Term Investment—Eastgate Financial Co. Common Shares	28,000	
	Cash		28,000
	To record purchase of strategic investment in common shares of Eastgate Financial.		
June 1	Trading Securities—Sanburg Common Shares	14,700	
	Cash (600 × $24.50)		14,700
	To record purchase of 600 Sanburg common shares.		
29	Short-Term Investment—Treasury Bills	50	
	Interest revenue		50
	Cash	10,050	
	Short-Term Investment—Treasury Bills		10,050
	To record maturity of treasury bills.		
July 1	Long-Term Investment—Lower Corporation Bonds	98,000	
	Cash		98,000
	To record purchase of long-term investment in Lower Corporation bonds.		
1	Trading Securities—Cey Common Shares	27,000	
	Cash (800 × $33.75)		27,000
	To record purchase of 800 Cey common shares.		

Action Plan

• Keep a running balance of the number of shares purchased and sold.

• Calculate the gain or loss on sale by subtracting the securities' carrying value from the proceeds.

• Determine the adjustment to fair value based on the difference between the securities' total cost and total fair value.

• Calculate the interest revenue on the bonds by adding the amortization of the discount to the semi-annual interest payment.

• Determine the equity method investment income by multiplying the investee company's profit by the percent of the common shares the investor company owns.

• Determine the profit before income tax by adding the other revenues and expenses to profit from operations.

• Calculate income tax expense by multiplying profit before income tax by the tax rate.

• Calculate the other comprehensive income reported in the comprehensive income statement by deducting the income tax on the fair value adjustment from the fair value adjustment.

• Calculate the accumulated other comprehensive income by adding the opening balance (zero in the first year of operations) and the fair value adjustment net of tax.

Sept. 1	Cash (800 × $1)	800	
	Dividend Revenue		800
	To record receipt of $1 per share dividend from Cey.		
Oct. 8	Cash	5,000	
	Equity Method Investment—Southview Finance Co.		5,000
	To record receipt of $5,000 dividends from Southview Finance Co.		
Nov. 1	Cash (200 × $26.25)	5,250	
	Trading Securities—Sanburg Common Shares [(200 ÷ 600) × $14,700)]		4,900
	Gain on Sale of Trading Securities		350
	To record sale of 200 Sanburg common shares.		
Dec. 15	Cash [(600 − 200) × $0.50]	200	
	Dividend Revenue		200
	To record receipt of $0.50 per share dividend from Sanburg.		

(b)

Trading Securities	Cost	Fair Value	Gain (Loss) on Fair Value Adjustment
Sanburg common shares (400)	$ 9,800	$10,000	$ 200
Cey common shares (800)	27,000	24,000	(3,000)
Total	$36,800	$34,000	$(2,800)

Dec. 31	Loss on Fair Value Adjustment—Trading Securities	2,800	
	Trading Securities—Sanburg Common Shares	200	
	Trading Securities—Cey Common Shares		3,000
	To record fair value adjustment on trading securities.		
31	Interest receivable	3,000	
	Long-Term Investment—Lower Corporation Bonds	73	
	Interest revenue ($3,000 + $73)		3,073
	To record the accrual of interest on the Lower Corporation bonds.		
31	Other Comprehensive Income—		
	Loss on Fair Value Adjustment ($28,000 − $26,000)	2,000	
	Long-Term Investment—Eastgate Financial Co. Common Shares		2,000
	To record loss on fair value adjustment on long-term investment.		
31	Equity Method Investment—Southview Finance Co. ($90,000 × 25%)	22,500	
	Revenue from Equity Investment—Southview Finance Co.		22,500
	To record 25% equity in Southview Finance Co.'s profit.		

(c)

NORTHSTAR FINANCE CORPORATION
Balance Sheet (partial)
December 31, 2011

Assets

Current assets	
Trading securities—at fair value	$ 34,000
Long-term investments	
Bond investment—amortized cost	98,073
Equity investment—fair value	26,000
Equity investment—equity method	142,500
Total long-term investments	266,573

Liabilities and Shareholders' Equity	
Shareholders' equity	
Accumulated other comprehensive income (loss)	(1,400)

(d)

NORTHSTAR FINANCE CORPORATION
Statement of Comprehensive Income
Year Ended December 31, 2011

Profit from operations	$250,000
Other revenues and expenses	
Other revenue	
Revenue from equity method investment	22,500
Interest revenue	3,123
Dividend revenue ($800 + $200)	1,000
Gain on sale of trading securities	350
	26,973
Other expenses	
Loss on fair value adjustment on trading securities	2,800
Total other revenues and expenses	24,173
Profit before income tax	274,173
Income tax ($274,173 × 30%)	82,252
Profit	191,921
Other comprehensive income	
Loss on fair value adjustment, net of $600 income tax	
[$2,000 – ($2,000 × 30%)]	1,400
Comprehensive income	$ 190,521

The Navigator

Summary of Study Objectives

1. *Identify reasons to invest, and classify investments.* Companies purchase debt and equity securities of other companies for two main reasons: (1) for non-strategic reasons as a source of investment income, and (2) for strategic reasons, such as gaining control of a competitor, influencing strategic alliances, or moving into a new line of business.

Non-strategic investments are debt and equity securities that are purchased for purposes of earning interest or dividend revenue or for the purpose of selling them in the short term at a gain. Investments purchased for selling in the short term are referred to as trading securities and are reported at fair value. Debt securities purchased for the purpose of earning interest income are reported at amortized cost and may be short-term or long-term. Strategic investments are always investments in equity securities and are classified as long-term investments.

2. *Account for debt investments that are reported at amortized cost.* Debt investments purchased for the purposes of earning interest revenue are reported at amortized cost. Debt investments include money-market instruments, bonds, commercial paper, and similar items. Entries are required to record the (1) acquisition, (2) interest revenue, and (3) maturity or sale. Interest revenue is recognized as it accrues and any discount or premium is amortized using the effective-interest method.

3. *Account for trading investments.* Trading investments can be either debt or equity securities that are purchased for the purpose of selling in the short term at a gain. An equity investment may be in either preferred or common shares of another corporation. Trading investments are reported at fair value and the gains and losses resulting from the fair value adjustments are reported in profit. Entries are required to record the (1) acquisition, (2) investment revenue, (3) fair value adjustments, and (4) sale.

4. *Account for strategic investments.* Strategic investments are long-term investments in common shares of another company. The accounting for strategic investments is based on how much influence the investor has over the operating and financial affairs of the issuing corporation (the investee). When the investor company does not have significant influence (ownership is usually less than 20%) over the investee company, the investment is reported at fair value. Gains and losses resulting from fair value adjustments can be reported in other comprehensive income.

When there is significant influence (ownership is usually 20% or more), the equity method should be used. The equity method records investment revenue when profit is reported by the investee and increases the investor's investment account accordingly. Dividends that are received reduce the value of the investment account.

5. *Indicate how investments are reported in the financial statements.* Trading securities are presented in the current assets section of the balance sheet. This includes equity investments and short- and long-term debt investments as long as they have been purchased for trading. Debt investments maturing within 12 months of the balance sheet date that are purchased to earn interest are also reported in current assets at amortized cost. Debt instruments purchased for purposes of earning interest revenue with maturity dates of longer than 12 months from the date of the balance sheet and equity investments that are purchased for strategic purposes are reported in long-term investments. Gains and losses resulting from fair value adjustments that are reported in the income statement are presented in other revenues or other expenses. If any gains and losses resulting from fair value adjustments on strategic equity investments are reported in other comprehensive income, then this is added to accumulated other comprehensive income in the shareholders' equity section of the balance sheet.

When a company controls the common shares of another company (that is, its ownership is usually greater than 50%), consolidated financial statements that give details about the financial position of the combined entity must also be prepared.

The Navigator

Glossary

WILEY PLUS Glossary
Key Term Matching Activity

Available-for-sale investments Debt or equity securities that are held with the intention of selling them sometime in the future and are neither trading securities nor held to maturity for the purpose of earning interest income. (p. 900)

Consolidated financial statements Financial statements that present the assets and liabilities controlled by the parent company, and the total profitability of the combined companies. (p. 893)

Debt instruments Debt obligations such as money-market instruments, bonds, commercial paper, or similar items that can be bought and sold. Also called *debt securities.* (p. 878)

Equity instruments An ownership interest in a corporation such as preferred and common shares. Also called *equity securities.* (p. 878)

Equity method An accounting method in which the investment in common shares is initially recorded at cost. The investment account is then adjusted annually to show the investor's equity in the investee. (p. 895)

Fair value The amount of cash that is expected to be collected if the investment is sold. (p. 880)

Fair value adjustment An accounting entry to adjust the carrying value of the investment, for any increases or decreases in its fair value. (p. 887)

Investee The corporation that issues (sells) the debt or equity securities. (p. 884)

Investor The corporation that buys (owns) the debt or equity securities. (p. 884)

Long-term debt instruments Debt instruments with a maturity of longer than 12 months after the balance sheet date. (p. 881)

Money-market instruments Short-term debt instruments that are low-risk and highly liquid, such as money-market funds, banker's acceptances, term deposits, and treasury bills. (p. 879)

Non-strategic investment An investment that is purchased mainly to generate investment income. (p. 878)

Parent company A company that controls, or owns more than 50% of the common shares of, another company. (p. 893)

Securities Debt or equity instruments that a company may invest in. (p. 878)

Short-term debt instruments Debt instruments that mature within 12 months of the balance sheet date. (p. 881)

Strategic investment An investment in equity securities that is purchased to maintain a long-term operating relationship with another company. (p. 878)

Subsidiary company A company whose common shares are controlled by another company (usually more than 50% of its common shares are owned by the other company). (p. 893)

Trading investments or **trading securities** Debt or equity securities that are bought and held for sale in the near term, mainly to generate earnings from short-term price differences. (p. 879)

Self-Study Questions

WILEY
PLUS Quizzes

Answers are at the end of the chapter.

(SO 1) K 1. Which of the following is not a reason that corporations purchase debt or equity securities as non-strategic investments?
   (a) They want to exert influence over the decisions of another company.
   (b) They want to invest excess cash for short periods of time to earn a greater return than would be earned if the funds were simply held in the company's chequing account.
   (c) They want to invest excess cash for the long term to generate investment income.
   (d) They speculate that the investment will increase in value and result in a gain when sold.

(SO 1) K 2. Which of the following statements is true?
   (a) Trading securities are purchased as a strategic investment.
   (b) Investments in debt instruments can be either non-strategic or strategic investments.
   (c) Investments in debt instruments can be reported at amortized cost or fair value.
   (d) Investments in equity instruments can be reported at amortized cost or fair value.

(SO 2) K 3. Which of the following statements is false?
   (a) Money-market instruments purchased to earn interest are reported at amortized cost.
   (b) Money-market instruments that mature within 12 months of the balance sheet are reported in long-term investments.
   (c) Money-market instruments include term deposits, treasury bills, money-market funds, and banker's acceptances.
   (d) The discount or premium on bonds reported at amortized cost is amortized using the effective interest method.

(SO 2) AP 4. The accounting entry to record the accrual of interest on a treasury bill is:
   (a) Debit interest revenue and credit short-term investment in treasury bill.

   (b) Debit interest revenue and credit cash.
   (c) Debit short-term investment in treasury bill and credit interest revenue.
   (d) Debit cash and credit short-term investment in treasury bill.

(SO 3, 4) AP 5. Which securities are valued at fair value in public companies?
   (a) Trading securities
   (b) Long-term investment in 15% of the common shares of the investee
   (c) Long-term investment in bonds held to earn interest
   (d) Both (a) and (b)

(SO 3) AP 6. During 2010, Gosch Ltd. purchased common shares in International Corp. for $120,000 for purposes of trading. At December 31, the fair value of the shares is $125,000. The journal entry to adjust the trading securities at year end is which one of the following?
   (a) Gain on Fair Value Adjustment—
       Trading Securities | 5,000 |
         Trading Securities—
         International Corp. | | 5,000
   (b) Trading Securities—
       International Corp. | 5,000 |
         Gain on Fair Value Adjustment—
         Trading Securities | | 5,000
   (c) Trading Securities—
       International Corp. | 5,000 |
         Other Comprehensive Income—
         Gain on Fair Value Adjustment | | 5,000
   (d) No journal entry is required because gains are not recorded until the investment is sold.

(SO 4) K 7. The equity method of accounting for an investment in common shares is normally used when the investor owns:
   (a) less than 20% of the investee's common shares.
   (b) 20% or more of the investee's common shares.
   (c) 20% or more of the investee's preferred shares.
   (d) more than 50% of the investee's common shares.

(SO 4) AP 8. The Big K Ranch owns 20% of the Little L Ranch's common shares. The Little L Ranch reported profit of $150,000 and paid dividends of $40,000 this year. How much investment revenue would the Big K Ranch report if it used the equity method?
(a) $22,000
(b) $30,000
(c) $110,000
(d) $8,000

(SO 5) K 9. When the fair value of trading securities is less than the carrying value, the loss is reported in:
(a) the liability section of the balance sheet.
(b) the other revenues section of the income statement.
(c) other comprehensive income.
(d) the other expenses section of the income statement.

10. Which of the following is *false*? Canadian GAAP (SO 5) K for Private Enterprises requires that:
(a) investments in debt instruments be reported at amortized cost.
(b) all investments in equity instruments be reported at cost.
(c) no gains and losses be reported in other comprehensive income.
(d) if there is not a quoted market price for an equity investment of less than 20%, it must be reported at cost.

The Navigator

Questions

(SO 1) C 1. What are the differences between non-strategic and strategic investments?

(SO 1) C 2. On October 5, 2009, Transalta (a power generation and marketing company) and Canadian Hydro Developers Inc. announced that Canadian Hydro's board of directors unanimously recommended that its shareholders accept Transalta's offer to acquire Canadian Hydro at $5.25 per share. Canadian Hydro is the largest and most diversified owner of renewable energy generation facilities in Canada. Is this a non-strategic investment or a strategic investment by Transalta? Explain.

(SO 1) K 3. What are the differences between trading investments and investments held to earn interest income?

(SO 2, 3) C 4. For public companies, what are the differences between the accounting for bonds purchased for trading and bonds held to earn interest revenue?

(SO 2, 3) C 5. Osborne Corp., a public company, is considering making an investment in Bank of Canada bonds. If Osborne considers this to be a long-term investment made to earn interest income instead of an investment purchased for trading, will this have an impact on Osborne's recognition of interest revenue from the investment? Explain why or why not.

(SO 2, 3) C 6. What is the difference between recording interest revenue on a treasury bill and interest on a bond purchased for trading?

(SO 3, 4) C 7. For public companies, what is the difference in reporting (a) gains and losses for fair value adjust-

ments on trading investments and (b) gains and losses for fair value adjustments on long-term equity investments reported at fair value?

8. What constitutes "significant influence"? Is it safe (SO 4) K to conclude that there is significant influence when a company owns 20% of the common shares of another company?

9. When should a strategic investment be (a) reported (SO 4) K at fair value and (b) accounted for using the equity method?

10. Explain why the equity method cannot be applied to (SO 4) C strategic investments without significant influence.

11. Identify what is included in the carrying value of a (SO 4) C strategic investment (a) reported at fair value and (b) accounted for using the equity method.

12. Onex Corporation owns 100% of the common (SO 4) C shares of Celestica Inc. (a) Which company is the parent? Which one is the subsidiary? (b) What kind of financial statements should Onex prepare to properly present this investment?

13. Assad says, "I understand why fair value is used to (SO 2, report certain investments—it is more relevant to 3, 4) C statement users. But I don't understand why fair value is only used to report certain investments and not all investments." Identify which investments are not reported at fair value and explain to Assad why they are reported this way and others are not.

14. Explain why trading securities are reported as cur- (SO 5) K rents assets.

(SO 5) K 15. Identify the proper statement presentation of the following investments: (a) trading securities, (b) short-term debt investments purchased to earn interest, (c) debt investments purchased to earn interest with maturities longer than 12 months, (d) strategic investments reported at fair value, and (e) strategic investments accounted for using the equity method.

(SO 5) K 16. For public companies, identify the proper statement presentation of the following accounts: (a) Gains (Losses) on Fair Value Adjustments on Trading Securities, (b) Gains (Losses) on Sale of Trading Securities, (c) Gains (Losses) on Fair Value Adjustments on Long-Term Equity Investments, (d) Dividend Revenue, and (e) Interest Revenue.

17. Indicate at what amount investments in (a) debt instruments and (b) non-strategic equity investments would be reported under Canadian GAAP for Private Enterprises. (SO 5) AP

Brief Exercises

Identify terminology.
(SO 1) K

BE16–1 The following terms were introduced in this chapter:

1. Strategic investments
2. Non-strategic investments
3. Trading securities
4. Debt investments reported at amortized cost

Match each term with the following definitions:

(a) _____ Debt securities that are held to earn interest income
(b) _____ Investments purchased to influence or control another company
(c) _____ Debt or equity securities that are bought and held for sale in the near term at a profit
(d) _____ Investments purchased mainly to generate investment income

Classify investments.
(SO 1) C

BE16–2 For each of the following investments, identify (a) whether it is most likely a non-strategic or strategic investment, (b) whether it is most likely a current asset or long-term investment, and (c) the valuation reported on the balance sheet. Assume that the investor is a public company. The first one has been done for you as an example.

Investment	(a) Non-Strategic or Strategic Investment	(b) Current Asset or Long-Term Investment	(c) Valuation
1. Purchased 120-day treasury bill with excess cash	Non-strategic	Current asset	Amortized cost
2. Common shares purchased by a bank for resale in the near future at a gain			
3. 15% of the common shares of a company purchased to hold with the intent of acquiring control of the company			
4. 10-year bonds purchased to hold and earn interest revenue			
5. 10-year bonds purchased to sell in the near future at a gain			

Account for debt investments reported at amortized cost.
(SO 2) AP

BE16–3 On December 2, 2010, Toyworks Ltd. invested $100,000 in a Canadian government 90-day treasury bill. On December 31, $500 of interest had accrued on the treasury bill. On March 1, 2011, the treasury bill matured and Toyworks received $101,500 in cash. Prepare the journal entries to record (a) the purchase of the treasury bill; (b) the accrual of interest on December 31, 2010; and (c) the receipt of cash on March 1, 2011.

BE16-4 On January 1, 2010, Phelps Corporation purchased $400,000 of 10-year, 5% bonds at par from Cullen Ltd. Interest is received semi-annually on July 1 and January 1. Phelps purchased the bonds to hold and earn interest. At December 31, 2010, the bonds were trading at 97. Prepare the journal entries to record (a) the purchase of the bonds on January 1, (b) the receipt of interest on July 1, and (c) any adjusting entries required at December 31.

Account for debt investment reported at amortized cost.
(SO 2) AP

BE16-5 On June 30, $150,000 of five-year, 5% Plaza bonds are purchased at 101. Interest is receivable semi-annually each June 30 and December 31 by Coast Corp. The semi-annual amortization amount for the first interest period is $135. Coast Corp. purchased the bonds to hold and earn interest. At December 31, the bonds were trading at 102. Prepare the journal entries to record (a) the purchase of the bonds on June 30 and (b) the receipt of the first interest payment on December 31.

Account for debt investment reported at amortized cost.
(SO 2) AP

BE16-6 Using the data presented in BE 16-5, assume that Coast Corp. is a public company and that it purchased Plaza's bonds to sell in the near future at a gain. Prepare the journal entries to record (a) the purchase of the bonds on June 30, (b) the receipt of the first interest payment on December 31, and (c) any required adjusting journal entries on December 31 on the books of the investor. (d) Prepare the journal entries to record the issue of the bonds on June 30 and the first interest payment on December 31 on the books of the investee.

Account for trading investment and liability.
(SO 3) AP

BE16-7 On August 1, McLain Finance Inc. buys 2,000 Datawave common shares as a trading investment for $72,000 cash. On October 15, McLain receives a cash dividend of $2 per share from Datawave. On December 1, McLain sells the shares for $70,000 cash. Record these three transactions.

Account for trading investment.
(SO 3) AP

BE16-8 The carrying value of Deal Inc.'s common shares at November 30, 2010, is $64,000. The fair value of the investment at November 30 and December 31, 2010, is $68,000 and $66,000, respectively. The company prepares adjusting journal entries monthly. Prepare the required adjusting entries to record the securities at fair value at November 30 and December 31.

Account for trading investments.
(SO 3) AP

BE16-9 Using the data presented in BE16-8, assume that the investment in Deal Inc.'s common shares is sold on January 15, 2011, for $67,000. Prepare the journal entry to record the sale of the investment.

Account for trading investments.
(SO 3) AP

BE16-10 On January 1, Loop Limited, a public company, purchases 20% of Hook Corporation's common shares for $150,000. For the year ended December 31, Hook reports profit of $180,000 and pays a $5,000 cash dividend. The fair value of Loop's investment in Hook at December 31 is $160,000. Prepare journal entries required assuming Loop (a) does not have significant influence over Hook, and (b) does have significant influence over Hook.

Account for strategic investment.
(SO 4) AP

BE16-11 Chan Inc., a public company, owns 20% of Dong Ltd.'s common shares. The carrying value of the investment at January 1, 2010, is $300,000. During the year, Dong reported profit of $250,000 and paid a dividend of $15,000. The investment's fair value on December 31, 2010, Chan's year end, is $315,000. Indicate the amount reported for the long-term investment at December 31, the amount of investment income reported in the income statement, and the amount of investment income reported in other comprehensive income assuming (a) the investment is reported at fair value and the company chooses to report gains and losses on fair value adjustments in other comprehensive income, and (b) the equity method is used to account for the investment.

Compare impact of reporting at fair value and using the equity method.
(SO 4) AP

BE16-12 Atwater Corporation, a public corporation, reported profit of $650,000, a gain on fair value adjustment of $46,000 net of tax on its strategic investment reported at fair value, and a loss on fair value adjustment of $50,000 on its trading securities for the year ended April 30, 2010. Where Atwater has the choice, it reports gains and losses in other comprehensive income. Prepare a statement of comprehensive income.

Prepare statement of comprehensive income.
(SO 5) AP

Classify accounts.
(SO 5) AP

BE16–13 Indicate on which financial statement (i.e., balance sheet, income statement, or statement of comprehensive income) each of the following accounts would be reported if the investor is a public company. Where the company has the choice, it reports gains and losses in other comprehensive income and the company presents the statement of comprehensive income separately from the income statement. Also give the appropriate financial statement classification (e.g., current assets, long-term investments, or other revenue).

Account	Financial Statement	Classification
Trading securities		
Dividend revenue		
Equity method investment		
Long-term investment—bonds		
Gain on sale of trading securities		
Gain on fair value adjustment for trading securities		
Loss on fair value adjustment for strategic investment		
Interest revenue on bonds purchased for trading		

Report investments on
balance sheet.
(SO 5) AP

BE16–14 Sabre Corporation, a public company, has the following investments at November 30, 2010:

1. Trading securities: common shares of National Bank, carrying value $25,000, fair value $26,000.
2. Strategic investment: 15% of the common shares of Sword Corp., carrying value $108,000, fair value $105,000.
3. Equity investment: common shares of Epee Inc. (30% ownership), carrying value $210,000, equity method balance $250,000.
4. Debt investment purchased to earn interest: bonds of Ghoti Ltd. maturing in four years, amortized cost $150,000, fair value $175,000.
5. Debt investment purchased to earn interest revenue: Canadian government 120-day treasury bill, purchased at $25,000, fair value $25,125 (fair value at date of issue plus interest accrued to November 30, 2010).

Show how the investments would be reported in the assets section of the balance sheet.

Exercises

Distinguish between
non-strategic and strategic
investments.
(SO 1) C

E16–1 Gleason Telecommunications Ltd. has several investments in debt and equity securities of other companies.

1. 15% of the common shares of Lewis Telecommunications Inc., with the intent of purchasing at least 10% more of the common shares and requesting a seat on Lewis's board of directors.
2. 100% of the 15-year bonds issued by Li Internet Ltd., intended to be held for 15 years to earn interest revenue.
3. 95% of the common shares of Barlow Internet Services Inc.
4. 120-day treasury bill.
5. 10% of the common shares of Talk to Us Ltd., to be sold if the share price increases.

Instructions

Indicate whether each of the above investments is a non-strategic or strategic investment and explain why.

Classify investments.
(SO 1) C

E16–2 Kroshka Holdings Corporation has several investments in the debt and equity securities of other companies:

1. 10-year BCE bonds, intended to be held to earn interest.
2. 10-year GE bonds, intended to be sold if interest rates go down.
3. 1-year Government of Canada bonds, intended to be held to earn interest.
4. 180-day treasury bill, intended to be held to earn interest.
5. Bank of Montreal preferred shares, purchased to be sold in the near term at a profit.
6. Tim Hortons common shares, purchased to sell in the near term at a profit.
7. 60% of the common shares of Kriska Holdings Corporation, a major competitor of Kroshka Holdings.

Instructions

(a) Indicate whether each of the above investments is a non-strategic or strategic investment.
(b) Indicate whether each of the above investments would be classified as a current asset or long-term investment on Kroshka Holdings' balance sheet.
(c) For each investment that you classified as non-strategic, indicate the value the investment will be reported at on the balance sheet assuming that the investor is a public company.

E16–3 During the year ended November 30, 2011, Jackson Corporation had the following transactions for money-market instruments that were held to earn interest revenue:

Record debt investments reported at amortized cost. (SO 2) AP

Jan. 2	Purchased a 120-day treasury bill maturing on May 1 for $9,900.
May 1	The treasury bill matured. Jackson received $10,000 cash.
June 1	Invested $50,000 in a money-market fund.
30	Received notification that $125 of interest had been earned and added to the fund.
July 31	Received notification that $125 of interest had been earned and added to the fund.
Aug. 15	Cashed the money-market fund and received $50,350.
Oct. 31	Purchased a three-month, 2.5% term deposit for $30,000.

Instructions

(a) Prepare the journal entries to record the above transactions.
(b) Prepare any required adjusting journal entries at November 30.

E16–4 On July 1, 2010, Imperial Inc. purchased $500,000 of Acme Corp. 10-year, 4% bonds at 98 for the purpose of holding and earning interest revenue. The bonds pay interest semi-annually on January 1 and July 1. Imperial Inc. has a December 31 year end. At December 31, 2010, the bonds are trading at 99.

Record debt investment reported at amortized cost and bond liability. (SO 2) AP

Instructions

(a) Assuming Imperial Inc. purchased the bonds from Acme Corp., record the purchase of the bonds on July 1 for (1) Imperial Inc., and (2) Acme Corp.
(b) Record any adjusting journal entries that are required at December 31 for (1) Imperial Inc., and (2) Acme Corp. The semi-annual amortization amount for the first interest period is $406.
(c) Record the receipt of the first interest payment on January 1, 2011, for (1) Imperial Inc., and (2) Acme Corp.
(d) Compare the accounting for the bond investment with that of the bond liability.

E16–5 Using the data presented in E16–4, assume that Imperial Inc. purchased the bonds to sell in the near future at a gain and that Imperial Inc. is a public company.

Record debt investment for trading purposes. (SO 3) AP

Instructions

(a) Record the purchase of the bonds on July 1, 2010.
(b) Record any adjusting journal entries that are required at December 31, 2010.
(c) Indicate if the investment is presented in current assets or long-term investments on Imperial Inc.'s December 31, 2010, balance sheet.
(d) Record the receipt of the first interest payment on January 1, 2011.
(e) Assume the bonds are sold at 99.5 on July 1, 2011, after the semi-annual interest payment has been received and recorded. Record the sale of the bonds.

Record debt trading
investment transactions.
(SO 3) AP

E16-6 Piper Corporation had the following transactions with trading securities:

Jan. 1 Purchased $120,000 of Harris Corp. 6% bonds at 101. Interest is payable semi-annually on July 1 and January 1.

July 1 Received semi-annual interest on Harris bonds.

1 Sold half of the Harris bonds for $64,000.

Dec. 31 Accrued interest at Piper's year end.

31 Piper's bonds were trading at 100.

Instructions

Record the above transactions.

Record debt and equity
trading investments.
(SO 3) AP

E16-7 On November 1, 2010, Lalonde Lteé, a public company, buys 4,000 shares of Lyman Corporation for $35 per share and $200,000 of Kaur Inc. 6% bonds at face value as trading investments. The bonds pay interest semi-annually on May 1 and November 1. On December 15, 2010, Lalonde sells 1,600 Lyman shares for $50 per share. At December 31, 2010, Lalonde's year end, the Lyman shares are trading at $45 per share and the Kaur bonds are trading at 98. On March 31, 2011, Lalonde sells the remaining Lyman shares for $40 per share. On December 31, 2011, the Kaur bonds are trading at 100 again.

Instructions

Record the above transactions, including any required adjusting entries, for 2010 and 2011.

Record adjusting entry for
trading securities; show
statement presentation.
(SO 3) AP

E16-8 At December 31, 2010, the trading securities for Yanik, Inc., are as follows:

Security	Carrying Value	Fair Value
Co. A Common shares	$18,500	$16,000
Co. B Preferred shares	12,500	14,000
Co. C Five-year, 4% bonds	23,000	19,000
Totals	$54,000	$49,000

Instructions

(a) Prepare the adjusting entries required at December 31 to report the investment portfolio at fair value.

(b) Show the financial statement presentation of the trading securities and the gains and losses on fair value adjustments at December 31, 2010.

Record equity trading
investment.
(SO 3) AP

E16-9 McCormick Inc. had the following investment transactions:

Jan. 1 Purchased 1,000 Starr Corporation $5, non-cumulative, preferred shares for trading purposes for $110,000.

Apr. 1 Received the quarterly cash dividend.

July 1 Received the quarterly cash dividend.

2 Sold 500 Starr shares for $58,000.

Oct. 1 Received the quarterly cash dividend.

Dec. 31 The shares were trading at $60 per share.

Instructions

Record the above transactions and any required journal entries at December 31.

Record strategic equity
investments.
(SO 4) AP

E16-10 Visage Cosmetics is a public company and where it has the choice, it reports gains and losses in other comprehensive income. Visage had the following transactions in 2010:

1. Visage Cosmetics acquires 40% of Diner Limited's 30,000 common shares for $18 per share on January 2, 2010. On June 15, Diner pays a cash dividend of $30,000. On December 31, Diner reports profit of $380,000 for the year.

2. Visage Cosmetics acquires 10% of Image Fashion Inc.'s 400,000 common shares for $12 per share on March 18, 2010. On June 30, Image Fashion pays a cash dividend of $44,000. On December 31, Image Fashion reports profit of $252,000 for the year. At December 31, Image Fashion shares are trading at $11 per share.

Instructions

Record the above transactions and any required adjusting journal entries for the year ended December 31, 2010, assuming Visage Cosmetics intends to hold both investments for strategic purposes.

E16–11   On January 1, 2011, Diversity Corporation, a public company, buys 20% of Bellingham Corporation's 200,000 common shares for $360,000. At December 31, 2011, Bellingham pays a $30,000 cash dividend and reports profit of $200,000. At December 31, 2011, Bellingham Corporation shares are trading at $19 per share. Assume Diversity has significant influence over Bellingham. Both companies have a December 31 year end. Where Diversity has the choice, it reports gains and losses in other comprehensive income.

Record strategic equity investment; determine balance sheet presentation. (SO 4) AP

Instructions

(a) Record the above transactions.
(b) Determine the amount to be reported on Diversity's balance sheet and income statement for the investment in Bellingham shares at December 31.
(c) Repeat (a) and (b) assuming Diversity has purchased Bellingham's shares as a strategic investment but does not have significant influence over Bellingham.

E16–12   In January 2009, Bank of America Corporation took over Merrill Lynch & Co. through a share exchange with Merrill Lynch's shareholders. The shareholders of Merrill Lynch received .8595 of a share of Bank of America in exchange for each of their Merrill Lynch common shares. The total purchase price of Bank of America's investment in Merrill Lynch was $29.1 billion.

Explain accounting for consolidation. (SO 4) AP

Instructions

(a) Which company is the parent company and which is the subsidiary company?
(b) After the acquisition, Merrill Lynch continued to operate under the Merrill Lynch name. But Merrill Lynch shares are no longer traded on the stock exchange and the company's financial results have been consolidated with Bank of America's for reporting purposes. Explain why.

E16–13   Lai Inc., a public company, had the following investment transactions:

Identify impact of investment transactions. (SO 2, 3, 4, 5) AP

1. Purchased 16% of Regina Corporation's common shares for cash as a strategic investment.
2. Received a cash dividend on Regina common shares.
3. Purchased Saskatoon Ltd.'s bonds for cash for the purpose of trading.
4. Bought Government of Canada bonds for cash for the purpose of holding them to earn interest.
5. Accrued interest on Government of Canada bonds.
6. The Government of Canada bonds matured. Interest was previously accrued.
7. Purchased Victoria Ltd. preferred shares as a trading investment.
8. Received dividend on Victoria Ltd.'s preferred shares.
9. Bought 30% of Black Tackle Ltd. common shares for cash as an investment with significant influence.
10. Received Black Tackle's financial statements, which reported a loss for the year.
11. Black Tackle paid a cash dividend.
12. Accrued interest on Saskatoon Ltd.'s bonds.
13. Prepared an adjusting entry to record an increase in the fair value of Regina Corporation's common shares.

14. Prepared an adjusting entry to record a decrease in the fair value of Victoria Ltd.'s preferred shares.
15. Prepared an adjusting entry to record an increase in the fair value of the Saskatoon Ltd. bonds.

Instructions

Using the following table format, indicate whether each of the above transactions would result in an increase (+), decrease (–), or no effect (NE) in each category. The first one has been done for you as an example. Assume that, where Lai Inc. has the choice, it reports gains and losses in other comprehensive income.

	Balance Sheet			Income Statement			Statement of Comprehensive Income
			Shareholders'				Other Comprehensive
Assets	Liabilities		Equity	Revenues	Expenses	Profit	Income
1. NE (+/–)	NE		NE	NE	NE	NE	NE

Prepare balance sheet.
(SO 5) AP

E16–14 You are provided with the following balance sheet accounts of New Bay Inc., a public company, as at December 31, 2011:

Accounts payable	$ 35,000	Computers and equipment	$ 66,000
Accounts receivable	60,000	Equity method investment—	
Accumulated depreciation—		Hemosol Inc. common shares	55,000
computers and equipment	40,000	Interest payable	10,000
Accumulated other		Interest receivable	1,500
comprehensive income	2,000	Long-term equity investment,	
Allowance for doubtful accounts	10,000	fair value	25,000
Bond interest payable	8,000	Long-term investment—	
Bonds payable, 8%, due 2015	268,000	Aliant Inc. bonds	180,000
Cash	22,000	Note receivable, 5%, due	
Common shares, 10,000,		April 21, 2014	60,000
no par value	100,000	Retained earnings	45,000
		Trading securities, at fair value	48,500

Instructions

Prepare New Bay's balance sheet at December 31, 2011.

Statement of comprehensive income.
(SO 5) AP

E16–15 You are provided with the following income accounts of Oakridge Ltd. for the year ended December 31, 2011. Oakridge reported profit from operations of $125,000 for the year ended December 31, 2011. Oakridge's income tax rate is 30%.

Interest revenue	$5,000
Loss on sale—trading securities	1,500
Other comprehensive income—loss on fair value	3,000
Gain on fair value adjustment—trading securities	7,500
Interest expense	8,000

Instructions

Prepare a statement of comprehensive income starting with profit from operations.

Problems: Set A

P16–1A On January 1, 2010, Morrison Inc., a public company, purchased $400,000 of Pearl Corporation's 10-year, 6% bonds for $385,460. Interest is received semi-annually on July 1 and January 1. Morrison's year end is December 31. Morrison intends to hold Pearl's bonds until January 1, 2020, the date the bonds mature, to earn interest revenue. The bonds' fair value on December 31, 2010, was $395,000.

Record debt investments; show statement presentation. (SO 2, 3, 5) AP

Instructions

(a) Record the purchase of the bonds on January 1, 2010.
(b) Prepare the entry to record the receipt of interest on July 1, 2010. The semi-annual amortization of the discount is $527.
(c) Prepare the adjusting entries required at December 31, 2010. The semi-annual amortization of the discount at January 1, 2011, is $544.
(d) Show the financial presentation of the bonds for Morrison on December 31, 2010.
(e) Prepare the entry to record the receipt of interest on January 1, 2011.
(f) Prepare the entry to record the repayment of the bonds on January 1, 2020. Assume the entry to record the last interest payment has been recorded.
(g) How would your answers to (b) through (e) change if the bonds were purchased for the purpose of trading?

Taking It Further What was the market rate of interest on January 1, 2010, when the bonds were purchased?

P16–2A Liu Corporation had the following transactions in debt instruments held for purposes of earning interest revenue during the year ended December 31, 2010:

Record debt investments at amortized cost; show statement presentation. (SO 2, 5) AP

Jan. 1   Purchased a 180-day (six-month) Canadian government treasury bill for $98,039.
June 30   Treasury bill matured. Received $100,000 cash.
July 5   Purchased a money-market fund for $25,000.
Oct. 1   Cashed in the money-market fund, receiving $25,185.
    1   Purchased six-month, 3%, term deposit for $75,000.
Dec. 31   Accrued semi-annual interest on the term deposit.

Instructions

(a) Record the transactions.
(b) Show the financial statement presentation of the investment at December 31 and any related accounts.

Taking It Further What was the annual rate of interest earned on the treasury bill?

P16–3A The following bond transactions occurred during 2010 for CASB Incorporated and Densmore Consulting Ltd. Both companies have a December 31 year end. Both companies are public.

Record debt investment at fair value and liability; show statement presentation. (SO 2, 3, 5) AP

Jan. 1   CASB issued $1 million of 10-year, 7% bonds at 98. The bonds pay interest semi-annually on June 30 and December 31.
    1   Densmore Consulting purchased $200,000 of CASB's bonds at 98 on the TSX.
June 30   The semi-annual interest on the bonds was paid. The semi-annual amortization was $672.
Dec. 31   The semi-annual interest on the bonds was paid. The semi-annual amortization amount was $696.
    31   The bonds were trading at 99 on this date.

Instructions

(a) Prepare the journal entries for CASB (investee) to record the above transactions.

(b) Show how the bond liability and related income statement accounts would be presented in CASB's financial statements for the year ended December 31, 2010.

(c) Prepare the journal entries and any required adjusting journal entries for Densmore Consulting to record the above transactions assuming that it purchased the bonds for purposes of earning interest.

(d) Show how the debt investment and related income statement accounts would be presented in Densmore Consulting's financial statements for the year ended December 31, 2010.

(e) Assume instead that Densmore purchased the bonds for purposes of trading. Prepare the journal entries and any required adjusting journal entries for Densmore Consulting to record the above transactions.

(f) Assuming Densmore purchased the bonds for purposes of trading, show how the debt investment and related income statement accounts would be presented in Densmore Consulting's financial statements for the year ended December 31, 2010.

Taking It Further Assume that Densmore needed cash and sold the bonds on the open market on January 1, 2011, for 99.5 after receiving and recording the semi-annual interest payment. Indicate the amount of gain or loss that Densmore would record if the bonds were purchased (1) to hold and earn interest, and (2) for purposes of trading. Explain why CASB does not record an entry to reflect the transaction.

Record equity and debt trading investments; show statement presentation.
(SO 3, 5) AP

P16–4A During the year ended December 31, 2010, Rakai Corporation, a public company, had the following transactions in trading securities:

Feb. 1 Purchased 425 IBF common shares for $20,400.

Mar. 1 Purchased 1,000 RST common shares for $36,000.

Apr. 1 Purchased $140,000 of CRT 5% bonds for $138,000. Interest is payable semi-annually on April 1 and October 1.

July 1 Received a cash dividend of $1 per share on the IBF common shares.

Aug. 1 Sold 125 IBF common shares at $45 per share.

Oct. 1 Received the semi-annual interest on the CRT bonds.

1 Sold the CRT bonds for $140,000.

Dec. 31 The fair values of the IBF and RST common shares were $43 and $39 per share, respectively.

Instructions

(a) Record the transactions.

(b) Show the financial statement presentation of the trading securities and any related accounts in the financial statements for the year ended December 31.

Taking It Further If Rakai Corporation anticipated that it would need the cash that was used to invest in the trading securities in the near future, should the company have invested in equity securities? What would you recommend to the company?

Record equity trading investments; show statement presentation.
(SO 3, 5) AP

P16–5A The following are in Hi-Tech Inc.'s portfolio of trading securities at December 31, 2010:

	Quantity	Carrying Value
Aglar Corporation common shares	500	$26,000
BAL Corporation common shares	700	42,000
Hicks Corporation preferred shares	600	16,800
		$84,800

On December 31, 2010, the investments' carrying value equalled their fair value. Hi-Tech had the following transactions related to the securities during 2011:

Jan. 7   Sold 500 Aglar common shares at $55 per share.
       10   Purchased 200 common shares of Miley Corporation at $78 per share.
Feb. 2   Received a cash dividend of $1 per share on the Hicks preferred shares.
       10   Sold all 600 Hicks preferred shares at $27 per share.
Apr. 30   Received 700 additional BAL common shares as a result of a 2-for-1 stock split.
Aug. 3   Received 20 additional Miley common shares as the result of a 10% stock dividend.
Sept. 1   Purchased an additional 800 common shares of Miley at $70 per share.
Dec. 31   The fair value of the BAL common shares was $32 per share and the fair value of
          the Miley common shares was $72 per share.

Instructions

(a) Record the transactions.
(b) Show the financial statement presentation of the securities and any related accounts at December 31, 2011.
(c) On January 31, 2012, the company sold 510 shares of Miley for $74 per share. Record the sale of the shares.

Taking It Further   Assume that at December 31, 2012, Hi-Tech held 510 shares of Miley and 1,400 shares of BAL. If Miley shares were trading at $69 per share and BAL shares were trading at $29 per share at December 31, 2012, indicate the gain or loss resulting from the fair value adjustment that would be reported in Hi-Tech's income statement.

P16–6A   Olsztyn Inc., a public company, had the following investment transactions:

1. Purchased Arichat Corporation common shares as a trading security.
2. Received a cash dividend on Arichat common shares.
3. Purchased Bombardier bonds to hold and earn interest revenue.
4. Received interest on Bombardier bonds.
5. Purchased 10% of Havenot's common shares. The company intends to bid on Havenot's remaining common shares.
6. Purchased 40% of LaHave Ltd.'s common shares as a long-term equity investment, with significant influence.
7. Received LaHave's financial statements, which reported profit for the year.
8. LaHave paid a cash dividend.
9. The fair value of Arichat's common shares was higher than carrying value at year end.
10. The fair value of Bombardier's bonds was lower than carrying value at year end.
11. The fair value of Havenot's common shares was lower than carrying value at year end.
12. The fair value of LaHave Ltd.'s common shares was higher than carrying value at year end.

Identify impact of investments on financial statements.
(SO 2, 3, 4, 5) AP

Instructions

Using the following table format, indicate whether each of the above transactions would result in an increase (+), a decrease (−), or no effect (NE) in each category. The first one has been done for you as an example. Where Olsztyn has the choice, it reports gains and losses in other comprehensive income.

Balance Sheet			Income Statement			Statement of Comprehensive Income
Assets	Liabilities	Shareholders' Equity	Revenues	Expenses	Profit	Other Comprehensive Income
1. NE (+/−)	NE	NE	NE	NE	NE	NE

Taking It Further   Assume instead that Olsztyn Inc. is a Canadian private company. How would your response to the question differ if the company reported under Canadian GAAP for Private Enterprises?

Record strategic equity
investment, using fair value
and equity methods;
compare balances.
(SO 4) AP

P16–7A Cardinal Concrete Limited, a public company, acquired 20% of the common shares of Edra Inc. on January 1, 2010, by paying $2.4 million for 100,000 shares. Edra paid a $0.60 per share semi-annual cash dividend on June 30 and again on December 31. Edra reported profit of $1.5 million for the year. The shares' fair value at year end was $25 per share. Where Cardinal has a choice, it reports gains and losses in other comprehensive income.

Instructions

(a) Prepare the journal entries for Cardinal Concrete for 2010, assuming Cardinal (1) does not have significant influence, and (2) has significant influence.

(b) Compare the investment and revenue account balances at December 31, 2010, under each method of accounting used in (a).

Taking It Further What are the potential advantages to a company of having significant influence over another company? Explain.

Record strategic equity
investments, using fair value
and equity methods. Show
statement presentation.
(SO 4, 5) AP

P16–8A Sub Corporation has 1 million common shares issued. On January 10, 2011, Par Inc. purchased a block of these shares on the open market at $10 per share to hold as a strategic investment. Sub reported profit of $260,000 for the year ended December 31, 2011, and paid a $0.35 per share dividend. Sub's common shares were trading at $12 per share on December 31, 2011.

This problem assumes three independent situations that relate to how Par, a public company, would report its investment:

Situation 1: Par purchased 100,000 Sub common shares.
Situation 2: Par purchased 300,000 Sub common shares.
Situation 3: Par purchased 1 million Sub common shares.

Instructions

(a) For each situation, identify how Par would report its investment in Sub common shares in the financial statements.

(b) Record all transactions for Par related to the investment for the year ended December 31, 2011, if (1) the investment is reported at fair value, and (2) the equity method is used to account for the investment. Assume that, where Par has a choice, it reports gains and losses in other comprehensive income.

(c) Compare Par's nonconsolidated balance sheet and income statement accounts that relate to this investment at December 31 if (1) the investment is reported at fair value, and (2) the equity method is used to account for the investment.

Taking It Further Assuming that Sub's shares were trading at $13 on December 31, 2012, and Par owned 100,000 common shares of Sub, what amount would be reported in accumulated other comprehensive income at December 31, 2012, relating to this investment? Assume that Par's income tax rate is 30%.

Prepare income statement
and statement of
comprehensive income.
(SO 5) AP

P16–9A Silver Lining Corporation, a public company, is a large silver producer. Selected condensed information (in millions) for Silver Lining Corporation follows for the year ended December 31, 2011:

Cost of sales	$2,214	Operating expenses	$639
Equity (loss) in investee earnings	(6)	Other expenses	67
Silver sales	3,350	Other revenues	6
Income tax expense	60	Gains on fair value adjustments—	
Interest expense	7	strategic investment (net of tax)	12
Interest income	38		

Instructions

(a) Prepare an income statement and a separate statement of comprehensive income for the year ended December 31, 2011.

(b) Silver Lining Corporation had an opening balance in its Accumulated Other Comprehensive Income account of $49 million. What is the ending balance it would report in the shareholders' equity section of its balance sheet at December 31, 2011?

Taking It Further If a company has purchased common shares of another company as a trading investment, IFRS generally does not allow the investor to reclassify the trading securities as long-term investments where the fair value adjustments are reported in other comprehensive income. Why do standard setters want to prevent companies from reclassifying investments?

P16–10A Presented in alphabetical order, the following data are from the accounting records of Stinson Corporation, a public company, at April 30, 2011:

Prepare statement of comprehensive income and balance sheet.
(SO 5) AP

Accounts payable	$ 65,000	Income tax expense	$ 82,860
Accounts receivable	48,000	Income tax payable	25,000
Accumulated depreciation—		Interest expense	7,500
equipment	72,000	Interest revenue	1,200
Accumulated other comprehensive		Long-term investment—	
income	18,000	bonds due 2015	24,000
Bonds payable	150,000	Long-term investment—	
Cash	100,000	Verma common shares	220,000
Common shares (no par value,		Other comprehensive	
unlimited authorized, 200,000 issued)	300,000	income—loss on fair value	
Depreciation expense	27,500	adjustment, net of $3,600 tax	12,000
Dividend revenue	11,000	Rent expense	79,000
Equipment	275,000	Retained earnings	161,660
Equity method investment—		Salary expense	235,000
Indura common shares	170,000	Service revenues	550,000
Gain on fair value adjustment		Supplies	5,000
on trading securities	1,500	Supplies expense	7,500
Gain on sale of trading securities	3,000	Trading securities—	
Goodwill	50,000	Anderson common shares	15,000

Instructions
Prepare a statement of comprehensive income and balance sheet at April 30, 2011.

Taking It Further How would the balance sheet and income statement differ with respect to Stinson's investments if it was a private company and it reported under Canadian GAAP for Private Enterprises?

Problems: Set B

P16–1B On January 1, 2010, Givarz Corporation, a public company, purchased $100,000 of Schuett Corp. five-year, 9% bonds at 104. Interest is received semi-annually on July 1 and January 1. Givarz's year end is December 31. Givarz intends to hold the bonds until January 1, 2015, the date the bonds mature, to earn interest revenue. The bonds were trading at 101 on December 31, 2010.

Record debt investments; show statement presentation.
(SO 2, 3, 5) AP

Instructions
(a) Record the purchase of the bonds on January 1, 2010.
(b) Prepare the entry to record the receipt of interest on July 1, 2010. The semi-annual amortization of the premium is $340.

(c) Prepare the adjusting entries required at December 31, 2010. The semi-annual amortization of the premium at February 1, 2011, is $354.

(d) Show the financial presentation of the investment in Schuett Corp.'s bonds on December 31, 2010.

(e) Prepare the entry to record the receipt of interest on January 1, 2011.

(f) Prepare the entry to record the repayment of the bonds on January 1, 2015. Assume the entry to record the last interest payment has been recorded.

(g) How would your answers to (b) through (e) change if the bonds were purchased for the purpose of trading?

Taking It Further What was the market rate of interest on February 1, 2010, when the bonds were purchased?

Record debt investments; show statement presentation. (SO 2, 5) AP

P16–2B Lannan Corp. had the following debt instrument transactions during the year ended December 31, 2010. The debt instruments were purchased to earn interest revenue.

Feb. 1 Purchased six-month term deposit for $50,000.
Aug. 1 Term deposit matured and $51,250 cash was received.
    1 Purchased a money-market fund for $55,000.
Dec. 1 Cashed in money market fund and received $55,735 cash.
    1 Purchased a 90-day (three-month) treasury bill for $99,260.
    31 The treasury bill's value with accrued interest was $99,508.

Instructions

(a) Record the transactions.

(b) Show the financial statement presentation of the debt investments and any related accounts at December 31.

Taking It Further What was the annual rate of interest on the term deposit that Lannan Corp. purchased on February 1, 2010?

Record debt investment at fair value and liability; show statement presentation. (SO 2, 3, 5) AP

P16–3B The following bond transactions occurred during 2010 for College of Higher Learning (CHL) and Otutye Ltd. Both companies have a July 31 year end. Assume that both companies are public enterprises.

Feb. 1 CHL issued $10 million of five-year, 6% bonds at 101. The bonds pay interest semi-annually on August 1 and February 1.
    1 Otutye purchased $2 million of CHL's bonds at 101 on the TSX.
July 31 Both companies prepared entries to accrue the bond interest. The semi-annual amortization amount was $8,110.
    31 The bonds were trading at 100 on this date.
Aug. 1 The semi-annual interest on the bonds was paid.

Instructions

(a) Prepare the journal entries for CHL (investee) to record the above transactions.

(b) Show how the bond liability and related accounts would be presented in CHL's financial statements for the year ended July 31, 2010.

(c) Prepare the journal entries for Otutye to record the above transactions, assuming that it purchased the bonds for purposes of earning interest.

(d) Show how the debt investment and related accounts would be presented in Otutye's financial statements for the year ended July 31, 2010.

(e) Prepare the journal entries and any required adjusting journal entries for Otutye to record the above transactions assuming that it purchased the bonds for purposes of trading.

(f) Assuming the bonds were purchased to trade, show how the debt investment and related income statement accounts would be presented in Otutye's financial statements for the year ended July 31, 2010.

Taking It Further   Did the market interest rate on the bonds increase or decrease between February 1 and July 31, 2010? Will Otutye want the market interest rate on the bonds to increase or decrease? Explain.

P16–4B   During the year ended December 31, 2010, Mead Investment Corporation, a public company, had the following transactions in trading securities:

Record debt and equity trading investments; show statement presentation.
(SO 3, 5) AP

Feb. 1	Purchased 1,200 CBF common shares for $63,600.
Mar. 1	Purchased 400 RSD common shares for $10,000.
Apr. 1	Purchased $100,000 of MRT 6% bonds at 100. Interest is payable semi-annually on April 1 and October 1.
July 1	Received a cash dividend of $1 per share on the CBF common shares.
Aug. 1	Sold 400 CBF common shares at $50 per share.
Oct. 1	Received the semi-annual interest on the MRT bonds.
2	Sold the MRT bonds for 102.
Dec. 31	The fair values of the CBF and RSD common shares were $45 and $27 per share, respectively.

Instructions

(a) Record the transactions.
(b) Show the financial statement presentation of the trading securities and any related accounts in Mead's financial statements for the year ended December 31.

Taking It Further   If Mead Investment Corporation anticipated that it would need the cash that was used to invest in the trading securities in the near future, should the company have invested in equity securities? What would you recommend to the company?

P16–5B   The following investments are in Head Financial Corporation's portfolio of trading securities at December 31, 2010:

Record equity trading investments; show statement presentation.
(SO 3, 5) AP

	Quantity	Carrying Value
Alta Corporation common shares	500	$18,500
Brunswick Corporation common shares	700	35,000
Flon Corporation preferred shares	300	27,000
		$80,500

On December 31, 2010, the portfolio's total cost equalled its total fair value. Head Financial had the following transactions for the securities during 2011:

Jan. 7	Sold all 500 Alta common shares for $41 per share.
10	Purchased 200 common shares of Econo Corporation at $53 per share.
Feb. 2	Received a cash dividend of $6 per share on Flon preferred shares.
10	Sold all 300 Flon preferred shares at $85 per share.
Mar. 15	Received 70 additional Brunswick common shares as a result of a 10% stock dividend when the shares were trading at $45 per share.
June 23	Received 400 additional Econo common shares as a result of a 3-for-1 stock split.
Dec. 31	The fair value of the Brunswick common shares was $42 per share and the fair value of the Econo common shares was $18 per share.

Instructions

(a) Record the transactions.
(b) Show the financial statement presentation of the securities and any related accounts in the financial statements for the year ended December 31, 2011.
(c) Assume that on February 15, 2012, the company sold 385 Brunswick shares for $45 per share. Record the sale of the shares.

Taking It Further Assume that at December 31, 2012, Head Financial held 385 shares of Brunswick and 600 shares of Econo. If Brunswick shares were trading at $46 per share and Econo shares were trading at $19 per share at December 31, 2012, indicate the gain or loss resulting from the fair value adjustment that would be reported in Head Financial's income statement.

Identify impact of investments on financial statements.
(SO 2, 3, 4, 5) AP

P16–6B Abioye Inc., a public company, had the following investment transactions:

1. Purchased Chang Corporation preferred shares as trading security.
2. Received a stock dividend on the Chang preferred shares.
3. Purchased Government of Canada bonds for cash as a trading security.
4. Accrued interest on the Government of Canada bonds.
5. Purchased Micmac Inc.'s bonds to be held to earn interest.
6. Sold half of the Chang preferred shares at a price less than originally paid.
7. Purchased 25% of Xing Ltd.'s common shares as a long-term equity investment, with significant influence.
8. Received Xing's financial statements, which reported a loss for the year.
9. Accrued interest on Micmac Inc. bonds.
10. Xing paid a cash dividend.
11. Purchased 12% of the common shares of Sarolta Ltd. Abioye has made a hostile bid to acquire Sarolta's remaining common shares.
12. The fair value of Chang's preferred shares was lower than carrying value at year end.
13. The fair value of the Government of Canada bonds was higher than carrying value at year end.
14. The fair value of Sarolta's common shares was higher than carrying value at year end.
15. The fair value of Micmac Inc.'s bonds was lower than carrying value at year end.

Instructions

Using the following table format, indicate whether each of the above transactions would result in an increase (+), a decrease (−), or no effect (NE) in each category. The first one has been done for you as an example. Where Abioye has a choice, it reports gains and losses in other comprehensive income.

Balance Sheet			Income Statement			Statement of Comprehensive Income
Assets	Liabilities	Shareholders' Equity	Revenues	Expenses	Profit	Other Comprehensive Income
NE (+/−)	NE	NE	NE	NE	NE	NE

Taking It Further Assume instead that Abioye Inc. is a Canadian private company. How would your response to the question differ if the company reported under Canadian GAAP for Private Enterprises?

Record strategic equity investment, using fair value and equity methods; compare balances.
(SO 4) AP

P16–7B DFM Services Ltd. acquired 20% of the common shares of BNA Corporation on January 1, 2010, by paying $1.6 million for 100,000 shares. BNA paid a $0.40 per share semi-annual cash dividend on June 15 and December 15. BNA reported profit of $800,000 for the year ended December 31, 2010. The shares' fair value was $1,650,000 at year end. Where DFM has a choice, it reports gains and losses in other comprehensive income.

Instructions

(a) Prepare the journal entries for DFM Services for 2010, assuming DFM (1) does not have significant influence, and (2) has significant influence.
(b) Compare the investment and revenue account balances at December 31, 2010, under each method of accounting used in (a).

Taking It Further   What factors should be considered when determining whether a company has significant influence over another company? Could a company have significant influence over another company if it owned 19% of the common shares of the investee? Explain.

P16–8B   Hat Limited has 300,000 common shares issued. On October 1, 2010, Cat Inc. purchased a block of these shares on the open market at $40 per share to hold as a strategic equity investment. Hat reported profit of $675,000 for the year ended September 30, 2011, and paid a $0.40 per share dividend. Hat's shares were trading at $43 per share on September 30, 2011.

Record strategic equity investments, using fair value and equity methods. Show statement presentation. (SO 4, 5) AP

 This problem assumes three independent situations that relate to how Cat, a public company, would report its investment:

Situation 1: Cat purchased 30,000 Hat common shares.
Situation 2: Cat purchased 90,000 Hat common shares.
Situation 3: Cat purchased 300,000 Hat common shares.

Instructions

(a) For each situation, identify how Cat Inc. should report its investment in Hat Limited in its financial statements.
(b) Record all transactions for Cat related to the investment for the year ended September 30, 2011, if (1) the investment is reported at fair value, and (2) the equity method is used to account for the investment. Assume that, where Cat has a choice, it reports gains and losses in other comprehensive income.
(c) Compare Cat's nonconsolidated balance sheet and income statement accounts that relate to this investment at September 30 if (1) the investment is reported at fair value, and (2) the equity method is used to account for the investment.

Taking It Further   Assuming that Hat's shares were trading at $45 on September 30, 2012, and Cat owned 30,000 common shares of Hat, what amount would be reported in accumulated other comprehensive income at September 30, 2012, relating to this investment? Assume that Cat has a 30% tax rate.

P16–9B   Selected condensed information (in millions) for Investments R Us Company follows for the year ended December 31, 2011:

Prepare income statement and statement of comprehensive income. (SO 5) AP

Equity in earnings of Speed Railway	$ 4	Dividend income	$	3
Gain on fair value adjustment of		Operating expenses		4,616
trading securities	2	Loss on sale of trading investments		194
Gain on disposal of land	26	Loss on fair value adjustment—		
Income tax expense	781	strategic equity investment		
Interest expense	299	(net of tax)		68
Interest revenue	6	Other expenses		21
		Revenues		7,240

Instructions

(a) Prepare an income statement and separate statement of comprehensive income for the year ended December 31, 2011.
(b) Investments R Us Company had an opening balance in its Accumulated Other Comprehensive Loss account of $150 million. What is the ending balance it would report in the shareholders' equity section of its balance sheet at December 31, 2011?

Taking It Further   Explain why a company may want to report gains and losses on fair value adjustments for its investments in other comprehensive income instead of including them in profit.

Prepare statement of
comprehensive income and
balance sheet.
(SO 5) AP

P16–10B Presented in alphabetical order, the following data are from the accounting records of Vladimir Corporation at December 31, 2010:

Accounts payable	$ 85,000	Interest expense	$ 12,500
Accounts receivable	68,000	Interest revenue	1,800
Accumulated depreciation—		Long-term investment—	
equipment	92,000	bonds due 2015	36,000
Accumulated other		Long-term investment—	
comprehensive income	28,000	Burma common shares	185,000
Allowance for doubtful accounts	4,000	Loss on fair value adjustment	
Bonds payable	250,000	on trading securities	1,500
Cash	150,000	Notes receivable—due 2013	75,000
Common shares (no par value,		Other comprehensive income—	
unlimited authorized,		gain on fair value adjustment,	
200,000 issued)	250,000	net of $3,600 tax	12,000
Depreciation expense	28,000	Rent expense	45,000
Dividend revenue	9,000	Retained earnings	?
Equipment	288,000	Revenue from equity investment	31,000
Equity method investment—		Salary expense	335,000
RIBI common shares	215,000	Service revenues	651,000
Gain on sale of trading securities	2,500	Supplies	2,500
Goodwill	75,000	Supplies expense	6,500
Income tax expense	79,290	Trading securities—	
Income tax payable	16,000	common shares	37,000

Instructions

Prepare a statement of comprehensive income and balance sheet at December 31, 2010.

Taking It Further   Indicate if there would be any differences in reporting Vladimir's investments if it was a private company and it reported under Canadian GAAP for Private Enterprises. Explain.

Continuing Cookie Chronicle

(*Note*: This is a continuation of the Cookie Chronicle from Chapters 1 through 15.)

Natalie and Curtis have been approached by Ken Thornton, a shareholder of The Beanery Coffee Ltd. Ken wants to retire and would like to sell his 1,000 shares in The Beanery Coffee, which represent 20% of all shares issued. The Beanery is currently operated by Ken's twin daughters, who each own 40% of the common shares. The Beanery not only operates a coffee shop but also roasts and sells beans to retailers under the name Rocky Mountain Beanery.

The business has been operating for approximately five years, and in the last two years Ken has lost interest and left the day-to-day operations to his daughters. Both daughters at times find the work at the coffee shop overwhelming. They would like to have a third shareholder involved to take over some of the responsibilities of running a small business. Both feel that Natalie and Curtis are entrepreneurial in spirit and that their expertise would be a welcome addition to the business operation. The twins have also said that they plan to operate this business for another 10 years and then retire.

Ken has met with Curtis and Natalie to discuss the business operation. All have concluded that there would be many advantages for Cookie & Coffee Creations Ltd. to acquire an interest in The Beanery Coffee. One of the major advantages would be volume discounts for purchases of coffee bean inventory.

Despite the apparent advantages, Natalie and Curtis are still not convinced that they should participate in this business venture. They come to you with the following questions:

1. We are a little concerned about how much influence we would have in the decision-making process for The Beanery Coffee. Would the amount of influence we have affect how we would account for this investment?
2. Can you think of other advantages of going ahead with this investment?
3. Can you think of any disadvantages of going ahead with this investment?

Instructions

(a) Answer Natalie and Curtis's questions.
(b) Identify how you think this investment should be classified and reported on the balance sheet of Cookie & Coffee Creations Ltd. and explain why.
(c) What other information would you likely obtain before you recommend whether this investment should be accounted for using the equity method?

Cumulative Coverage—Chapters 13 to 16

Plankton Corporation's trial balance at December 31, 2011, is presented on p. 926. All transactions and adjustments for 2011 have been recorded except for the items described below.

Jan. 7 Issued 1,000 preferred shares for $25,000. In total, 100,000 $2, non-cumulative, convertible, preferred shares are authorized. Each preferred share is convertible into five common shares.

Mar. 16 Purchased 800 common shares of Osborne Inc. for $24 per share. This investment is intended to be held as a trading investment.

Aug. 2 Sold the Osborne common shares for $25 per share (see March 16 transaction).
     5 Invested $20,000 in a money-market fund.

Sept. 25 Five hundred of the preferred shares issued on January 7 were converted into common shares (see January 7 transaction).

Oct. 24 Cashed in the money-market fund, receiving $20,000 plus $200 interest (see August 5 transaction).

Nov. 30 Obtained a $50,000 bank loan by issuing a three-year, 6% note payable. Plankton is required to make equal blended principal and interest instalment payments of $1,521 at the end of each month. The first payment was made on December 31. Note that at December 31, $15,757 of the note payable is due within the next year.

Dec. 1 Declared the annual dividend on the preferred shares on December 1 to shareholders of record on December 23, payable on January 15.

    31 Plankton owns 40% of RES, which it has accounted for using the equity method. RES earned $20,000 and paid dividends of $1,200 in 2011.

    31 Semi-annual interest of $300 is receivable on the Sontag Corporation bonds on January 1, 2012. The bonds were purchased at par.

    31 The annual interest is due on the bonds payable on January 1, 2012. The par value of the bonds is $130,000 and the amortization of the discount for this period is $200.

    31 The fair value of the company's investment in BCB common shares was $28,000.

Instructions

(a) Record the transactions.
(b) Prepare an updated trial balance at December 31, 2011, that includes these transactions.
(c) Using the income statement accounts in the trial balance, calculate income before income tax. Assuming Plankton has a 27% income tax rate, prepare the journal entry to adjust income taxes for the year. Note that Plankton has recorded $50,000 of income tax expense for the year to date. Update the trial balance for this additional entry. For purposes of this question ignore the income tax relating to Other Comprehensive Income.
(d) Prepare the following financial statements for Plankton: (1) income statement, (2) statement of comprehensive income, (3) statement of changes in shareholders' equity, and (4) balance sheet. For purposes of this question ignore the income tax on Other Comprehensive Income and Accumulated Other Comprehensive Income.

PLANKTON CORPORATION
Trial Balance
December 31, 2011

	Debit	Credit
Cash	$ 18,000	
Accounts receivable	51,000	
Allowance for doubtful accounts		$ 2,550
Merchandise inventory	22,700	
Equity method investment—RES common shares	85,000	
Long-term debt investment—Sontag bonds	10,000	
Long-term equity investment—BCB common shares	30,000	
Land	120,000	
Building	200,000	
Accumulated depreciation—building		40,000
Equipment	40,000	
Accumulated depreciation—equipment		15,000
Accounts payable		18,775
Income tax payable		4,500
Bonds payable (6%, due January 1, 2019)		126,250
Common shares, unlimited number of no par value shares authorized, 100,000 issued		100,000
Retained earnings		120,500
Accumulated other comprehensive income		5,000
Sales		750,000
Cost of goods sold	370,000	
Operating expenses	180,000	
Interest revenue		375
Interest expense	6,250	
Income tax expense	50,000	
Total	$1,182,950	$1,182,950

BROADENING YOUR PERSPECTIVE

Financial Reporting and Analysis

Financial Reporting Problem

BYP16–1 Refer to the financial statements and accompanying notes for The Forzani Group Ltd. presented in Appendix A.

Instructions

(a) Did Forzani report any non-strategic investments in its 2009 financial statements?
(b) How were Forzani's strategic investments reported in its 2009 financial statements? Why were the strategic investments reported this way?

Interpreting Financial Statements

BYP16–2 Royal Bank of Canada is one of the largest banks in Canada. According to its 2009 annual report, it had approximately 80,000 employees serving 17 million customers in

48 countries. The bank's business largely involves borrowing money and lending it to others, but at any given time it will have a large amount of money invested in securities when it is not out on loan. It also acts as an investment dealer, buying investments from one client and selling them to another, sometimes as a principal and sometimes as an agent. The company reported the following information in its 2009 financial statements (in millions of dollars):

	2009	2008
Trading securities, at fair value	$140,062	$122,508
Available-for-sale securities, at fair value	46,210	48,626

The available-for-sale securities are investments in debt and equity instruments that are not held for trading. The gains and losses on fair value adjustments on these investments are reported in other comprehensive income. Any gains and losses on sale of these investments are reported in net income.

Instructions

(a) Why does Royal Bank most likely have an investment portfolio consisting of both trading and available-for-sale securities?

(b) The available-for-sale classification for investments has been eliminated in the IFRS standard issued in November 2009, effective January 1, 2013. However, as we learned in this chapter, companies may decide for equity investments (other than trading investments) to report all gains and losses in other comprehensive income. What are the advantages of reporting gains and losses in other comprehensive income instead of profit? What are the disadvantages? Do you think the Royal Bank will choose this option for some of its investments? Why?

(c) The majority of the Royal Bank's investments are trading securities. In your opinion, why does it have such a high percentage of its portfolio invested in trading securities?

Critical Thinking

Collaborative Learning Activity

Note to instructor: Additional instructions and material for this group activity can be found on the Instructor Resource Site.

BYP16–3 In this group activity, you will compare the accounting for long-term debt investments to that for long-term bonds payable (Chapter 15).

Instructions

(a) Your instructor will divide the class into groups of two and distribute a package to each. With your partner, determine who will be the investor and who will be the issuer (borrower). Select the pages associated with your role from the package. Review the notes and complete the requirements.

(b) With your partner, compare your answers and, when they are different, explain how your answers were determined.

Communication Activity

BYP16–4 Under International Financial Reporting Standards, investments in debt instruments are reported at either amortized cost or fair value. The president of Lunn Financial Enterprises does not understand why there are two methods and wonders why all debt investments are not reported at amortized cost.

Instructions

Write a memo to the president of Lunn Financial Enterprises, explaining when it is appropriate to report debt investments at amortized cost and when it is appropriate to report debt investments at fair value. Discuss in your memo why reporting different debt investments using different methods gives better information for investors and creditors to evaluate the performance of the company's investment portfolio.

Ethics Case

Ethics in Accounting

BYP16–5 Kreiter Financial Services Limited purchased a large portfolio of debt and equity investments during 2011. The portfolio's total fair value at December 31, 2011, is greater than its total cost. Some securities have increased in value and others have decreased. Vicki Lemke, the financial vice-president, and Ula Greenwood, the controller, are busy classifying the securities in the portfolio for the first time.

Lemke suggests classifying the securities that have increased in value as trading securities in order to increase profit for the year. She wants to classify the equity securities that have decreased in value as strategic investments without significant influence and record the fair value adjustments on these securities in other comprehensive income. She wants to classify the debt securities that have decreased in value as debt investments held to earn interest and record them at amortized cost. She argues that this way, decreases in value will not affect profit.

Greenwood disagrees. She says that classifying investments based on their performance is not consistent with GAAP.

Instructions

(a) Will classifying the securities as Lemke suggests actually affect income the way the pair think it will?
(b) Is there anything unethical in what Lemke proposes?
(c) Who are the stakeholders affected by their proposals?
(d) Is Greenwood correct? Explain.
(e) Which qualitative characteristics of financial reporting are not met if the investments are classified based on performance?
(f) How should the investments be classified?

"All About You" Activity

BYP16–6 As indicated in the "All About You" feature in this chapter, any Canadian aged 18 or older can save up to $5,000 every year in a tax-free savings account (TFSA). TFSA savings can be used for any purpose, including to go on vacation, to buy a car, or to start a small business. The goal of TFSAs is to allow Canadians to save more and achieve their goals quicker.

Instructions

Go to http://www.tfsa.gc.ca.
(a) Click on "TFSA vs. RRSP." What is the purpose of an RRSP? Is an investment in an RRSP a strategic or non-strategic investment? Is an investment in a TFSA a strategic or non-strategic investment?
(b) Click on the link "TFSA calculator." What type of investments can be made in a TFSA?
(c) Click on the link "TFSA calculator." Scroll down to the heading "TFSA Calculator" and click on the on-line "TFSA calculator." Assume the following:

1. Your income range for income tax purposes:	$10,000 – $39,999
2. Monthly investment in a TFSA:	$200
3. Rate of return:	6%
4. Term of investment:	20 years

How much more will you save in a TFSA than in a taxable savings account?

(d) Assume the same as in (c) except assume that your income range for income tax purposes is $40,000. How much more will you save in a TFSA than in a taxable savings account?

(e) What assumptions are used in the TFSA calculator with respect to:

1. When the annual investment is made?   3. The investment portfolio?
2. Provincial tax rates?

ANSWERS TO CHAPTER QUESTIONS

Answers to Accounting in Action Insight Questions

Business Insight, p. 880

Q: Was the merger of Suncor and Petro-Canada a non-strategic or strategic investment? What are some of the advantages the combined company might have now that it will be the largest energy company in Canada and the fifth largest in North America?

A: The merger of Suncor and Petro-Canada was a strategic investment. The merger will result in a larger company that should be able to compete better in the global marketplace. The value and performance of the two companies combined is expected to be greater than the sum of them operating individually. The new combined company should be insulated from potential foreign takeovers.

Across the Organization, p. 893

Q: Why should a company's management and the board of directors have to consult with their own shareholders if they are planning on issuing shares to take over another company?

A: If a company issues its own shares to purchase the shares of another company, the percentage of shares owned by the current shareholders may be significantly reduced. In fact, the shareholders of the company being acquired may end up owning the majority of the shares of the combined company after the exchange. As a result, the shareholders of the company issuing shares may lose control of the company.

All About You, p. 900

Q: Assume that you are an 18-year-old student with no taxable income and, through the generosity of your grandparents, you will be able to save $2,000 a year while you are a student. Is it beneficial for you to contribute to a TFSA? Would you classify your investment in a TFSA as a long-term or short-term investment?

A: Yes, investments earn investment income. By contributing to a TFSA sooner than later, you will be able to protect more investment income from being taxed. The investment in a TFSA will be a long-term investment.

Answer to Forzani Review It Question 4, p. 896

The Forzani Group's financial statements are consolidated. It owns 100% of all of its subsidiary companies (see Note 2 (a)).

Answers to Self-Study Questions

1. a   2. c   3. b   4. c   5. d   6. b   7. b   8. b   9. d   10. b

Remember to go back to the beginning of the chapter to check off your completed work!

CHAPTER 17
THE CASH FLOW STATEMENT

clearwater.ca

✔ THE NAVIGATOR

- ☐ Understand *Concepts for Review*
- ☐ Read *Feature Story*
- ☐ Scan *Study Objectives*
- ☐ Read *Chapter Preview*
- ☐ Read text and answer *Before You Go On*
- ☐ Work *Demonstration Problem*
- ☐ Review *Summary of Study Objectives*
- ☐ Answer *Self-Study Questions*
- ☐ Complete assignments

CONCEPTS FOR REVIEW:

Before studying this chapter, you should understand or, if necessary, review:

a. The difference between the accrual basis and the cash basis of accounting. (Ch. 3, pp. 119–120)

b. The major items included in a corporation's balance sheet. (Ch. 4, pp. 191–199 and Ch. 13, pp. 734–737)

c. The major items included in a corporation's income statement. (Ch. 14, pp. 775–778)

Cash Management Keeps Clearwater Sailing

Bedford, N.S.—Clearwater Seafoods is a leader in the global seafood industry, recognized for its consistent quality, wide diversity, and commitment to preserving the environment. Having provided quality seafood products for more than 30 years, Clearwater operates a large fleet of vessels in Canada and Argentina and owns several processing plants throughout Eastern Canada.

The company weathered tough economic times in 2008 to report an overall decrease in cash of $55 million in 2008, compared with an increase in cash of $60 million in 2007. Significant foreign exchange losses caused a large shortfall in cash flows from operating activities. The company also made large investments in property, plant, and equipment in 2008, which were only partially funded through an increase in cash from financing activities.

With a diminished borrowing capacity due to lower earnings and the current difficult borrowing environment, the company has a focused strategy for maintaining liquidity. "There are fewer lenders extending credit and therefore the conditions attached to new loans are more restrictive and the cost of borrowing has increased," says Tyrone Cotie, director of corporate finance and investor relations at the company. "This requires the company to become more focused on maintaining healthy liquidity."

Clearwater expected to negotiate new debt with similar terms for approximately $99 million in near-term debt maturities and foreign exchange lines. As well, using its cash flow to reduce debt levels, the company planned to refinance convertible debentures from the Clearwater Seafoods Income Fund, due in 2010.

The company was also limiting cash distributions to unitholders. It paid no distributions in 2008 and didn't expect to pay any in 2009 or 2010. In addition, it planned to review alternative lending arrangements, including asset-backed lending arrangements and other financing structures available to more highly leveraged borrowers.

Clearwater's plans to tightly manage its working capital included lowering its trade receivables balance. It will tighten its collection terms and discounting, and limit its investment in inventories, reviewing any slow-moving items and improving integration of its fleet and sales force. The company will also limit capital spending, focusing on maintaining its existing fleet and completing any necessary repairs and maintenance. Clearwater has completed its current multi-year fleet renewal program and has no planned expenditures in the coming few years. It expected the fleet renewal program to result in a more efficient fleet with lower costs, improved quality, and greater catch volumes, all of which would improve profitability.

Clearwater also planned to liquidate underperforming assets and sell non-core assets. "A lower investment in working capital will improve the company's cash flows, which it can use to pay down debt and improve overall leverage and liquidity," explains Cotie.

The cash flows generated from operations are a key indicator of the company's health. "The sustainability of a business is ultimately linked to your ability to generate cash," Cotie says.

The Navigator

STUDY OBJECTIVES:

After studying this chapter, you should be able to:

1. Describe the purpose and content of the cash flow statement.

2. Prepare a cash flow statement using either the indirect or the direct method.

3. Analyze the cash flow statement.

The Navigator

As Tyrone Cotie in our feature story states, the sustainability of a business is ultimately linked to its ability to generate cash. So how do companies generate cash? How do they use cash? How is this information presented in the financial statements so users can assess a company's ability to generate cash? This chapter, which presents the cash flow statement, will answer these and similar questions.

The chapter is organized as follows:

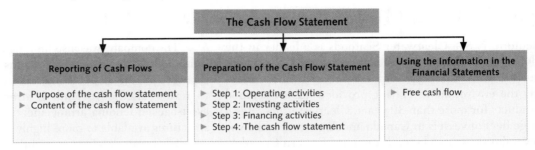

The Cash Flow Statement

Reporting of Cash Flows	Preparation of the Cash Flow Statement	Using the Information in the Financial Statements
► Purpose of the cash flow statement ► Content of the cash flow statement	► Step 1: Operating activities ► Step 2: Investing activities ► Step 3: Financing activities ► Step 4: The cash flow statement	► Free cash flow

Reporting of Cash Flows

STUDY OBJECTIVE 1

Describe the purpose and content of the cash flow statement.

The financial statements we have studied so far present only partial information about a company's cash flows (cash receipts and cash payments). For example, comparative balance sheets show the increase in property, plant, and equipment during the year, but they do not show how the additions were financed or paid for. The income statement shows profit, but it does not indicate the amount of cash that was generated by operating activities. The statement of comprehensive income reports changes in fair values of certain equity investments, but not the cash generated from the sale of these investments. Similarly, the statement of retained earnings or the statement of changes in shareholders' equity shows the amount of cash dividends that was declared, but not the amount of cash dividends that was actually paid during the year.

Purpose of the Cash Flow Statement

Alternative terminology
Under IFRS, the cash flow statement is commonly referred to as the *statement of cash flows.*

The **cash flow statement** gives information about the cash receipts, cash payments, and net change in cash that result from operating, investing, and financing activities during a period. Reporting the causes of changes in cash helps investors, creditors, and other interested parties understand what is happening to a company's most liquid resource—its cash. As the feature story indicates, in order to determine whether a company is financially sound or not, it is essential to understand its cash flows.

The information in a cash flow statement should help investors, creditors, and others evaluate the following aspects of the company's financial position:

1. **Ability to generate future cash flows.** Investors and others examine the relationships between items in the cash flow statement. From these, users can predict the amounts, timing, and uncertainty of future cash flows better than they can from accrual-based data.
2. **Ability to pay dividends and meet obligations.** If a company does not have enough cash, employees cannot be paid, debts settled, or dividends paid. Employees, creditors, and shareholders are particularly interested in this statement because it is the only one that shows the flow of cash in a company.
3. **Investing and financing transactions during the period.** By examining a company's investing and financing transactions, users can better understand why assets and liabilities changed during the period.

4. **Difference between profit and cash provided (used) by operating activities.** Profit gives information about the success or failure of a business. However, some people are critical of accrual-based profit because it requires many estimates, allocations, and assumptions. As a result, the reliability of the profit amount is often challenged. This is not true of cash. If readers of the cash flow statement understand the reasons for the difference between profit and net cash provided by operating activities, they can then decide for themselves how reliable the profit amount is.

Content of the Cash Flow Statement

Before we can start preparing the cash flow statement, we must first understand what it includes and why. We will begin by reviewing the definition of cash used in the cash flow statement and then discuss how cash receipts and payments are classified within the statement.

Definition of Cash

The cash flow statement is often prepared using "cash and cash equivalents" as its basis. You will recall from Chapter 7 that cash equivalents are short-term, highly liquid investments that are readily convertible to known amounts of cash. Cash equivalents are held for the purpose of meeting short-term cash commitments rather than for investing or other purposes. Generally, only money-market instruments that are due within three months can be considered cash equivalents. Because of the varying definitions of "cash" that can be used in this statement, companies must clearly define cash as it is used in their particular statement.

The International Accounting Standards Board and the Financial Accounting Standards Board were working on a project to improve the presentation of information in certain financial statements, including the cash flow statements. One of the recommendations under consideration was to exclude "cash equivalents" from the definition of cash. In other words, the cash flow statement would present information about the changes in cash only, and not cash and cash equivalents. In the meantime, you will find that many public companies, including The Forzani Group, include cash equivalents in their definition of cash. It should also be noted that Canadian GAAP for Private Enterprises allows companies to include cash equivalents with cash in preparing the cash flow statement.

We have chosen to present the cash flow statement in this chapter using cash only because including cash equivalents in the definition of cash increases the complexity of preparing the statement. You will learn more about preparing a cash flow statement using "cash and cash equivalents" in more advanced accounting courses.

Classification of Cash Flows

The cash flow statement classifies cash receipts and cash payments into three types of activities: (1) operating, (2) investing, and (3) financing activities. The transactions and other events for each kind of activity are as follows:

1. **Operating activities** include the cash effects of transactions that create revenues and expenses. They affect profit.
2. **Investing activities** include (a) purchasing and disposing of investments and long-lived assets, and (b) lending money and collecting the loans. They generally affect long-term asset accounts.
3. **Financing activities** include (a) obtaining cash from issuing debt and repaying the amounts borrowed, and (b) obtaining cash from shareholders and paying them dividends. Financing activities generally affect long-term liability and shareholders' equity accounts.

Illustration 17-1 lists typical cash receipts and cash payments in each of the three classifications.

Illustration 17-1 ➡

Cash receipts and payments
classified by activity

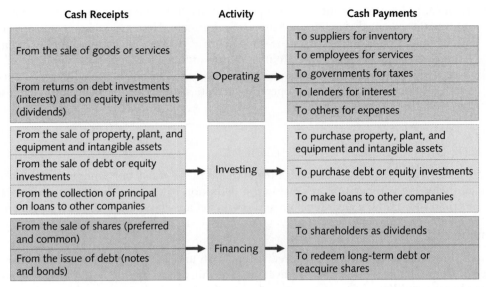

There are always exceptions to general guidelines such as those shown above. For example,

Illustration 17-2 ⬇

Operating, investing, and
financing activities

As you can see, some cash flows that are related to investing or financing activities are classified as operating activities. For example, receipts of investment revenue (interest and dividends) earned from debt or equity securities are classified as operating activities. So are payments of interest to lenders of debt. Why are these considered operating activities? It is because these items are reported in the income statement where results of operations are shown.

Note the following general guidelines:

1. **Operating activities** involve income statement items and noncash working capital accounts (current assets and current liabilities) on the balance sheet.
2. **Investing activities** involve cash flows resulting from changes in long-term asset accounts.
3. **Financing activities** involve cash flows resulting from changes in long-term liability and shareholders' equity accounts.

Illustration 17-2 shows these general guidelines.

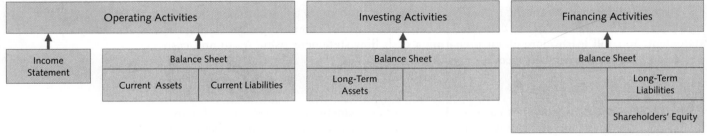

There are always exceptions to general guidelines such as those shown above. For example, changes in short-term investments that are not cash equivalents are reported as investing activities. Changes in short-term notes receivable that result from non-trade (i.e., lending) transactions are also reported as investing activities rather than as operating activities. And changes in short-term notes payable that result from non-trade (i.e., borrowing) transactions are reported as financing activities.

Under IFRS, companies currently have a choice as to whether to classify interest and dividends received (and paid) as an operating, investing, or financing activity. But once they make a choice, it must be followed consistently. For simplicity's sake, in this textbook we have consistently classified interest paid or received as an operating activity, and dividends paid as a financing activity.

Significant Noncash Activities. Not all of a company's significant investing and financing activities involve cash. The following are examples of significant noncash activities:

1. An issue of debt to purchase assets
2. An issue of common shares to purchase assets

3. A conversion of debt or preferred shares to common shares
4. Exchanges of property, plant, and equipment

Significant investing and financing activities that do not affect cash are not reported in the body of the cash flow statement. These noncash activities are reported in a separate note, which satisfies the full disclosure principle. This disclosure requirement also includes the noncash portion of a partial cash transaction.

To illustrate the disclosure of a transaction that includes both cash and noncash activities, assume that a building is purchased for $10 million with a $1-million cash down payment, and the remainder financed with a mortgage note payable. The cash flow statement would disclose only the $1 million cash paid (as an investing activity). The acquisition of the building (a $10-million investing activity) by a mortgage note payable (a $9-million financing activity) would be disclosed in the notes and cross-referenced to the $1-million cash outflow reported in the investing activities section of the cash flow statement.

 ## ACCOUNTING IN ACTION: ALL ABOUT YOU

Similar to a business, you need to consider your cash situation. How much can you afford to spend, and what are your sources of cash? And how well are others doing in that regard? In August 2009, the Office of the Superintendent of Bankruptcy Canada reported that personal bankruptcies in Canada were up 54.3% from the year before, with 106,933 Canadians filing for bankruptcy over the previous 12 months. Canadians were ill prepared for the economic downturn in 2008 because the amount of debt they were carrying was astronomical. Credit cards are largely the problem. Since credit cards were introduced in the 1960s, debt levels have increased to the point that the average Canadian has a debt level that is 131% of their income. Many Canadians are spending more than they are making. "If Canadians were to think of themselves as businesses, many would have negative cash flow," the *National Post* reported. "With negative cash flow, how long can a business stay afloat?"

Source: Garry Marr, "You Can Be Born Again Financially," *National Post*, August 15, 2009.

Is it appropriate to use your credit card to pay for your operating activities such as your groceries, clothes, and entertainment? Is it appropriate to use your credit card to finance your investment activities such as tuition or, if you have a large enough limit, a car?

BEFORE YOU GO ON . . .

→ Review It

1. How does the cash flow statement help users understand a company's financial position?
2. What are the three types of activities reported in the cash flow statement? Give an example of each.
3. What are significant noncash activities and how are they reported?
4. In its cash flow statement for the year ended February 1, 2009, what amounts are reported by The Forzani Group for (a) cash provided by operating activities, (b) cash used by investing activities, and (c) cash used by financing activities? The answer to this question is at the end of the chapter.

→ Do It

During its first week of existence, Carrier Moulding Ltd. had the following transactions:

1. Issued common shares for cash.
2. Sold a long-term equity investment.
3. Purchased a tractor-trailer truck. Made a cash down payment, and financed the remainder with a mortgage note payable.
4. Paid for inventory purchases.
5. Collected cash for services provided.

Classify each of these transactions by type of cash flow activity. Indicate whether the transaction would be reported as a cash inflow or cash outflow.

Action Plan

- Identify the three types of activities that are used to report all cash inflows and outflows.
- Report as operating activities the cash effects of transactions that create revenues and expenses, and which are included when profit is determined.
- Report as investing activities transactions to (a) acquire and dispose of investments and long-lived assets, and (b) lend money and collect loans.
- Report as financing activities transactions to (a) obtain cash by issuing debt and repay the amounts borrowed, and (b) obtain cash from shareholders and pay them dividends.

Solution

1. Financing activity; cash inflow
2. Investing activity; cash inflow
3. Investing activity; cash outflow for down payment. The remainder is a noncash investing (tractor-trailer truck) and financing (mortgage note payable) activity.
4. Operating activity; cash outflow
5. Operating activity; cash inflow

The Navigator

Related exercise material: BE17–1, BE17–2, E17–1, and E17–2.

Preparation of the Cash Flow Statement

STUDY OBJECTIVE 2

Prepare a cash flow statement using either the indirect or the direct method.

You may recall that we first illustrated the cash flow statement in Chapter 1, in Illustration 1-11. The cash flow statement covers the same period of time as the income statement and statements of comprehensive income, retained earnings, and changes in shareholders' equity (e.g., for the year ended). All of these statements, including the cash flow statement, report activities that happened during a specific period of time. Only the balance sheet reports information at a specific point in time.

The general format of the cash flow statement focuses on the three types of activities (operating, investing, and financing) that we discussed in the preceding section. The operating activities section is always presented first. It is followed by the investing activities and financing activities sections. Any significant noncash investing and financing activities are reported in a note to the financial statements.

A total of the cash receipts and cash payments for each of the three activities—operating, investing, and financing—is calculated to determine the net increase or decrease in cash from each activity. If there was a net increase in cash, we say that cash was "provided by" that activity. If there was a net decrease in cash, we say that cash was "used by" that activity. The totals for each activity are then calculated to determine the overall net increase (decrease) in cash for the period. The overall net increase is then added to (or the net decrease is subtracted from) the beginning-of-period cash balance. This gives the end-of-period cash balance. The end-of-period cash balance must agree with the cash balance reported on the balance sheet. If it doesn't, then you know you have made a mistake in preparing the cash flow statement and you need to find and correct your error(s).

Now that we understand the content and format of a cash flow statement, where do we find the information to prepare it? We could examine the cash account in the general ledger and sort each cash receipt and payment into the different types of operating activities, investing activities, or financing activities shown in Illustration 17-1. But this is not practical or necessary because, for every cash receipt or payment, we have already recorded the reason for the receipt or payment in other general ledger accounts as a result of the double-entry bookkeeping system you learned in Chapter 2. Therefore, when we prepare the cash flow statement, we examine the changes in all of the other accounts to explain the changes in cash.

Note that this is different from how the other financial statements are prepared. The other financial statements are prepared from the account balances listed in the adjusted trial balance. The cash flow statement, on the other hand, requires detailed information about the changes in account balances that occurred between two periods of time. An adjusted trial balance will not provide the necessary data. Also remember that the accrual basis of accounting is followed in preparing the other financial statements. The cash flow statement deals with cash receipts and payments and, as a result, the accrual basis of accounting is not used in the preparation of a cash flow statement.

The information to prepare this statement usually comes from three sources:

1. The **comparative balance sheet** shows the balances at the beginning and end of the period for each asset, liability, and shareholders' equity item. This information is used to determine the changes in each asset, liability, and shareholders' equity item during that period.
2. The **income statement** helps us determine the amount of cash provided or used by operating activities during the period.
3. **Additional information** includes transaction data that are needed to determine how cash was provided or used during the period. The statement of comprehensive income and the statements of retained earnings or changes in shareholders' equity also provide information about cash receipts and payments.

The four steps to prepare the cash flow statement from these data sources are shown in Illustration 17-3.

| Step 1: | Determine the net cash provided (used) by operating activities by converting profit from an accrual basis to a cash basis. |

The current year's income statement is analyzed, as well as the relevant current assets and current liabilities accounts from the comparative balance sheet, and selected additional information.

| Step 2: | Determine the net cash provided (used) by investing activities by analyzing changes in long-term asset accounts. |

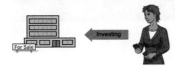

Comparative balance sheet data and selected additional information are analyzed for their effects on cash.

| Step 3: | Determine the net cash provided (used) by financing activities by analyzing changes in long-term liability and equity accounts. |

Comparative balance sheet data and selected additional information are analyzed for their effects on cash.

| Step 4: | Prepare the cash flow statement and determine the net increase (decrease) in cash. |

Compare the net change in cash reported on the cash flow statement with the change in cash reported on the balance sheet to make sure the amounts agree.

← Illustration 17-3

Steps in preparing the cash flow statement

To explain and illustrate the preparation of a cash flow statement, we will use financial information from Computer Services Corporation. Illustration 17-4 presents Computer Services' current- and prior-year balance sheets, its current-year income statement, and related financial information.

Illustration 17-4 ➜

Computer Services' financial information

COMPUTER SERVICES CORPORATION Balance Sheets December 31			
Assets	2011	2010	Increase (Decrease)
Current assets			
Cash	$ 55,000	$ 33,000	$ 22,000
Accounts receivable	20,000	30,000	(10,000)
Inventory	15,000	10,000	5,000
Prepaid expenses	5,000	1,000	4,000
Property, plant, and equipment			
Land	130,000	20,000	110,000
Building	160,000	40,000	120,000
Accumulated depreciation—building	(11,000)	(5,000)	6,000
Equipment	27,000	10,000	17,000
Accumulated depreciation—equipment	(3,000)	(1,000)	2,000
Total assets	$398,000	$138,000	
Liabilities and Shareholders' Equity			
Current liabilities			
Accounts payable	$ 28,000	$ 12,000	$ 16,000
Income tax payable	6,000	8,000	(2,000)
Long-term liabilities			
Bonds payable	130,000	20,000	110,000
Shareholders' equity			
Common shares	70,000	50,000	20,000
Retained earnings	164,000	48,000	116,000
Total liabilities and shareholders' equity	$398,000	$138,000	

COMPUTER SERVICES CORPORATION Income Statement Year Ended December 31, 2011		
Sales revenue		$507,000
Cost of goods sold		150,000
Gross profit		357,000
Operating expenses	$111,000	
Depreciation expense	9,000	
Loss on sale of equipment	3,000	123,000
Profit from operations		234,000
Other expenses		
Interest expense		42,000
Profit before income tax		192,000
Income tax expense		47,000
Profit		$145,000

Additional information for 2011:

1. A $29,000 cash dividend was paid.
2. Land was acquired by issuing $110,000 of long-term bonds.
3. Equipment costing $25,000 was purchased for cash.
4. Equipment with a carrying amount of $7,000 (cost of $8,000, less accumulated depreciation of $1,000) was sold for $4,000 cash.
5. Depreciation expense consists of $6,000 for the building and $3,000 for equipment.

We will now apply the four steps using the above information for Computer Services Corporation.

STEP 1: OPERATING ACTIVITIES

Determine the Net Cash Provided (Used) by Operating Activities by Converting Profit from an Accrual Basis to a Cash Basis

In order to perform this step and determine the cash provided (used) by operating activities, profit must be converted from an accrual basis to a cash basis. Why is this necessary? Under generally accepted accounting principles, companies use the accrual basis of accounting. As you have learned, this basis requires that revenue be recorded when it is earned and that expenses be matched against the revenue that they helped generate. Earned revenues may include credit sales that have not been collected in cash. Some expenses incurred, such as depreciation, are not paid in cash. Other expenses incurred are paid in cash either before or after they are recognized as an expense. Thus, under the accrual basis of accounting, profit is not the same as net cash provided by operating activities.

Profit can be converted to net cash provided (used) by operating activities by one of two methods: (1) the indirect method or (2) the direct method. The **indirect method** converts total profit from an accrual basis to a cash basis. The **direct method** converts each individual revenue and expense account from an accrual basis to a cash basis, identifying specific cash receipts and payments. Both methods arrive at the same total amount for "Net cash provided (used) by operating activities." The difference is which items they disclose.

On the following pages, in two separate sections, we describe the use of the two methods. Section 1 explains the indirect method. Section 2 explains the direct method. Both methods are included because both are accepted under Canadian and international accounting standards. Your instructor may ask you to learn only one of these methods. If so, when you have finished the section assigned by your instructor, turn to the next topic after these sections, "Step 2: Investing Activities."

Section 1: Indirect Method

Most companies use the indirect method. They prefer this method for three reasons: (1) it is easier to prepare, (2) it focuses on the differences between profit and net cash flow from operating activities, and (3) it reveals less detail to competitors. To determine net cash provided (used) by operating activities under the indirect method, profit is adjusted for items that did not affect cash.

Illustration 17-5 shows three types of adjustments that are made to adjust profit for items that affect accrual-based profit but do not affect cash. The first two types of adjustments are found on the income statement. The last type of adjustment—changes to current asset and current liability accounts—is found on the balance sheet.

| Profit | ± | Adjustments | = | Net Cash Provided (Used) by Operating Activities |

+ Add back noncash expenses, such as depreciation expense.

± Add back losses and deduct gains that result from investing and financing activities.

± Add decreases in current asset and increases in current liability accounts. Deduct increases in current asset and decreases in current liability accounts.

← Illustration 17-5

Adjustments to convert profit to net cash provided (used) by operating activities

The next three subsections explain each type of adjustment.

Noncash Expenses

Helpful hint Expenses with no cash outflows are added back to profit in the indirect method.

A	=	L	+	SE
−6,000				−9,000
−3,000				

Cash flows: no effect

The income statement includes expenses that do not use cash, such as depreciation expense. For example, Computer Services' income statement reports a depreciation expense of $9,000. Recall that the entry to record depreciation is:

Depreciation Expense	9,000	
Accumulated Depreciation—Building		6,000
Accumulated Depreciation—Equipment		3,000

This entry has no effect on cash, so depreciation expense is added back to profit in order to arrive at net cash provided (used) by operating activities. It is important to understand that depreciation expense is not added to operating activities as if it were a source of cash. As shown in the journal entry above, depreciation does not involve cash. It is added to cancel the deduction that was created by the depreciation expense when profit was determined.

A partial operating activities section of the cash flow statement for Computer Services is shown below, with the addition of the noncash expense to profit highlighted in red.

Operating activities	
Profit	$145,000
Adjustments to reconcile profit to net cash provided (used) by operating activities:	
Depreciation expense	9,000

Other examples of noncash expenses include the amortization of bond discounts and premiums for a bond issuer. The amortization of a bond discount results in interest expense being higher than the cash paid to the bond investors. Recall from Chapter 15 that the journal entry to amortize a bond discount for the issuer results in a debit to the Interest Expense account and a credit to the Bonds Payable account. So the amortization of a bond discount must be added back to profit to determine the net cash provided (used) by operating activities.

The amortization of a bond premium for the issuer results in interest expense being lower than the cash payment to the bond investors. The journal entry to amortize a bond premium results in a debit to the Bonds Payable account and a credit to the Interest Expense account. So the amortization of a bond premium must also be deducted from profit to determine the net cash provided (used) by operating activities.

Just as a bond issuer amortizes bond discounts or premiums, so does a bond investor who is holding bonds as a long-term investment. You will recall that we learned about accounting for long-term debt investments at amortized cost in Chapter 16. Profit must be adjusted for the effects of the amortization on bond discounts and premiums for investors to determine cash provided (used) by operating activities. Recall that amortization of a bond discount for an investor results in interest revenue being greater than cash receipts. Thus the bond investor will deduct the amortization of the bond discount. Amortization of a bond premium for a bond investor results in interest revenue being less than the cash receipts. Thus the bond investor will add the amortization of the bond premium to determine cash provided by operations.

Gains and Losses

Illustration 17-1 states that cash received from the sale of long-lived assets should be reported in the investing activities section of the cash flow statement. Consequently, all gains and losses from investing activities must be eliminated from profit to arrive at net cash from operating activities.

Helpful hint Gains are deducted from, and losses are added to, profit in the indirect method.

Why is this necessary? Perhaps it will help if we review the accounting for the sale of a long-lived asset. The sale of a long-lived asset is recorded by (1) recognizing the cash proceeds that are received, (2) removing the asset and accumulated depreciation account, and (3) recognizing any gain or loss on the sale.

To illustrate, recall that Computer Services' income statement reported a $3,000 loss on the sale of equipment. With the additional information provided in Illustration 17-4, we can reconstruct the journal entry to record the sale of equipment:

Cash	4,000	
Accumulated Depreciation	1,000	
Loss on Sale of Equipment	3,000	
Equipment		8,000

A	=	L	+	SE
+4,000				−3,000
+1,000				
−8,000				

⬆ Cash flows: +4,000

The cash proceeds of $4,000 that are received are not considered part of operating activities; rather they are part of investing activities. Selling long-lived assets is not part of a company's primary activities. *There is therefore no cash inflow (or outflow) from operating activities.* Logically, then, to calculate the net cash provided (used) by operating activities, we have to eliminate the gain or loss on the sale of an asset from profit.

To eliminate the $3,000 loss on the sale of equipment, we have to add it back to profit to arrive at net cash provided (used) by operating activities. Adding back the loss cancels the original deduction. This is illustrated in the following partial cash flow statement for Computer Services:

Operating activities	
Profit	$145,000
Adjustments to reconcile profit to net cash provided (used) by operating activities:	
Depreciation expense	9,000
Loss on sale of equipment	3,000

If a gain on sale occurs, the gain is deducted from profit in order to determine net cash provided (used) by operating activities. For both a gain and a loss, the actual amount of cash received from the sale of the asset is reported as a source of cash in the investing activities section of the cash flow statement.

Gains and losses are also possible in other circumstances, such as when debt is retired. The same adjustment guidelines apply to debt as described for gains and losses on the sale of assets, except that the other side of the transaction is reported in financing activities, rather than investing activities.

Changes in Noncash Current Asset and Current Liability Accounts

Another type of adjustment in converting profit to net cash provided (used) by operating activities involves changes in noncash current asset and current liability accounts. Most current asset and current liability accounts include transactions that result in revenues or expenses. For example, the Accounts Receivable account includes credit sales recorded as revenue before the cash has actually been received. Prepaid expenses include assets that have been paid in advance, but which have not yet expired or been used up, and have therefore not yet been recorded as an expense. An example is Prepaid Insurance, which is only recorded as Insurance Expense at the end of each month as it expires. Similarly, Income Tax Payable includes income tax expense that a company has incurred but not yet paid.

Thus, because these accruals and prepayments change asset and liability accounts but the changes do not involve cash, we need to adjust profit to determine the net cash provided (used) by operating activities. We do this by analyzing the change in each current asset and current liability account to determine each change's impact on profit and cash.

As was mentioned previously in the chapter, there are situations when current asset and current liability accounts do not result from operating activities. Short-term equity investments are an example of a current asset that does not relate to operating activities. The purchase and sale of investments are shown in the investing activities section of the cash flow statement. Short-term notes receivable that do not relate to sales transactions are another example of a current asset shown in the investing activities section. Similarly, short-term notes payable that do not relate to purchase transactions are an example of a current liability that does not relate to operating activities. These are shown instead in the financing activities section of the cash flow statement.

Helpful hint Increases in current assets are deducted from, and decreases in current assets are added to, profit in the indirect method.

Changes in Noncash Current Assets

The adjustments that are required for changes in noncash current asset accounts are as follows: increases in these accounts are deducted from profit and decreases in these accounts are added to profit, to arrive at net cash provided (used) by operating activities. We will look at these relationships by analyzing Computer Services' current asset accounts.

Decrease in Accounts Receivable. When accounts receivable decrease during the year, revenues on an accrual basis are lower than revenues on a cash basis. In other words, more cash was collected during the period than was recorded as revenue. Computer Services' accounts receivable decreased by $10,000 (from $30,000 to $20,000) during the year. For Computer Services, this means that cash receipts were $10,000 higher than revenues.

Illustration 17-4 indicated that Computer Services had $507,000 in sales revenue reported on its income statement. To determine how much cash was collected in connection with this revenue, it is useful to analyze the Accounts Receivable account:

	Accounts Receivable			
Jan. 1 Balance	30,000			
Sales revenue	507,000	Receipts from customers		517,000
Dec. 31 Balance	20,000			

$10,000 net decrease {

If sales revenue (assumed to be sales on account) journalized during the period was $507,000 (Dr. Accounts Receivable; Cr. Sales Revenue), and the change in Accounts Receivable during the period was a decrease of $10,000, then cash receipts from customers must have been $517,000 (Dr. Cash; Cr. Accounts Receivable).

Consequently, revenue as reported on the accrual-based income statement was less than cash collections. To convert profit to net cash provided (used) by operating activities, the $10,000 decrease in accounts receivable must be added to profit on the cash flow statement because $10,000 more cash was collected than was reported as accrual-based revenue in the income statement.

Showing a decrease in accounts receivable as an addition on the cash flow statement implies that a company can increase its cash by collecting its receivables. In fact, this is true. One of the strategies that Clearwater Seafoods in our feature story is using to manage its cash is to tighten its collection terms in order to lower its trade receivables balance. Showing a deduction in accounts receivable as an increase in cash in the cash flow statement should seem logical.

When the accounts receivable balance increases during the year, revenues on an accrual basis are higher than cash receipts. Therefore, the amount of the increase in accounts receivable is deducted from profit to arrive at net cash provided (used) by operating activities.

Increase in Inventory. Assuming a perpetual inventory system is being used, the Inventory account is increased by the cost of goods purchased and decreased by the cost of goods sold. When the Inventory account increases during the year, that means the cost of goods purchased is greater than the cost of goods sold expense recorded in the income statement. Therefore, when converting profit to cash provided (used) by operating activities, any increase in the Inventory account must be deducted from profit because the cash-based expense is greater than the accrual-based cost of goods sold deducted on the income statement.

During 2011, Computer Services Corporation's Inventory account increased by $5,000. We know from the income statement that cost of goods sold, which decreases inventory (Dr. Cost of Goods Sold; Cr. Inventory), was $150,000. If the Inventory account had an increase of $5,000, this means the company must have purchased (Dr. Inventory; Cr. Accounts Payable) $5,000 more than it sold. Therefore, purchases of inventory during the year must have been $155,000 ($150,000 + $5,000), as shown below:

	Inventory			
Jan. 1 Balance	10,000			
Purchases	155,000	Cost of goods sold		150,000
Dec. 31 Balance	15,000			

$5,000 net increase {

Since the cost of goods sold of $150,000 has already been deducted on the income statement, we simply deduct the extra $5,000 on the cash flow statement to convert profit to net cash provided (used) by operating activities. Note that if inventory had decreased, this would mean that the cost of goods purchased was less than the cost of goods sold and we would add the decrease back to profit when calculating cash provided (used) by operating activities.

This adjustment does not completely convert an accrual-based expense (cost of goods sold) to a cash-based figure (cash payments made to suppliers). It just converts the cost of goods sold to the cost of goods purchased during the year. It does not tell us how much cash was paid to suppliers for the goods purchased. The analysis of accounts payable—shown later—completes the calculation of payments made to suppliers by converting the cost of goods purchased from an accrual basis to a cash basis.

Increase in Prepaid Expenses. Prepaid expenses increased during the period by $4,000. This means that the cash paid for expenses is higher than the expenses reported on the accrual basis. In other words, cash payments were made in the current period, but expenses will not be recorded until future periods. To determine how much cash was paid for operating expenses, it is useful to analyze the Prepaid Expenses account. Operating expenses, as reported on the income statement, were $111,000. Accordingly, payments for expenses must have been $115,000:

Prepaid Expenses				
Jan. 1 Balance	1,000			
Payments for expenses	115,000	Operating expenses	111,000	} $4,000 net increase
Dec. 31 Balance	5,000			

To adjust profit to net cash provided (used) by operating activities, the $4,000 increase in prepaid expenses must be deducted from profit to determine the cash paid for expenses. If prepaid expenses decrease, reported expenses are higher than the expenses paid. Therefore, the decrease in prepaid expenses is added to profit to arrive at net cash provided (used) by operating activities.

These adjustments may not completely convert accrual-based expenses to cash-based expenses. For example, if Computer Services Corporation had any accrued expenses payable, these would also have to be considered before we could completely determine the amount of cash paid for operating expenses. We will look at changes in current liability accounts in the next section.

You should also check if depreciation expense has been combined and reported in the operating expenses category rather than reported separately. If Computer Services had combined depreciation expense with operating expenses for reporting purposes, you would have to analyze the accumulated depreciation accounts to determine the depreciation expense that needs to be added back to profit, as discussed earlier. As Computer Services reported depreciation expense separately from its operating expenses on its income statement in Illustration 17-4, we did not need to perform this separate analysis.

Changes in Current Liabilities

The adjustments that are required for changes in current liability accounts are as follows: increases in these accounts are added to profit, and decreases are deducted from profit, to arrive at net cash provided (used) by operating activities. We will observe these relationships by analyzing Computer Services' current liability accounts: Accounts Payable and Income Tax Payable.

Helpful hint Increases in current liabilities are added to and decreases in current liabilities are deducted from profit in the indirect method.

Increase in Accounts Payable. In some companies, the Accounts Payable account is used only to record purchases of inventory on account. An accrued expenses payable account is used to record other credit purchases. In other companies, the Accounts Payable account is used to record all credit purchases.

For simplicity, in this chapter we have assumed that Accounts Payable is used only to record purchases of inventory on account. Computer Services' Accounts Payable account is therefore increased by purchases of inventory (Dr. Inventory; Cr. Accounts Payable) and decreased by payments to suppliers (Dr. Accounts Payable; Cr. Cash). We determined the amount of purchases made by Computer Services in the analysis of the Inventory account earlier: $155,000. Using this figure, we can now determine that payments to suppliers must have been $139,000:

$16,000 net increase {

Accounts Payable			
	Jan. 1 Balance		12,000
Payments to suppliers 139,000	Purchases		155,000
	Dec. 31 Balance		28,000

To convert profit to net cash provided (used) by operating activities, the $16,000 increase in accounts payable must be added to profit. The increase in accounts payable means that less cash was paid for the purchases than was deducted in the accrual-based expenses section of the income statement. The addition of $16,000 completes the adjustment that is required to convert the cost of goods purchased to the cash paid for these goods.

In summary, the conversion of the cost of goods sold on the accrual-based income statement to the cash paid for goods purchased involves two steps: (1) The change in the Inventory account adjusts the cost of goods sold to the accrual-based figure cost of goods purchased. (2) The change in the Accounts Payable account adjusts the accrual-based cost of goods purchased to the cash-based payments to suppliers. These changes for Computer Services are summarized as follows:

Cost of goods sold	$150,000
Add: Increase in inventory	5,000
Cost of goods purchased	155,000
Less: Increase in accounts payable	16,000
Cash payments to suppliers	$139,000

If a periodic inventory system was used instead of a perpetual inventory system, the accounts for purchases and related expenses, rather than cost of goods sold, would be adjusted in the same way for any change in accounts payable. There would be no change in the Inventory account throughout the period in a periodic inventory system.

Decrease in Income Tax Payable. When a company incurs income tax expense but has not yet paid its taxes, it records income tax payable. A change in the Income Tax Payable account is due to the difference between the income tax expense incurred and the income tax actually paid during the year.

Computer Services' Income Tax Payable account decreased by $2,000. This means that the $47,000 of income tax expense reported on the income statement was $2,000 less than the amount of taxes actually paid during the period ($49,000), as shown in the following T account:

$2,000 net decrease {

Income Tax Payable			
	Jan. 1 Balance		8,000
Payments for income tax 49,000	Income tax expense		47,000
	Dec. 31 Balance		6,000

To adjust profit to net cash provided (used) by operating activities, the $2,000 decrease in income tax payable must be deducted from profit. If the amount of income tax payable had increased during the year, the increase would be added back to profit because the income tax expense deducted on the accrual-based income statement was higher than the cash paid during the period.

If Computer Services had any accrued expenses payable, they would be treated just as income tax payable was. Income tax payable is actually an example of an accrued expense payable; however, it is dealt with separately because income tax expense is reported by itself on the income statement.

Helpful hint Whether the indirect or direct method (Section 2) is used, net cash provided (used) by operating activities will be the same.

The partial cash flow statement that follows in Illustration 17-6 shows the impact on operating activities of the changes in current asset and current liability accounts (the changes are highlighted in red). It also shows the adjustments that were described earlier for noncash expenses and gains and losses. The operating activities section of the cash flow statement is now complete.

COMPUTER SERVICES CORPORATION Cash Flow Statement (partial) Year Ended December 31, 2011		
Operating activities		
Profit		$145,000
Adjustments to reconcile profit to net cash provided (used) by operating activities:		
Depreciation expense	$ 9,000	
Loss on sale of equipment	3,000	
Decrease in accounts receivable	10,000	
Increase in inventory	(5,000)	
Increase in prepaid expenses	(4,000)	
Increase in accounts payable	16,000	
Decrease in income tax payable	(2,000)	27,000
Net cash provided by operating activities		172,000

In summary, the operating activities section of Computer Services' cash flow statement shows that the accrual-based profit of $145,000 resulted in net cash provided by operating activities of $172,000, after adjustments for noncash items.

Summary of Conversion to Net Cash Provided (Used) by Operating Activities—Indirect Method

As shown in the previous pages, the cash flow statement prepared by the indirect method starts with profit. It then adds or deducts items to arrive at net cash provided (used) by operating activities. The adjustments are generally for three types of items: (1) noncash expenses, (2) gains and losses, and (3) changes in related noncash current asset and current liability accounts. The required adjustments to profit to determine cash provided (used) by operating activities are summarized as follows:

Noncash expenses	Depreciation expense	Add
	Amortization expense (intangible assets)	Add
	Amortization of discount on bond payable	Add
	Amortization of premium on bond payable	Deduct
Gains and losses	Gain on sale of asset	Deduct
	Loss on sale of asset	Add
Changes in noncash current asset and current liability accounts	Increase in current asset account	Deduct
	Decrease in current asset account	Add
	Increase in current liability account	Add
	Decrease in current liability account	Deduct

BEFORE YOU GO ON . . .

→ Review It

1. What is the format of the operating activities section of the cash flow statement when the indirect method is used?
2. Why are depreciation expense and losses added to profit in the operating activities section when the indirect method is used?
3. Explain why increases in noncash current asset account balances are deducted from profit and increases in noncash current liability account balances are added to profit when preparing the operating activities section using the indirect method.

→ Do It

Selected financial information follows for Reynolds Ltd. at December 31. Prepare the operating activities section of the cash flow statement using the indirect method.

	2011	2010	Increase (Decrease)
Current assets			
Cash	$54,000	$37,000	$ 17,000
Accounts receivable	68,000	26,000	42,000
Inventories	54,000	10,000	44,000
Prepaid expenses	4,000	6,000	(2,000)
Current liabilities			
Accounts payable	23,000	50,000	(27,000)
Accrued expenses payable	10,000	0	10,000

REYNOLDS LTD.		
Income Statement		
Year Ended December 31, 2011		
Sales revenue		$890,000
Cost of goods sold		465,000
Gross profit		425,000
Operating expenses	$188,000	
Depreciation expense	33,000	
Loss on sale of equipment	2,000	223,000
Profit from operations		202,000
Other expenses		
Interest expense		12,000
Profit before income tax		190,000
Income tax expense		65,000
Profit		$125,000

Action Plan

- Operating activities relate to items shown on the income statement, which are generally affected by changes in the related noncash current assets and current liabilities in the balance sheet, and noncash items in the income statement.
- Start with profit to determine the net cash provided (used) by operating activities. Add noncash expenses, losses, decreases in noncash current asset accounts, and increases in noncash current liability accounts. Deduct gains, increases in noncash current asset accounts, and decreases in noncash current liability accounts.

Solution

REYNOLDS LTD.		
Cash Flow Statement (partial)		
Year Ended December 31, 2011		
Operating activities		
Profit		$125,000
Adjustments to reconcile profit to net cash provided (used) by operating activities:		
Depreciation expense	$ 33,000	
Loss on sale of equipment	2,000	
Increase in accounts receivable	(42,000)	
Increase in inventories	(44,000)	
Decrease in prepaid expenses	2,000	
Decrease in accounts payable	(27,000)	
Increase in accrued expenses payable	10,000	(66,000)
Net cash provided by operating activities		59,000

The Navigator   *Related exercise material*: BE17–3, BE17–4, BE17–5, E17–3, E17–4, and E17–5.

Section 2: Direct Method

Although both the indirect and direct methods of determining cash provided (used) by operating activities are acceptable choices under IFRS and Canadian GAAP for Private Enterprises, the direct method is encouraged by Canadian standard setters. Under the direct method, net cash provided (used) by operating activities is calculated by adjusting each individual revenue and expense item in the income statement from the accrual basis to the cash basis.

To simplify and condense the operating activities section, only major classes of operating cash receipts and cash payments are reported. The difference between these cash receipts and cash payments for these major classes is the net cash provided (used) by operating activities. These relationships are shown in Illustration 17-7.

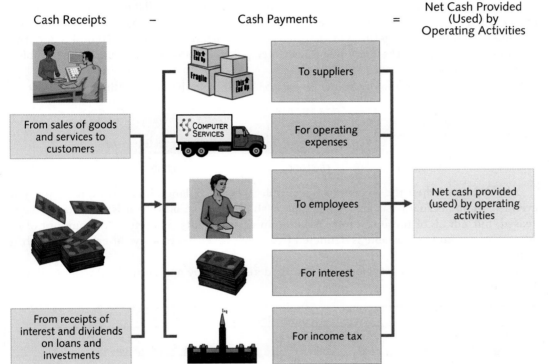

Illustration 17-7

Major classes of operating cash receipts and payments

An efficient way to apply the direct method is to analyze the items reported in the income statement in the order in which they are listed. The cash receipts and cash payments that relate to these revenues and expenses are then determined by adjusting for changes in the related current asset and current liability accounts. The adjustments that are required to convert the related revenues and expenses from an accrual system to a cash system are summarized in Illustration 17-8.

	Revenues	Expenses
Current assets		
Increase in account balance	Deduct	Add
Decrease in account balance	Add	Deduct
Current liabilities		
Increase in account balance	Add	Deduct
Decrease in account balance	Deduct	Add

Illustration 17-8

Summary of adjustments required to convert from accrual to cash

Note that Illustration 17-8 shows the adjustments to the related revenue and expense accounts. Under the indirect method, in the previous section, we showed the adjustments to profit. Note that the results are the same. For example, an increase in a current asset results in a deduction from revenue, or an increase in expenses, both of which result in a reduction of profit. In the previous section, we also learned that an increase in current assets results in a deduction from profit to determine cash provided (used) by operating activities.

We further explain the reasoning behind these adjustments for Computer Services Corporation, first for cash receipts and then for cash payments, in the following subsections.

Cash Receipts

Computer Services has only one source of cash receipts: its customers.

Cash Receipts from Customers

The income statement for Computer Services reported sales revenue from customers of $507,000. But how much was received in cash from customers? To answer that, it is necessary to look at the change in accounts receivable during the year.

When accounts receivable decrease during the year, revenues on an accrual basis are lower than revenues on a cash basis. In other words, more cash was collected during the period than was recorded as revenue. Computer Services' accounts receivable decreased by $10,000 (from $30,000 to $20,000) during the year. This means that cash receipts were $10,000 higher than revenues. To determine the amount of cash receipts, the decrease in accounts receivable is added to sales revenue.

Thus, cash receipts from customers were $517,000, calculated as in Illustration 17-9.

Illustration 17-9 ➡

Formula to calculate cash receipts from customers—direct method

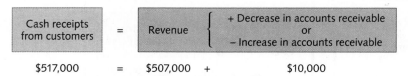

Cash receipts from customers	=	Revenue	+ Decrease in accounts receivable or − Increase in accounts receivable
$517,000	=	$507,000 +	$10,000

Alternatively, when the Accounts Receivable account balance increases during the year, revenues on an accrual basis are higher than cash receipts. In other words, revenues have increased, but not all of these revenues resulted in cash receipts. Therefore, the amount of the increase in accounts receivable is deducted from sales revenues to arrive at cash receipts from customers.

Cash receipts from customers can also be determined by analyzing the Accounts Receivable account as follows:

	Accounts Receivable			
Jan. 1 Balance	30,000			
Sales revenue	507,000	Receipts from customers	517,000
Dec. 31 Balance	20,000			

$10,000 net decrease

Note that this is basically the same analysis that we illustrated in the previous section on the indirect method. We will see that the difference between the two methods is in the presentation of the information on the cash flow statement.

Cash Receipts from Interest and Dividends

Computer Services does not have cash receipts from any source other than customers. If an income statement details other revenue, such as interest and/or dividend revenue, these amounts must be adjusted for any accrued amounts receivable to determine the actual cash receipts. As in Illustration 17-9, increases in accrued receivables would be deducted from accrual-based revenues. Decreases in accrued receivable accounts would be added to accrual-based revenues.

Cash Payments

Computer Services has many sources of cash payments: to suppliers and for operating expenses, interest, and income taxes. We will analyze each of these in the next sections.

Cash Payments to Suppliers

Computer Services reported a cost of goods sold of $150,000 on its income statement. But how much of that was paid in cash to suppliers? To answer that, two steps are required:

1. Determine the cost of goods purchased for the year by adjusting the cost of goods sold by the change in inventory. When the Inventory account increases during the year, the cost of goods purchased is higher than the cost of goods sold. To determine the cost of goods purchased, the increase in inventory is added to the cost of goods sold. Computer Services' inventory increased by $5,000 so its cost of goods purchased is $155,000 ($150,000 + $5,000). If Inventory had decreased, that amount would be deducted from the cost of goods sold to determine the cost of goods purchased.

2. Then determine cash payments to suppliers by adjusting the cost of goods purchased by the change in accounts payable. When accounts payable increase during the year, that means purchases on an accrual basis are higher than they are on a cash basis. To determine cash payments to suppliers, an increase in accounts payable is deducted from the cost of goods purchased. For Computer Services, accounts payable increased by $16,000. Thus cash payments to suppliers were $139,000 ($155,000 – $16,000). If Accounts Payable had decreased, that means cash payments to suppliers amounted to more than the purchases. In that case, the decrease in accounts payable is added to the cost of goods purchased to determine the cash payments to suppliers.

These two steps are shown in Illustration 17-10.

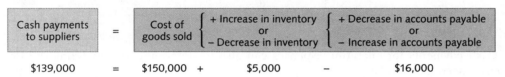

$139,000 = $150,000 + $5,000 – $16,000

Illustration 17-10

Formula to calculate cash payments to suppliers—direct method

The two steps in adjusting cost of goods sold to cash payments to suppliers (also known as creditors) can also be performed by an analysis of the Inventory and Accounts Payable accounts, as follows:

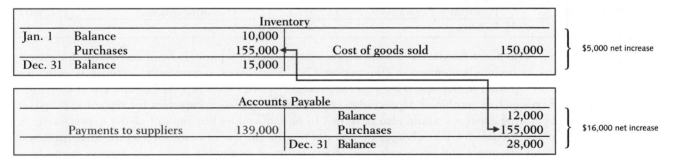

In some companies, the Accounts Payable account is used only to record purchases of inventory on account. An accrued expenses payable account is used to record other credit purchases. In other companies, the Accounts Payable account is used to record all credit purchases. For simplicity, we have assumed in this chapter that Accounts Payable is only used to record purchases of inventory on account.

Cash Payments for Operating Expenses

Computer Services' income statement includes $111,000 of operating expenses. To determine the cash paid for operating expenses, we need to adjust this amount for any changes in prepaid expenses and accrued liabilities.

If prepaid expenses increase during the year, the cash paid for operating expenses will be higher than the operating expenses reported on the income statement. To adjust operating expenses to cash payments for services, any increase in prepaid expenses must be added to operating expenses. On the other hand, if prepaid expenses decrease during the year, the decrease must be deducted from operating expenses.

Operating expenses must also be adjusted for changes in accrued liability accounts (e.g., accrued expenses payable). While for simplicity we have assumed in this chapter that accrued liabilities are recorded separately from accounts payable, some companies combine them with accounts payable. This is one reason that using the direct method can be difficult in reality. If accrued liabilities and accounts payable are combined and recorded in one account, you have to figure out what proportion of accounts payable relates to purchases of inventory, and what relates to other payables, in order to determine the cash payments to suppliers and cash payments for operating expenses.

At this point, Computer Services does not have any accrued expenses payable related to its operating expenses. If it did, any changes in the Accrued Expenses Payable account would affect operating expenses as follows: When accrued expenses payable increase during the year, operating expenses on an accrual basis are higher than they are on a cash basis. To determine cash payments for operating expenses, an increase in accrued expenses payable is deducted from operating expenses. On the other hand, a decrease in accrued expenses payable is added to operating expenses because the cash payments are greater than the operating expenses.

Computer Services' cash payments for operating expenses were $115,000, calculated as in Illustration 17-11.

Illustration 17-11 ➡

Formula to calculate cash payments for operating expenses—direct method

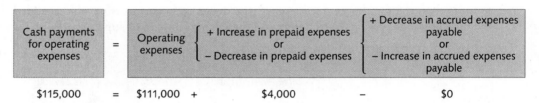

| Cash payments for operating expenses | = | Operating expenses | { + Increase in prepaid expenses or − Decrease in prepaid expenses | { + Decrease in accrued expenses payable or − Increase in accrued expenses payable |

$115,000 = $111,000 + $4,000 − $0

Cash payments for operating expenses can also be determined by analyzing the Prepaid Expenses account as follows:

$4,000 net increase {

Prepaid Expenses				
Jan. 1	Balance	1,000		
	Payments for expenses	115,000	Operating expenses	111,000
Dec. 31	Balance	5,000		

Computer Services reported depreciation expense separately from its operating expenses on its income statement in Illustration 17-4. Sometimes, depreciation expense is combined and reported in the operating expenses category rather than reported separately. If Computer Services had combined depreciation expense with operating expenses for reporting purposes, operating expenses would also have had to be reduced by the amount of the depreciation expense included. Other charges that do not require the use of cash, such as the amortization of bond discounts and premiums, and amortization of intangible assets, are treated in the same way as depreciation of property, plant, and equipment.

Cash Payments to Employees

Some companies report payments to employees separately, removing these payments from their operating expenses. To determine payments to employees, you would have to know the salary expense amount on the income statement and any salaries payable on the comparative balance sheets. Cash payments to employees would equal the salary expense, plus any decrease (or less any increase) during the period in salaries payable.

Other companies condense their income statements in such a way that cash payments to suppliers and employees cannot be separated from cash payments for operating expenses (i.e., they do not disclose their cost of goods sold or salary expense separately). Although the disclosure will not be as informative, for reporting purposes it is acceptable to combine these sources of cash payments.

Cash Payments for Interest

Computer Services reports $42,000 of interest expense on its income statement in Illustration 17-4. This amount equals the cash paid, since the comparative balance sheet indicated no interest payable at the beginning or end of the year. The relationship among cash payments for interest, interest expense, and changes in interest payable (if any) is shown in Illustration 17-12.

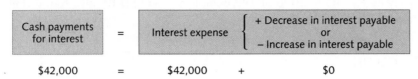

Cash payments for interest	=	Interest expense	{ + Decrease in interest payable or − Increase in interest payable
$42,000	=	$42,000	+ $0

Illustration 17-12

Formula to calculate cash payments for interest—direct method

Cash Payments for Income Tax

The income statement for Computer Services shows an income tax expense of $47,000 and a decrease in income tax payable of $2,000. When a company incurs income tax expense but has not yet paid its taxes, it records income tax payable. A change in the Income Tax Payable account is due to the difference between the income tax expense that was incurred and the income tax that was actually paid during the year.

The relationship among cash payments for income tax, income tax expense, and changes in income tax payable is shown in Illustration 17-13.

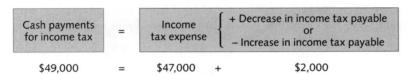

Cash payments for income tax	=	Income tax expense	{ + Decrease in income tax payable or − Increase in income tax payable
$49,000	=	$47,000	+ $2,000

Illustration 17-13

Formula to calculate cash payments for income tax—direct method

Computer Services' Income Tax Payable account decreased by $2,000. This means that the $47,000 of income tax expense reported on the income statement was $2,000 less than the $49,000 of taxes paid during the period, as detailed in the following T account:

Income Tax Payable			
Payments for income tax	49,000	Jan. 1 Balance	8,000
		Income tax expense	47,000
		Dec. 31 Balance	6,000

} $2,000 net decrease

All of the revenues and expenses in the income statement have now been adjusted to a cash basis. This information is put together in Illustration 17-14, which shows the operating activities section of the cash flow statement using the direct method.

Helpful hint Note that in the operating activities section, positive numbers indicate cash inflows (receipts) and negative numbers indicate cash outflows (payments). As well, whether the direct or indirect method is used, net cash provided (used) by operating activities will be the same.

COMPUTER SERVICES CORPORATION
Cash Flow Statement (partial)
Year Ended December 31, 2011

Operating activities		
Cash receipts from customers		$517,000
Cash payments		
To suppliers	$(139,000)	
For operating expenses	(115,000)	
For interest	(42,000)	
For income tax	(49,000)	(345,000)
Net cash provided by operating activities		172,000

Illustration 17-14

Net cash provided by operating activities—direct method

As mentioned earlier, while both international and Canadian accounting standards allow the use of both the indirect and direct methods, Canadian GAAP for Private Enterprises encourages companies to use the direct method of reporting operating activities. To understand why the direct method is encouraged for private companies, we recommend that you compare Illustration 17-6 with Illustration 17-14. Both methods show the identical amount of net cash provided by operating activities. But which method would be more understandable to you if you were a user of this information?

There is no correct answer to this question, but Canadian standard setters have long believed that investors would find information on the various functional cash flows (e.g., payments to employees) more useful than the information on adjustments required to convert profit into cash flows from operating activities (e.g., depreciation expense). Nevertheless, in Canada, the vast majority of companies, including The Forzani Group Ltd., use the indirect method. A study by KPMG in 2006 of 199 companies using IFRS also found that 92% of the companies used the indirect method.

BEFORE YOU GO ON . . .

→ Review It

1. What is the format of the operating activities section of the cash flow statement for the direct method?
2. Give the formulae to calculate cash receipts from customers, cash payments to suppliers, and cash payments for operating expenses.
3. If both the indirect and direct methods arrive at the same net cash provided (used) by operating activities, why does it matter which method is used?

→ Do It

Selected financial information follows for Reynolds Ltd. at December 31. Prepare the operating activities section of the cash flow statement using the direct method.

	2011	2010	Increase (Decrease)
Current assets			
Cash	$54,000	$37,000	$ 17,000
Accounts receivable	68,000	26,000	42,000
Inventories	54,000	10,000	44,000
Prepaid expenses	4,000	6,000	(2,000)
Current liabilities			
Accounts payable	23,000	50,000	(27,000)
Accrued expenses payable	10,000	0	10,000

REYNOLDS LTD.
Income Statement
Year Ended December 31, 2011

Sales revenue		$890,000
Cost of goods sold		465,000
Gross profit		425,000
Operating expenses	$188,000	
Depreciation expense	33,000	
Loss on sale of equipment	2,000	223,000
Profit from operations		202,000
Other expenses		
Interest expense		12,000
Profit before income tax		190,000
Income tax expense		65,000
Profit		$125,000

Action Plan

• Determine the net cash provided (used) by operating activities by adjusting each revenue and expense item for changes in the related current asset and current liability account.
• Report cash receipts and cash payments by major sources and uses: cash receipts from customers and cash payments to suppliers, for operating expenses, to employees, for interest, and for income taxes.

Solution

REYNOLDS LTD. Cash Flow Statement (partial) Year Ended December 31, 2011		
Operating activities		
Cash receipts from customers		$848,000[1]
Cash payments		
To suppliers	$(536,000)[2]	
For operating expenses	(176,000)[3]	
For interest	(12,000)	
For income tax	(65,000)	(789,000)
Net cash provided by operating activities		59,000

Calculations:
[1] Cash receipts from customers: $890,000 − $42,000 = $848,000
[2] Payments to suppliers: $465,000 + $44,000 + $27,000 = $536,000
[3] Payments for operating expenses: $188,000 − $2,000 − $10,000 = $176,000

Related exercise material: BE17–6, BE17–7, BE17–8, BE17–9, BE17–10, BE17–11, E17–6, E17–7, E17–8, and E17–9.

The Navigator

STEP 2: INVESTING ACTIVITIES

Determine the Net Cash Provided (Used) by Investing Activities by Analyzing Changes in Long-Term Asset Accounts

Regardless of whether the indirect or direct method is used to calculate operating activities, investing and financing activities are measured and reported in the same way. Investing activities affect long-term asset accounts, such as long-term investments; property, plant, and equipment; and intangible assets. There are, of course, exceptions. Short-term investments are generally reported as investing activities as are short-term notes receivable issued for loans rather than for trade transactions.

To determine the investing activities, the balance sheet and additional information in Illustration 17-4 must be examined. The change in each long-term asset account (and the short-term investment accounts) is analyzed to determine what effect, if any, it had on cash. Computer Services has no short-term investments or notes receivable but does have three long-term asset accounts that must be analyzed: Land, Building, and Equipment.

Land

Land increased by $110,000 during the year, as reported in Computer Services' balance sheet. The additional information in Illustration 17-4 states that this land was purchased by issuing long-term bonds. Issuing bonds for land has no effect on cash, but it is a significant noncash investing and financing activity that must be disclosed in a note to the statement.

Building

The Building account increased by $120,000 during the year. What caused this increase? No additional information has been given for this change. Whenever unexplained differences in accounts occur, we assume the transaction was for cash. That is, we would assume in this case that a building was acquired, or expanded, for $120,000 cash.

Accumulated Depreciation—Building

Accumulated Depreciation increased by $6,000 during the year. As explained in the additional information in Illustration 17-4, this increase resulted from the depreciation expense reported on the income statement for the building:

$6,000 net increase

Accumulated Depreciation—Building		
	Jan. 1 Balance	5,000
	Depreciation expense	6,000
	Dec. 31 Balance	11,000

As was explained earlier, depreciation expense is a noncash charge and does not affect the cash flow statement.

Equipment

Computer Services' Equipment account increased by $17,000. The additional information in Illustration 17-4 explains that this was a net increase resulting from two different transactions: (1) a purchase of equipment for $25,000 cash, and (2) a sale of equipment with a carrying amount of $7,000 (cost of $8,000, less accumulated depreciation of $1,000) for $4,000 cash. The T account below shows the reasons for the change in the equipment account during the year:

$17,000 net increase

Equipment				
Jan. 1 Balance	10,000			
Purchase of equipment	25,000	Cost of equipment sold	8,000	
Dec. 31 Balance	27,000			

In the above example, you were given additional information about both the purchase and the sale of equipment. Often, in analyzing accounts, you will be given just one piece of information and are expected to deduce the information that is missing. For example, if you knew the beginning and ending balances of the Equipment account as well as the fact that the cost of the equipment sold was $8,000, you could determine that the cost of the equipment purchased must have been $25,000.

The following entries show the details of the equipment transactions shown in the above T account:

A	=	L	+	SE
+25,000				
−25,000				

↓ Cash flows: −25,000

A	=	L	+	SE
+4,000				−3,000
+1,000				
−8,000				

↑ Cash flows: +4,000

Equipment	25,000	
Cash		25,000
Cash	4,000	
Accumulated Depreciation	1,000	
Loss on Sale of Equipment	3,000	
Equipment		8,000

Each transaction, both the purchase and the sale, should be reported separately on the cash flow statement. It is not correct to report the net change in a long-term balance sheet account as simply an increase or decrease in that account. This is different than current asset and current liability accounts, where we report only the net change.

In this particular case, the purchase of equipment should be reported as a $25,000 outflow of cash. The sale of equipment should be reported as a $4,000 inflow of cash. Note that it is the cash proceeds that are reported on the cash flow statement, not the cost of the equipment sold.

Accumulated Depreciation—Equipment

The accumulated depreciation for equipment increased by $2,000. This change does not represent the depreciation expense for the year. In fact, the additional information in Illustration 17-4 told us that there was $3,000 of depreciation expense for the equipment and that the equipment sold had $1,000 of accumulated depreciation.

The T account below for Accumulated Depreciation—Equipment shows that these two items explain the overall net increase of $2,000. The balance was decreased (debited $1,000) as a result of the sale of equipment and was increased by $3,000 of depreciation expense for the current period, for a net increase of $2,000.

Accumulated Depreciation—Equipment				
		Jan. 1	Balance	1,000
Sale of equipment	1,000		Depreciation expense	3,000
		Dec. 31	Balance	3,000

$2,000 net decrease

As we have seen, the sale of the equipment affects one account on Computer Services' income statement (Loss on Sale of Equipment) and three accounts on its balance sheet (Cash, Equipment, and Accumulated Depreciation). In the cash flow statement, it is important to report the effects of this sale in one place: the investing activities section. The overall result is that the sale of the equipment ends up having no impact on the operating activities section of the cash flow statement. Instead, the cash proceeds received from the sale of the equipment are shown fully in the investing activities section.

The investing activities section of Computer Services' cash flow statement is shown in Illustration 17-15 and reports the changes in the three accounts: Land, Building, and Equipment.

COMPUTER SERVICES CORPORATION Cash Flow Statement (partial) Year Ended December 31, 2011		
Investing activities		
Purchase of building	$(120,000)	
Purchase of equipment	(25,000)	
Sale of equipment	4,000	
Net cash used by investing activities		$(141,000)
Note x: Significant noncash investing and financing activities		
Issue of bonds to purchase land		$110,000

◀ **Illustration 17-15**

Net cash used by investing activities

In a healthy and growing company, we will normally expect that the company will use cash for investing activities each year. Providing cash by selling significant portions of long-term assets can mean the company is strapped for cash and in financial difficulties. On the other hand, when the economic environment makes it difficult to borrow, as it was for Clearwater Seafoods in our feature story, liquidating underperforming assets and selling non-core assets can be a prudent strategy.

Helpful hint Note that in the investing activities section, positive numbers indicate cash inflows (receipts) and negative numbers indicate cash outflows (payments).

BEFORE YOU GO ON . . .

➡ Review It

1. What are some examples of items reported in the investing activities section of the cash flow statement?
2. Since short-term investments are a current asset, why aren't they reported in the operating activities section rather than the investing activities section of the cash flow statement?
3. Why isn't the gain or loss on the sale of equipment reported in the operating activities section and the change in the carrying amount of equipment reported in the investing activities section of the cash flow statement?

➡ Do It

Umiujaq Corporation reported an opening balance of $146,000 and an ending balance of $135,000 in its Equipment account; and an opening balance of $47,000 and an ending balance of $62,000 in its Accumulated Depreciation—Equipment account. During the year, it sold equipment with a cost of $21,000 for cash at a gain on the sale of $1,000. It also purchased equipment for cash. It recorded depreciation expense of $31,000. Calculate (a) the cash paid for equipment purchased, and (b) the cash received from the sale of equipment.

Action Plan

- Prepare a T account for Equipment and record the beginning and ending balances and the cost of the equipment sold. Use this information to calculate the cost of equipment purchased during the year.
- Prepare a T account for Accumulated Depreciation—Equipment and record the beginning and ending balances and the depreciation expense. Recall that depreciation expense increases accumulated depreciation. Use this information to calculate the accumulated depreciation of the equipment sold during the year.
- Calculate the carrying amount of the equipment sold. Since there was a gain on the sale, the equipment sold for more than its carrying amount. Therefore, add the gain on sale to the carrying amount to determine the cash received from the sale of the equipment.

Solution

(a) Cash paid for equipment = $10,000

Equipment			
Opening bal.	146,000		
Purchase of equipment	10,000*	Sale of equipment	21,000
Ending bal.	135,000		

* $10,000 = $135,000 + $21,000 − $146,000

(b) Cash received from sale of equipment = $6,000

Accumulated Depreciation—Equipment			
		Opening balance	47,000
Sale of equipment	16,000**	Depreciation expense	31,000
		Ending balance	62,000

** $16,000 = $47,000 + $31,000 − $62,000

Carrying amount of equipment sold: $21,000 − $16,000 = $5,000
Carrying amount of the equipment sold plus the gain on sale = $5,000 + $1,000 = $6,000

The Navigator

Related exercise material: BE17–12 and BE17–13.

STEP 3: FINANCING ACTIVITIES

Determine the Net Cash Provided (Used) by Financing Activities by Analyzing Changes in Long-Term Liability and Equity Accounts

The third step in preparing a cash flow statement is to analyze the changes in long-term liability and equity accounts. If short-term notes payable are issued for lending purposes rather than for trade, they should also be reported in the financing activities section. Computer Services has no notes payable but has one long-term liability account, Bonds Payable, and two shareholders' equity accounts, Common Shares and Retained Earnings.

Bonds Payable

Bonds Payable increased by $110,000. As indicated earlier, land was acquired from the issue of these bonds. This noncash transaction is reported as a note to the cash flow statement because it is a significant financing activity.

Common Shares

Computer Services' Common Shares account increased by $20,000. Since there is no additional information about any reacquisition of shares, we assume that this change is due entirely to the issue of additional common shares for cash. This cash inflow is reported in the financing activities section of the cash flow statement. If the company had also reacquired shares as well as issued new common shares, both of these transactions would be reported in the cash flow statement.

Retained Earnings

What caused the net increase of $116,000 in Retained Earnings? This increase can be explained by two factors. First, profit increased retained earnings by $145,000. Second, the additional information in Illustration 17-4 indicates that a cash dividend of $29,000 was paid. This information could have also been deduced by analyzing the T account:

Retained Earnings				
		Jan. 1	Balance	48,000
Cash dividend	29,000		Profit	145,000
		Dec. 31	Balance	164,000

$116,000 net increase

The cash dividend paid is reported as a cash outflow in the financing activities section of the cash flow statement. Note that the Retained Earnings account above only reports the dividend declared. This amount must be adjusted to determine the dividend paid, if there is any change in the balance of the Dividends Payable account reported in the current liabilities section of the balance sheet. There was none in the case of Computer Services.

If you were told the beginning and ending balances in the Retained Earnings account as well as the amount of the profit, you could have calculated the amount of the cash dividend, or vice versa. In this case, both the profit and cash dividend were described in Illustration 17-4. You will often be asked to deduce missing information in the end-of-chapter material, which will help you determine how well you understand account relationships.

The financing activities section of Computer Services' cash flow statement is shown in Illustration 17-16 and reports the issue of common shares and payment of a dividend. The information on the significant noncash financing activity of bonds being issued to purchase land has already been illustrated and is not included here.

Helpful hint Note that in the financing activities section, positive numbers indicate cash inflows (receipts) and negative numbers indicate cash outflows (payments).

◀ **Illustration 17-16**

Net cash used by financing activities

COMPUTER SERVICES CORPORATION		
Cash Flow Statement (partial)		
Year Ended December 31, 2011		
Financing activities		
Issue of common shares	$ 20,000	
Payment of cash dividend	(29,000)	
Net cash used by financing activities		$(9,000)

ACCOUNTING IN ACTION: ACROSS THE ORGANIZATION

Microsoft Corp. took advantage of record low interest rates to issue its first-ever long-term bond offering in 2009, adding $3.75 billion to its already swelling cash reserves. The sale included $2 billion in bonds maturing in five years, $1 billion in bonds maturing in 10 years, and $750 million in 30-year bonds. The company will be paying yields of between 3% and 5.24%. Microsoft did not need the financing. As at March 31, 2009, it had $25.3 billion in cash, cash equivalents, and short-term investments. Instead, it was taking advantage of good market conditions and the company's great credit rating. Microsoft carries the highest possible credit rating of AAA. The company said it plans to use the proceeds from the sale for "general corporate purposes," which could include working capital, share buybacks, and acquisitions.

Source: Dan Gallagher, Deborah Levine, and John Letzing, "Microsoft Raises $3.75 Billion in First-Ever Bond Offering," *Market-Watch*, May 11, 2009, available at www.marketwatch.com.

Typically, which department in a company is responsible for making decisions about whether to issue bonds? What would that department consider when making this decision?

BEFORE YOU GO ON . . .

➜ Review It

1. What are some examples of items reported in the financing activities section of the cash flow statement?
2. When should short-term notes payable be reported in the operating activities section and when should they be reported in the financing activities section of the cash flow statement?
3. If you know the opening and ending retained earnings balances and the amount of profit, explain how you can figure out the amount of dividends paid to report in the financing activities section of the cash flow statement.
4. What are some significant noncash investing and financing activities shown in a cash flow statement? Give some examples.

➜ Do It

La Tuque Corporation reported an opening balance of $80,000 and an ending balance of $95,000 in its Common Shares account and an opening balance of $15,000 and an ending balance of $20,000 in its Contributed Capital—Reacquisition of Common Shares account. During the year, it issued $50,000 of common shares for cash and reacquired common shares for cash. Calculate the cash paid to reacquire the shares.

Action Plan

- Prepare a T account for Common Shares and record the beginning and ending balances and the cost of the new shares issued. Use this information to determine the cost of the shares reacquired.
- Prepare a T account for Contributed Capital—Reacquisition of Common Shares and record the beginning and ending balances. Use this information to determine the increase in the account as a result of the reacquisition of the shares.
- An increase in contributed capital indicates that the company paid less than the cost of the common shares to reacquire them. Deduct this increase from the cost of the shares to determine the cash paid.

Solution

Cash paid to reacquire shares = $30,000

	Common Shares		
		Opening balance	80,000
Reacquisition of shares	35,000*	Issue of shares	50,000
		Ending balance	95,000

* $35,000 = $80,000 + $50,000 − $95,000

	Contributed Capital—Reacquisition of Common Shares		
		Opening balance	15,000
		Reacquisition of shares	5,000**
		Ending balance	20,000

** $5,000 = $20,000 − $15,000

Cash paid for reacquisition of shares: $35,000 − $5,000 = $30,000

Related exercise material: BE17–14, BE17–15, and E17–10.

The Navigator

STEP 4: THE CASH FLOW STATEMENT

Prepare the Cash Flow Statement and Determine the Net Increase (Decrease) in Cash

The final step is to calculate the overall net increase or decrease in cash for the year by adding cash provided or used in each of the three sections of the cash flow statement. Computer Services' net increase in cash of $22,000 is calculated as follows:

Net cash provided by operating activities	$172,000
Net cash used by investing activities	(141,000)
Net cash used by financing activities	(9,000)
Net increase in cash	$ 22,000

The $22,000 net increase in cash is then added to cash at the beginning of the year of $33,000 to equal $55,000 of cash at the end of the year. This number is compared with the cash account balance in the end-of-the-year balance sheet, which also shows that cash is $55,000 at the end of the year. This is known as proving the cash balance. If cash at the end of the year on the cash flow statement is not equal to cash on the balance sheet, there is an error in the cash flow statement, which will need to be found and corrected.

Using this information and the partial cash flow statements shown in Illustrations 17-6, 17-14, 17-15, and 17-16, we can now present a complete cash flow statement for Computer Services Corporation. Illustration 17-17 presents the statement using the indirect method of preparing the operating activities section from Illustration 17-6. Illustration 17-18 presents the statement using the direct method of preparing the operating activities section from Illustration 17-14. Notice that while the operating activities sections differ in the indirect and direct methods, the investing (Illustration 17-15) and financing (Illustration 17-16) activities sections are exactly the same in the two following statements.

← **Illustration 17-17**

Cash flow statement— indirect method

COMPUTER SERVICES CORPORATION
Cash Flow Statement
Year Ended December 31, 2011

Operating activities		
Profit		$145,000
Adjustments to reconcile profit to net cash		
provided (used) by operating activities:		
Depreciation expense	$ 9,000	
Loss on sale of equipment	3,000	
Decrease in accounts receivable	10,000	
Increase in inventory	(5,000)	
Increase in prepaid expenses	(4,000)	
Increase in accounts payable	16,000	
Decrease in income tax payable	(2,000)	27,000
Net cash provided by operating activities		172,000
Investing activities		
Purchase of building	$(120,000)	
Purchase of equipment	(25,000)	
Sale of equipment	4,000	
Net cash used by investing activities		(141,000)
Financing activities		
Issue of common shares	$ 20,000	
Payment of cash dividend	(29,000)	
Net cash used by financing activities		(9,000)
Net increase in cash		22,000
Cash, January 1		33,000
Cash, December 31		$ 55,000
Note x: Significant noncash investing and financing activities		
Issue of bonds to purchase land		$110,000

Illustration 17-18 ➡

Cash flow statement—
direct method

COMPUTER SERVICES CORPORATION Cash Flow Statement Year Ended December 31, 2011		
Operating activities		
Cash receipts from customers		$517,000
Cash payments		
To suppliers	$(139,000)	
For operating expenses	(115,000)	
For interest	(42,000)	
For income tax	(49,000)	(345,000)
Net cash provided by operating activities		172,000
Investing activities		
Purchase of building	$(120,000)	
Purchase of equipment	(25,000)	
Sale of equipment	4,000	
Net cash used by investing activities		(141,000)
Financing activities		
Issue of common shares	$ 20,000	
Payment of cash dividend	(29,000)	
Net cash used by financing activities		(9,000)
Net increase in cash		22,000
Cash, January 1		33,000
Cash, December 31		$ 55,000
Note x: Significant noncash investing and financing activities		
Issue of bonds to purchase land		$110,000

BEFORE YOU GO ON . . .

➡ Review It

1. How do you determine the net increase or decrease in cash?
2. Explain how the income statement, statement of retained earnings or statement of changes in shareholders' equity, and balance sheet are interrelated with the cash flow statement.

➡ Do It

Selected information follows for Reynolds Ltd. at December 31. Prepare a cash flow statement.

	2011	2010	Increase (Decrease)
Cash	$ 54,000	$ 37,000	$ 17,000
Property, plant, and equipment			
Land	45,000	70,000	(25,000)
Buildings	200,000	200,000	0
Accumulated depreciation—buildings	(21,000)	(11,000)	10,000
Equipment	193,000	68,000	125,000
Accumulated depreciation—equipment	(28,000)	(10,000)	18,000
Long-term liabilities and shareholders' equity			
Bonds payable	110,000	150,000	(40,000)
Common shares	220,000	60,000	160,000
Retained earnings	206,000	136,000	70,000

Additional information:
1. Cash provided from operating activities was $59,000 as shown in the "Do Its" on pages 946 and 953.
2. Equipment was bought for cash. Equipment with a cost of $41,000 and a carrying amount of $36,000 was sold at a loss of $2,000.
3. Bonds of $40,000 were redeemed at their face value for cash.
4. Profit was $125,000 and a cash dividend was paid.

Action Plan

- Determine the net cash provided (used) by investing activities. Investing activities generally relate to changes in long-term asset accounts.
- Determine the net cash provided (used) by financing activities. Financing activities generally relate to changes in long-term liability and shareholders' equity accounts.
- Determine the net increase (decrease) in cash and add it to the beginning of period cash. Verify that this amount agrees with the end-of-period cash balance reported on the balance sheet.

Solution

REYNOLDS LTD.
Cash Flow Statement
Year Ended December 31, 2011

Operating activities		
Net cash provided by operating activities		$ 59,000
Investing activities		
Sale of land	$ 25,000	
Sale of equipment	34,000[1]	
Purchase of equipment	(166,000)[2]	
Net cash used by investing activities		(107,000)
Financing activities		
Redemption of bonds	$ (40,000)	
Issue of common shares	160,000	
Payment of dividends	(55,000)[3]	
Net cash provided by financing activities		65,000
Net increase in cash		17,000
Cash, January 1		37,000
Cash, December 31		$ 54,000

[1] $36,000 – $2,000 = $34,000
[2] $68,000 – $41,000 – $193,000 = $166,000
[3] $136,000 + $125,000 – $206,000 = $55,000

Related exercise material: BE17–16, E17–11, E17–12, and E17–13.

The Navigator

Using the Information in the Financial Statements

The cash flow statement gives information about a company's financial health that cannot be found in the other financial statements. None of the other financial statements give enough information for decision-making by themselves. The income statement, statements of comprehensive income, retained earnings, and changes in shareholders' equity, and the balance sheet must be read along with the cash flow statement in order to fully understand a company's financial situation.

For example, the income statement might show a profitable company. However, a rapidly growing company might also find it difficult to pay its current liabilities because its cash is being used to finance its growth. Both successful and unsuccessful companies can have problems with cash flow. According to Clearwater Seafoods in our feature story, the sustainability of a business is linked to its ability to generate cash. Clearwater considers cash flows generated from operations as a key indicator of the company's health.

Consider the condensed income and cash flow data shown below for three different companies, each operating in the same industry.

> STUDY OBJECTIVE 3
>
> Analyze the cash flow statement.

	Company A	Company B	Company C
Profit (loss)	$ 75,000	$ 25,000	$ (50,000)
Cash provided (used) by operating activities	$100,000	$(25,000)	$ (25,000)
Cash provided (used) by investing activities	(50,000)	(25,000)	35,000
Cash provided (used) by financing activities	(25,000)	75,000	15,000
Net increase in cash	$ 25,000	$ 25,000	$ 25,000

In this example, we have assumed that each company has the same change in cash, an increase of $25,000. However, this increase in cash is generated quite differently by each company. Company A reports profit of $75,000 and a positive cash flow from operating activities of $100,000. How can Company A's cash provided by operating activities be higher than its profit? This could occur in any of these three situations: if it has noncash expenses such as depreciation, reduced current assets such as receivables or inventory, or increased current liabilities such as accounts payable. It is important to analyze the components of each section as well as the net result, along with the information in the other financial statements. Depending on which of the situations created Company's A higher cash flow from operating activities, there could be different implications. For example, if receivables are lower, this could be because the company is collecting them faster. If so, this is a good thing. Alternatively, receivables could have decreased because sales decreased. This is not good, and has implications for future profitability.

For now, we know that Company A's operating activities produced a positive cash flow of $100,000, which allowed it to invest $50,000 in its long-lived assets and repay $25,000 of its debt and/or pay dividends. Based only on this information, Company A appears to be in a strong financial position.

Company B, which also produced a positive profit, used $25,000 in its operating activities. How could Company B's profit result in a negative operating cash flow? Company B may be in the early start-up stages of its development. It may have quickly increasing receivables and inventories, with lower amounts of noncash expenses. It was able to end up with the same cash balance as Company A only because it borrowed money. If Company B is indeed a new and rapidly growing company, this is fine. If not, this type of cash flow pattern would not be sustainable in the long run.

Assuming Company B is a start-up company, its cash flow figures appear to be reasonable. For example, early in its operations, during its growth stage, one would expect a company to generate a small amount of profit (or a loss) and negative cash from its operating activities. It will likely also be spending large amounts to purchase productive assets, and will finance these purchases by issuing debt or equity securities. Thus, during its early years, cash from operating and investing activities will likely be negative, while cash from financing activities will be positive.

Company C, which reported both a loss and a negative cash flow from operating activities, is able to produce a positive change in cash only by selling long-lived assets and borrowing additional debt. A company that generates cash mainly from investing activities is usually in a downsizing or restructuring situation. This is fine if the assets being disposed of are unnecessary or unprofitable. However, if the company is in a position where it must sell off income-producing assets to generate cash, then this will affect future revenue and profitability.

As you can see from the above example, analyzing cash flows from different activities along with the information in the other financial statements can provide significant information about a company's overall financial health and activities.

Free Cash Flow

Another way of evaluating cash flows is to determine how much discretionary cash flow a company has—in other words, how much cash it has available to expand, repay debt, pay dividends, or do whatever it best determines. This discretionary cash flow is a measure of solvency known as "free cash flow."

Free cash flow describes the cash remaining from operating activities after making cash outlays for capital expenditures. Using net cash provided by operating activities as a proxy for free cash flow is not sufficient as it does not take into account the fact that a company must invest in productive assets, such as property, plant, and equipment, just to maintain its current level of operations. However, the cash flow statement rarely separates investing activities into those required for maintenance and those used for expansion. So we are often forced to use the net cash used by investing activities rather than capital expenditures incurred to maintain productive capacity when calculating free cash flow.

To calculate free cash flow, the net cash used for investing activities is deducted from the net cash provided by operating activities. Illustration 17-19 uses data from Forzani's cash flow statement (in thousands) to illustrate the calculation of free cash flow.

Cash Provided (Used) by Operating Activities	–	Cash Used (Provided) by Investing Activities	=	Free Cash Flow
$95,743	–	$57,814	=	$37,929

← Illustration 17-19

Free cash flow

Forzani had positive free cash flow of $37,929 thousand. The cash Forzani produced from operating activities was more than sufficient to cover its current year's investing activities. We are not able to determine whether these investing activities were incurred by Forzani to maintain its existing productive capacity, to expand, or for both purposes. However, we do know from the cash flow statement that Forzani used all of its free cash flow, as well as cash on hand from the previous year, to repurchase shares and pay long-term debt and dividends. This resulted in an overall cash reduction.

 ## ACCOUNTING IN ACTION: BUSINESS INSIGHT

Amazon.com, Inc., which used to be just the Earth's biggest bookstore, now prides itself on offering Earth's biggest selection of just about anything. Amazon.com's website offers millions of books and videos (which still account for most of the company's sales), not to mention toys, tools, electronics, home furnishings, apparel, health and beauty goods, prescription drugs, and gourmet foods.

The company states in its annual report: "Our financial focus is on long-term, sustainable growth in free cash flow." In fact, Amazon.com considers free cash flow to be so important that it includes a reconciliation of net cash provided (used) by operating activities to free cash flow in its annual report. Amazon reports that: "Free cash flow reflects an additional way of viewing our liquidity that, when viewed with our GAAP results, provides a more complete understanding of factors and trends affecting our cash flows." It uses "free cash flow, and ratios based on it, to conduct and evaluate our business because, although it is similar to cash flow from operations, we believe it is a more conservative measure of cash flows since purchases of fixed assets are a necessary component of ongoing operations."

What is the likely reason that free cash flow so important to Amazon.com?

BEFORE YOU GO ON . . .

➡ **Review It**

1. How is it possible for a company to report a profit but report a negative cash flow from operating activities?
2. How is it possible for different companies to report the same net change in cash but different amounts for cash provided (used) by operating activities?
3. What is free cash flow?
4. What does it mean if a company has a negative free cash flow?

Related exercise material: BE17–17, BE17–18, E17–14, and E17–15.

The Navigator

Demonstration Problem

Demonstration Problems

The income statement for the year ended December 31, 2011, for Kosinski Manufacturing Ltd. contains the following condensed information:

KOSINSKI MANUFACTURING LTD. Income Statement Year Ended December 31, 2011		
Sales		$6,583,000
Cost of goods sold		3,572,000
Gross profit		3,011,000
Operating expenses	$2,289,000	
Gain on sale of machinery	(24,000)	2,265,000
Profit from operations		746,000
Other expenses		
Interest expense		85,000
Profit before income tax		661,000
Income tax expense		298,000
Profit		$ 363,000

Kosinski's comparative balance sheet at December 31 contained the following account balances:

	2011	2010
Cash	$ 204,500	$ 180,000
Accounts receivable	775,000	610,000
Inventories	834,000	917,000
Prepaid expenses	29,000	25,000
Machinery	6,906,000	7,065,000
Accumulated depreciation—machinery	(2,497,000)	(2,355,000)
Total assets	$6,251,500	$6,442,000
Accounts payable	$ 517,000	$ 601,000
Interest payable	6,000	0
Income taxes payable	24,500	20,000
Dividends payable	5,000	10,000
Long-term notes payable	1,500,000	2,000,000
Common shares	3,075,000	3,000,000
Retained earnings	1,124,000	811,000
Total liabilities and shareholders' equity	$6,251,500	$6,442,000

Additional information:

1. Operating expenses include depreciation expense of $880,000.
2. Accounts payable relate to the purchase of inventory.
3. Machinery that cost $984,000 was sold at a gain of $24,000.
4. New machinery was purchased during the year for $825,000.
5. Dividends declared in 2011 totalled $50,000.
6. Common shares were sold for $75,000 cash.

Instructions

Prepare the cash flow statement using (a) the indirect method or (b) the direct method, as assigned by your instructor.

Solution to Demonstration Problem

(a) Indirect Method

Action Plan

KOSINSKI MANUFACTURING LTD.
Cash Flow Statement
Year Ended December 31, 2011

Operating activities		
Profit		$ 363,000
Adjustments to reconcile profit to net cash		
provided by operating activities:		
Depreciation expense	$ 880,000	
Gain on sale of machinery	(24,000)	
Increase in accounts receivable	(165,000)	
Decrease in inventories	83,000	
Increase in prepaid expenses	(4,000)	
Decrease in accounts payable	(84,000)	
Increase in interest payable	6,000	
Increase in income taxes payable	4,500	696,500
Net cash provided by operating activities		1,059,500
Investing activities		
Sale of machinery	$ 270,000	
Purchase of machinery	(825,000)	
Net cash used by investing activities		(555,000)
Financing activities		
Repayment of notes payable ($2,000,000 − $1,500,000)	$(500,000)	
Issue of common shares	75,000	
Payment of cash dividends ($50,000 + $10,000 − $5,000)	(55,000)	
Net cash used by financing activities		(480,000)
Net increase in cash		24,500
Cash, January 1		180,000
Cash, December 31		$ 204,500

Calculations:

Accumulated depreciation on machinery sold: $2,355,000 + $880,000 − $2,497,000 = $738,000
Carrying amount of machinery sold: $984,000 − $738,000 = $246,000
Proceeds on sale = Carrying amount + Gain = $246,000 + $24,000 = $270,000

(b) Direct Method

KOSINSKI MANUFACTURING LTD.
Cash Flow Statement
Year Ended December 31, 2011

Operating activities		
Cash receipts from customers		$6,418,000 [1]
Cash payments to suppliers		(3,573,000)[2]
Cash payments for operating expenses		(1,413,000)[3]
Cash payments for interest		(79,000)[4]
Cash payment for income tax		(293,500)[5]
Net cash provided by operating activities		1,059,500
Investing activities		
Sale of machinery	$ 270,000	
Purchase of machinery	(825,000)	
Net cash used by investing activities		(555,000)
Financing activities		
Repayment of note payable	$(500,000)	
Issue of common shares	75,000	
Payment of cash dividends	(55,000)	
Net cash used by financing activities		(480,000)

Action Plan

- Determine the net cash provided (used) by operating activities. Operating activities generally relate to revenues and expenses shown on the income statement, which are affected by changes in related noncash current assets and current liabilities in the balance sheet, and noncash items in the income statement.
- Determine the net cash provided (used) by investing activities. Investing activities generally relate to changes in long-term assets.
- Determine the proceeds on sale of machinery by analyzing the accumulated depreciation account to determine the accumulated depreciation on the asset sold. Then calculate the carrying amount, which is then added to the gain to determine proceeds.
- Determine the net cash provided (used) by financing activities. Financing activities generally relate to changes in long-term liability and shareholders' equity accounts.
- Dividends paid are equal to dividends declared plus a decrease in dividends payable or minus an increase in dividends payable.
- Determine the net increase (decrease) in cash and add it to the beginning of period cash balance. Verify that this amount agrees with the end-of-period cash balance reported on the balance sheet.
- Note the similarities and differences between the indirect and direct methods: Both methods report the same total amount of cash provided (used) by operating activities but report different detail in this section. The information in the investing and financing sections is the same in both methods.

Net increase in cash	24,500
Cash, January 1	180,000
Cash, December 31	$ 204,500

Calculations:
[1] $6,583,000 − $165,000 = $6,418,000   [4] $85,000 − $6,000 = $79,000
[2] $3,572,000 − $83,000 + $84,000 = $3,573,000   [5] $298,000 − $4,500 = $293,500
[3] $2,289,000 − $880,000 + $4,000 = $1,413,000

The Navigator

Summary of Study Objectives

1. *Describe the purpose and content of the cash flow statement.* The cash flow statement gives information about the cash receipts and cash payments resulting from the operating, investing, and financing activities of a company during the period.

In general, operating activities include the cash effects of transactions that affect profit. Investing activities generally include cash flows resulting from changes in long-term asset items. Financing activities generally include cash flows resulting from changes in long-term liability and shareholders' equity items.

2. *Prepare a cash flow statement using either the indirect or the direct method.* There are four steps to prepare a cash flow statement: (1) Determine the net cash provided (used) by operating activities. In the indirect method, this is done by converting profit from an accrual basis to a cash basis. In the direct method, this is done by converting each revenue and expense from an accrual basis to a cash basis. (2) Analyze the changes in long-term asset accounts and record them as investing activities,

or as significant noncash transactions. (3) Analyze the changes in long-term liability and equity accounts and record them as financing activities, or as significant noncash transactions. (4) Prepare the cash flow statement and determine the net increase or decrease in cash.

3. *Analyze the cash flow statement.* The cash flow statement must be read along with the other financial statements in order to adequately assess a company's financial position. In addition, it is important to understand how the net change in cash is affected by each type of activity—operating, investing, and financing—especially when different companies are being compared. Free cash flow is a measure of solvency: it indicates how much of the cash that was generated from operating activities during the current year is available after making necessary payments for capital expenditures. It is calculated by subtracting the cash used by investing activities from the cash provided by operating activities.

The Navigator

Glossary

WILEY PLUS   Glossary   Key Term Matching Activity

Cash flow statement A financial statement that gives information about a company's cash receipts and cash payments during a period and classifies them as operating, investing, and financing activities. (p. 932)

Direct method A method of determining the net cash provided (used) by operating activities by adjusting each item in the income statement from the accrual basis to the cash basis. (p. 939)

Financing activities Cash flow activities from long-term liability and equity accounts. These include (a) obtaining cash by issuing debt and repaying the amounts borrowed, and (b) obtaining cash from shareholders and providing them with a return on their investment. (p. 933)

Free cash flow Cash provided by operating activities less cash used by investing activities. (p. 963)

Indirect method A method of preparing a cash flow statement in which profit is adjusted for items that did not affect cash, to determine net cash provided (used) by operating activities. (p. 939)

Investing activities Cash flow activities from long-term asset accounts. These include (a) acquiring and disposing of investments and long-lived assets, and (b) lending money and collecting on those loans. (p. 933)

Operating activities Cash flow activities that include the cash effects of transactions that create revenues and expenses, and thus affect profit. (p. 933)

Self-Study Questions

WILEY PLUS Quizzes

Answers are at the end of the chapter.

(SO 1) C **1.** Which of the following is an example of a cash flow from an operating activity?
(a) A payment of cash to lenders for interest
(b) A receipt of cash from the sale of common shares
(c) A payment of cash dividends to shareholders
(d) A receipt of cash from the issue of a mortgage payable

(SO 1) C **2.** Which of the following is an example of a cash flow from an investing activity?
(a) A receipt of cash from the issue of bonds
(b) A payment of cash to purchase common shares
(c) A receipt of cash from the sale of equipment
(d) The acquisition of land by issuing bonds

(SO 1) C **3.** Which of the following is an example of a cash flow from a financing activity?
(a) A receipt of cash from the sale of land
(b) An issue of debt for land
(c) A payment of dividends
(d) A cash purchase of inventory

(SO 2) AP **4.** Profit is $132,000. During the year, accounts payable increased by $10,000, inventory decreased by $6,000, and accounts receivable increased by $12,000. Under the indirect method, net cash provided by operating activities is:
(a) $104,000.
(b) $128,000.
(c) $136,000.
(d) $146,000.

(SO 2) K **5.** In determining cash provided (used) by operating activities under the indirect method, the items that are added to profit do not include:
(a) depreciation expense.
(b) a gain on the sale of equipment.
(c) a decrease in inventory.
(d) an increase in accounts payable.

(SO 2) AP **6.** The beginning balance in Accounts Receivable is $44,000. The ending balance is $42,000. Sales during the period are $129,000. Cash receipts from customers are:

(a) $127,000.
(b) $129,000.
(c) $131,000.
(d) $130,000.

(SO 2) AP **7.** Retained earnings were $197,000 at the beginning of the year and $386,500 at the end of the year, and profit was $200,000. Dividends payable were $2,000 at the beginning of the year and $2,500 at the end of the year. What amount should be reported in the financing activities section of the cash flow statement for dividend payments?
(a) $500
(b) $10,000
(c) $10,500
(d) $11,000

(SO 2) C **8.** Which of the following items is an example of a noncash investing and financing activity?
(a) A loss on the sale of a building
(b) The purchase of a building, financed by a mortgage payable
(c) Depreciation expense on the building
(d) The refinancing of the interest rate on the mortgage

(SO 3) C **9.** If a company is in its first year of business and is rapidly growing, it would be normal to see:
(a) negative cash from operating and investing activities, and positive cash from financing activities.
(b) negative cash from operating activities, and positive cash from investing and financing activities.
(c) positive cash from operating activities, and negative cash from investing and financing activities.
(d) positive cash from operating and financing activities, and negative cash from investing activities.

(SO 3) K **10.** Free cash flow gives an indication of a company's ability to:
(a) generate sales.
(b) generate profit.
(c) generate cash for discretionary uses.
(d) generate cash for investments.

The Navigator

Questions

(SO 1) C **1.** What is a cash flow statement and how is it useful to investors and creditors?

(SO 1) C **2.** Elisa Botelho maintains that the cash flow statement is an optional financial statement. Do you agree? Explain.

(SO 1) C **3.** What are "cash equivalents"? Should a company include cash equivalents with cash when preparing its cash flow statement?

(SO 1) C **4.** Identify, and describe the differences among, the three types of activities reported in the cash flow statement.

(SO 1) K   5. What are the general guidelines in terms of the re-lating income statement and balance sheet items to operating, investing, and financing activities?

(SO 1) K   6. What are some examples of significant noncash investing and financing transactions? How should they be disclosed?

(SO 1) C   7. At a shareholders' meeting, one of Osman Corpo-ration's shareholders asks why the company's cash flow statement ends with cash at the end of the pe-riod on the balance sheet date and yet the date on the cash flow statement is not the same as the one on the balance sheet—it seems to cover the entire year. Explain why the dates of the two statements are not the same.

(SO 2) C   8. What are the basic differences in how the cash flow statement is prepared in contrast to an income statement or balance sheet? What information is used in preparing the cash flow statement?

(SO 2) C   9. How can a company's cash balance decrease when the company has earned profit? Conversely, how can cash increase when a company has incurred a loss?

(SO 2) C   10. Describe the indirect method for determining net cash provided (used) by operating activities.

(SO 2) K   11. Identify three items under the indirect method that could be adjustments to reconcile profit to net cash provided (used) by operating activities.

(SO 2) C   12. Why and how is depreciation expense reported in a cash flow statement prepared using the indirect method?

(SO 2) C   13. Gail doesn't understand why losses are added and gains are deducted from profit when calculating cash provided (used) by operating activities in the indirect method. She argues that losses must be deducted and gains added as they are on the in-come statement. Explain to Gail why she is wrong.

(SO 2) C   14. Describe the direct method for determining net cash provided (used) by operating activities.

(SO 2) C   15. If a company reports $500,000 of cash collected from customers on its cash flow statement, would it also report $500,000 of sales on its income state-ment? Explain why or why not.

(SO 2) C   16. Under the direct method, why is depreciation ex-pense not reported in the operating activities sec-tion?

(SO 2) C   17. Contrast the advantages and disadvantages of the direct and indirect methods of preparing the cash flow statement. Are both methods acceptable? Which method is preferred by standard setters? Which method is more popular? Why?

(SO 2) C   18. Goh Corporation changed its method of reporting operating activities from the indirect method to the direct method in order to make its cash flow statement more informative to its readers. Will this change increase, decrease, or not affect the net cash provided (used) by operating activities?

(SO 2) C   19. Explain how the sale of equipment at a gain is re-ported on a cash flow statement. Do the same for the sale of equipment at a loss.

(SO 2) C   20. Explain how the redemption of bonds payable at a loss is reported on a cash flow statement. Do the same for the redemption of bonds payable at a gain.

(SO 2) C   21. Explain why changes in short-term notes receivable and notes payable are sometimes reported as operat-ing activities and sometimes as financing activities.

(SO 2) AP   22. David, Barbara, and Zofia were discussing the prep-aration of the cash flow statement of Rock Candy Corp. Rock Candy had purchased $25,000 of ma-chinery during the year. It paid for it with $10,000 cash and financed the remainder with a note pay-able. David thinks that the purchase of the machin-ery should be disclosed as a cash outflow of $25,000 in the investing activities section of the cash flow statement and the note payable should be disclosed as a cash inflow of $15,000 in the financing activi-ties section. Barbara thinks this transaction should be recorded as a cash outflow of $10,000 in the in-vesting activities section for the purchase of equip-ment and the remainder as a significant noncash investing and financing activity in the notes to the statement. Zofia thinks that this transaction should only be disclosed as a significant noncash investing and financing activity in the notes to the statement. Who is correct? Explain.

(SO 3) C   23. In general, should a financially healthy, growing company be providing or using cash in each of the three activities in the cash flow statement? Explain why this would normally be expected.

(SO 3) C   24. Explain how a company's cash flows can indicate whether it is in the early stages of its development or not.

(SO 3) C   25. What does free cash flow indicate, and how is it calculated?

(SO 3) C   26. How is it possible for a company to report positive net cash from operating activities but have a nega-tive free cash flow?

Brief Exercises

BE17–1 For each of the following transactions, indicate whether it will increase (+), decrease (–), or have no effect (NE) on a company's cash flows:

Indicate impact of transactions on cash.
(SO 1) AP

(a) ___ Repayment of a short-term note payable
(b) ___ Sale of land for cash at a loss
(c) ___ Reacquisition of common shares
(d) ___ Purchase of a long-term equity investment
(e) ___ Acquisition of equipment by an issue of common shares
(f) ___ Issuing preferred shares for cash
(g) ___ Distribution of a previously declared stock dividend
(h) ___ Collection of accounts receivable
(i) ___ Recording depreciation expense
(j) ___ Declaring cash dividends

BE17–2 Classify each of the transactions listed in BE17–1 as an operating, investing, financing, or significant noncash investing and financing activity. If a transaction does not belong in any of these classifications, explain why.

Classify transactions by activity.
(SO 1) C

BE17–3 Indicate whether each of the following transactions would be added to (+) or subtracted from (–) profit in determining the cash provided (used) by operating activities using the indirect method:

Indicate impact on cash from operating activities—indirect method.
(SO 2) AP

(a) ___ Depreciation expense
(b) ___ Increase in accounts receivable
(c) ___ Decrease in inventory
(d) ___ Increase in accounts payable
(e) ___ Decrease in income tax payable
(f) ___ Gain on sale of equipment
(g) ___ Loss on the sale of long-term equity investment
(h) ___ Impairment loss for goodwill
(i) ___ Amortization of a premium on a long-term investment in bonds

BE17–4 Crystal Inc. reported profit of $775,000 for the year ended November 30, 2011. Depreciation expense for the year was $250,000, accounts receivable increased by $150,000, prepaid expenses decreased by $95,000, accounts payable increased by $280,000, and the company incurred a gain on sale of equipment of $25,000. Calculate the net cash provided (used) by operating activities using the indirect method.

Calculate cash from operating activities—indirect method.
(SO 2) AP

BE17–5 The comparative balance sheet for Dupigne Corporation shows the following noncash current asset and current liability accounts at March 31:

Calculate cash from operating activities—indirect method.
(SO 2) AP

	2011	2010
Accounts receivable	$40,000	$60,000
Inventory	70,000	63,000
Prepaid expenses	6,000	4,000
Accounts payable	40,000	35,000
Income tax payable	10,000	16,000

Dupigne's income statement reported the following selected information for the year ended March 31, 2011: profit was $250,000, depreciation expense was $60,000, and there was a loss on sale of equipment of $24,500. Calculate the net cash provided (used) by operating activities using the indirect method.

BE17–6   Westcoast Corporation has accounts receivable of $28,000 at December 31, 2010, and of $19,000 at December 31, 2011. Sales revenues were $275,000 for 2011. Calculate the cash receipts from customers.

BE17–7   Winter Sportswear Inc. reported a cost of goods sold of $89,500 on its income statement. It also reported an increase in inventory of $5,600 and an increase in accounts payable of $7,200 for the same period. Calculate the cash payments to suppliers.

BE17–8   For the current year, Linus Corporation reports operating expenses of $100,000, including depreciation expense of $15,000. At the beginning of the year, prepaid expenses were $12,500 and accrued expenses payable were $8,500. At the end of the year, prepaid expenses were $23,400 and accrued expenses payable were $14,900. Calculate the cash payments for operating expenses.

BE17–9   ICE Inc. reported salary expense of $198,000 on its 2011 income statement. It also reported salaries payable of $2,500 at December 31, 2010, and of $3,000 at December 31, 2011. Calculate the cash payments to employees.

BE17–10   Home Grocery Corporation reported income tax expense of $90,000 in its 2011 income statement. It also reported income tax payable of $17,000 at December 31, 2010, and of $8,000 at December 31, 2011. Calculate the cash payments for income tax.

BE17–11   Angus Meat Corporation reported the following information for the year ended December 31:

Balance sheet accounts:	2011	2010	Income statement accounts:	
Accounts receivable	$85,000	$60,000	Sales	$375,000
Inventory	62,000	55,000	Gain on sale of land	15,000
Prepaid expenses	5,000	9,000	Cost of goods sold	150,000
Accounts payable	35,000	42,000	Operating expenses	75,000
Income tax payable	14,000	9,000	Depreciation expense	20,000
			Income tax expense	50,000

Calculate the net cash provided (used) by operating activities using the direct method.

BE17–12   The T accounts for equipment and the related accumulated depreciation for Trevis Corporation are as follows:

Equipment				Accumulated Depreciation—Equipment			
Beg. Bal.	80,000					Beg. bal.	44,500
Acquisitions	41,600	Disposals	24,000	Disposals	5,500	Depreciation	12,000
End. Bal.	97,600					End. bal.	51,000

In addition, Trevis's income statement reported a loss on the sale of equipment of $1,500. (a) What will be reported on the cash flow statement with regard to the sale of equipment if Trevis uses the indirect method? (b) If Trevis uses the direct method?

BE17–13   Select information follows for Cathrea Select Corporation at December 31:

	2011	2010
Land	$ 95,000	$180,000
Buildings	250,000	250,000
Accumulated depreciation—buildings	(55,000)	(45,000)
Equipment	237,000	148,000
Accumulated depreciation—equipment	(86,000)	(78,000)

Additional information:

1. Land was sold for cash at a gain of $35,000.
2. Equipment was bought for cash.

3. Equipment with a cost of $58,000 and a carrying amount of $18,000 was sold at a gain of $5,000.

Calculate cash provided (used) by investing activities.

BE17–14 Canadian Tire Corporation, Limited reported profit of $374.2 million for the year ended December 31, 2008. Its retained earnings were $2,455.1 million on December 31, 2007, and $2,755.5 million on December 31, 2008. It also repurchased shares, which resulted in a $5.4-million reduction to retained earnings in 2008. Calculate the dividends paid by Canadian Tire in 2008, assuming there were no dividends payable at the beginning or end of the year.

Calculate cash paid for dividends.
(SO 2) AP

BE17–15 Select information follows for Cathrea Select Corporation at December 31:

Calculate cash provided (used) by financing activities.
(SO 2) AP

	2011	2010
Dividends payable	$ 20,000	$ 15,000
Bonds payable	995,000	990,000
Mortgage notes payable	475,000	200,000
Common shares	55,000	45,000
Retained earnings	165,000	85,000

Additional information:

1. Interest expense on the bonds payable was $55,000, which included $5,000 of amortization of the bond discount.
2. Principal payments on the mortgage payable were $25,000.
3. A building was purchased for $500,000 by paying $200,000 cash and signing a mortgage note payable for the balance.
4. Profit for the year was $145,000.

Calculate cash provided (used) by financing activities.

BE17–16 The following information is available for Baker Corporation for the year ended April 30, 2011:

Prepare cash flow statement.
(SO 2) AP

Cash, May 1, 2010	$ 8,500
Cash provided by operating activities	49,000
Cash receipts	
Sale of equipment at a loss of $1,200	6,000
Issue of non-trade note payable	20,000
Issue of $75,000 mortgage note payable to partially finance purchase of land for $100,000	75,000
Cash payments	
Dividends	25,000
Reacquisition of common shares	19,000
Purchase of land for $100,000, partially financed by issuing a $75,000 mortgage note payable	100,000

Prepare a cash flow statement for the year, including any required note disclosure.

BE17–17 Two companies reported the following information.

Use cash flows to identify new company.
(SO 3) AN

	Company A	Company B
Profit (loss)	$ (5,000)	$100,000
Cash provided (used) by operating activities	(10,000)	50,000
Cash provided (used) by investing activities	(70,000)	30,000
Cash provided (used) by financing activities	120,000	(100,000)

Which company is more likely to be in the early stages of its development? Explain.

Calculate free cash flow.
(SO 3) AP

BE17–18   Svetlana Limited reported cash provided by operating activities of $300,000, cash used by investing activities of $250,000, and cash provided by financing activities of $70,000. Calculate Svetlana's free cash flow.

Exercises

Classify transactions.
(SO 1) AP

E17–1   A list of cash transactions follows:

Transaction	(a)	(b)	(c)
1. Purchased land.	– Cash	Land	Investing
2. Paid dividends.			
3. Sold a building.			
4. Retired bonds at maturity.			
5. Sold a long-term equity investment.			
6. Paid employee salaries.			
7. Paid interest on a mortgage note payable.			
8. Sold inventory on account.			
9. Collected an account receivable.			
10. Paid an account payable.			
11. Provided services to a customer.			
12. Paid income taxes owing.			

Instructions

Compete the above table indicating for each transaction (a) whether it increases (+) or decreases (–) cash, (b) what other account is affected in the transactions besides cash, and (c) where the transaction should be classified on the cash flow statement. The first one has been completed for you as an example.

Classify transactions.
(SO 1) AP

E17–2   Eng Corporation had the following transactions:

Transaction	(a) Classification	(b) Cash Inflow or Outflow
1. Sold inventory for $1,000 cash.	O	+$1,000
2. Purchased a machine for $30,000. Made a $5,000 down payment and issued a long-term note for the remainder.		
3. Issued common shares for $50,000.		
4. Collected $16,000 of accounts receivable.		
5. Paid a $25,000 cash dividend.		
6. Sold a long-term equity investment with a carrying value of $15,000 for $10,000.		
7. Redeemed bonds having an amortized cost of $200,000 for $175,000.		
8. Paid $18,000 on accounts payable.		
9. Purchased inventory for $28,000 on account.		
10. Purchased a long-term investment in bonds for $100,000.		
11. Sold equipment with a carrying amount of $16,000 for $13,000.		
12. Paid $12,000 interest expense on long-term notes payable.		

Instructions

Complete the above table indicating whether each transaction (a) should be classified as an operating activity (O), investing activity (I), financing activity (F), or noncash transaction (NC); and (b) represents a cash inflow (+), cash outflow (−), or has no effect (NE) on cash, and in what amount. The first one has been done for you as an example.

E17–3   IROC Corporation had the following transactions.

Indicate impact on profit and cash from operating activities.
(SO 2) AP

Transaction	(a) Profit	(b) Cash Provided (Used) by Operating Activities
1. Sold inventory for cash at a price higher than cost.	+	+
2. Sold inventory on account at a price less than cost.		
3. Purchased inventory on account.		
4. Accrued income tax payable.		
5. Paid income taxes.		
6. Purchased supplies for cash.		
7. Recorded depreciation expense.		
8. Paid an amount owing on account.		
9. Collected an amount owing from a customer.		
10. Paid a one-year insurance policy in advance.		
11. Sold land for cash at a price higher than cost.		
12. Paid a cash dividend.		

Instructions

Identify whether each of the above transactions will increase (+), decrease (−), or have no effect (NE) on (a) profit and (b) net cash provided (used) by operating activities. The first one has been completed for you as an example.

E17–4   Pesci Ltd.'s income statement and changes in current assets and current liabilities for the year are reported below:

Prepare operating activities section—indirect method.
(SO 2) AP

PESCI LTD. Income Statement Year Ended November 30, 2011		
Sales		$948,000
Cost of goods sold		490,000
Gross profit		458,000
Operating expenses	$310,000	
Depreciation expense	50,000	
Loss on sale of equipment	10,000	370,000
Profit before income tax		88,000
Income tax expense		30,000
Profit		$ 58,000
Changes in current assets and current liabilities were as follows:		
Accounts receivable	$36,000	increase
Inventory	19,000	decrease
Prepaid expense	2,000	decrease
Accounts payable	12,000	increase
Dividends payable	5,000	decrease
Income taxes payable	4,000	decrease

Instructions

Prepare the operating activities section of the cash flow statement, using the indirect method.

Prepare operating activities
section—indirect method.
(SO 2) AP

E17–5 The current assets and liabilities sections of Barth Inc.'s comparative balance sheets at December 31 are presented below:

BARTH INC.		
Comparative Balance Sheet Accounts		
	2011	2010
Cash	$105,000	$ 99,000
Accounts receivable	89,000	120,000
Inventory	126,000	95,000
Prepaid expenses	27,000	32,000
Accounts payable	65,000	73,000
Accrued expenses payable	15,000	5,000
Dividends payable	85,000	92,000
Income taxes payable	14,000	10,500

BARTH INC.		
Income Statement		
Year Ended December 31, 2011		
Sales		$565,000
Cost of goods sold		310,000
Gross profit		255,000
Operating expenses	$95,000	
Depreciation expense	42,000	
Gain on sale of land	(12,000)	125,000
Profit before income taxes		130,000
Income taxes		32,500
Profit		$ 97,500

Instructions

Prepare the operating activities section of the cash flow statement, using the indirect method.

Indicate impact on cash
from operating activities—
direct method.
(SO 2) AP

E17–6 You are provided with the following transactions:

	(a)	(b)	(c)
		Add to (+) or Deduct	
	Related Income	from (−) Income	Related Cash
Transaction	Statement Account(s)	Statement Account	Receipt or Payment
1. Increase in accounts receivable	Sales revenue	−	Cash receipts from customers
2. Decrease in accounts receivable	_____	_____	_____
3. Increase in accounts payable	_____	_____	_____
4. Decrease in interest payable	_____	_____	_____
5. Increase in prepaid expenses	_____	_____	_____
6. Increase in inventory	_____	_____	_____
7. Decrease in inventory	_____	_____	_____
8. Increase in income tax payable	_____	_____	_____
9. Increase in salaries payable	_____	_____	_____
10. Decrease in accrued expenses payable	_____	_____	_____

Instructions

Under the direct method, net cash provided (used) by operating activities is calculated by adjusting each item in the income statement from the accrual basis to the cash basis. For each transaction, do the following: (a) Identify the related income statement account. (b) Indicate if the transaction should be added to or deducted from the related income statement account to convert profit to cash from operating activities. (c) State the title of the resulting cash receipt or payment category that is reported on the cash flow statement. The first transaction has been done for you as an example.

E17–7 The following information is taken from the general ledger of Robinson Limited:

Calculate operating cash flows—direct method.
(SO 2) AP

(a) Sales revenue | $275,000
Accounts receivable, January 1 | 22,900
Accounts receivable, December 31 | 37,000

(b) Cost of goods sold | $110,000
Inventory, January 1 | 9,200
Inventory, December 31 | 5,900
Accounts payable, January 1 | 12,400
Accounts payable, December 31 | 13,750

(c) Operating expenses | $ 50,000
Depreciation expense | 15,000
Prepaid expenses, January 1 | 5,500
Prepaid expenses, December 31 | 3,000
Accrued expenses payable, January 1 | 4,500
Accrued expenses payable, December 31 | 6,500

(d) Interest expense | $ 18,000
Interest payable, January 1 | 4,000
Interest payable, December 31 | 4,000
Bonds payable, January 1 | 395,000
Bonds payable, December 31 | 397,000

Instructions

Using the direct method, calculate (a) the cash receipts from customers, (b) the cash payments to suppliers, (c) the cash payments for operating expenses, and (d) the cash payments for interest expense.

E17–8 McGillis Ltd. completed its first year of operations on October 31, 2011. McGillis reported the following information at October 31, 2011:

Prepare operating activities section—direct method.
(SO 2) AP

McGILLIS LTD.
Income Statement
Year Ended October 31, 2011

Service revenue | | $182,000
Operating expenses | $88,000 |
Depreciation expense | 14,500 |
Loss on sale of equipment | 5,750 | 108,250
Profit from operations | | 73,750
Interest expense | | 10,000
Profit before income tax | | 63,750
Income tax expense | | 15,000
Profit | | $ 48,750

McGILLIS LTD.
Selected Account Balances at October 31, 2011

Accounts receivable | $42,000
Prepaid expenses | 4,400
Accounts payable | 33,000
Interest payable | 1,100
Dividends payable | 2,500
Income taxes payable | 1,500

Instructions

Assuming that the accounts payable related to operating expenses, prepare the operating section of a cash flow statement using the direct method.

Prepare operating activities
section—direct method.
(SO 2) AP

E17–9   The income statement and account balances for Barth Inc. are presented in E17–5.

Instructions

Prepare the operating section of a cash flow statement using the direct method.

Determine investing and
financing activities.
(SO 2) AP

E17–10   The following selected accounts are from Dupré Corp.'s general ledger for the year ended December 31, 2011:

Equipment				Accumulated Depreciation—Equipment			
Jan. 1	160,000					Jan. 1	71,000
July 31	70,000	Nov. 10	39,000	Nov. 10	30,000		
Sept. 2	53,000					Dec. 31	28,000
Dec. 31	244,000					Dec. 31	69,000

Notes Payable				Retained Earnings			
		Jan. 1	0			Jan. 1	105,000
Dec. 2	5,000	Sept. 2	45,000	Aug. 23	4,000	Dec. 31	67,000
		Dec. 31	40,000			Dec. 31	168,000

Additional information:

July 31   Equipment was purchased for cash.
Sept. 2   Equipment was purchased and partially financed through the issue of a note.
Aug. 23   A cash dividend was paid.
Nov. 10   A loss of $3,000 was incurred on the sale of equipment.
Dec. 2   A partial payment on the note payable was made plus $375 of interest.
Dec. 31   Depreciation expense was recorded for the year.
Dec. 31   Closing entries were recorded.

Instructions

From the postings in the above accounts and additional information provided, indicate what information would be reported in the investing and/or financing activities sections of the cash flow statement, including any required note disclosure.

Prepare cash flow statement—
indirect method.
(SO 2) AP

E17–11   Savary Limited's comparative balance sheet at December 31 is as follows:

SAVARY LIMITED Balance Sheet December 31		
Assets	2011	2010
Cash	$ 114,000	$ 85,000
Accounts receivable	750,000	600,000
Inventory	500,000	330,000
Prepaid insurance	18,000	25,000
Equipment and vehicles	1,250,000	1,000,000
Accumulated depreciation	(350,000)	(280,000)
Total assets	$2,282,000	$1,760,000
Liabilities and Shareholders' Equity		
Accounts payable	$ 226,000	$ 200,000
Salaries payable	30,000	40,000
Interest payable	26,000	20,000
Notes payable (non-trade)	500,000	350,000
Preferred shares	200,000	0
Common shares	400,000	400,000
Retained earnings	900,000	750,000
Total liabilities and shareholders' equity	$2,282,000	$1,760,000

Additional information:

1. Profit for 2011 was $200,000.
2. Equipment was purchased during the year. No equipment was sold.
3. Cash dividends were paid to the preferred shareholders during the year.

Instructions

Prepare the cash flow statement, using the indirect method.

E17–12   The accounting records of Flypaper Airlines Inc. reveal the following transactions and events for the year ended March 31, 2011:

Payment of interest	$ 10,000	Payment of salaries	$ 53,000
Cash sales	48,000	Depreciation expense	16,000
Receipt of dividend revenue	14,000	Proceeds from sale of aircraft	212,000
Payment of income tax	7,500	Purchase of equipment for cash	22,000
Profit	38,000	Loss on sale of aircraft	3,000
Payment of accounts payable	110,000	Payment of dividends	14,000
Payment for land	174,000	Payment of operating expenses	28,000
Collection of accounts receivable	192,000		

Prepare cash flow statement—direct method.
(SO 2) AP

Additional information:
Flypaper Airlines' cash on April 1, 2010, was $35,000.

Instructions

Prepare a cash flow statement, using the direct method.

E17–13   The comparative balance sheet for Puffy Ltd. follows:

Prepare cash flow statement—indirect and direct methods.
(SO 2) AP

PUFFY LTD. Balance Sheet December 31		
Assets	**2011**	**2010**
Cash	$ 69,000	$ 24,500
Accounts receivable	85,000	76,000
Inventories	180,000	189,000
Land	75,000	100,000
Equipment	260,000	200,000
Accumulated depreciation	(66,000)	(32,000)
Total assets	$603,000	$557,500
Liabilities and Shareholders' Equity		
Accounts payable	$ 38,000	$ 47,000
Income taxes payable	6,000	2,500
Bonds payable	120,000	200,000
Common shares	209,000	174,000
Retained earnings	230,000	134,000
Total liabilities and shareholders' equity	$603,000	$557,500

Additional information:

1. Profit for 2011 was $115,000.
2. Bonds payable amounting to $80,000 were retired at maturity.
3. Common shares were issued for $35,000.
4. Land was sold at a gain of $5,000.
5. No equipment was sold during 2011.
6. Net sales for the year were $978,000.
7. Cost of goods sold for the year was $751,000.
8. Operating expenses (not including depreciation expense) were $43,000.
9. Income tax expense was $40,000.

Instructions

Prepare a cash flow statement using (a) the indirect method or (b) the direct method, as assigned by your instructor.

Compare cash flows for two companies.
(SO 3) AN

E17–14   Condensed cash flow statements are as follows for two companies operating in the same industry:

	Company A	Company B
Cash provided (used) by operating activities	$200,000	$(180,000)
Cash provided (used) by investing activities	(20,000)	(20,000)
Cash provided (used) by financing activities	(60,000)	320,000
Increase in cash	120,000	120,000
Cash, beginning of period	30,000	30,000
Cash, end of period	$150,000	$ 150,000

Instructions

Which company is in a better financial position? Explain why.

Calculate and discuss free cash flow.
(SO 3) AN

E17–15   Selected information follows for Bank of Montreal and Scotiabank (in millions):

	Bank of Montreal	Scotiabank
Profit	$ 1,978	$ 3,140
Cash provided (used) by operating activities	4,246	20,112
Cash provided (used) by investing activities	11,047	(51,740)

Instructions

(a) Calculate the free cash flow for each company.

(b) Which company appears to be in a stronger financial position? Explain.

(c) In what way might a bank's free cash flow be different from the free cash flow of a manufacturing company?

Problems: Set A

Classify transactions by activity. Indicate impact on cash and profit.
(SO 1) AP

P17–1A   You are provided with the following transactions that took place during a recent fiscal year:

Transaction	(a) Classification	(b) Cash	(c) Profit
1. Paid telephone bill for the month.	O	–	–
2. Sold equipment for cash, at a loss.			
3. Sold a short-term equity investment, at a gain.			
4. Acquired a building by paying 10% in cash and signing a mortgage payable for the balance.			
5. Made principal repayments on the mortgage.			
6. Paid interest on the mortgage.			
7. Sold inventory on account, at a price greater than cost.			
8. Paid wages owing (previously accrued) to employees.			
9. Declared and distributed a stock dividend to common shareholders.			
10. Paid rent in advance.			

11. Sold inventory for cash, at a price greater
    than cost.   _____ _____ _____
12. Wrote down the value of inventory to net
    realizable value, which was lower than cost. _____ _____ _____
13. Received semi-annual bond interest.   _____ _____ _____
14. Received dividends on an equity method
    investment.   _____ _____ _____
15. Issued common shares.   _____ _____ _____
16. Paid a cash dividend to common shareholders. _____ _____ _____
17. Collected cash from customers on account. _____ _____ _____
18. Collected service revenue in advance.   _____ _____ _____

Instructions

Complete the above table for each of the following requirements. The first one has been done for you as an example.

(a) Classify each transaction as an operating activity (O), an investing activity (I), a financing activity (F), or a noncash transaction (NC) on the cash flow statement.

(b) Specify whether the transaction will increase (+), decrease (–), or have no effect (NE) on cash reported on the balance sheet.

(c) Specify whether the transaction will increase (+), decrease (–), or have no effect (NE) on profit reported on the income statement.

Taking It Further Explain how an operating activity can increase cash but not increase profit.

P17–2A The income statement of Breckenridge Ltd. follows:

Prepare operating activities section—indirect and direct methods.
(SO 2) AP

BRECKENRIDGE LTD. Income Statement Year Ended November 30, 2011		
Sales		$820,000
Cost of goods sold		490,000
Gross profit		330,000
Operating expenses	$206,000	
Depreciation expense	25,000	
Loss on sale of land	35,000	266,000
Profit before income tax		64,000
Income tax expense		16,000
Profit		$ 48,000

Additional information:

1. Accounts receivable increased by $20,000 during the year.
2. Prepaid expenses increased by $15,000 during the year.
3. Accounts payable to suppliers decreased by $30,000 during the year.
4. Accrued expenses payable decreased by $10,000 during the year.
5. Income tax payable increased by $2,000 during the year.

Instructions

Prepare the operating activities section of the cash flow statement, using (a) the indirect method or (b) the direct method, as assigned by your instructor.

Taking It Further In what circumstances will the direct method result in a different amount of cash provided (used) by operations than the indirect method?

Prepare operating activities
section—indirect and
direct methods.
(SO 2) AP

P17–3A   The income statement of Hanalei International Inc. contained the following condensed information:

HANALEI INTERNATIONAL INC. Income Statement Year Ended December 31, 2011		
Service revenue		$480,000
Operating expenses	$245,000	
Depreciation expense	35,000	
Gain on sale of equipment	(25,000)	255,000
Profit from operations		225,000
Other revenues and expenses		
Interest expense		10,000
Profit before income taxes		215,000
Income tax expense		53,750
Profit		$ 161,250

Hanalei's balance sheet contained the following comparative data at December 31:

	2011	2010
Accounts receivable	$40,000	$52,000
Prepaid insurance	8,000	5,000
Accounts payable	30,000	41,000
Interest payable	2,000	1,250
Income tax payable	4,500	3,000
Unearned revenue	12,000	8,000

Additional information: Accounts payable relate to operating expenses.

Instructions

Prepare the operating activities section of the cash flow statement, using (a) the indirect method or (b) the direct method, as assigned by your instructor.

Taking It Further   What are the advantages and disadvantages of the direct method of determining cash provided (used) by operating activities?

Calculate cash flows for
investing activities.
(SO 2) AP

P17–4A   The following selected account balances relate to the property, plant, and equipment accounts of Trudeau Inc. at year end:

	2011	2010
Accumulated depreciation—buildings	$307,500	$300,000
Accumulated depreciation—equipment	124,000	94,000
Depreciation expense—buildings	25,000	42,500
Depreciation expense—equipment	49,125	27,000
Gain on sale of equipment	1,000	0
Loss on sale of building	10,000	0
Buildings	850,000	750,000
Equipment	393,000	340,000
Land	100,000	60,000

Additional information:

1. Purchased $75,000 of equipment for $10,000 cash and a note payable for the remainder.
2. Equipment was also sold during the year.
3. Sold a building that originally cost $50,000.
4. Used cash to purchase land and a building.

Instructions

Determine the amount of any cash inflows or outflows related to investing activities in 2011.

Taking It Further   Is it unfavourable for a company to have a net cash outflow from investing activities?

P17–5A   The following selected account balances relate to the shareholders' equity accounts of Valerio Corp. at year end:

Calculate cash flows for financing activities.
(SO 2) AP

	2011	2010
Dividends payable	$ 6,250	$ 2,500
Bonds payable	590,000	585,000
Mortgage notes payable	375,000	310,000
Preferred shares: 2,250 shares in 2011; 2,750 in 2010	225,000	275,000
Common shares: 54,000 shares in 2011; 40,000 in 2010	540,000	410,000
Contributed capital—reacquisition of common shares	2,000	0
Retained earnings	200,000	100,000
Cash dividends declared	25,000	10,000
Interest expense	48,250	44,750

Additional information for 2011:

1. Included in interest expense is amortization of the bond payable discount, $5,000.
2. A mortgage note payable for $100,000 was issued for the purchase of equipment.
3. Mortgage payments included interest and principal amounts.
4. Converted 500 preferred shares to 5,000 common shares.
5. Common shares were issued for cash.
6. Reacquired 1,000 common shares with an average cost of $10/share for cash during the year.

Instructions

(a) What was the amount of profit reported by Valerio in 2011?
(b) Determine the amount of any cash inflows or outflows related to financing activities in 2011.
(c) Identify and determine the amount of any noncash financing activities in 2011.

Taking It Further   Is it unfavourable for a company to have a net cash outflow from financing activities?

P17–6A   Condensed financial data follow for E-Perform Ltd.:

Prepare cash flow statement—indirect method.
(SO 2) AP

E-PERFORM LTD.
Balance Sheet
December 31

Assets	2011	2010
Cash	$ 97,800	$ 48,400
Accounts receivable	75,800	43,000
Inventory	122,500	92,850
Prepaid expenses	38,400	26,000
Long-term equity investment	128,000	114,000
Property, plant, and equipment	270,000	242,500
Accumulated depreciation	(50,000)	(52,000)
Total assets	$682,500	$514,750
Liabilities and Shareholders' Equity		
Accounts payable	$ 93,000	$ 77,300
Accrued expenses payable	11,500	7,000
Notes payable (non-trade)	110,000	150,000
Common shares	220,000	175,000
Retained earnings	234,000	105,450
Accumulated other comprehensive income	14,000	0
Total liabilities and shareholders' equity	$682,500	$514,750

```
                              E-PERFORM LTD.
                              Income Statement
                        Year Ended December 31, 2011
  Sales                                                          $492,780
  Cost of goods sold                                              185,460
  Gross profit                                                    307,320
  Operating expenses                              $62,410
  Depreciation expense                             46,500
  Loss on sale of equipment                         7,500         116,410
  Profit from operations                                          190,910
  Other expenses
  Interest expense                                                  4,730
  Profit before income tax                                        186,180
  Income tax expense                                               45,000
  Profit                                                        $ 141,180
```

Additional information:

1. New equipment costing $85,000 was purchased for $25,000 cash and a $60,000 note payable.
2. Equipment with an original cost of $57,500 was sold at a loss of $7,500.
3. Notes payable matured during the year and were repaid.
4. E-Perform records any gains and losses on its long-term equity investment as other comprehensive income. There were no purchases or sales of long-term equity investments during the year.

Instructions

Prepare a cash flow statement for the year using the indirect method.

Taking It Further   If a company has a loss, does that also mean that there has been a net reduction in cash from operating activities? Explain.

Prepare cash flow statement— direct method.
(SO 2) AP

P17–7A   Refer to the information presented for E-Perform Ltd. in P17–6A.

Additional information:

1. Accounts payable relate only to merchandise creditors.
2. Accrued expenses payable and prepaid expenses relate to operating expenses.

Instructions

Prepare a cash flow statement for the year using the direct method.

Taking It Further   E-Perform Ltd.'s cash balance more than doubled in 2011. Briefly explain what caused this, using the cash flow statement.

Prepare cash flow statement— indirect method.
(SO 2) AP

P17–8A   The financial statements of Wetaskiwin Ltd. follow:

WETASKIWIN LTD. Balance Sheet December 31		
Assets	2011	2010
Cash	$ 9,000	$ 10,000
Short-term notes receivable	14,000	23,000
Accounts receivable	28,000	14,000
Inventory	29,000	25,000
Property, plant, and equipment	73,000	78,000
Accumulated depreciation	(30,000)	(24,000)
Total assets	$123,000	$126,000

Liabilities and Shareholders' Equity		
Accounts payable	$ 25,000	$ 43,000
Income tax payable	3,000	20,000
Notes payable	15,000	10,000
Common shares	25,000	25,000
Retained earnings	55,000	28,000
Total liabilities and shareholders' equity	$123,000	$126,000

WETASKIWIN LTD.
Income Statement
Year Ended December 31, 2011

Sales		$286,000
Cost of goods sold		194,000
Gross profit		92,000
Operating expenses	$38,000	
Loss on sale of equipment	2,000	40,000
Profit from operations		52,000
Other revenues and expenses		
Interest revenue	$(1,000)	
Interest expense	2,000	1,000
Profit before income tax		51,000
Income tax expense		15,000
Profit		$ 36,000

Additional information:

1. Short-term notes receivable are from loans to other companies. During the year, the company collected the outstanding balance at December 31, 2010, and made new loans in the amount of $14,000.
2. Equipment was sold during the year. This equipment cost $15,000 originally and had a carrying amount of $10,000 at the time of sale.
3. Equipment costing $10,000 was purchased in exchange for a $10,000 note payable.
4. Depreciation expense is included in operating expenses.

Instructions

Prepare a cash flow statement for the year using the indirect method.

Taking It Further Wetaskiwin Ltd. had a relatively small change in its cash balance in 2011; cash decreased by only $1,000. Is it still necessary or important to prepare a cash flow statement? Explain.

P17–9A   Refer to the information presented Wetaskiwin Ltd. in P17–8A.

Additional information:

1. Accounts receivable are from the sale of merchandise on credit.
2. Accounts payable relate to the purchase of merchandise on credit.

Instructions

Prepare a cash flow statement for the year using the direct method.

Taking It Further Wetaskiwin Ltd. had a positive cash balance at the beginning and end of 2011. Given that, is it possible that the company could have had a negative cash balance at one or more points during the year? Explain.

Prepare cash flow statement—direct method.
(SO 2) AP

Prepare cash flow statement—
indirect method.
(SO 2) AP

P17–10A   Presented below is the comparative balance sheet for Diatessaron Inc. at December 31, 2011, and 2010:

DIATESSARON INC.
Balance Sheet
December 31

Assets	2011	2010
Cash	$ 67,000	$ 98,000
Accounts receivable	101,000	75,000
Inventory	205,000	143,000
Long-term debt investment	98,000	0
Property, plant and equipment	560,000	460,000
Less: Accumulated depreciation	(162,500)	(140,000)
	$868,500	$636,000
Liabilities and Shareholders' Equity		
Accounts payable	$ 87,500	$ 65,000
Dividends payable	6,000	0
Income tax payable	14,000	16,000
Long-term notes payable	45,000	0
Common shares	650,000	525,000
Retained earnings	66,000	30,000
	$868,500	$636,000

DIATESSARON INC.
Income Statement
Year Ended December 31, 2011

Sales		$632,000
Cost of goods sold		429,000
Gross profit		203,000
Operating expenses	$147,500	
Loss on sale of equipment	2,000	149,500
Profit from operations		53,500
Interest expense	$ 3,000	
Interest revenue	(5,500)	(2,500)
Profit before income tax		56,000
Income tax expense		14,000
Profit		$ 42,000

Additional information:

1. Cash dividends of $6,000 were declared on December 30, 2011, payable on January 15, 2012.
2. A long-term debt investment was acquired for cash at a cost of $97,500.
3. Depreciation expense is included in the operating expenses.
4. The company issued 12,500 common shares for cash on March 2, 2011. The fair value of the shares was $10 per share. The proceeds were used to purchase additional equipment.
5. Equipment that originally cost $25,000 was sold during the year for cash. The equipment had a net book value of $9,000 at the time of sale.
6. The company issued a note payable for $50,000 and repaid $5,000 by year end.

Instructions

Prepare a cash flow statement for the year using the indirect method.

Taking It Further   Is it necessary to show both the proceeds from issuing a new note payable and the partial repayment of notes payable? Or is it sufficient to simply show the net increase or decrease in notes payable, as is done with accounts payable? Explain.

P17–11A Refer to the information presented for Diatessaron Inc. in P17–10A.

Prepare cash flow statement—direct method.
(SO 2) AP

Additional information:

1. All purchases of inventory are on credit.
2. Accounts payable is used only to record purchases of inventory.

Instructions

Prepare a cash flow statement for the year using the direct method.

Taking It Further Why is it necessary to know that accounts payable is used for purchases of inventory when using the direct method, but not the indirect method?

P17–12A Selected information (in US$ millions) for two close competitors, Potash Corporation of Saskatchewan Inc. and Agrium Inc., follows for the year ended December 31, 2008:

Calculate free cash flow and evaluate cash.
(SO 3) AN

	Potash	Agrium
Profit	$3,495	$ 1,322
Cash provided by operating activities	3,013	1,044
Cash used by investing activities	(1,647)	(3,375)
Cash used by financing activities	(1,809)	1,196
Cash and cash equivalents, end of period	277	374

Instructions

(a) Calculate the free cash flow for each company.
(b) Which company appears to be in the stronger financial position?

Taking It Further By comparing the companies' cash flows, can you tell which company is likely in a growth stage? Explain.

Problems: Set B

P17–1B You are provided with the following transactions that took place during a recent fiscal year:

Classify transactions by activity. Indicate impact on cash and profit.
(SO 1) AP

Transaction	(a) Classification	(b) Cash	(c) Profit
1. Paid wages to employees.	O	–	–
2. Sold land for cash, at a gain.			
3. Acquired land by issuing common shares.			
4. Paid a cash dividend to preferred shareholders.			
5. Performed services for cash.			
6. Performed services on account.			
7. Purchased inventory for cash.			
8. Purchased inventory on account.			
9. Paid income tax.			
10. Made principal repayment on a trade note payable.			
11. Paid semi-annual bond interest.			
12. Received rent from a tenant in advance.			
13. Recorded depreciation expense.			
14. Reacquired common shares at a price greater than the average cost of the shares.			

15. Sold preferred shares for cash. ___ ___ ___
16. Collected cash from customers on account. ___ ___ ___
17. Issued a non-trade note payable. ___ ___ ___
18. Paid insurance for the month. ___ ___ ___

Instructions

Complete the above table for each of the following requirements, assuming none of the transactions were previously accrued. The first one has been done for you as an example.

(a) Classify each transaction as an operating activity (O), an investing activity (I), a financing activity (F), or a noncash transaction (NC) on the cash flow statement.

(b) Specify whether the transaction will increase (+), decrease (−), or have no effect (NE) on cash reported on the balance sheet.

(c) Specify whether the transaction will increase (+), decrease (−), or have no effect (NE) on profit reported on the income statement.

Taking It Further   Explain how an operating activity can decrease cash but not decrease profit.

Prepare operating activities section—indirect and direct methods.
(SO 2) AP

P17–2B   The income statement of Gum San Ltd. follows:

GUM SAN LTD.
Income Statement
Year Ended April 30, 2011

Sales		$540,000
Cost of goods sold		329,000
Gross profit		211,000
Operating expenses	$92,500	
Depreciation expense	14,500	
Gain on sale of equipment	(9,500)	97,500
Profit from operations		113,500
Other revenues		
Interest revenue		7,500
Profit before income taxes		121,000
Income tax expense		36,300
Profit		$ 84,700

Additional information:

1. Accounts receivable increased by $31,000 during the year.
2. Inventory decreased by $22,000 during the year.
3. Prepaid expenses increased by $17,000 during the year.
4. Accounts payable to suppliers increased by $25,000 during the year.
5. Accrued expenses payable decreased by $16,500 during the year.
6. Income tax payable increased by $3,300 during the year.

Instructions

Prepare the operating activities section of the cash flow statement, using (a) the indirect method or (b) the direct method, as assigned by your instructor.

Taking It Further   Will the amount of cash provided (used) by operations always be the same amount if it is determined by using the direct method or the indirect method? Explain.

P17–3B Sable Island Ltd.'s income statement contained the following condensed information:

Prepare operating activities section—indirect and direct methods.
(SO 2) AP

SABLE ISLAND LTD. Income Statement Year Ended December 31, 2011		
Fee revenue		$900,000
Operating expenses	$642,000	
Depreciation expense	50,000	
Loss on sale of equipment	23,000	715,000
Profit from operations		185,000
Other expenses		
Interest expense		5,000
Profit before income tax		180,000
Income tax expense		45,000
Profit		$ 135,000

Sable Island's balance sheet contained the following comparative data at December 31:

	2011	2010
Accounts receivable	$56,000	$48,000
Prepaid expenses	14,000	11,500
Accounts payable	41,000	36,000
Income tax payable	4,000	9,250
Interest payable	1,000	550
Unearned revenue	10,000	13,750

Additional information: Accounts payable relate to operating expenses.

Instructions

Prepare the operating activities section of the cash flow statement, using (a) the indirect method or (b) the direct method, as assigned by your instructor.

Taking It Further What are the advantages and disadvantages of the indirect method of determining cash provided (used) by operating activities?

P17–4B The following selected account balances relate to the property, plant, and equipment accounts of Bird Corp. at year end:

Calculate cash flows for investing activities.
(SO 2) AP

	2011	2010
Accumulated depreciation—buildings	$ 578,750	$ 600,000
Accumulated depreciation—equipment	218,000	192,000
Depreciation expense—buildings	31,250	30,000
Depreciation expense—equipment	48,000	45,000
Buildings	1,310,000	1,250,000
Equipment	492,000	480,000
Land	250,000	200,000
Loss on sale of equipment	5,000	0
Gain on sale of building	18,000	0

Additional information:
1. Purchased land for $50,000 and buildings for $130,000, by making a $25,000 down payment and financing the remainder with a mortgage note payable.
2. A building was sold during the year.
3. Cash was used to purchase equipment.
4. Equipment with an original cost of $28,000 was sold during the year.

Instructions

Determine the amount of any cash inflows or outflows related to investing activities in 2011.

Taking It Further   Is it favourable for a company to have a net cash inflow from investing activities?

Calculate cash flows for
financing activities.
(SO 2) AP

P17–5B   The following selected account balances relate to the shareholders' equity accounts of Wood Corp. at year end:

	2011	2010
Bond payable	$214,000	$216,000
Long-term notes payable	240,000	350,000
Preferred shares: 7,000 shares in 2011; 5,000 in 2010	175,000	125,000
Common shares: 9,000 shares in 2011; 10,000 in 2010	126,000	140,000
Contributed capital—reacquisition of common shares	1,500	0
Cash dividends—preferred	6,250	6,250
Stock dividends—common	14,000	0
Retained earnings	300,000	240,000
Interest expense	23,000	28,000

Additional information:

1. Interest expense includes amortization of the bond premium.
2. The company paid $170,000 of notes payable that matured during the year.
3. The company reacquired 2,000 common shares in 2011, with an average cost of $28,000.
4. During the year, 1,000 common shares were issued as a stock dividend.
5. Preferred shares were sold for cash.

Instructions

(a) What was the amount of profit reported by Wood Corp. in 2011?
(b) Determine the amount of any cash inflows or outflows related to financing activities in 2011.
(c) Identify and determine the amount of any noncash financing activities in 2011.

Taking It Further   Is it favourable for a company to have a net cash inflow from financing activities?

Prepare cash flow statement—
indirect method.
(SO 2) AP

P17–6B   Presented below is the comparative balance sheet for Wayfarer Inc. at December 31, 2011, and 2010:

<table>
<tr><td colspan="3" align="center">WAYFARER INC.
Balance Sheet
December 31</td></tr>
<tr><td>Assets</td><td>2011</td><td>2010</td></tr>
<tr><td>Cash</td><td>$ 120,600</td><td>$ 176,400</td></tr>
<tr><td>Accounts receivable</td><td>181,800</td><td>135,000</td></tr>
<tr><td>Inventory</td><td>369,000</td><td>257,400</td></tr>
<tr><td>Long-term debt investment</td><td>176,400</td><td>0</td></tr>
<tr><td>Property, plant, and equipment</td><td>1,008,000</td><td>828,000</td></tr>
<tr><td>Less: Accumulated depreciation</td><td>(292,500)</td><td>(252,000)</td></tr>
<tr><td></td><td>$1,563,300</td><td>$1,144,800</td></tr>
<tr><td>Liabilities and Shareholders' Equity</td><td></td><td></td></tr>
<tr><td>Accounts payable</td><td>$ 157,500</td><td>$ 117,000</td></tr>
<tr><td>Dividends payable</td><td>10,800</td><td>0</td></tr>
<tr><td>Income tax payable</td><td>25,200</td><td>28,800</td></tr>
<tr><td>Long-term notes payable</td><td>81,000</td><td>0</td></tr>
<tr><td>Common shares</td><td>1,170,000</td><td>945,000</td></tr>
<tr><td>Retained earnings</td><td>118,800</td><td>54,000</td></tr>
<tr><td></td><td>$1,563,300</td><td>$1,144,800</td></tr>
</table>

WAYFARER INC.
Income Statement
Year Ended December 31, 2011

Sales		$1,137,600
Cost of goods sold		772,200
Gross profit		365,400
Operating expenses	$265,500	
Loss on sale of equipment	3,600	269,100
Profit from operations		96,300
Interest expense	$ 5,400	
Interest revenue	(9,900)	(4,500)
Profit before income tax		100,800
Income tax expense		25,200
Profit		$ 75,600

Additional information:

1. Cash dividends of $10,800 were declared on December 30, 2011, payable on January 15, 2012.
2. A long-term debt investment was acquired for cash at a cost of $175,500.
3. Depreciation expense is included in the operating expenses.
4. The company issued 22,500 common shares for cash on March 2, 2011. The fair value of the shares was $10 per share. The proceeds were used to purchase additional equipment.
5. Equipment that originally cost $45,000 was sold during the year for cash. The equipment had a net book value of $16,200 at the time of sale.
6. The company issued a note payable for $90,000 and repaid $9,000 of it by year end.

Instructions

Prepare a cash flow statement for the year using the indirect method.

Taking It Further   If a company earns a profit during the year, does that always mean that there has been a net increase in cash from operating activities? Explain.

P17–7B   Refer to the information presented for Wayfarer Inc. in P17–6B.

Additional information:

1. Accounts payable is used for merchandise purchases.
2. Accounts receivable relate to merchandise sales.

Instructions

Prepare a cash flow statement for the year using the direct method.

Taking It Further   Wayfarer Inc.'s cash balance decreased by $55,800 in 2011. Briefly explain what caused this, using the cash flow statement. Should management be concerned about this decrease?

P17–8B   Condensed financial data follow for Galenti, Inc.

Prepare cash flow statement—direct method. (SO 2) AP

Prepare cash flow statement—indirect method. (SO 2) AP

GALENTI, INC.
Balance Sheet
December 31

Assets	2011	2010
Cash	$ 102,700	$ 47,250
Trading securities	94,500	107,000
Accounts receivable	80,800	37,000
Inventory	111,900	102,650
Prepaid expenses	10,000	16,000
Property, plant, and equipment	290,000	205,000
Accumulated depreciation	(49,500)	(40,000)
Total assets	$640,400	$474,900

Liabilities and Shareholders' Equity

Accounts payable	$ 62,700	$ 54,280
Accrued expenses payable	12,100	18,830
Notes payable	140,000	80,000
Common shares	250,000	200,000
Retained earnings	175,600	121,790
Total liabilities and shareholders' equity	$640,400	$474,900

GALENTI, INC.
Income Statement
Year Ended December 31, 2011

Revenues		
Sales		$307,500
Gain on sale of equipment		8,750
		316,250
Expenses		
Cost of goods sold	$99,460	
Operating expenses	24,670	
Depreciation expense	58,700	
Interest expense	2,940	
Loss on sale of trading securities	7,500	193,270
Profit before income tax		122,980
Income tax expense		32,670
Profit		$ 90,310

Additional information:

1. Trading securities were sold for $15,000, resulting in a realized loss of $7,500. There were no unrealized gains or losses in 2011. Assume Galenti, Inc. includes changes in trading securities in operating activities.
2. New equipment costing $141,000 was purchased for $71,000 cash and a $70,000 note payable.
3. Equipment with an original cost of $56,000 was sold, resulting in a gain of $8,750.
4. Notes payable that matured during the year were paid in cash.

Instructions

Prepare a cash flow statement for the year using the indirect method.

Taking It Further   In terms of the information included on the cash flow statement, is it important to differentiate between realized and unrealized gains and losses on investments?

Prepare cash flow statement—direct method.

(SO 2) AP

P17–9B   Refer to the information presented for Galenti, Inc. in P17–8B.

Additional information:

1. Accounts payable is used for merchandise purchases.
2. Prepaid expenses and accrued expenses payable relate to operating expenses.
3. Accounts receivable relate to merchandise sales.

Instructions

Prepare a cash flow statement for the year using the direct method.

Taking It Further   Inventory and accounts payable both increased during 2011. Explain how these changes are reported on the cash flow statement when using the direct method.

P17–10B   The financial statements of Milk River Ltd. follow:

Prepare cash flow statement—indirect method.
(SO 2) AP

MILK RIVER LTD.
Balance Sheet
December 31

Assets	2011	2010
Cash	$ 13,000	$ 5,000
Accounts receivable	38,000	24,000
Inventory	27,000	20,000
Property, plant, and equipment	80,000	78,000
Accumulated depreciation	(30,000)	(24,000)
Goodwill	5,000	16,000
Total assets	$133,000	$119,000
Liabilities and Shareholders' Equity		
Accounts payable	$ 17,000	$ 15,000
Income taxes payable	1,000	4,000
Notes payable	36,000	52,750
Common shares	18,000	14,000
Retained earnings	61,000	33,250
Total liabilities and shareholders' equity	$133,000	$119,000

MILK RIVER LTD.
Income Statement
Year Ended December 31, 2011

Sales		$256,000
Cost of goods sold		140,000
Gross profit		116,000
Operating expenses	$64,000	
Impairment loss on goodwill	11,000	75,000
Profit from operations		41,000
Other revenues and expenses		
Interest expense		4,000
Profit before income tax		37,000
Income tax expense		9,250
Profit		$ 27,750

Additional information:

1. Equipment costing $14,000 was purchased with a $4,000 down payment and the remainder was financed with a note payable.
2. During the year, equipment was sold for $8,500 cash. This equipment had cost $12,000 originally and had a carrying amount of $8,500 at the time of sale.
3. All depreciation expenses are in the operating expenses category.
4. Notes payable were also repaid during the year.

Instructions

Prepare a cash flow statement for the year using the indirect method.

Taking It Further   If equipment was both purchased and sold during the year, is it important to show both of these transactions? Or is it sufficient to show only the net increase or decrease in equipment, similar to how increases and decreases in inventory are shown?

P17–11B   Refer to the information presented for Milk River Ltd. in P17–10B. Further analysis reveals that accounts payable relate to purchases of merchandise inventory.

Prepare cash flow statement—direct method.
(SO 2) AP

Instructions

Prepare a cash flow statement for the year using the direct method.

Taking It Further   Explain why it is important to know if the company paid cash or financed the purchase of equipment and how this is shown on the cash flow statement.

Calculate free cash flow and evaluate cash.

(SO 3) AN

P17–12B   Selected information (in thousands) for two close competitors, Reitmans (Canada) Limited and Le Château Inc., follows for fiscal 2009:

	Reitmans	Le Château
Profit	$ 85,806	$ 38,621
Cash provided by operating activities	128,995	41,821
Cash used by investing activities	(70,913)	(11,756)
Cash used by financing activities	(59,700)	(23,877)
Cash and cash equivalents, end of period	214,054	10,034

Instructions

(a) Calculate the free cash flow for each company.

(b) Which company appears to be in the stronger financial position?

Taking It Further   By comparing the companies' cash flows, can you tell which company is likely in a growth stage? Explain.

Continuing Cookie Chronicle

(*Note:* This is a continuation of the Cookie Chronicle from Chapters 1 through 16.)

Natalie has prepared the balance sheet and income statement of Cookie & Coffee Creations Ltd. for the first year of operations, shown on the following page, but does not understand how to prepare the cash flow statement. Recall that the company started operations on November 1, 2011, so all of the opening balances are nil (zero).

Additional information:

1. Recall from Chapter 15 that kitchen equipment (a commercial oven) was bought for $15,000 on May 1, 2012, and a $10,500 note payable was signed to help pay for it. The terms provide for semi-annual fixed principal payments of $1,750 on May 1 and November 1 of each year, plus interest of 4%.
2. Recall from Chapter 13 that 23,550 common shares were originally issued for the following:

Number of Shares	Asset Acquired	Fair Value
17,500	Cash	$17,500
900	Accounts receivable	900
1,650	Merchandise inventory	1,650
3,500	Kitchen Equipment	3,500

All other furniture, fixtures, and equipment were purchased during the year for cash.

3. Recall from chapter 13 that 1,300 common shares were issued as payment for $1,200 of legal expenses and that these were later repurchased from the lawyer for $1,300 cash.
4. Recall from Chapter 14 that a semi-annual dividend was declared to the preferred shareholders on April 30 and was paid on June 1. The second semi-annual dividend was declared to the preferred shareholders on October 31, to be paid on December 1.
5. Prepaid expenses relate only to operating expenses.

Instructions

Prepare a cash flow statement, using (a) the indirect method or (b) the direct method, as assigned by your instructor.

COOKIE & COFFEE CREATIONS LTD.
Income Statement
Year Ended October 31, 2012

Sales		$475,000
Cost of goods sold		237,500
Gross profit		237,500
Operating expenses		
Depreciation expense	$ 9,850	
Salaries and wages expense	92,500	
Other operating expenses	44,940	147,290
Profit from operations		90,210
Other expenses		
Interest expense		210
Profit before income tax		90,000
Income tax expense		18,000
Profit		$ 72,000

COOKIE & COFFEE CREATIONS LTD.
Balance Sheet
October 31, 2012

Assets

Current assets			
Cash		$29,294	
Accounts receivable		3,250	
Inventory		17,897	
Prepaid expenses		6,300	$ 56,741
Property, plant, and equipment			
Furniture and fixtures	$ 12,500		
Less: Accumulated depreciation	1,250	$11,250	
Computer equipment	$ 4,200		
Less: Accumulated depreciation	600	3,600	
Kitchen equipment	$80,000		
Less: Accumulated depreciation	8,000	72,000	86,850
Total assets			$143,591

Liabilities and Shareholders' Equity

Current liabilities			
Accounts payable		$ 5,306	
Income tax payable		18,000	
Dividends payable		625	
Salaries payable		2,250	
Interest payable		210	
Note payable—current portion		3,500	$ 29,891
Long-term liabilities			
Note payable—long-term portion			7,000
Total liabilities			36,891
Shareholders' equity			
Contributed capital			
Preferred shares, 2,500 shares issued	$12,500		
Common shares, 23,550 shares issued	23,455		
Total contributed capital		$35,955	
Retained earnings		70,745	
Total shareholders' equity			106,700
Total liabilities and shareholders' equity			$143,591

Financial Reporting and Analysis

Financial Reporting Problem

BYP17–1   Refer to the consolidated financial statements for The Forzani Group Ltd., which are reproduced in Appendix A at the end of the textbook.

Instructions

(a) How does Forzani define "cash" for the purpose of its cash flow statement?

(b) What was the increase or decrease in cash for the year ended February 1, 2009?

(c) What were the significant investing activities reported in Forzani's 2009 cash flow statement?

(d) What were the significant financing activities reported in Forzani's 2009 cash flow statement?

(e) Did Forzani report any significant noncash investing and financing activities in 2009?

Interpreting Financial Statements

BYP17–2   Andrew Peller Limited is a leading producer and marketer of quality wines in Canada, with wineries in British Columbia, Ontario, and Nova Scotia. The company's March 31, 2009, balance sheet reported current assets of $134.8 million and current liabilities of $105.6 million, including bank indebtedness (negative cash balance) of $52.2 million. Andrew Peller Limited had a loss for fiscal 2009 of $125,000, which was a significant decline from a profit of $11.4 million in 2008. In spite of this, the company reported on its cash flow statement for 2009 that it generated $13.7 million of cash from operating activities and increased its cash by $10.4 million from financing activities, both of which were greater than in 2008. The company also used $24.1 million in cash for investing activities including $13.7 million in the acquisition of several other businesses during the year.

Instructions

(a) Do you believe that Andrew Peller Limited's creditors should be worried about its lack of cash? Explain why or why not.

(b) How is it possible for a company to generate $13.7 million of cash from its operating activities when it had a loss for the year?

(c) Calculate Andrew Peller Limited's free cash flow for fiscal 2009. Explain what this free cash flow means.

Critical Thinking

Collaborative Learning Activity

Note to instructor: Additional instructions and handout material for this group activity can be found on the Instructor Resource Site.

BYP17–3 In this group activity you will prepare cash flow statements using (1) the indirect method and (2) the direct method.

Instructions

(a) Your instructor will divide the class into groups. Each group will split into two smaller groups. Using information provided by your instructor, one of these groups will prepare a cash flow statement using the indirect method; the other will prepare one using the direct method. Record the results of your small group discussion.

(b) In your larger group, compare the subtotals of the two cash flow statements. If any subtotals are different, explain how the statements were prepared and correct any error(s).

(c) Based on the cash flow statements, answer the following questions about the company:

1. Will the company be able to meet its current obligations in the next 12 months?
2. Where did the major portion of cash come from during the year?
3. Where was the major portion of cash spent during the year?

Communication Activity

BYP17–4 Many investors today prefer the cash flow statement over the income statement. They believe that cash-based data are a better measure of performance than accrual-based data because they believe that it is harder to manage profit using cash-based data.

Instructions

Write a brief memo explaining whether or not it is harder for management to manage income using cash-based data than accrual-based data. In your answer, say which financial statement, in your opinion, is the best measure of a company's performance, and explain why.

Ethics Case

BYP17–5 Paradis Corporation is a wholesaler of automotive parts. It has 10 shareholders who have been paid a total of $1 million in cash dividends for eight years in a row. In order for this dividend to be declared, the board of directors' policy requires that net cash provided by operating activities, as reported in Paradis's cash flow statement, must be more than $1 million. President and CEO Phil Monat's job is secure as long as he produces annual operating cash flows to support the usual dividend.

At the end of the current year, controller Rick Rodgers presents president Monat with some disappointing news. The net cash provided by operating activities is only $970,000. The president says to Rick, "We must get that amount above $1 million. Isn't there some way to increase operating cash flow by another $30,000?" Rick answers, "These figures were prepared by my assistant. I'll go back to my office and see what I can do." The president replies, "I know you won't let me down, Rick."

After examining the cash flow statement carefully, Rick concludes that he can get the operating cash flows above $1 million by reclassifying a two-year, $60,000 non-trade note payable that is listed in the financing activities section as "Proceeds from bank loan—$60,000." He will report the note as a note arising from trade transactions in the operating activities section instead. He returns to the president, saying, "You can tell the board to declare its usual dividend. Our net cash flow provided by operating activities is $1.03 million." "Good man, Rick! I knew I could count on you," exclaims the president.

Instructions

(a) Who are the stakeholders in this situation?

(b) Was there anything unethical about the president's actions? Was there anything unethical about the controller's actions?

(c) Are the board members or anyone else likely to discover the misclassification?

"All About You" Activity

BYP17–6   In the "All About You" feature, you read that many Canadians have big debt loads and negative cash flows. Assume you are a student enrolled in your second year of college and have just learned about the importance of managing cash flows and how to prepare a cash flow statement. You want to use your knowledge to prepare a cash budget, for the upcoming year, September 1, 2010, to August 31, 2011. To help you prepare next year's cash budget, you have prepared a cash flow statement for the past year, September 1, 2009, to August 31, 2010.

My Cash Flow Statement Year Ended August 31, 2010	
Operating Activities	
Cash received from summer job	$ 8,000
Cash contribution from parents	3,600
Cash paid for rent, utilities, cable, Internet	(4,000)
Cash paid for groceries	(3,200)
Cash paid for clothes	(3,000)
Cash paid for gas, insurance, parking	(4,420)
Cash paid for miscellaneous	(500)
Cash paid for interest on credit card	(180)
Cash used in operating activities	(3,700)
Investing Activities	
Tuition and books	(7,000)
Laptop and printer	(1,200)
Cash used in investing activities	(8,200)
Financing Activities	
Student loan	7,500
Loan from parents	1,500
Purchases on credit card	1,000
Cash provided from financing activities	10,000
Decrease in cash	(1,900)
Cash, September 1, 2009	4,000
Cash, August 31, 2010	$ 2,100

Instructions

(a) Comment on your cash position on August 31, 2010, compared with September 1, 2009.

(b) Prepare a cash flow forecast for September 1, 2010, to August 31, 2011, based on the following estimates and assumptions:

1. Tuition and books $7,500
2. Student loan $7,500
3. Your parents will contribute $4,000 toward your rent, utilities, cable, and Internet. You will not have to pay your parents back for this contribution.
4. Rent, utilities, cable, and Internet $4,000
5. Groceries $3,600
6. Gas, insurance, and parking $4,600
7. Clothes $3,000
8. Miscellaneous $500
9. You plan to pay off the amount owed on your credit card.
10. Your parents will lend you an additional $1,500 if you need it.
11. You plan to pay off the amount owed on your credit card right away.
12. You are pretty sure that you will be rehired by the same company next summer; however, you do not think you will get a raise in pay.

(c) What is the amount of cash you forecast you will have at August 31, 2011?

(d) Will you need to borrow the additional $1,500 from your parents?

(e) Will you be able to pay off the $1,000 owed on your credit card? Should you try to do so?

(f) What actions may you be able to take to improve your cash flow?

ANSWERS TO CHAPTER QUESTIONS

Answers to Accounting in Action Insight Questions

All About You, p. 935

Q: Is it appropriate to use your credit card to pay for your operating activities such as your groceries, clothes, and entertainment? Is it appropriate to use your credit card to finance your investment activities such as tuition or, if you have a large enough limit, a car?

A: Credit cards should never be used for a long-term financing activity because they have an average interest rate of 18%. They can be effectively used for short-term operating activities such as paying for your groceries, clothes, and entertainment, provided that you are able to pay off the full amount of your credit card balance when the payment is due and avoid any interest charges. And credit cards should only be used for long-term investing activities if you will have enough cash to pay off the credit card bill before its due date and avoid interest charges. Long-term investment activities should be financed with long-term financing. If you are buying a car or financing your education, you need either a long-term bank loan or a student loan where your payment schedule will match your long-term use of that car or education.

Across the Organization, p. 957

Q: Typically, which department in a company is responsible for making decisions about whether to issue bonds? What would that department consider when making this decision?

A: Either the treasury or finance department (depending on how the company is organized) is responsible for making decisions about whether to issue bonds. It would be responsible for forecasting future cash inflows and outflows and would use that information to determine if and when the company needs to increase cash through financing activities. It would also be responsible for determining whether it was better to borrow by issuing bonds or if the company should sell shares, by evaluating such things as interest rates, current share prices, and general market conditions.

Business Insight, p. 963

Q: What is the likely reason that free cash flow is so important to Amazon.com?

A: Free cash flow results from cash generated by operating activities (through increases in sales and/or decreases in operating costs), and from effective management of capital expenditures to maintain productivity. Free cash flow is important to Amazon.com because it measures the discretionary cash flow that is available for it to expand operations, repay debt, pay dividends, or use for other purposes.

Answer to Forzani Review It Question 4, p. 935

Forzani reports the following (in thousands): (a) $95,743 cash provided by operating activities, (b) $57,814 cash used by investing activities, and (c) $81,939 cash used by financing activities.

Answers to Self-Study Questions

1. a   2. c   3. c   4. c   5. b   6. c   7. b   8. b   9. a   10. c

Remember to go back to the beginning of the chapter to check off your completed work!

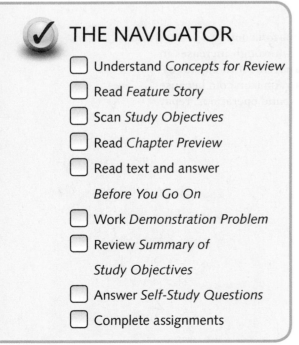

CONCEPTS FOR REVIEW:

Before studying this chapter, you should understand or, if necessary, review:

a. The various types of users of financial statement information. (Ch. 1, pp. 3–4)

b. The content and classification of a balance sheet. (Ch. 4, pp. 191–199, and Ch. 16, pp. 897–898)

c. The content and classification of an income statement. (Ch. 5, pp. 263–267)

d. The effects of discontinued operations. (Ch. 14, pp. 776–777)

e. The content and classification of a statement of changes in shareholders' equity. (Ch. 14, pp. 783–785)

f. The content of a statement of comprehensive income. (Ch. 14, pp. 777–778)

g. The ratios introduced in previous chapters: working capital, current ratio, acid-test (Ch. 4, pp. 200–201); gross profit margin, profit margin (Ch. 5, pp. 268–269); inventory turnover, days sales in inventory (Ch. 6, p. 332); receivables turnover, collection period, operating cycle (Ch. 8, pp. 453–454); asset turnover, return on assets (Ch. 9, pp. 521–522); return on equity (Ch. 13, p. 737); earnings per share, price-earnings, payout (Ch. 14, pp. 787-789); debt to total assets, interest coverage (Ch. 15, pp. 843–844); and free cash flow (Ch. 17, pp. 962–963).

Presenting the Whole Picture

TORONTO, ON—In the high-stakes world of investing and lending, it's not "who you know" that counts, but "what you know." Effective communication enables investors, lenders, and others to know whether a company is doing well, what its past performance has been, and what its future prospects are. The annual report plays a significant role in keeping a company's stakeholders informed.

While most annual reports follow the same basic format, they vary widely in their presentation, content, and most importantly, the quality of the information they provide. That's where the annual Corporate Reporting Awards play an important role. Jointly sponsored by the Canadian Institute of Chartered Accountants (CICA), CNW Group, Fasken Martineau, PricewaterhouseCoopers, and the Toronto Stock Exchange, the awards aim to recognize the best reporting models in Canada and thereby strengthen corporate reporting in this country.

"It is important that we acknowledge excellent examples of corporate reporting, especially in these unsettled times," said CICA's president and CEO, Kevin Dancey. "It is encouraging to see so many companies dedicated to providing corporate reports that are relevant, clear, and easily understood. All of the entrants are dedicated to continuous improvement and raising the bar each year for even better reporting."

Canadian Tire Corporation, Limited has been among CICA's Corporate Reporting Award winners for a number of years, most recently in the 2009 awards as the industry winner in the Consumer Products category. In the feature photo on page 998, Brian Fiedler, VP, Finance and Administration of Canadian Tire (left) is seen accepting his award from Bill Buchanan, FCA, Overall Judging Coordinator, CICA.

Most annual reports feature a message from the chair and CEO, the year's financial statements, a management discussion and analysis (MD&A), and information about the company directors. The judges described Canadian Tire's financial statements as "well prepared and easy to read." The judges also consider things like a statement of objectives, a discussion of the company's performance relative to those objectives, some comparative industry information, and information on corporate governance. The judges commented that Canadian Tire's MD&A has "good in-depth information with an excellent presentation of strategic goals. [It] also includes excellent discussion of strategies, what has been accomplished, and plans for the future." They also commended Canadian Tire's disclosure of information on board members, including "biographies with details concerning independence status, attendance at board meetings, share ownership, and public board memberships during the past five years."

The judges also liked the layout and design of the retailer's annual report. They noted in their remarks that "the physical design of the report, with a pocket on the back page, is good as it allows the Annual Report and the Financial Information to be kept together." And they highlighted Canadian Tire's electronic disclosure, saying "information loads quickly and there is consistent navigation across the site."

Communication is, after all, what it's all about. Full disclosure is more important now than ever. That means communicating everything—both good news and bad—so the users of the financial information can make well-informed decisions.

The Navigator

STUDY OBJECTIVES:

After studying this chapter, you should be able to:

1. Identify the need for, and tools of, financial statement analysis.
2. Explain and apply horizontal analysis.
3. Explain and apply vertical analysis.
4. Identify and use ratios to analyze a company's liquidity, solvency, and profitability.
5. Recognize the limitations of financial statement analysis.

The Navigator

An important lesson can be learned from Canadian Tire's annual report described in our feature story. Effective communication is the key to decision-making. The purpose of this chapter is to introduce the tools used in financial analysis to help users evaluate, and make decisions about, a company's financial performance and position.

We will use three commonly used tools of analysis—horizontal, vertical, and ratio—to analyze the financial statements of a hypothetical publicly-traded, regional chain of stores called Hometown Tires and More. We will then compare this analysis to Canadian Tire, one of Hometown Tires and More's competitors, and their industry where appropriate. We will conclude our discussion with some of the limiting factors users should be aware of in their analysis of financial information.

The chapter is organized as follows:

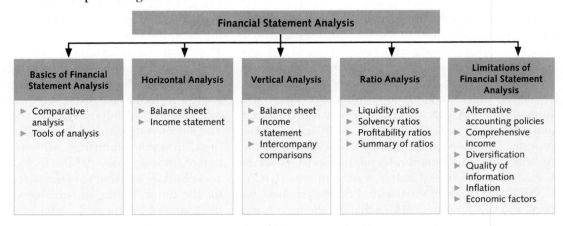

Basics of Financial Statement Analysis

STUDY OBJECTIVE 1

Identify the need for, and tools of, financial statement analysis.

Financial statement analysis involves evaluating three characteristics of a company: its liquidity, solvency, and profitability. We learned in Chapter 11 that the objective of financial reporting is to give capital providers (i.e., investors and lenders) information useful for decision-making. Each of these user groups has an interest in a company's liquidity, solvency, and/or profitability depending on their decision needs. For example, a short-term lender, such as a bank, is primarily interested in liquidity—the ability of a borrower to pay its obligations when they come due. The borrower's liquidity is extremely important in evaluating the safety of a short-term loan. A long-term lender, such as a bondholder, looks at solvency measures to determine the company's ability to survive over a long period of time. Long-term lenders consider such measures as the amount of debt in the company's capital structure and its ability to meet interest payments. Investors (current and potential shareholders) look at the company's profitability. They want to assess the probability of receiving dividend income and the growth potential of the share price.

Alternative terminology
Lenders are also commonly known as *creditors*, and *investors* are commonly known as *shareholders*.

Comparative Analysis

In analyzing financial statements, the users of financial information must make comparisons in order to evaluate a company's past and current performance and position, and to use this information to help determine future expectations. Comparisons are needed because, although every item reported in a financial statement has significance, it has limited value on its own. When Canadian Tire reported accounts receivable of $824.1 million on its balance sheet dated January 3, 2009, we know that the company had that amount of accounts receivable on that date. However, we do not know if the amount is an increase or decrease compared with past years, or if Canadian Tire is collecting its receivables on a timely basis. To get this information, the amount of receivables must be compared with other financial statement data.

When you compare any one financial statement item with a related financial statement item or items, the value and usefulness of the information increases for analysis purposes. Comparisons can be made on several different bases. The following three are illustrated in this chapter:

1. **Intracompany basis.** This basis compares an item or financial relationship inside or within a company in the current year with one or more prior years. Intracompany comparisons are useful for finding changes in financial relationships and discovering significant trends. For example, Canadian Tire can compare its accounts receivable balance at the end of the current year with last year's balance to find the amount of the increase or decrease. Likewise, Canadian Tire can compare the percentage of accounts receivable to total assets at the end of the current year with the percentage in one or more prior years.

2. **Intercompany basis.** This basis compares an item or financial relationship of one company with the same item or relationship in one or more competing companies. Intercompany comparisons are useful for understanding a company's competitive position. For example, Canadian Tire's total sales for the year can be compared with the total sales of one of its major competitors.

   Who are its competitors? Don't be fooled by the name: Canadian Tire sells much more than tires. It sells a wide range of home, car, sports, and food products in its retail stores, in addition to apparel, gasoline, and financial services in some of its other businesses. Consequently, although it has a number of competitors, its primary competition can be found in the consumer products industry, which includes companies such as RONA, Sears, and Walmart.

3. **Industry averages.** This basis compares an item or financial relationship of a company with industry averages. These averages are determined and published by organizations that provide financial ratings, such as Statistics Canada, Financial Post Infomart, Dun & Bradstreet, Standard and Poor's, and RMA Annual Statement Studies. Comparisons with industry averages give information about how well a company is performing within its industry. For example, Canadian Tire's profit can be compared with the average profit of all companies in the consumer products industry.

To analyze a company, we usually start with its financial statements. As mentioned in our feature story, Canadian Tire's financial statements were judged to be "well prepared and easy to read." However, it is just as important to review other financial and non-financial information in a company's annual report besides the financial statements. Other financial information includes a management discussion and analysis of the company's financial position and a summary of key financial figures and ratios from prior years. Canadian Tire's annual report includes a 10-year summary of financial highlights comparing the current and prior years.

Non-financial information includes a discussion of the company's mission, goals, and objectives, and its market position, people, and products. Some analysts argue that non-financial, or qualitative, information is even more important than financial, or quantitative, information in determining how successful a company will be. Financial information can only evaluate past performance. Non-financial information may help predict future performance better. For example, the section on "Where We're Headed" in Canadian Tire's annual report was considered to be very useful by the judges for the Corporate Reporting Awards, in conjunction with its MD&A, which included an "excellent discussion of strategies, what has been accomplished, and plans for the future."

We must also consider the economic circumstances in which a company is operating. Economic measures such as the rates of interest, inflation, unemployment, and changes in supply and demand can have a significant impact on a company's performance. For example, suppose a company's performance has been declining and it is operating in an industry that is being affected by declining commodity prices. An analyst can not reach a proper conclusion about the reasons for the company's weaker results if the analyst does not know about the declining prices.

Analyzing financial information will be challenging for companies like Canadian Tire in 2008 and subsequent years. In 2008 and 2009, much of the industrialized world entered into a

Tutorials:
Annual Report Walkthrough

global recession. This recession is expected to have a significant impact on consumer spending for many years to come. Consequently, when one is comparing financial data over time, it will be important to try to assess what changes relate solely to the economy and what changes relate to factors that management can control. This will not be an easy task. And, as we will learn later, analyzing data that include losses adds yet another complexity to financial analysis.

Tools of Analysis

We use various tools to evaluate the significance of financial statement data for decision-making. Three commonly used tools include:

1. **Horizontal analysis.** This tool evaluates a series of financial statement data over different periods of time.
2. **Vertical analysis.** This tool evaluates financial statement data by expressing each item in a financial statement as a percentage of a base amount that covers the same period of time as the item.
3. **Ratio analysis.** This tool expresses the relationship among selected items of financial statement data.

Horizontal analysis is used mainly in intracompany comparisons. As we learned earlier, an intracompany analysis involves financial data *within* a company. Two features in annual reports make horizontal comparisons easier. First, the data in each of the financial statements found in the annual report are presented in comparison with data for one or more previous years. For example, Canadian Tire reports comparative data in its financial statements for the year ended January 3, 2009 (2008 fiscal year), and the year ended December 29, 2007 (2007 fiscal year). Canadian Tire's year end is the Saturday closest to December 31. Second, a summary of selected financial data is presented in the annual report for a series of five to 10 years or more.

Vertical analysis is used in both intracompany and intercompany comparisons. Vertical analysis is helpful to compare financial data both *within* a company and between two or more companies. Ratio analysis is used in all three types of comparison: intracompany, intercompany, and industry.

While horizontal and vertical analysis are being introduced for the first time in this chapter, you should already have some familiarity with ratio analysis, which was introduced in past chapters. In the following sections, we will explain and illustrate each of the three types of analysis.

BEFORE YOU GO ON . . .

→ Review It

1. Identify some of the users of financial statement analysis.
2. What are the differences between intracompany, intercompany, and industry comparisons?
3. What are the three different tools that are used to compare financial information?

The Navigator

Related exercise material: BE18–1.

Horizontal Analysis

STUDY OBJECTIVE 2

Explain and apply horizontal analysis.

Horizontal analysis, also called **trend analysis**, is a technique for comparing a series of financial statement data over a period of time. The term "horizontal analysis" means that we view financial statement data from left to right (or right to left) across time.

The purpose of horizontal analysis is to determine the increase or decrease that has taken place over time. This change may be expressed as a percentage of a base period or as a percentage change between periods. For example, operating revenue figures and horizontal analysis percentages for Canadian Tire for the most recent five-year period are shown in Illustration 18-1.

CANADIAN TIRE CORPORATION, LIMITED Year Ended December 31 (in millions)					
	2008	2007	2006	2005	2004
Operating revenue	$9,121.3	$8,606.1	$8,252.9	$7,713.9	$7,062.1
% of base-year amount	129.2%	121.9%	116.9%	109.2%	100.0%
% change for year	6.0%	4.3%	7.0%	9.2%	—

← Illustration 18-1

Horizontal analysis for Canadian Tire

If we assume that 2004 is the base year, we can express operating revenue as a percentage of the base-year amount. We call this a **horizontal percentage of base-period amount**. It is calculated by dividing the amount for the specific year we are analyzing by the base-year amount, as shown in Illustration 18-2.

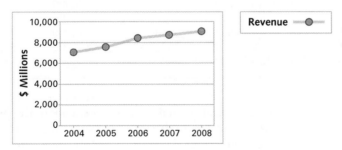

← Illustration 18-2

Horizontal percentage of base-period amount formula

We can determine that Canadian Tire's operating revenue in 2008 is 129.2% of the operating revenue in 2004 by dividing $9,121.3 million by $7,062.1 million. In other words, operating revenue in 2008 is 29.2% greater than sales four years earlier, in 2004. From this horizontal analysis, shown in the second row of Illustration 18-1, we can easily see Canadian Tire's revenue trend. Revenue has increased each year since 2004.

Graphic displays often aid in horizontal analysis, allowing quick identification of trends and changes in direction or magnitude. Canadian Tire's revenue is graphed below for the five-year period. We have chosen to chart dollar amounts, but percentages can also be charted and will provide the same information.

We can also use horizontal analysis to measure the percentage change for any one specific period. This is known as a **horizontal percentage change for period**. It is calculated by dividing the dollar amount of the change between the specific year under analysis and the base year by the base-year amount, as shown in Illustration 18-3.

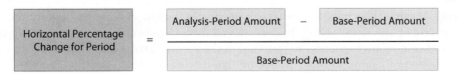

← Illustration 18-3

Horizontal percentage change for period formula

For example, if we set the previous year, 2007 in this case, as our base year, we can determine that Canadian Tire's operating revenue increased by $515.2 million ($9,121.3 million − $8,606.1 million) between 2007 and 2008. This increase can then be expressed as a percentage, 6%, by dividing the amount of the change between the two years, $515.2 million, by the amount in the prior, or base, year, $8,606.1 million. That is, in 2008, operating revenue increased by 6% compared with 2007. The percentage change in operating revenues for each of the five years is presented in the last row of Illustration 18-1.

Balance Sheet

To further illustrate horizontal analysis, we will use the hypothetical financial statements of Hometown Tires and More Inc. Its two-year condensed balance sheet, which shows dollar and percentage changes, is presented in Illustration 18-4.

Illustration 18-4 →

Horizontal analysis of balance sheet

HOMETOWN TIRES AND MORE INC. Balance Sheet December 31				
			Increase (Decrease)	
Assets	2008	2007	Amount	Percentage
Current assets				
Cash	$ 50,000	$ 55,000	$ (5,000)	(9.1%)
Trading investments, at fair value	20,000	35,000	(15,000)	(42.9%)
Accounts receivable	72,500	50,000	22,500	45.0%
Inventory	372,500	340,000	32,500	9.6%
Prepaid expenses	30,000	20,000	10,000	50.0%
Total current assets	545,000	500,000	45,000	9.0%
Property, plant, and equipment	400,000	450,000	(50,000)	(11.1%)
Intangible assets	55,000	65,000	(10,000)	(15.4%)
Total assets	$1,000,000	$1,015,000	$(15,000)	(1.5%)
Liabilities and Shareholders' Equity				
Liabilities				
Current liabilities	$ 337,700	$ 333,500	$ 4,200	1.3%
Long-term liabilities	400,000	475,000	(75,000)	(15.8%)
Total liabilities	737,700	808,500	(70,800)	(8.8%)
Shareholders' equity				
Common shares (300,000 shares issued)	90,000	90,000	0	0.0%
Retained earnings	152,300	96,500	55,800	57.8%
Accumulated other comprehensive income	20,000	20,000	0	0.0%
Total shareholders' equity	262,300	206,500	55,800	27.0%
Total liabilities and shareholders' equity	$1,000,000	$1,015,000	$(15,000)	(1.5%)

The above horizontal percentages are an example of a percentage change for a period, and not a percentage of a base-period amount. It makes sense to calculate the percentage change for a period above since only two periods are under analysis. Note that, in a horizontal analysis, while the amount column of the increase or decrease is additive (e.g., the change in total liabilities of $70,800 is equal to $4,200 − $75,000), the percentage column is not additive (8.8% is not equal to 1.3% − 15.8%).

The horizontal analysis of Hometown Tires and More's comparative balance sheet shows that several changes have occurred between 2007 and 2008. In the current assets section, trading investments decreased by $15,000, or 42.9%. We will learn when we look at the income statement later that this change was due to a decline in the fair value of the investments and not due to the sale of any of these investments. Recall from Chapter 16 that losses on fair value adjustments of trading investments are reported in the income statement and not in the statement of comprehensive income. This is why accumulated other comprehensive income, shown in the shareholders' equity section of the balance sheet, did not change between 2007 and 2008.

Accounts receivable increased by $22,500, or 45%. We will look at the income statement in the next section to determine whether sales increased by the same proportion as receivables. If not, this may indicate that the receivables are slow-moving.

Inventory increased by a larger dollar amount, $32,500, than did accounts receivable but not by as large a percentage: 9.6% for inventory compared with 45% for accounts receivable. Inventory may have changed because of increased sales; we will investigate this further when we analyze the income statement. Prepaid expenses also increased by 50% in 2008. One has to be careful in interpreting percentage changes like this. Because it is a proportionately large change ($10,000) on a small amount ($20,000), the percentage change is not as meaningful as it first appears. Overall, total assets decreased $15,000, or 1.5%, from 2007 to 2008.

Current liabilities increased by 1.3%. Changes in current assets and current liabilities usually move in the same direction; that is, normally both will increase or both will decrease. In this case, both have risen, although current assets have increased more than current liabilities. This is better than the inverse—or current liabilities increasing more than current assets.

Long-term liabilities decreased by $75,000, or 15.8%, in 2008. Hometown Tires and More appears to be using some of its profits to repay its debt. Retained earnings in the shareholders' equity section of the balance sheet increased significantly in 2008, by 57.8%. This suggests that Hometown Tires and More is financing its business by retaining profit, rather than by adding to its long-term debt.

Income Statement

Illustration 18-5 presents a horizontal analysis of Hometown Tires and More's condensed income statement for the years 2007 and 2008.

Illustration 18-5

Horizontal analysis of income statement

HOMETOWN TIRES AND MORE INC.
Income Statement
Years Ended December 31

	2008	2007	Increase (Decrease) Amount	Percentage
Sales	$2,095,000	$1,960,000	$135,000	6.9%
Sales returns and allowances	98,000	123,000	(25,000)	(20.3%)
Net sales	1,997,000	1,837,000	160,000	8.7%
Cost of goods sold	1,381,000	1,240,000	141,000	11.4%
Gross profit	616,000	597,000	19,000	3.2%
Operating expenses	457,000	440,000	17,000	3.9%
Profit from operations	159,000	157,000	2,000	1.3%
Other expenses				
Interest expense	27,000	29,500	(2,500)	(8.5%)
Loss on fair value adjustment– trading investments	15,000	0	15,000	n/a
Profit before income tax	117,000	127,500	(10,500)	(8.2%)
Income tax expense	23,400	25,500	(2,100)	(8.2%)
Profit	$ 93,600	$ 102,000	$ (8,400)	(8.2%)

Horizontal analysis of the income statement, illustrating percentage changes for the period, shows the following changes: Net sales increased by 8.7%, while the cost of goods sold increased by 11.4%.

Sales do not appear to have increased at the same rate as receivables. Recall from Illustration 18-4 that receivables increased by 45%. Here we learn that net sales increased by only 8.7%. Later in the chapter, we will look at the receivables turnover ratio to determine whether receivables are being collected more slowly or not. However, we must be cautious in over-interpreting this increase. This type of business relies a lot on cash sales, not credit sales.

Recall also that in Illustration 18-4 we observed that inventory increased by 9.6%. The cost of goods sold reported on the income statement also appears to have increased, by 11.4%, even though net sales only increased by 8.7%. We will look at the inventory turnover ratio later in the chapter to determine whether these increases are reasonable.

To continue with our horizontal analysis of the income statement, we note that gross profit increased by 3.2%. Operating expenses outpaced this percentage increase at 3.9%. Normally, management tries to control operating expenses wherever possible, so we would hope to see operating expenses change at the same rate, or a lower rate, than gross profit.

Other expenses increased, primarily because of the loss on fair value adjustment related to the trading investments that was mentioned in the last section. Note that profit declined by the same amount as profit before income tax, 8.2%. This indicates that although income tax expense declined in 2008, its decline was proportionate to net sales in each year (that is, income tax expense is unchanged at 20% of profit before income tax in each year).

A horizontal analysis of changes from period to period is pretty straightforward and is quite useful. But complications can occur in making the calculations. If an item has a small value in a base year and a large value in the next year, the percentage change may not be meaningful. In addition, if a negative amount appears in the base year and there is a positive amount the following year, or vice versa, no percentage change can be calculated. Or, if an item has no value in a base year and a value in the next year, no percentage change can be calculated. That was the case with the loss on fair value adjustment reported in 2008. Because there was no loss reported in 2007, no percentage change could be calculated.

We have not included a horizontal analysis of Hometown Tires and More's statement of changes in shareholders' equity or cash flow statement. An analysis of these statements is not as useful as the horizontal analyses performed on the balance sheet and income statement. The amounts presented in the statement of changes in shareholders' equity and cash flow statement give details about the changes between two periods. The value of these statements comes from the analysis of the changes during the year, and not from percentage comparisons of these changes against a base amount.

Hometown Tires and More did not have any other comprehensive income in 2008, so it did not present a separate statement of comprehensive income. However, if it had, it might have been useful to analyze the changes in its sources of other comprehensive income. It should be cautioned, however, that these changes can vary widely from year to year, which can result in a horizontal analysis having limited value.

BEFORE YOU GO ON . . .

→ Review It

1. What is horizontal analysis?
2. How is a percentage of a base period amount calculated? How is a percentage change for a period calculated?
3. How can graphs aid in interpreting a horizontal analysis?
4. How do negative amounts affect the calculation of horizontal analysis percentages?

→ Do It

Selected, condensed information (in thousands) from Bonora Ltd.'s income statements for four years ended June 30 follows:

	2011	2010	2009	2008
Revenues	$5,035	$6,294	$9,468	$8,646
Gross profit	936	1,077	2,146	1,900
Profit	251	110	546	428

(a) Using horizontal analysis, calculate the percentage of the base-year amount for 2008 to 2011, assuming that 2008 is the base year.
(b) Using horizontal analysis, calculate the percentage change between the following years: 2008 and 2009; 2009 and 2010; and 2010 and 2011.

Action Plan

• Set the base-year (2008) dollar amounts at 100. Express each later year's amount as a percentage of the base year by dividing the dollar amount for the year under analysis by

the base-year amount.
- Find the percentage change between two periods by dividing the dollar amount of the change between the prior year and the current year by the prior-year amount.

Solution

(a) Horizontal percentage of the base-year amount

	2011	2010	2009	2008
Revenues	58.2%	72.8%	109.5%	100%
Gross profit	49.3%	56.7%	112.9%	100%
Profit	58.6%	25.7%	127.6%	100%

(b) Horizontal percentage change for each year

	2010 to 2011	2009 to 2010	2008 to 2009
Revenues	(20.0%)	(33.5%)	9.5%
Gross profit	(13.1%)	(49.8%)	12.9%
Profit	128.2%	(80.0%)	27.6%

Related exercise material: BE18–2, BE18–3, BE18–4, BE18–5, E18–1, E18–3, and E18–4.

The Navigator

Vertical Analysis

STUDY OBJECTIVE 3

Explain and apply vertical analysis.

Vertical analysis, also called **common size analysis**, is a technique for evaluating financial statement data that expresses each amount under analysis as a percentage of a base amount within a period. The term "vertical analysis" means that we view financial statement data from up to down (or down to up) within the same period of time.

Note that while horizontal analysis compares data across more than one year, vertical analysis compares data within the same year. These data are expressed as a percentage, known as the **vertical percentage**. It is calculated by dividing the financial statement amount under analysis by the base amount for that particular financial statement, as shown in Illustration 18-6.

← Illustration 18-6

Vertical percentage formula

The base amount commonly used for the balance sheet is *total assets*. For example, using vertical analysis on Canadian Tire's balance sheet (not shown here), we would say that accounts receivable are 11% of total assets (total assets being the base amount).

The base amount for the income statement is usually *revenues* for a service company and *net sales* for a merchandising company. Using vertical analysis on Canadian Tire's income statement (not shown here), we would say that operating expenses are 94% of revenues.

Balance Sheet

Illustration 18-7 shows a vertical analysis of Hometown Tires and More's comparative balance sheet. This analysis uses *total assets* as the base amount for the asset items and *total liabilities and shareholders' equity* (which equals total assets) as the base amount for the liability and shareholders' equity items.

Illustration 18-7 →

Vertical analysis of
balance sheet

HOMETOWN TIRES AND MORE INC. Balance Sheet December 31				
	2008		**2007**	
Assets	Amount	Percentage	Amount	Percentage
Current assets				
Cash	$ 50,000	5.0%	$ 55,000	5.4%
Trading investments, at fair value	20,000	2.0%	35,000	3.5%
Accounts receivable	72,500	7.2%	50,000	4.9%
Inventory	372,500	37.3%	340,000	33.5%
Prepaid expenses	30,000	3.0%	20,000	2.0%
Total current assets	545,000	54.5%	500,000	49.3%
Property, plant, and equipment	400,000	40.0%	450,000	44.3%
Intangible assets	55,000	5.5%	65,000	6.4%
Total assets	$1,000,000	100.0%	$1,015,000	100.0%
Liabilities and Shareholders' Equity				
Liabilities				
Current liabilities	$ 337,700	33.8%	$ 333,500	32.9%
Long-term liabilities	400,000	40.0%	475,000	46.8%
Total liabilities	737,700	73.8%	808,500	79.7%
Shareholders' equity				
Common shares (300,000 shares issued)	90,000	9.0%	90,000	8.8%
Retained earnings	152,300	15.2%	96,500	9.5%
Accumulated other comprehensive income	20,000	2.0%	20,000	2.0%
Total shareholders' equity	262,300	26.2%	206,500	20.3%
Total liabilities and shareholders' equity	$1,000,000	100.0%	$1,015,000	100.0%

Vertical analysis shows the size of each item in the balance sheet compared with a base amount. It can also show the percentage change in the individual asset, liability, and shareholders' equity items. For example, we can see that current assets increased from 49.3% of total assets in 2007 to 54.5% of total assets in 2008. We can also see that the biggest change was in inventory, which increased from 33.5% of total assets in 2007 to 37.3% in 2008. This is contrary to what we first observed in Illustration 18-4, where it appeared that prepaid expenses had the greatest percentage increase in the current assets category. In Illustration 18-7, prepaid expenses increased only by one percentage point of total assets, from 2% in 2007 to 3% in 2008. You will recall our earlier words of caution about interpreting such a large percentage change as was presented for prepaid expenses in Illustration 18-4.

Property, plant, and equipment and intangible assets both decreased as relative percentages of total assets: 44.3% in 2007 to 40% in 2008 for property, plant, and equipment and 6.4% in 2007 to 5.5% in 2008 for intangible assets. Although it is not separately detailed, property, plant, and equipment increased by $40,000 as a result of new equipment purchases and decreased by $90,000 as a result of an increase in accumulated depreciation, for a net decrease of $50,000. Intangible assets decreased solely due to a change in accumulated amortization.

Long-term liabilities decreased from 46.8% to 40%, while retained earnings increased from 9.5% to 15.2% of total liabilities and shareholders' equity between 2007 and 2008. These results reinforce the earlier observation that Hometown Tires and More is financing its growth by retaining earnings, rather than by issuing additional debt.

Note that Hometown Tires and More only has one class of share capital—common shares—issued. Its common shares didn't actually change between 2007 and 2008, yet common shares are a different percentage of total assets in each year (8.8% in 2007 and 9.0% in 2008). This is because the base (total assets) has changed in each year while the amount of common shares has not.

Income Statement

A vertical analysis of Hometown Tires and More's income statement is shown in Illustration 18-8, with *net sales* used as the base amount.

	2008		2007	
HOMETOWN TIRES AND MORE INC. Income Statement Year Ended December 31				
	Amount	Percentage	Amount	Percentage
Sales	$2,095,000	104.9%	$1,960,000	106.7%
Sales returns and allowances	98,000	4.9%	123,000	6.7%
Net sales	1,997,000	100.0%	1,837,000	100.0%
Cost of goods sold	1,381,000	69.2%	1,240,000	67.5%
Gross profit	616,000	30.8%	597,000	32.5%
Operating expenses	457,000	22.9%	440,000	24.0%
Profit from operations	159,000	7.9%	157,000	8.5%
Other expenses				
Interest expense	27,000	1.3%	29,500	1.6%
Loss on fair value adjustment— trading investments	15,000	0.7%	0	0.0%
Profit before income tax	117,000	5.9%	127,500	6.9%
Income tax expense	23,400	1.2%	25,500	1.4%
Profit	$ 93,600	4.7%	$ 102,000	5.5%

◀ Illustration 18-8

Vertical analysis of income statement

We can see that the cost of goods sold as a percentage of net sales increased by 1.7 percentage points (from 67.5% to 69.2%). Operating expenses declined as a percentage of net sales by 1.1 percentage points (from 24.0% to 22.9%). As a result, profit from operations did not change substantially between 2007 and 2008: it declined by 0.6 percentage points (from 8.5% to 7.9%). Profit before income tax declined between 2007 and 2008 from 6.9% to 5.9%, primarily because of the loss on fair value adjustment reported in 2008. Profit declined as well as a percentage of net sales from 2007 to 2008: it decreased by 0.8 percentage points. Although we saw Hometown Tires and More's profit decrease by 8.2% in Illustration 18-5, its profitability is relatively unchanged (less than 1%) in comparison with net sales.

Vertical analysis can also be depicted graphically. For example, Hometown Tires and More's key components of net sales in 2008, represented as 100% above in Illustration 18-8, could be shown using a pie chart. The chart enables one to determine proportions far more quickly. When viewing the graph, it is easy to see that cost of goods sold at 69.2% of net sales is the largest expense for Hometown Tires and More in 2008.

A vertical analysis can also be performed on the statement of comprehensive income, statement of changes in shareholders' equity, and cash flow statement. However, this is rarely done. For a statement of comprehensive income, there is no logical base amount and the changes in other comprehensive income can vary widely each year. The statement of changes in shareholders' equity and cash flow statement already give details that show changes between two periods.

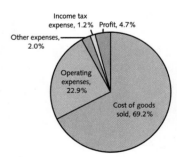

Intercompany Comparisons

Another benefit of vertical analysis is that it makes it possible to compare companies of different sizes. For example, Hometown Tires and More's main competitor is Canadian Tire. Using vertical analysis, the condensed balance sheet (or the income statement) of the small local retail company Hometown Tires and More can be more meaningfully compared with the balance sheet (or income statement) of the giant retailer Canadian Tire, as shown in Illustration 18-9.

Illustration 18-9 ➡

Intercompany balance sheet
comparison—vertical analysis

	BALANCE SHEETS December 31, 2008 (in thousands)			
	Hometown Tires and More		Canadian Tire	
Assets	Amount (in thousands)	Percentage	Amount (in millions)	Percentage
Current assets	$ 545.0	54.5%	$3,978.6	51.1%
Long-term receivables and other assets	0.0	0.0%	290.6	3.7%
Property, plant, and equipment	400.0	40.0%	3,389.8	43.5%
Intangible assets	55.0	5.5%	129.1	1.7%
Total assets	$1,000.0	100.0%	$7,788.1	100.0%
Liabilities and Shareholders' Equity				
Liabilities				
Current liabilities	$ 337.7	33.8%	$1,999.7	25.7%
Long-term liabilities	400.0	40.0%	2,220.3	28.5%
Total liabilities	737.7	73.8%	4,220.0	54.2%
Shareholders' equity				
Share capital	90.0	9.0%	715.4	9.2%
Retained earnings	152.3	15.2%	2,755.5	35.4%
Accumulated other comprehensive income	20.0	2.0%	97.2	1.2%
Total shareholders' equity	262.3	26.2%	3,568.1	45.8%
Total liabilities and shareholders' equity	$1,000.0	100.0%	$7,788.1	100.0%

Canadian Tire's total assets are more than 7,700 times greater than the total assets of the much smaller Hometown Tires and More. Vertical analysis helps eliminate this difference in size. For example, although Hometown Tires and More has fewer dollars of property, plant, and equipment compared with Canadian Tire ($400,000 compared with $3,389.8 million), using percentages, the proportion of property, plant, and equipment for each company is relatively similar (40% compared with 43.5%).

Although Hometown Tires and More has fewer dollars of debt than Canadian Tire ($737,700 compared with $4,220 million), it has a higher debt percentage than does Canadian Tire (73.8% compared with 54.2%). This is not surprising given that Hometown Tires and More does not have the same access to equity financing as does Canadian Tire. Hometown Tires and More is a much smaller company, whose shares trade (not very often) on the TSX Venture Exchange, whereas Canadian Tire's shares trade daily on the much larger Toronto Stock Exchange. Accordingly, Hometown Tires and More has a lower equity base than Canadian Tire (26.2% compared with 45.8%).

As you can see from this limited example, there are many things that can be learned by looking at vertically analyzed financial statements even when comparing companies of vastly different sizes.

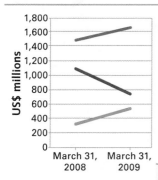

 ### ACCOUNTING IN ACTION: BUSINESS INSIGHT

Many companies report financial information using percentages. For example, Visa Inc. reported that its revenue for the quarter ended March 31, 2009, rose 13% to US$1.64 billion compared with the same quarter a year earlier. Operating expenses dropped 31% to US$766 million, the result of an expense-cutting campaign to help offset tighter consumer spending. Due to increasing revenues and decreasing expenses, its profit for the quarter rose nearly 71% to US$536 million.

Sources: "Visa Profit Surges Nearly 71 Percent," *The Globe and Mail*, April 29, 2009.

Are the percentage changes for Visa based on horizontal or vertical analysis?

BEFORE YOU GO ON . . .

→ Review It

1. What is vertical analysis?
2. How is vertical analysis different from horizontal analysis?
3. How can graphs aid in interpreting vertical analysis?
4. What base amount is used to calculate the percentage size of an amount reported in a vertically analyzed balance sheet? Income statement?
5. Can vertical analysis be used to compare two companies of differing size?

→ Do It

Summary financial information for Boyko Corporation at May 31 is as follows:

	2011	2010
Current assets	$ 234,000	$180,000
Property, plant, and equipment	756,000	420,000
Intangible assets	75,000	75,000
Total assets	$1,065,000	$675,000

Calculate the vertical percentages for each category, for each year, using vertical analysis.

Action Plan

- The base amount is total assets in a balance sheet.
- Find the relative percentage by dividing the specific asset amount by the base amount for each year.

Solution

	2011		2010	
	Amount	Percentage	Amount	Percentage
Current assets	$ 234,000	22.0%	$180,000	26.7%
Property, plant, and equipment	756,000	71.0%	420,000	62.2%
Intangible assets	75,000	7.0%	75,000	11.1%
Total assets	$1,065,000	100.0%	$675,000	100.0%

Related exercise material: BE18–5, BE18–6, BE18–7, E18–2, E18–3, and E18–4.

The Navigator

Ratio Analysis

Ratio analysis expresses the relationships between selected financial statement items and is the most widely used tool of financial analysis. Ratios are generally classified into three types:

STUDY OBJECTIVE 4

Identify and use ratios to analyze a company's liquidity, solvency, and profitability.

1. Liquidity ratios. These measure a company's short-term ability to pay its maturing obligations and to meet unexpected needs for cash.
2. Solvency ratios. These measure a company's ability to survive over a long period of time.
3. Profitability ratios. These measure a company's operating success for a specific period of time.

In earlier chapters, we presented liquidity, solvency, and profitability ratios for evaluating a company's financial condition. In this section, we provide an example of a comprehensive financial analysis using these ratios.

This analysis uses three bases for comparisons: (1) intracompany, comparing two years of data (2007 and 2008) for Hometown Tires and More; (2) intercompany, comparing Hometown Tires and More with Canadian Tire, its main competitor, for the year ended December 31, 2008; and (3) industry, comparing both companies with averages for the consumer products industry. For some of the ratios that we use, industry comparisons are not available. These are indicated by "n/a."

You will recall that Hometown Tires and More's balance sheet was presented earlier in the chapter in Illustration 18-4 and its income statement in Illustration 18-5. We will use the information in these two financial statements, plus additional data which will be introduced as required, to calculate Hometown Tires and More's ratios in the next three sections. You can use these data to review the calculations for each 2008 ratio calculated for Hometown Tires and More to make sure you understand where the numbers came from. Detailed calculations are not shown for the ratios presented for Hometown Tires and More for 2007, or for Canadian Tire or the industry for 2008.

Liquidity Ratios

Liquidity ratios measure a company's short-term ability to pay its maturing obligations and to meet unexpected needs for cash. Short-term lenders, such as bankers and suppliers, are particularly interested in assessing liquidity. Liquidity ratios include working capital, the current ratio, the acid-test ratio, receivables turnover, collection period, inventory turnover, days sales in inventory, and the operating cycle.

Working Capital

Working capital is the difference between current assets and current liabilities. The 2008 and 2007 working capital figures for Hometown Tires and More, and 2008 intercompany data for comparison, are shown below.

Working capital = Current assets – Current liabilities		
Hometown Tires and More **2008** $545,000 – $337,700 = $207,300	Hometown Tires and More **2007** $166,500	Intracompany
	Canadian Tire **2008** $1,978.9 million	Intercompany
	Industry Average **2008** n/a	Industry

Hometown Tires and More has a positive and increasing working capital: $207,300 in 2008 and $166,500 in 2007. It is not very meaningful to compare this amount with that of the much larger Canadian Tire. In addition, no industry average is available for working capital, and working capital amounts are not comparable within the industry.

It is difficult to compare absolute dollar amounts. As we learned in Chapter 4, the current ratio—which expresses current assets and current liabilities as a ratio rather than as an amount—is a more useful indicator of liquidity. In addition, two companies with the same amount of working capital may have very different current ratios.

Current Ratio

The current ratio is a widely used measure of a company's liquidity and short-term debt-paying ability. The ratio is calculated by dividing current assets by current liabilities. The 2008 and 2007 current ratios for Hometown Tires and More, and 2008 intercompany and industry data for comparison, are shown below.

Current ratio = $\dfrac{\text{Current assets}}{\text{Current liabilities}}$		
Hometown Tires and More **2008** $\dfrac{\$545,000}{\$337,700} = 1.6:1$	Hometown Tires and More **2007** 1.5:1	Intracompany
	Canadian Tire **2008** 2.0:1	Intercompany
	Industry Average **2008** 2.5:1	Industry

What does the ratio actually mean? The 2008 ratio of 1.6:1 means that for every dollar of current liabilities, Hometown Tires and More has $1.60 of current assets. Hometown Tires and More's current ratio increased slightly between 2007 and 2008. Its 2008 ratio is lower than Canadian Tire's current ratio of 2.0:1 and quite a bit lower than the industry average of 2.5:1. Despite this, Hometown Tires and More appears to have more than enough current assets to pay its current liabilities.

Acid-Test Ratio

The current ratio is only one measure of liquidity. It does not consider what the current assets are composed of. For example, a satisfactory current ratio does not disclose the fact that a portion of the current assets may be tied up in inventory or prepayments. The acid-test ratio differs from the current ratio by excluding assets that are less liquid, such as inventory, which takes longer to be converted to cash. For merchandising companies, inventory must be sold before any accounts receivable can be created, which must subsequently be collected before cash is available. The acid-test ratio also excludes prepaid expenses, which will not be converted to cash.

The acid-test ratio is calculated by dividing the sum of cash, short-term investments (trading investments in Hometown Tires and More's case), and receivables by current liabilities. The 2008 and 2007 acid-test ratios for Hometown Tires and More, and 2008 intercompany and industry data for comparison, are shown below.

Acid-test ratio $= \dfrac{\text{Cash + Short-term investments + Receivables}}{\text{Current liabilities}}$		
Hometown Tires and More **2008** $\dfrac{\$50,000 + \$20,000 + \$72,500}{\$337,700} = 0.4{:}1$	Hometown Tires and More **2007** **0.4:1**	Intracompany
	Canadian Tire **2008** **0.6:1**	Intercompany
	Industry Average **2008** **1.2:1**	Industry

What does the ratio actually mean? The 2008 ratio of 0.4:1 means that for every dollar of current liabilities, Hometown Tires and More has $0.40 of highly liquid current assets. The company's acid-test ratio is unchanged from 2007. However, it is much lower than its current ratio. This likely means that Hometown Tires and More has a large balance in its inventory and/or prepaid accounts. In addition, given that the current ratio increased while the acid-test ratio did not change in 2008, inventory and/or prepaid expenses likely increased. We will investigate the liquidity of both companies' inventory shortly, as this is the more significant account of the two.

Hometown Tires and More's acid-test ratio is lower than that of Canadian Tire but not as much lower as its current ratio was. Both Hometown Tires and More and Canadian Tire have acid-test ratios significantly below that of the industry average of 1.2:1.

Receivables Turnover

The acid-test ratio does not consider the impact of uncollectible receivables on liquidity. A dollar of cash is more available to pay bills than a dollar of an overdue account receivable. The receivables turnover ratio is used to assess the liquidity of the receivables. It measures the number of times, on average, that receivables are collected during the period. The receivables turnover is calculated by dividing net credit sales (net sales less cash sales) by the average gross accounts receivable.

You will recall from earlier chapters that when a figure from the income statement is compared with a figure from the balance sheet in a ratio, the balance sheet figure is averaged by adding together the beginning and ending balances and dividing them by 2. That is because income statement figures cover a period of time and balance sheet figures are at a point in time—in this case, the beginning and the end of the period. That is why average receivables are used in the calculation of the receivables turnover ratio shown below. Comparisons of end-of-period figures with end-of-period figures, or period figures to period figures, do not require averaging, as we saw in the current ratio and acid-test ratios calculated above.

Assuming that all sales are credit sales and that there is no allowance for doubtful accounts, the 2008 and 2007 receivables turnover figures for Hometown Tires and More, and 2008 intercompany and industry data for comparison, are shown below.

Receivables turnover = $\dfrac{\text{Net credit sales}}{\text{Average gross accounts receivable}}$		
Hometown Tires and More **2008** $\dfrac{\$1,997,000}{(\$72,500 + \$50,000) \div 2}$ = 32.6 times	Hometown Tires and More **2007** **38.7 times**	Intracompany
	Canadian Tire **2008** **11.8 times**	Intercompany
	Industry Average **2008** **18.3 times**	Industry

Hometown Tires and More's receivables turn over (i.e., they are collected) 32.6 times a year. In general, the faster the turnover, the more reliable the current ratio is for assessing liquidity.

Hometown Tires and More's receivables turnover declined from 38.7 times in 2007 to 32.6 times in 2008. It is still much higher than Canadian Tire's receivables turnover of 11.8 times a year and the industry average of 18.3 times in 2008.

Why is Hometown Tires and More's receivables turnover so much higher than those of Canadian Tire and of the industry? Hometown Tires and More likely has fewer credit sales and therefore fewer receivables. More of its sales are for cash. Canadian Tire, on the other hand, has receivables from its franchise stores and company credit card, which may take longer to collect than a trade receivable.

It is important to be careful in interpreting this ratio. We assumed that all sales were credit sales, when in fact, this is not a reasonable assumption. Companies do not separately disclose their credit and cash sales. However, intracompany, intercompany, and industry comparisons can still be made, since the same assumption—all sales were credit sales—was applied to Canadian Tire and the industry average.

Collection Period. A popular variation of the receivables turnover is to convert it into a collection period stated in days. This is done by dividing the number of days in a year (365 days) by the receivables turnover, as shown below.

Collection period = $\dfrac{\text{Days in year}}{\text{Receivables turnover}}$		
Hometown Tires and More **2008** $\dfrac{365 \text{ days}}{32.6}$ = 11 days	Hometown Tires and More **2007** **9 days**	Intracompany
	Canadian Tire **2008** **31 days**	Intercompany
	Industry Average **2008** **20 days**	Industry

The effectiveness of a company's credit and collection policies is much easier to interpret using the collection period, rather than the receivables turnover ratio. Hometown Tires and More's receivables were collected every 11 days in 2008. Although weaker than in 2007, they are still being collected faster than both Canadian Tire and the industry average. In addition, this collection period is well under the normal 30-day payment period. The general rule is that the collection period should not be more than the credit-term period (the time allowed for payment). Even Canadian Tire's collection period of 31 days is still a reasonable one. So, despite earlier concerns, receivables management appears to be in good shape for both companies, and the industry.

ACCOUNTING IN ACTION: ACROSS THE ORGANIZATION

The receivables turnover and collection period ratios are closely watched by the credit and collections department in most companies. Wyeth Consumer Healthcare, a Canadian subsidiary of global pharmaceutical company Pfizer, reviews its ratios monthly in order to check whether receivables are being collected on a timely basis. In Wyeth's case, its terms of sale are net 30 days, so it wants to see a receivables turnover of 12 times or more and a collection period of 30 days or less.

Wyeth
Consumer Healthcare

What other liquidity ratios should be monitored, and by what department(s), across the organization?

Inventory Turnover

Inventory turnover measures the average number of times that the inventory is sold during the period. Its purpose is to measure the liquidity of the inventory. The inventory turnover is calculated by dividing the cost of goods sold by the average inventory.

Hometown Tires and More's 2008 and 2007 inventory turnover figures, and 2008 intercompany and industry data for comparison, are shown below.

$\text{Inventory turnover} = \dfrac{\text{Cost of goods sold}}{\text{Average inventory}}$		
Hometown Tires and More **2008** $\dfrac{\$1,381,000}{(\$372,500 + \$340,000) \div 2} = 3.9 \text{ times}$	Hometown Tires and More **2007** **3.9 times**	Intracompany
	Canadian Tire **2008** **7.6 times**	Intercompany
	Industry Average **2008** **7.6 times**	Industry

Hometown Tires and More turns over (sells) its entire inventory 3.9 times a year. Its inventory turnover was unchanged between 2007 and 2008. Hometown Tires and More's turnover ratio of 3.9 times is low compared with that of Canadian Tire and the industry of 7.6 times. Generally, the faster inventory is sold, the less cash there is tied up in inventory and the less chance there is of inventory becoming obsolete.

Days Sales in Inventory. A variant of inventory turnover is the days sales in inventory. This is calculated by dividing the inventory turnover into the number of days in a year (365 days). Hometown Tires and More's days sales in inventory ratios for 2008 and 2007, and 2008 intercompany and industry data for comparison, are shown below.

$\text{Days sales in inventory} = \dfrac{\text{Days in year}}{\text{Inventory turnover}}$		
Hometown Tires and More **2008** $\dfrac{365 \text{ days}}{3.9} = 94 \text{ days}$	Hometown Tires and More **2007** **94 days**	Intracompany
	Canadian Tire **2008** **48 days**	Intercompany
	Industry Average **2008** **48 days**	Industry

Hometown Tires and More's inventory turnover of 3.9 times divided into 365 days is approximately 94 days. In other words, Hometown Tires and More has 94 days' (more than three months') worth of inventory on hand. This is relatively slow compared with that of Canadian Tire and the industry of 48 days.

It is important to use judgement in interpreting both the inventory turnover and days sales in inventory ratios. Remember that Hometown Tires and More is comprised of only a few stores, while Canadian Tire has more than 1,100 stores and the industry is composed of large box stores. Canadian Tire, and other stores in the industry, are large enough to take advantage of just-in-time and other computerized inventory management techniques, whereas Hometown Tires and More likely does not have such sophisticated inventory options.

Nonetheless, Hometown Tires and More must keep a close eye on its inventory. It runs the risk of being left with unsaleable inventory, not to mention the additional costs of financing and carrying this inventory over a longer period of time.

Operating Cycle

The operating cycle measures the average time it takes to purchase inventory, sell it on account, and the collect the cash from customers. It is calculated by adding the days sales in inventory and the collection period together. The 2008 and 2007 operating cycle figures for Hometown Tires and More, and 2008 intercompany and industry data for comparison, are shown below.

Operating cycle = Days sales in inventory + Collection period		
Hometown Tires and More **2008** 94 days + 11 days = 105 days	Hometown Tires and More **2007** **103 days**	Intracompany
	Canadian Tire **2008** **79 days**	Intercompany
	Industry Average **2008** **68 days**	Industry

In 2008, it took Hometown Tires and More an average of 105 days (more than three months) from the time it purchased its inventory, sold it on account, and collected the cash. This was two days slower than its operating cycle in 2007. Both Canadian Tire's and the industry's operating cycles were much faster than Hometown Tires and More's in 2008.

Liquidity Conclusion

On an intracompany comparison, Hometown Tires and More's current ratio increased slightly while its acid-test and inventory turnover ratios remained unchanged from 2007 to 2008. Although its receivables turnover ratio declined, it is still a strong result, and well within the normal collection period. And while its inventory turnover ratio did not change between 2007 and 2008, it is taking a long time to sell its inventory, which could be problematic in future, especially in difficult economic conditions. Because Hometown Tires and More's receivables turnover ratio declined, its operating cycle—comprised of both receivables and inventory—also declined in 2008.

On an intercompany comparison, Hometown Tires and More's current and acid-test ratios are lower (worse) than that of Canadian Tire. Its receivables turnover is better but its inventory turnover and operating cycle are significantly worse than Canadian Tire's. Hometown Tires and More's liquidity is worse than the industry's on all measures, except for its receivables ratios.

Solvency Ratios

Solvency ratios measure a company's ability to survive over a long period of time. Long-term lenders and investors are interested in a company's long-term solvency, particularly its ability to pay interest as it comes due and to repay the face value of debt at maturity. Solvency ratios include debt to total assets, interest coverage, and free cash flow.

Debt to Total Assets

Debt to total assets measures the percentage of the total assets that is provided by lenders. It is calculated by dividing total liabilities (both current and long-term) by total assets. This ratio indicates the company's degree of leverage. It also gives some indication of the company's ability to absorb losses without hurting the interests of its lenders. The higher the percentage of total debt to total assets, the greater the risk that the company may be unable to meet its maturing obligations. The lower the debt to total assets ratio, the more net assets there are to repay lenders if the company becomes insolvent. So, from a lender's point of view, a low ratio of debt to total assets is desirable.

Hometown Tires and More's 2008 and 2007 debt to total assets ratios, and 2008 intercompany and industry data for comparison, are shown below.

Debt to total assets = $\dfrac{\text{Total liabilities}}{\text{Total assets}}$		
Hometown Tires and More **2008** $\dfrac{\$737,700}{\$1,000,000} = 73.8\%$	Hometown Tires and More **2007** 79.7%	Intracompany
	Canadian Tire **2008** 54.2%	Intercompany
	Industry Average **2008** 37.1%	Industry

Helpful hint A popular variation of the debt to total assets ratio is the debt to equity ratio. It is calculated by dividing total debt by shareholders' equity. It compares the percentage of assets provided by lenders with that provided by shareholders.

A ratio of 73.8% means that lenders have provided 73.8% of Hometown Tires and More's total assets. Although its ratio improved in 2008, Hometown Tires and More's debt to total assets ratio is much higher than Canadian Tire's 54.2%, and that of the industry, 37.1%.

However, as mentioned in the chapter, Hometown Tires and More does not have the same access to the equity markets as does Canadian Tire, since Hometown Tires and More is smaller with limited share trading. Consequently, it is not surprising that it relies on debt financing. A more relevant calculation is whether or not it can afford this level of debt. The debt to total assets ratio should never be interpreted without also looking at the interest coverage ratio, discussed in the next section. A company may have a low debt to total assets ratio but be unable to cover its interest obligations. Alternatively, a company may have a high debt to total assets ratio but be easily able to cover its interest.

Interest Coverage

The interest coverage ratio gives an indication of the company's ability to make its interest payments as they come due. It is calculated by dividing profit before interest expense and income tax expense by interest expense. Note that the interest coverage ratio uses profit before interest expense and income tax expense. This is often abbreviated as EBIT, which stands for earnings before interest and tax. The term "earnings" is used instead of "profit" in this phrase—both are commonly used and mean the same thing. EBIT represents the amount that is available to cover interest.

The 2008 and 2007 interest coverage ratios for Hometown Tires and More, and 2008 intercompany and industry data for comparison, are shown below.

Alternative terminology The interest coverage ratio is also called the *times interest earned ratio*.

Interest coverage = $\dfrac{\text{Profit} + \text{Interest expense} + \text{Income tax expense}}{\text{Interest expense}}$		
Hometown Tires and More **2008** $\dfrac{\$93,600 + \$27,000 + \$23,400}{\$27,000} = 5.3$ times	Hometown Tires and More **2007** 5.3 times	Intracompany
	Canadian Tire **2008** 5.4 times	Intercompany
	Industry Average **2008** 14.0 times	Industry

Despite Hometown Tires and More's high debt to total assets ratio, it is able to cover its interest payments. Its profit before interest and taxes was 5.3 times the amount needed for interest expense in 2008 and 2007. Hometown Tires and More's interest coverage remained unchanged in 2008, despite the improvement in its debt to total assets ratio. It is below that of Canadian Tire at 5.4 times and that of the industry at 14 times. It is interesting to note that, although Hometown Tires and More's debt to total assets ratio was significantly higher than that of Canadian Tire, its interest coverage ratio is only slightly below that of Canadian Tire.

Free Cash Flow

One indication of a company's solvency, as well as of its ability to expand operations, repay debt, or pay dividends, is the amount of excess cash it generates after paying to maintain its current productive capacity. This amount is referred to as free cash flow.

Hometown Tires and More's cash flow statement was not included in the illustrations shown earlier in the chapter. For your information and for the purpose of the calculation below, its cash provided by operating activities for the year ended December 31, 2008 was $122,800 and its cash used by investing activities was $40,000 for the same period. The company's free cash flow figures for 2008 and 2007, and 2008 intercompany data for comparison, are shown below.

Free cash flow = Cash provided (used) by operating activities – Cash used (provided) by investing activities		
Hometown Tires and More **2008** $122,800 – $40,000 = $82,800	Hometown Tires and More **2007** **$100,000**	Intracompany
	Canadian Tire **2008** **$(274.1) million**	Intercompany
	Industry Average **2008** **n/a**	Industry

Hometown Tires and More used $40,000 in its investing activities in 2008 to purchase additional property, plant, and equipment. Hometown Tires and More has $82,800 of "free" cash to invest in additional property, plant, and equipment; repay debt; and pay its dividends. This is less than the $100,000 it had available in 2007 primarily because of an increase in investing activities in 2008.

In contrast, Canadian Tire reported a negative amount of free cash in 2008. It spent $274.1 million more on investing activities than it generated from operating activities. There is no industry average available for free cash flow. And, as noted earlier, it is hard to make a meaningful comparison of absolute dollar amounts for two companies of such different sizes.

Solvency Conclusion

In an intracompany comparison, Hometown Tires and More's solvency generally improved in 2008, as its debt to total assets ratio improved and its interest coverage ratio remained unchanged. Its free cash flow declined because of an increase in cash used by investing activities.

Despite this improvement inside the company, in intercompany and industry comparisons, Hometown Tires and More's solvency was lower (worse) than that of Canadian Tire and the industry. It is important to distinguish between Hometown Tires and More and Canadian Tire in this analysis, as they are very different types of companies. Hometown Tires and More, as a small regional company, relies mainly on debt for its financing and has to generate enough profit to cover its interest payments. In contrast, Canadian Tire, a large national company, relies more on equity for its financing needs.

Profitability Ratios

Profitability ratios measure a company's operating success for a specific period of time. A company's profit, or lack of it, affects its ability to obtain debt and equity financing, its liquidity position, and its growth. Both lenders and investors are therefore interested in evaluating profitability. Profitability ratios include the gross profit margin, profit margin, asset turnover, return on assets, return on equity, earnings per share, price-earnings, and payout ratios.

Gross Profit Margin

The gross profit margin is determined by dividing gross profit (net sales less cost of goods sold) by net sales. This ratio indicates the relative relationship between net sales and cost of goods sold. Gross profit margins should be watched closely over time. If the gross profit margin is too high, the company may lose sales if its pricing is not competitive. If the gross profit margin is too low, the company may not have enough margin to cover its expenses.

Hometown Tires and More's gross profit margin figures for 2008 and 2007, and 2008 intercompany data for comparison, are shown below.

Gross profit margin = $\dfrac{\text{Gross profit}}{\text{Net sales}}$		
Hometown Tires and More **2008** $\dfrac{\$616,000}{\$1,997,000} = 30.8\%$	Hometown Tires and More **2007** 32.5%	Intracompany
	Canadian Tire **2008** 10.1%	Intercompany
	Industry Average **2008** n/a	Industry

Hometown Tires and More's gross profit margin for 2008 means that 30.8 cents of each dollar of its sales that year went to cover operating expenses and generate a profit. Hometown Tires and More's gross profit margin declined slightly, from 32.5% in 2007 to 30.8% in 2008.

Hometown Tires and More's gross profit margin is higher than Canadian Tire's. This could be the result of several factors. It may be that Hometown Tires and More sells a different mix of merchandise than do Canadian Tire and other competitors. In addition, Hometown Tires and More's prices may be higher in general not only because of increased costs, but also because the company offers a higher level of personal service.

There is no industry average for the gross profit margin because very few Canadian companies reported this information in 2008.

Profit Margin

Profit margin is a measure of the percentage of each dollar of sales that results in profit. It is calculated by dividing profit by net sales. Hometown Tires and More's 2008 and 2007 profit margin figures, and 2008 intercompany and industry data for comparison, are shown below.

Profit margin = $\dfrac{\text{Profit}}{\text{Net sales}}$		
Hometown Tires and More **2008** $\dfrac{\$93,600}{\$1,997,000} = 4.7\%$	Hometown Tires and More **2007** 5.6%	Intracompany
	Canadian Tire **2008** 4.1%	Intercompany
	Industry Average **2008** 4.2%	Industry

Alternative terminology
Profit margin is also called the *return on sales*.

Hometown Tires and More's profit margin declined between 2007 and 2008, at 4.7% of net sales, primarily because of the loss on fair value adjustment related to the trading investments. The profit margin is above that of both Canadian Tire and the industry.

Asset Turnover

Asset turnover measures how efficiently a company uses its assets to generate sales. It is determined by dividing net sales by average total assets. The resulting number shows the dollars of sales produced by each dollar of assets. The 2008 and 2007 asset turnover ratios for Hometown Tires and More, and 2008 intercompany and industry data for comparison, are shown below.

$$\text{Asset turnover} = \frac{\text{Net sales}}{\text{Average total assets}}$$		
Hometown Tires and More **2008** $$\frac{\$1,997,000}{(\$1,000,000 + \$1,015,000) \div 2} = 2.0 \text{ times}$$	Hometown Tires and More **2007** **1.7 times**	Intracompany
	Canadian Tire **2008** **1.3 times**	Intercompany
	Industry Average **2008** **1.8 times**	Industry

In 2008, Hometown Tires and More generated $2 of sales for each dollar it had invested in assets. This ratio improved from 2007, when its asset turnover was 1.7 times, or $1.70 of sales for each dollar of assets. Its 2008 asset turnover is also higher than that of Canadian Tire and the industry. As a small operation, its assets may have a carrying amount that is less than newer and larger operations.

Return on Assets

An overall measure of profitability is return on assets. This ratio is calculated by dividing profit by average total assets. Hometown Tires and More's return on assets figures for 2008 and 2007, and 2008 intercompany and industry data for comparison, are shown below.

$$\text{Return on assets} = \frac{\text{Profit}}{\text{Average total assets}}$$		
Hometown Tires and More **2008** $$\frac{\$93,600}{(\$1,000,000 + \$1,015,000) \div 2} = 9.3\%$$	Hometown Tires and More **2007** **9.7%**	Intracompany
	Canadian Tire **2008** **5.1%**	Intercompany
	Industry Average **2008** **6.9%**	Industry

Hometown Tires and More's return on assets declined from 2007 to 2008. Its 2008 return of 9.3% is higher than that of Canadian Tire and the industry. Although the percentage is high, it must be analyzed in perspective. Hometown Tires and More's profit was high to begin with, relatively speaking. And, it is being compared with a relatively small asset base, so it results in a higher percentage, proportionately.

The return on assets can be further analyzed by looking at the profit margin and asset turnover ratios in combination, as shown below.

	Profit Margin $$\frac{\text{Profit}}{\text{Net sales}}$$	×	**Asset Turnover** $$\frac{\text{Net sales}}{\text{Average total assets}}$$	=	**Return on Assets** $$\frac{\text{Profit}}{\text{Average total assets}}$$
2008	4.7%	×	2.0 times	=	9.3%
2007	5.6%	×	1.7 times	=	9.7%

The above amounts do not work out precisely because of rounding. If we use Hometown Tires and More's unrounded profit margin and asset turnover instead of the amounts rounded to one decimal place, we can prove the above calculation.

Even with the slight discrepancies resulting because of rounding, we can clearly see that Hometown Tires and More's return on assets declined because of the decrease in profitability. That is, while Hometown Tires and More's assets generated more efficient sales in 2008, the profitability of each dollar of sales declined significantly, which resulted in a reduced return on assets.

Return on Equity

Alternative terminology
Return on equity is also known as *return on investment*.

A popular measure of profitability is the return on equity ratio. This ratio shows how many dollars of profit were earned for each dollar invested by the shareholders. It is calculated by dividing profit by average total shareholders' equity.

Although we calculate this ratio using total shareholders' equity below, it can also be calculated using only the common shareholders' equity if there is more than one class of shares. In such cases, the numerator, profit, is reduced by any preferred dividends to determine the profit available for common shareholders. The denominator, average total shareholders' equity, is reduced by any share capital belonging to the preferred shareholders to determine average common shareholders' equity. You will recall that Hometown Tires and More only has one class of share capital—common shares—so it has no preferred shares or preferred dividends.

The return on equity figures for Hometown Tires and More for 2008 and 2007, and 2008 intercompany and industry data for comparison, are shown below.

Return on equity = $\dfrac{\text{Profit}}{\text{Average shareholders' equity}}$		
Hometown Tires and More **2008** $\dfrac{\$93,600}{(\$262,300 + \$206,500) \div 2} = 40.0\%$	Hometown Tires and More **2007** 50.9%	Intracompany
	Canadian Tire **2008** 11.2%	Intercompany
	Industry Average **2008** 10.6%	Industry

Although it declined in 2008, Hometown Tires and More's return on equity is unusually high at 40%. The return on equity figures for Canadian Tire and the industry are much lower at 11.2% and 10.6%, respectively.

Note that Hometown Tires and More's 2008 return on equity of 40% is much higher than its return on assets of 9.3%. The reason is that Hometown Tires and More has made effective use of leveraging, or trading on the equity. Trading on the equity means that the company can earn a higher return by using borrowed money in its operations than it has to pay on the borrowed money. This enables Hometown Tires and More to use money supplied by lenders to increase the return to the shareholders. Recall that Hometown Tires and More has proportionately more debt than Canadian Tire, so it is not surprising that its return on equity is higher than Canadian Tire's.

A comparison of the rate of return on total assets to the rate of interest paid for borrowed money indicates the profitability of trading on the equity. Note, however, that trading on the equity is a two-way street. For example, if you borrow money at 5% and earn only 2% on it, you're trading on the equity at a loss rather than at a gain. Hometown Tires and More earns more on its borrowed funds than it has to pay in the form of interest. Thus, the return to shareholders is higher than the return on assets, which indicates that shareholders are benefiting from positive leveraging or trading on the equity.

Earnings Per Share (EPS)

Earnings per share is a measure of the profit earned on each common share. Shareholders usually think in terms of the number of shares they own or plan to buy or sell. Reducing profit to a per share basis gives a useful measure of profitability. This measure is widely used and reported. Because of the importance of the earnings per share ratio, publicly traded companies are required to present it directly on the income statement.

Earnings per share is calculated by dividing the profit available to common shareholders (profit less preferred dividends) by the weighted average number of common shares. Hometown Tires and More's profit was reported in Illustration 18-5 and its number of common shares was reported in Illustration 18-4. You will recall that Hometown Tires and More does not have any preferred shares, so there are no preferred dividends to consider in this calculation. There has been no change in the number of common shares over the past three years; consequently, the weighted average number of shares is the same as the issued number—300,000.

The earnings per share figures for Hometown Tires and More for 2008 and 2007, and 2008 intercompany data for comparison, are shown below.

Earnings per share = $\dfrac{\text{Profit} - \text{Preferred dividends}}{\text{Weighted average number of common shares}}$		
Hometown Tires and More 2008 $\dfrac{\$93,600 - \$0}{300,000} = \$0.31$	Hometown Tires and More **2007** **$0.34**	Intracompany
	Canadian Tire **2008** **$4.59**	Intercompany
	Industry Average **2008** n/a	Industry

Hometown Tires and More's earnings per share declined by $0.03 per share ($0.34 − $0.31) in 2008. Comparisons with the industry average or Canadian Tire are not meaningful, because of the large differences in the number of shares issued by companies for different purposes. The only meaningful EPS comparison is an intracompany one.

Price-Earnings (PE) Ratio

The price-earnings (PE) ratio is an often-quoted measure of the ratio of the market price of each common share to the earnings per share. The price-earnings ratio reflects investors' assessments of a company's future earnings. It is calculated by dividing the market price per share by earnings per share. The current value of Hometown Tires and More's shares is $1.40/share. Earnings per share were calculated above.

The price-earnings ratios for Hometown Tires and More for 2008 and 2007, and 2008 intercompany and industry data for comparison, are shown below.

Price-earnings ratio = $\dfrac{\text{Market price per share}}{\text{Earnings per share}}$		
Hometown Tires and More 2008 $\dfrac{\$1.40}{\$0.31} = 4.5 \text{ times}$	Hometown Tires and More **2007** **3.5 times**	Intracompany
	Canadian Tire **2008** **9.8 times**	Intercompany
	Industry Average **2008** **11.5 times**	Industry

In 2008, Hometown Tires and More's shares were valued at 4.5 times its earnings. The earnings per share, although declining, are still strong and the price of the shares has increased, indicating investors believe the company has expectations of future increases in profitability.

Canadian Tire's 2008 price-earnings ratio is 9.8 times, which is higher than Hometown Tires and More's average of 4.5 times but lower than that of the industry.

In general, a higher price-earnings ratio means that investors favour the company. They are willing to pay more for the shares because they believe the company has good prospects for long-term growth and profit in the future.

Some investors carefully study price-earnings ratios over time to help them determine when to buy or sell shares. If the highs and lows of a particular share's PE ratio remain constant over several stock market cycles, then these highs and lows can indicate selling (shares are overpriced) and buying (shares are underpriced) points for the shares. They could also mean other things, however, so investors should be very cautious in interpreting PE ratios.

Payout Ratio

The payout ratio measures the percentage of profit distributed as cash dividends. It is calculated by dividing cash dividends by profit. Hometown Tires and More paid $37,800 in dividends in 2008. Its profit was reported earlier in Illustration 18-5. The 2008 and 2007 payout ratios for Hometown Tires and More, and 2008 intercompany data for comparison, are shown below.

Payout ratio = $\dfrac{\text{Cash dividends}}{\text{Profit}}$		
Hometown Tires and More 2008 $\dfrac{\$37,800}{\$93,600} = 40.4\%$	Hometown Tires and More **2007** 35.3%	Intracompany
	Canadian Tire **2008** 18.3%	Intercompany
	Industry Average **2008** n/a	Industry

No information is available for the industry, but Hometown Tires and More's 2008 payout ratio of 40.4% is more than double the payout ratio of Canadian Tire. Hometown Tires and More is a small regional company, and has a few controlling shareholders who exercise discretion as to how much it pays in dividends.

Many companies with stable earnings have high payout ratios. For example, BCE Inc. recently had a 66% payout ratio. Companies that are expanding rapidly normally have low, or no, payout ratios. Research In Motion, for example, had a zero payout ratio.

Profitability Conclusion

In an intracompany comparison, except for the asset turnover ratio, Hometown Tires and More's profitability measures declined between 2007 and 2008. Some of its market-based ratios increased, such as the price-earnings and payout ratios. However, these ratios do not really say much because of the limited trading of Hometown Tires and More's shares. We therefore ignore these market-based ratios in our intercompany and industry comparisons.

In an intercompany comparison, Hometown Tires and More's profitability measures were all better than those of Canadian Tire. In an industry comparison, Hometown Tires and More's profitability was better than that of the industry for all ratios that were available.

Summary of Ratios

The following three illustrations summarize the liquidity, solvency, and profitability ratios we have seen in this textbook. In addition to the ratio formula and purpose, the desired direction (higher or lower) of the result is included.

Illustration 18-10

Liquidity ratios

Ratio	Formula	Purpose	Desired Result
Working capital	Current assets − Current liabilities	Measures short-term debt-paying ability.	Higher
Current ratio	$\dfrac{\text{Current assets}}{\text{Current liabilities}}$	Measures short-term debt-paying ability.	Higher
Acid-test	$\dfrac{\text{Cash + Short-term investments + Accounts receivable}}{\text{Current liabilities}}$	Measures immediate short-term debt-paying ability.	Higher
Receivables turnover	$\dfrac{\text{Net credit sales}}{\text{Average gross accounts receivable}}$	Measures liquidity of receivables.	Higher
Collection period	$\dfrac{\text{Days in year}}{\text{Receivables turnover}}$	Measures number of days receivables are outstanding.	Lower
Inventory turnover	$\dfrac{\text{Cost of goods sold}}{\text{Average inventory}}$	Measures liquidity of inventory.	Higher
Days sales in inventory	$\dfrac{\text{Days in year}}{\text{Inventory turnover}}$	Measures number of days inventory is on hand.	Lower
Operating cycle	Days sales in inventory + Collection period	Measures number of days to purchase inventory, sell it on account, and collect the cash.	Lower

To summarize, a higher result is generally considered to be better for the working capital, current, acid-test, inventory turnover, and receivables turnover ratios. For those ratios that use turnover ratios in their denominators—the days sales in inventory and collection period—as well as the operating cycle which is the combination of both of these, a lower result is better. That is, you want to have fewer days of inventory on hand and take fewer days to collect receivables—a lower operating cycle—than the opposite situation.

Of course, there are exceptions. A current ratio can be high at times because of higher balances of inventory and receivables included in current assets that are the result of slow-moving inventory or uncollectible receivables. This is why it is important never to conclude an assessment of liquidity based only on one ratio. In the case of the current ratio, it should always be interpreted along with the acid-test, inventory, and receivables turnover ratios. Likewise, the acid-test ratio should always be interpreted along with the receivables turnover ratio.

Illustration 18-11 ↓

Solvency ratios

Ratio	Formula	Purpose	Desired Result
Debt to total assets	$\dfrac{\text{Total liabilities}}{\text{Total assets}}$	Measures percentage of total assets provided by lenders.	Lower
Interest coverage	$\dfrac{\text{Profit + Interest expense + Income tax expense (EBIT)}}{\text{Interest expense}}$	Measures ability to meet interest payments.	Higher
Free cash flow	Cash provided (used) by operating activities – Cash used (provided) by investing activities	Measures cash available operating activities that management can use after paying capital expenditures.	Higher

For the debt to total assets ratio, a lower result is generally considered to be better. Having less debt reduces a company's dependence on debt financing and offers more flexibility for future financing alternatives. For the interest coverage ratio and free cash flow measure, a higher result is better.

It is important to interpret the debt to total assets and interest coverage ratios together. For example, a company may have a high debt to total assets ratio and a high interest coverage ratio, which indicates that it is able to handle a high level of debt. Or, it may have a low debt to total assets ratio and a low interest coverage ratio, indicating it has difficulty in paying its interest even for a low amount of debt. Consequently, one should always interpret a company's solvency after considering the interrelationship of these two ratios.

Illustration 18-12 ↓

Profitability ratios

Ratio	Formula	Purpose	Desired Result
Gross profit margin	$\dfrac{\text{Gross profit}}{\text{Net sales}}$	Measures margin between selling price and cost of goods sold.	Higher
Profit margin	$\dfrac{\text{Profit}}{\text{Net sales}}$	Measures amount of profit generated by each dollar of sales.	Higher
Asset turnover	$\dfrac{\text{Net sales}}{\text{Average total assets}}$	Measures how efficiently assets are used to generate sales.	Higher
Return on assets	$\dfrac{\text{Profit}}{\text{Average total assets}}$	Measures overall profitability of assets.	Higher
Return on equity	$\dfrac{\text{Profit}}{\text{Average shareholders' equity}}$	Measures profitability of shareholders' investment.	Higher
Earnings per share	$\dfrac{\text{Profit – Preferred dividends}}{\text{Weighted average number of common shares}}$	Measures amount of profit earned on each common share.	Higher
Price-earnings ratio	$\dfrac{\text{Market price per share}}{\text{Earnings per share}}$	Measures relationship between market price per share and earnings per share.	Higher
Payout ratio	$\dfrac{\text{Cash dividends}}{\text{Profit}}$	Measures percentage of profit distributed as cash dividends.	Higher

For the profitability ratios shown above, a higher result is generally considered to be better. However, there are some user-related considerations with respect to the price-earnings and payout ratios that must be understood. A higher price-earnings ratio generally means that investors favour that company and have high expectations of future profitability. However, some investors avoid shares with high PE ratios in the belief that they are overpriced, so not everyone prefers a high PE ratio.

Investors interested in purchasing a company's shares for income purposes (in the form of a dividend) are interested in companies with a high payout ratio. Investors more interested in purchasing a company's shares for growth purposes (for the share price's appreciation) are interested in a low payout ratio. They would prefer to see the company retain its earnings rather than pay them out.

We have shown liquidity, solvency, and profitability ratios in separate sections in this chapter. However, it is important to recognize that analysis should not focus on one section in isolation of the others. Liquidity, solvency, and profitability are closely interrelated in most companies. For example, a company's profitability is affected by the availability of financing and short-term liquidity. Similarly, a company's solvency not only requires satisfactory liquidity but is also affected by its profitability.

It is also important to recognize that the ratios shown in Illustrations 18-10, 18-11, and 18-12 are only examples of commonly used ratios. You will find more examples as you learn more about financial analysis.

 ## ACCOUNTING IN ACTION: ALL ABOUT YOU

More Canadians are investing in the stock market largely because of the increasing ease of trading stocks online. Traders range from students like you tracking their investments to seniors making adjustments to their retirement savings. Everybody wants to buy and sell stocks just at the right time. How do investors predict what stock prices will do and when to buy and sell stock? Some people use scientific methods while others make predictions by means that border on the occult, including basing their decisions on the phases of the moon or the activity of sunspots. However, there are generally two methods of predicting stock prices: fundamental and technical analysis. Fundamental analysts believe that market activity is 90% logical and 10% psychological. By that, they mean that most stock trading stems from investors making logical decisions based on company information. Fundamental analysts make their decisions based on their estimate of the future profits and dividends. They estimate future earnings by analyzing the historical financial statements, the industry, and the management team. In contrast, technical analysts believe the market is only 10% logical and 90% psychological, meaning that most investors base their decisions on perceptions and intuition. Technical analysts study the movements of stock prices and the volume traded for clues to future changes in prices. Basically, they study how investors have reacted to the market in the past and try to predict their future behaviour. How does analysis relate to accounting? By learning ratio analysis, you are well on your way to understanding what fundamental analysts use in their stock market investment decisions.

Sources: Burton G. Malkiel, *A Random Walk Down Wall Street,* New York: W. W. Norton & Company Inc., 2003, pp. 126–7 and 147; "Online Trading Goes Mainstream," *Financial Post,* September 9, 2009.

Taking a job with a company is in many ways similar to deciding whether or not to buy shares of that company. If you are offered a job at two companies when you graduate, what type of analysis would be appropriate—fundamental or technical—in making your decision?

BEFORE YOU GO ON . . .

➜ Review It

1. What are liquidity ratios? Explain working capital, current ratio, acid-test, receivables turnover, collection period, inventory turnover, days sales in inventory, and operating cycle.
2. What are solvency ratios? Explain debt to total assets, interest coverage, and free cash flow.
3. What are profitability ratios? Explain gross profit margin, profit margin, asset turnover, return on assets, return on equity, earnings per share, price-earnings ratio, and payout ratio.
4. Identify for which ratios a lower result may be better, and explain why.

➜ Do It

The following liquidity ratios are available for two fast food companies:

	Grab 'N Gab	Chick 'N Lick
Current ratio	1.3:1	1.5:1
Acid-test ratio	1.0:1	0.8:1
Receivables turnover	52 times	73 times
Inventory turnover	40 times	26 times
Operating cycle	16 days	19 days

Which of the two companies is more liquid? Explain.

Action Plan

- Review the formula for each ratio so you understand how it is calculated and how to interpret it.
- Remember that for liquidity ratios, a higher result is usually better except for the collection period, days sales in inventory, and operating cycle ratios.
- Review the impact of the receivables and inventory turnover ratios on the current ratio before concluding your analysis.
- Consider any industry factors that may affect your analysis.

Solution

Grab 'N Gab is the more liquid of the two companies. Although its receivables turnover is not as strong as that of Chick 'N Lick (52 times compared with 73 times), the collection period is still only 7 days (365 ÷ 52), which is an excellent collection period by any standard. Of course, you wouldn't expect a fast food business to have many receivables anyway.

Grab 'N Gab's inventory turnover, which is more important for a fast food business, is stronger than that of Chick 'N Lick. This slower inventory turnover may be artificially making Chick 'N Lick's current ratio look better than that of Grab 'N Gab. This hunch is proven by the fact that although Chick 'N Lick has the (apparently) better current ratio, Grab 'N Gab has the better acid-test ratio, which excludes the effect of inventory. In addition, Grab 'N Gab has the better operating cycle of the two companies.

➜ Do It Again

Selected information from the financial statements of two companies competing in the same industry follows:

	Papa Corporation	Bear Limited
Total assets, beginning of year	$388,000	$372,000
Total assets, end of year	434,000	536,000
Total shareholders' equity, beginning of year	269,000	296,000
Total shareholders' equity, end of year	294,000	344,000
Net sales	660,000	780,000
Gross profit	175,000	248,000
Profit	68,000	105,000

(a) For each company, calculate the following ratios: gross profit margin, profit margin, asset turnover, return on assets, and return on equity.

(b) Which company has the better return on assets ratio? What is the key driver of this return on assets ratio—profitability or turnover?

(c) Which company is more profitable? Explain.

Action Plan

- Review the formula for each ratio so you understand how it is calculated and how to interpret it.
- Don't forget to average the balance sheet figures [(beginning of period + end of period) ÷ 2] when comparing them with a period figure (e.g., asset turnover, return on assets, and return on equity ratios).
- Recall that the profit margin and the asset turnover ratio combine to explain the return on assets ratio.
- Remember that for profitability ratios, a higher result is usually better.

Solution

(a)

	Papa	Bear
Gross profit margin	$\dfrac{\$175,000}{\$660,000} = 26.5\%$	$\dfrac{\$248,000}{\$780,000} = 31.8\%$
Profit margin	$\dfrac{\$68,000}{\$660,000} = 10.3\%$	$\dfrac{\$105,000}{\$780,000} = 13.5\%$
Asset turnover	$\dfrac{\$660,000}{(\$388,000 + \$434,000) \div 2} = 1.6 \text{ times}$	$\dfrac{\$780,000}{(\$372,000 + \$536,000) \div 2} = 1.7 \text{ times}$
Return on assets	$\dfrac{\$68,000}{(\$388,000 + \$434,000) \div 2} = 16.5\%$	$\dfrac{\$105,000}{(\$372,000 + \$536,000) \div 2} = 23.1\%$
Return on equity	$\dfrac{\$68,000}{(\$269,000 + \$294,000) \div 2} = 24.2\%$	$\dfrac{\$105,000}{(\$296,000 + \$344,000) \div 2} = 32.8\%$

(b) Bear Limited has the higher return on assets ratio. The key driver of this higher ratio is the profit margin. Bear has the higher profit margin of the two companies. It also has a slightly higher asset turnover. These two ratios combine to result in a significantly higher return on assets ratio for Bear.

(c) Bear Limited is more profitable than Papa Corporation on all profitability ratios.

Related exercise material: BE18–8, BE18–9, BE18–10, BE18–11, BE18–12, BE18–13, BE18–14, E18–5, E18–6, E18–7, E18–8, E18–9, E18–10, E18–11, and E18–12.

The Navigator

Limitations of Financial Statement Analysis

Business decisions are frequently made by using one or more of the analytical tools illustrated in this chapter. But you should be aware of the limitations of these tools and of the financial statements they are based on.

STUDY OBJECTIVE 5

Recognize the limitations of financial statement analysis.

Alternative Accounting Policies

There are a wide variety of different accounting policies and practices that companies can use. For example, companies may use different inventory cost determination methods (specific identification, FIFO, or average) or different depreciation methods (straight-line, diminishing-balance, or units-of-production) depending on the pattern of the revenues (economic benefits) their assets produce. Different methods result in differing financial positions and performance, which will reduce comparability.

For example, Canadian Tire uses the diminishing-balance method of depreciation for much of its property, plant, and equipment. Both RONA and Sears, two of its competitors, use the straight-line method of depreciation. Consequently, profit and total assets could be different—depending on the amount of property, plant, and equipment and at what point in its useful life it is—simply because of the use of different depreciation methods. This would affect a number of solvency and profitability ratios.

Recall, however, that although depreciation expense and the carrying amount of property, plant, and equipment may be different in one or more periods because of the choice of depreciation methods, in total, over the life of the assets, there is no difference. We call differences created from alternative accounting policies "artificial" or timing differences. Although it might be possible to detect differences in accounting policies by reading the notes to the financial statements, adjusting the financial data to compensate for the use of different policies can be difficult for the average user. In real life, analysts spend a great deal of time adjusting financial statement data for these types of differences in order to improve the comparability of the ratios.

Also, as has been highlighted throughout this text, publicly traded companies are transitioning to International Financial Reporting Standards (IFRS). One eventual benefit of this transition is improved comparability of companies across the globe. During the period when companies in Canada are changing to IFRS, comparability may be a challenge. As we learned in Chapter 14, changes in accounting policies normally involve retroactive adjustments to ensure comparability between years. However, in some cases, retroactive adjustment will not be feasible or practical.

Comparability may also be hindered by the accounting policy options available for private companies. While publicly traded companies must adopt IFRS, private companies have the choice of adopting IFRS or adopting Canadian GAAP for Private Enterprises. If a private company chooses not to adopt IFRS, which is the most likely scenario, further complications will arise in trying to compare a private company with a public company for certain accounting policies.

Comprehensive Income

Most financial analysis ratios exclude other comprehensive income from the analysis. Profitability ratios, including industry averages, generally use data from the income statement and not the statement of comprehensive income, which includes both profit and other comprehensive income. In addition, there are no standard ratio formulas incorporating comprehensive income.

Nonetheless, it is important to review a company's sources of other comprehensive income in any financial analysis. In particular, gains and losses from fair value adjustments of strategic equity investments (with no significant influence) can be significant. You will recall that while gains and losses from non-strategic equity (trading) investments are included in profit, gains and losses from fair value adjustments of strategic equity investments (without significant influence) normally are reported on the statement of comprehensive income as other comprehensive income. You will also recall from Chapter 16 that this is an area currently in flux with the standard setters.

For example, Canadian Tire reported a profit of $374.2 million for the year ended January 3, 2009. During the same year, it reported other comprehensive income of $147.2 million, which resulted in total comprehensive income of $521.4 million ($374.2 + $147.2). Canadian Tire's profit margin was 41%. However, if a profit margin was calculated using total comprehensive income rather than just profit, it would have been 57% instead of 41%.

In cases like this, where other comprehensive income is significant, and depending on the source of the income, some analysts will adjust profitability ratios to incorporate the effect of total comprehensive income.

Diversification

Diversification in Canadian industry can also limit the usefulness of financial analysis. Many companies today are so diversified that they cannot be classified by industry. Canadian Tire, for example, sells home, food, car, sports, and leisure products. In addition, it is the country's largest independent gasoline retailer. It offers banking, credit, and other financial services. Canadian Tire also sells work clothes and casual attire through its subsidiary, Mark's Work Wearhouse. Consequently, one of the limitations of our analysis of Canadian Tire is to try to interpret ratios based on the consolidated results of so many different types of businesses. In addition, deciding what industry a company is in and comparing its results with an industry average can also pose challenges to an effective evaluation of its financial performance and position.

When companies have significant operations in different lines of business, they are required to report additional disclosures in a segmented information note to their financial statements. Many analysts say that segmented information is the most important data in the financial statements. Without it, a comparison of diversified companies is very difficult. Canadian Tire has four operating segments representing different lines of business: Canadian Tire Retail, Canadian Tire Financial Services, Canadian Tire Petroleum, and Mark's Work Wearhouse. It reports selected financial data such as gross operating revenue, profit before income taxes, interest revenue, depreciation and amortization, total assets, and capital expenditures for each of these segments in the notes to its statements.

Quality of Information

In evaluating a company's financial performance, the quality of the information provided is extremely important. A company that has a high quality index includes full and transparent information that will not confuse or mislead users of the financial statements. In our feature story, CICA's president and CEO, Kevin Dancey, said: "It is encouraging to see so many companies dedicated to providing corporate reports that are relevant, clear, and easily understood … especially in these unsettled times."

Financial statements for companies like Canadian Tire, with fulsome and transparent disclosure practices, have a high quality of information value. Other companies may limit the information they disclose. In such cases, the quality of the information will decrease.

Fortunately, the chief executive officer and chief financial officer of a publicly traded company must ensure, and personally declare, that the reported financial information is accurate, relevant, and understandable. In addition, audit committees are held responsible for quizzing management on the degree of aggressiveness or conservatism applied to the information and the quality of the underlying estimates, accounting policies, and judgements.

A strong corporate governance process, including an active board of directors and audit committee, is essential to ensuring the quality of information. Canadian Tire received commendations from the Corporate Reporting Awards judges for its corporate governance disclosure.

Inflation

Our accounting information system does not adjust data for price-level changes. For example, a five-year comparison of Canadian Tire's operating revenues shows growth of 129.2%. But this growth trend would be misleading if the general price level had increased or decreased greatly during the same period. In actuality, the inflation rates added up to 8.4% during this same period, so while Canadian Tire's revenues have indeed increased, they have not increased as much as it first appears. Still, our comparisons are relevant because data that have not been adjusted for inflation are being used consistently for both revenues and expenses, and for each period.

In Canada, inflation has not been very significant of late. The Bank of Canada has a stated policy to maintain an inflation rate at an average of 2% (within a 1% to 3% range). As noted above, inflation was 8.4% over the period 2004 to 2008 used to compare Canadian Tire's operating revenues, or an average of less than 2% a year.

Some countries experience "hyper," or extremely rapid, inflation. Hyperinflation occurs where the cumulative inflation rate, over a three-year period, reaches or exceeds 100%. One such example is Zimbabwe, where inflation reached an annual rate of 89.7 sextillion percent (that's 89,7 followed by 20 zeros) in 2008—the highest in the world. In 2009, Zimbabwe abandoned printing of the Zimbabwean dollar, and the South African rand and U.S. dollar became the standard currencies for exchange.

Some economists predict that hyperinflation may become a risk in the future for the United States because of the falling economy and government interventions to try to correct the situation. In countries where hyperinflation exists, financial statements are adjusted for the effects of inflation in order to make the financial information more meaningful for decision-making.

Economic Factors

The recession of 2008 and 2009 in much of the industrialized world has impacted the financial results of most companies. A report released by the Canadian Centre for Policy Alternatives said that this particular recession has hit Canada harder and faster than any previous downturn and Canadian companies were more exposed to economic ruin than they had been since the Great Depression of the 1930s. In 2008 and 2009, we saw many companies restructure or downsize their operations; others closed or were bought by other companies; and still others were evaluating their options to operate effectively in the new economic situation.

We can expect to see many more discontinued operations included in financial statements than we have in past years. You will recall learning about discontinued operations in Chapter 14. Irregular items, such as discontinued operations, must be segregated from any analyses because discontinued operations are not indicative of a company's sustainable earnings.

During times like an economic recession, horizontal analyses and ratios compared across years lose much of their relevance. When losses result in negative numbers, it is difficult to calculate percentages and ratios, much less interpret them. Vertical analyses become more useful in such times. If a company has losses, they must be assessed based on the factors driving the loss in the current period. Less attention should be paid to comparing the losses with results from prior periods.

One must use this information, along with non-financial information, to try to assess what changes relate to the economic situation and what changes relate to factors that management can, or should be able to, control. For example, have operating expenses increased faster than revenues? Why? Are consumers not spending? Are prices too high? Have expenses not been adequately controlled or adjusted for the current marketplace? Particular attention must be paid to the company's results compared with those of its competitors and the entire industry.

Never has it been more important to analyze a company's own financial information in light of external information. For example, how do economic indicators such as the unemployment rate, interest rates, currency rates, and the like affect the business under analysis? One analyst recently said: "In many cases, the Canadian Tire of today stacks up well against prior recessions (newer store base, stronger credit business, productivity initiatives); however, it will not be immune to the recession and certain elements are more challenging today (competitive environment, consumer credit behaviour, currency." It is understanding what impact these elements have on the financial results—anticipating and correcting for them—that will help companies survive in these challenging times.

BEFORE YOU GO ON . . .

→ Review It

1. What are some of the limitations of financial analysis?
2. Will the transition to International Financial Reporting Standards or Canadian GAAP for Private Enterprises facilitate or limit financial analysis?
3. How much other comprehensive income does the Forzani Group report for the year ended February 1, 2009? What percentage is this comprehensive income of its profit for the same year? Should other comprehensive income be incorporated into a financial analysis of Forzani? The answer to this question is at the end of the chapter.
4. How might the economic recession of 2008 and 2009 be expected to affect financial analysis in future years?

Related exercise material: BE18–15 and E18–13.

The Navigator

WILEY PLUS

Demonstration Problems

Demonstration Problem

A vertical analysis of the condensed financial statements of Mukhin Inc. for the years 2008 to 2011 follows.

MUKHIN INC. Percentage Balance Sheet May 31				
Assets	2011	2010	2009	2008
Current assets	11.1%	11.1%	13.9%	11.4%
Current assets of discontinued operations	0.2%	2.1%	0.6%	4.2%
Non-current assets	88.0%	77.0%	84.8%	81.2%
Non-current assets of discontinued operations	0.7%	9.8%	0.7%	3.2%
Total assets	100.0%	100.0%	100.0%	100.0%

Liabilities and Shareholders' Equity

Current liabilities	19.3%	17.5%	19.0%	15.0%
Current liabilities of discontinued operations	0.0%	1.4%	0.2%	4.1%
Non-current liabilities	52.4%	52.1%	46.0%	45.3%
Non-current liabilities of discontinued operations	2.3%	4.8%	1.8%	3.4%
Total liabilities	74.0%	75.8%	67.0%	67.8%
Shareholders' equity	26.0%	24.2%	33.0%	32.2%
Total liabilities and shareholders' equity	100.0%	100.0%	100.0%	100.0%

MUKHIN INC. Percentage Balance Sheet May 31				
	2011	**2010**	**2009**	**2008**
Revenues	100.0%	100.0%	100.0%	100.0%
Expenses	87.8%	89.5%	104.0%	96.0%
Profit (loss) before income taxes	12.2%	10.5%	(4.0%)	4.0%
Income tax expense (recovery)	3.8%	3.1%	(0.3%)	2.3%
Profit (loss) from continuing operations	8.4%	7.4%	(3.7%)	1.7%
Profit (loss) from discontinued operations	0.0%	(0.2%)	1.4%	9.0%
Profit (loss)	8.4%	7.2%	(2.3%)	10.7%

Instructions

(a) How should discontinued operations be treated in a financial analysis?

(b) Discuss the significant changes between 2008 and 2011 for the company, with and without the impact of discontinued operations.

Solution to Demonstration Problem

(a) Nonrecurring items, such as discontinued operations, should be excluded from any comparative analysis because these items are not expected to recur and do not reflect sustainable profit going forward.

(b) Current assets increased in 2009, declined in 2010, and remained stable in 2011. Mukhin's current liabilities are a higher percentage of total assets than are its current assets. Current liabilities have generally been increasing, except for in 2010. Except for during that same year, 2010, Mukhin's non-current assets have also been increasing as a percentage of total assets. Non-current liabilities have been increasing. The company likely increased its long-term liabilities to help finance increasing purchases of non-current assets.

Mukhin's liquidity and solvency appear to be declining over recent years, with increasing percentages of liabilities. We would have to perform further analyses (e.g., ratio analysis) to determine the reasons for this decline.

In terms of profitability, Mukhin appears to be controlling its expenses, which have declined, except in 2009. Except for this same year, its profitability (profit from continuing operations) also appears to be on the increase.

It is interesting to note the impact that discontinued operations have on Mukhin's financial position. While these should be excluded from our comparative analysis, one might question whether they are a nonrecurring item or not since over the last four years, discontinued operations appear to be the norm rather than the exception. However, except in 2008, the discontinued operations have not significantly impacted Mukhin's profitability.

Action Plan

• Exclude the impact of irregular items in your analysis.

• Look at the percentage comparisons both vertically (within the year) and horizontally (across the years).

The Navigator

Summary of Study Objectives

1. Identify the need for, and tools of, financial statement analysis. Users of financial statements make comparisons in order to evaluate a company's past, current, and future performance and position. There are three bases of comparison: (1) intracompany, (2) intercompany, and (3) industry. The tools of financial analysis include horizontal, vertical, and ratio analysis.

2. Explain and apply horizontal analysis. Horizontal analysis is a technique for evaluating a series of data over a period of time. The increase or decrease that has taken place is determined, and is expressed as either an amount or a percentage. It is calculated by dividing the amount in a specific period (or the change between periods) by a base-period amount.

3. Explain and apply vertical analysis. Vertical analysis is a technique for expressing each item in a financial statement as a percentage of a relevant total (base amount) in the same financial statement. It is calculated by dividing the financial statement amount under analysis by the base amount for that particular financial statement, which is usually total assets for the balance sheet and revenues for the income statement.

4. Identify and use ratios to analyze a company's liquidity, solvency, and profitability. Liquidity ratios include working capital, current ratio, acid-test ratio, receivables turnover, collection period, inventory turnover, days sales in inventory, and operating cycle. Solvency ratios include debt to total assets, interest coverage, and free cash flow. Profitability ratios include the gross profit margin, profit margin, asset turnover, return on assets, return on equity, earnings per share, price-earnings, and payout ratios. The formula, purpose, and desired result for each ratio are presented in Illustrations 18-10 (liquidity), 18-11 (solvency), and 18-12 (profitability).

5. Recognize the limitations of financial statement analysis. The usefulness of analytical tools can be limited by (1) the use of alternative accounting policies, (2) significant amounts of other comprehensive income, (3) diversification within a company or industry, (4) the quality of the information provided, (5) inflation, and (6) economic factors.

Glossary

WILEY PLUS Glossary
Key Term Matching Activity

Horizontal analysis A technique for evaluating a series of financial statement data over a period of time to determine the increase (decrease) that has taken place. This increase (decrease) is expressed as either an amount or a percentage. Also known as trend analysis. (p. 1002)

Horizontal percentage change for period A percentage measuring the change from one period to the next period. It is calculated by dividing the dollar amount of the change between the specific period under analysis and the base (prior) period by the base-period amount. (p. 1003)

Horizontal percentage of base-period amount A percentage measuring the change since a base period, normally involving more than one period. It is calculated by dividing the amount for the specific period under analysis by the base-period amount. (p. 1003)

Liquidity ratios Measures of a company's short-term ability to pay its maturing obligations and to meet unexpected needs for cash. (p. 1012)

Profitability ratios Measures of a company's operating success for a specific period of time. (p. 1018)

Ratio analysis A technique for evaluating financial statements that expresses the relationship between selected financial statement data. (p. 1011)

Solvency ratios Measures of a company's ability to survive over a long period of time. (p. 1016)

Vertical analysis A technique for evaluating financial statement data within a period. Each item in a financial statement is expressed as a percentage of the base amount. Also known as common size analysis. (p. 1007)

Vertical percentage A percentage measuring the proportion of an amount in a financial statement within a period. It is calculated by dividing the financial statement amount under analysis by the base amount for that particular financial statement. (p. 1007)

Self-Study Questions

WILEY PLUS Quizzes

Answers are at the end of the chapter.

(SO 1) K 1. Comparisons of data within a company are an example of which of the following comparative bases?
   (a) Intracompany
   (b) Intercompany
   (c) Industry
   (d) Horizontal

(SO 2) AP 2. Rankin Inlet Corporation reported net sales of $300,000, $330,000, and $360,000 in the years 2009, 2010, and 2011, respectively. If 2009 is the base year, what is the horizontal percentage of the base-period amount for 2011?
   (a) 77%
   (b) 108%
   (c) 120%
   (d) 130%

(SO 2) AP 3. As indicated in Question 2 above, Rankin Inlet Corporation reported net sales of $300,000, $330,000, and $360,000 in the years 2009, 2010, and 2011, respectively. What is the horizontal percentage change for each period?
   (a) 110% and 120%
   (b) 110% and 109%
   (c) 10% and 9%
   (d) 10% and 20%

(SO 3) K 4. In a vertical analysis, the base amount for depreciation expense is generally:
   (a) net sales.
   (b) depreciation expense in a previous year.
   (c) total assets.
   (d) total property, plant, and equipment.

(SO 2, 3) C 5. The following schedule shows what type of analysis?

	2011		2010	
	Amount	Percentage	Amount	Percentage
Current assets	$200,000	25%	$175,000	21%
Property, plant, and equipment	600,000	75%	650,000	79%
Total assets	$800,000	100%	$825,000	100%

   (a) Horizontal analysis
   (b) Differential analysis
   (c) Vertical analysis
   (d) Intercompany analysis

(SO 4) K 6. Which of the following is *not* a liquidity ratio?
   (a) Acid-test ratio
   (b) Asset turnover
   (c) Inventory turnover
   (d) Collection period

(SO 4) AN 7. Which of the following situations would be the most likely indicator that a company might have a solvency problem?
   (a) Increasing debt to total assets and interest coverage ratios
   (b) Increasing debt to total assets and decreasing interest coverage ratios
   (c) Decreasing debt to total assets and interest coverage ratios
   (d) Decreasing debt to total assets and increasing interest coverage ratios

(SO 4) AN 8. Which of the following situations is a likely indicator of profitability?
   (a) An increasing price-earnings ratio
   (b) Increasing return on assets, asset turnover, and profit margin ratios
   (c) Decreasing return on equity and payout ratios
   (d) A decreasing gross profit margin and increasing profit margin

(SO 5) C 9. Which of the following situations most likely indicates that a financial analysis should be interpreted with caution?
   (a) Different inventory cost formulas are being used by competing companies with similar inventory.
   (b) A company had no other comprehensive income.
   (c) Inflation is low.
   (d) The quality of information is high.

(SO 5) K 10. When a company operates in significantly different lines of business, which of the following statements is *not* true?
   (a) A financial analysis cannot be performed.
   (b) The company must report selected financial information about each line of business in the notes to its financial statements.
   (c) Consolidated financial statements can limit the usefulness of financial analysis.
   (d) It will be difficult to compare its ratios with the industry average.

Questions

(SO 1) C 1. (a) What are the differences among the following bases of comparison: (1) intracompany, (2) intercompany, and (3) industry averages? (b) Explain whether these three bases of comparison should be used individually or together.

(SO 1) C 2. (a) Identify the three commonly used tools of analysis. (b) Explain whether each is normally used in an intracompany, intercompany, and/or industry comparison.

(SO 2) K 3. Explain how the percentage of a base-period amount and the percentage change for a period are calculated in horizontal analysis.

(SO 2) C 4. Explain how a horizontal analysis is affected if an account (a) has no value in a base year and a value in the next year, or (b) has a negative value in the base year and a positive value in the next year.

(SO 2, 3) C 5. Horizontal analysis and vertical analysis are two methods of financial statement analysis. Explain the difference between these two methods.

(SO 2, 3) C 6. Visa Inc. became a public corporation in March 2008. Can a meaningful horizontal and vertical analysis be prepared for its first full year of operations as a public company, the year ended March 31, 2009? Explain.

(SO 2, 3) C 7. Explain how graphs can benefit horizontal and vertical analyses.

(SO 3) K 8. What items are usually assigned a 100% value in a vertical analysis of (a) the balance sheet and (b) the income statement?

(SO 3) C 9. Can vertical analysis be used to compare two companies of different sizes, such as Walmart, the world's largest retailer, and Costco, the eighth-largest retailer in the world? Explain.

(SO 4) K 10. What do the following classes of ratios measure: (a) liquidity ratios, (b) solvency ratios, and (c) profitability ratios?

(SO 4) C 11. Which ratio(s) should be used to help answer each of the following questions?
   (a) How efficient is a company at using its assets to produce sales?
   (b) What is the company's ability to pay its obligations immediately without selling inventory?
   (c) How long does it take to purchase inventory, sell it on account, and collect the cash?
   (d) How many dollars of profit were earned for each dollar invested by the shareholders?
   (e) How able is a company to pay interest charges as they come due?

(SO 4) AN 12. Does a high current ratio always indicate that a company has a strong liquidity position? Describe two situations in which a high current ratio might be hiding liquidity problems.

(SO 4) AN 13. Aubut Corporation, a retail store, has a receivables turnover of 4.5 times. The industry average is 6.5 times. Does Aubut have a collection problem with its receivables?

(SO 4) C 14. Wong Ltd. reported debt to total assets of 37% and an interest coverage ratio of 3 times in the current year. The industry average is 39% for debt to total assets and 2.5 times for interest coverage. Is Wong's solvency better or worse than that of the industry?

(SO 4) AN 15. Explain how the profit margin and asset turnover are related to the return on assets ratio.

(SO 4) C 16. The return on assets for McDonald's is 8.2%. During the same year, it reported a return on equity of 15.6%. Has McDonald's made effective use of leverage? Explain.

(SO 4) AN 17. If you were an investor interested in buying the shares of a company with growth potential, would you look for a company that had high or low price-earnings and payout ratios? If you were interested in buying the shares of a company with income potential, would your answer change? Explain why.

(SO 5) C 18. Identify and briefly explain the limitations of financial analysis.

(SO 5) C 19. Explain how the move from Canadian accounting standards to international accounting standards will likely affect financial analysis during the years 2010 to 2012.

(SO 5) C 20. If Irving, a private company, chooses to move to Canadian GAAP for Private Enterprises rather than IFRS, what impact might this have for financial analysis purposes?

(SO 5) AN 21. McCain Foods and Cavendish Farms are close competitors in the frozen potato product field. Both are private companies. Yet, McCain produces other frozen food products besides french fries, such as appetizers, pizzas, vegetables, desserts, juices, and dinner entrees. Assuming you were able to access each company's financial statements, in what way(s) would their differing product lines affect your financial analysis?

(SO 5) AN 22. Explain how the use of the different accounting policies or reporting situations outlined below will affect a comparative analysis of two competing companies. In your answer, identify specifically which ratios you anticipate will be affected.

(a) One company uses FIFO; the other uses average cost for its inventory cost formula.

(b) One company uses straight-line depreciation; the other uses diminishing-balance depreciation.

(c) One company reports a loss from discontinued operations; the other has no discontinued operations.

23. In what ways do you anticipate the global economic recession that started in 2008 will affect financial analysis for subsequent years? (SO 5) C

Brief Exercises

BE18–1 Match each of the following terms with the most appropriate description.

Match terms with descriptions. (SO 1) K

Terms	Description
_____ 1. Intracompany	(a) Analysis-period amount ÷ Base-period amount
_____ 2. Horizontal percentage	(b) Comparison with averages calculated by financial rating organizations
_____ 3. Intercompany	(c) An analysis tool that evaluates financial statement data within a period of time
_____ 4. Industry	(d) Comparisons made between companies
_____ 5. Horizontal analysis	(e) (Analysis-period amount – base-period amount) ÷ base-period amount
_____ 6. Horizontal percentage change for period	(f) An analysis tool that evaluates financial statement data over time
_____ 7. Vertical analysis	(g) Comparisons made within a company
_____ 8. Ratio analysis	(h) An analysis tool used in all three types of comparisons (intracompany, intercompany, and industry)

BE18–2 Comparative data (in thousands) from the balance sheet of Federer Ltd. are shown below. Using horizontal analysis, calculate the percentage of the base year, assuming 2009 is the base year.

Prepare horizontal analysis. (SO 2) AP

	2011	2010	2009
Cash	$ 24	$ 45	$ 30
Accounts receivable	268	227	197
Inventory	499	481	395
Prepaid expenses	22	0	10
Property, plant, and equipment	3,216	3,150	2,990
Intangible assets	532	432	332
Total assets	$4,561	$4,335	$3,954

BE18–3 Refer to BE18–2. Using horizontal analysis, calculate the percentage change for each year.

Prepare horizontal analysis. (SO 2) AP

BE18–4 A graph of the horizontal analysis percentages of the base-year amount for selected components from Tilden Ltd.'s income statement is shown below. Did Tilden's profit increase, decrease, or remain unchanged over the three-year period, or is it not determinable from the information provided in the graph? Explain.

Use horizontal analysis to determine change in profit. (SO 2) AN

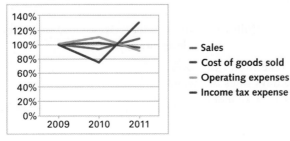

Prepare horizontal and vertical analyses.
(SO 2, 3) AP

BE18–5 Comparative data from the balance sheet of Rioux Ltd. are shown below. (a) Using horizontal analysis, calculate the percentage of the base-year amount, using 2009 as the base year. (b) Prepare a vertical analysis for each year.

	2011	2010	2009
Cash	$ 150,000	$ 175,000	$ 75,000
Accounts receivable	600,000	400,000	450,000
Inventory	780,000	600,000	700,000
Property, plant, and equipment	3,130,000	2,800,000	2,850,000
Total assets	$4,660,000	$3,975,000	$4,075,000

Prepare vertical analysis.
(SO 3) AP

BE18–6 Comparative data (in thousands) from the income statement of JTI Inc. are shown below. Prepare a vertical analysis for each year.

	2011	2010
Net sales	$1,934	$2,073
Cost of goods sold	1,612	1,674
Gross profit	322	399
Operating expenses	218	240
Profit before income tax	104	159
Income tax expense	31	48
Profit	$ 73	$ 111

Use vertical analysis to determine change in profit.
(SO 3) AP

BE18–7 A graph of the vertical analysis percentages for selected components from Waubons Corp.'s income statement is shown below. (a) Did Waubons' profit as a percentage of sales increase, decrease, or remain unchanged over the three-year period? (b) What was (were) the primary reason(s) for this change?

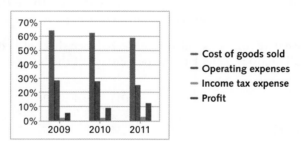

Classify ratios.
(SO 4) K

BE18–8 Indicate whether each of the following ratios is a liquidity (L) ratio, a solvency (S) ratio, or a profitability (P) ratio.

_____ (a) Return on assets
_____ (b) Receivables turnover
_____ (c) Earnings per share
_____ (d) Payout ratio
_____ (e) Acid-test ratio
_____ (f) Debt to total assets
_____ (g) Free cash flow
_____ (h) Inventory turnover
_____ (i) Return on equity
_____ (j) Interest coverage

Interpret changes in ratios.
(SO 4) C

BE18–9 For each of the following independent situations, indicate whether the change would be viewed as an improvement or deterioration:

(a) A decrease in the receivables turnover
(b) An increase in the days sales in inventory
(c) A decrease in debt to total assets

(d) A decrease in interest coverage
(e) An increase in the gross profit margin
(f) A decrease in asset turnover
(g) An increase in return on equity
(h) A decrease in the acid-test ratio

BE18–10 Holysh Inc. reported a current ratio of 1.5:1 in the current year, which is higher than last year's current ratio of 1.3:1. It also reported an acid-test ratio of 1:1, which is higher than last year's acid-test ratio of 0.6:1; receivables turnover of 8 times, which is less than last year's receivables turnover of 9 times; and an inventory turnover of 6 times, which is less than last year's inventory turnover of 7 times. Is Holysh's liquidity improving or deteriorating? Explain.

Evaluate liquidity.
(SO 4) AN

BE18–11 Selected financial data for Shumway Ltd. are shown below. (a) Calculate for each of 2011 and 2010 the inventory turnover and the days sales in inventory ratios. (b) Calculate for each of 2011 and 2010 the receivables turnover and collection period ratios. (c) Calculate for each of 2011 and 2010 the operating cycle. (d) Based on these ratios, what conclusion(s) can be drawn about the management of the inventory and receivables?

Calculate and evaluate inventory, receivables, and operating cycle ratios.
(SO 4) AN

	2011	2010	2009
Sales	$6,420,000	$6,240,000	$5,430,000
Cost of goods sold	4,540,000	4,550,000	3,950,000
Accounts receivable (gross)	850,000	750,000	650,000
Inventory	1,020,000	980,000	840,000

BE18–12 Shoppers Drug Mart reported the following selected financial data (in thousands) for a recent year:

Calculate solvency ratios.
(SO 4) AP

Interest expense	$ 63,952
Income tax expense	253,338
Profit	565,212
Total assets	6,419,306
Total liabilities	2,841,215
Cash provided by operating activities	478,989
Cash used by investing activities	664,566

Calculate the following: (a) debt to total assets, (b) interest coverage, and (c) free cash flow.

BE18–13 Loblaw reported sales of $6,718 million and profit of $109 million for a recent quarter. Its total assets were $13,943 million at the beginning of the quarter and $13,814 million at the end of the quarter. (a) Calculate the profit margin, asset turnover, and return on assets for the quarter. (b) Explain how these three ratios are interrelated.

Calculate profitability ratios.
(SO 4) AP

BE18–14 Recently, the price-earnings ratio of Research In Motion was 20 times and the price-earnings ratio of the Bank of Montreal was 12 times. The payout ratio of each company was 0% and 74%, respectively. Which company's shares would you purchase for growth? For income? Explain.

Evaluate investor ratios.
(SO 4) AN

BE18–15 Stirling Corporation and Apple Inc. have similar types of inventory. Each company uses a different inventory cost formula—FIFO and average—during a period of falling prices. At the end of the current year, Stirling reported an average inventory amount of $10,000, while Apple reported an average inventory amount of $12,000. Stirling reported cost of goods sold of $200,000, while Apple reported cost of goods sold of $180,000. (a) Identify which company is using the FIFO cost formula and which is using the average formula. (b) Calculate the inventory turnover ratio for each company. Explain the effect the differing amounts—cost of goods sold and inventory—have on the resulting inventory turnover ratio. (c) How would you treat any differences in the inventory turnover ratio between the two companies for analysis purposes?

Evaluate impact of alternative cost formulas on inventory turnover.
(SO 4, 5) AN

Exercises

Prepare horizontal analysis.
(SO 2) AP

E18–1 Comparative data from the balance sheet of Dressaire Inc. are shown below:

	2011	2010	2009
Current assets	$120,000	$ 80,000	$100,000
Non-current assets	400,000	350,000	300,000
Current liabilities	90,000	70,000	65,000
Long-term liabilities	145,000	125,000	150,000
Common shares	150,000	115,000	100,000
Retained earnings	135,000	120,000	85,000

Instructions

(a) Using horizontal analysis, calculate the percentage of the base-year amount, using 2009 as the base year.

(b) Using horizontal analysis, calculate the percentage change for each year.

Prepare vertical analysis.
(SO 3) AP

E18–2 Comparative data from the income statement of Fleetwood Corporation are shown below:

	2011	2010
Sales	$800,000	$600,000
Cost of goods sold	550,000	375,000
Gross profit	250,000	225,000
Operating expenses	175,000	125,000
Profit before income tax	75,000	100,000
Income tax expense	18,750	25,000
Profit	$ 56,250	$ 75,000

Instructions

Prepare a vertical analysis for each year.

Prepare horizontal and vertical analyses.
(SO 2, 3) AP

E18–3 Comparative data from the income statement of Olympic Corporation are shown below:

	2011	2010
Net sales	$610,000	$540,000
Cost of goods sold	460,000	400,000
Gross profit	150,000	140,000
Operating expenses	55,000	50,000
Profit before income tax	95,000	90,000
Income tax	32,000	30,000
Profit	$ 63,000	$ 60,000

Instructions

(a) Prepare a horizontal analysis, calculating the percentage of the base-year amount, assuming 2010 is the base year.

(b) Prepare a vertical analysis for each year.

Prepare horizontal and vertical analyses and identify changes.
(SO 2, 3) AN

E18–4 Comparative data from the balance sheet of Mountain Equipment Co-operative, an outdoor equipment supplier, are shown on the following page:

MOUNTAIN EQUIPMENT CO-OPERATIVE
Balance Sheet
December 28 (in thousands)

Assets	2008	2007
Current assets	$ 67,525	$ 62,437
Property, plant, and equipment	104,920	83,782
Total assets	$172,445	$146,219
Liabilities and Members' Equity		
Current liabilities	$ 33,786	$ 29,167
Long-term liabilities	3,439	1,684
Total liabilities	37,225	30,851
Members' equity	135,220	115,368
Total liabilities and members' equity	$172,445	$146,219

Instructions

(a) Prepare a horizontal analysis, calculating the percentage of the base-year amount, assuming 2007 is the base year.
(b) Prepare a vertical analysis for each year.
(c) Identify any significant changes from 2007 to 2008.

E18–5 The following is a selected list of ratios:

_____ Acid-test	_____ Gross profit margin
_____ Asset turnover	_____ Interest coverage
_____ Collection period	_____ Inventory turnover
_____ Current ratio	_____ Price-earnings ratio
_____ Days sales in inventory	_____ Profit margin
_____ Debt to total assets	_____ Receivables turnover
_____ Earnings per share	_____ Return on assets
_____ Free cash flow	_____ Return on equity

Classify and compare ratios.
(SO 4) C

Instructions

(a) Classify each of the above ratios as a liquidity (L), solvency (S), or profitability (P) ratio.
(b) For each of the above ratios, indicate whether a higher result is generally considered better (B) or worse (W).

E18–6 Nordstar, Inc. operates hardware stores in several provinces. Selected comparative financial statement data are shown below:

Calculate and evaluate liquidity ratios.
(SO 4) AN

NORDSTAR, INC.
Balance Sheet (partial)
December 31 (in millions)

	2008	2007
Current assets		
Cash	$ 30	$ 91
Short-term investments	55	60
Accounts receivable	676	586
Inventory	628	525
Prepaid expenses	41	52
Total current assets	$1,430	$1,314
Total current liabilities	$ 890	$ 825

For the year ended December 31, 2008, net credit sales were $4,190 million and the cost of goods sold was $2,900 million.

Instructions

(a) Calculate the liquidity ratios for 2008.
(b) Using the data in the chapter, compare Nordstar's liquidity to the liquidity of (1) Canadian Tire Corporation, Limited, and (2) the industry averages for the consumer products industry for 2008.

Evaluate liquidity.
(SO 4) AN

E18–7 The following selected ratios are available for Pampered Pets Inc. for the most recent three years:

	2011	2010	2009
Current ratio	2.6:1	1.4:1	2.1:1
Acid-test	0.8:1	0.6:1	0.7:1
Receivables turnover	6.7 times	7.4 times	8.2 times
Inventory turnover	7.5 times	8.7 times	9.9 times
Operating cycle	103 days	91 days	81 days

Instructions

(a) Has the company's collection of its receivables improved or weakened over the last three years?
(b) Is the company selling its inventory faster or slower than in past years?
(c) Overall, has the company's liquidity improved or weakened over the last three years? Explain.

Evaluate solvency.
(SO 4) AN

E18–8 The following selected ratios are available for Ice-T Inc. for the three most recent years:

	2011	2010	2009
Debt to total assets	50%	45%	40%
Interest coverage	2.0 times	1.5 times	1.0 times

Instructions

(a) Has the debt to assets improved or weakened over the last three years?
(b) Has the interest coverage improved or weakened over the last three years?
(c) Overall, has the company's solvency improved or weakened over the last three years?

Calculate and compare profitability ratios.
(SO 4) AP

E18–9 Selected information for Xtreme Corporation and its industry follow:

Total assets, beginning of year	$275,000
Total assets, end of year	350,000
Total shareholders' equity, beginning of year	100,000
Total shareholders' equity, end of year	133,500
Preferred shares	25,000
Sales	500,000
Cost of goods sold	375,000
Profit	33,500

Industry averages: Gross profit margin, 27.5%; profit margin, 7.5%; asset turnover, 1.5 times; return on assets, 12%; and return on equity, 40%.

Instructions

(a) Calculate the gross profit margin, profit margin, asset turnover, return on assets, and return on equity ratios for Xtreme Corporation.
(b) For each ratio, indicate whether Xtreme's ratio compares favourably (F) or unfavourably (U) with that of the industry.

Evaluate profitability
(SO 4) AN

E18–10 Imperial Oil and Suncor Energy reported the following investor-related information recently:

	Imperial Oil	Suncor Energy
Earnings per share	$4.39	$2.29
Payout ratio	8.7%	8.7%
Price-earnings ratio	9.4 times	10.4 times
Profit margin	12.4%	7.1%
Return on equity	45.7%	16.2%

Instructions

(a) Based on the above information, can you tell which company is more profitable?

(b) Which company do investors favour?

(c) Would investors purchase shares in these companies mainly for growth or for dividend income?

E18–11 Selected comparative financial data (in thousands, except for share price) of Canada's number one bookseller, Indigo Books & Music, are shown below:

Calculate and classify ratios. (SO 4) AP

	2009	2008
Revenue	$940,399	$922,878
Interest expense	309	786
Income tax expense (recovery)	15,077	(8,755)
Profit	30,650	52,808
Total assets	487,506	421,004
Total liabilities	256,616	217,250
Total shareholders' equity	230,890	203,754
Cash provided by operating activities	93,907	76,880
Cash used by investing activities	(49,149)	(18,841)
Market price per share	11.00	12.62
Weighted average number of common shares	24,675	24,744

Instructions

(a) Calculate the following ratios for 2009:

1. Asset turnover
2. Debt to total assets
3. Earnings per share
4. Free cash flow
5. Interest coverage

6. Price-earnings ratio
7. Profit margin
8. Return on assets
9. Return on equity

(b) Indicate whether each of the above ratios is a measure of liquidity (L), solvency (S), or profitability (P).

E18–12 The following selected ratios are available for a recent year for Suncor Energy and Husky Energy:

Analyze ratios. (SO 4) AN

	Suncor	Husky
Liquidity		
Current ratio	0.9:1	1.2:1
Acid-test	0.6:1	0.9:1
Receivables turnover	19.5 times	16.7 times
Solvency		
Debt to total assets	35.1%	12.3%
Interest coverage	8.9 times	24.2 times
Profitability		
Profit margin	7.1%	15.2%
Asset turnover	0.9 times	0.9 times
Return on equity	16.2%	28.8%
Price-earnings ratio	10.4 times	9.1 times

Instructions

(a) Which company is more liquid? Explain.
(b) Which company is more solvent? Explain.
(c) Which company is more profitable? Explain.
(d) Which company do investors favour? Is this consistent with your findings in (a) to (c)? Explain.

Determine effect of different situations on ratios.
(SO 4, 5) E

E18–13 Several different situations are outlined below that may affect the financial results of two different companies operating in the same industry.

Situation	Ratio
1. Company A reported an operating loss from discontinued operations; Company B had no discontinued operations.	Profit margin
2. Company A uses the straight-line depreciation method and an estimated useful life of 5 years; Company B uses the straight-line depreciation method and an estimated useful life of 8 years for similar equipment.	Asset turnover
3. Company A is experiencing a high level of inflation in its primary country of operation; Company B is operating in a country with little or no inflation.	Return on equity
4. Company A sells most of its merchandise for cash; Company B sells most of its merchandise on account.	Receivables turnover
5. Company A capitalized development costs; Company B expensed all of its costs for the R&D incurred on a similar invention.	Debt to total assets

Instructions

(a) For each of the situations described above, explain how it would affect the ratio given beside it. For example, in item 1, an operating loss would affect (reduce) the profit but would not affect the net sales in the calculation of the profit margin.

(b) For each of the situations described above, indicate which company will appear to have the "better" ratio result, all other things being equal. For example, in item 1, Company B would appear to have the better (higher) profit margin as Company A's profit would be lower while net sales are unchanged in the calculation of the profit margin.

Problems: Set A

Prepare horizontal analysis and identify changes.
(SO 2) E

P18–1A The following condensed financial information is available for Big Rock Brewery, Canada's largest craft brewer.

BIG ROCK BREWERY INCOME TRUST Income Statement Year Ended December 31 (in thousands)				
	2008	2007	2006	2005
Net revenue	$37,633	$36,451	$38,701	$40,563
Cost of goods sold	14,905	14,192	13,773	15,255
Gross profit	22,728	22,259	24,928	25,308
Operating expenses	18,523	17,422	16,183	17,561
Profit from operations	4,205	4,837	8,745	7,747
Other income	220	462	–	–
Profit before income taxes	4,425	5,299	8,745	7,747
Income tax expense (recovery)	(530)	(169)	365	1,127
Profit	$ 4,955	$ 5,468	$ 8,380	$ 6,620

BIG ROCK BREWERY INCOME TRUST Balance Sheet December 31 (in thousands)				
Assets	2008	2007	2006	2005
Current assets	$ 6,683	$ 5,598	$11,554	$12,770
Non-current assets	29,216	30,263	30,617	29,016
Total assets	$35,899	$35,861	$42,171	$41,786
Liabilities and Unitholders' Equity				
Current liabilities	$ 4,675	$ 5,511	$ 4,377	$ 3,896
Non-current liabilities	6,228	3,202	7,427	8,060
Total liabilities	10,903	8,713	11,804	11,956
Unitholders' equity	24,996	27,148	30,367	29,830
Total liabilities and unitholders' equity	$35,899	$35,861	$42,171	$41,786

Instructions

(a) Prepare a horizontal analysis, calculating the percentage of the base-year amount for the income statement and balance sheet, assuming 2005 is the base year.

(b) Identify the key components in Big Rock's income statement and balance sheet that are primarily responsible for the change in the company's financial position and performance over the four-year period.

Taking It Further   How has Big Rock primarily financed its assets—through debt or equity—over the last four years?

P18–2A   A horizontal and vertical analysis of the income statement for a retail company selling a wide variety of general merchandise is shown below:

Interpret horizontal and vertical analysis.
(SO 2, 3) E

RETAIL CORPORATION Horizontal Income Statement Year Ended January 30				
	2011	2010	2009	2008
Revenue	140.0%	111.0%	114.0%	100.0%
Cost of goods sold	148.3%	113.3%	116.7%	100.0%
Gross profit	127.5%	107.5%	110.0%	100.0%
Operating expenses	171.4%	133.1%	126.9%	100.0%
Profit from operations	93.3%	87.6%	96.9%	100.0%
Other revenues and expenses				
Interest expense	40.0%	60.0%	80.0%	100.0%
Other revenue	240.0%	140.0%	200.0%	100.0%
Profit before income tax	140.0%	110.8%	113.8%	100.0%
Income tax expense	160.0%	116.0%	124.0%	100.0%
Profit	135.2%	109.5%	111.4%	100.0%

RETAIL CORPORATION Vertical Income Statement Year Ended January 30				
	2011	2010	2009	2008
Revenue	100.0%	100.0%	100.0%	100.0%
Cost of goods sold	63.6%	61.2%	61.4%	60.0%
Gross profit	36.4%	38.8%	38.6%	40.0%
Operating expenses	21.4%	21.0%	19.5%	17.5%
Profit from operations	15.0%	17.8%	19.1%	22.5%
Other revenues and expenses				
Interest expense	(2.9%)	(5.4%)	(7.0%)	(10.0%)
Other revenue	0.9%	0.6%	0.9%	0.5%
Profit before income tax	13.0%	13.0%	13.0%	13.0%
Income tax expense	2.9%	2.6%	2.7%	2.5%
Profit	10.1%	10.4%	10.3%	10.5%

Instructions

(a) How effectively has the company controlled its cost of goods sold over the four-year period?

(b) In a vertical analysis, the company's profit before income tax has remained unchanged at 13% of revenue over the four-year period. Yet, in a horizontal analysis, profit before income tax has grown 40% over that period of time. Explain how this is possible.

(c) Identify any other key financial statement components that have changed over the four-year period for the company.

Taking It Further Identify any additional information that might be helpful to you in your analysis of this company over the four-year period.

Prepare vertical analysis, calculate profitability ratios, and compare.
(SO 3, 4) AN

P18–3A Comparative income statement data for Chen Inc. and Chuan Ltd., two competitors, are shown below for the year ended December 31, 2011:

	Chen	Chuan
Net sales	$1,849,035	$539,038
Cost of goods sold	1,060,490	338,006
Gross profit	788,545	201,032
Operating expenses	502,275	89,000
Profit from operations	286,270	112,032
Interest expense	6,800	1,252
Profit before income tax	279,470	110,780
Income tax expense	103,800	38,300
Profit	$ 175,670	$ 72,480

Additional information:

	Chen		Chuan	
	2011	2010	2011	2010
Total assets	$977,090	$812,410	$297,346	$205,279
Total shareholders' equity	802,265	646,595	222,478	149,998

Instructions

(a) Prepare a vertical analysis of the income statement for each company.

(b) Calculate the gross profit margin, profit margin, asset turnover, return on assets, and return on equity ratios for 2011 for each company.

(c) Using the information calculated in (a) and (b), compare the profitability of each company.

Taking It Further How is your assessment of profitability affected by the differing sizes of the two companies, if at all? Explain.

Determine impact of transactions on liquidity ratios.
(SO 4) AN

P18–4A The following selected liquidity ratios are available for Yami Corporation:

Current ratio	1.5:1
Acid-test	1.0:1
Receivables turnover	15 times
Inventory turnover	10 times

Instructions

Indicate whether each of the above ratios would increase, decrease, or remain unchanged as a result of each of the following independent transactions, assuming the company uses a perpetual inventory system:

(a) Yami buys merchandise on account.

(b) Yami pays an account payable.

(c) Yami sells merchandise on account at a profit.

(d) Yami collects an account receivable.

Taking It Further Would you expect the impact of each of the above transactions on the current ratio to change if the current ratio were 0.5:1 instead of 1.5:1? Explain.

P18–5A Comparative financial statements for Johnson Cables Ltd. are shown below:

Calculate ratios.
(SO 4) AP

JOHNSON CABLES LTD.
Income Statement
Year Ended December 31

	2011	2010
Net sales	$1,948,500	$1,700,500
Cost of goods sold	1,025,500	946,000
Gross profit	923,000	754,500
Operating expenses	516,000	449,000
Profit from operations	407,000	305,500
Interest expense (net)	28,000	19,000
Profit before income tax	379,000	286,500
Income tax expense	113,700	86,000
Profit	$ 265,300	$ 200,500

JOHNSON CABLES LTD.
Balance Sheet
December 31

Assets	2011	2010
Current assets		
Cash	$ 68,100	$ 64,200
Accounts receivable	107,800	102,800
Inventory	143,000	115,500
Total current assets	318,900	282,500
Debt investments, at amortized cost	54,000	50,000
Property, plant, and equipment	625,300	520,300
Total assets	$998,200	$852,800
Liabilities and Shareholders' Equity		
Current liabilities		
Accounts payable	$155,000	$125,400
Income tax payable	43,500	42,000
Current portion of mortgage payable	10,000	20,000
Total current liabilities	208,500	187,400
Mortgage payable	104,000	200,000
Total liabilities	312,500	387,400
Shareholders' equity		
Common shares (56,000 issued in 2011; 60,000 in 2010)	168,000	180,000
Contributed capital—reacquired common shares	2,000	–
Retained earnings	515,700	285,400
Total shareholders' equity	685,700	465,400
Total liabilities and shareholders' equity	$998,200	$852,800

Additional information:
1. All sales were on account.
2. The allowance for doubtful accounts was $5,400 in 2011 and $5,100 in 2010.
3. On July 1, 2011, 4,000 shares were reacquired and cancelled.
4. In 2011, $15,000 of dividends were paid to the common shareholders.
5. Cash provided by operating activities was $313,900.
6. Cash used by investing activities was $161,000.

Instructions

Calculate all possible liquidity, solvency, and profitability ratios for 2011.

Taking It Further Based on the ratios you have calculated for 2011, can you determine whether Johnson Cables' liquidity, solvency, and profitability is strong or weak? If not, what additional information would you require?

Calculate and compare ratios.
(SO 4) AN

P18–6A Comparative financial statements for Click and Clack Ltd. are shown below:

CLICK AND CLACK LTD.
Income Statement
Year Ended December 31

	2011	2010
Sales	$900,000	$840,000
Cost of goods sold	620,000	575,000
Gross profit	280,000	265,000
Operating expenses	164,000	160,000
Profit from operations	116,000	105,000
Other revenues and expenses		
Interest expense	(35,000)	(20,000)
Gain on fair value adjustment—trading investments	5,000	0
Profit before income tax	86,000	85,000
Income tax expense	22,000	20,000
Profit	$ 64,000	$ 65,000

CLICK AND CLACK LTD.
Balance Sheet
December 31

Assets	2011	2010
Cash	$ 70,000	$ 65,000
Trading investments, at fair value	45,000	40,000
Accounts receivable	94,000	90,000
Inventories	130,000	125,000
Prepaid expenses	25,000	23,000
Land, buildings, and equipment	390,000	305,000
Total assets	$754,000	$648,000

Liabilities and Shareholders' Equity	2011	2010
Notes payable	$110,000	$100,000
Accounts payable	45,000	42,000
Accrued liabilities	32,000	40,000
Bonds payable, due 2015	190,000	150,000
Common shares (20,000 issued)	200,000	200,000
Retained earnings	177,000	116,000
Total liabilities and shareholders' equity	$754,000	$648,000

Additional information:
1. The allowance for doubtful accounts was $4,000 in 2011 and $5,000 in 2010.
2. Accounts receivable at the beginning of 2010 were $88,000, net of an allowance for doubtful accounts of $3,000.
3. Inventories at the beginning of 2010 were $115,000.
4. Total assets at the beginning of 2010 were $630,000.
5. Total current liabilities at the beginning of 2010 were $180,000.
6. Total liabilities at the beginning of 2010 were $361,000.
7. Total shareholders' equity at the beginning of 2010 was $259,000.
8. Seventy-five percent of the sales were on account.
9. In each of 2010 and 2011, $8,000 of dividends were paid to the common shareholders.
10. Cash provided by operating activities was $68,000 in 2011 and $60,000 in 2010.
11. Cash used by investing activities was $120,000 in 2011 and $50,000 in 2010.

Instructions

(a) Calculate all possible liquidity, solvency, and profitability ratios for 2011 and 2010.
(b) Identify whether the change in each ratio from 2010 to 2011 was favourable (F), unfavourable (U), or no change (NC).

Taking It Further Explain whether overall (a) liquidity, (b) solvency, and (c) profitability improved, deteriorated, or remained the same between 2010 and 2011.

P18–7A Selected financial data for Tim Hortons and Starbucks are presented below for a recent year:

Calculate and evaluate ratios for two companies. (SO 4) E

	Tim Hortons (in CAD$ millions)	Starbucks (in US$ millions)
Income Statement		
Total revenue	$2,043.7	$10,383.0
Cost of sales	1,181.0	4,645.3
Gross profit	862.7	5,737.7
Operating expenses	419.1	5,233.8
Profit from operations	443.6	503.9
Other expenses	19.6	44.4
Profit before income tax	424.0	459.5
Income tax expense	139.3	144.0
Profit	$ 284.7	$ 315.5
Balance Sheet		
Current assets	$ 465.0	$1,748.0
Non-current assets	1,527.6	3,924.6
Total assets	$1,992.6	$5,672.6
Current liabilities	$ 366.0	$2,189.7
Long-term liabilities	486.2	992.0
Total liabilities	852.2	3,181.7
Shareholders' equity	1,140.4	2,490.9
Total liabilities and shareholders' equity	$1,992.6	$5,672.6
Additional information:		
Average accounts receivable	$ 132.2	$ 308.7
Average inventories	65.9	692.3
Average total assets	1,894.9	5,508.3
Average total shareholders' equity	1,071.2	2,387.5

Instructions

(a) For each company, calculate the following ratios. Industry averages are given in parentheses after each ratio, where available.

  1. Current ratio (1.8:1)
  2. Receivables turnover (36.1 times)
  3. Collection period (10 days)
  4. Inventory turnover (51.9 times)
  5. Days sales in inventory (7 days)
  6. Operating cycle (17 days)
  7. Debt to total assets (36.7%)
  8. Gross profit margin (26.6%)
  9. Profit margin (3.5%)
  10. Asset turnover (1.5 times)
  11. Return on assets (5.2%)
  12. Return on equity (9.7%)

(b) Compare the liquidity, solvency, and profitability of the two companies with each other and their industry.

Taking It Further Tim Hortons' year end is December 28, 2008, and Starbucks' year end is September 28, 2008. How do these differing year ends affect your comparative analysis, if at all?

Evaluate ratios for two companies.
(SO 4) E

P18–8A Selected ratios for two companies operating in the office supply industry follow. Industry ratios, where available, have also been included.

Ratio	Paperclip Co.	Stapler Co.	Industry Average
Acid-test	0.6:1	0.8:1	0.6:1
Asset turnover	2.6 times	2.2 times	2.5 times
Current ratio	1.7:1	3.0:1	1.6:1
Debt to total assets	50%	30%	50%
Gross profit margin	23%	40%	27%
Interest coverage	4.2 times	8.6 times	7.1 times
Inventory turnover	6 times	3 times	5 times
Payout ratio	8%	22%	10%
Price-earnings ratio	29 times	45 times	38 times
Profit margin	5%	4%	4%
Receivables turnover	11.8 times	9.1 times	10.2 times
Return on assets	13%	8.8%	10%
Return on equity	25%	13%	16%

Instructions

(a) Both companies offer their customers credit terms of net 30 days. Indicate the ratio(s) that should be used to assess how well the accounts receivable are managed. Comment on how well each company appears to be managing its accounts receivable.

(b) How well does each company appear to be managing its inventory? Indicate the ratio(s) that should be used to assess inventory management.

(c) Which company, Paperclip or Stapler, is more solvent? Identify the ratio(s) that should be used to determine this and defend your choice.

(d) To your surprise, you notice that Paperclip's gross profit margin is significantly less than Stapler's and somewhat less than the industry average. Identify two possible reasons for this.

(e) Which company do investors appear to believe has greater prospects for growing its income and dividends? Indicate the ratio(s) you used to reach this conclusion and explain your reasoning.

Taking It Further What is primarily responsible for the difference in the two companies return on assets ratios—profitability or turnover? Explain.

Evaluate ratios for two companies.
(SO 4) E

P18–9A The following ratios are available for agricultural chemicals competitors Potash Corporation of Saskatchewan (PotashCorp) and Agrium for a recent year:

	PotashCorp	Agrium	Industry
Liquidity			
Current ratio	0.9:1	1.8:1	2.6:1
Acid-test	0.6:1	0.6:1	0.9:1
Receivables turnover	10.0 times	10.0 times	6.3 times
Inventory turnover	7.1 times	3.3 times	3.4 times
Operating cycle	87 days	147 days	165 days
Solvency			
Debt to total assets	55.2%	58.1%	30.5%
Interest coverage	37.7 times	19.2 times	29.2 times
Profitability			
Gross profit margin	51.9%	31.4%	63.9%
Profit margin	38.8%	12.9%	13.3%
Asset turnover	0.9 times	1.0 times	0.5 times
Return on assets	35.1%	17.2%	13.9%
Return on equity	65.9%	36.7%	20.1%
Price-earnings ratio	8.4 times	8.1 times	9.9 times
Payout ratio	3.0%	1.3%	n/a

Instructions

(a) Which company is more liquid? Explain.
(b) Which company is more solvent? Explain.
(c) Which company is more profitable? Explain.

Taking It Further Which company do investors favour? Is your answer consistent with your findings above?

P18–10A You are in the process of analyzing two similar companies in the same industry. This is the first year of operations for both companies. You learn that they have different accounting practices and policies as follows:

Identify impact of different accounting policies.
(SO 5) AN

1. Company A, which has the same type of equipment as Company B, uses the straight-line method of depreciation while Company B uses the diminishing-balance method.
2. Company A invests its excess cash in short-term debt investments held for trading, carried at fair value. Company B invests its excess cash in long-term debt investments held to earn interest income, carried at amortized cost. Both companies have invested exactly the same amount of cash and prices have been generally rising for these investments.

Instructions

(a) Considering only the impact of the choice of depreciation method, determine which company will report a higher (1) current ratio, (2) debt to total assets ratio, and (3) profit margin ratio, or if there will be no impact.
(b) Considering only the impact of the classification of securities, determine which company will report a higher (1) current ratio, (2) debt to total assets ratio, and (3) profit margin ratio, or if there will be no impact.
(c) Identify two other limitations of financial analysis that an analyst should watch for when analyzing financial statements.

Taking It Further How should an analyst account for different accounting policies and practices in an intercompany comparison of these two companies? Explain.

Problems: Set B

P18–1B The following condensed financial information is available for WestJet Airlines.

Prepare horizontal analysis and identify changes.
(SO 2) E

WESTJET AIRLINES LTD.
Income Statement
Year Ended December 31 (in millions)

	2008	2007	2006	2005
Revenue	$2,550	$2,127	$1,765	$1,389
Operating expenses	2,257	1,826	1,566	1,288
Profit from operations	293	301	199	101
Other expenses	38	64	35	49
Profit before income taxes	255	237	164	52
Income tax expense	77	44	49	28
Profit	$ 178	$ 193	$ 115	$ 24

WESTJET AIRLINES LTD. Balance Sheet December 31 (in thousands)				
Assets	2008	2007	2006	2005
Current assets	$ 926	$ 718	$ 456	$ 320
Non-current assets	2,353	2,266	2,271	1,893
Total assets	$3,279	$2,984	$2,727	$2,213
Liabilities and Shareholders' Equity				
Current liabilities	$ 740	$ 591	$ 464	$ 377
Non-current liabilities	1,453	1,443	1,457	1,166
Total liabilities	2,193	2,034	1,921	1,543
Shareholders' equity	1,086	950	806	670
Total liabilities and shareholders' equity	$3,279	$2,984	$2,727	$2,213

Instructions

(a) Prepare a horizontal analysis, calculating the percentage of the base-year amount for the income statement and balance sheet, assuming 2005 is the base year.

(b) Identify the key components in WestJet's income statement and balance sheet that are primarily responsible for the change in the company's financial position and performance over the four-year period.

Taking It Further   How has WestJet primarily financed its assets—through debt or equity—over the last four years?

Interpret horizontal and vertical analysis.
(SO 2, 3) E

P18–2B   A horizontal and vertical analysis of the income statement for a service company providing consulting services is shown below:

SERVICE CORPORATION Horizontal Income Statement Year Ended December 31				
	2011	2010	2009	2008
Revenue	120.0%	110.0%	114.0%	100.0%
Operating expenses	118.6%	111.4%	114.3%	100.0%
Profit from operations	123.3%	106.7%	113.3%	100.0%
Other revenues and expenses				
Interest expense	40.0%	60.0%	80.0%	100.0%
Other revenue	240.0%	140.0%	200.0%	100.0%
Profit before income tax	166.8%	130.2%	131.7%	100.0%
Income tax expense	166.8%	130.2%	131.7%	100.0%
Profit	166.8%	130.2%	131.7%	100.0%

SERVICE CORPORATION Vertical Income Statement Year Ended January 30				
	2011	2010	2009	2008
Revenue	100.0%	100.0%	100.0%	100.0%
Operating expenses	69.2%	70.9%	70.2%	70.0%
Profit from operations	30.8%	29.1%	29.8%	30.0%
Other revenues and expenses				
Interest expense	(3.3%)	(5.4%)	(7.0%)	(10.0%)
Other revenue	1.0%	0.6%	0.9%	0.5%
Profit before income tax	28.5%	24.3%	23.7%	20.5%
Income tax expense	5.7%	4.9%	4.8%	4.1%
Profit	22.8%	19.4%	18.9%	16.4%

Instructions

(a) How effectively has the company controlled its operating expenses over the four-year period?

(b) In a horizontal analysis, the company's income tax expense has changed exactly as much as profit (66.8%) over the four-year period. Yet, in a vertical analysis, the income tax percentage is different than the profit percentage in each period. Explain how this is possible.

(c) Identify any other key financial statement components that have changed over the four-year period for the company.

Taking It Further   Identify any additional information that might be helpful to you in your analysis of this company over the four-year period.

P18–3B   Comparative income statement data for Manitou Ltd. and Muskoka Ltd., two competitors, are shown below for the year ended June 30, 2011:

Prepare vertical analysis, calculate profitability ratios, and compare.
(SO 3, 4) AN

	Manitou	Muskoka
Net sales	$360,000	$1,400,000
Cost of goods sold	200,000	720,000
Gross profit	160,000	680,000
Operating expenses	60,000	272,000
Profit from operations	100,000	408,000
Rental income	12,000	24,000
Profit before income tax	112,000	432,000
Income tax expense	22,400	95,040
Profit	$ 89,600	$ 336,960

Additional information:

	Manitou		Muskoka	
	2011	2010	2011	2010
Total assets	$535,000	$380,000	$1,900,000	$1,550,000
Total shareholders' equity	249,600	160,000	911,960	575,000

Instructions

(a) Prepare a vertical analysis of the income statement for each company.

(b) Calculate the gross profit margin, profit margin, asset turnover, return on assets, and return on equity ratios for 2011 for each company.

(c) Using the information calculated in (a) and (b), compare the profitability of each company.

Taking It Further   How is your assessment of profitability affected by the differing sizes of the two companies, if at all? Explain.

P18–4B   The following selected profitability ratios are available for Hubei Corporation:

Determine impact of transactions on profitability ratios.
(SO 4) AN

Profit margin	10%
Asset turnover	1.5 times
Earnings per share	$2
Price-earnings ratio	8 times

Instructions

Indicate whether each of the above ratios would increase, decrease, or remain unchanged as a result of each of the following independent transactions:

(a) Hubei issues common shares for cash.

(b) Hubei sells equipment at a loss.

(c) Hubei pays the principal on a mortgage note payable.

(d) Hubei's share price decreases from $16 per share to $12 per share.

Taking It Further   Would the answers to any of the above change if the profit margin was negative and the earnings per share was a loss per share?

Calculate ratios.
(SO 4) AP

P18–5B   Comparative financial statements for Rosen Inc. are shown below:

ROSEN INC.
Income Statement
Year Ended December 31

	2011	2010
Net sales	$790,000	$624,000
Cost of goods sold	540,000	405,600
Gross profit	250,000	218,400
Operating expenses	153,880	149,760
Profit from operations	96,120	68,640
Interest expense	3,200	1,200
Loss on fair value adjustment—trading investments	6,720	6,000
Profit before income tax	86,200	61,440
Income tax expense	12,930	9,216
Profit	$ 73,270	$ 52,224

ROSEN INC.
Balance Sheet
December 31

Assets	2011	2010
Current assets		
Cash	$ 23,100	$ 11,600
Trading investments, at fair value	24,800	33,000
Accounts receivable	106,200	93,800
Inventory	96,400	74,000
Total current assets	250,500	212,400
Property, plant, and equipment	465,300	459,600
Total assets	$715,800	$672,000
Liabilities and Shareholders' Equity		
Current liabilities		
Accounts payable	$164,850	$130,000
Income tax payable	2,500	4,000
Other payables and accruals	12,800	22,000
Total current liabilities	180,150	156,000
Bonds payable	90,000	120,000
Total liabilities	270,150	276,000
Shareholders' equity		
Common shares (15,000 issued)	150,000	150,000
Retained earnings	295,650	246,000
Total shareholders' equity	445,650	396,000
Total liabilities and shareholders' equity	$715,800	$672,000

Additional information:
1. All sales were on account.
2. The allowance for doubtful accounts was $5,500 in 2011 and $4,500 in 2010.
3. In 2011, $15,420 of dividends were paid to the common shareholders.
4. Cash provided by operating activities was $110,420.
5. Cash used by investing activities was $53,500.

Instructions

Calculate all possible liquidity, solvency, and profitability ratios for 2011.

Taking It Further Based on the ratios you have calculated for 2011, can you determine whether Rosen's liquidity, solvency, and profitability are strong or weak? If not, what additional information would you require?

P18–6B Comparative financial statements for Star Track Ltd. are shown below:

Calculate and compare ratios. (SO 4) AN

STAR TRACK LTD.
Balance Sheet
December 31

Assets	2011	2010
Cash	$ 50,000	$ 42,000
Accounts receivable	100,000	87,000
Inventories	240,000	200,000
Prepaid expenses	25,000	31,000
Long-term debt investments, at amortized cost	180,000	100,000
Land	75,000	75,000
Building and equipment	570,000	600,000
Total assets	$1,240,000	$1,135,000
Liabilities and Shareholders' Equity		
Notes payable	$ 125,000	$ 125,000
Accounts payable	160,750	140,000
Accrued liabilities	52,000	50,000
Bonds payable, due 2014	100,000	100,000
Preferred shares	200,000	200,000
Common shares (100,000 issued)	300,000	300,000
Retained earnings	302,250	220,000
Total liabilities and shareholders' equity	$1,240,000	$1,135,000

STAR TRACK LTD.
Income Statement
Year Ended December 31

	2011	2010
Sales	$1,000,000	$940,000
Cost of goods sold	650,000	635,000
Gross profit	350,000	305,000
Operating expenses	200,000	180,000
Profit from operations	150,000	125,000
Interest expense (net)	35,000	35,000
Profit before income taxes	115,000	90,000
Income tax expense	17,250	13,500
Profit	$ 97,750	$ 76,500

Additional information:
1. The allowance for doubtful accounts was $5,000 in 2011 and $4,000 in 2010.
2. Accounts receivable at the beginning of 2010 were $80,000, net of an allowance for doubtful accounts of $3,000.
3. Inventories at the beginning of 2010 were $250,000.
4. Total assets at the beginning of 2010 were $1,075,000.
5. The current liabilities at the beginning of 2010 were $300,000.
6. Total liabilities at the beginning of 2010 were $500,000.
7. Total shareholders' equity at the beginning of 2010 was $659,000.
8. All sales were on account.
9. In each of 2010 and 2011, $15,500 of dividends were paid to the preferred shareholders.
10. Cash provided by operating activities was $92,000 in 2011 and $65,000 in 2010.
11. Cash used by investing activities was $80,000 in 2011 and $50,000 in 2010.

Instructions

(a) Calculate all possible liquidity, solvency, and profitability ratios for 2011 and 2010.

(b) Identify whether the change in each ratio from 2010 to 2011 was favourable (F), unfavourable (U), or no change (NC).

Taking It Further Explain whether overall (a) liquidity, (b) solvency, and (c) profitability improved, deteriorated, or remained the same between 2010 and 2011.

Calculate and evaluate ratios for two companies.
(SO 4) E

P18–7B Selected financial data (in thousands) for The Brick Group Income Fund and Leon's Furniture are presented below for a recent year:

	The Brick	Leon's
Income Statement		
Net sales	$1,427,113	$740,376
Cost of goods sold	846,577	440,360
Gross profit	580,536	300,016
Operating expenses	511,473	205,880
Profit from operations	69,063	94,136
Other expense	279,751	0
Profit (loss) before income tax	(210,688)	94,136
Income tax expense (recovery)	(9,932)	30,746
Profit (loss)	$(200,756)	$63,390
Balance Sheet		
Current assets	$ 296,029	$264,777
Non-current assets	408,510	248,631
Total assets	$ 704,539	$513,408
Current liabilities	$ 307,509	$129,585
Long-term liabilities	258,050	30,465
Total liabilities	565,559	160,050
Shareholders' equity	138,980	353,358
Total liabilities and shareholders' equity	$ 704,539	$513,408
Additional information:		
Average accounts receivable	$ 71,186	$ 31,988
Average inventories	222,165	84,272
Average total assets	835,494	494,317
Average total shareholders' equity	269,900	337,682
Interest expense	5,588	0

Instructions

(a) For each company, calculate the following ratios. Industry averages are given in parentheses after each ratio, where available.

1. Current ratio (2.3:1)
2. Receivables turnover (23.1 times)
3. Collection period (16 days)
4. Inventory turnover (7.2 times)
5. Days sales in inventory (51 days)
6. Operating cycle (67 days)

7. Debt to total assets (17.4%)
8. Interest coverage (55.7 times)
9. Profit margin (4.3%)
10. Asset turnover (1.9 times)
11. Return on assets (8.2%)
12. Return on equity (17.7%)

(b) Compare the liquidity, solvency, and profitability of the two companies with each other and their industry.

Taking It Further The Brick is an income fund, reporting unitholders' equity rather than shareholders' equity, which Leon's reports. How could these differing forms of business affect your comparative analysis, if at all?

P18–8B Selected ratios for two companies operating in the beverage industry follow. Industry ratios, where available, have also been included.

Evaluate ratios for two companies.
(SO 4) E

Ratio	Refresh	Flavour	Industry Average
Acid-test	0.2:1	0.4:1	0.3:1
Asset turnover	1.0 times	1.0 times	0.9 times
Current ratio	0.6:1.0	1.1:1.0	0.8:1.0
Debt to total assets	56.0%	72.0%	n/a
Gross profit margin	73.8%	60.0%	57.7%
Interest coverage	12.3 times	6.9 times	5.3 times
Inventory turnover	5.8 times	9.9 times	8.3 times
Payout ratio	15.0%	20.4%	18.0%
Price-earnings ratio	50.3 times	24.3 times	32.2 times
Profit margin	11.3%	10.2%	8.1%
Receivables turnover	10.4 times	9.8 times	9.3 times
Return on assets	11.2%	9.3%	7.2%
Return on equity	25.7%	29.8%	26.4%

Instructions

(a) Both companies offer their customers credit terms of net 30 days. Indicate the ratio(s) that should be used to assess how well the accounts receivable are managed. Comment on how well each company appears to be managing its accounts receivable.

(b) How well does each company appear to be managing its inventory? Indicate the ratio(s) that should be used to assess inventory management.

(c) Which company, Refresh or Flavour, is more solvent? Identify the ratio(s) that should be used to determine this and defend your choice.

(d) To your surprise, you notice that Refresh's gross profit margin is significantly more than both Flavour's and the industry average. Identify two possible reasons for this.

(e) Which company do investors appear to believe has greater prospects for growing its income and dividends? Indicate the ratio(s) you used to reach this conclusion and explain your reasoning.

Taking It Further What is primarily responsible for the difference in the two companies' return on assets ratios—profitability or turnover? Explain.

P18–9B The following ratios are available for toolmakers Black & Decker and Snap-on for a recent year:

Evaluate ratios for two companies.
(SO 4) E

Liquidity	Black & Decker	Snap-on	Industry
Current ratio	1.7:1	2.2:1	2.0:1
Acid-test	1.1:1	1.7:1	1.4:1
Receivables turnover	5.2 times	5.1 times	5.5 times
Inventory turnover	3.6 times	4.3 times	4.6 times
Operating cycle	172 days	156 days	146 days
Solvency			
Debt to total assets	52.4%	41.5%	31.5%
Interest coverage	6.7 times	9.8 times	12.6 times
Profitability			
Gross profit margin	32.8%	45.0%	33.7%
Profit margin	6.9%	8.2%	3.2%
Asset turnover	1.1 times	0.9 times	0.6 times
Return on assets	7.8%	7.6%	3.7%
Return on equity	18.9%	16.9%	11.2%
Price-earnings ratio	8.4 times	8.5 times	8.1 times
Payout ratio	43.9%	32.1%	3.3%

Instructions

(a) Which company is more liquid? Explain.

(b) Which company is more solvent? Explain.

(c) Which company is more profitable? Explain.

Taking It Further Which company do investors favour? Is your answer consistent with your findings above?

Identify impact of different accounting policies.
(SO 5) AN

P18–10B You are in the process of analyzing two similar companies in the same industry. This is the first year of operations for both companies. You learn that they have different accounting policies as follows:

1. Company A, which has the same type of inventory as Company B, uses the first-in, first-out inventory cost formula, while Company B uses the average cost formula. The cost of merchandise has generally been rising throughout the year.
2. Company A primarily uses operating leases while Company B primarily uses finance leases.

Instructions

(a) Considering only the impact of the choice of inventory cost formula, determine which company will report a higher (1) current ratio, (2) debt to total assets ratio, and (3) gross profit margin ratio, or if there will be no impact.

(b) Considering only the impact of the choice of lease, determine which company will report a higher (1) current ratio, (2) debt to total assets ratio, and (3) gross profit margin ratio, or if there will be no impact.

(c) Identify two other limitations of financial analysis that an analyst should watch for when analyzing financial statements.

Taking It Further How should an analyst account for different accounting policies in an intercompany comparison of these two companies? Explain.

Continuing Cookie Chronicle

(*Note:* This is a continuation of the Cookie Chronicle from Chapters 1 through 17.)

The balance sheet and income statement of Cookie & Coffee Creations Ltd. for its first year of operations, the year ended October 31, 2012, follow:

COOKIE & COFFEE CREATIONS LTD.
Balance Sheet
October 31, 2012

Assets			
Current assets			
Cash		$29,294	
Accounts receivable		3,250	
Inventory		17,897	
Prepaid expenses		6,300	$ 56,741
Property, plant, and equipment			
Furniture and fixtures	$12,500		
Less: Accumulated depreciation	1,250	$11,250	
Computer equipment	$ 4,200		
Less: Accumulated depreciation	600	3,600	
Kitchen equipment	$80,000		
Less: Accumulated depreciation	8,000	72,000	86,850
Total assets			$143,591

Liabilities and Shareholders' Equity
Current liabilities

Accounts payable	$ 5,306	
Income tax payable	18,000	
Dividends payable	625	
Salaries payable	2,250	
Interest payable	210	
Note payable—current portion	3,500	$ 29,891
Long-term liabilities		
Note payable—long-term portion		7,000
Total liabilities		36,891

Shareholders' equity
Contributed capital

Preferred shares, 2,500 shares issued	$12,500		
Common shares, 23,550 shares issued	23,455		
Total contributed capital		$35,955	
Retained earnings		70,745	106,700
Total liabilities and shareholders' equity			$143,591

COOKIE & COFFEE CREATIONS LTD.
Income Statement
Year Ended October 31, 2012

Sales		$475,000
Cost of goods sold		237,500
Gross profit		237,500
Operating expenses		
Depreciation expense	$ 9,850	
Salaries and wages expense	92,500	
Other operating expenses	44,940	147,290
Profit from operations		90,210
Other expenses		
Interest expense		210
Profit before income tax		90,000
Income tax expense		18,000
Profit		$ 72,000

Additional information:

Natalie and Curtis are thinking about borrowing an additional $25,000 to buy more kitchen equipment. The loan would be repaid over a four-year period. The terms of the loan provide for equal semi-annual instalment payments of $3,125 on May 1 and November 1 of each year, plus interest of 4% on the outstanding balance.

Instructions

(a) Calculate the following ratios, using ending balances where appropriate rather than average balances:

1. Current ratio	8. Debt to total assets
2. Acid-test ratio	9. Interest coverage
3. Receivables turnover	10. Gross profit margin
4. Collection period	11. Profit margin
5. Inventory turnover	12. Asset turnover
6. Days sales in inventory	13. Return on assets
7. Operating cycle	14. Return on equity

(b) Comment on your findings from part (a).

(c) Based on your analysis in parts (a) and (b), do you think a bank would lend Cookie & Coffee Creations Ltd. $25,000 to buy the additional equipment? Explain your reasoning.

(d) What alternatives could Cookie & Coffee Creations consider instead of bank financing?

Financial Reporting and Analysis

Financial Reporting Problem

BYP18–1 The financial statements of The Forzani Group Ltd. are presented in Appendix A at the end of this textbook.

Instructions

(a) Prepare a horizontal analysis, calculating the percentage change for 2009 compared with 2008, for Forzani's balance sheets and income statements, similar to the examples shown in Illustrations 18-4 and 18-5.

(b) Prepare a vertical analysis for 2009 and 2008 for Forzani's balance sheets and income statements, similar to the examples in Illustrations 18-7 and 18-8.

(c) Identify and comment on any significant items or trends you observe from your horizontal and vertical analyses in (a) and (b).

Interpreting Financial Statements

BYP18–2 Selected financial ratios for the Canadian National Railway Company (CN), the Canadian Pacific Railway Limited (CP), and their industry are presented here for a recent year:

	CN	CP	Industry
Liquidity			
Current ratio	0.9:1	0.9:1	0.9:1
Acid-test ratio	0.7:1	0.6:1	0.7:1
Receivables turnover	13.2 times	7.9 times	8.4 times
Solvency			
Debt to total assets	60%	61%	42.9%
Interest coverage	7.8 times	3.8 times	6.8 times
Free cash flow	$631 million	$223 million	n/a
Profitability			
Profit margin	22.3%	12.6%	12.1%
Asset turnover	0.3 times	0.3 times	0.4 times
Return on assets	8.7%	5.8%	5.7%
Return on equity	18.3%	10.8%	13.9%

Instructions

(a) Comment on the relative liquidity of the two companies.

(b) Comment on the relative solvency of the two companies.

(c) Comment on the relative profitability of the two companies.

(d) CN prepares its financial statements using U.S. generally accepted accounting principles while CP uses Canadian generally accepted accounting principles. What impact might the use of different accounting principles have on your assessment above?

Critical Thinking

Collaborative Learning Activity

Note to instructor: Additional instructions and material for this group activity can be found on the Instructor Resource Site.

BYP18–3 In this group activity, you will analyze Rogers Communications Inc. and BCE Inc. on an intracompany, intercompany, and industry basis.

Working in Groups

Instructions

(a) Your instructor will divide the class into groups and distribute selected financial and ratio information for each company and their industry. Your group will review the liquidity, solvency, and profitability of the company you are assigned and its industry for a two-year period.

(b) You will be asked to compare your results on an intercompany basis to those of a group assigned the other company.

Communication Activity

BYP18–4 You are a new member of the board of directors and audit committee of Easy-Mix Cement Inc. EasyMix is a publicly traded company producing cement in 10 different countries worldwide. You are about to attend your first meeting of the audit committee, at which ratios will be presented to help members better understand the year-end financial results.

Writing Handbook

Instructions

Identify any of the limitations of financial statement analysis that you believe may apply to EasyMix's ratios. Prioritize your list and prepare questions that you should raise at the audit committee meeting to help you better understand the implications of the ratios presented.

Ethics Case

BYP18–5 Sabra Surkis, president of Surkis Industries, wants to issue a press release to improve her company's image and boost its share price, which has been gradually falling. As controller, you have been asked to provide a list of financial ratios along with some other operating statistics from Surkis Industries' first-quarter operations.

Two days after you provide the ratios and data requested, Carol Dunn, the public relations director of Surkis, asks you to review the financial and operating data contained in the press release written by the president and edited by Carol. In the news release, the president highlights the sales increase of 5% over last year's first quarter and the positive change in the current ratio from 1.1:1 last year to 1.5:1 this year. She also emphasizes that production was up 10% over the prior year's first quarter.

You note that the release contains only positive or improved ratios, and none of the negative or weakened ratios. For instance, there is no mention that the debt to total assets ratio has increased from 35% to 45%. Nor was it mentioned that the operating cycle has increased by 19%. There was also no indication that the reported profit for the quarter would have been a loss if the estimated lives of Surkis's machinery had not been increased by 30%.

Instructions

(a) Who are the stakeholders in this situation?
(b) Is there anything unethical in president Surkis's actions?
(c) Should you as controller remain silent? Does Carol have any responsibility?

Ethics in Accounting

"All About You" Activity

BYP18–6 In the "All About You" feature, you learned that there are two general approaches — fundamental and technical analysis—to deciding when to buy and sell shares. You have recently inherited $5,000 cash and you are considering investing in Canadian Tire's shares.

Instructions

Go to Canadian Tire Corporation's website at http://corp.canadiantire.ca and click on "Annual Reports." Go to the 2009 annual report.

(a) Included in the annual report is the Management Discussion and Analysis (MD&A). What is the purpose of Canadian Tire's MD&A? Do you think the MD&A provides useful information for your investment decision?

(b) Calculate the following ratios for 2009 (the year ended January 2, 2010). Compare these to the 2008 ratios shown in the Ratio Analysis section of the chapter for Canadian Tire and reproduced in parentheses after each ratio below. For each ratio, comment on the change between the two years:

1. Current ratio (2.0:1)
2. Inventory turnover (7.6 times)
3. Debt to total assets (54.2%)
4. Interest coverage (5.4 times)
5. Gross profit margin (10.1%)
6. Profit margin (4.1%)
7. Return on assets (5.1%)
8. Return on equity (11.2%)
9. Price-earnings ratio (9.8 times)
10. Payout ratio (18.3%)

(c) On Canadian Tire's website, go to the "Investors" section and then select "Stock/Shareholder Information" and click on "Historical Price Lookup." What were Canadian Tire's shares trading at on the following dates?

1. January 4, 2008
2. December 31, 2008
3. January 5, 2009
4. December 31, 2009

(d) Under "Stock/Shareholder Information," click on "Stock Chart" and input 5 years into the time range. Comment on the changes in the price of Canadian Tire's shares over the five years.

(e) Based on your brief analysis of Canadian Tire's ratios and share prices, do you think buying Canadian Tire's shares is a good investment for you? Explain.

(f) If you are investing in the stock market, will you rely solely on fundamental analysis? On technical analysis? Or do you think you might use both fundamental analysis and technical analysis? Explain.

ANSWERS TO CHAPTER QUESTIONS

Answers to Accounting in Action Insight Questions

Business Insight, p. 1010

Q: Are the percentage changes for Visa based on horizontal or vertical analysis?

A: The trend percentages reported in the press release are an example of horizontal analysis, which calculates the percentage changes for the period—the quarters ended March 31, 2009, and March 31, 2008, in this case. Vertical analysis reports percentages within the same year.

Across the Organization, p. 1015

Q: What other liquidity ratios should be monitored, and by what department(s), across the organization?

A: The inventory turnover and days sales in inventory ratios would be monitored closely by both the purchasing and sales departments to make sure that the inventory is saleable. The finance department will also monitor these ratios to ensure that the cost of carrying the inventory is not unreasonable. The finance department would also watch the acid-test ratio in order to assess its cash flow requirements.

All About You, p. 1025

Q: Taking a job with a company is in many ways similar to deciding whether or not to buy shares of that company. If you are offered a job at two companies when you graduate, what type of analysis would be appropriate—fundamental or technical—in making your decision?

A: If you are looking for a company that can meet its obligations to you and provide you with a career, you will be interested in the company's ability to meet its short- and long-term obligations and to grow. Fundamental analysis will help you predict the company's earnings potential and cash flows. In choosing a job you will also want to have information on the reputation of the management team. Looking at the company's share prices over the last couple of years might be helpful in getting an overall picture of how the company has been performing. But since technical analysis is typically about short-term directional changes in value, it would not be as useful as functional analysis.

Answer to Forzani Review It Question 3, p. 1030

Forzani reported other comprehensive income of $871 thousand for the year ended February 1, 2009. This amount is 3% of its profit of $29,325 thousand for the same period. Comprehensive income should be considered in a financial statement analysis, if its omission would significantly skew the interpretation of the results. Three percent does not appear to be very significant, although it is a significant change from the prior year when Forzani reported an other comprehensive loss of $87 thousand.

Answers to Self-Study Questions

1. a   2. c   3. c   4. a   5. c   6. b   7. b   8. b   9. a   10. a

Remember to go back to the beginning of the chapter to check off your completed work!

←

The Forzani Group Ltd.

In this appendix we illustrate current financial reporting with a comprehensive set of corporate financial statements that are prepared in accordance with generally accepted accounting principles. We are grateful for permission to use the actual financial statements of The Forzani Group Ltd.—Canada's largest sporting goods retailer.

Forzani's financial statement package features a balance sheet, statement of operations (or income statement as we know it), statements of retained earnings, comprehensive earnings and accumulated other comprehensive earnings (loss), cash flow statement, and notes to the financial statements. The financial statements are preceded by two reports: a statement of management's responsibilities for financial reporting and the auditors' report.

We encourage students to use these financial statements in conjunction with relevant material in the textbook. As well, these statements can be used to solve the Review It questions in the Before You Go On section within the chapter and the Financial Reporting Problem in the Broadening Your Perspective section of the end-of-chapter material.

Annual reports, including the financial statements, are reviewed in detail on the companion website to this textbook.

Management's Responsibilities For Financial Reporting

The Annual Report, including the consolidated financial statements, is the responsibility of the management of the Company. The consolidated financial statements were prepared by management in accordance with generally accepted accounting principles. The significant accounting policies used are described in Note 2 to the consolidated financial statements. The integrity of the information presented in the financial statements, including estimates and judgments relating to matters not concluded by year-end, is the responsibility of management. Financial information presented elsewhere in this Annual Report has been prepared by management and is consistent with the information in the consolidated financial statements.

Management is responsible for the development and maintenance of systems of internal accounting and administrative controls. Such systems are designed to provide reasonable assurance that the financial information is accurate, relevant and reliable, and that the Company's assets are appropriately accounted for and adequately safeguarded (refer also to page 55 under "internal control over financial reporting"). The Board of Directors is responsible for ensuring that management fulfils its responsibilities for final approval of the annual consolidated financial statements. The Board appoints an Audit Committee consisting of three directors, none of whom is an officer or employee of the Company or its subsidiaries. The Audit Committee meets at least four times each year to discharge its responsibilities under a written mandate from the Board of Directors. The Audit Committee meets with management and with the independent auditors to satisfy itself that they are properly discharging their responsibilities, reviews the consolidated financial statements and the Auditors' Report, and examines other auditing, accounting and financial reporting matters. The consolidated financial statements have been reviewed by the Audit Committee and approved by the Board of Directors of The Forzani Group Ltd. The consolidated financial statements have been examined by the shareholders' auditors, Ernst & Young, LLP, Chartered Accountants. The Auditors' Report outlines the nature of their examination and their opinion on the consolidated financial statements of the Company. The independent auditors have full and unrestricted access to the Audit Committee, with and without management present.

Robert Sartor
Chief Executive Officer

Micheal R. Lambert, CA
Chief Financial Officer

Auditor's Report

To the Shareholders of
The Forzani Group Ltd.

We have audited the consolidated balance sheets of The Forzani Group Ltd. as at February 1, 2009 and February 3, 2008 and the consolidated statements of operations, retained earnings, comprehensive earnings, accumulated other comprehensive earnings (loss) and cash flows for the 52 week period ended February 1, 2009 and the 53 week period ended February 3, 2008. These financial statements are the responsibility of the Company's management. Our responsibility is to express an opinion on these financial statements based on our audits.

We conducted our audits in accordance with Canadian generally accepted auditing standards. Those standards require that we plan and perform an audit to obtain reasonable assurance whether the financial statements are free of material misstatement. An audit includes examining, on a test basis, evidence supporting the amounts and disclosures in the financial statements. An audit also includes assessing the accounting principles used and significant estimates made by management, as well as evaluating the overall financial statement presentation.

In our opinion, these consolidated financial statements present fairly, in all material respects, the financial position of the Company as at February 1, 2009 and February 3, 2008 and the results of its operations and its cash flows for the 52 week period ended February 1, 2009 and the 53 week period ended February 3, 2008 in accordance with Canadian generally accepted accounting principles.

Ernst & Young LLP

Calgary, Canada
April 7, 2009

Ernst & Young LLP
Chartered Accountants

The Forzani Group Ltd.
Consolidated Balance Sheets
(in thousands)

As at		February 1, 2009		February 3, 2008
ASSETS				
Current				
Cash	$	3,474	$	47,484
Accounts receivable		84,455		75,506
Inventory (Note 3)		291,497		319,445
Prepaid expenses (Note 4)		2,827		14,501
		382,253		456,936
Capital assets (Note 5)		196,765		188,621
Goodwill and other intangibles (Note 6)		91,481		89,335
Other assets (Note 7)		9,280		3,863
Future income tax asset (Note 12)		9,681		16,209
	$	689,460	$	754,964
LIABILITIES				
Current				
Indebtedness under revolving credit facility (Note 8)	$	17,130	$	-
Accounts payable and accrued liabilities		277,820		279,910
Current portion of long-term debt (Note 8)		7,501		51,863
		302,451		331,773
Long-term debt (Note 8)		126		6,586
Deferred lease inducements		47,811		55,089
Deferred rent liability		5,893		6,033
		356,281		399,481
SHAREHOLDERS' EQUITY				
Share capital (Note 11)		147,161		157,105
Contributed surplus		6,401		7,210
Accumulated other comprehensive earnings (loss)		863		(8)
Retained earnings		178,754		191,176
		333,179		355,483
	$	689,460	$	754,964

See accompanying notes to the consolidated financial statements
Approved on behalf of the Board:

Roman Doroniuk, CA

John M. Forzani

The Forzani Group Ltd.
Consolidated Statements of Operations
(in thousands, except per share data)

	For the 52 weeks ended February 1, 2009	For the 53 weeks ended February 3, 2008
Revenue		
Retail	$ 994,043	$ 969,256
Wholesale	352,715	361,753
	1,346,758	1,331,009
Cost of sales	863,239	852,608
Gross margin	483,519	478,401
Operating and administrative expenses		
Store operating	277,089	251,630
General and administrative	109,328	103,801
	386,417	355,431
Operating earnings before undernoted items	97,102	122,970
Amortization of capital assets	47,613	44,468
Interest	5,175	5,797
Loss on sale of investment (Note 21)	-	864
	52,788	51,129
Earnings before income taxes	44,314	71,841
Income tax expense (recovery) (Note 12)		
Current	6,273	27,439
Future	8,716	(3,049)
	14,989	24,390
Net earnings	$ 29,325	$ 47,451
Earnings per share (Note 11(c))	$ 0.94	$ 1.40
Diluted earnings per share (Note 11(c))	$ 0.93	$ 1.39

See accompanying notes to the consolidated financial statements

The Forzani Group Ltd.
Consolidated Statements of Retained Earnings, Comprehensive Earnings and Accumulated Other Comprehensive Earnings (Loss)
(in thousands)

Consolidated Statements of Retained Earnings	For the 52 weeks ended February 1, 2009		For the 53 weeks ended February 3, 2008	
Retained earnings, beginning of period	$	191,176	$	171,095
Adjustment arising from adoption of new accounting policy (Note 2)		(1,357)		-
Adjusted Retained earnings, beginning of period	$	189,819	$	171,095
Net earnings		29,325		47,451
Dividends paid (Note 11(f))		(9,327)		(2,472)
Adjustment arising from shares purchased under a normal course issuer bid (Note 11(e))		(31,063)		(24,898)
Retained earnings, end of period	$	178,754	$	191,176

Consolidated Statements of Comprehensive Earnings				
Net earnings	$	29,325	$	47,451
Other comprehensive earnings (loss):				
Unrealized foreign currency gains and (losses) on cash flow hedges		1,340		(138)
Tax impact		(469)		51
Other comprehensive earnings (loss)		871		(87)
Comprehensive earnings	$	30,196	$	47,364

Consolidated Statements of Accumulated Other Comprehensive Earnings (Loss) ("AOCE")				
Accumulated other comprehensive earnings (loss), beginning of period	$	(8)	$	-
Transitional adjustment upon adoption of new financial instruments standard		-		79
Accumulated other comprehensive earnings (loss), beginning of period, as restated		(8)		79
Other comprehensive earnings (loss)		871		(87)
Accumulated other comprehensive earnings (loss), end of period	$	863	$	(8)

See accompanying notes to the consolidated financial statements

The Forzani Group Ltd.
Consolidated Statements of Cash Flows
(in thousands)

		For the 52 weeks ended February 1, 2009		For the 53 weeks ended February 3, 2008
Cash provided by (used in) operating activities				
Net earnings	$	29,325	$	47,451
Items not involving cash:				
Amortization of capital assets		47,613		44,468
Amortization of deferred finance charges		377		738
Amortization of deferred lease inducements		(11,500)		(11,109)
Rent expense (Note 9)		152		524
Stock-based compensation (Note 11(d))		(174)		2,756
Future income tax expense (recovery)		8,716		(3,049)
Loss on sale of investment (Note 21)		-		864
Unrealized loss on ineffective hedges		321		44
		74,830		82,687
Changes in non-cash elements of working capital related to operating activities (Note 9)		20,913		23,737
		95,743		106,424
Cash provided by (used in) financing activities				
Net proceeds from issuance of share capital (Note 11(b))		2,384		13,273
Share repurchase via normal course issuer bid (Note 11(e))		(44,027)		(33,331)
Long-term debt		(51,199)		(19,198)
Revolving credit facility		17,130		-
Lease inducements received		4,221		7,648
Dividends paid (Note 11(f))		(9,327)		(2,472)
		(80,818)		(34,080)
Changes in non-cash elements of financing activities (Note 9)		(1,121)		(1,698)
		(81,939)		(35,778)
Cash provided by (used in) investing activities				
Capital assets		(52,139)		(40,660)
Other assets		(2,998)		2,151
Acquisition of wholly-owned subsidiaries (Note 17)		-		(8,774)
		(55,137)		(47,283)
Changes in non-cash elements of investing activities (Note 9)		(2,677)		1,363
		(57,814)		(45,920)
Increase (decrease) in cash		(44,010)		24,726
Net cash position, opening		47,484		22,758
Net cash position, closing	$	3,474	$	47,484

See accompanying notes to the consolidated financial statements

The Forzani Group Ltd.
Notes to Consolidated Financial Statements (tabular amounts in thousands)

1.   Nature of Operations

The Forzani Group Ltd. ("FGL" or "the Company") is Canada's largest national retailer of sporting goods, offering a comprehensive assortment of brand-name and private-brand products, operating stores from coast to coast, under the following corporate and franchise banners: Sport Chek, Coast Mountain Sports, Sport Mart, National Sports, Athletes World, Sports Experts, Intersport, Econosports, Atmosphere, RnR, Tech Shop, Pegasus, Nevada Bob's Golf, Hockey Experts, S3 and The Fitness Source.

2.   Significant Accounting Policies

The preparation of the financial statements in conformity with Canadian generally accepted accounting principles ("GAAP") requires management to make estimates and assumptions that affect the reported amounts of assets and liabilities and disclosures of contingent assets and liabilities at the date of the consolidated financial statements and the reported amounts of revenue and expenses during the reporting period. Actual results could differ materially from these estimates. Estimates are used when accounting for items such as employee benefits, product warranties, inventory provisions, amortization and assessment for impairment, uncollectible receivables and the liability for the Company's loyalty program. The financial statements have, in management's opinion, been prepared within reasonable limits of materiality and within the framework of the accounting policies summarized below:

(a)   Organization

The consolidated financial statements include the accounts of The Forzani Group Ltd. and its subsidiaries, all of which are wholly owned.

(b)   Inventory valuation

Inventory is valued at the lower of laid-down cost and net realizable value. Laid-down cost is determined using the weighted average cost method and includes invoice cost, duties, freight, and distribution costs. Net realizable value is defined as the expected selling price.

Volume rebates and other supplier discounts are included in income when earned. Volume rebates are accounted for as a reduction of the cost of the related inventory and are "earned" when the inventory is sold. All other rebates and discounts are "earned" when the related expense is incurred.

(c)   *Capital assets*

Capital assets are recorded at cost and are amortized using the following methods and rates:

Asset	Basis	Rate
Building	Declining balance	4%
Building and leased land	Straight-line	Lesser of the term of the lease or estimated useful life, not exceeding 20 years
Furniture, fixtures, equipment, software and automotive	Straight-line	3-8 years
Leasehold improvements	Straight-line	Lesser of the term of the lease and estimated useful life, not exceeding 10 years

The carrying value of long-lived assets is reviewed at least annually or whenever events indicate a potential impairment has occurred. An impairment loss is recorded if and when a long-lived asset's carrying value exceeds the sum of the undiscounted cash flows expected from its use and eventual disposition. The impairment loss is measured as the amount by which the carrying value exceeds its fair value.

(d)   *Variable interest entities*

Variable interest entities ("VIE") are consolidated by the Company if and when the Company is the primary beneficiary of the VIE, as described in Canadian Institute of Chartered Accountants ("CICA") Accounting Guideline 15, *Consolidation of Variable Interest Entities.*

(e)   *Goodwill and other intangibles*

Goodwill represents the excess of the purchase price of entities acquired over the fair market value of the identifiable net assets acquired.

Goodwill and other intangible assets with indefinite lives are not amortized, but tested for impairment at year end or more frequently if events or changes in circumstances indicate the asset might be impaired and, if required, asset values reduced accordingly. The method used to assess impairment is a review of the fair value of the asset based on expected present value of future cash flows.

Non-competition agreement costs are amortized, on a straight-line basis, over the life of the agreements, not exceeding five years.

(f)   *Other assets*

Other assets include system and interactive development costs, long-term receivables and other deferred charges.

System development costs relate to the implementation of computer software. Upon activation, costs are amortized over the estimated useful lives of the systems (3 – 8 years).

Long-term receivables are carried at cost less a valuation allowance, if applicable.

(g)   Deferred lease inducements and property leases

Deferred lease inducements represent cash and non-cash benefits that the Company has received from landlords pursuant to store lease agreements. These lease inducements are amortized against rent expense over the term of the lease.

The Company capitalizes any rent expense during a related fixturing period as a cost of leasehold improvements. Such expense is recognized on a straight-line basis over the life of the lease.

(h)   Revenue recognition

Revenue includes sales to customers through corporate stores operated by the Company and sales to, and service fees from, franchise stores and others. Sales to customers through corporate stores operated by the Company are recognized at the point of sale, net of an estimated allowance for sales returns. Sales of merchandise to franchise stores and others are recognized at the time of shipment. Royalties and administration fees are recognized when earned, in accordance with the terms of the franchise/license agreements.

(i)   Store opening expenses

Operating costs incurred prior to the opening of new stores, other than rent incurred during the fixturing period, are expensed as incurred.

(j)   Fiscal year

The Company's fiscal year follows a retail calendar. The fiscal years for the consolidated financial statements presented are the 52-week period ended February 1, 2009 and the 53-week period ended February 3, 2008.

(k)   Foreign currency translation

Foreign currency accounts are translated to Canadian dollars. At the transaction date, each asset, liability, revenue or expense is translated into Canadian dollars using the exchange rate in effect at that date. At the year-end date, monetary assets and liabilities are translated into Canadian dollars using the exchange rate in effect at that date, and the resulting foreign exchange gains and losses are included in income.

(l)   Stock-based compensation

The Company accounts for stock-based compensation using the fair value method. The fair value of the options granted are estimated at the date of grant using the Black-Scholes valuation model and recognized as an expense over the option-vesting period.

(m)   Income taxes

The Company follows the liability method under which future income tax assets and liabilities are determined based on differences between the financial reporting and tax basis of assets and liabilities, measured using tax rates substantively enacted at the balance sheet dates.

Changes in tax rates are reflected in the consolidated statements of operations in the period in which they are substantively enacted.

(n)   *Asset retirement obligations*

The Company recognizes asset retirement obligations in the period in which a reasonable estimate of the fair value can be determined. The liability is measured at fair value and is adjusted to its present value in subsequent periods through accretion expense. The associated asset retirement costs are capitalized as part of the carrying value of the related asset and amortized over its useful life.

(o)   *Financial Instruments - Recognition and Measurement – CICA Section 3855*

Section 3855 establishes standards for recognizing and measuring financial assets, financial liabilities, and non-financial derivatives. It requires that financial assets and financial liabilities, including derivatives, be recognized on the consolidated balance sheet when the Company becomes a party to the contractual provisions of the financial instrument or non-financial derivative contract. It also requires that all financial assets and liabilities are to be classified as either a) Held for Trading, b) Available for Sale, c) Held to Maturity, d) Loans/Receivables, or e) Other Financial Liabilities, depending on the Company's stated intention and/or historical practice. Under this standard, all financial instruments are required to be measured at fair value (or amortized cost) upon initial recognition, except for certain related party transactions. Treatment of the fair value of each financial instrument is determined by its classification.

In accordance with the standard, the Company's financial assets and liabilities are generally classified as follows:

Asset/Liability	Category	Measurement
Assets		
Cash	Held for trading	Fair value
Accounts receivable	Loans/Receivables	Amortized cost
Long-term receivables	Loans/Receivables	Amortized cost
Liabilities		
Indebtedness under revolving credit facility	Other financial liabilities	Amortized cost
Accounts payable and accrued liabilities	Other financial liabilities	Amortized cost
Long-term debt	Other financial liabilities	Amortized cost

Foreign currency options and forward exchange contracts, which are included in accounts receivable, have been classified as held for trading and measured at fair value. Fair value is determined by reference to published price quotations.

New Accounting Policies

Effective February 4, 2008 the Company adopted the following accounting standards issued by the CICA:

Capital Disclosures – CICA Section 1535

The standard establishes disclosure requirements about an entity's capital and how it is managed. The new standard requires disclosure of an entity's objectives, policies and processes for managing capital, quantitative data about what an entity regards as capital and whether the entity has complied with any externally imposed capital requirements and the consequences of any non-compliance. Additional disclosure required as a result of the adoption of this standard is contained in Note 10.

Financial Instruments - Disclosures (CICA Section 3862) and Financial Instruments – Presentation (CICA Section 3863)

The standards replace Section 3861, *Financial Instruments - Disclosure and Presentation*, revising and enhancing disclosure requirements while carrying forward, substantially unchanged, its presentation requirements. These new sections place increased emphasis on disclosure about the nature and extent of risks arising from financial instruments and how the entity manages those risks. Additional disclosure required as a result of the adoption of this standard is contained in Note 16.

Inventory - CICA Section 3031

The standard introduces significant changes to the measurement and disclosure of inventories, including the allocation of overhead based on normal capacity, the use of the specific cost method for inventories that are not ordinarily interchangeable for goods and services produced for specific purposes, and the reversal of previous write-downs to net realizable value when there is a subsequent increase in the value of inventories. Inventory policies, carrying amounts, amounts recognized as an expense, write-downs and the reversals of write-downs are required to be disclosed.

Under the prior guidance, the Company included storage costs in the cost of inventory. This is no longer permitted, resulting in a $1,357,000 adjustment to opening inventory for the year and a corresponding adjustment to opening retained earnings. Prior periods have not been restated.

Future Accounting Pronouncements

The following are new standards that have been issued by the CICA that are not yet effective but may impact the Company:

Goodwill and Intangible Assets

In November 2007, the CICA issued Section 3064, *Goodwill and Intangible Assets* ("Section 3064"). Section 3064, which replaces Section 3062, *Goodwill and Intangible Assets*, and Section 3450, *Research and Development Costs*, establishes standards for the recognition, measurement and disclosure of goodwill and intangible assets. This standard is effective for the Company for interim and annual consolidated financial statements relating to fiscal years beginning on or after October 1, 2008. The Company is currently assessing the impact that this section will have on its financial position and results of operations. Any adjustment required will be recorded through opening retained earnings in the first quarter of the Company's fiscal 2010 year.

Business Combinations and Consolidated Financial Statements – CICA Section 1582 and 1601

As of January 30, 2011, the Company will be required to adopt new CICA standards with respect to business combinations and consolidated financial statements. The new CICA Section 1582 will replace CICA Section 1581 and is meant to align the accounting for business combinations under Canadian GAAP with the requirements of International Financial Reporting Standards. Likewise, CICA Section 1601 will replace CICA Section 1600 with respect to consolidated financial statements.

Under sections 1582 and 1601 the definition of a business is expanded and is described as an integrated set of activities and assets that are capable of being managed to provide a return to investors or economic benefits to owners, members or participants. In addition, acquisition costs are not part of the purchase consideration and are to be expensed when incurred. With the adoption of these standards, the Company expects that all acquisition related costs will be expensed through the statement of operations. These standards will be applied on a prospective basis.

International Financial Reporting Standards ("IFRS")

In February 2008, the CICA announced that GAAP for publicly accountable enterprises will be replaced by IFRS for fiscal years beginning on or after January 1, 2011. Companies will be required to provide IFRS comparative information for the previous fiscal year. Accordingly, the conversion from GAAP to IFRS will be applicable to the Company's reporting for the first quarter of fiscal 2012 for which the current and comparative information will be prepared under IFRS.

The Company is in the process of completing the scoping and assessment phase of the transition. This phase identified a number of topics possibly impacting either the Company's financial results and/or the Company's effort necessary to changeover to IFRS. This phase is ongoing, as the Company will continue to assess future International Accounting Standards Board ("IASB") pronouncements for transitional impacts.

The Company has started the key elements phase of implementation which includes the identification, evaluation and selection of accounting policies necessary for the Company to transition to IFRS. Consideration of impacts on operational elements such as information technology and internal control over financial reporting are integral to this process.

Although the Company's impact assessment activities are underway and progressing according to plan, continued progress is necessary before the Company can prudently increase the specificity of the disclosure of pre- and post-IFRS changeover accounting policy differences.

3. Inventory

Included within cost of sales for the period ended February 1, 2009, are normal course charges to inventory made throughout the year, of $12,265,000 (2008 – $12,514,000). These charges include the disposal of obsolete and damaged product, inventory shrinkage and permanent markdowns to net realizable values.

4. Prepaid Expenses

	2009	2008
Prepaid rent	$ -	$ 10,200
Advertising	1,348	1,720
Service contracts	785	773
Other	694	1,808
	$ 2,827	$ 14,501

5. Capital Assets

	2009			2008		
	Cost	Accumulated Amortization	Net Book Value	Cost	Accumulated Amortization	Net Book Value
Land	$ 3,173	$ -	$ 3,173	$ 3,173	$ -	$ 3,173
Buildings	20,928	5,382	15,546	20,928	4,680	16,248
Building on leased land	4,583	3,114	1,469	4,583	2,852	1,731
Furniture, fixtures, equipment, software and automotive	243,564	173,611	69,953	217,365	149,386	67,979
Leasehold improvements	260,030	167,435	92,595	239,439	146,003	93,436
Construction in progress	14,029	-	14,029	6,054	-	6,054
	$ 546,307	$ 349,542	$ 196,765	$ 491,542	$ 302,921	$ 188,621

6. Goodwill and Other Intangibles

	2009			2008		
	Cost	Accumulated Amortization	Net Book Value	Cost	Accumulated Amortization	Net Book Value
Goodwill	$ 61,162	$ 1,178	$ 59,984	$ 61,162	$ 1,178	$ 59,984
Trademarks/Trade names	32,359	934	31,425	30,140	934	29,206
Non-competition agreements	4,000	3,928	72	4,000	3,855	145
	$ 97,521	$ 6,040	$ 91,481	$ 95,302	$ 5,967	$ 89,335

7. Other Assets

	2009			2008		
	Cost	Accumulated Amortization	Net Book Value	Cost	Accumulated Amortization	Net Book Value
Interactive development	$ 2,649	$ 2,649	$ -	$ 2,649	$ 2,649	$ -
System development	1,641	1,641	-	1,641	1,641	-
Other deferred charges	6,967	3,153	3,814	4,176	2,094	2,082
	$ 11,257	$ 7,443	$ 3,814	$ 8,466	$ 6,384	$ 2,082

	2009	2008
Depreciable other assets net book value (see above)	$ 3,814	$ 2,082
Deferred advertising charges	2,566	-
Long-term receivables (at interest rates of prime plus 1% and expiring between September 2010 and July 2011)	2,900	1,781
	$ 9,280	$ 3,863

8.   Long Term Debt

	2009	2008
G.E. term loan	$ -	$ 49,744
Mortgage with monthly payments of $58,000 and an interest rate of 6.2% compounded semi-annually, secured by land and building, expiring October 2009.	5,458	5,782
Vendor take-back, unsecured with implied interest rate of 4.8% and payments due March 2009	2,043	2,792
Asset retirement obligation	126	113
Other	-	18
	7,627	58,449
Less current portion	7,501	51,863
	$ 126	$ 6,586

Principal payments on the above, due in the next five years, are as follows:

2010	$ 7,501
2011	$ -
2012	$ -
2013	$ -
2014	$ -

Effective June 11, 2008, the Company renewed its credit agreement with GE Canada Finance Holding Company. The renewed agreement increased the $235 million credit facility, which was comprised of a $185 million revolving loan and a $50 million term loan, to a $250 million facility, comprised entirely of a revolving loan and having a June 11, 2013 expiry date. Under the terms of the credit agreement, the interest rate payable on the revolving loan is based on the Company's financial performance as determined by its interest coverage ratio. As at February 1, 2009, the interest rate paid was bank prime less 0.45%. The facility is collateralized by general security agreements against all existing and future acquired assets of the Company. As at February 1, 2009, the Company is in compliance with its financial covenant.

Based on estimated interest rates currently available to the Company for mortgages with similar terms and maturities, the fair value of the mortgage at February 1, 2009 amounted to approximately $6,119,000 (2008 - $5,274,000). Interest costs incurred for the 52-week period ended February 1, 2009 on long-term debt amounted to $851,000 (2008 - $3,178,000). The fair value of the other long-term debt components above approximates book value given their short terms to maturity and floating interest rates.

9.   Supplementary Cash Flow Information

	For the 52 weeks ended February 1, 2009		For the 53 weeks ended February 3, 2008	
Rent expense				
Straight-line rent expense	$	(140)	$	228
Non-cash free rent		292		296
	$	152	$	524
Change in non-cash elements of working capital related to operating activities				
Accounts receivable	$	(11,137)	$	(9,963)
Inventory		21,753		13,772
Prepaid expenses		11,674		(11,813)
Financial Instruments		764		-
Accounts payable and accrued liabilities		(2,141)		31,741
	$	20,913	$	23,737
Change in non-cash elements of financing activities				
Lease inducements	$	(907)	$	(1,115)
Long-term debt		-		(568)
Change in fair value of cash flow hedge		871		-
Net financial assets		(1,085)		(15)
	$	(1,121)	$	(1,698)
Change in non-cash elements of investing activities				
Capital assets	$	668	$	795
Other assets		(3,345)		568
	$	(2,677)	$	1,363
Net cash interest paid	$	4,648	$	5,017
Net cash taxes paid	$	26,109	$	29,509

10. Capital Disclosures

The Company's objectives in managing capital are to ensure sufficient liquidity to pursue its strategy of organic growth combined with strategic acquisitions and to deploy capital to provide an appropriate return on investment to its shareholders. The Company's overall strategy remains unchanged from the prior year. The capital structure of the Company consists of cash, short and long-term debt and shareholders' equity comprised of retained earnings and share capital. The Company manages its capital structure and makes adjustments to it in light of economic conditions and the risk characteristics of the underlying assets. The Company's primary uses of capital are to finance non-cash working capital requirements, capital expenditures and acquisitions, which are currently funded from its internally-generated cash flows. The Company is in compliance with all externally imposed capital requirements, including its debt covenant.

11. Share Capital

(a) *Authorized*

An unlimited number of Class A shares (no par value)

An unlimited number of Preferred shares, issuable in series

(b) *Issued*

Class A shares	Number	Consideration
Balance, January 28, 2007	33,696	$ 148,424
Shares issued upon employees exercising stock options	1,077	13,273
Stock-based compensation related to options exercised	-	3,841
Shares repurchased via normal course issuer bid	(1,803)	(8,433)
Balance, February 3, 2008	32,970	157,105
Shares issued upon employees exercising stock options	192	2,384
Stock-based compensation related to options exercised	-	636
Shares repurchased via normal course issuer bid	(2,694)	(12,964)
Balance, February 1, 2009	30,468	$ 147,161

(c) *Earnings Per Share*

	2009	2008
Basic	$ 0.94	$ 1.40
Diluted	$ 0.93	$ 1.39

The Company uses the treasury stock method to calculate diluted earnings per share. Under the treasury stock method, the numerator remains unchanged from the basic earnings per share calculation, as the assumed exercise of the Company's stock options does not result in an adjustment to earnings. Diluted calculations assume that options under the stock option plan have been exercised at the later of the beginning of the year or date of issuance, and that the funds derived therefrom would have been used to repurchase shares at the average market value of the Company's stock, 2009 – $13.11 (2008 - $19.91). Anti-dilutive options, 2009 – 1,264,000 (2008 – 26,000) are excluded from the effect of dilutive securities. The reconciliation of the denominator in calculating diluted earnings per share is as follows:

	2009	2008
Weighted average number of Class A shares outstanding (basic)	31,298	33,787
Effect of dilutive options	67	370
Weighted average number of common shares outstanding (diluted)	31,365	34,157

(d)   Stock Option and Unit Plans

The Company has granted stock options to directors, officers and employees to purchase Class A shares at prices between $7.70 and $23.00 per share. These options expire on dates between February 2009 and June 2013.

The Company has three stock option plans. The first plan has the following general terms: options vest over a period ranging from 2 to 5 years and the maximum term of the options granted is 5 years. During the year, no options (2008 – Nil) were issued under this plan. The related stock-based compensation expense was $25,000 (2008 - $323,000).

The second plan has the following general terms: options vest over a period ranging from 2 to 5 years dependent on the Company achieving certain performance targets (in 2007 these targets were met thereby causing the options to become fully vested by the first quarter of fiscal 2008), and the maximum term of the options granted is 5 years. During the year, 120,000 (2008 – 200,000 options) were issued under this plan. The related stock-based compensation expense of $383,000 was recognized immediately (2008 - $1,886,000) as the Company met the targets in fiscal 2007.

The third plan, which forms part of a Long Term Incentive Plan ("LTIP"), has the following general terms: option grants are made annually and options vest over 3 years with a maximum term of 5 years. Under the terms of the plan, options issued carry a tandem share appreciation right ("TSAR") which allows holders to exercise vested options in either the traditional fashion, where shares are issued from treasury, or surrender their option in exchange for an amount of cash equaling the difference between the market price for a common share on the date of surrender and the strike price of the option. The final details of this plan were approved by the Company in the third quarter of fiscal 2008. During the year, as a result of the TSAR exercise history being predominantly for cash, the Company deemed the plan to be cash-settled and accounted for it as a liability-classified award with TSARs measured at their fair value on the date of issuance, and re-measured at each reporting period, until settlement. During the year ended February 1, 2009, 309,590 options (2008 – 388,710) were issued under this plan and a credit of $582,000 to stock-based compensation expense was recognized (2008 - $547,000 expensed).

The total number of shares authorized for option grants under all option plans is 3,406,622.

During the 52-weeks ended February 1, 2009, the following options were granted:

Options issued	Weighted average fair value per option	Weighted average risk-free rate	Weighted average expected option life	Weighted average expected volatility	Weighted average expected dividend yield
429,590	$2.99	2.93%	3.00	27.41%	2.01%

A summary of the status of the Company's stock option plans as of February 1, 2009 and February 3, 2008, and any changes during the period ending on those dates is presented below:

| | 2009 | | 2008 | |
Stock Options	Options	Weighted Average Exercise Price	Options	Weighted Average Exercise Price
Outstanding, beginning of year	1,658	$15.04	2,157	$12.85
Granted	430	$15.85	589	$18.08
Exercised	(204)	$12.39	(1,077)	$12.33
Forfeited	(189)	$14.93	(11)	$13.32
Outstanding, end of year	1,695	$15.56	1,658	$15.04
Options exercisable at year end	1,174		1,254	

The following table summarizes information about stock options outstanding at February 1, 2009:

| | Options Outstanding | | | Options Exercisable | |
Range of Exercise Prices	Number Outstanding	Weighted Average Remaining Contractual Life	Weighted Average Exercise Price	Number of Shares Exercisable	Weighted Average Exercise Price
$7.70 - $15.98	769	1.80	$13.01	718	$13.33
$16.00 - $23.00	926	3.55	$17.57	456	$18.07
	1,695	2.76	$15.56	1,174	$15.17

The Company issues director stock units ("DSU"), restricted stock units ("RSU") and performance stock units ("PSU") from time to time. These units are accounted for as liability-classified awards and are measured at their intrinsic value on the date of issuance, and re-measured at each reporting period, until settlement.

During the year, 166,865 (2008 – 168,390) PSUs were issued and an expense of $1,710,000 (2008 – $2,428,000) was charged to compensation expense.

During the year, 46,622 (2008 – 49,520) RSUs were issued and an expense of $580,000 (2008 - $137,000) was charged to compensation expense.

During the year, 20,327 (2008 – 16,049) DSUs were issued and $630,000 (2008 - $154,000 expense) was credited to compensation expense due to a reduction in the fair value of units.

As at February 1, 2009, the Company has recorded a total amount payable for all units outstanding of $2,149,000 (2008 - $2,172,000) of which $1,346,000 (2008 - $1,976,000) relates to DSUs, paid when a director leaves the Board of Directors.

(e) *Normal Course Issuer Bid*

For the year ended February 1, 2009, 2,694,376 (2008 – 1,802,900) Class A shares were repurchased pursuant to the Company's Normal Course Issuer Bid for a total expenditure of $44,027,000 (2008 - $33,331,000) or $16.34 (2008 - $18.49) per share. The consideration in excess of the stated value of $31,063,000 (2008 – $24,898,000) was changed to retained earnings.

(f) *Dividends*

On April 7, 2009 the Company declared a dividend of $0.075 per Class A common share, payable on May 4, 2009 to shareholders of record on April 20, 2009. The Company's stated intention is to declare annual dividends of $0.30 per share, payable quarterly, subject to the Board of Directors discretion.

The Company has declared quarterly dividends of $0.075 per Class A common share, payable to shareholders of record as follows:

Date Declared	For Shareholders of Record Dated
December 7, 2007	January 21, 2008
April 9, 2008	April 21, 2008
June 10, 2008	July 21, 2008
September 2, 2008	October 20, 2008
December 12, 2008	January 19, 2008
April 7, 2009	April 20, 2009

All dividends paid by the Company are, pursuant to subsection 89 (14) of the Income Tax Act (Canada), designated as eligible dividends. An eligible dividend paid to a Canadian resident is entitled to the enhanced dividend tax credit.

12. Income Taxes

The components of the future income tax asset amounts as at February 1, 2009 and February 3, 2008 are as follows:

	2009	2008
Current assets	$ (1,286)	$ (2,401)
Capital and other assets	(10,885)	(14,957)
Tax benefit of share issuance and financing costs	87	167
Deferred lease inducements	14,198	16,863
Non-capital loss carry forward	3,156	13,345
Accruals and deferred liabilities	4,411	3,192
Future income tax asset	$ 9,681	$ 16,209

A reconciliation of income taxes, at the combined statutory federal and provincial tax rate to the actual income tax rate, is as follows:

	2009		2008	
Federal and provincial income taxes	$ 13,471	30.4%	$ 24,354	33.9%
Increase (decrease) resulting from:				
Non deductible expenses	615	1.4%	1,796	2.5%
Effect of substantively enacted tax rate changes	-	-	(2,155)	(3.0%)
Other, net	903	2.0%	395	0.5%
Provision for income taxes	$ 14,989	33.8%	$ 24,390	33.9%

The Company has non-capital losses available to be carried forward of $9,804,000 expiring in 2028.

For the period ending February 1,2009, the Company has recorded a tax receivable balance of $11,125,000 (2008 - ($3,944,000)) which is included within accounts receivable.

13. Commitments

(a)   The Company is committed, at February 1, 2009, to minimum payments under long-term real property and data processing hardware and software equipment leases, for future years, as follows:

Year	Gross
2010	$ 87,523
2011	$ 77,283
2012	$ 65,083
2013	$ 52,753
2014	$ 40,403
Thereafter	$ 86,471

In addition, the Company may be obligated to pay percentage rent under certain of the leases.

(b)   As at February 1, 2009, the Company has open letters of credit for purchases of inventory of approximately $1,961,000 (2008 - $1,890,000).

14.   Employee Benefit Plans

The Company has a defined contribution plan and an employee profit sharing plan (replaces the previous deferred profit sharing plan). Defined contributions are paid to employee retirement savings plans and are expensed when incurred.

Under the employee profit sharing plan, the Company creates a pool of funds to distribute to participating employees on a predetermined basis. Distributions are tied to the value of the Company's common shares and the employees' achievement of individual financial and operational targets. Payouts under the employee profit sharing plan are made annually. The deferred profit sharing plan contributions were previously paid to a Trustee for the purchase of shares of the Company and then distributed to participating employees on a predetermined basis, upon retirement from the Company. Contributions to both the employee profit sharing plan and previously to the deferred profit sharing plan are recognized as an expense when incurred.

For the period ended February 1, 2009, the Company has expensed $1,090,000 (2008 - $1,095,000) to the defined contribution plan and has accrued $504,000 for the employee profit sharing plan (2008 - $150,000).

15.   Contingencies and Guarantees

In the normal course of business, the Company enters into numerous agreements that may contain features that meet the Accounting Guideline ("AcG") 14 definition of a guarantee. AcG-14 defines a guarantee to be a contract (including an indemnity) that contingently requires the Company to make payments to the guaranteed party based on (i) failure of another party to perform under an obligating agreement or (ii) failure of a third party to pay its indebtedness when due.

The Company has provided the following guarantees to third parties:

(a)   The Company has provided guarantees to franchisees' banks pursuant to which it has agreed to buy back inventory from the franchisee in the event that the bank realizes on the related security. The Company has provided securitization guarantees for certain franchisees to repay equity loans in the event of franchisee default. The terms of the guarantees range from less than a year to the lifetime of the particular underlying franchise agreement, with an average guarantee term of 4 years. Should a franchisee default on its bank loan, the Company would be required to purchase between 50% – 100%, with a weighted average of 65%, of the franchisee's inventory up to the value of the franchisee's bank indebtedness. As at February 1, 2009, the Company's maximum exposure is $43,707,000 (2008 - $37,174,000). Should the Company be required to purchase the inventory of a specific franchisee, it is expected that the full value of the inventory would be recovered. Historically, the Company has not had to repurchase significant inventory from franchisees pursuant to these guarantees. The Company has not recognized the guarantee in its consolidated financial statements.

(b)   In the ordinary course of business, the Company has agreed to indemnify its lenders under its credit facilities against certain costs or losses resulting from changes in laws and regulations and from any legal action brought against the lenders related to the use, by the Company, of the loan proceeds, or to the lenders having extended credit thereunder. These indemnifications extend for the term of the credit facilities and do not provide any limit on the maximum potential liability. Historically, the Company has not made any indemnification payments under such agreements and no amount has been accrued in the consolidated financial statements with respect to these indemnification agreements.

(c)   In the ordinary course of business, the Company has provided indemnification commitments to certain counterparties in matters such as real estate leasing transactions, securitization agreements, director and officer indemnification agreements and certain purchases of assets (not inventory in the normal course). These indemnification agreements generally require the Company to compensate the counterparties for costs or losses resulting from any legal action brought against the counterparties related to the actions of the Company or any of the obligors under any of the aforementioned matters or failure of the obligors under any of the aforementioned matters to fulfill contractual obligations thereunder. The terms of these indemnification agreements will vary based on the contract and generally do not provide any limit on the maximum potential liability. Historically, the Company has not made any payments under such indemnifications and no amount has been accrued in the consolidated financial statements with respect to these indemnification commitments.

(d)   Claims and suits have been brought against the Company in the ordinary course of business. In the opinion of management, all such claims and suits are adequately covered by insurance, or if not so covered, the results are not expected to materially affect the Company's financial position.

16.   Financial Instruments and Hedges

(a)   Fair Value of Financial Assets and Liabilities

The following table details carrying values and fair values of financial assets and liabilities by financial instrument classification:

	As at February 1, 2009	
	Carrying Value	Fair Value
Loans and Receivables:		
Trade and accrued receivables	$ 84,455	$ 84,455
Long-term receivables	$ 2,900	$ 2,900
Other Financial Liabilities:		
Revolving credit facility	$ 17,130	$ 17,130
Trade payables and accrued liabilities	$ 277,820	$ 277,820
Current and long-term debt	$ 7,627	$ 8,288

The fair value of a financial instrument is the estimated amount that the Company would receive or pay to settle the financial assets and financial liabilities as at the reporting date. The fair values of cash, trade and accrued receivables, revolving credit facilities, trade payables and accrued liabilities, approximate their carrying values given their short-term maturities. The fair values of long-term receivables and long-term debt approximate their carrying values given the current market rates associated with these instruments. The fair value of the interest rates is determined based on current market rates and on information received from the Company's counterparties to these agreements.

b) **Interest Income and Expense, and Gains or Losses by Class of Financial Asset and Financial Liability**

All interest income and expense, regardless of the class of financial asset or financial liability, is recorded in the consolidated statement of operations as interest.

All foreign exchange gains and losses, regardless of the class of financial asset or financial liability, are recorded in the consolidated statement of operations in cost of sales (realized) or general and administrative expense (unrealized).

c) **Risks**

Exposure to credit risk and interest rate risk arises in the normal course of the Company's business. The Company does not currently enter into derivative financial instruments to reduce exposure to fluctuations in any credit or interest risks impacting the operations of the Company.

i. Credit risk

The Company is exposed to credit risk on its accounts receivable from franchisees. The accounts receivable are net of applicable allowances for doubtful accounts, which are established based on the specific credit risks associated with individual franchisees and other relevant information. Concentration of credit risk with respect to receivables is limited, due to the large number of franchisees.

As at February 1, 2009, the aging of the Accounts receivable is as follows:

Current	$	74,924
Past due 0 - 60 days		4,190
Past due over 61 days		6,102
Accounts receivable		85,216
Less: allowance for doubtful accounts		(761)
	$	84,455

ii. Interest rate risk

The Company is exposed to interest rate risk on the credit facility as the rate is based on an index rate and on the Company's financial performance as determined by its interest coverage ratio. As at February 1, 2009, the interest rate paid was bank prime less 0.45%.

On February 1, 2009, a 25 basis point increase or decrease in interest rates, assuming that all other variables are constant, would have resulted in a $157,000 decrease or increase in the Company's net earnings for the period ended February 1, 2009.

The Company is not exposed to interest rate risk on long-term receivables, mortgages and vendor take-back loans as the rates are fixed.

iii. Asset-backed exposures

The Company has no exposure to asset-backed securities.

iv. Exchange risk

The Company currently uses forward currency contracts and options to hedge anticipated transactions whose terms do not exceed one year.

The Company has recorded an unrealized gain in the consolidated statement of comprehensive earnings for the fiscal year ended February 1, 2009 of $1,340,000 (net of tax - $871,000) (2008 - ($138,000), net of tax -($87,000)) relating to forward foreign currency contracts that qualify for hedge accounting.

The outstanding forward foreign exchange contracts to which hedge accounting was applied at February 1, 2009 have notional amounts of $3,629,000 (2008 - $6,208,000) and terms ranging from February 6, 2009 to August 21, 2009 at forward rates ranging from $1.021 to $1.2695.

Items currently reported in AOCE will be reclassified to net earnings when the hedged item is settled and the related non-financial asset is expensed or when a hedge is deemed ineffective and the hedged item has settled.

On February 1, 2009, a 1% increase or decrease in the exchange rate of the Canadian dollar compared to the U.S dollar, assuming that all other variables are constant, would have resulted in a $85,000 decrease or increase in the Company's net earnings for the period ended February 1, 2009.

v. Liquidity Risk

Liquidity risk is the risk the Company will encounter difficulties in meeting it's financial liability obligations. The Company manages its liquidity risk through cash and debt management. See Note 10 for a more detailed discussion.

17. Acquisitions

(a)   Effective September 9, 2007, the Company acquired select net assets of Al DiMarco's Custom Golf Shop Ltd. and various other related entities ("DiMarco"). The acquisition was accounted for using the purchase method as net assets acquired encompass the necessary inputs, processes and outputs to sustain the business, thereby meeting the definition of a business and accordingly the consolidated financial statements include the results of operations since the date of the acquisition.

The consideration for the transaction was $1,039,000 in cash and the settlement of an outstanding account receivable by the Company from DiMarco of $3,095,000.

The assigned fair values of the underlying assets and liabilities acquired by the Company as at September 9, 2007 are summarized as follows:

Cash	$	3
Inventory		3,755
Prepaid expenses		39
Capital assets		425
Total assets acquired		4,222
Less: amounts due to others		(88)
Net assets acquired	$	4,134

(b)   Effective November 26, 2007, the Company acquired 100% of the outstanding shares of Athletes World Limited ("AWL") which was operating under Companies' Creditors Arrangement Act ("CCAA") protection. While under CCAA protection, FGL maintained its usual role in the management of the day-to-day operation of Athletes World under the supervision of a court-appointed monitor who was responsible for reviewing Athletes World's ongoing operations, assisting with the development and filing of the Court documents, liaising with creditors and other stakeholders and reporting to the Court. On June 30, 2008 AWL successfully exited from CCAA protection.

The acquisition was accounted for using the purchase method and accordingly the consolidated financial statements include the results of operations since the date of acquisition.

The assigned fair values of the underlying assets and liabilities acquired by the Company as at November 26, 2007, are summarized as follows:

Inventory	$	26,171
Capital assets		2,626
Intangible asset - trademark		2,212
Future income tax asset		13,215
Total assets acquired		44,224
Bank indebtedness		108
Accounts payable		17,254
Long-term debt		18,196
Total liabilities acquired		35,558
Net assets acquired	$	8,666
Consideration given:		
Cash	$	1,500
Acquisition costs		7,166
Total Consideration	$	8,666

18. Segmented Financial Information

The Company operates principally in two business segments: corporately-owned and operated retail stores and as a wholesale business selling to franchisees and others. Amortization and interest expense are not disclosed by segment as they are substantially retail in nature.

In determining the reportable segments, the Company considered the distinct business models of the retail and wholesale operations, the division of responsibilities, and the reporting to the CEO and Board of Directors.

	For the 52 weeks ended February 1, 2009	For the 53 weeks ended February 3, 2008
Revenues:		
Retail	$ 994,043	$ 969,256
Wholesale	352,715	361,753
	1,346,758	1,331,009
Operating Profit:		
Retail	115,431	143,517
Wholesale	37,229	35,296
	152,660	178,813
Non-segment specific administrative expenses	55,558	55,843
Operating profit before under noted items	97,102	122,970
Amortization of capital assets	47,613	44,468
Interest expense	5,175	5,797
Loss on sale of investment	-	864
	52,788	51,129
Earnings before income taxes	44,314	71,841
Income tax expense	14,989	24,390
Net earnings	$ 29,325	$ 47,451

As at	February 1, 2009		February 3, 2008	
Accounts receivable				
Retail	$	617	$	2,796
Wholesale		74,031		71,036
Non-segment specific		9,807		1,674
	$	84,455	$	75,506
Capital assets				
Retail	$	172,146	$	164,740
Wholesale		21,262		20,596
Non-segment specific		3,357		3,285
	$	196,765	$	188,621
Goodwill and other intangibles/Other assets				
Retail	$	73,162	$	63,291
Wholesale		23,263		20,336
Non-segment specific		4,336		9,571
	$	100,761	$	93,198
Total assets				
Retail	$	476,711	$	515,739
Wholesale		169,915		164,541
Non-segment specific		42,834		74,684
	$	689,460	$	754,964

19. Related Party Transaction

An officer of the Company holds an interest in franchise store operations. During the year, the franchise operations transacted business, in the normal course and at fair market value, with the Company, purchasing product in the amount of $11,438,000 (2008 - $7,660,000). At the year end, accounts receivable from the franchise operation were $4,404,000 (2008 – $1,821,000).

20. Variable Interest Entities

At February 1, 2009, the Company had a long-term receivable due from an entity which is considered a variable interest entity VIE under CICA AcG 15. The entity operates several franchise stores. The Company has received guarantees for the full amount of the receivable from the shareholders of the entity. The Company has concluded that it is not the primary beneficiary of the VIE and that it is not required to consolidate this VIE in its consolidated financial statements. The Company has no exposure to loss related to the long-term receivable.

21. Sale of Investment

During fiscal 2008, the Company sold its investment in a trademark licensing company. The investment had a cost of $3,088,000 and was sold for $2,224,000 with a one-time loss of $864,000 recognized during the period ended February 3, 2008.

22. Subsequent Events

Effective February 18, 2009, the Company completed an asset purchase from Access Distribution Inc., for total expected consideration of $4,000,000, payable over 5 years on the completion of certain performance measures.

23. Comparative Figures

Certain comparative figures have been reclassified to conform to the presentation adopted for the current period.

Present value concepts are widely used by accountants in the preparation of financial statements. In fact, under International Financial Reporting Standards (IFRS), these concepts are more widely applied than under traditional Canadian GAAP. This appendix will explain the basics that you must be aware of to understand related topics in this text.

Interest Rates

Interest is payment for the use of money. It is the difference between the amount borrowed or invested (the principal) and the amount repaid or collected. The amount of interest to be paid or collected is usually stated as a rate over a specific period of time. The rate of interest is generally stated as an annual rate.

The amount of interest involved in any financing transaction is based on three elements:

1. **Principal** (p): The original amount borrowed or invested
2. **Interest rate** (i): An annual percentage of the principal
3. **Number of periods** (n): The time period that the principal is borrowed or invested

Simple Interest

Simple interest is calculated on the principal amount only. It is the return on the principal for one period. Simple interest is usually expressed as shown in Illustration PV-1.

$$\text{Interest} = \text{Principal } (p) \times \text{Interest Rate } (i) \times \text{Number of Periods } (n)$$

◄ **Illustration PV-1**
Simple interest formula

For example, if you borrowed $1,000 for 3 years at a simple interest rate of 9% annually, you would pay $270 in total interest, calculated as follows:

$$
\begin{aligned}
\text{Interest} &= p \times i \times n \\
&= \$1{,}000 \times 9\% \times 3 \\
&= \$270
\end{aligned}
$$

Year 1		Year 2		Year 3		
$90	+	$90	+	$90	=	$270

Compound Interest

Compound interest is the return on (or growth of) the principal for two or more time periods. Compounding calculates interest not only on the principal but also on the interest earned to date on that principal, assuming the interest is left on deposit (i.e., added to the original principal amount).

To illustrate the difference between simple and compound interest, assume that you deposit $1,000 in the Last Canadian Bank, where it will earn simple interest of 9% per year, and you deposit another $1,000 in the First Canadian Bank, where it will earn interest of 9% per year compounded annually. Also assume that in both cases you will not withdraw any interest until three years from the date of deposit. The calculation of interest to be received and the accumulated year-end balances are given in Illustration PV-2.

Illustration PV-2 ▾
Simple versus compound interest

LAST CANADIAN BANK			
Simple Interest Calculation	Simple Interest	Accumulated Year-End Balance	
Year 1 $1,000.00 × 9%	$ 90.00	$1,090.00	
Year 2 $1,000.00 × 9%	90.00	$1,180.00	
Year 3 $1,000.00 × 9%	90.00	$1,270.00	
	$270.00		

FIRST CANADIAN BANK		
Compound Interest Calculation	Compound Interest	Accumulated Year-End Balance
Year 1 $1,000.00 × 9%	$ 90.00	$1,090.00
Year 2 $1,090.00 × 9%	98.10	$1,188.10
Year 3 $1,188.10 × 9%	106.93	$1,295.03
	$295.03	

$25.03 Difference

Note in Illustration PV-2 that simple interest uses the initial principal of $1,000 to calculate the interest in all three years. Compound interest uses the accumulated balance (principal plus interest to date) at each year end to calculate interest in the following year. This explains why your compound interest account is larger: you are earning interest on interest. For practical purposes, compounding assumes that unpaid interest earned becomes a part of the principal. The accumulated balance at the end of each year becomes the new principal on which interest is earned during the next year.

Assuming all else is equal (especially risk), if you had a choice between investing your money at simple interest or at compound interest, you would choose compound interest. In the example, compounding provides $25.03 of additional interest income.

Compound interest is used in most business situations. Simple interest is generally applicable only to short-term situations of one year or less. Present value concepts use compound interest.

Calculating Present Values

In the previous section on compound and simple interest, the initial principal was given. It was used to calculate the interest earned and the value of the investment at the end of three years. **The initial principal, invested at the beginning of year one, is the present value of the investment. The value of the investment at the end of three years is the future value** of the investment.

You are probably more accustomed to being given the present value and then calculating the future value. But in business, there are many situations in which the future value is given, and it is necessary to calculate the present value. For example, we determine the market price of a bond by calculating the present value of the principal and interest payments. Calculating the amount to be reported for fixed and intangible assets, notes payable, pensions, and finance lease liabilities can also involve present value calculations.

Present value calculations are always based on three variables:

1. The *dollar amount* to be received (the future amount or future value)
2. The *length of time* until the amount is received (the number of periods)
3. The *interest rate* (the discount rate) per period

The process of determining the present value is often referred to as **discounting the future cash flows**. The word "discount" has many meanings in accounting, each of which varies with the context in which it is being used. Be careful not to confuse the use of this term.

Present Value of a Single Future Amount

In the following section, we will show three methods of calculating the present value of a single future amount: present value formula, present value tables, and financial calculators.

Present Value Formula

To illustrate present value concepts, assume that you want to invest a sum of money at 5% in order to have $1,000 at the end of one year. The amount that you would need to invest today is called the present value of $1,000 discounted for one year at 5%.

The variables in this example are shown in the time diagram in Illustration PV-3.

Present Value = $952.38   **Future Amount = $1,000**

Illustration PV-3 ➡

Time diagram for the present value of $1,000 discounted for one period at 5%

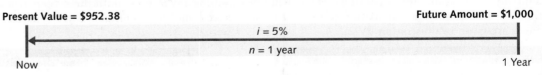

$i = 5\%$

$n = 1$ year

Now   1 Year

The formula used to determine the present value for any interest (discount) rate (i), number of periods (n), and future amount (FV) is shown in Illustration PV-4.

Illustration PV-4

Present value of a single future amount formula

$$\text{Present value } (PV) = \frac{\text{Future value } (FV)}{(1 + i)^n}$$
$$= FV \div (1 + i)^n$$

Alternative terminology
The present value of a single future amount formula is also called the *present value of 1 formula*.

In applying this formula to calculate the present value (PV) for the above example, the future value (FV) of $1,000, the interest (discount) rate (i) of 5%, and the number of periods (n) of one are used as follows:

PV $= \$1,000 \div (1 + 5\%)^1$
$= \$1,000 \div 1.05$
$= \$952.38$

If the single future cash flow of $1,000 is to be received in two years and discounted at 5%, its present value is calculated as follows:

PV $= \$1,000 \div (1 + 5\%)^2$
$= \$1,000 \div 1.05^2$ or $[(\$1,000 \div 1.05) \div 1.05]$
$= \$907.03$

The time diagram in Illustration PV-5 shows the variables used to calculate the present value when cash is received in two years.

Present Value = $907.03 **Future Amount = $1,000**

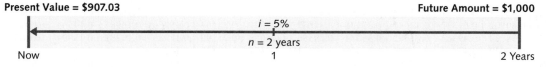

Illustration PV-5

Time diagram for present value of $1,000 discounted for two periods at 5%

Present Value Tables

The present value may also be determined through tables that show the present value of 1 for n periods for different periodic interest rates or discount rates. In Table PV-1, the rows represent the number of discounting periods and the columns the periodic interest or discount rates. The five-digit decimal numbers in the respective rows and columns are the factors for the present value of 1.

When present value tables are used, the present value is calculated by multiplying the future cash amount by the present value factor specified at the intersection of the number of periods and the discount rate. For example, if the discount rate is 5% and the number of periods is 1, Table PV-1 shows that the present value factor is 0.95238. Then the present value of $1,000 discounted at 5% for one period is calculated as follows:

PV $= \$1,000 \times 0.95238$
$= \$952.38$

For two periods at a discount rate of 5%, the present value factor is 0.90703. The present value of $1,000 discounted at 5% for two periods is calculated as follows:

PV $= \$1,000 \times 0.90703$
$= \$907.03$

Note that the present values in these two examples are identical to the amounts determined previously when using the present value formula. This is because the factors in a present value table have been calculated using the present value formula. The benefit of using a present value table is that it can be quicker than using the formula. If you are using a simple calculator (not a financial calculator) or doing the calculations by hand, there are more calculations involved as the number of periods increase, making it more tedious than using the present value tables.

Table PV-1 can also be used if you know the present value and wish to determine the future cash flow. The present value amount is divided by the present value factor specified at the intersection of the number of periods and the discount rate in Table PV-1. For example, it can easily be determined that an initial investment of $907.03 will grow to yield a future amount of $1,000 in two periods, at an annual discount rate of 5% ($1,000 = $907.03 ÷ 0.90703).

| | | | | | | TABLE PV-1
PRESENT VALUE OF 1
$PV = \dfrac{1}{(1+i)^n}$ | | | | | | | |

(n) Periods	2%	2½%	3%	4%	5%	6%	7%	8%	9%	10%	11%	12%	15%
1	0.98039	0.97561	0.97087	0.96154	0.95238	0.94340	0.93458	0.92593	0.91743	0.90909	0.90090	0.89286	0.86957
2	0.96117	0.95181	0.94260	0.92456	0.90703	0.89000	0.87344	0.85734	0.84168	0.82645	0.81162	0.79719	0.75614
3	0.94232	0.92860	0.91514	0.88900	0.86384	0.83962	0.81630	0.79383	0.77218	0.75131	0.73119	0.71178	0.65752
4	0.92385	0.90595	0.88849	0.85480	0.82270	0.79209	0.76290	0.73503	0.70843	0.68301	0.65873	0.63552	0.57175
5	0.90573	0.88385	0.86261	0.82193	0.78353	0.74726	0.71299	0.68058	0.64993	0.62092	0.59345	0.56743	0.49718
6	0.88797	0.86230	0.83748	0.79031	0.74622	0.70496	0.66634	0.63017	0.59627	0.56447	0.53464	0.50663	0.43233
7	0.87056	0.84127	0.81309	0.75992	0.71068	0.66506	0.62275	0.58349	0.54703	0.51316	0.48166	0.45235	0.37594
8	0.85349	0.82075	0.78941	0.73069	0.67684	0.62741	0.58201	0.54027	0.50187	0.46651	0.43393	0.40388	0.32690
9	0.83676	0.80073	0.76642	0.70259	0.64461	0.59190	0.54393	0.50025	0.46043	0.42410	0.39092	0.36061	0.28426
10	0.82035	0.78120	0.74409	0.67556	0.61391	0.55839	0.50835	0.46319	0.42241	0.38554	0.35218	0.32197	0.24718
11	0.80426	0.76214	0.72242	0.64958	0.58468	0.52679	0.47509	0.42888	0.38753	0.35049	0.31728	0.28748	0.21494
12	0.78849	0.74356	0.70138	0.62460	0.55684	0.49697	0.44401	0.39711	0.35553	0.31863	0.28584	0.25668	0.18691
13	0.77303	0.72542	0.68095	0.60057	0.53032	0.46884	0.41496	0.36770	0.32618	0.28966	0.25751	0.22917	0.16253
14	0.75788	0.70773	0.66112	0.57748	0.50507	0.44230	0.38782	0.34046	0.29925	0.26333	0.23199	0.20462	0.14133
15	0.74301	0.69047	0.64186	0.55526	0.48102	0.41727	0.36245	0.31524	0.27454	0.23939	0.20900	0.18270	0.12289
16	0.72845	0.67362	0.62317	0.53391	0.45811	0.39365	0.33873	0.29189	0.25187	0.21763	0.18829	0.16312	0.10686
17	0.71416	0.65720	0.60502	0.51337	0.43630	0.37136	0.31657	0.27027	0.23107	0.19784	0.16963	0.14564	0.09293
18	0.70016	0.64117	0.58739	0.49363	0.41552	0.35034	0.29586	0.25025	0.21199	0.17986	0.15282	0.13004	0.08081
19	0.68643	0.62553	0.57029	0.47464	0.39573	0.33051	0.27651	0.23171	0.19449	0.16351	0.13768	0.11611	0.07027
20	0.67297	0.61027	0.55368	0.45639	0.37689	0.31180	0.25842	0.21455	0.17843	0.14864	0.12403	0.10367	0.06110

Financial Calculators

Present values can also be calculated using financial calculators. A financial calculator will perform the same calculation as a simple calculator, but it requires fewer steps and less input. Basically, with a financial calculator, you input the future value, the discount rate, and the number of periods, and then tell it to calculate the present value. We will not illustrate how to use a financial calculator because the details vary with different financial calculators.

But you should know that the present value amounts calculated with a financial calculator can be slightly different than those calculated with present value tables. That is because the numbers in a present value table are rounded. For example, in Table PV-1 the factors are rounded to five digits. In a financial calculator, only the final answer is rounded to the number of digits you have specified.

A major benefit of using a financial calculator is that you are not restricted to the interest rates or numbers of periods on a present value table. In Table PV-1, present value factors have been calculated for 13 interest rates (there are 13 columns in that table) and the maximum number of periods is 20. With a financial calculator you could, for example, calculate the present value of a future amount to be received in 25 periods using 5.75% as the discount rate. Later in this appendix, we will illustrate how to partly overcome this limitation of present value tables through a method called interpolation.

Regardless of the method used in calculating present values, **a higher discount rate produces a smaller present value**. For example, using an 8% discount rate, the present value of $1,000 due one year from now is $925.93 versus $952.38 at 5%. It should also be recognized that **the further away from the present the future cash flow is, the smaller the present value**. For example, using the same discount rate of 5%, the present value of $1,000 due in five years is $783.53. The present value of $1,000 due in one year is $952.38.

BEFORE YOU GO ON . . .

➡ Review It

1. Distinguish between simple and compound interest.
2. Distinguish between present value and future value.
3. What are the three variables used in calculating present value?
4. When calculating present value, what are the benefits of using present value tables and of using financial calculators?

➜ Do It

Suppose you have a winning lottery ticket and the lottery commission gives you the option of taking $10,000 three years from now, or taking the present value of $10,000 now. If an 8% discount rate is used, what is the present value of your winnings if you take the option of receiving $10,000 three years from now? Show the calculation using either (a) the present value formula or (b) Table PV-1.

Action Plan
- Note that $10,000 is the future value, the number of periods is 3, and the discount rate is 8%.
- Recall that the present value of $10,000 to be received in 3 years is less than $10,000 because interest can be earned on an amount invested today (i.e., the present value) over the next three years.
- Understand that the discount rate used to calculate the present value is the compound interest rate that would be used to earn $10,000 in 3 years if the present value is invested today.
- Draw a time diagram showing when the future value will be received, the discount rate, and the number of periods.

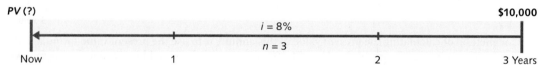

PV (?) $i = 8\%$ **$10,000**

$n = 3$

Now   1   2   3 Years

Solution

(a) Using the present value formula:
$$PV = \$10,000 \div (1 + 8\%)^3$$
$$= \$10,000 \div 1.08^3 \text{ or } \{[(\$10,000 \div 1.08) \div 1.08] \div 1.08\}$$
$$= \$7,938.30$$

(b) Using the present value factor from Table PV-1:
The present value factor for three periods at 8% is 0.79383.
$$PV = \$10,000 \times 0.79383$$
$$= \$7,938.30$$

➜ Do It Again

Determine the amount you must deposit now in your savings account, paying 3% interest, in order to accumulate $5,000 for a down payment on a hybrid electric car four years from now, when you graduate. Show the calculation using either (a) present value formula, or (b) Table PV-1.

Action Plan
- Note that $5,000 is the future value, $n = 4$, and $i = 3\%$.
- Draw a time diagram showing when the future value will be received, the discount rate, and the number of periods.

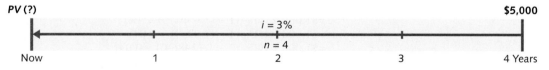

PV (?) $i = 3\%$ **$5,000**

$n = 4$

Now   1   2   3   4 Years

Solution
The amount you must deposit now in your savings account is the present value calculated as follows:

(a) Using the present value formula:
$$PV = \$5,000 \div (1 + 3\%)^4$$
$$= \$5,000 \div 1.03^4 \text{ or } (\{[(\$5,000 \div 1.03) \div 1.03] \div 1.03\} \div 1.03)$$
$$= \$4,442.43$$

(b) Using the present value factor from Table PV-1:
The present value factor for four periods at 3% is 0.88849.
$$PV = \$5,000 \times 0.88849$$
$$PV = \$4,442.45$$

Note: The difference in the two answers is due to rounding the factors in Table PV-1.

Related exercise material: BEPV-1, BEPV-2, BEPV-3, BEPV-4, and BEPV-5.

The Navigator

Present Value of a Series of Future Cash Flows (Annuities)

The preceding discussion was for the discounting of only a single future amount. Businesses and individuals frequently engage in transactions in which a series of equal dollar amounts are to be received or paid periodically. Examples of a series of periodic receipts or payments are loan agreements, instalment sales, mortgage notes, lease (rental) contracts, and pension obligations. These series of periodic receipts or payments are called **annuities**. In calculating the present value of an annuity, it is necessary to know (1) the discount rate (i), (2) the number of discount periods (n), and (3) the amount of the periodic receipts or payments (FV).

To illustrate the calculation of the present value of an annuity, assume that you will receive $1,000 cash annually for three years, and that the discount rate is 4%. This situation is shown in the time diagram in Illustration B-6.

Illustration PV-6 ➡️

Time diagram for a three-year annuity

PV (?)		$1,000		$1,000		$1,000
			$i = 4\%$			
			$n=3$			
Now		1		2		3 Years

One method of calculating the present value of this annuity is to use the present value formula to determine the present value of each of the three $1,000 payments and then add those amounts as follows:

$$PV = [\$1{,}000 \div (1 + 4\%)^1] + [\$1{,}000 \div (1 + 4\%)^2] + [\$1{,}000 \div (1 + 4\%)^3]$$
$$= \$961.54 + \$924.56 + \$889.00$$
$$= \$2{,}775.10$$

The same result is achieved by using present value factors from Table PV-1, as shown in Illustration PV-7.

Illustration PV-7 ➡️

Present value of a series of future cash flows

Future Value	×	Present Value of 1 Factor at 4%	=	Present Value
$1,000 (one year away)		0.96154		$ 961.54
1,000 (two years away)		0.92456		924.56
1,000 (three years away)		0.88900		889.00
		2.77510		$2,775.10

Determining the present value of each single future cash flow, and then adding the present values, is required when the periodic cash flows are not the same in each period. But when the future receipts are the same in each period, there are three other ways to calculate present value.

The first is to use the present value of an ordinary annuity formula, as shown in Illustration PV-8.

Illustration PV-8 ➡️

Present value of an ordinary annuity of 1 formula

$$\text{Present value } (PV) = \text{Future value } (FV) \times \frac{1 - \dfrac{1}{(1 + i)^n}}{i}$$

$$=\$1{,}000 \times [(1 - (1 \div (1 + 4\%)^3)) \div 4\%]$$
$$=\$1{,}000 \times [(1 - (1 \div (1.04)^3)) \div 0.04]$$
$$=\$1{,}000 \times [(1 - (1 \div 1.124864)) \div 0.04]$$
$$=\$1{,}000 \times [(1 - 0.888996358) \div 0.04]$$
$$=\$1{,}000 \times 2.77509$$
$$=\$2{,}775.09$$

TABLE PV-2
PRESENT VALUE OF AN ANNUITY OF 1
$PV= \dfrac{1 - \dfrac{1}{(1+i)^n}}{i}$

(n) Periods	2%	2½%	3%	4%	5%	6%	7%	8%	9%	10%	11%	12%	15%
1	0.98039	0.97561	0.97087	0.96154	0.95238	0.94340	0.93458	0.92593	0.91743	0.90909	0.90090	0.89286	0.86957
2	1.94156	1.92742	1.91347	1.88609	1.85941	1.83339	1.80802	1.78326	1.75911	1.73554	1.71252	1.69005	1.62571
3	2.88388	2.85602	2.82861	2.77509	2.72325	2.67301	2.62432	2.57710	2.53129	2.48685	2.44371	2.40183	2.28323
4	3.80773	3.76197	3.71710	3.62990	3.54595	3.46511	3.38721	3.31213	3.23972	3.16987	3.10245	3.03735	2.85498
5	4.71346	4.64583	4.57971	4.45182	4.32948	4.21236	4.10020	3.99271	3.88965	3.79079	3.69590	3.60478	3.35216

(n) Periods	2%	2½%	3%	4%	5%	6%	7%	8%	9%	10%	11%	12%	15%
6	5.60143	5.50813	5.41719	5.24214	5.07569	4.91732	4.76654	4.62288	4.48592	4.35526	4.23054	4.11141	3.78448
7	6.47199	6.34939	6.23028	6.00205	5.78637	5.58238	5.38929	5.20637	5.03295	4.86842	4.71220	4.56376	4.16042
8	7.32548	7.17014	7.01969	6.73274	6.46321	6.20979	5.97130	5.74664	5.53482	5.33493	5.14612	4.96764	4.48732
9	8.16224	7.97087	7.78611	7.43533	7.10782	6.80169	6.51523	6.24689	5.99525	5.75902	5.53705	5.32825	4.77158
10	8.98259	8.75206	8.53020	8.11090	7.72173	7.36009	7.02358	6.71008	6.41766	6.14457	5.88923	5.65022	5.01877
11	9.78685	9.51421	9.25262	8.76048	8.30641	7.88687	7.49867	7.13896	6.80519	6.49506	6.20652	5.93770	5.23371
12	10.57534	10.25776	9.95400	9.38507	8.86325	8.38384	7.94269	7.53608	7.16073	6.81369	6.49236	6.19437	5.42062
13	11.34837	10.98319	10.63496	9.98565	9.39357	8.85268	8.35765	7.90378	7.48690	7.10336	6.74987	6.42355	5.58315
14	12.10625	11.69091	11.29607	10.56312	9.89864	9.29498	8.74547	8.24424	7.78615	7.36669	6.98187	6.62817	5.72448
15	12.84926	12.38138	11.93794	11.11839	10.37966	9.71225	9.10791	8.55948	8.06069	7.60608	7.19087	6.81086	5.84737
16	13.57771	13.05500	12.56110	11.65230	10.83777	10.10590	9.44665	8.85137	8.31256	7.82371	7.37916	6.97399	5.95423
17	14.29187	13.71220	13.16612	12.16567	11.27407	10.47726	9.76322	9.12164	8.54363	8.02155	7.54879	7.11963	6.04716
18	14.99203	14.35336	13.75351	12.65930	11.68959	10.82760	10.05909	9.37189	8.75563	8.20141	7.70162	7.24967	6.12797
19	15.67846	14.97889	14.32380	13.13394	12.08532	11.15812	10.33560	9.60360	8.95011	8.36492	7.83929	7.36578	6.19823
20	16.35143	15.58916	14.87747	13.59033	12.46221	11.46992	10.59401	9.81815	9.12855	8.51356	7.96333	7.46944	6.25933

The second is to use a present value of an annuity table. As illustrated in Table PV-2, these tables show the present value of 1 to be received periodically for a given number of periods. From Table PV-2, it can be seen that the present value factor of an annuity of 1 for three periods at 4% is 2.77509. This present value factor is the total of the three individual present value factors, as shown in Illustration PV-7.[1] Applying this present value factor to the annual cash flow of $1,000 produces a present value of $2,775.09 ($1,000 × 2.77509).

The third method is to use a financial calculator and input the number of periods, the interest rate, and the amount of the annual payment. When using a financial calculator to calculate the present value of an annuity, it is also necessary to specify if the annual cash flow is an ordinary annuity or an annuity in arrears. In **an ordinary annuity, the first payment is at the end of the first period**, as in our example. In **an annuity in arrears, the first payment starts immediately, at the beginning of the first period**. In this appendix and textbook, all of the annuity examples are ordinary annuities.

Interest Rates and Time Periods

In the preceding calculations, the discounting has been done on an annual basis using an annual interest rate. There are situations where adjustments may be required to the interest rate, the time period, or both.

Using Time Periods of Less Than One Year

Discounting may be done over shorter periods of time than one year, such as monthly, quarterly, or semi-annually. When the time frame is less than one year, it is necessary to convert the annual interest rate to the applicable time frame. Assume, for example, that the investor in Illustration PV-6 received $500 semi-annually for three years instead of $1,000 annually. In this case, the number of periods (n) becomes six (three annual periods × 2), and the discount rate (i) is 2% (4% × $^6/_{12}$ months).

If present value tables are used to determine the present value, the appropriate present value factor from Table PV-2 is 5.60143. The present value of the future cash flows is $2,800.72 (5.60143 × $500). This amount is slightly higher than the $2,775.09 calculated in Illustration PV-8 because interest is calculated twice during the same year. Thus, interest is compounded on the first half-year's interest.

Interpolation

As previously discussed, one of the limitations of the present value tables is that the tables contain a limited number of interest rates. But in certain situations where the factor for a certain interest rate is not available, it can be deduced or **interpolated** from the tables. For example, if you wished to find the factor to determine the present value of 1 for a 3½% interest rate and five periods, it would be difficult to use Table PV-1 to do so. Table PV-1 (or Table PV-2 for that matter) does not have a 3½% interest rate column. We can, however, average the factors for the 3% and 4% interest rates to approximate the factor for a 3½% interest rate.

Factor, $n = 5$, $i = 3\%$		0.86261
Factor, $n = 5$, $i = 4\%$	+	0.82193
Sum of two factors	=	1.68454
Average two factors	÷	2
Factor, $n = 5$, $i = 3\frac{1}{2}\%$	=	0.84227

← Illustration PV-9

Interpolation of 3½% interest rate factor

[1] The difference of 0.00001 between 2.77509 and 2.77510 is due to rounding.

As previously mentioned, interpolation is only necessary when using present value tables. If a financial calculator is used, any interest rate can be used in the calculations.

BEFORE YOU GO ON . . .

➔ Review It

1. What is an annuity?
2. How is Table PV-2 used to calculate the present value of an annuity?
3. If an annuity is paid every three months for five years and 8% is the annual discount rate, what are the number of periods (n) and the interest rate (i) used in the present value calculation?
4. When is it necessary to interpolate an interest rate?

➔ Do It

Corkum Company has just signed a capital lease contract for equipment that requires rental payments of $6,000 each, to be paid at the end of each of the next five years. The appropriate discount rate is 6%. What is the present value of the rental payments; that is, the amount used to capitalize the leased equipment? Show the calculation using either (a) the present value of an annuity formula or (b) Table PV-2.

Action Plan

- Draw a time diagram showing when the future value will be received, the discount rate, and the number of periods.

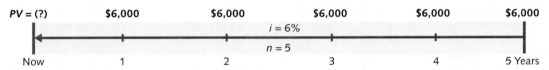

- Note that each of the future payments is the same amount paid at even intervals; therefore, use present value of an annuity calculations to determine the present value (i = 6% and n = 5).

Solution
The present value of lease rental payments of $6,000 paid at the end of each year for five years, discounted at 6%, is calculated as follows:

(a) Using the present value of an annuity formula:
$\quad$ PV $= \$6,000 \times [(1 - (1 \div (1 + 6\%)^5) \div 6\%]$
$\quad = \$6,000 \times [(1 - (1 \div (1.06)^5) \div 0.06]$
$\quad = \$6,000 \times [(1 - (1 \div 1.33823) \div 0.06]$
$\quad = \$6,000 \times [(1 - .747256) \div 0.06]$
$\quad = \$6,000 \times 4.21236$
$\quad = \$25,274.16$

(b) Using the present value factor from Table PV-2:
$\quad$ The present value factor from Table PV-2 is 4.21236 (five periods at 6%).
$\quad$ PV $= \$6,000 \times 4.21236$
$\quad$ PV $= \$25,274.16$

Related exercise material: BEPV-6, BEPV-7, and BEPV-8.

The Navigator

Applying Present Value Concepts

Calculating the Market Price or Present Value of a Bond

The present value (or market price) of a bond is a function of three variables: (1) the payment amounts, (2) the length of time until the amounts are paid, and (3) the market interest rate, also known as the discount rate.

The first variable (dollars to be paid) is made up of two elements: (1) the principal amount (a single sum), and (2) a series of interest payments (an annuity). To calculate the present value of the bond, both the principal amount and the interest payments must be discounted, which requires two different calculations. The present value of a bond can be calculated using present value formulas, factors from the two present value tables, or a financial calculator. We will illustrate only present value tables.

It is important to note that **the interest rate used to determine the annual or semi-annual interest payments is fixed over the life of a bond.** This is the **bond's contractual interest rate.** The company issuing the bond chooses the specific interest rate before issuing the bonds. But investors may use a different interest rate when determining how much they are willing to pay (the present value) for the bonds. Investors are influenced by both general economic conditions and their assessment of the company issuing the bonds. **Investors use the market interest rate to determine the present value of the bonds.** In the following sections, we will illustrate how to calculate the present value of the bonds using a market interest rate that is equal to, greater than, or less than the contractual interest rate.

Market Interest Rate Equals the Contractual Interest Rate

When the investor's market interest rate is equal to the bond's contractual interest rate, the bonds' present value will equal their face value. To illustrate, assume there is a bond issue of five-year, 6% bonds with a face value of $100,000. Interest is payable **semi-annually** on January 1 and July 1. In this case, the investor will receive (1) $100,000 at maturity, and (2) a series of 10 $3,000 interest payments [($100,000 × 6%) × $\frac{6}{12}$ months] over the term of the bonds. The length of time (n) is the total number of interest periods (10 periods = 5 years × 2 payments per year), and the discount rate (i) is the rate per semi-annual interest period (3% = 6% × $\frac{6}{12}$ months). The time diagram in Illustration PV-10 shows the variables involved in this discounting situation.

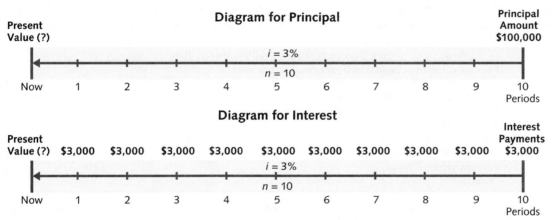

← Illustration PV-10

Time diagram for the present value of a five-year, 6% bond paying interest semi-annually

The calculation of the present value of these bonds using factors from the appropriate present value tables is shown in Illustration PV-11.

6% Contractual Rate and 6% Market Rate	
Present value of principal to be received at maturity	
$100,000 × PV of 1 due in 10 periods (n) at 3% (i)	
$100,000 × 0.74409 (Table PV-1)	$ 74,409
Present value of interest to be received periodically	
over the term of the bonds	
$3,000 × PV of 1 due periodically for 10 periods (n) at 3% (i)	
$3,000 × 8.53020 (Table PV-2)	25,591*
Present value of bonds	$100,000
* Rounded	

← Illustration PV-11

Present value of principal and interest (face value)

Thus, when the market rate is the same as the contractual rate, the bonds will sell at face value.

Market Interest Rate Is Greater Than the Contractual Interest Rate

Now assume that the investor's market rate of return is 8%, not 6%. The future cash flows are again $100,000 and $3,000, respectively. **These cash flows are based on the bond contract and do not vary with the investor's rate of return.** But the investor's rate of return can vary, depending on available rates in the marketplace. If the market interest rate is 8%, then the present value is calculated using this rate. In this case, 4% (8% × $^{6}/_{12}$ months) will be used because the bonds pay interest semi-annually. The present value of the bonds is $91,889, as calculated in Illustration PV-12.

Illustration PV-12 ➡️

Present value of principal and interest (discount)

6% Contractual Rate and 8% Market Rate	
Present value of principal to be received at maturity	
$100,000 × PV of 1 due in 10 periods (n) at 4% (i)	
$100,000 × 0.67556 (Table PV-1)	$67,556
Present value of interest to be received periodically	
over the term of the bonds	
$3,000 × PV of 1 due periodically for 10 periods (n) at 4% (i)	
$3,000 × 8.11090 (Table PV-2)	24,333*
Present value of bonds	$91,889
*Rounded	

In this situation, the bonds will sell for $91,889, at a discount of $8,111. **If the market interest rate is greater than the contract interest rate, the bonds will always sell at a discount.** If investors determine that the bond's contract interest rate is too low, they will compensate by paying less for the bonds. Note that they will still collect the full $100,000 at the maturity date.

Market Interest Rate Is Less Than the Contractual Interest Rate

On the other hand, the market rate might be lower than the contract interest rate. In this case, the interest paid on the bonds is higher than what investors expected to earn. As a result, they will compensate by paying more for the bonds. If the market interest rate is 5%, the present value will be calculated using 2.5% (5% × $^{6}/_{12}$ months) as the discount rate. The cash payments and number of periods remain the same. In this case, the present value of the bonds is $104,376, calculated as in Illustration PV-13.

Illustration PV-13 ➡️

Present value of principal and interest (premium)

6% Contractual Rate and 5% Market Rate	
Present value of principal to be received at maturity	
$100,000 × PV of 1 due in 10 periods (n) at 2.5% (i)	
$100,000 × 0.78120 (Table PV-1)	$ 78,120
Present value of interest to be received periodically	
over the term of the bonds	
$3,000 × PV of 1 due periodically for 10 periods (n) at 2.5% (i)	
$3,000 × 8.75206 (Table PV-2)	26,256*
Present value of bonds	$104,376
*Rounded	

These bonds will sell at a $4,376 premium for $104,376. **If the market interest rate is less than the contract interest rate, the bonds will always sell at a premium.**

The above discussion relied on present value tables to solve present value problems. As previously discussed, financial calculators may also be used to calculate present values without the use of these tables. In addition, most computer spreadsheets and programs also have built-in formulas to perform the discounting functions.

BEFORE YOU GO ON . . .

➡️ Review It

1. Explain how the present value of a bond is determined.
2. Distinguish between the market rate of interest and the contractual rate of interest. How is each of these used in determining the present value of a bond?
3. If the bonds have interest payable semi-annually, how is the discount rate (i) determined? How is the number of periods (n) determined?
4. If the market rate is greater than the contract rate, will the bonds sell at a premium or a discount? Explain.

➡️ Do It

Forest Lake Enterprises issued $1 million of six-year, 4.5% bonds that pay interest semi-annually. The market rate of interest for the bonds at the issue date is 4%. What cash proceeds did Forest Lake Enterprises receive from the issue of the bonds?

Action Plan

- Note that Forest Lake will be able to sell these bonds at a premium because the bonds pay higher interest (4.5%) than the current market interest rate (4%).
- Recall that the contractual interest rate is used to determine the interest payment; the market rate is used to determine the present value.
- Adjust the interest rates and number of periods for the effect of the semi-annual periods.
- Use Table PV-1 to determine the present value of the principal.
- Use Table PV-2 to determine the present value of the interest payments.

Solution

1. Amount to be received at maturity is the face value of the bonds, $1,000,000
2. Semi-annual interest payment = $22,500 ($1,000,000 × 4.5% × $^6/_{12}$ months)
3. Number of periods $n = 12$ (6 years × 2 payments a year)
4. Discount rate $i = 2\%$ (4% ÷ 2 payments a year)

The cash proceeds that Forest Lake will receive from issuing the bonds is the present value of principal to be received at maturity plus the present value of the interest received periodically, calculated as follows:

Present value of principal to be received at maturity:
$1,000,000 × 0.78849 (PV of $1 due in 12
periods at 2% from Table PV-1) $ 788,490

Present value of interest to be received periodically
over the term of the bonds: $22,500 × 10.57534
(PV of $1 due each period for 12 periods at 2% from Table PV-2)   237,945
Present value of bonds $1,026,435

Related exercise material: BEPV-9 and BEPV-10.

The Navigator

Calculating the Present Value of Notes Payable

Long-term notes payable are normally repayable in a series of periodic payments. These payments may be fixed principal payments plus interest, or blended principal and interest payments. The accounting treatment of notes is similar to that for bonds. The present value of a note is a function of the same three variables: (1) the payment amounts, (2) the length of time until the amounts are paid (time to maturity date), and (3) the market interest rate. Examples of long-term notes payable include unsecured notes, mortgages (which are secured notes on real property, such as a house), and loans (e.g., student or car).

Note Payable: Fixed Principal Payments Plus Interest

Let's assume Heathcote Company obtains a five-year note payable, with an 8% interest rate, to purchase a piece of equipment costing $25,000. If we first assume that repayment is to be in fixed principal payments plus interest, paid annually, then the payment amount would be $5,000 ($25,000 ÷ 5 years) plus 8% interest on the outstanding balance. Illustration PV-14 details the total cost of this loan over the five-year period.

	Year 1	Year 2	Year 3	Year 4	Year 5	Total
Principal	$5,000	$5,000	$5,000	$5,000	$5,000	$25,000
Interest[1]	2,000	1,600	1,200	800	400	6,000
Total	7,000	6,600	6,200	5,800	5,400	$31,000
Present value factor[2]	0.92593	0.85734	0.79383	0.73503	0.68058	
Present value	$6,482	$5,658	$4,922	$4,263	$3,675	$25,000

◀ Illustration PV-14

Cost of equipment loan—fixed principal payments plus interest

[1] Interest is calculated on the outstanding principal balance at the beginning of the year. In Year 1, it is $25,000 × 8% = $2,000. In Year 2, it is $20,000 ($25,000 − $5,000) × 8% = $1,600, and so on.
[2] These factors are taken from Table PV-1, for $i = 8\%$ and the appropriate n, or number of periods.

Note Payable: Blended Principal Plus Interest Payments

In the case of blended principal and interest payments, present value concepts are used to calculate the amount of the annual payment.

If we divide the total loan amount of $25,000 by the present value factor for an annuity from Table PV-2 for $i = 8\%$ and $n = 5$, then we can determine that the annual payment is $6,261 ($25,000 ÷ 3.99271). Illustration PV-15 details the total cost of this loan over the five-year period.

Illustration PV-15 ➔

Cost of equipment loan—blended principal and interest payments

	Year 1	Year 2	Year 3	Year 4	Year 5	Total
Payment	$6,261	$6,261	$6,261	$6,261	$6,261	$31,305
Present value factor[1]	0.92593	0.85734	0.79383	0.73503	0.68058	
Present value[2]	$5,797	$5,368	$4,970	$4,602	$4,261	$25,000

[1] These factors are taken from Table PV-1, for $i = 8\%$ and the appropriate n, or number of periods.
[2] The sum of the annual present values is not exactly equal to $25,000 because of rounding. If full digits were used, the total would be $25,000.

Comparison of Notes Payable with Fixed Principal versus Blended Payments

Both options result in a present value cost of $25,000, but the blended principal and interest payment option results in a higher total cash outflow, $31,305, compared with $31,000 for the fixed principal payments plus interest option. Note the difference also in the annual cash flows required under each option. For example, the fixed principal and interest payment option results in a higher cash outflow in the first two years and lower cash outflow in the last three years.

These examples illustrate the effect of the timing and amount of cash flows on the present value. Basically, payments made further away from the present are worth less in present value terms, and payments made closer to the present are worth more.

Notes Payable: Stated Interest Rate below Market Interest Rate

In the previous two examples, the stated (contract) interest rate and the market (discount) interest rate were both 8%. As a result of these rates being equal, the present value and the principal amount of the loan were both $25,000. We found the same result in the previous section on bonds payable.

Businesses sometimes offer financing with stated interest rates below market interest rates to stimulate sales. Examples of notes with stated interest rates below market are seen in advertisements offering no payment for two years. These zero- interest-bearing notes do not specify an interest rate to be applied, but the face value is greater than the present value. The present value of these notes is determined by discounting the repayment stream at the market interest rate.

As an example, assume that a furniture retailer is offering "No payment for two years, or $150 off on items with a sticker price of $2,000." The implicit interest cost over the two years is $150, and the present value of the asset is then $1,850 ($2,000 − $150). From Table PV-1, the effective interest rate can be determined:

PV ÷ FV = discount factor $1,850 ÷ $2,000 = 0.925

Looking at the n = 2 row, this would represent an interest rate of approximately 4%. Most notes have an interest cost, whether explicitly stated or not.

If a financial calculator is used, the exact interest rate can be determined by inputting $1,850 as the present value, $2,000 as the future value, 2 as the number of periods, and then instructing the calculator to compute the interest rate. The result is an interest rate of 3.975%, which is very close to the 4% estimated by using the present value tables.

Also note that the purchaser should record the furniture at a cost of $1,850 even if the purchaser chose the option of no payment for two years. In this case, the purchaser will recognize interest expense of $74 ($1,850 × 4%) in the first year and $76 [($1,850 + $74) × 4%] in the second year (numbers have been rounded so total interest expense over two years is equal to $150).

Canada Student Loans

The Canadian federal government, in an effort to encourage post-secondary education, offers loans to eligible students with no interest accruing while they maintain their student status. When schooling is complete, the entire loan must be repaid within 10 years. Repayment of the loan can be at a fixed rate of prime + 5%, or a floating rate of prime + 2.5%. Let's assume that you attend school for four years and borrow $2,500 at the end of each year. Upon graduation, you have a total debt of $10,000.

If you had not been eligible for the student loan, and had borrowed the money as needed through a conventional lender who agreed to let the interest accrue at 9% over the four years, with no payments required, how much would you owe upon graduation? Compound interest would accrue as shown in Illustration PV-16.

	Year 1	Year 2	Year 3	Year 4
Balance, beginning of period	$ 0	$2,500	$5,225	$8,195
Interest (@ 9%)	0	225	470	738
	0	2,725	5,695	8,933
Increase in borrowings	2,500	2,500	2,500	2,500
Balance, end of period	$2,500	$5,225	$8,195	$11,433

← Illustration PV-16

Cost of student loan with a conventional lender

The loan would total $11,433 at the end of Year 4. Note that this is the future value of the loan at an interest rate of 9%. This amount can also be determined using present value concepts as shown in Illustration PV-17.

	Year 1	Year 2	Year 3	Year 4
Balance, beginning of period (PV)	$ 0	$2,500	$5,225	$8,195
From Table PV-1; FV = PV / 0.91743[1]	0	2,725	5,695	8,933
Increase in borrowings	2,500	2,500	2,500	2,500
Balance, end of period	$2,500	$5,225	$8,195	$11,433

← Illustration PV-17

Cost of student loan with a conventional lender using PV calculations

[1] $n = 1$, $i = 9\%$; calculation done for each year separately, based on the balance at the beginning of each period.

A third way of calculating this future value is to first calculate the PV of an annuity of $2,500 over four years at 9%, and to then calculate the FV of this figure, as follows:

- From Table PV-2, the present value of an annuity of $2,500 per year for 4 years at 9% is:
  $2,500 × 3.23972 = $8,099.30.
- From Table PV-1, the future value (4 years at 9%) of $8,099.30 is:
  $8,099.30 ÷ 0.70843 = $11,432.75.

The benefit of having a Canada Student Loan, as opposed a loan with a conventional lender, is shown in Illustration PV-18 by comparing the cost of repaying these two types of loans.

	Canada Student Loan	Conventional Loan
Value of loan at the end of 4 years	$ 10,000	$ 11,433
PV factor from Table PV-2: $n = 10$; $i = 9\%$	6.41766	6.41766
Annual annuity required to pay the loan	$ 1,558.20	$ 1,781.49

← Illustration PV-18

Calculation of annuity required to repay two loans

Under the Canada Student Loan, there is a nominal savings of $2,232.90 [10 × ($1,781.49 − $1,558.20)] over the life of the loan. This example uses present value calculations to illustrate the effect of not incurring interest while you are in school.

BEFORE YOU GO ON . . .

➔ Review It

1. Explain how calculating the present value of a note is similar to, or different from, calculating the present value of a bond.
2. Differentiate between the two kinds of payment options on a note payable.
3. What are the benefits of having a Canada Student Loan instead of a conventional bank loan?

➔ Do It

You are about to purchase your first car. You decide to finance the car at an annual interest rate of 7% over a period of 48 months. If your monthly payment is $574.71, how much is the car worth today?

Action Plan

- The present value factor of an annuity for $n = 48$ and $i = 0.58\%$ (7% ÷ 12 months) is 41.76019.

Solution

The day the car is purchased, it is worth the present value of the future cash payments. The present value of $574.71 to be paid monthly for four years, discounted at 7%, is $24,000 ($574.71 × 41.76019).

Related exercise material: BEPV-11, BEPV-12, BEPV-13, BEPV-14, BEPV-15, BEPV-16, and BEPV-17.

The Navigator

Assets–Estimating Value in Use Using Future Cash Flows

As we have learned in a previous section, a bond can be valued based on future cash flows. So too can an asset. In Chapter 9, you learned that companies are required to regularly determine whether the value of property, plant, and equipment has been impaired. Recall that an asset is impaired if the carrying amount reported on the balance sheet is greater than its recoverable amount. The recoverable amount is either the asset's fair value or its *value in use*. Determining the value in use requires the application of present value concepts. The computation of value in use is a two-step process: (1) future cash flows are estimated, and (2) the present value of these cash flows is calculated.

For example, assume JB Company owns a specialized piece of equipment used in its manufacturing process. JB needs to determine the asset's value in use to test for impairment. As the first step in determining value in use, JB's management estimates that the equipment will last for another five years and that it will generate the following future cash flows at the end of each year:

Year 1	Year 2	Year 3	Year 4	Year 5
$9,000	$10,000	$13,000	$10,000	$7,000

In the second step of determining value in use, JB calculates the present value of each of these future cash flows. Using a discount rate of 8%, the present value of each future cash flow is shown in Illustration PV-19.

Illustration PV-19 ➡

Present value of estimated future cash flows of specialized equipment

	Year 1	Year 2	Year 3	Year 4	Year 5
Future cash flows	$9,000	$10,000	$13,000	$10,000	$7,000
Present value factor[1]	0.92593	0.85734	0.79383	0.73503	0.68058
Present value amount	$8,333	$ 8,573	$10,320	$ 7,350	$4,764

[1] The appropriate interest rate to be used is based on current market rates; however, adjustments for uncertainties related to the specific asset may be made. Further discussion on this topic is covered in more advanced texts.

The value in use of JB's specialized equipment is the sum of the present value of each year's cash flow, $39,340 ($8,333 + $8,573 + $10,320 + $7,350 + $4,764). If this amount is less than the asset's carrying amount, JB will be required to record an impairment as shown in Chapter 9.

The present value method of estimating the value in use of an asset can also be used for intangible assets. For example, assume JB purchases a licence from Redo Industries for the right to manufacture and sell products using Redo's processes and technologies. JB estimates it will earn $6,000 per year from this licence over the next 10 years. What is the value in use to JB of this licence?

Since JB expects to earn the same amount each year, Table PV-2 is used to find the present value factor of the annuity after determining the appropriate discount rate. As pointed out in the previous example, JB should choose a rate based on current market rates; however, adjustments for uncertainties related to the specific asset may be required. Assuming JB uses 8% as the discount rate, the present value factor from Table PV-2 for 10 periods is 6.71008. The value in use of the licence is $40,260 ($6,000 × 6.71008).

BEFORE YOU GO ON . . .

➡ **Review It**

1. When is it necessary to calculate the value in use of an asset?
2. Explain the two steps in calculating the value in use of an asset.

➡ **Do It**

You are attempting to estimate the value in use of your company's production equipment, which you estimate will be used in operations for another eight years. You estimate that the equipment will generate annual cash flows of $16,000, at the end of each year, for the remainder of its productive life, and that 9% is the appropriate discount rate. What is the value in use of this equipment?

Action Plan
- Identify future cash flows.
- Use Table PV-2 to determine the present value of an annuity factor for $n = 8$ and $i = 9\%$ and calculate the present value.

Solution

The value in use is equal to the present value of the estimated annual future cash flows for the remaining life of the asset discounted at an appropriate discount rate.

Future annual cash flows:	$16,000
Number of periods:	8
Discount rate:	9%
Present value annuity factor ($n = 8$, $i = 9\%$):	5.53482
Present value:	$88,557 = $16,000 \times 5.53482$

Related exercise material: BEPV-18, BEPV-19, and BEPV-20.

The Navigator

Brief Exercises

BEPV–1 Determine the amount of interest that will be earned on each of the following investments:

	Investment	(i) Interest Rate	(n) Number of Periods	Type of Interest
(a)	$100	5%	1	Simple
(b)	$500	6%	2	Simple
(c)	$500	6%	2	Compound

Calculate simple and compound interest.

BEPV–2 Smolinski Company is considering an investment that will return a lump sum of $500,000 five years from now. What amount should Smolinski Company pay for this investment in order to earn a 4% return?

Calculate present value of a single-sum investment.

BEPV–3 Mehmet's parents invest $8,000 in a 10-year guaranteed investment certificate (GIC) in his name. The investment pays 4% annually. How much will the GIC yield when it matures? Compare the interest earned in the first and second five-year periods, and provide an explanation for the difference.

Calculate future value of a single-sum investment and demonstrate the effect of compounding.

BEPV–4 Janet Bryden has been offered the opportunity to invest $44,401 now. The investment will earn 7% per year, and at the end of that time will return Janet $100,000. How many years must Janet wait to receive $100,000?

Calculate number of periods of a single investment sum.

BEPV–5 If Kerry Dahl invests $3,152 now, she will receive $10,000 at the end of 15 years. What annual rate of interest will Kerry earn on her investment? Round your answer to the nearest whole number.

Calculate interest rate on single sum.

BEPV–6 Kilarny Company is considering investing in an annuity contract that will return $25,000 at the end of each year for 15 years. What amount should Kilarny Company pay for this investment if it earns a 6% return?

Calculate present value of an annuity investment.

BEPV–7 For each of the following cases, indicate in the chart below the appropriate discount rate (i) and the appropriate number of periods (n) to be used in present value calculations. Show calculations. The first one has been completed as an example.

Determine number of periods and discount rate.

	Annual Interest Rate	Number of Years	Frequency of Payments	(n) Number of periods	(i) Discount Rate
1.	8%	3	Quarterly	$3 \times 4 = 12$	$8\% \div 4 = 2\%$
2.	5%	4	Semi-annually		
3.	7%	5	Annually		
4.	4%	3	Quarterly		
5.	6%	6	Semi-annually		
6.	6%	15	Monthly		

BEPV–8 Insert the appropriate discount factor into the table below for each of the situations given. These factors have to be interpolated from Tables PV-1 and PV-2.

Interpolate discount factors.

	PV of 1 (Table PV-1)	PV of an Annuity of 1 (Table PV-2)

(a) $n = 4$, $i = 4\frac{1}{2}\%$
(b) $n = 6$, $i = 6\frac{1}{2}\%$

Calculate present value of bonds.

BEPV–9 Cross Country Railroad Co. is about to issue $100,000 of 10-year bonds that pay a 5.5% annual interest rate, with interest payable semi-annually. The market interest rate is 5%. How much can Cross Country expect to receive for the sale of these bonds?

Calculate present value of bonds.

BEPV–10 Assume the same information as BEPV–9, except that the market interest rate is 6% instead of 5%. In this case, how much can Cross Country expect to receive from the sale of these bonds?

Calculate present value of note.

BEPV–11 Caledonian Company receives a six-year, $50,000 note that bears interest at 8% (paid annually) from a customer at a time when the market interest rate is 7%. What is the present value of the note received by Caledonian?

Calculate present value of note.

BEPV–12 Hung-Chao Yu Company issues a six-year, 8% mortgage note on January 1, 2011, to obtain financing for new equipment. The terms provide for semi-annual instalment payments of $112,825. What were the cash proceeds received from the issue of the note?

Determine interest and principal payments.

BEPV–13 You are told that a note has repayment terms of $4,000 per year for five years, with a stated interest rate of 4%. How much of the total payment is for principal, and how much is for interest?

Calculate annual payments.

BEPV–14 You would like to purchase a car with a list price of $30,000, and the dealer offers financing over a five-year period at 8%. If repayments are to be made annually, what would your annual payments be?

Calculate trade-in value of car.

BEPV–15 Assume the same information as in BEPV–14, except that you can only afford to make annual payments of $6,000. If you decide to trade in your present car to help reduce the amount of financing required, what trade-in value would you need to negotiate to ensure your annual payment is $6,000?

Compare financing options.

BEPV–16 As CFO of a small manufacturing firm, you have been asked to determine the best financing for the purchase of a new piece of equipment. If the vendor is offering repayment options of $10,000 per year for five years, or no payment for two years followed by one payment of $46,000, which option would you recommend? The current market rate of interest is 8%.

Compare financing options.

BEPV–17 If the market rate of interest in BEPV–16 is 10%, would you choose the same option?

Calculate value of machine for purchase decision.

BEPV–18 Barney Googal owns a garage and is contemplating purchasing a tire retreading machine for $16,100. After estimating costs and revenues, Barney projects a net cash flow from the retreading machine of $2,690 annually for eight years. Barney hopes to earn a return of 11% on such investments. What is the present value of the retreading operation? Should Barney Googal purchase the retreading machine?

Calculate value in use for a machine.

BEPV–19 Chang Company must perform an impairment test on its equipment. The equipment will produce the following cash flows: Year 1, $35,000; Year 2, $45,000; Year 3, $55,000. Chang requires a minimum rate of return of 10%. What is the value in use for this equipment?

Calculate value in use of a patent.

BEPV–20 ABC Company signs a contract to sell the use of its patented manufacturing technology to DEF Corp for 15 years. The contract for this transaction stipulates that DEF Corp pays ABC $18,000 at the end of each year for the use of this technology. Using a discount rate of 9%, what is the value in use of the patented manufacturing technology?

Company Index

Subject Index

A cumulative index appears at the end of each Part.

Photo Credits

All images are copyright © iStockphoto unless otherwise noted.

Logos are registered trademarks of the respective companies and are reprinted with permission.

Chapter 1 Opener: Courtesy The Forzani Group Ltd.; Page 4: Courtesy Great Little Box Company. **Chapter 2** Opener: Courtesy Prestige Dance Academy; Page 69: Courtesy Goodyear Tire and Rubber Company. **Chapter 3** Opener: Courtesy Seneca College of Applied Arts and Technology; Page 124: PhotoDisc/Getty Images. **Chapter 4** Opener: Courtesy Moulé. Page 190: The Canadian Press/Adrian Wyld. **Chapter 5** Opener: Courtesy The Forzani Group Ltd.; Page 257: Courtesy Liquidation World. **Chapter 6** Opener: Courtesy The Forzani Group Ltd. **Chapter 7** Opener: Courtesy Barrett & Mackay Photography. **Chapter 8** Opener: Cindy Wilson/Telegraph-Journal. **Chapter 9** Opener: Courtesy Dawson College. **Chapter 10** Page 569: The Canadian Press/Marcos Townsend. Pages 582-583: Reproduced with permission of the Minister of Public Works and Government Services Canada, 2009. **Chapter 11** Page 619: The Canadian Press/Frank Gunn. **Chapter 12** Opener: Courtesy Bailey Altrogge Matchett LLP; Page 667: Courtesy Assiniboia Capital Corporation. Page 691: The Canadian Press/Ben Margot. **Chapter 13** Opener: Courtesy ZENN Motor Inc.; Page 721: PhotoDisc, Inc. **Chapter 14** Opener: Courtesy Sun Life Financial; Page 789: Courtesy WestJet. **Chapter 15** Opener: Courtesy Hydro-Québec; Page 834: The Canadian Press/John Woods. **Chapter 16** Opener: Courtesy Scotiabank; Page 880: Courtesy Suncor Energy Inc. **Chapter 17** Opener: Courtesy Clearwater Foods; Page 963: The Canadian Press/Elaine Thompson. **Chapter 18** Opener: Courtesy The Canadian Institute of Chartered Accountants; Page 1015: Reproduced with Permission from Wyeth Consumer Healthcare.